The Latin American Fashion Reader

Dress, Body, Culture

Series Editor: **Joanne B. Eicher**, *Regents' Professor, University of Minnesota*

Advisory Board:

Ruth Barnes, *Ashmolean Museum, University of Oxford*
Helen Callaway, *CCCRW, University of Oxford*
James Hall, *University of Illinois at Chicago*
Beatrice Medicine, *California State University, Northridge*
Ted Polhemus, *Curator, "Street Style" Exhibition, Victoria and Albert Museum*
Griselda Pollock, *University of Leeds*
Valerie Steele, *The Museum at the Fashion Institute of Technology*
Lou Taylor, *University of Brighton*
John Wright, *University of Minnesota*

Books in this provocative series seek to articulate the connections between culture and dress, which is defined here in its broadest possible sense as any modification or supplement to the body. Interdisciplinary in approach, the series highlights the dialog between identity and dress, cosmetics, coiffure and body alternations as manifested in practices as varied as plastic surgery, tattooing, and ritual scarification. The series aims, in particular, to analyse the meaning of dress in relation to popular culture and gender issues and will include works grounded in anthropology, sociology, history, art history, literature, and folklore.

ISSN: 1360-466X

Previously published in the Series

Helen Bradley Foster, *"New Raiments of Self": African American Clothing in the Antebellum South*
Claudine Griggs, *S/he: Changing Sex and Changing Clothes*
Michaele Thurgood Haynes, *Dressing Up Debutantes: Pageantry and Glitz in Texas*
Anne Brydon and Sandra Niessen, *Consuming Fashion: Adorning the Transnational Body*
Dani Cavallaro and Alexandra Warwick, *Fashioning the Frame: Boundaries, Dress and the Body*
Judith Perani and Norma H. Wolff, *Cloth, Dress and Art Patronage in Africa*
Linda B. Arthur, Religion, *Dress and the Body*
Paul Jobling, *Fashion Spreads: Word and Image in Fashion Photography*
Fadwa El Guindi, *Veil: Modesty, Privacy and Resistance*
Thomas S. Abler, *Hinterland Warriors and Military Dress: European Empires and Exotic Uniforms*
Linda Welters, *Folk Dress in Europe and Anatolia: Beliefs about Protection and Fertility*
Kim K.P. Johnson and Sharron J. Lennon, *Appearance and Power*
Barbara Burman, *The Culture of Sewing*
Annette Lynch, *Dress, Gender and Cultural Change*
Antonia Young, *Women Who Become Men*
David Muggleton, *Inside Subculture: The Postmodern Meaning of Style*
Nicola White, *Reconstructing Italian Fashion: America and the Development of the Italian Fashion Industry*
Brian J. McVeigh, *Wearing Ideology: The Uniformity of Self-Preservation in Japan*
Shaun Cole, *Don We Now Our Gay Apparel: Gay Men's Dress in the Twentieth Century*
Kate Ince, *Orlan: Millennial Female*
Nicola White and Ian Griffiths, *The Fashion Business: Theory, Practice, Image*
Ali Guy, Eileen Green and Maura Banim, *Through the Wardrobe: Women's Relationships with their Clothes*
Linda B. Arthur, *Undressing Religion: Commitment and Conversion from a Cross-Cultural Perspective*
William J.F. Keenan, *Dressed to Impress: Looking the Part*
Joanne Entwistle and Elizabeth Wilson, *Body Dressing*
Leigh Summers, *Bound to Please: A History of the Victorian Corset*
Paul Hodkinson, *Goth: Identity, Style and Subculture*
Michael Carter, *Fashion Classics from Carlyle to Barthes*
Sandra Niessen, Ann Marie Leshkowich and Carla Jones, *Re-Orienting Fashion: The Globalization of Asian Dress*
Kim K.P. Johnson, Susan J. Torntore and Joanne B. Eicher, *Fashion Foundations: Early Writings on Fashion and Dress*
Helen Bradley Foster and Donald Clay Johnson, *Wedding Dress Across Cultures*
Eugenia Paulicelli, *Fashion under Fascism: Beyond the Black Skirt*
Charlotte Suthrell, *Unzipping Gender: Sex, Cross-Dressing and Culture*
Yuniya Kawamura, *The Japanese Revolution in Paris Fashion*
Ruth Barcan, *Nudity: A Cultural Anatomy*
Samantha Holland, *Alternative Femininities: Body, Age and Identity*
Alexandra Palmer and Hazel Clark, *Old Clothes, New Looks: Second Hand Fashion*
Yuniya Kawamura, *Fashion-ology: An Introduction to Fashion Studies*

DRESS, BODY, CULTURE

The Latin American Fashion Reader

Edited by

Regina A. Root

Oxford • New York

English edition
First published in 2005 by
Berg
Editorial offices:
1st Floor, Angel Court, 81 St Clements Street, Oxford OX4 1AW, UK
175 Fifth Avenue, New York, NY 10010, USA

© Regina A. Root 2005

All rights reserved.
No part of this publication may be reproduced in any form
or by any means without the written permission of
Berg.

Berg is the imprint of Oxford International Publishers Ltd.

Library of Congress Cataloging-in-Publication Data
The Latin American fashion reader / edited by Regina A. Root.
    p. cm. — (Dress, body, culture)
  Includes bibliographical references and index.
    ISBN 1-85973-888-5 (cloth : alk. paper) — ISBN 1-85973-893-1 (pbk. : alk. paper) 1. Clothing and dress—Latin America—History. 2. Fashion—Latin America—History. 3. Latin America—Social life and customs. I. Root, Regina A. II. Series.

  GT623.L38 2005
  391′.0098—dc22
                                                                  2004029771

British Library Cataloguing-in-Publication Data
A catalogue record for this book is available from the British Library.

ISBN-13   978 1 85973 888 7 (Cloth)
                978 1 85973 893 1 (Paper)

ISBN-10   1 85973 888 5 (Cloth)
                1 85973 893 1 (Paper)

Typeset by JS Typesetting Ltd, Porthcawl, Wales
Printed in the United Kingdom by Biddles Ltd, King's Lynn.

www.bergpublishers.com

To Audrey

Contents

List of Figures	ix
Notes on Contributors	xi
Acknowledgments	xv
Introduction Regina A. Root	1

Part 1: Unraveling History

1 Visualizing Difference: The Rhetoric of Clothing in Colonial Spanish America
Mariselle Meléndez ... 17

2 Fashioning Independence: Gender, Dress and Social Space in Postcolonial Argentina
Regina A. Root ... 31

3 The Traveler's Eye: *Chinas Poblanas* and European-Inspired Costume in Postcolonial Mexico
Kimberly Randall ... 44

4 Far Eastern Influences in Latin American Fashions
Araceli Tinajero ... 66

Part 2: Altered Traditions

5 Ixcacles: Maguey-fiber Sandals in Modern Mexico
Pamela Scheinman ... 79

6 "Why do Gringos Like Black?" Mourning, Tourism, and Changing Fashions in Peru
Blenda Femenías ... 93

7 Dressed to Kill: The Embroidered Fashion Industry of the Sakaka of Highland Bolivia
Elayne Zorn ... 114

8 Representations of Tradition in Latin American Boundary
Textile Art
Elyse Demaray, Melody Keim-Shenk, and Mary A. Littrell   142

Part 3: Fashion and the Cultural Imaginary

9 Ponchos of the River Plate: Nostalgia for Eden
Ruth Corcuera   163

10 Mappin Stores: Adding an English Touch to the São Paulo
Fashion Scene
Rita Andrade   176

11 As She Walks to the Sea: A Semiology of Rio de Janeiro
Nizia Villaça   188

12 "Every Girl had a Fan which she Kept Always in Motion":
Puerto Rican Women's Dress at a Time of Social and Cultural
Transition
Dilia López Gydosh and Marsha A. Dickson   198

Part 4: Mediation and Consumption

13 *Guayaberismo* and the Essence of Cool
Marilyn Miller   213

14 Transvestite Pedagogy: Jacqueline and Cuban Culture
James Pancrazio   232

15 Frida and Evita: Latin American Icons for Export
María Claudia André   247

16 Fashioning United States Salvadoranness: Unveiling the Faces
of Christy Turlington and Rosa López
Claudia M. Milian Arias   263

Part 5: In Search of Fashion

17 Scattered Bodies, Unfashionable Flesh
Fabricio Forastelli   283

Notes   290

Bibliography   310

Index   337

List of Figures

1.1. Black slaves working the mines on the island of Hispaniola. Benzoni, Girolamo. "Americae, das fu[e]nffte Buch". Frankfurt a. M.: E. Kempfer 1613. (Theodor de Bry's "America". Pt. 5. German.) Courtesy of the Rare Book and Special Collections Library at the University of Illinois at Urbana-Champaign. 19

1.2. On the left: Spanish woman with mantle. On the right: Mestiza. Both images are by Baltazar Martínez de Compañon as published in *Trujillo del Perú (1779–1789)*. Copyright Patrimonio Nacional. 27

2.1. On the left: "Woman from Buenos Aires: Summer Dress." On the right: "Woman from Buenos Aires: Ball gown." Both lithographs are from César Hipólito Bacle's *Trajes y costumbres de la provincia de Buenos Aires* (Buenos Aires: Bacle y Compañía, 1833). 37

2.2. "Peinetones on the Street." Satirical caricature from César Hipólito Bacle's *Trajes y costumbres de la provincia de Buenos Aires* (Buenos Aires: Bacle y Compañía, 1833). 38

3.1. *China poblana* costume in Mexico. Between 1829 and 1834, the German artist Carl Nebel traveled through Mexico, where he produced a series of lithographs depicting Mexican customs and important archaeological sites. His depiction of *china poblanas* reinforced traveler's impressions of their seductive qualities and spirited independence. First published in Paris as *Voyage pittoresque et archeologique dans la partie la plus interessante du Mexique* (1836), this image also appeared in the Spanish translation entitled *Viaje pintoresco y arqueológico sobre la parte más interesante de la República Mexicana, en los años transcurridos desde 1829 hasta 1834* (Mexico City: Porrúa, 1963). Reprinted courtesy of the General Research Division, The New York Public Library, Astor, Lenox and Tilden Foundations. 55

5.1. A pair of maguey-fiber sandals from San Felipe Tepemaxalco, Puebla. 83

List of Figures

5.2.	On the left: Doña Angela Escobar (age 80) wearing the traditional *traje* of Hueyapan, Morelos. On the right: Hueyapan shop owner Doña Camila Perez Zamudio (age 87) in her *ixcacles*. Photographs by Pamela Scheinman.	84
6.1.	Nilda Bernal holds a shawl embroidered by her and Juan Condori, Coporaque, Peru, 1992. Photograph by Patricia Jurewicz.	94
7.1.	Two young women, from ayllu Sakaka, pose in the central plaza of the town of Sacaca on a Sunday market day. Photograph by Elayne Zorn, 1988.	116
7.2.	A young man, playing charango, and two young women singers, perform in the Samkha ayllu folklore festival. Photograph by Elayne Zorn, 1989.	127
9.1.	Nineteenth-century poncho from the Argentine Pampas that belonged to Chief Cayupán. Poncho stitch with the ikat and its lines. Note that the warp helps shape the Spanish flag. Made of sheep's wool, it measures 1.95 m long and 1.54 m wide. Courtesy of the José Hernández Museum.	172
10.1.	Advertisement for the opening of Mappin Stores. From the 29 November 1913 issue of O *Estado de S. Paulo*.	183
12.1.	Left: "Untucked" shirtwaist look, porta-abanico and eyelet "lace" with ribbon trim, circa 1898. Reprinted from W. S. Bryan, Our Islands and Their People as Seen with Camera and Pencil (St. Louis, 1899, p. 269). Right: Extremely wide flat brim hats trimmed with feathers and flowers, porta-abanico and eyelet "lace" with ribbon-trim, circa 1909–10. From "La moda en Puerto Rico, una mirada al pasado" Museo de Arte de Ponce, Puerto Rico.	205
17.1.	On the sidelines of the Argentine Worker's Movement mobilization on 6 September 1996. Photograph by Regina A. Root.	287

Notes on Contributors

Rita Andrade edits the Brazilian edition of *Fashion Theory*. She coordinates the undergraduate program in Fashion Design at the Universidade Anhembi Morumbi in São Paulo. She holds a Master's degree in History of Textiles and Dress from the University of Southampton and is a doctoral candidate in history at the Pontifícia Universidade Católica de São Paulo. A member of the editorial board of the Sociedade Brasileira de Estudos da Moda, her research focuses on Brazilian fashion history and the couture of the 1920s and 1930s.

María Claudia André is Associate Professor of Hispanic American Literature at Hope College. She is the editor of *Chicanas and Latin American Women Writers: Exploring the Realm of the Kitchen as a Self-Empowering Site* (Edwin Mellen Press, 2001) and *Antología de escritoras argentinas contemporáneas* (Editorial Biblos, 2004).

Ruth Corcuera is the director of the cultural anthropology section of the Argentine Centro de Investigaciones en Antropología Filosófica y Cultural (CIAFIC). She is the author of several books, including *Herencia textil andina* (Dupont, 1987) and *Ponchos de las tierras del Plata* (Verstraeten Editores, 1999). She holds a Ph.D. from the Pontificia Universidad Católica in Lima.

Elyse Demaray holds a Ph.D. in American literature and Women's Studies from Indiana University as well as a Master's degree in Textiles and Clothing from Iowa State University where she currently teaches literature, Women's Studies and writing. Her research interests center on gender identity as it relates to the body and its adornment.

Marsha A. Dickson is Associate Professor in Apparel and Textiles at Kansas State University. Her scholarly work focuses on challenges and opportunities in the global apparel industry. She has conducted research in several international locations, including India, China and Guatemala. With Mary A. Littrell, she is the co-author of *Social Responsibility in the Global Market: Fair Trade of Cultural Products* (Sage Publications, 1999).

Blenda Femenías is a Visiting Assistant Professor in the Department of Anthropology at the University of Pittsburgh and a Research Associate at the Haffenreffer

Museum of Anthropology at Brown University. She is the author of *Gender and the Boundaries of Dress in Contemporary Peru* (University of Texas Press, 2004). She has been a Fulbright Scholar in Peru twice and holds a Ph.D. in cultural anthropology from the University of Wisconsin at Madison.

Fabricio Forastelli is Visiting Assistant Professor in the Department of Spanish and Portuguese at Emory University. His research interests are nineteenth- and twentieth-century Latin American literature, cultural critique and political discourse analysis. He has edited a collection of essays entitled *Las marcas del género* (Universidad Nacional de Córdoba, 1999).

Melody Keim-Shenk received her Masters of Family and Consumer Services with a specialization in Textiles and Clothing from Iowa State University. Her areas of interest include alternative trade, cultural anthropology, and definitions of tradition. She previously worked for Ten Thousand Villages, an alternative trading company, and currently works with the YWCA of Lancaster, Pennsylvania.

Mary A. Littrell, Professor and Head of the Department of Design and Merchandising at Colorado State University in Fort Collins, received her Ph.D. from Indiana University. Her research focuses on the marketing of artisinal products across cultures, with recent field research in India and Central Asia. With Marsha A. Dickson, she is co-author of *Social Responsibility in the Global Market: Fair Trade of Cultural Products* (Sage Publications, 1999).

Dilia López-Gydosh, a doctoral candidate in textiles and clothing at The Ohio State University, is currently a Visiting Assistant Professor of Textiles, Apparel and Merchandising at West Virginia University. Her research interests center on the historical and cultural aspects of Puerto Rican dress.

Mariselle Meléndez is Associate Professor of Colonial Latin American Literature and Culture at the University of Illinois, Urbana-Champaign. She is the author of *Raza, género e hibridez en El lazarillo de ciegos caminantes* (University of North Carolina Studies in the Romance Languages and Literatures, 1999) and the co-editor with Santa Arias of *Mapping Colonial Spanish America: Places and Commonplaces of Identity, Culture and Experience* (Bucknell University Press, 2002). Her articles have appeared in *Latin American Literary Review, Revista Iberoamericana, Revista de Crítica Literaria Latinoamericana, Revista de Estudios Hispánicos,* and *Dieciocho/Hispanic Enlightenment,* among others.

Claudia M. Milian Arias is Visiting Assistant Professor of Africana Studies and American Civilization at Brown University. Her work is comparative in scope, exploring the intersections between Latina, Latino, Central American, and African American literatures, and has been published in *A Companion to Racial and Ethnic Studies, Nepantla, The Americas Review,* and *Callaloo*.

Notes on Contributors

Marilyn Miller is Assistant Professor of Caribbean and Latin American Studies at Tulane University in New Orleans. She has published several essays on African diasporic poetics, performance, and intellectual history in the Spanish Caribbean. She is the author of *Rise and Fall of the Cosmic Race. The Cult of Mestizaje in Latin America* (University of Texas Press, 2004).

James Pancrazio is an Associate Professor of Latin American literature and culture at Illinois State University. He is the author of *The Logic of Fetishism: Alejo Carpentier and the Cuban Tradition* (Bucknell University Press, 2004) and is currently working on a book-length project on the relationship between pleasure and transculturation in Cuban literature and culture. His articles have appeared in *Cuban Studies*, *Revista Iberoamericana*, and *Bulletin of Hispanic Studies*.

Kimberly Randall is a recent graduate of the Fashion Institute of Technology's Museum Studies program for Costume and Textiles. Her chapter is drawn from her thesis research. She is currently researching how elements of Latin American ethnic dress and textiles were used to promote fashion in the United States during the early decades of the twentieth century.

Regina A. Root holds a Ph.D. in Hispanic Languages and Literatures from the University of California at Berkeley and is Assistant Professor of Hispanic Studies in the Department of Modern Languages and Literature at the College of William and Mary. Her research focuses on the interrelationship between fashion and politics in Latin America, with publications having appeared in *Fashion Theory*, *DeSigniS*, *Folios*, and *The Americas*, among others. Her book on *Couture and Consensus: Fashion and Political Culture in Postcolonial Argentina* is forthcoming with the University of Minnesota Press.

Pamela Scheinman earned a Masters of Fine Arts in Textiles from Indiana University in Bloomington and teaches in the Department of Art and Design at Montclair State University in New Jersey. Her publications, curatorial work, and lectures focus on Latin American popular art, contemporary fiber and Mexican folk photography (while under the auspices of a Fulbright grant). She is currently researching a history of the *Alpargatería Española* in Mexico City.

Araceli Tinajero received her Ph.D. from Rutgers University and teaches Japanese, Spanish, and Hispanic literatures. She is Assistant Professor of Spanish at the City College of the City University of New York and the author of *Orientalismo en el modernismo hispanomericano* (Purdue University Press, 2004). Currently is finishing a book on reading practices in Spain, the Caribbean and the United States.

Nizia Villaça holds a Ph. D. in anthropology from Paris V, Sorbonne. She is a Full Professor of Communications at the Federal University of Rio de Janeiro and a member of the Brazilian National Council of Researchers. She is the author of several articles and books on body communication and human behavior, including *En nome do corpo* with Fred Goes (Editorial Rocco, 1998) and *Impresso electrônico?* (Rio Mauad, 2002).

Elayne Zorn received her Ph.D. in anthropology from Cornell University and is Associate Professor of Anthropology at the University of Central Florida. Her publications include articles and book chapters about diverse aspects of highland Peruvian and Bolivian culture, art, and political economy, and a book on community-controlled tourism in Peru entitled *Weaving a Future: Tourism, Cloth, and Culture on an Andean Island* (University of Iowa, 2004).

Acknowledgments

There are several people who have played an important role at every stage of this volume's development. Kathryn Earle, the managing director of Berg Publishers, has been a most patient visionary, generous with her time and advice. I am grateful to Joanne B. Eicher, the series editor, for her invaluable comments. Hannah Shakespeare, Ken Bruce, Felicity Howlett, and Caroline McCarthy – all members of the Berg team – were always helpful and supportive.

As we assembled the volume, the Latin American Studies Association offered its support for the project, granting the 2003 panel on "Dress, Body and Culture in Latin America" a traveling fellowship that enabled us to bring together contributors for an engaging discussion on the emerging field of Latin American fashion studies. The Wendy and Emery Reves Center for International Studies at the College of William and Mary provided additional funding for this endeavor. *Moda Brasil* granted first page to the conference panel, applauding the transnational approach to fashion studies at a time of world discord.

Numerous readers have also contributed to the success of this project at various stages of its development. My contributors have offered their wholehearted commitment to this project at every stage. In the process, they have helped create a genuinely thoughtful and ever growing community of scholars who work on Latin American dress, body and culture. Catherine Barrera, Gwen Kirkpatrick, Francine Masiello, Laura Novik, and Barbara Weissberger shared great insight and offered moral support in more ways than they probably know. Yosi Anaya, Virginia Davis, Rachel DiNitto, Bill Fisher, Christopher Larkosh, Silvia Tandeciarz, Sibel Zandi-Sayek and several anonymous readers provided engaging reader comments. While at Old Dominion University, Anita Fellman, Luisa Igloria, Sujata Moorti and Carolyn Rhodes of the Women's Studies program were the most encouraging colleagues I could have had.

I am grateful to have had the opportunity to participate in a 2000 workshop organized by Laura Novik for faculty and students of the University of Buenos Aires Facultad de Arquitectura, Diseño y Urbanismo. This workshop, along with the stimulating dialogue with designers and merchandisers at the Centro de Estudios de la Moda in Argentina, helped me formulate the parameters of this project in its earliest stages. From that point on I have been fortunate to work with colleagues and designers in many countries. As we finalized the volume, the vision of Rita Andrade and the talented fashion photographer Jaques Faing of Brazil helped make the cover a reality.

Acknowledgments

My colleagues at the College of William and Mary also deserve great thanks. In particular, the generous advice of Georgia Greenia, the technological savvy of Michael Blum, the kind spirit of Shelia Eubank, the advice of Cathy Reed, the dedication of Sarah Smith to the consolidation of the bibliography, and the translation expertise of Silvia Tandeciarz helped the final stages move along with ease. Alexis Wichowski of Jebudas Communications created the most thoughtful and thorough index for this volume.

I have been blessed with an extremely supportive family. My mother Heidi made summer trips to Virginia to help make my writing life easier. My father Jim and sister Kristina offered steadfast encouragement. And to my David and Audrey, who make all of it possible, let's go outside and enjoy the day!

Regina A. Root

Introduction

The word is out: Latin American fashion is hot. Itsy bitsy Brazilian underwear modeled by Giselle Bündchen and sold in the pages of *Victoria's Secret*. Sueded ponchos for an elegant overlayer in Paris. Handwoven bags from Chiapas with pre-Columbian motifs carried in Buenos Aires with the spirit of resistance. Designers affiliated with the Color Marketing Group have created a palette of so-called "Latin tones" – from romantic pinks to "earth-connected hues" – for the fashions targeting United States Baby Boomers over the next decade. From the rainbow that adorns Mayan women to the tango-inspired dress of Argentina, Latin American dress has long been a source of inspiration to designers from around the world. Surprisingly, however, scholars continue to overlook the influences, scope and diversity of dress within this world culture region. Bringing together an international community of scholars whose research focuses on the interrelationship between dress, body and culture, this volume reveals a diverse set of responses that aim to unravel the history and significance of Latin American fashion.

What, then, *is* Latin American fashion? The very term, which refers to the dress, body and culture of a large and heterogeneous world culture region, might seem all too impractical for the scholar wishing to compare and contrast the fashions of Mexico, Central America, the Caribbean and South America. Given that the nature of dress in Latin America is highly diversified, the chapters of this volume look to overlapping socio-historical influences that have shaped the pursuit of elegance and transformed cultural dynamics to elucidate some general characteristics for the region. As a cultural process, fashion is a profoundly social experience that invites individual and collective bodies to assume certain identities and, at times, also to transgress limits and create new ones. Taking into consideration the transnational flows and multicultural influences of dress and material culture, this volume aims to initiate an interdisciplinary discussion on the paths for research in the field. Crossing boundaries to attain a more integrated approach, the *Latin American Fashion Reader* maps the multivalent nature of fashion's discursive and visual registers.

To address the transformative qualities of Latin American fashion, this volume is organized into five parts. Relying heavily on archival research, the first part unravels Latin American fashion history through the examination of the region's colonial legacy and the power of dress. A section on altered traditions turns to ethnographic fieldwork to rethink the points of contact

Introduction

between local knowledge and the global context. At first glance, the resonances of fashion might seem limitless, as if the local were constantly remade for a world market. Despite the aggressive interactions of world trade, there also appear to exist clear boundaries that allow for individual – in this case indigenous – communities to preserve the sacred attributes of their traditional rites and dress. The essays of the third part address the role of the cultural imaginary, situating the articulations of dress within and beyond the parameters of urban and national spaces. From the Argentine ponchos confectioned for Parisian collections to the Brazilian bikinis shown on Cable News Network (CNN), the cultural imaginary links individual styles and collective fantasies to the historical understandings of myth and national identity. The fourth part further informs the mediation and consumption of culture through the study of fashion icons; final words in search of fashion expose the contested territories negotiated by Latin American fashion scholars to politicize and make over the realm of the quotidian.

Unraveling History[1]

When Christopher Columbus claimed the islands of Cuba, the Dominican Republic and Haiti for Spain in 1492, he initiated the conquest of the indigenous populations living in the region known today as Latin America and the Caribbean. The first images and accounts of American natives that circulated throughout Europe reveal much about a sense of awe experienced by the first colonizers. They viewed the natives' "nakedness" with bewilderment and marveled at the presence of material goods such as cotton cloth, intricate feather work and weavings. This "New World" would provide Europe with material goods as varied as silver, gold, sugar, chocolate, textiles and dye. Portugal, involved in its own push for colonial power, would successfully challenge Spain for the region that makes up today's Brazil. As Spain and Portugal quickly established colonial governments, the native populations suffered the effects of brutal conquest, incurable disease, and forced conversion to Christianity. Friar Bartolomé de Las Casas would coin the term "black legend" to describe the exploitative practices of conquistadors and settlers who had turned to slavery and other forms of systematic violence to establish ranches, mines and textile industries.

To maintain a sense of hierarchy and respond to increasing *mestizaje*, or racial mixing, a caste system was established throughout the region. Prior to colonization, dress and textiles had often served as indicators of social and religious identity and as mediums of exchange, a fact that European authors of the period often disregarded. The caste system forced natives and African slaves to wear Western styles of dress, thereby reinforcing the authority of the Spanish and Portuguese and, over time, their creole descendants. Some indigenous communities gave voice to their history and religious beliefs with the help of intricate color coding systems as found in woven textiles or the compilations of strings used in traditional narratives. In this way, the *huipil* of Guatemala and the highlands of Mexico placed deities of the sun and the underworld in dialogue with the Christian faith. Still worn today by Mayan women, the traditional blouse component of their *traje*, or dress, reveals information about the wearer's village, status, heritage, and personal beliefs. Recent excavations in Argentina and Brazil point to the African and Islamic origins of some pieces of jewelry found near the sites of plantations and urban mansions, suggesting that accessories may not have been censored by colonial authorities in the same way as dress. Colonial powers often allowed one to wear almost any design provided that it was gender specific. The selection of fabric, however, was a highly serious matter. Depending on her social status, a Mexican woman of the eighteenth century would have purchased either a silk or cotton *rebozo*, or scarf. Decrees prohibited the use of certain textiles by those whom the caste system deemed as inferiors, thus leading to the prohibition of velvet or taffeta for specially fashioned Incan *unku*s, or tunics, in the Andean region.

In the first part of the volume, Mariselle Meléndez analyzes the construction of cultural, racial and ethnic differences as mediated by the rhetoric of clothing in colonial Spanish America. In the colonial visual register, nakedness marked the "barbarian" Other while clothing served to privilege the more powerful, "civilized" Europeans. To reach a more complete understanding of the nuances of dress in this period, Meléndez investigates the contradictory identity of the shipwrecked conquistador, whose unfortunate circumstances often forced him into a state of nakedness, and the subaltern of the late eighteenth century who manipulated dress codes to challenge the caste system. Once the lack of clothing was no longer the issue and racial miscegenation challenged the very categories of the caste system, the aura of colonial power began to disintegrate. In this light, these disruptive performances of dress serve as early cultural indicators of the crisis that would lead to a region-wide independence movement and the subsequent fragmentation of the Spanish Empire.

By the early nineteenth century, the region experienced several calls for independence from Spain and Portugal that deeply affected the way people consumed fashion. For Cuba and Puerto Rico, this struggle for independence would not materialize until the end of the nineteenth century, although the description of fashion and dance in several literary works began to plot the demise of Spanish rule and construct alternate political identities. In the visual imaginary of this period, creole political leaders such as Simón Bolívar (Venezuela) and José de San Martín (Argentina) appear in wind-swept capes and uniforms of their own design. Many women found themselves called upon to sew the accessories of war, their products in view and their identities concealed. A few, like Juana de Azurduy (Bolivia) and Josefa de Tenorio (Argentina), took on male uniforms in order to fight on the battlefield, later arguing that they merited equal status in postcolonial society.

Introduction

Distancing themselves from the customs of Spain, the fashionable women of Buenos Aires would transform the Spanish *peineta*, or hair comb, into the three-feet by three-feet Argentine *peinetón* in order to assert their presences and at times obstruct the very public sphere that professed independence from oppression but which, ironically, had not yet granted all inhabitants of the River Plate region the privilege of citizenship. My essay explores the metonymy of this fashionable style in order to elucidate its cultural significance in the postcolonial period: The *peinetón*, which in the early 1800s categorized an odd-looking but highly fashionable hair comb, was later used as a term to describe the politically conscious woman whose crowned head granted her a great deal of significance in the public sphere. In satirical caricatures from the 1830s, the enlarged crests of women's combs invade downtown Buenos Aires and over-power the top hats of men. By 1837, government-sponsored popular poetry would equate the *peinetón*-wearing woman with the prostitute, reminding all that fashionable crowns granted women reign over their domestic obligations but not over the political life of the emerging Argentine republic.

In nineteenth-century Mexico, the unique dress of working class women – embroidered white blouses, fine woven scarves and brightly colored skirts – caught the eye of the foreign traveler. Rich with symbolism and folklore, this so-called *china poblana* costume referred to the servant dress of a woman from Puebla while at the same time evoking the legendary *china poblana*, an Asian woman brought to Mexico as a slave in the seventeenth century. Just as important as the Spanish *maja* and Parisian *grisette*, the costume of the *china poblana* has been transformed over the centuries into a national archetype for the Mexican woman. As Mexico struggled to define itself as a nation in the nineteenth and early twentieth centuries, this dress evolved as well, later versions colored with the green, red and white hues of the flag that evoke patriotic sentiments in native Mexicans. In the United States, the elected queen who presides over the Cinco de Mayo festivities, often wears *china poblana* to celebrate her Mexican American heritage. In the next essay, Kimberly Randall analyzes the information provided in travel diaries and foreign correspondence to reconstruct what the *china poblana* looked like at the pinnacle of her expression. Costume histories have often categorized Latin America as a region where outmoded styles prevail long after they have circulated elsewhere, thereby privileging the status of European fashion centers. Randall focuses her study on the contrast between elite Mexican fashions, which tended to follow styles espoused by the fashion presses of France, Great Britain and Spain, and the dynamic configurations under way in the more popular sectors. Taking another look at the very narratives that have informed traditional costume historians' assessments of Latin American design – and which contemporary scholars have often disregarded for their racist descriptions – Randall's work exposes the layered segments and multicultural fusions of this intricate dress.

Araceli Tinajero's essay extends the categories of Latin American fashion to include the Far Eastern influences that were brought to the region as a result of Spanish imperialistic expansion. During the colonial period, Spanish mercantilist trade routes brought silks from the Philippines, porcelain from China, and cotton from India to various Latin American ports. Tinajero reviews colonial shipping news and finds that samples of these goods remained in Latin America and influenced the behavior of all sectors of the population, but especially the colonizers who cherished these items and the colonized artisans who began to integrate Far Eastern designs in their work. Looking to the Asian artifacts that inform the late nineteenth-century writings of Rubén Darío (the prominent Nicaraguan author whose works initiated the first uniquely Latin American literary movement) and contemporary Feng Shui practices, Tinajero explains that Orientalism has informed and shaped the region's fashions for centuries. While contemporary scholars must still link the consumption of these fashions to exoticism and the neo-colonial relationships that govern the trade of Far Eastern goods, it is clear that the impact of Asian immigrants on contemporary Latin American material culture has also brought about a significant, and positive, shift in attitudes. The popularity of Chinatowns and *Sayonara* sandals in contemporary Peru, Tinajero argues, may very well be part of a process – however contradictory – that will lead to a greater acceptance of multicultural values in the region.

Altered Traditions

Rapid modernization, tourism, globalization . . . In recent years, these phenomena have altered significantly the ways in which artisans create, consume and market traditional ritual clothes and "ethnic" dress. When indigenous garments are sold to the tourist who seeks an authentic version of "native costume," a process that anthropologists often analyze as the consumption of ethnicity, these artifacts are severed from their ceremonial origins as they enter into a secular world consisting of market-driven forces and, at times, contradictory political economies. Each of the four essays in this part deals with a different aspect of the alteration of "traditional" indigenous dress for sale in the marketplace. Pamela Scheinman asks if modernization imposes "inevitable and irreversible conditions, in effect coercing conservative subsistence farmers into a cash economy and *mestizo* culture" or if marginalized social groups can find a way in which to mediate this process. To investigate this question, she turns to the case of *ixcacles*, handmade agave fiber sandals that Nahua society invests with magical powers in curing rituals and for walking into the afterlife. Turning to historical documents and interviews with craftswomen, Scheinman perceptively explores the abandonment of indigenous languages and dress through the lens of Mexican cultural history and the making of *ixcacles*. While traditional wearers still abound, young people have discarded their *ixcacles* in favor of more modern – and less indigenous – styles. In recent years, Scheinman writes, craftspeople have modified their designs to appeal to tourists who will use them as beachwear or a souvenir, thereby perpetuating their income *and* their cultural heritage.

Introduction

"Why do gringos like black?" an artisan asked Blenda Femenías when she was studying the alterations of traditional ritual clothes into commodities no longer primarily invested with sacred meaning. For the inhabitants of Caylloma, Peru, black signifies a state of mourning, while for tourists it often represents a fashion statement that they can wear for special occasions back home. Furthermore, many tourists request specially designed embroideries that natives associate with festival styles. How, then, does the artisan fashion a garment that combines mourning and festival styles, as in the case of a commissioned vest that Femenías discusses, and simultaneously maintain the integrity of the artisan's role in society? After all, sacred cloths and designs are indeed for sale; what differs is that they are being sold to people who will not use them for the reasons they were created. At the same time, we are reminded that "outside influences" do not solely determine these transformations; "local artisans have also initiated change for local customers," the author explains. Combining original ethnographic research with a narrative of personal experiences, Femenías maps the increasingly secularized trading places of Caylloma, demonstrating the multi-layered negotiations an ethnic artisan addresses in the creation of "authentic native costume" and the marketing of his or her "Indian" identity.

Drawing on two years of ethnographic fieldwork and apprenticeship, Elayne Zorn takes us to the coca-growing region of Bolivia to analyze a regional fashion industry – independent of but parallel to Western commercial fashion enterprises – that provides embroidered ethnic dress to the people of Northern Potosí. The Sakaka *ayllu*, a community of about 21,000 people who themselves combine distinctive clothes of their own design with factory-produced garments to signal their cultural heritage, create "traditional" clothes that will reach wearers of different markets and ethnic backgrounds. Because Bolivian society is highly polarized along racial and ethnic lines, indigenous styles, while symbolically poetic for the wearer, imply a low social status. Western-style dress grants the wearer a higher status in society; a change in fashion is thus a matter of great significance, as the wearer must forge a new identity that detracts from his or her ethnic affiliations. The Sakaka, many of whom sold heirloom textiles during the "ethnic art" boom of the 1980s to survive, now use wages earned from seasonal labor in the coca/cocaine economy to create new "traditional" designs that reaffirm their sense of community despite the numerous forces, such as modernization or racism, working against them.

If the previous essays reveal how artisans have altered their traditions in response to market demands, then Elyse Demaray, Melody Keim-Shenk and Mary Littrell provide an important perspective on how foreign businesses rely on varying concepts of "tradition" to market "boundary textile art" to customers who reside in developed countries. Boundary art, as the authors define it, is produced by an ethnic group for sale to outsiders and "crosses the boundary where . . . two cultures meet" (Baizerman 1987: 5). Turning to field research, on-site interviews and observations, the authors analyze two United

States-based businesses with differing goals that ultimately determine their approach to tradition, which in turn affect the ways in which artisans fashion their goods and interact with the global market economy. As a fair trade enterprise, Maya Traditions carefully balances the traditional techniques and designs of Mayan weavers while changing colors and styles according to market demands. The upscale, for-profit Peruvian Connection, which has excelled in an extremely competitive market while granting its employees more than subsistence wages, emphasizes Peruvian cultural heritage but not motifs. Tradition, as the authors of this and the other essays demonstrate, varies according to each culture and exists apart from its representation in the global economy. While grounded in the past through meaning, the idea of what constitutes "tradition" finds itself subject to continuous negotiations in the present, as the interaction between artisans, consumers (both native and foreign), and the businesses that market these commodities attests.

Fashion and the Cultural Imaginary

For some scholars, aspects of Latin American fashion – whether the garment or department store – serve as a point of entry into questions of national identity as determined by economic, socio-political and cultural transformations. In her meditation on the Argentine poncho, Ruth Corcuera delves into the garment's mythical past, revealing its semi-nomadic indigenous origins and explaining its subsequent appropriation by the *gauchos* who roamed the country's interior. Sometimes an individual's sole material possession, the poncho could serve its owner as a bed, a pillow, a card table, and even a house. Corcuera, whose studies of textiles and ponchos have helped shape the field of cultural anthropology in her native Argentina, reveals here the form and symbolic complexity of this garment. The poncho, she argues, while associated in the Argentine cultural imaginary with freedom and geographical expanse, also serves as a testament to cultural integration. Reading the history of Argentina's frontier through the poncho, her essay valorizes the indigenous roots of the garment and brings to light the socio political transformations that have made this very garment a symbol of Argentine national identity. The poncho may exist in many forms throughout Latin America and the world, but for many Argentines its messages and meanings remit to an Edenic past.

Rita Andrade's chapter examines the social impact that Mappin Stores, a British department store launched in Brazil in 1913, would have on the lives of *paulistas*, or the inhabitants of São Paulo. Referred to endearingly as Casa Mappin, this department store relied heavily on class-based hierarchies prevalent in city life to market its vision of sophistication and modernity at a moment of urban expansion and massive immigration. In her essay, Andrade uncovers the documents and advertisements once housed in the Mappin Historical Archive, now closed to the public, to elucidate how five- o'clock tea,

Introduction

red brick buildings and even British libraries infused São Paulo, today Brazil's largest city, with a certain "Englishness." This extensive study on the dissemination and consumption of English style reveals the irony with which European ideas and fashions eventually merged into an urban experience of "Brazilianness."

If the previous chapter explores the dynamics of foreign fashion consumption in Brazil, Nizia Villaça explores the influences of the beach fashions of Rio de Janeiro on national and global culture. In the media and on tourist postcards, attention to a stereotypical Copacabana "way of life" has neglected to address issues of socio-economic disparity and political resistance. "In the window of being and seeming," she reminds us, "fashion is a kind of record keeper that reveals aspects of individual and collective appearance." Approaching Brazilian beachwear in a semiotic fashion, Villaça places the trend-setting garments that helped establish Rio de Janeiro as the body's "cultural capital" in dialogue with their respective moments of creation. The stress on bodily freedom at the beach, for instance, might be read as a form of resistance that addressed the sexual, racial and political divisions imposed on Brazilians from 1965 to 1984, a period plagued by military dictatorship. Unisex thongs and flower-power designs represented, to borrow the words of cultural critic Luiz Carlos Maciel, the only free territory in a dictatorial country. In later decades, within the context of a globalized economy, beach fashions have reflected an increasingly fragmented – and tribal – set of ethical stands and approaches to leisure in Rio de Janeiro. Beach fashions, Villaça reveals, are as complex as the city that has continuously witnessed their emergence from the waves of the sea.

Dilia López-Gydosh and Marsha A. Dickson highlight the transformations in Puerto Rican women's dress immediately following the Spanish American War of 1898, chronicling the presence of cross-cultural fusions in dress that remit to the legacy of Spanish and later United States colonialism. Grounded in the analysis of fashion magazines, photographic representations of women, records of fashion imports to the island, as well as religious and travel narratives, this essay suggests that women discarded some Spanish fashions for those of the United States in order to push for their rights to self-expression in a traditional society that did not favor their political participation. With the opening of department stores and the publication of weekly fashion magazines in Puerto Rico, women discarded the Spanish elements of their styles, such as the *mantilla* for the hat, and their fashions increasingly reflected the push towards cultural assimilation. López-Gydosh and Dickson point out that some, mostly understated, forms of Spanish dress persisted through the early part of the twentieth century, like eyelet "lace" with ribbon trim or the "untucked" shirtwaist. Nostalgic revivals of "empire" dress appeared in the 1910s. Eventually, however, the only remnant of Spanish colonialism found in women's dress was the *porta-abanico*, a long necklace that carried a folded fan. Because "every girl had a fan which she kept always in motion," as one American visitor to the island would observe in 1899, the authors suggest that women may have engaged a subtle language of resistance. With their seemingly restrained fan waves, captured indelibly in early twentieth-century photographs, several women quietly undermined the recent transference of power as they contemplated more personalized paths to liberation.

Cultural Mediation and Consumption

Into the twentieth century, Latin American dress would inspire several fashions in Europe and the United States, from the blouse with lace ruffles inspired by the Afro-Cuban *rhumba* to the well-known Mexican *huaraches* (or woven leather sandals) to the straw Panama hat actually created in Ecuador. *Vogue* and *Look* turned attention to trendsetting Latin American women whose visions of *haute couture*, as in the case of Eva Perón (Argentina), and native designs, as in the case of surrealist painter Frida Kahlo (Mexico), would continue to resonate in the popular imaginary until the present day. Other, more contemporary, fashion statements have tended to revisit the past for a retro-effect, such as the young Cuban American donning the *guayabera*, a lightweight, embroidered cotton shirt worn outside the pants throughout the Caribbean; or the Chicano *Zoot-suiter*, whose wartime appropriations of his father's suits inspired ethnic pride in the face of racism and brutality; or the teenage club kid wearing *Inca-techno* styles while discotheque-dancing. The final chapters in this volume deal with the cultural mediation and consumption of fashionable Latin(o) American identities.

In her essay on the *guayabera*, Marilyn Miller examines the multivalent manifestations of this icon of Caribbean cultural identity and fashion. "The guayabera *invests* its wearer with Cubanness," she writes, even if its style has become more popular outside Cuba than on the island. Soldiers who fought for Cuban independence in 1898 wore the simply cut shirt; following the revolution of 1959, Fidel Castro and government officials adapted the *guayabera* as a kind of professional uniform, conveying a relaxed attitude that many associated with the *guajiros*, or people from rural areas, rather than the "civilized" elite of Havana. While the *guayabera* is no longer ubiquitous as everyday wear in Cuba, it provides nightclub waiters and bartenders who cater to foreign tourists with a touch of *cubanía*, or Cubanness. Many Hispanics living in the United States find that the breezy shirt brings "the Latin back to their (Latin) American identity," as Miller explains, adding that the garment has also become the "costume of the financially successful but perpetually nostalgic Cuban American." In recent years, United States-based labels, including Banana Republic and Donna Karan, have created elegant, unisex versions of this Caribbean fashion, signaling the garment's integration beyond nationalist and regionalist discourses and into contemporary crossover cultures.

Because fashion can be so highly charged culturally, its representation in writing also signals a carefully constructed symbolic order. Grounded in psychoanalytic theory and gender studies, James Pancrazio's chapter on

Introduction

"Transvestite Pedagogy" investigates the complexities of (literary) transvestism in fashionable discourse as published in popular magazines two decades after Cuban independence, in the 1920s. Following the retreat of Spanish colonialism, the rhetoric of fashion provided a forum for discussions on the configuration of national identity, even if that identity came to the shores of the island from afar. At a time of postcolonial renovation, Cuban fashion writing plotted ways in which the public might consume fashion and its newly emancipated cultural identity. In this meditation on cultural crisis, Pancrazio uncovers the early fashion writings of renowned Cuban author Alejo Carpentier, penned under the female pseudonym of Jacqueline in the pages of Havana's *Social* magazine. Jacqueline, who most readers associated with a fashionable French or United States identity, helped sell seemingly elitist magazines – and its ideas – to a popular readership. At the same time, fashion descriptions rendered Jacqueline's identity elusive and fluid, as if to mediate the cultural discourse of an emerging Cuban nation. The tensions at play in these chronicles hinged on the idea of insularity, which entailed resisting external influences in the nation-building process, and the idea of instrumentality, which implied the appropriation of foreign models for the island's cultural development. If "transvestism is a textual act," as Pancrazio suggests, then Carpentier's cross-dressing initiates a "play of masks" that modernity itself would seem to represent. After all, the self that writes cannot be the self that is represented, and the writing self must become absent if it is to appear as representation. Thus, a didactic language based on the power of fantasy and self-transformation encouraged readers to consider individualized designs alongside the more collective visions of Cuba's political and cultural future.

Cultural mediation also affects the ways in which we consume and perceive Latin American icons, their images "seducing" an interpretive global community of consumers that seems forever fascinated with the lives and looks of some celebrities. Among the more cult-like icons, we find Ernesto "Che" Guevara, Frida Kahlo, Eva Perón, their stylized images found screenprinted on T-shirts worldwide, mass-merchandised to the point of erasing their cultural significance. María Claudia André describes the historical roles and revisions of Kahlo and Perón, two "Latin American icons for export" who actively engaged the self-conscious construction and reproduction of their own images and who "sought to construct an ideal of themselves that paradoxically both matches and mismatches most of the consumer theories and practices that have made icons out of them." In their lifetimes, both women used their status as the wives of famous men to challenge patriarchal domination at historical junctures that limited women's political participation. In her art and in real life, Frida Kahlo emphasized her *mestiza* heritage, asserting a post-revolutionary Mexican cultural identity through the use of traditional costumes. Her self-portraits represent dress as a source of resistance against the legacy of colonialism and twentieth-century brands of cultural imperialism. Ultimately, the very machine of mass production and consumption that Kahlo resisted during her

Introduction

lifetime ended up absorbing – and even marketing – her message. As André's essay demonstrates, designers have consistently reworked Kahlo's style since her canonization as a Mexican surrealist in the 1930s. Elsa Schiaparelli honored her with the creation of a dress in her name in the 1930s, and several decades later, Jean Paul Gaultier promoted a seductive Frida vamp to "update" the artist's image for the new millenium. In contrast, Eva Perón wore *haute couture* designs (she was one of Christian Dior's main customers) while also confirming the status of the working classes, who understood her fashion motivations because she shared their humble origins. Like Kahlo's image, the style of the woman who the Argentine masses endearingly referred to as "Evita" has been packaged and repackaged in numerous cultural productions, with Madonna's fashion-conscious portrayal of the Argentine political leader in the 1996 film *Evita* providing just one of many examples. Today, the images of Frida and Evita appear on jacket designs and thematic earrings and handbags throughout the world. The postmodern cultural fetish for self-defining consumption in a global economy, André argues powerfully, is gradually erasing the meaning of these historical figures, "attenuating the urgency of radical social change and displacing it into cultural dilettantism and quietism" (cited in André).

How are fashionable "Latin American" and "Latino" identities mediated in popular culture? Claudia M. Milian Arias explores the fashioning and consumption of "Salvadoranness" in the United States by unveiling the faces of domestic servant Rosa López and supermodel Christy Turlington. López, a political refugee from El Salvador who represents explicit Salvadoranness, gained prominence in the mid-1990s when she served as a defense witness for the O.J. Simpson trial. Turlington, to whom the Metropolitan Museum of Art awarded the *Face of the Twentieth Century Award* and upon whom its Costume Institute's models are modeled, dedicates much energy to Salvadoran American causes and serves as the chairwoman of the *International Committee for Intercambios Culturales* (Cultural Exchanges) of El Salvador. Yet her Salvadoran identity is difficult to place, for the media has "unracialized" and then "reracialized" her ethnic roots, creating an entirely new category in a celebrity-style caste system that projects a "whitened" American ideal. This is "Christy-turlingtonicity," reads *Media Week*. "Maybe she's born with it, maybe it's Maybelline," claim many commercials for the make-up line that Turlington represents. Grounded in critical race theory and fashion studies, Milian Arias' essay demonstrates how cultural mediations of image – and ultimately fashion – are in perpetual motion, highlighting and erasing differences that the media creates and the public consumes.

In Search of Fashion

In the final essay to this volume, cultural critic Fabricio Forastelli returns to his native Argentina to uncover the status of fashion. He arrives on 18 December

Introduction

2003, during an intense political moment that commemorates the victims of police brutality following Argentina's economic collapse in 2001. Just two years later, Forastelli discovers that the state of Latin American fashion is in flux, as individual and collective forms of dress disclose some very powerful emotions. His essay remembers the latter part of the twentieth century, which witnessed a horrifying backlash against democratic values when countries such as Argentina, Chile and Uruguay installed military governments. Strict gender codes imposed clean-cut looks for men and feminine styles for women. Responding to human rights abuses and the plight of the "disappeared" (which refers to the tens of thousands of victims who were killed or whose whereabouts still remain unknown), the Mothers of the Plaza de Mayo in Argentina began to protest near important national monuments in their morning robes and house slippers, as if to state visually that they had no one at home to care for as the regime had taken away their sons and daughters. Today, the Mothers wear a white scarf, embroidered with the names of their missing loved ones, during their weekly marches.

Around this same period, in other parts of the region, the revolutionary movements of Cuba (1959–present) and Nicaragua (1979–90) signaled a turn towards socialist anti-fashion, which associated the elitist pursuit of luxury with the kind of capitalist domination that created dependencies on foreign goods and which exploited the working classes. Indeed, much of Latin America had experienced uneven economic development throughout the twentieth century. In the garment industry, multinationals relied on the cheap labor of native workers for the weaving, assembly and sewing of garments. Yet in recent years, even revolutionary Fidel Castro (Cuba) has occasionally shed his camouflage for the sartorial pleasures of a dark blue designer suit. A heightened awareness of the sweatshop conditions of the *maquiladora* industry, or the export-processing zones established in the 1960s and which still operate today under the North American Free Trade Agreement (NAFTA), sometimes led consumers to boycott specific collections and push for a more socially conscious fashion system. Some designers, such as Carlos Miele (Brazil), have worked with women of the *favelas*, or shantytowns, and various indigenous communities to establish cooperatives that will ensure fair-trade wages for their creations.

Situated in a transnational context, Forastelli's chapter links local forms of knowledge in the urban setting to the global forces at play in Latin American fashions. During a recent visit to Argentina, the author met with university intellectuals and queer activists to find that they have aligned themselves politically with those disenfranchised by neoliberal economic policies. What to wear in such a context?, he asks. "In a city where one out of every two people is unemployed or underemployed, dressing like a Subcomondante Marcos would be a bit of an overstatement," Forastelli writes. At the university, fashionable dress is regarded as a kind of "narcissistic projection," one in which perhaps only visiting scholars dare partake. Furthermore, scholarly interventions deemed fashionable in Europe and the United States may not offer the

Introduction

radical message that Argentine academics, negotiating the promise of the future while facing the memory of dictatorships past, hope to hear. Following a lecture by Gayatri Spivak at the University of Buenos Aires in 2003, firmly grounded in postcolonial theories on cultural imperialism, some members of the audience were known to have joked mockingly amongst themselves – saying "Shut up!" as if to indicate a false surprise – in the months that followed. These days, Forastelli suggests, Argentines want more help deciphering contemporary economic discourses that seem as mysteriously encoded as pre-Colombian hieroglyphs. "As economic recipes after Argentina's deluge become more and more impossible to read in the discourses of transnational financial bodies," he explains, "dress may be the very performance that helps us calculate the ruins of the local amidst the ashes of the economic global market." Even transvestites have modified their dress to reflect the dynamics of everyday life in Argentina. "You would expect Argentine transvestites to dress with glamour," Lohana Berkins explains at a mass protest. "Wrong. Now we dress without glamour, like any other sweaty worker in the streets."

What *is* Latin American fashion and how might we approach the power of its messages and transformations? This volume represents but a star on a larger map, as the very object of our study ultimately reveals whole worlds of culture. Crossing the boundaries of academic disciplines, the transnational scope of this emerging field offers many exciting possibilities for an integrated discussion of dress as it relates to cultural process, identity formation and social change in Latin America. As fashion interprets the present and plots the future, the answer to the question posed above will certainly depend on whom you decide to ask.

Part 1

Unraveling History

Visualizing Difference: The Rhetoric of Clothing in Colonial Spanish America[1]

Mariselle Meléndez

Clothing has played a vital role in the process of identity construction of different ethnic and racial groups. Corporeal decorations, accessories, jewelry, costume, and types of fabrics, for example, have been historically used by diverse social groups to distinguish themselves and visually express particular cultural identities.[2] Clothing has also constituted a rhetorical vehicle to establish power relationships, social categorizations, and degrees of civilization among societies. As Pierre Bourdieu (1984: 7) suggests, systems of domination can find expression in the preferences for certain kind of clothing by fulfilling "a social function of legitimating social differences." In the case of colonial Spanish America, the absence or lack of clothing functioned as a determinant factor to classify and categorize others. Difference was visually and discursively constructed through the rhetoric of clothing.

This chapter examines the importance of clothing as a social marker and a rhetorical strategy in the process of identity construction in colonial Spanish America. First, I discuss the role that lack of clothing played in the narratives of conquest and colonization as well as its importance for some Amerindian societies previous to the Spanish arrival in the so-called New World." Taking into consideration European authors such as Fray Ramón Pané, Cristóbal Colón, Alvar Núñez Cabeza de Vaca, Bernal Díaz del Castillo, Pedro Cieza de León as well as *mestizo* and indigenous writers such as Guaman Poma de Ayala and Inca Garcilaso, I indicate the significance of clothes as a sign of cultural, racial and ethnic superiority. The second part of the chapter is devoted to the role that clothing played as a symbolic tool of recognition as seen in legal and literary texts of the late colonial period.[3] I examine how eighteenth-century remarks by colonial authorities and male writers responded to the importance that clothing played in the visual categorization of the colonial citizens. Within this context, clothing functioned as a "strategic cultural practice" (Pratt 1992:

167) that aimed to express superiority and distinction. As a sign of visual recognition, clothing was manipulated by subaltern groups to challenge the social categorizations that were once imposed by Spaniards to limit social movement. This chapter contends that in the eighteenth century, clothing was considered a dangerous sign of cultural transgression and a destabilizing factor in the colonial social order due to its dynamic nature of appropriation.

Lack of Clothing and the Differentiation of the "Other" in Early Colonial Texts

Walter Mignolo observes that the lack of writing along with the lack of clothing and cannibalism constituted three crucial elements often used in the construction of Amerindian images: "Not having it yet or having it in excess were two cognitive moves used by Europeans in constructing the identity of the self-same by constructing at the same time, the image of the other" (Mignolo 1992: 312). Written as well as visual texts usually contrasted the nakedness of the indigenous people with the presence of clothing in the European to emphasize the superiority of the latter over the former.[4] This was also true for the case of visual representations of the African slaves in the Americas, as early engravings reveal (see Figure 1). Naked bodies symbolized within colonial discourse lack of civilization and social inferiority.

Christopher Columbus offers us the first written accounts in which lack of clothing worked as a visual reminder of the native disposition to be mastered and civilized. In his "Carta a Santángel" (1493/1978: 6), Columbus comments:

> The inhabitant of both sexes in this island, and in all the others which I have seen, or of which I have received information, go always naked as they were born, with the exception of some of the women, who use the covering of a leaf, or a small bough, or an apron of cotton which they prepare for that purpose. None of them, as I have already said, are possessed of any iron, neither have they weapons, being unacquainted with, and indeed incompetent to use them, not from any deformity of body (for they are well-formed), but because they are timid and full of fear.

Native identity was articulated in terms of lack of clothing and weapons that make them inferior but not dangerous.[5] For Europeans, moral and physical nakedness justified their presence in foreign lands as fully civilized clothed men. They were "to dress" the Amerindians in a literal and figurative manner, covering their bodies and their souls with fabric, religion, and reason. From the very beginning of the encounter, clothing came to be understood as a sign of difference and a symbol of power. Even the natives according to Columbus, came to be aware of this fact:

Visualizing Difference

Figure 1.1. Black slaves working the mines on the island of Hispaniola. Benzoni, Girolamo. "Americae, das fu[e]nffte Buch." Frankfurt a. M.: E. Kempfer 1613. (Theodor de Bry's "America." Pt. 5. German.) Courtesy of the Rare Book and Special Collections Library at the University of Illinois at Urbana-Champaign.

[The Indians] have a firm belief that all strength and power, and indeed all good things, are in heaven, and that I descended from thence with these ships and sailors, and under this impression was I received after they had thrown aside their fears . . . and those men who have crossed to the neighboring islands give an admirable description of everything they observed; *but they never saw any people clothed*, nor any ship like ours. (Colon 1978: 8–9, emphasis mine)

This fact was confirmed by Fray Ramón Pané in his *Relación acerca de las antigüedades de los indios* (circa 1498) when he writes that the main *cacique* in the island of *Hispaniola* had foretold the dominion of the natives there by foreigners fully clothed: "And they say this *cacique* affirmed he had spoken with Yucahuguamá, who had told him that those who remained alive after his death would enjoy their dominion for but a brief time because a clothed people would come to their land who would overcome them and kill them, and they would die of hunger" (Pané 1498/1999: 31).[6] Early narratives of the encounter showed how nakedness became an immediate tool to articulate difference.

Natives as well as Spaniards recognized visually what set them apart: the lack of or presence of clothing. Early illustrations of the encounter published between the sixteenth and seventeenth centuries reiterated that fact very clearly. For Europeans, this lack became a social parameter that justified the power to change the other.

Nakedness as a trope of barbarism suffered a twist in 1542 when Alvar Núñez Cabeza de Vaca in his book *Naufragios* presented the Spaniard in a state of nakedness. However, what he considered part of the common nature of the indigenous groups: "All this people of this land go about naked" (Núñez Cabeza de Vaca 1542/1999: 117), became for the Spaniards an accidental result of the shipwreck: "and since we were naked and the cold was very great . . . Those of us who escaped [were] naked as the day we were born and [we had] lost everything we carried with us" (Núñez Cabeza de Vaca 1542/1999: 97, 99). Extreme weather did not seem to affect the rustic nature of the native but it did have traumatic consequences for the civilized/clothed men for whom nakedness was not the norm. Compassion underlies the scenes in which Alvar Núñez highlighted the pain and suffering of their vulnerable bodies, which was so visibly apparent even to the indigenous people: "And with the great grief and pity they felt on seeing us in such a state, they all began to weep loudly and so sincerely, that they could be heard a great distance away" (Núñez Cabeza de Vaca 1542/1999: 101).

Spaniards unaware of Alvar Núñez's disastrous expedition were unable to recognize their civilized fellow countryman, "who experienced great shock upon seeing me so strangely dressed . . . They remained looking at me a long time, so astonished that they neither spoke to me nor managed to ask me anything" (Núñez Cabeza de Vaca 1542/1999: 245). An internalized Western assumption of "nakedness as symbol of barbarism" became, in this passage, an equivocal sign of identification. At this instant, Cabeza de Vaca had become an "Other". Clothing as a sign of civilization would lose its meaning in the eyes of the Amerindians who associated the fully clothed Spaniards with barbaric acts of violence. In this respect Núñez Cabeza de Vaca comments, ". . . saying that the Christians were lying, because we came from where the sun rose, and they from where it set; and that we cured the sick, and they killed those who were well; *and that we came naked and barefoot, and they went about dressed and on horses and with lances*" (Núñez Cabeza de Vaca 1542/1999: 249, 251; emphasis mine).

The above passages show the ambivalent and dynamic nature of the ideology of clothing and nakedness. As instruments of knowledge about others, they depended upon the cultural context in which they were manipulated. In the case of Cabeza de Vaca's persona, both "misrecognitions" functioned discursively as mechanisms to stress Alvar Núñez's suffering, exceptional survival skills, and his lack of uncivilized behavior. Nakedness made the European extra superior while leaving the natives in a fixed state of primitivism.

Bernal Díaz del Castillo, in his *Historia verdadera de la conquista de la Nueva España* (1568), discusses a similar passage to the one described by Núñez

Cabeza de Vaca. Bernal narrates the story of two Spaniards, Jerónimo de Aguilar and Gonzalo Guerrero, who were captured by indigenous tribes and turned into slaves. When found by Spaniards again their physical transformation was outstanding due to an altered physical appearance. Guerrero was so aware of the transformation that, when Hernán Cortés offered to rescue him, he said to his newly freed companion Aguilar, "You go, and God be with you, but I have my face tattooed and my ears pierced, *what would the Spaniards say should they see me in this guise*?" (Díaz del Castillo 1568/1969: 43, emphasis mine). Fear of rejection by his countrymen forced Guerrero to make a decision to stay with his new Indian wife. Guerrero was very well aware of how physical transformation could visually bring rejection. "Seeing" and "being seen," as Homi Bhabha (1994: 76) reminds us, became in colonial discourse crucial elements in the process of subjectification of others.

Guerrero's friend Aguilar, on the other hand, decided to return with the Spaniards. In that first encounter, Aguilar realized how physical appearance was so embedded in the Spanish mentality about the Other. When they saw him they could not recognize Aguilar as one of their own due to his physical transformation: "because Aguilar was nothing other than an Indian." He was finally recognized when he pronounced the following words: "God and Saint Mary and Seville" (Díaz del Castillo 1568/1969: 69). After cultural recognition, clothing worked as a material tool to reinscribe their own "Other" to his former state of civilization: "Cortés at once *ordered him to be given a shirt and doublet and drawers and a cape and sandals, for he had no other clothes*, and asked him about himself and what his name was and when he came to this country" (Díaz del Castillo 1568/1969: 45, emphasis mine). Clothing as a tool of reinstatement was crucial in the ordering and visual recognition in the European civilized world.

The visualization of nakedness and clothing as ordering markers of civilization is also seen in the work of the *mestizo* writer Inca Garcilaso de la Vega, *Comentarios reales* (1609). In Chapter VIII, Book One, he introduces the episode of Pedro el Serrano, a Spaniard who ended up shipwrecked on a deserted island and suffered all kind of adversities. Vega mentions that, after two months, Serrano "saw himself naked as when he was born, and due to the amount of rain, heat and humidity in the region, the few clothes he possesed became rotten. The sun, with its great heat, tired him a lot, because he had neither clothes nor shade to protect him" (Vega 1609/1984: 19, emphasis mine). His physical transformation as a result of the harshness of the weather made him look like a wild boar, his skin all covered with hair. After three years, another Spaniard landed on the island and found Pedro Serrano. The mutual lack of recognition left them in a state of shock: "When they saw each other, it was difficult to determine who was in greater shock. Serrano thought that the other man was the devil disguised as a man, who had come to tempt him in some desperation. The guest understood that Serrano was the devil himself." Both started fleeing from each other out of fear and in the process Serrano screamed: "Jesus, Jesus, deliver me, oh Lord, from the devil!" (Vega 1609/1984: 19–20). The other man finally recognized Serrano as a Christian and convinced him that he was a Christian too. This passage underscores how nakedness and also clothing could potentially become visual misleading tools when categorizing others. Appearance carried within itself deceptiveness inasmuch as clothing as well as nakedness functioned as ambiguous visual artifacts to judge difference.

Nakedness as a manipulative tool of differentiation became evident when Serrano returned to Europe. He decided to travel from Spain to Germany in the same physical state that he found himself on the island: almost naked. He saw the opportunity to financially benefit from this: "for this to be proof of his shipwreck" and "to earn a lot of money" (1984: 20). Lack of clothing was seen as an opportunity to make money and not necessarily as a negative aspect of differentiation. Although lack of clothing was still considered the abnormal, when seen in the European body it became a symbol of admiration and superiority. Even the Royal Majesty was impressed and convinced: ". . . and the Royal Majesty having heard and seen [Pedro Serrano], awarded him four thousand pesos of income" (Vega 1609/1984: 20). Through nakedness, Serrano was able to demonstrate his physical ability to survive in a hostile environment; an act that enabled him to gain respect from his fellow "civilized" men.

Some European authors seemed to disregard how important clothing was within the native societies they encountered. Clothing, for some indigenous societies in Peru and Mexico, was also considered a sign of distinction. In certain native societies clothing was used as an important complement to cultural practices such as celebrations. Pedro Cieza de León in *La crónica del Perú* (1540–50) recalls one Andean celebration '. . . [the Indians] went to the square, where, in different areas, blankets similar to tapestries had been thrown upon the ground for the *caciques* and persons of rank and authority to sit. These men were very well adorned and dressed with their best clothes" (Cieza de León 1540–50/2000: 375). For the indigenous nobility, clothing served as a tool to state visually a cultural affiliation as well as social status. Cieza was in awe when he commented on the luxurious clothes worn by the Inca rulers:

> The clothes of these Incas consisted of short shirts with wide sleeves, extremely adorned with bright embroidery made of gold, while others [shirts] had emeralds and precious stones . . . In order to make these clothes, [the Indians] had and still have perfect colors such as crimson, blue, yellow, black and other sorts, which are really superior to the ones in Spain. (Cieza de León 1540–50/2000: 370)

Garcilaso de la Vega devoted passages to emphasize the importance of clothes in Andean societies. Clothing according to him, was the second most important tax that Inca subalterns paid to the Inca: "In addition to the first tribute which consisted of sowing and harvesting the Sun's lands as well as those of the Inca, the Indians offered another tribute, which was to furnish the clothes, shoes, and weapons for the army as well as for needy people" (Vega 1609/1984: 176). How clothes were made, what kind of fabric was used for a specific social status and who was chosen to make them, offered evidence on how in Inca society clothes represented a symbol of distinction and social class.

The Amerindian writer Felipe Guaman Poma de Ayala in his *Nueva Coronica y Buen Gobierno* (1615) explains in detail how the lineages of the Inca rulers were expressed in their attire. He describes the type of adornments, weapons, fabric, colors and accessories that the Incas chose to mark their lineages. The pictures he included in his chronicle reiterated visually the importance of clothing as a sign of distinction. In these illustrations one can notice easily the differences between the second and the fourth Inca rulers just by the manner in which they wore the mantle, the type of shield (*rodela*) and the style of shirt (*camiseta*). Colors worn by them also corroborated their difference. The second Inca Sinche Roca "wore a red *llauto* (Indian head-dress) decorated with feathers as a sunshade, and his shirt was pink" (Guaman Poma de Ayala 1615/1993: 71), while the fourth Inca had "his coat of arms and sallet (*uma chuco*) were dark blue (*yanas pacra*) . . . His mantle was red, and his shirt was blue in the top, and was decorated with three stripes of adornment (*tocapo*) in the middle, and the ornament (*caxane*) of the lower part was white and green" (Guaman Poma de Ayala 1615/1993: 79). As Guaman Poma de Ayala illustrates, the Incas had their own sophisticated system of social classification based on their style of dress. Clothing worked in their society as visual reminders of power and civilization.[8]

Vega also made clear how even within Inca society, lack of clothing was interpreted as a sign of barbarism. Referring to the pre-Inca society, he explains: "The Indians of that first age dressed like animals, because the only clothes they had was what nature gave them: their own skin" (Vega 1609/1984: 26). Vega reiterates that in that barbaric period "the Indians are so uncivilized that they do not want to get dressed" (Vega 1609/1984: 26). He views the lack of clothing as one of the main elements that distinguished the barbaric pre-Inca Andean society versus the civilized "clothed" Inca culture. For European societies and highly developed Amerindians societies, clothing was not only a social marker but also a tool with which to measure one's degree of civilization.

Andean societies were not the only ones for whom clothing played an important role in the establishment of distinction. Patricia Anawalt reminds us that in Aztec society, indigenous nobility assigned the kind of clothes that each social group was allowed to wear according to their social status (Anawalt 1981: 27). Fabrics such as cotton were designated only for the noble class whereas fabric made of maguey or yucca was intended for the lower class. Aztec nobility strictly controlled what an individual was allowed to wear including color, accessories, and number of feathers. On this issue Hernán Cortés recalled in his "Segunda Carta de Relación" (1520): "In addition to this Mutezuma gave me many garments belonging to himself which, considering that they were woven of cotton without any admixture of silk, could not, I think, be matched in all the world" (Cortés 1520/1962: 85). He also noted that the presence of certain clothes made clear the distinction between Montezuma and others. In his famous encounter with the Aztec ruler, Cortés commented on the visual appearance of Montezuma and his companions: "All three were dressed in similar fashion except that Mutezuma wore shoes whereas the others were barefoot" (Cortés 1520/1962: 69). Again, lack or presence of certain clothing items served as signs of distinction for both societies. Bernal Díaz del Castillo recognized this when he commented in more detail on Montezuma's appearance: "The Great Montezuma was richly attired according to his usage, and he was shod with sandals, the soles were of gold and the upper part adorned with precious stones" (Díaz del Castillo 1568/1969: 193). Both authors seem to have valued Montezuma because of the clothing commodities that the Aztec ruler wore. He is recognized as "different" by the Spaniards solely on the fact that Montezuma had more valuable clothes.

The written and visual accounts of the authors discussed above illustrate the importance of clothing as a symbolic visual item that denoted distinction and connoted civilization. Lack of clothing was associated with barbarism and served as a rhetorical device to justify power over others. Clothing and nakedness as signs of difference constituted exemplary discursive strategies to judge others visually and to impose fixed identities that would fit within specific political agendas.

However, what happened in the eighteenth century when lack of clothing did not seem to be an issue? What role did the rhetoric of clothing play in the process of identity constructions? What role did race, gender, and social class play in the interpretation of dressing habits? In the second part of this chapter I would like to examine the cultural implications of adapting and transforming clothing as a social marker of categorization. I will also discuss how dressing habits for members of the marginalized sectors of the society became destabilizing practices that blurred the social classifications imposed by the colonial order.

The Culture of Excesses: The Symbolic Appropriation of Clothes

In colonial Spanish America, the eighteenth century was a period of profound transformations that affected all sectors of society. Miscegenation had produced a multiracial society that was constantly under the surveillance of colonial authorities. Racial groups were being categorized not only by color but also by their dressing habits, hairstyle, social behavior, cultural practices and eating habits. Social mobility was always a concern for a colonial system that was obsessed with social hierarchies. In a time when color had become an equivocal and misleading sign of differentiation, colonial authorities struggled to legally establish transparent practices of differentiation.

Dressing habits played a vital role in the desire by all sectors of the society to distinguish themselves from the others. Clothing was used not only by the Spanish and Creole aristocracy to visually state their social power and distinction over the rest but it was also used by lower sectors of the society to gain social access to places that were prohibited to them. This practice was very common in the urban centers of the Viceroyalties such as Mexico and Lima.

Jean Descola (1968: 127) observed that during the eighteenth century, people were judged and valued by the luxury of their clothes.[9] Clothing in the late colonial period constituted a symbol of social status and it was used as a determinant visual factor to ascertain who was who in society. The value of what a woman could contribute in her dowry was also determined by the kind of fabric, dresses and jewelry that she owned. These items were used by their husbands as if future objects of investment. The quality of fabric, their places of origin and the color, were important factors in determining how much money a woman had and to what social class she belonged.[10] But clothing as Daniel Roche (1994: 186) suggests, was not only "a way of demonstrating rank and acquiring prestige," for it could also be considered an "essential element in the representations and the realities of a system."

Sumptuary laws enacted by the Crown in the eighteenth century are a perfect example of the importance that dressing habits had in the daily lives of people in the colonies. The Royal decrees aimed to establish racial and social divisions legally by controlling and imposing the use of certain clothes throughout their domains. A *Real Pragmática* enacted in 1716 clearly stated the type of fabric that lower sectors of the population such as mestizos, mulattos, blacks and other *casta* groups were allowed to use. Individuals such as

> blacksmiths, tanners, *esparto* workers, those who work in the spice business, and other people that have similar or even worse jobs, as well as unskilled workers, farm workers and day laborers, are not allowed to wear clothes made of silk, or any other fabric mixed with silk. They are only allowed to wear or bring clothes made of wool, linen or cotton. (Konetzke 1962: 130)[11]

Visual items of clothing became indicators of the social status of colonial individuals. "Seeing" as a way of "interpreting" (Mirzoeff 1999: 13) was to become intrinsically related to the act of classifying and containing the other.

Other royal decrees intended to limit the racial transformation under way in the late colonial period. In 1725, the Viceroy of Peru imposed a royal decree that aimed to control "the outrageous excess of the clothes worn by blacks, mulattos, Indians and *mestizos* of both sexes" (Konetzke 1962: 187). According to the Viceroy, it was crucial to stop these sectors of the population from dressing in such a manner due to "the frequent thefts committed in order to be able to afford such expensive attires" (Konetzke 1962: 187). Controlling the type of clothes that lower sectors of the society could wear was a way to make visually clear the racial and social distinctions necessary in a profoundly hierarchical society.

The control of dressing habits was important because for colonial authorities of the time, color was not a clear factor of distinction. For example, when the skin of a mestizo woman looked lighter or about the same color as that of Spanish woman, it was difficult for the authorities to deny access to racially marginalized women (and men) to spaces that were reserved for whites. If one studies the depiction of a Spaniard woman and the picture of a *mestizo* woman (both shown in Figure 1.2), it is very difficult to differentiate them racially as both are depicted with similar skin tones. What finally determined their racial and social status was the type of dress, hairstyle and jewelry they wore. The wealth of the Spanish woman was expressed with the luxury of her fabric, the detail in her embroidery, and the presence of jewelry and many accessories in her hair. If women from different racial groups, but similar skin color, dressed in similar fashion, as happened in colonial Latin America, the authorities were unable to judge according to visual appearance. Furthermore, a *mestiza* or a *mulata* could end up enjoying rights that were the exclusive domain of white women, a dangerous factor that could threaten the colonial order.

El lazarillo de ciegos caminantes (1775–76) offers us an interesting anecdote that illustrates how pervasive was the association between clothing and social status in the mentality of some sectors of the society. In chapter IV, the narrator who journeyed from Buenos Aires to Lima comments on the good taste of the women from Córdoba when it came to dressing. He emphasizes that for these women, clothing was considered an important fact in their lives. As an example, he mentions the case of a mulatto woman who despite many warnings from the Creole women in town, insisted in exhibiting herself in a "very embellished" fashion (Carrió de la Vandera 1980: 113). She was told several times to dress according to her racial and social status (calidad).[12] One day, one of the *cordobesas* asked the *mulata* to stop by her house. Once inside and in the presence of other Creole women, the *cordobesa* gave the following order to the servants: "to take the mulatto woman's clothes off of her, to whip her, to burn her expensive attire while she watched and then to dress her *with clothes appropriate for her birth status*" (1980: 113, emphasis mine).

The mulatto woman was violently stripped from her clothes and physically punished as a reminder of her social status. In such acts one can observe how clothing in colonial society was considered a threatening element, especially when it enabled women from lower sectors of the society to look like their superiors in the caste system. To restore the "correct" social status, the *cordobesa* made the *mulata* wear clothing that was considered to be appropriate for her race. In this passage race becomes an unstable instrument of categorization and a sign of fear. Racial categories ended up constantly threatened by the manipulation of what to wear. Race as "an organizing principle" and a way of "interpreting the world" (Winant 1994: 2) was challenged by the manipulation of those for whom racial categories of exclusion had been created. The mulatto woman understood the symbolic meaning of clothing as a sign of distinction, and although her transgression was finally suppressed by the *cordobesas*, it did not change the fact that racial categories represented malleable constructions that were usually contested. Colonial authorities were very aware of that when they enacted laws that aimed to control dressing habits:

Visualizing Difference

Figure 2.1. On the left: Spanish woman with mantle. On the right: Mestiza. Both images are by Baltazar Martínez de Compañon as published in *Trujillo del Perú (1779–1789)*. Copyright Patrimonio Nacional.

And because the observance of what is included in this *Pragmática* aims to maintain a good public government in our kingdoms, a government which could find itself disturbed by a multiplicity of jurisdictions, with punishments decided and executed not by the hands of the *Justicias Ordinarias* (Ordinary Justice) alone, we grant them [the Ordinary Justice] with exclusive jurisdiction to inquire about specific cases that merit punishment, and to execute the penalties committed. The punishments against transgressors are to be executed inviolably. (Konetzke 1962: 133)

Clothing was not only a visual parameter with which to categorize race; it also played a crucial role in discourses that attempted to control women's mobility within the public space. Male authorities engaged in a criticism of women as an excessive consumer of clothes made connections between the use of luxurious clothes and women's visibility outside the domestic space. This criticism was not evidence only in literary texts but also in colonial legislation. The decree pronounced in 1716 "Contra el abuso de trages y gastos superfluos" ("Against the abuse of superfluous dresses and expenses") offers solid evidence of the anxiety that colonial authorities felt towards women's control over their own bodies when deciding what to wear and how much to spend for it. The problem for the authorities relied also in the excessive public display of luxurious accessories and the material of the dresses, especially when they were made with fabrics not bought from Spain and its dominions. Referring to people who attended and participated in the *comedias* in the Viceroyalty of New Spain the Crown stated:

> ... and only black and colored silk dresses without embroideries and decorative trimmings will only be permitted, and only if they come from our own Kingdoms' factories,[13] its dominions or our friendly provinces, and we will give as a deadline the day of the celebration of Corpus Christi ... to wear these types of dresses that are already currently worn and *that exceed the regulations that are given now*, with the declaration that this regulation has to be made clear and also inviolably executed starting the same day of Corpus Christi. (Konetzke 1962: 127)

Clothing in colonial legislation served as a mechanism of control that assured Spain's monopoly over the textiles trade. According to authorities, colonial citizens, especially women, had become active consumers of goods such as textiles. For legal authorities, the quality and value displayed in the fabrics were dangerous reminders of the impact of illegal foreign trade in the colonies.[14] The visual display of what was not considered part of Spain's economic hegemony was viewed as a transgression against the colonial order: it was deemed "excessive." Regulating the public display of what to wear constituted a desperate mechanism of social control for a society that had started to distinguish itself by its own sense of fashion and consumption.

The negative repercussions of the excessive display of clothing can also be noted in the letter addressed to the Academic Society of the Lovers of the Country published in the newspaper *Mercurio Peruano* in 1791, entitled "Carta escrita a la Sociedad sobre los gastos excesivos de una Tapada" ("Letter written to the Society about the excessive expenses of a Tapada"). The letter came from an overwhelmed husband who has found himself in a precarious economic situation due to his wife's excessive expenses. He complained how, because of his beautiful wife's fashion taste, he was almost broke. He also protested her insistence and strong desire to attend every public and social event in town, and her need to have a different dress for each occasion. Her exquisite fashion taste had gained the admiration of all of those who attended the same social events. In the process, however, the husband had found himself unable to pay his debts.

There were two elements of his wife's behavior that concerned him: the fact that she demanded to attend every social event in town, and second, her strong belief that a different dress was needed. The husband commented that expenses just in shoes and food surpassed his income of one thousand pesos a year. When it came to dresses, the situation was worse. She demanded "four summer short skirts, and at least two winter ones, because of this we have one thousand fights (that causes her to kick up a fuss), for according to her, the skirt that worked for one social event is not to be used again for the near future. With what money is all this going to be paid?" (Mercurio Peruano 1964: 113). Her obsession with good appearances and quality of clothes was also emphasized in the husband's complaints: "And finally, from where am I going to obtain the money to pay for the services of the Silversmith, who renews all the fashion, and the Tailor, who invents it, and the Merchant who sells on credit to my Wife the lace, the satin, the fetlock, and the lamé?" (Mercurio Peruano 1964: 133–4). Acknowledging a situation beyond his control, the husband concluded his letter by asking for help and expressing fear of the consequences should his wife figure out what he had done: "I beg you to help me with great discretion because she is very clever and acute, and if she finds out that I have written this letter there will be *hell to pay* as she often says" (Mercurio Peruano 1964: 114).

The above letter offers a good depiction of the symbolic implications clothing had for certain women and men in the late colonial period. For the wife, clothing had become a vehicle to express social freedom by making her visible in a society in which "looks" had become a measure for social status and prestige. The opportunity to acquire a new dress enabled her to attend as many public events as she wanted transgressing the traditional role bestowed upon her as a mother and wife circumscribed to the domestic space. Also, through the act of ordering and buying clothes, she exercised power and became an integral part of a local economy that existed because of women's desire to dress well. The business of the silversmith, merchant and tailor depended exclusively on clients like her who were willing to buy a lot and often.

For the husband, on the other hand, clothing represented a dangerous and disruptive factor in his responsibility of "governing" and "managing" the household. He was unable to control her "excesses" that consequently affected his ability to provide and pay others. His social status and reputation was being damaged by her obsession with being well dressed publicly at all times. However, what it seems more bothersome to him was his failure and inability to control her, stating how afraid he was of the possibility of his wife finding out that he had written such letter. Excessiveness in dressing habits had become in the eighteenth century a powerful tool of self-expression, especially for marginalized sectors of the society that were trying to gain visual and social recognition in a male and racially dominated world.

Final Remarks: Clothing as a Visual System of Representation

The colonial texts that I analyze in this essay offer us the opportunity to understand the role of clothing in the process of identity construction in colonial Spanish America. In the early colonial period, the lack versus the presence of clothing became dominant factors in the categorization of the self and the other. It contributed to the establishment of ethnic and racial categories centered on ideas of power, control and domination. Clothing constituted a visual tool to establish differences and to justify superiority over other cultures. Visuality as a "system of representation" (Sturken and Cartwright 2002: 12),[15] played a central role in the desire to know other cultures. In this dynamic process of creating an image of others through the act of looking, clothing became the quintessential paradigm of ethnic, racial and cultural distinction.

In the eighteenth century, however, colonial society had assimilated well the importance of clothing as a symbolic mark of distinction. Clothing was seen as an avenue of self-expression and was manipulated by marginal sectors of the society such as mestizos, blacks, mulattos, and women who wanted to find a space of their own in a society governed by the categories of race, gender and birthplace. The problem for colonial authorities consisted now not on the lack of, but on the obsession with clothes. Sumptuary laws like those discussed before offered a glimpse of the relevant role that clothing was playing in the process of social control and categorization. Regulations regarding what to wear, how to wear it, who was allowed to dress in certain manner and use of a certain fabric, represented crucial mechanisms of control. Clothing as a dynamic process of self-expression was evident in all sectors of the colonial society. Social acceptance through clothing became a tangible possibility of mobility in a highly hierarchical colonial world.

If clothing served as a clear indicator of superiority between European and Amerindian societies, now in the late colonial period it had become an ambivalent indicator of superiority. Racially subordinated subjects manipulated clothing to achieve recognition and in the process, they managed to blur racial and social categorizations that had seemed so transparent in the early colonial period. Clothing complicated the visual process of recognition of the other. Those who were supposed to be different were becoming almost the same. Within this context, clothing would become an obsession. Creoles and Spaniards added more luxurious fabrics and accessories to their styles in order to defeat attempts by marginal sectors of the society that – attempting to ascend socially and economically – dressed like them. Meanwhile, indigenous groups, mestizos, mulattos, blacks, and other castes continued their attempt to look like those who were more socially, economically, politically, and culturally recognized and accepted. The symbolic appropriation of clothing entailed the crossing of legal boundaries and social categorizations that seemed so transparent at an earlier time. Mechanisms of control such as laws and, on some occasions, physical violence, were to become extreme tools to halt the dangerous and dynamic process of social, gender and racial mobility that was underway in a society in which clothing was seen as a visual expression of recognition and as the possibility for social freedom. Spanish American colonial texts thus clearly demonstrate the dynamic nature of clothing and its impact upon processes of identity construction and differentiation.

2

Fashioning Independence: Gender, Dress and Social Space in Postcolonial Argentina[1]

Regina A. Root

The clothing choices of the fashionable few can have a profound impact on the political discourse of a country. The word coined for an item of clothing or a particular style may resonate in the public conscience as a sign of the times or as a symbol of national identity. In Latin American countries today, many women have found their fashion in the *funda*, a special purse for the cellular telephone sold in various colors and designs. At the same time it places the wearer within the multinational paradigm of neoliberal capitalism, the *funda* also remits to the space of the home. Appropriating the vocabulary of the home, the cellular telephone cover becomes a meaning transferred, a term of high fashion that once was used to describe mattress covers. In the late 1990s in the United States, the Zoot-suit experienced a revival along with the nostalgia for the dynamic nightlife of big cities.[2] In the 1940s, *Zoot-suiters*, a term applied to rebellious Chicano males struggling against police brutality and the racism of sailors in Los Angeles, marked their presence in the city by wearing the clothing of their fathers in extra-large sizes.

In the nineteenth century, during the regime of Juan Manuel de Rosas, one's style of dress served to identify different ideologies at a time when the emerging nation's political panorama was dominated by two tendencies: the Unitarians and the Federals. Governed by an intellectual elite based in Buenos Aires, the Unitarians espoused progressive, liberal and European ideas. The Federals, on the other hand, had the support of the fortunate soldiers, or *caudillos*, whose wealth had been acquired following the war for independence from Spain and who ruled Argentina's interior and the lands outside Buenos Aires. Federal authorities, who were in power from 1829 to 1852, issued decrees that legalized a scarlet insignia that ordered and unified all Argentines under the pledge of Federal power, regardless of sex, race or class. The official literature of the period intensified these distinctions, delineating the Federal patriotic subject and implicating the Unitarian in a drama of national betrayal. Because Juan Manuel de Rosas had pushed so vehemently for an ordered and more homogenous society, the vocabulary of fashion made it possible to identify the ideology of the wearer. These enforced dress codes thus enabled authors and bystanders to "read" a person or group in the same way that a twenty-first century North American might read the "suits" on Wall Street.

A combination of seemingly disparate elements joined into a kind of referential union. In real life, a Federal could be identified, if not out of fervor alone, by his scarlet vests, insignias and hair accessories. Anonymous letters to the editor in newspapers of the period employed patriotic metonyms instead of signatures, alluding to these Federal characteristics, such as elongated sideburns in "Patillas" ("Sideburns") or "Los Patilludos" ("Sideburned Ones"). Aristocratic Unitarians, on the other hand, showed a predilection for high French fashions and risked their lives while donning U-shaped (for Unitarian) beards or shades of light blue and green. The mere mention of the word *celeste* (light blue) no longer evoked the colors of the flag for independence but instead remitted to an illegal political position. The usage of metonymical terms that denoted particular styles of uniforms and dress solidified hierarchies that posited Federalists as Argentines and Unitarians as marginalized *afrancesados*.[3]

Drawing from the vocabulary of uniform and fashion, postcolonial Argentine literature relied on a series of associations that can only be explained from a sociopolitical context. Metonymical digression, Roman Jakobson (1990: 130) explains, involves culturally based transfers of meaning in the expression of relational concepts that a given "speech community" finds pertinent to its existence and experiences. According to *The New Princeton Encyclopedia of Poetry and Poetics* (1993: 783), metonymy is "a figure in which one word is substituted for another on the basis of some material, causal or conceptual relation." As a rhetorical device, metonymy forces us to unravel the origins of a word in a diachronic fashion, only to arrive at another object or idea that we wish to express.[4] Michel Le Guern (1973: 104) argues that metonymy can indicate the points of intersection between the history of civilization and language. He cites an example from French, the word *bureau*, used to identify a desk or an office. The term, however, was originally a term for the piece of cloth that covered a desk. When the cloth disappeared from fashion, a transfer in meaning occurred and the *bureau* became the desk itself (Le Guern 1973: 105). In order to capture the cultural and historical context of a metonym, the reader must engage in a study of the subtle transference process and the final shift in language. A metonym, after all, does not disclose the reason for its emergence.[5]

In this chapter, I will analyze the transference of a uniquely Argentine word, the *peinetón*, used to describe a comb worn by women in the region. In the process, I hope to demonstrate how an historical study of dress must ground itself in metonymical process – that is, fashion theorists and historians need to address the linguistic registers describing the accessory or garment to elucidate the significance of its production. First created as a term to designate a fashionable

Argentine style for a tortoiseshell comb worn following the retreat of Spanish colonialism, the *peinetón* became a symbol for the early nineteenth-century woman who, seeking her independence in postcolonial society, participated with more freedom in the public sphere. In this meditation on nineteenth-century gender politics, we will bring into our discussion the vocabulary of fashion and its subsequent treatment in satirical caricatures and the modern poetry of an emerging Argentine nation.

Derived from *peine* ("comb" in Spanish) and later, the *peineta*, the *peinetón* might translate into English as something more elaborate than a "grandiose comb." Not likely to be found in dictionaries of Spanish, one pronounces the Argentine word as if to underline it and proclaim a statement. The accent on its final syllable demands the listener's most undivided attention. At the cusp of its popularity, the *peinetón* would measure up to 3 feet in height and width.

The *peinetón* has often appeared in twentieth century historical and literary works as a mere anecdote, a testimony to an earlier, more distinct Argentine aesthetic. Numerous travelogs feature this art of head dressing, with reactions from foreign visitors ranging from graceful praise to dumbfounded marvel, "the ponderous yet not inelegant comb giving to their little heads a great deal of importance" (*British Packet*, no. 216: 1). Alcides D'Orvigny likened the combs to large convex fans that followed *porteñas*, or port-dwelling residents of Buenos Aires, throughout the city. With dramatic tension, Arsène Isabelle equated the *peinetón* to an elaborate building or fortress in the air (López and Botalla 1983: 191). In New York, words did not suffice. *The British Packet* (no. 348: 2–3) reports that New Yorkers admired the beauty, while contemplating the oddity, of an exhibited Argentine comb. Many writers made associations between the *peinetón* and growing nationalist sentiment. The expressive styles of Argentine ladies, or so it was believed, distinguished them aesthetically from the women of other countries. Even though the *peinetón* now appears only in museums, one may still hear this partisan declaration in prominent designer circles or on the nationally televised Roberto Giordano fashion hour.[6]

Emergence of the *Peinetón*

We can trace the evolution of the European hair comb into an elaborate and enlarged *peinetón* to the move for independence from Spain. The Spanish brought the first hair combs to Argentina in the eighteenth century. By the nineteenth century, Argentines looked to the fashions of France in an attempt to distance themselves from the customs they shared with the Spanish.[7] The romantic rebellion in Europe had brought about several changes in fashion and had affected women's hairstyles most markedly. The intricately woven hair designs of courtly Versailles, having reached dramatic heights, evolved with revolution into more free-flowing styles. By 1820, perhaps as a nostalgic revisit of monarchical times, one popular style, the *chignon*, appeared in French fashion plates. This style incorporated tortoise-shell combs that secured ornately woven hair atop a woman's head, its extended height leading to the style's portrayal as a hair fashion for giraffes. While it seems possible for the Argentine *peinetón* to have evolved from the *chignon*, it is likely that a cross of influences ultimately formed this unique hair fashion.

According to British ship captain E. E. Vidal, a hybrid of foreign styles marked the 1820s, especially when it concerned women's clothing. The women of Buenos Aires, he writes, "adopted a style of dress between the English and French," while retaining the Spanish *mantilla*, a kind of shawl (Vidal 1820: 49).[8] The essentials of female dress during this period included, "a head-dress, consisting either of a handkerchief of gold gauze with braids of diamonds, or of chains of gold, twisted in and out of their shining black hair..." (Vidal 1820: 49). Even with meticulous descriptions such as this one, it is difficult to know just how similar the early Argentine headdress was to its French counterpart. By 1823, however, the crown-like *peineta* began its decade-long transformation into the lofty *peinetón*. When the word *peinetón* appeared for the first time in the advertising section of *La Gazeta Mercantil* in 1830, it would also have begun to distance itself from any European comb in size alone (López and Botalla 1983: 11–12). An instant commercial success, the Argentine comb would monopolize the sidewalks of Buenos Aires through 1837.

When attempting to describe the *peinetón*, most reporters admitted to a loss of words. A reporter from *The British Packet* would recount:

> How shall we describe the immense comb, which now forms so prominent a part of the head-dress of the fashionable fair of Buenos Ayres, its fretwork with ornaments, and the graceful mode in which it is arranged in the hair – truly we might exclaim with the "noble Poet,"
> "I can't describe it, though so much it strike,
> Nor liken it, – I never saw the like." (no. 271: 3)

More than with any other fashion of the nineteenth century, male reporters attempted to "capture" the essence of the immense comb, desiring to crystallize its most outstanding characteristics while calling for the end of its popularity. The fashion chronicles of *El Monitor* describe the comb as "an exaggeration so exaggerated that it exceeds the limits of the exaggerated; and if women believe that the enormity of the combs favors them, they are mistaken."[9] The newspaper found no practical use for the *peinetón*, only to quip that a woman with such a monstrous head could best serve her family as a walking parasol (no. 152: 2).

The Pursuit of Space

With great artistic license, contemporary author Eduardo Gudiño Kieffer tantalizes us with the idea that the *peinetón* is as Argentine as the pampas, its exaggerated size perhaps inspired by the horizon of geographic expanse. He writes:

> I think, with the fantasy afforded me as a writer, that the vastness of the horizons of the pampas transformed the Spanish *peineta* into a *peinetón*. Why not think that a river-ocean, that a land apparently without limits, would enlarge not only ideas but also the simplest of "things"? (Gudiño Kieffer 1986: 10)

The seemingly limitless national boundaries – from the continuous grazing lands of the pampa to the River Plate – contributes to a feeling of infinite space and promise. The vast Argentine landscape, as Gudiño Kieffer proposes, engenders ideas and brings about the transformation of the simplest things into larger-than-life objects, allusions to national pride.

Following the thread of this creative proposal, one might propose that the *peinetón* served to demarcate symbolically the national boundaries of the Argentine nation under a new flag. Gudiño Kieffer's assertion that the comb emerges alongside the quest for independence and the development of unique, national customs proves most useful. At this time, however, Argentina seemed anything but united. Following independence in 1810, the region was divided and fragmented. The tumultuous evolution of the United Provinces of the River Plate into an Argentine Confederation saw its share of power-driven personalities, contradictory political poses, and territorial disputes (both internal and international).[10] Tensions escalated between arrogant city leaders in Buenos Aires and the *caudillos* of the interior who believed themselves independent from their political decisions. Despite the ebbs and flows of civil war, the move to forge the underpinnings of a national identity began. It was during the years of the Argentine Confederation, and not independence, that the native comb finally grew into the outlandish *peinetón*.

Francine Masiello notes that postcolonial Argentina experienced a temporary repositioning of gender roles, due in part to the domestic role attributed to women in raising young, upstanding patriots, and to the shift in the representation of the sexes. She writes:

> The emphasis on nuclear family life, childbearing, and female participation in civil society was subject to shifting interpretations and uses, and the feeble separation of spheres of activity – in which the masculine domain was identified with the public sphere and the feminine with the private – already showed signs of wear. Indeed, the cultural documents of the period indicate a less stable set of gender assignments than one might have expected. (Masiello 1991: 20)

In this uncharted moment in the public sphere, women stood to gain a more pronounced access, despite numerous obstacles and male anti-sentiments regarding their political participation. The Generation of 1837, a literary society comprised mostly of Unitarian males, would capitalize on these gender shifts and spatial transformations in their literary work. When voicing resistance to Federalist power, these writers assumed women's pseudonyms and the rhetoric of fashion writing, thereby initiating "the possibility of feminine discourse as a way to structure the space of the imagination" (Masiello 1991: 23). With the possibility of a feminine discourse, combined with the spatial flux underway in the public sphere, a woman and her *peinetón* could not go unnoticed.[11]

At the core of headdressing lay the quest for co-existence in the public arena. When worn in public, the seemingly frivolous, exuberant *peinetón* commanded from all observers the special acknowledgment of its wearer. Despite the fact that a woman faced several obstacles, among them legal limitations imposed on her *because* of her gender, the *peinetón* endowed her with the status of a conceivable, almost unavoidable, public participant. Even though the period's documents suggest that the comb caused headaches and hair loss, women still sought to claim public space of their own with the help of this fashion accessory.[12] Undoubtedly, the *peinetón* served as a symbolic gesture, a visual demonstration of what was on a woman's mind.

Women who aspired to wear the *peinetón* received much comment in the national press, provoking several unfavorable comments. Many men complained about the aesthetic of the comb in letters to the editor, denouncing what they saw as the ghastliest proportions ever concocted, the monstrous height of the comb contrasting too sharply with women's delicate attributes. Out of concern for domestic peace and prosperity, one military officer, *El Oficial*, sent a series of provocative letters regarding headdressing trends to the editors of *La Argentina*. Likening the enormous superstructures in women's hair to a national landmark, he writes, "All of you women are walking around so weighed down that you have lost a lot of your natural grace, for each of you wears the tower of the School on her head" (no. 19: 14). Referring to today's Colegio Nacional de Buenos Aires, the official envisions, with horror, the weight of an all-male institution flaunted atop women's heads.

In the push to arrange the public arena, men found themselves obstructed by the very presence of women. With the comb, women had the ability to shift the directions of men, or, in some cases, to run them off the street. *The British Packet* portrayed the woman and her comb as a military paratrooper, her potentially explosive *peinetón* endowing her with a "grenadier-like appearance" (no. 356: 3). These allusions to battle and a volatile public sphere in the wake of invading females, prompted many to implore that women desert their combs and regroup within a more "appropriate" domain, the home.

Conspiring against the *peinetón*, the visual arts anticipated a change in roles and the redistribution of public spaces, a process that ultimately led to the headdress's disappearance. Like the warriors before her, the *peinetón*-wearing woman was dressed to kill and prey to the Look.[13] Her towering comb linked the "sight of something" to the terror of castration, with effects not unlike those produced by the snakes on Medusa's head.[14] The sardonic caricatures in César Hipólito Bacle's "Extravagances of 1834" illustrate this shift beautifully. As women's combs take to downtown Buenos Aires, a man swears out of the desperation, "Damn the *peinetones*!" His exclamation serves as a heated response to the exaggerated proportions and oblique angles of the headdress that seemed to invade sidewalks. Having successfully generated her own expanse in the public arena, one woman parades down the middle of the street and right through two men. She injures one in the groin and permanently maims the other, who cries, "Ouch, she has gouged my eye!" The enlarged crests of women seem to overpower the top hats of men. With a confident stride, the woman at center responds in a demanding tone, "Disperse yourselves, gentlemen!"

In response to such disturbing scenarios and the perceived onslaught of traffic jams, the city of Buenos Aires adopted a set of social codes that required men

Figure 2.1. On the left: "Woman from Buenos Aires: Summer Dress." On the right: "Woman from Buenos Aires: Ball gown." Both lithographs are from César Hipólito Bacle's *Trajes y costumbres de la provincia de Buenos Aires* (Buenos Aires: Bacle y Compañía, 1833).

Figure 2.2. "Peinetones on the Street." Satirical caricature from César Hipólito Bacle's *Trajes y costumbres de la provincia de Buenos Aires* (Buenos Aires: Bacle y Compañía, 1833).

to pass comb-wearing women on the left. "Men with Sideburns" responded to what they viewed as an unjust distribution of space in a heated letter to the government-sponsored *La Gazeta Mercantil* (The Mercantile Gazette). These supporters of Rosas insisted that women discard their immense combs and puffed-up sleeves for a more graceful appearance, as their current fashion accessories had them monopolizing city sidewalks (*Gazeta Mercantil* no. 1962: 2). A group of mothers responded in agreement with such male critiques, arguing that the *peinetón* symbolized the modern-day demise of family values. Claiming that some fashionable ladies deprived their families of bread so as to flaunt expensive combs, they also criticized women for storming through areas designated solely for men. "Pro-Family Mothers" curtly reprimanded the *peinetón*-wearing women who invaded spaces off limits to them. They write, "Our friendly countrywomen can not be happy when they assume the fashionable *peinetón* and the ambition of men" (*Gazeta Mercantil* no. 2923: 2). Moved by the high volume of responses, the editor of *La Gazeta Mercantil* "cut the matter short, (all Editors being arbitrary) and declared the affair to have been sufficiently discussed," yet another indicator that the *peinetón* seemed to take up much too much space.[15]

Another indignant reader, who called himself a "Poor Christian," called on ecclesiastical authorities to mandate the removal of the distracting devices. In the wake of a solemn sermon, one congregation witnessed with alarm a man who crossed himself when some women – and their large combs – passed his pew. If women focused instead on the realm of the unseen and the devout virtues inherent to their sex, the Poor Christian argued, then men might dedicate their thoughts to matters of spirit and not to the *peinetón*. In a letter to *El Lucero*, he denounced the invasion of females in the Church. *The British Packet* would translate into English this summons for prompt clerical action:

> *To those who can remedy it*: – Is there any ecclesiastical or secular authority in the Capital of the United Provinces of the River Plate, who will unsheath a sword of fire against the want of reverence to the house of God? If there be, they ought to put forth a ray of their authority against those who are forgetful of that sacred place. What great irreverence can there be, in a people the most Catholic and religious of the Christian world, than to see a crowd of females enter the temple of God with castles and towers upon their heads, horrifying even the least religious among us? Some of these females, in addition to their large combs, have high *banderas* [flags] on each side, so that when they enter by the door they appear as if wishing to dispute the homage due to the God of Majesty. Is it not horrible to the Catholic possessing the least piety, to see a female who, not being able to enter the narrow passage to these temples passes through the Sacristy with these imperial crowns, and by the High Altar, to take her place in the church? Is it not painful to the pious Christian to be a spectator of these things occurring as they do every moment? . . .
>
> The females come with diadems of such an enormous height, that the religion of Jesus Christ imperiously demands a reform or a prohibition against their entering the Church.

Because the crown awaits in heaven, the author suggests, it must not be flaunted here on Earth. The presence of *peinetón*-wearing women and the "distractive" qualities of their fashion obsessions competed with more than higher ground. The Poor Christian's letter insists that voguish women were wreaking havoc with the hierarchy of religious ceremony on Earth. Because of the large size of their combs, women sidestepped the narrow passageways that they had used traditionally and barged through those entrances reserved for clergyman. In the eyes of the congregation, women appeared to have invaded the Sacristy, when in reality the sermon had not yet begun. With this change in movement and spatial allocation, it appeared that a woman could go wherever she pleased, a sacrilegious act in the eyes of many. If not controlled, the *peinetón* threatened to besiege all vestiges of power with its demands for space, both physically and symbolically.

A Change in Language

Within the context of spatial and social relations, the *peinetón* had brought about a consciousness of women's rise to prominence in public life. The comb would continue to evoke both criticism and admiration. I would argue that, as the struggle between Unitarians and Federalists intensified, the *peinetón* became a kind of political billboard that women carried when making a public show of support of Confederate power. One advertisement found in several daily newspapers announces the sale of combs engraved with a miniature portrait of Rosas.[16] As political tensions grew, so did the *peinetón*, until it measured one yard in width and another in height, an ample span for lengthy patriotic slogans. By 1833, the very year that Rosas was granted dictatorial powers, some combs proclaimed, "Confederation or Death" and "Long live the Argentine Confederation!"

In due time, the *peinetón* became an ambiguous term, subsequently undergoing a catachresis. That is to say, the term underwent a change in meaning that concluded with its canonization as a metonym. Speakers thus misapplied one word for another on a consistent basis. In addition to identifying the comb that women wore in public, the pronouncement of the word *peinetón* now held other connotations. In news accounts and popular poetry, the *peinetón* became a shorthand term used to tie women to the events of the public arena. Reserved for third-person accounts, the word classified the woman whose public presence and signature comb had to be taken into account. In order to clarify this shift for its English readers, *The British Packet* issued an editorial statement regarding the *peinetón*. Reporting the presence of four hundred large combs at a political gathering, one journalist prepared the ground for future readings with a special note. From that point on, he writes, the newspaper would view the *peinetón* as "a new figure of speech to designate the ladies" (no. 417: 3).

The Limits of Representation

Playing with the indisputable associations drawn from the association of gender, fashion and politics, authors and artists alike incorporated the metonymical *peinetón* into their portrayals of women and public spaces. However, as the metonymy of fashion evolved in popular literature and fashion caricatures, it presented women in an increasingly degraded light. Ridiculing their potential subjectivity so as to better serve male political interests, artistic pretense turned the very symbol of female presence against women. Out of her presence and implied ambition alone, the public *peinetón* became nothing short of a prostitute. Poetic gestures encouraged the need for male protectionism in the effort to curtail women's questionable circulation in public and to encourage their return to a morally enhanced domestic lifestyle.

In her study of *Sex and Danger in Buenos Aires*, Donna Guy maintains that a national discourse on prostitution has served as a means of social control in Argentina at numerous historical junctures. Within this context, the designation of strict gender roles became a method with which to force women out of the public sphere and into the home. She writes, "If women's social and economic roles linked family and nation, then women who existed outside traditional family structures threatened the nation" (Guy 1991: 2–3). Some premises regarding the public woman argued that the psycho-sexual impulse for fashionable clothing and expensive jewelry helped lead to her demise (Guy 1991: 49). The link between a woman and fashion revealed a most difficult paradox: while expected to follow the fashions of the day, a woman also ran the risk of others speculating undesirably about her moral character.

In the annals of popular literature, a unique poetic discourse developed in response to the at once desired and despised *peinetón*. By appealing to widespread sexist attitudes and poking fun at the new roles women had assumed, disdainful depictions of the "beautiful sex" delineated new perimeters of public and artistic representation. A series of verses published in the 1830s by the government-sponsored Imprenta del Comercio illustrates this point. "Lo que cuesta un peinetón" (What a Peinetón Costs"), which as a result of catachresis would have read "What a Woman Costs," details the precarious lives of men who find themselves at the whims of female fashion dictators. The poem's title, repeated throughout the poem for rhythmic and humorous effect, serves as an anaphora. Throughout, the reader cannot help but notice the high price of the *peinetón* and the warning to men of their imminent fall.

A complementary poem, "El que paga el peinetón" ("He Who Pays for the *Peinetón*"), suggests that enemies of the Confederation could not possess the funds necessary to please a woman's tastes, their prospective mates resorting to immoral acts to satisfy the female vice for fashion. "He Who Pays the Peinetón" categorically identifies *peinetón*-touting women as prostitutes (and adulterers) who feel they must cheat on their lovers to obtain a comb, that ultimate prize for sexual conquest. Most importantly, women are cast as Unitarian sympathizers, a tactic that reproached the *peinetón* symbolically while also serving as propaganda against the State's most pronounced political enemy.

Throughout these verses, the poetic voice evokes the color green, also the color of the Unitarian uniform, in a denigrating fashion. In Spanish, to describe something as inherently "green" is to regard the object as potentially perverse and overtly sexual. When the poetic voice paints a section of Buenos Aires "green," it weaves the reader through the windows and alleys where desperate Unitarian women linger, awaiting their prospective buyers. The omniscient narrator observes Buenos Aires street life with a careful eye, noting the city's open spaces and describing the interaction between the sexes. Strangely enough, the poem offers few descriptions of the men who pay for the *peinetón*. Instead, the reader takes on a male gaze, observing silently the women who have strayed from their homes into the irredeemable domains of public circulation.

Glimpses into the sad appearance and lives of individual women reinforce the perverse context of the poem. Beautiful, ugly, young and old . . . In the spectacle of the public sphere, women parade themselves before men as if prized cattle in a show, the onlookers evaluating each of their poses and contemplating the investment. A young beauty initiates the game of illusion and deceit. Engaged in a starvation diet, she configures her body to appeal to the man who will make her *peinetón* payments. Another girl fakes tears to evoke her beau's pity and, should she be so successful, a marriage proposal. Marriage, however, seems the last of her desires; the poem implies that she desires a lavish comb for an engagement gift. Each of these young women appears at the crossroads between a virtuous life and irredeemable behavior. The penchant for fashion seems to push them into the first stages of a dishonest lifestyle, with the obsession for the comb providing the final transformation.

Every woman risks being "read" by others in a potentially unbecoming fashion, like the way in which a *piropo*, a flirtatious remark made by males, might address the clothing or body parts of a female passerby. Even if a woman is married, this does not shield her from others who regard her public character with suspicion. The extravagant *peinetón* does not necessarily represent the wealth of a woman's husband, the poem suggests. It can also serve as a kind of public revelation, alluding to the possibility that the wife is engaged in a clandestine affair. The poem presents a chain of gossip that, while calling into question the motives of the *peinetón*, also hopes to catch a glimpse of the man who might have paid her way.

The public spaces of "He Who Pays for the Peinetón" become the setting of a makeshift morality play, a place where the reader can explore the outrageous defects of Unitarian life and the prostituted body that predominates the cityscape. The poem forces the reader to assume the Federal gaze and, in the process, to view negatively the position of the Unitarian in postcolonial society. Identified as a Unitarian by her light blue dress, one woman described in the poem desperately searches the neighborhood for a suitor who will pity her impoverished state and reward her with a *peinetón*. Because she is a Unitarian, everyone avoids her like the plague, fearing that she might carry a transmittable disease (stanza 5: "That fiery beast of a girl/ Wearing a light blue dress/ All fear she may be infected..."). Through metonymy, the *peinetón* would represent the object of lust as well as its embodiment. By relegating fashionable women to the political margins of Unitarian politics, government propaganda pushed its own ideas on the redistribution of space and power in postcolonial society.

A glimmer of hope appears in the final stanza of "He Who Pays the Peinetón." Over the bustling street scene, a young woman stares out the second-story window of her family home, daydreaming of the prince who will buy her a *peinetón* (stanza 18). Though she desires so desperately to join in the freedoms below, her family has protected her from the ensuing clash of the sexes below. During the fleeting moment at which the poetic voice focuses on the young female, her image evokes neither pity nor fear, which separates her from the multiple, degraded visions of the *peinetón* below.

Having situated the comb within the framework of female prostitution and partisan discourse, government-sponsored propaganda established new boundaries of representation. Popular poetry advocated a more pronounced separation between the public and private spheres, while also mandating the elimination of women from political life. The word play inherent in the *peinetón*, or the public woman, sought to undermine the value of women in the political development of the nation. Having assigned the *peinetón* and Unitarians alike to fixed, undesirable positions within the public sphere, poetic discourse hinted at the desired alternative. The government could force women to return to the less politicized and more traditional spaces of the home.

In early nineteenth century Argentina, the notion of a female-dominated public arena remained an option suitable only for satirical caricatures and burlesque commentary. While postcolonial society called on women to help men reach their goal of independence from Spain, and later, to manifest their patriotic support for the Confederation, the roles designated to them limited their participation both spatially and politically. While the exuberant *peinetón* brought about some awareness of these roles, literary representations ultimately painted this newfound mobility in a degrading light and plotted the return of women to the family home. Authors and artists alike used the metonymical *peinetón*, which equated a woman's comb with public participation, to reflect on the breakdown of rigid gender roles and the transformation of public spaces. Appropriating fashion as metonymy in order to bar women from access to critical public events, popular poetry and caricatures reminded women that their fashionable crowns granted them reign over their domestic obligations and not over the streets of Buenos Aires.

3

The Traveler's Eye: Chinas Poblanas and European-inspired Costume in Postcolonial Mexico

Kimberly Randall

While recent scholarship has made great strides in writing the rich history of the indigenous costumes and textiles of Mesoamerica, comparatively little attention has been paid to the historical influence that women's European fashions had in the region, especially in Mexico. This chapter seeks to explore and illustrate the conditions that helped define female fashion and standards of beauty in the four decades following that nation's independence from Spain in 1821. As a former Spanish colony, Mexico at independence already presented a rich and unique cultural mix of Spanish, French, Indian and even Asian influences that was readily reflected in the clothes and their symbolic importance.

As a representative of both feminine beauty and Mexican nationalism, the *china poblana* helps us to understand how these seemingly diverse costume influences converged and evolved both during and after the colonial period. The *china poblana* with her costume of European petticoats and colorfully embroidered Spanish-style blouse figures predominantly, especially in the detailed descriptions provided by travel writers in the nineteenth century. For her inventive use of lace, sequins and embroidered embellishments, the *china poblana* was many times praised for her "taste" and "extraordinary beauty."

The seeming independence of the *china poblana* contrasted starkly with the more cloistered lives of Mexican elite women for their movements were often limited to a morning walk to mass dressed in traditional Spanish black with mantilla and an afternoon ride along the Paseo in a closed carriage. Because the *chinas poblanas* were highly visible, travel writers were quick to notice the throngs of these well dressed, independent and often attractive young women in Mexico's urban areas. Matters of economy often determined differences in their costume; therefore it was common to see skirts in both printed cotton and scarlet cashmere. Nevertheless, the *china poblana's* basic costume was comprised of a skirt in contrasting colors, a ruffled or embroidered blouse, and the ubiquitous shawl or *rebozo*, which could be artfully manipulated to cover and reveal the neck and arms. Spangles and sequins, silk shoes and white stockings, a neckerchief and sash, and layers of tinkling jewelry were added to complete the artful ensemble.

The early independence years are especially important to the costume historian for it is clear from visitors' observations that diverse examples of Mexican fashion converged on the Mexican capital and other urban areas. Porfirio Diaz (1830–1915), the Mexican dictator who looms largely over the final decades of the nineteenth century, effectively segregated the classes, reserving Mexico City's best neighborhoods for the wealthiest individuals. The ethnic and social diversity of the population became largely invisible in the capital, and travel writing confirms that undiluted French fashion predominated in many urban areas. Even important accessories like the Spanish *mantilla* waned in popularity by the end of the century.

A more complete picture of the diversity of styles that coexisted during the early independence period can be drawn from the commentary of travel writers who flooded Mexico during the nineteenth century. In the spirit of Romanticism, many Europeans and Americans traveled abroad to write and publish their observations about cultures seemingly different from their own, which were quickly modernizing. During the early decades of Mexico's independence, they were able to observe firsthand the adoption and interpretation of fashion – both native and foreign. In recent years, however, many scholars have examined the personal motivations and biased perspectives of travel writers in Mexico as many of their opinions were influenced by what they stood to gain either politically or financially in the region. Despite their many prejudices, the travel writers as a group display remarkable consistency in their descriptions of Mexico's many costumes.

Fashion and Identity in Early Colonial Society

Firstly, for a better understanding of the role that fashion played in the early independence period, a brief overview of colonial history and society is necessary. The personal experiences of those who participated in the conquest helped to shape the colonial experience, influencing the generations to come. These first Spanish settlers of Mexico or New Spain as it was known, included groups of lesser gentry, especially those young men who had been cut off from the family fortune by the rules of primogeniture (Kandell 1988: 87–8). Others who were too young to have reaped the riches of Spain's re-conquest of the Moorish lands in the southern peninsula were also attracted to the unique opportunity that the colonies presented (Kamen 1997: 23). Intent on making a better life for their families, these colonists had ambitions beyond serving for the greater glory of the Spanish crown. Anthony Pagden in *Lords of All the World* writes that the early settlers considered the colonies "as places where they might secure for themselves goods and a way of life which they could never have hoped to acquire at home" (Pagden 1995: 6). With the vast amounts of silver that were later discovered in the northern regions beyond Mexico City, colonists had access to more than enough resources to rival the courtly elegance of Madrid (Kandell 1988: 180). The importance of appearances was emphasized, and the outward manifestation of material success came to symbolize nobility and power in the colonial period (Cortina 1994: 74).

Racial Hierarchies: The Caste System

Along with their newly-found splendor, Spanish colonists created a highly stratified social system, which by the end of the sixteenth century had separated the population strictly by race, not just Spanish and Indian but African as well (Seed 1982: 572). Mexico City, the seat of viceregal power, became the stage for racial mingling on a large scale, and intermarriage created new groups of people, mixed races that the Spanish referred to as *mestizos* (Spanish-Indians) and *mulatos* (Spanish-blacks) and *zambos* (black-Indians) (Seed). By the seventeenth century, the three main racial categories (Spaniard, Indian and black) and their offspring were no longer identifiable in the kaleidoscopic society that had emerged. The Spanish felt threatened by the growing miscegenation, and a new model known as the *sistema de castas* was devised to impose hierarchical divisions that were based on the proportion of Spanish blood in one's family (Cope 1994: 24–5). The European-born Spaniards or *peninsulares*, the rulers of viceregal society, occupied the top tier and directly beneath them were the American-born Spaniards, the *creoles* (Stayton 1996: 71). Those with no Spanish blood, it was presumed, would take their place on the bottom rung of society.

At the same time luxurious European costume and the public parade of finery became a defining feature of city life during the colonial period. The Alameda, the fashionable promenade of Mexico City, was the site for the daily display of wealth; so firmly entrenched was the tradition that it remained in evidence in the postcolonial period (Stayton 1996: 73). While the church encouraged members of the indigenous population to cover themselves up, the adoption of European fashions by *mestizos* and *mulatos* was discouraged (Cope 1994: 22). In the eyes of the Spanish, many *castas* were simply social climbers, but more importantly, they also used costume to signal their unwillingness to take their assigned place in the hierarchy (Cope 1994: 6). Over the centuries, sumptuary laws were frequently passed to discourage the *castas* from going too far in their adoption of European dress, and parameters outlined the cut and color of their garments (Keleman 1965: 3).

Colonial Splendor

The desire for courtly grandeur and aristocratic greatness meant that the colonists required much in the way of material goods to achieve their vision. Colonists were able to import from Spain a myriad of products ranging from olive oil to leather goods, but textiles were by far the most highly coveted of all items (Boyd-Bowman 1973: 335). The demand was so great that Spain could barely begin to meet the colony's need for fashionable fabrics (Boyd-Bowman 1973: 334). Ida Altman's examination of New Spain's notarial records from the first half of the sixteenth century revealed that of all the artisans in Mexico City, those representing the clothing trade were most numerous (Altman 1991: 430).

Spanish colonial expansion soon extended to the Philippines, and before long, colonial inhabitants were clothed in the finest silks from China. All classes in colonial Mexico were dressed in fabrics from Asia; including the Indian population who were dressed in cottons from India while the *creoles* and *mestizos* kept the finest silks for themselves (Schurz 1918: 390). In the eighteenth century the trade with Manila was praised by the viceroyalty as these "Chinese goods form the ordinary dress of the natives of New Spain" (Schurz 1918).

Bourbon Reforms and the Wars of Independence

In the century before independence, several events conspired to bring about the end of Spanish domination in Mexico. The death of the sickly and emotionally unstable Charles II (1661–1700) signaled the end of Hapsburg rule (Kandell 1988: 235), marking a new period in which Spain would take a more active interest in colonial affairs (Rodríguez 1994: 2). A Bourbon successor was found in Philip V (1683–1746), grandson of the French monarch Louis XIV – the first indication that Spain was entering a new period of reform that found its best expression with Charles III (1716–88) (Kandell 1988: 236).

In 1793, Spain's Prime Minister Godoy declared war on France in retaliation for the execution of Louis XVI and was promptly defeated by Napoleon. Within Spain, the growing unpopularity of Charles IV (1748–1819), Queen María Luisa and Prime Minister Godoy led to a movement of support for the crown prince Ferdinand VII (1784–1833). A mutinous mob forced the abdication of Charles IV in 1808, but before Ferdinand VII could take power, Napoleon, already angry at Spain for trading with his enemy England, abducted Ferdinand and installed his brother Joseph as King of Spain (Fuentes 1992: 242).

These events created a great feeling of uncertainty in the colonies. If France now controlled Spain did the viceroyalty have the power to govern in the colonies? This question led to a long power struggle in Mexico City between the *peninsulares*, who felt it was in their best interest to remain loyal to Spain, and those *creoles* leaning towards independence (Kandell 1988: 268–9). In the years after 1808, parish priests from the outer provinces took up the cause for independence and were joined by groups of Indians and *castas* in the fight for freedom.

In 1821, after years of bloodshed, starvation and disease, Mexico emerged as an independent nation, but independence didn't make a marked improvement in the lives of the people. In the decades that followed, Mexico would fall under the control of a new military elite who would break apart the historical power bases of the *peninsulares* and *creoles* (Kandell 1988: 307). The Indians and lower-class *castas* remained outside governmental concerns, as ostracized as they had been before independence (Sayer 1985: 97).

Early Independence: A Passion for Dress

Many observers in the first decades following independence noted the passion for dress amongst Mexican women. This fondness for finery and a sophisticated understanding of the symbolic power of fashion had a long tradition that was not only limited to the upper classes. In a romantic adventure novel by Captain Marryat written in 1843, the author describes the importance of luxurious dress for the women of Monterey, California, which still belonged to Mexico during this period.

> The women dress richly and with an admirable taste; the unmarried girls in white satin, with their long black hair falling upon their shoulders; their brow ornamented with rich jewels when at home, and when out, their faces covered with a long white veil, through which their dark eyes will shine like diamonds. (Marryat 1843: 66)

Richard Henry Dana, a Boston sailor, while quite taken with the style of the women of Monterey, was quick to relate the reckless abandon of many in their pursuit of fashion.

> The fondness of dress among the women is excessive, and is often the ruin of many of them. A present of a fine mantle, or of a necklace or pair of ear-rings, gains favor of the greater part of them. Nothing is more common than to see a woman living in a house of only two rooms, and the ground for a floor, dressed in spangled satin shoes, silk gown, high comb and gilt, if not gold ear-rings and necklace. If their husbands do not dress them well enough, they will soon receive presents from others. They used to spend whole days on board our vessel, examining the fine clothes and ornaments, and frequently made purchases at a rate which would have made a sempstress or waiting-maid in Boston open her eyes. (Dana 1992: 89)

Dana also describes the very same brow ornament that Captain Marryat observed on the women of Monterey during the 1840s and says the following: "a band, also, about the top of the head, with a cross, star, or other ornament in front, is common" (Dana 1992: 89). Known as *ferronerie*, these delicate bands were a Romantic era adaptation of a Renaissance fashion accessory. A nineteenth-century portrait of a woman by the Spanish painter Antonio María Esquivel also shows such an accessory. The Parisian fashion publication, *Petit Courrier des Dames*, from the year 1835 and into the 1840s, has several fashion plates that depict a variety of delicate *ferroneries* adorning the brows of women. Adoption of such a seemingly minor accessory provides insight into the awareness the Mexican woman had of European fashion and the deprivations she would suffer to appear fashionable. During a carriage ride to Mexico City, the traveler Frances Calderón de la Barca, the Scottish wife of the Spanish Ambassador to Mexico, noted that when a clean dress was pulled from one of her trunks, it was "to the great amusement of the Indian women, who begged to know if my gown was the *last fashion*, and said it was *muy guapa*, very pretty" (Calderón de la Barca 1982: 59).

Mexico had experienced tremendous political and social upheaval in the years leading up to independence, but colonial notions based on the importance of family lineage and aristocratic greatness continued to exert their influence on the new nation. The obsession with luxurious clothing and adopting a lifestyle beyond one's means is well documented in colonial Mexico (Stayton 1996: 71). Although changes in government were frequent and cultural conflict was rampant, nineteenth-century Mexicans still valued the importance of appearances. José Joaquín Fernández de Lizardi, author of *The Itching Parrot* (1816), describes the follies of a young man consumed by a passion for fashionable living, but who is reluctant to work because he sees himself as a gentleman. The excessive taxation imposed by Spain before independence and the economic turmoil created by Independence Wars had deprived many great families of their fortunes. Undoubtedly the loss of wealth for these individuals was very unsettling as they tried desperately to retain the veneer of their former lives. Richard Henry Dana noted this when he wrote: "I have often seen a man with a fine figure, and courteous manners, dressed in broad-cloth and velvet, with a noble horse completely covered with trappings; without a *real* in his pockets, and absolutely suffering for something to eat" (Dana 1992: 87).

The perceived shortcomings of the *creole* personality were subject to criticism in the period following independence for outsiders were quick to observe this disinclination toward earning a living. Captain G. F. Lyon, a British visitor with a rigid work ethic, was harsh in his assessment of some of the *creoles* he encountered in 1826. While he quickly commended those engaged in a trade, he had the following remarks for the others:

> The Creoles, or descendants of Europeans, are by their circumstances the most eminent persons in New Spain, and, with the exception of those engaged in active commerce, are an indolent, over-bearing, haughty race, who, with the ignorance which the barbarous policy of Spain has entailed upon them, have preserved also the most profound contempt for the poor despised Indians; and in fact for every one without their own particular pale. (Lyon 1828: 231–2).

Fashion in the Early Years of Independence

It has been a general observation of costume historians that, in those regions far removed from the fashion centers of London and Paris, there was a tendency to cling to outdated modes. Mexico was no exception, and Santina Levey in *Lace: A History* observed that Spanish and Portuguese America were "notoriously conservative areas" (Levey 1983: 71) where older styles often remained popular. Late eighteenth-century dress and the neoclassical styles of European fashion persisted in various forms in Mexico well into the early nineteenth century. That the 1820s were especially lean and difficult years in Mexico is evident as the new nation was struggling to resurrect industry and develop its infrastructure. When the English traveler H. G. Ward visited Mexico City at the end of 1823, he noticed in the shops featuring European goods that "the supply was scanty, and the price enormous" (Ward 1828: 223). In postcolonial Mexico, fashion could lag behind the times, and many women chose to maintain older styles – from necessity in some cases – even though European fashion had dramatically evolved. It stands to reason that the elites, especially those who suffered a reversal of fortune during the Independence Wars, would cling to vestiges of fashionable dress to signal their former status. In his *Mexican Illustrations* of 1828, author Mark Beaufoy recalled such an encounter: "I do, by the bye, remember one good-humored lady, at Valladolid, who had squeezed her bosom up to her chin, and wore her waist between her shoulder blades, as ten years back used to be fashion in Paris" (Beaufoy 1828: 129).

The delay in up-to-date fashions during the 1820s can also be explained by external circumstances. Initially refusing to accept Mexican independence, the Spanish king Fernando VII blockaded the eastern port of Veracruz from the island of San Juan de Ulúa until 1825 thus halting trade in one of Mexico's busiest port cities (Kicza 1995: 119). So for daytime attire, women continued to dress in the traditional Spanish style as was observed in Mexico City during the 1820s where women attended morning mass dressed in their Spanish black gowns and black lace mantillas (Bullock 1824: 214). Fashionable attire may have been beyond the reach for some during this unsettled period, but one accessory remained constant – the lace mantilla.

The presence of outdated and traditional fashions cannot be construed as evidence of sartorial stagnation as some costume historians might suggest for that interpretation effectively negates what was happening outside the elite classes. Mexican women were actively and passionately interested in the latest European modes, as was proven in an experiment conducted by the British visitor William Bullock. During the early 1820s in Jalapa, Mexico he distributed copies of *Ackermanns'* fashion plates, a British publication, and upon his return 6 months later, he was happy to see that printed calicos and bonnets had usurped Spanish black (Leask 2002: 309).

Despite the success of Bullock's local experiment with English fashions in Jalapa, much of Mexico's upper classes continued to prefer many of the same sources for fashion that were highly regarded in the colonial period. Even if they remained in step with the current modes, many Mexican women, like their counterparts in Spain, continued to wear traditional Spanish attire for daytime and switched to French modes for the evening. For obvious cultural and religious reasons, Spanish black persisted but a relatively new influence from Spain also had an impact. One of the most important and influential Spanish costumes of the eighteenth century was that of the working class *maja*. Immortalized in the paintings of the Spanish artist Francisco Goya, elements of this female dandy's ensemble found their way over the Atlantic and can be seen in paintings and engravings of Mexican women in the eighteenth and nineteenth centuries. Enormously popular with Spanish aristocratic classes, *maja* fashion imitated and evolved from Andalusian styles of the eighteenth century and eventually came to symbolize the Spanish "look" (Worth and Sibley 1994: 51). When the Italian artist traveler Claudio Linati visited Mexico in the 1820s he produced a series of lithographs of Mexican types called *Trajes civiles, militares y religiosos de México* (The Civil, Military and Religious Dress of Mexico). His *Dama Joven* (Young Woman) depicts a fashionable young Mexican woman holding the hand of her young son. Her black dress reveals a variety of Andalusian influences, especially in the tiered ruffles trimming the bottom of her skirt and in the fastenings of her lower sleeves. Fashion plates of Spanish costume, in particular a plate by Hippolyte Lecomte of a woman in Andalusian dress from 1817, bears a remarkable resemblance to the dress of the fashionable Mexican woman of Linati's lithograph. The lower sleeves of the Andalusian bodice originally fastened with lacings, making the sleeve snug around the lower arm; these later evolved into decorative trimmings and embellishments made from ribbons and braids (Worth and Sibley 1994: 53). Linati's young woman has both the sleeve trimmings and tiered skirts of the Lecomte's young Andalusian. Also noteworthy is how the overall silhouette of her dress conforms to the fashionable silhouette of the 1820s, which by then had assumed a lower waistline, but had not yet arrived at the natural waist.

Mexico City: The Fashion Center

Following the lean years of the 1820s, Mexico City would once again become the backdrop for an impressive parade of finery – the established *creole* families, new military elites and provocative *mestizas* displayed their fashions for the first-time visitor. Upon their arrival in Mexico City in 1840, Scotswoman Frances Calderón de la Barca (1804–82) and her husband, the new Spanish minister to Mexico, were quickly set up in a residence they found quite agreeable. Soon after settling in, a busy schedule of church events, bullfights, balls and visits soon began. Calderón de la Barca was astonished by the lavish array of garments and jewels adorning the Mexican women for a simple morning visit and wrote: "For the last few days our rooms have been filled with visitors, and my eyes are scarcely yet accustomed to the display of diamonds, pearls, silks, satins, blondes, and velvets, in which the ladies have paid their first visits of etiquette" (Calderón de la Barca 1982: 95).

After several weeks in Mexico City, Calderón de la Barca considers the idea of having a weekly gathering or *tertulia* as they were called in Mexico City. She is quickly discouraged by an acquaintance that warns her against the notion "because hitherto such parties have failed" (Calderón de la Barca 1982: 149). An informal weekly meeting of Mexico's best society was not satisfactory to upper class women. Only those events that allowed them to wear an excess of finery and jewels were welcome. While simple day dresses were acceptable attire for the countryside, Mexico City's finest women looked upon such a toilette with horror. Only in the past, "during the reign of simplicity" (Calderón de la Barca 1982: 149) from the years 1800–21, was an informal gown like the muslin dress quite fashionable, and it was then that "half the men in Mexico were ruined . . . by the embroidered French and Indian muslins bought by their wives" (Calderón de la Barca: 149).

Mexico City was undisputedly the fashion center of Mexico, and high fashion continued to emulate those styles from England, Spain and especially France during the mid-nineteenth century. After the turmoil of the 1820s, elaborate dress was ready for a comeback by the time Frances Calderón de la Barca and husband had arrived in the capital. Chloë Sayer writes in *Costumes of Mexico* that during this period "women reclaimed their right to deck themselves out as they pleased" (Sayer 1985a: 99).

Mexico's Female Dandies: The *China Poblana*

A more detailed discussion about the fashions of nineteenth century Mexico might begin with the elite classes and their adoption of popular French and English styles. But for the travel writers of the period, one of Mexico's most eye-catching and memorable female costumes didn't come from either France or Spain and in fact dates back to late in the colonial period. While the costume of the *china poblana* was considered a costume of the *mestiza*, it was nevertheless widely admired. Its roots are uncertain and there is much folklore surrounding its inception although most agree that the costume of the *china poblana* is a fusion of styles – both Spanish and Indian (Olivera 1991: 37–8).

In recent years, scholars have uncovered and clarified many of the incongruous details surrounding the history and mythology of the *china poblana*; current thinking has effectively separated the original *china poblana* from the later development of the eye-catching costume archetype adopted by young *mestizas*. Many of the tales surrounding the original *china poblana* seem to converge around the arrival of a young Asian woman in the village of Puebla during the seventeenth century (Sayer 1985a: 108). Gauvin Bailey, in his essay "A Mughal Princess in Baroque New Spain," explains that the first *china poblana* was a princess from India who was captured by pirates and was eventually brought to New Spain as a slave (Bailey 1997: 47–8). Not long after her arrival in the city of Puebla during the early decades of the seventeenth century, she was baptized as Catarina de San Juan. Unlike the provocative *china poblana* who captured the imagination of nineteenth-century travel writers, Catarina de San Juan was extremely pious and devoted to the poor. As her Christian faith deepened, she became prone to vivid religious visions and dressed in ascetic black.

Jeanne Gillespie in her essay "Gender, Ethnicity and Piety: The Case of the China Poblana" makes it clear that semantic confusion has obscured the significance of the original *china poblana*, effectively merging her identity with that of the independent and fashionable *mestiza* women of the nineteenth century (Gillespie 1998: 20–1). The source of ambiguity lies with the designation *china poblana*. In the period between Catarina de San Juan's ascension as a public figure in Puebla during the seventeenth century and the appearance of her showy counterpart sometime during the late eighteenth century, some meaning and significance had been lost. *China* can refer to a woman of Chinese or Asian descent; but it can also mean maid or servant girl; the meaning of *poblana* is more straightforward, and simply describes a person from the village of Puebla. The confusion therefore lies with the word *china*; its meaning has evolved since the viceregal period and this chapter concerns itself with the fashionable women of the servant class, the working-class *mestiza* who became a national symbol.

Bailey writes that the *china poblana* who was known for her colorful sequined skirts, embroidered blouse and *rebozo* is a late nineteenth-century invention meant to embody an idealized image of womanhood in the republic. Travel writing, however, contradicts this notion. The *china poblana* was already a familiar figure, the elements of her costume well understood by the time Frances Calderón de la Barca wrote her observations in the 1840s. The art historian Manuel Toussaint, in his introduction to the 1946 edition of the *Compendio de la Vida y Virtudes de la Venerable Catarina de San Juan* (Compendium of the Life and Virtues of the Venerable Catarina de San Juan) speculates that *china poblana* costume evolved either in the late eighteenth or early nineteenth century (Castillo Grajeda 1946: 10). An eighteenth century *casta* painting by José Joaquin Magón entitled *Castizo Child* shows a woman dressed in a modest version of *china poblana* attire that consists of a skirt in contrasting colors, ruffled blouse and *rebozo*. The artist simply describes her as *española*, thus contradicting any notion of a *mestiza* monopoly on basic elements of this style; this is also evocative of the *majas* influence in Spain where aristocratic women strived to copy the modes and manners of their street dress. It can't be assumed that the woman in the painting is a *china poblana*, but placing the principal costume elements in the eighteenth century seems to support the idea that china poblana dress evolved sometime before the nineteenth century.

Some earlier sources do not make any distinction between the original *china poblana* of the seventeenth-century Puebla and her republican manifestation in the nineteenth century. In her foreword to *La China Poblana*, Louise Stinetorf writes that when the original *china poblana* was questioned about her vibrant costume, she replied "the white of her costume was for the snow-capped volcanoes of her adopted land, the green for its many palm trees and red for the spilled blood of its heroic sons, native and transplanted" (Stinetorf 1960: 9). This figure, outfitted in the colors of the Mexican flag, would support a nineteenth-century notion of the *china poblana* as a symbolic and patriotic figure.

A short-sleeved lace trimmed chemise with a low décolletage and two stiffly starched lace-trimmed petticoats worn underneath brightly colored skirts comprised the basic costume (Olivera 1991: 37–8); and a shawl or *rebozo* completed the ensemble. Chloë Sayer in *Costumes of Mexico* writes that the costume seems to have been "inspired by Spanish peasant styles from Andalusia and Lagartera in the province of Toledo" (Sayer 1985a: 109). Heavily embroidered and embellished with bands of metallic lace, ribbons and trimmings, the short layered skirts of the women of Lagartera, Spain are immediately recognizable. While the women of Lagartera favored dark-colored skirts heavily trimmed in gold and silver lace and ribbons, Mexico's *mestiza* women adopted skirts in brighter colors, embellishing patterned fabrics with beads and sequins and trimming them with rich lace. The square-necked blouse with colorful embroidery and lace-trimmed neck and sleeves is a defining feature of costumes in the small villages of Andalusia (Ortiz Echagüe 1947: 17), and is clearly evoked in the colorful embroidered blouses of Mexico. Teresa Castelló Yturbide writes in *La Chaquira en México* that the construction of the Mexican square-necked blouse, while Spanish in origin, also exhibits a Moorish influence as indicated by the small square under the arm, a pattern derived from the Arab *djellaba* (Castelló Yturbide and Mapelli Mozzi 1998: 65). Many peasant styles from Spain feature heavily embroidered yokes and shoulders that are worked in both multicolored and monochromatic designs that are floral or geometric. The Chinese embroideries brought to Mexico by the Manila galleon most likely served as further inspiration for the floral embroidery embellishing the necklines of the Mexican blouse. In copying these designs, *mestiza* and Indian women imbued these floral patterns with a distinctly Mexican style.

A skirt in contrasting colors also seems to be a defining feature of the ensemble, and traveler descriptions and paintings alike often indicate skirts in two colors – many times scarlet and yellow. Again Teresa Castelló Yturbide writes that skirts of the *china poblana* costume were first made from red Indian bandanas in a paisley print, stitched together so they formed a scarlet skirt; a waistband in a contrasting color was later added to give the proper length (Castelló Yturbide and Mapelli Mozzi 1998: 66). Manuel Toussaint notes that the *china poblana's* skirts were made of castor, otherwise known as beaver cloth (Castillo Grajeda 1946: 9). Popular in Europe and North America, this fabric was woven to simulate cloth made of beaver fur; thick and durable, some castors were heavily napped and could be made of wool or flannel. This castor-like

The Traveler's Eye

Figure 3.1. *China poblana* costume in Mexico. Between 1829 and 1834, the German artist Carl Nebel traveled through Mexico, where he produced a series of lithographs depicting Mexican customs and important archaeological sites. His depiction of *china poblanas* reinforced traveler's impressions of their seductive qualities and spirited independence. First published in Paris as *Voyage pittoresque et archeologique dans la partie la plus interessante du Mexique* (1836), this image also appeared in the Spanish translation entitled *Viaje pintoresco y arqueológico sobre la parte más interesante de la República Mexicana, en los años transcurridos desde 1829 hasta 1834* (Mexico City: Porrúa, 1963). Reprinted courtesy of the General Research Division, The New York Public Library, Astor, Lenox and Tilden Foundations.

fabric could have been manufactured locally and in narrow widths; additional fabric would have been added at the waist to give the proper length. In *La Historia de México a través de la Indumentaria*, the authors write that patterns were traced on the fabric in *huizache* dye, and these patterns were subsequently outlined in sequins (Armella de Aspe 1988: 84). During an 1839 visit to Puebla de los Angeles, Frances Calderón de la Barca reported that the skirts of the *china poblana's* ensemble were "divided into two colours, the lower part made generally of a scarlet and black stuff, a manufacture of the country, and the upper part of white or yellow satin" (Calderón de la Barca 1966: 82–3). Despite the different ideas about the inception of *china poblana* style, the skirt in contrasting colors seems to be an indigenous contribution. Although red was probably the traditional color for the lower half of the skirt, especially in Puebla de los Angeles, a nineteenth-century lithograph by Carlos Nebel depicts three *chinas poblanas* with skirts in a variety of color combinations. One wears the traditional red and white combination and the other two have skirts in blue and yellow patterned fabrics, possibly made from locally printed fabrics. The daughter of William Parish Robertson who visited Mexico in the 1850s noted that lower classes all wore the ubiquitous *rebozo*, and the petticoat was "generally white from the waist . . . the rest being some colour" (Robertson 1853: 144).

The *rebozo* was a type of head covering or shawl that completed the *china poblana's* ensemble. An important accessory for women of all social classes, its usage can be traced back to the early years of the colonial era. Its origins are uncertain and, while there is a Spanish *rebozo*, it bears little – if any – resemblance to the Mexican version (Foster 1960: 98). Given the traditional importance of head coverings in Spanish culture, it is not surprising that it gained widespread popularity amongst all classes. An embroidered China crepe shawl could be substituted for the *rebozo* as they were a popular fashion accessory dating from the Manila trade. Additional accessories included an open vest, a handkerchief worn around the neck or a brightly colored sash tied around the waist.

By the time Calderón de la Barca observed her first *china poblana* in the late 1830s, she was a well-known figure endowed with historical and sartorial significance, and the costume was considered by many to embody the feminine ideal of the *mestiza* (Sayer 1985a: 108). While the *china poblana* was not considered part of the fashionable and respectable elite of Mexico City, her costume nevertheless could be just as costly as European costume when made of sumptuous fabrics and fine quality metallic and silk lace. When a general's wife sent Calderón de la Barca a *china poblana* dress, she was impressed enough to consider wearing it to a ball in Mexico City:

> This morning a very handsome dress was forwarded to me with the compliments of a lady whom I do not know, the wife of General –; with a request that, if I should go to the fancy ball as a Poblana peasant, I may wear this costume. It is a Poblana dress, and very superb, consisting of a petticoat of maroon-coloured merino, with gold fringe, gold bands and spangles; an under-petticoat, embroidered and trimmed with rich lace, to come below it. The first petticoat is trimmed with gold up the sides, which are slit open, and tied up with coloured ribbon. With this must be worn a chemise, richly embroidered round the neck and sleeves, and trimmed with lace; a satin vest, open in front, and embroidered in gold; a silk sash tied behind, the ends fringed with gold, and a small silk handkerchief which crosses the neck, with gold fringe. I had already another dress prepared, but I think this is the handsomer of the two. (Calderón de la Barca 1982: 84)

When a Mexican official learns that Calderón de la Barca is seriously considering the costume, he advises her against it. "The dress of a Poblana is that of a woman of no character. The lady of the Spanish minister is a *lady* in every sense of the word. However much she may have compromised herself, she ought neither to go as a *Poblana,* nor in any other character but her own" (Calderón de la Barca 1982: 89).

Some of the most fashionable women of Mexico City chose to adopt this costume when visiting the countryside as it was seen as most appropriate to disguise oneself in the costume of the *china poblana* when outside of Mexico City. It is a curious phenomenon that mimics a fashionable European trend of the late eighteenth century in which upper class women dressed in simple white gowns and played at being young country shepherdesses (Boucher 1987: 303). Calderón de la Barca describes the ensemble and the ritual surrounding the adoption of this costume for the upper class Mexican woman:

> This evening the Señora A – – came after it was dark, in a Poblana dress, which she had just bought to wear at a *Jamaica,* which they are going to have in the country – a sort of fair, where all the girls disguise themselves in peasants' dresses, and go about selling fruit, lemonade, vegetables, etc., to each other – a very ancient Mexican amusement. This dress cost her some hundred dollars. The top of the petticoat is yellow satin; the rest, which is of scarlet cashmere, is embroidered in gold and silver. Her hair was fastened back with a thick silver comb, and her ornaments were very handsome, coral set in gold. Her shoes white satin, embroidered in gold; the sleeves and body of the chemise, which is of the finest cambric, trimmed with rich lace; and the petticoat, which comes below the dress, shows two flounces of Valenciennes. She looks beautiful in this dress, which will not be objected to in the country, though it might not suit a fancy ball in Mexico. (Calderón de la Barca 1982: 222)

Whether or not the character of the *china poblana* was a respectable one, the images of them in paintings and prints are typically imbued with an overtly sexual character. Free from the restraints imposed upon women from fashionable society, the *china poblana* could dress as boldly as she pleased. Her colorful attire incorporated the goods of Mexican trade, which included "silk from China, glass beads from Czechoslovakia, calamine sequins, gold or silver burrs, and lace from Flanders, Valencia or Chantilly" (Murrieta 1994: 23). This undoubtedly was part of the thrill for an upper class woman adopting the costume if only for a few days in the country, although it is interesting to note that Calderón de la Barca's acquaintance appeared in the costume only after it was dark. Ruth Olivera wonders if all the criticism "was inspired merely by envy of the frankly attractive and sensuous *chinas*" (Olivera 1991: 127)?

In Marcos Arróniz's *Manual del Viajero en Méjico (Guide for the Traveler in Mexico)* from 1858, the author praises the many talents of the *china poblana,* writing that she has skills beyond the ability to dress in a lively and engaging manner.

> The *china* does not allow her small foot to be encased in a satin shoe: she knows to wash the clothes with perfection, to stew a delicate *mole,* to season *quesadillas* most tastily, and to admirably make up the *pulque* with pineapple and almond or *tuna* [fruit of the prickly-pear cactus]: there is no street where she is not seen, graceful and

attractive, with the twirl of a petticoat from one sidewalk to another; and in the *jarabe*, a dance as boisterous as it is national, captivating with her lascivious movements, the glance of her brown or dark eyes. Her black hair is gracefully waved, and from it, her name has come without a doubt. (Arróniz 1858: 138)

In *Latin America: Its Cities and Ideas*, José Romero writes that the city marketplaces of the eighteenth century enabled women of different social classes to mingle freely when engaging in daily trade (Romero 1999: 112). In Mexico City, the main fruit and vegetable market was located in the *Plaza del Volador*, and its low prices attracted all social groups (Kandell 1988: 296). It was here that women observed each other's fashions closely. *Mestizas* and *mulatas* aspiring to ascend the caste system could study the dress and mannerisms of upper class women. From the *mestizas* and *mulatas,* an upper class woman could learn the language and banter of the marketplace. Romero also believes that many men found their mistresses amongst these working class women, making the *china poblana* that much more exciting and provocative (Romero 1999: 113). During Good Friday in Mexico City, as Calderón de la Barca recounts the apparel of the crowd, the *china poblana* shines brightly:

> And above all, here and there a flashing Poblana, with a dress of real value and much taste, and often with a face and figure of extraordinary beauty, especially the figure; large and yet élancée, with a bold coquettish eye, and a beautiful little brown foot, shown off by the white satin shoe; the petticoat of her dress frequently fringed and embroidered in real massive gold, and reboso either shot with gold, or a bright-coloured China crape shawl, coquettishly thrown over her head. We saw several whose dresses could not have cost less than five hundred dollars. (Calderón de la Barca 1982: 146)

Many Mexican women wore their dresses several inches shorter than was the fashion in Europe and the *china poblanas* were no exception. A beautiful *poblana* probably realized that her lovely skin would be shown to its best advantage without stockings especially next to a white satin shoe, and a low-cut white cotton chemise would also produce the same effect. If her figure was large, maybe it was because she opted to not wear a corset with her chemise. In most cases, the *chinas poblanas* were working women and probably not accustomed to the practice of wearing a corset; their daily tasks would have required them to move about unconstrained. Lieutenant Wise would comment on the fact that women appeared in public without corsets when he visited the city of Guadalajara in 1849. At an evening's entertainment in the main plaza, he observed: . . . I had a clear chance of observing the pretty throngs that swept by. They were so tastefully attired in full flowing and becoming skirts, with no awkward stays or corsets to cramp the grace of motion – the coquettish ribosa, never quiet an instant, but changing its silken folds, and half revealing the glancing neck and arm" (Wise 1850: 234).

French traveler Louis de Bellemare, who published an unusual volume entitled *Vagabond Life in Mexico* in 1856 under the name of Gabriel Ferry, seemed more interested in exploring the dark side of Mexican life and society. His account of the *china poblana*, narrated as he drifted about the country, emphasized the seductive powers of her costume. He writes:

> The long wavy hair, which escaped in plaits from her open rebozo, her complexion of a slight umber tint, the brown shoulders that her chemise of fine linen, fringed with lace, left almost bare, her slender figure, which had never been deformed by stays, and, above all, the three short petticoats of different colors, which fell in straight folds over her pliant haunches, all pointed out the young woman as a genuine specimen of the China. (Ferry 1856: 94–5)

Like the Spanish *maja*, Mexico's *china poblana* did not lack admirers. Certainly, they are connected by some similarities in dress as both derived their inspiration from the peasant styles of Andalusia and New Castile (Gillespie 1998: 29). Their ethnic flair and spirited independence fulfilled the traveler's desire for an exoticism that was in stark contrast to the modes and manners in the capital cities of Western Europe or in the United States. Luckily, for the costume historian these travelers recorded in great detail the most important aspects of *china poblana* dress. Some even went so far as to describe additional accessories, which they deemed important enough include in their observations.

For the Spanish *maja*, a tight-fitting bodice or jacket was a key part of the ensemble. (Puigarri 1886: 244), and Mexican women living in rural areas seem to have adopted a similar style, wearing a jacket with their blouse and petticoats. British traveler William Bullock noticed that women's dress in the countryside was "showy, but not elegant: worked shifts, with a light open jacket, and a richly embroidered or spangled petticoat" (Bullock 1824: 217–18) was the unvarying dress. The influence of peasant styles from Andalusia and Lagartera extend beyond the embellished skirt and embroidered blouse and it is entirely possible that some other costume accessories, like tight-fitting jackets and vests from these regions could have influenced *china poblana* dress. When Frances Calderón de la Barca observed her first *china poblana* in Puebla de los Angeles, she had noted an often overlooked detail of the *china poblana* costume. She wrote that the chemise and two-colored skirt could also be worn "with a satin vest of some bright colour, and all brochéed with gold or silver, open in front, and turned back. This vest may be worn or omitted, as suits the taste of the wearer. It is without sleeves, but has straps" (Calderón de la Barca 1966: 83). This rich vest, embroidered and trimmed, could be related to the vests worn by the women of Lagartera. Isabel de Palencia in *The Regional Costumes of Spain* noted that the gala dress of the women of Lagartera could be worn with a "corselet of gold braid and embroidered silk" (Palencia 1926: 87). The Lagartera corselet was rather short and falling just under the bust line, it gives the appearance of having straps such as Calderón de la Barca described. That the *china poblana*'s open vest was turned back is similar to the way eighteenth-centry *majas* in Madrid wore their jackets, as Italian traveler Baretti attests in his description of a *maja* wearing a tight jacket that remained open to form "hanging flaps under the breast" (Baretti 1770: 153). Cruz Cano's late eighteenth-century fashion plate of a Spanish *maja* features a jacket with both lapels turned back.

In her description of the *poblana* petticoat given to her by a general's wife, Calderón de la Barca noted that the "first petticoat is trimmed with gold up the sides, which are slit open, and tied up with coloured ribbon" (Calderón de la Barca 1982: 84). Again, the Italian traveler Baretti noted that neither the *maja* nor her male counterpart, the *majo*, had their garments sewn along the seams, but held their clothing "together by interlacing ribbands" (Baretti 1770: 153). While these are minor details, further research may confirm that the *poblana* vest and ribboned seams are related to these elements of Andalusian and Lagartera costume.

It is clear from the testimonials of nineteenth-century travelers that the *china poblana* resonated with visitors from afar. Today, one still can see this legacy celebrated and remembered as a representative of Mexico's *mestizo* heritage. The elements of the *china poblana's* costume – like the red and green sequined petticoat and white embroidered blouse – can be found at many public parades and celebrations of national holidays.

French *Modistes* and the Follies of the New Elite

After independence, a new military elite would emerge in the society of Mexico City, competing with the interests of the more established political leaders. This new and influential group, some of whom were *mestizos*, emerged from the military ranks and was able to use their career as a means for social advancement and personal wealth (Wasserman 2000: 53). No new administration could succeed without military support, and the inflated salaries of the officers guaranteed their temporary allegiance (Kandell 1988: 307). Naturally, the costume of the period played an important role as the new elite sought to assert itself in a society long dominated by the established upper classes. Despite this newly found status, the immediate conversion of economic success into fashion sense was not always entirely successful. The vulgar aspects of the garments worn by the military wives was not lost on Frances Calderón de la Barca, who was quick to discern the differences between Mexican and European evening dress and thereby chastise this new elite. After attending one of her first balls in Mexico City, she writes:

> The Mexican women are decidedly neither pretty nor graceful, and their dress is awful. The French *modistes* who come here, and who are in fact the very scum of the earth, persuade them into all sorts of follies. Their gowns have all a hunchy, loaded look, all velvet or satin . . . The dresses compared to the actual fashion, are made excessively, incredibly short, and sticking [out] all round at the bottom like hoops – so that when they stoop! Caramba. (Calderón de la Barca 1966: 133)

From her letters, it is revealed that a group of French *modistes* had taken up residence in Mexico City at this time. The French *modiste* was a relative newcomer to the world of fashion, which had long been the domain of men; she was the dressmaker who constructed women's gowns and added the finishing touches after a tailor cut the necessary materials. The new elite, lacking confidence and desiring to establish themselves through dress, seemed to have placed themselves at the mercy of style makers who, in turn, foisted ridiculous garments on unsuspecting clients (Kandell 1988: 308). Regarding a masked ball attended with her husband, Calderón de la Barca writes that several women appeared in men's attire, "chiefly French *modistes*, generally a most disreputable set here" (Calderón de la Barca 1982: 125).

The French Retail Trade in Mexico

While there is scant evidence about the French retail trade in Mexico, it is known that a small group of businessmen from Barcelonnette arrived in Mexico during the nineteenth century. Most of them worked as retailers selling French goods in the capital. Nancy Nichols Barker, in her book *The French Experience in Mexico, 1821–1861*, marks the beginning of French influence in the capital. She writes, "According to tradition, this trend began in 1821 when three brothers, Arnaud by name, spinners of silk, left their Alpine village (Department of Basses-Alpes) in the valley of Barcelonnette to establish a retail clothing shop in the Mexican capital" (Barker 1979: 19). According to Barker, the success of these hard-working Frenchmen inspired others from their same village to move into "the vacancies created by the emigration of many Spaniards after independence and especially after their expulsion from the republic in 1828" (Barker 1979: 20). Of all the dressmakers and *modistes* of the city, Silvia Arrom writes that only a small number were Mexican, as the preference for European fashions made the French retailers the most highly regarded and sought after (Arrom 1985: 169–70). French hairdressers also opened businesses throughout the capital, as noted by Calderón de la Barca when she alleges that the heads of Mexican women are "dressed by rascally Frenchmen, who make them pay an ounce each hairdressing" (Calderón de la Barca 1966: 133). While French businesses were primarily limited to Mexico City, many later moved into the city of Puebla around 1840. Here they dominated the retail trade in that city well into the era of the dictator Porfirio Diaz (Proal and Charpenal 1998, 176).

National Costume: The White Muslin Gown

Before their arrival in Mexico City, Frances Calderón de la Barca writes in a letter dated December 23, 1839 that she and her husband traveled from the port city of Vera Cruz – their point of entry into Mexico – to Manga de Clavo.

The purpose of this visit was to introduce Calderón de la Barca's husband, the new Spanish minister, to General de Santa Anna (1794–1876) and his wife Señora de Santa Anna. Despite their dawn arrival, Frances noted that the first lady was "dressed to receive us in clear white muslin, with white satin shoes, and with very splendid diamond earrings, brooch, and rings" (Calderón de la Barca 1982: 45). These white muslin gowns worn with lace-trimmed petticoats would become known as one of Mexico's costume types during the eighteenth century. A type of day dress for the affluent countrywoman, it was typically accompanied by an embroidered shawl from the China trade and a parasol. Later in her travels, Frances Calderón de la Barca again notes the popularity of the white gowns. She writes: "Some country ladies, who attended mass in the chapel this morning, were dressed in very short clear muslin gowns, very much starched, and so disposed as to show two under petticoats, also stiffly starched, and trimmed with lace, their shoes coloured satin. Considered to be costumes of their own, I begin to think it rather pretty" (Calderón de la Barca 1982: 173).

Calderón de la Barca was so taken with the white muslin gowns that, shortly thereafter, she adopted the style. For a trip to Real del Monte, she writes about her intentions "to adopt the fashion of the country tomorrow" (Calderón de la Barca 1982: 180) and to "try the effect of traveling with clear gown, satin petticoat, and shoes ditto" (Calderón de la Barca 1982: 181).

These white muslin gowns, worn with petticoats, have an uncertain origin. While some fashion historians link the fashionable French chemise gown to white cotton frocks of young girls (Ribeiro 1999: 66), others believe that the lightweight gowns were a colonial innovation brought back to France from the islands of the Caribbean (Boucher 1987: 303). As there is virtually no mention of them in Mexico before the mid to late-eighteenth century, the Mexican version could have derived from the French version, and accordingly, its shape changed as fashion changed – assuming a lower waistline and fuller skirt. In Mexico, the muslin gowns were so pervasive that they appear in the inventories of several wills dating from the late eighteenth and early nineteenth centuries, as shown in Carmen Espinosa's book *Shawls, Crinolines, Filigree*. She notes that the "gowns and accessories must not be considered typical of what the general public wore" (Espinosa 1970: 9). In the will of Micaela Baca from 1831, the following items are listed: "one muslin embroidered dress, one dress of thin muslin, one dress of muslin with ruffle" (Espinosa 1970: 22–3). It stands to reason that these gowns would be very popular; their light color and weight would be perfect for a hot climate while their shape retained the fashionable silhouette as dictated by European fashion designers. This dress was also adopted by women of lesser means: In Claudio Linati's book of lithographs from 1828, there is a simplified version of the gown with three tiers of ruffles that is "made from coarsely printed cotton" (Linati 1956: 71) worn with a mantle or *rebozo* and white satin slippers.

In his analysis of textiles from the viceregal period, José Benítez refers to eighteenth-century archives to examine the many types of textiles used in the

Mexican colony. Those textiles manufactured locally and those imported from overseas both appear in records from this period. While scant evidence of these textiles exists for study, the names of these important textiles could quite possibly refer to those used to manufacture Mexico's popular white gowns. From an archived document from Valladolid, Mexico the author refers to a particular textile; woven overseas it was intended for consumption in the Americas, and curiously enough, it was named *indianilla criolla de algodón* (Benítez 1946: 139). Previous discussion revealed how valuable India's cottons were to all members of colonial society; Mexico depended on imported textiles to keep people clothed. The *indianilla* could be a reference to the textiles of India rather than to those woven textiles produced by the local indigenous population – meaning that the textile was modeled after fine cottons of India and was intended for consumption by the Creole population of Mexico, similar to the French *indiennes* manufactured for consumption in that country.

Dress and the Fashion Press

Towards the end of her stay in Mexico, Calderón de la Barca observes a notable improvement in the costume of Mexico City's upper class women. It seems that the overloaded style of dress had given way to a simpler, yet nonetheless elegant toilette. Perhaps the new elite, more comfortably established in their new roles, had learned not to repeat the costume follies of previous years. In one entry she writes the following about a ball in Mexico City:

> We returned from Mexico this morning, having gone in to attend the ball given at the French Minister's, on the day of Louis Philippe. It was very pretty, and we stayed till it was very late. We met with such a cordial reception from all our friends, whom we have not seen for a month, that we are tempted to believe ourselves as much missed in Mexico as they say we are. The Señoras L– and E–s were amongst the best dressed Mexican ladies last night; the latter in white crape and diamonds, and the other in black blonde over rose-colour, also with diamonds. (Calderón de la Barca 1982: 379)

The change in fashion, especially in the adoption of rose-colored gowns, is very much in keeping with Paris fashions of the 1840s. Margarete Braun-Ronsdorf says of the dresses from this period "that there had been an important change in colour schemes" (Braun-Ronsdorf 1964: 73–4), meaning that the soft pale colors of the 1830s had been replaced stronger tones. Of pink satin, Aileen Ribeiro writes in *Ingres in Fashion* that "it was a popular color in the fashion world" (Ribeiro 1999: 153). Rose and lilac were especially fashionable, and an example of black blonde lace worn over a rose-colored gown can be seen in François-Xavier Winterhalter's portrait of Louise d'Orleans from 1846.

In order to read about the latest fashions, Mexican women of the middle and upper classes turned to the French fashion press. During the last decades of Spanish rule in the Americas the French fashion press was already well established in Europe. Colonial Spain had never published periodicals for a female audience (Herrick 1957: 135). The Spanish government, trying to discourage extravagance in dress in the eighteenth century, had encouraged with little avail the adoption of a national costume for women. Furthermore, it never would have actively promoted French fashion in the colonies (Kany 1932: 191). The influence of the United States and its fashions press grew, especially after Mexico lost most of its territory north of Rio Grande in the Mexican-American War. Jane Herrick notes that *Godey's Lady's Book*, an American publication, achieved great success from the 1830s until 1898; by mid-century, several Mexican publications were in circulation (Herrick 1957: 135). The growing awareness of how to wear high European fashion was soon disseminated further with the publication of the periodical *El Liceo Mexicano* in the 1840s. This periodical included poems, short stories, popular musical scores and the latest French fashion plates. Fashion plates were accompanied by flowery commentary on the latest styles and their suitability for Mexican women. One article reads:

> Simplicity is today the woman of fashion, and without her almost nothing is in good taste. The two figures in the fashion plate serve as an example. One costume is for at home and the other for day dress. The first, does it not reveal to us something of Constantinople? Does it not have the glimmer of an indolent Turk? Is it not certain that it gives off the scent of a divine and magnificent sultan? (El Liceo Mexicano 1844)

This new "spirit of elegance" is readily apparent in a portrait of Rosario Echeverría painted by the Mexican painter Pelegrín Clavé. The artist, in the spirit of Ingres, captured the simplicity of the silk satin gown, blonde bertha, and ubiquitous lace-trimmed handkerchief – all identifiably European – while retaining the loveliness of clearly Mexican features.

By the time Carl Sartorius visited in 1859 and wrote about his observations, Mexican women were well versed in the fashions of Europe and their applications. Sartorius reveals:

> In their toilettes, the ladies are guided more by Paris 'Journal des Modes' than the men. The new patterns in silk, woolen and cotton stuffs are seen sooner in Mexico than in Russia; and the daughter of the official in the distant mountain village, decks herself with showy productions of Lyons and Manchester, with the embroidery of St. Gall, and jewelry of Paris . . . (Sartorius 1859: 55).

American visitor Mary Ashley Townsend, who made repeated trips to Mexico several decades later, noted the few opportunities that existed for extravagant dress in the capital. Aware of the fact that Mexican women in the past had a predilection for lavish styles, she wrote: "The charge to which they were open some years few years ago of tasteless overdressing, even in making morning calls, no longer applies to them as they have in a great measure adopted and closely conformed to the French mode" (Townsend 2001: 290). That the attire of the upper classes did conform to a more restrained European standard of dress over the course of the nineteenth century is noteworthy. More opportunity for contact with foreign visitors, the impact of modernization and the influence of the fashion press undoubtedly had a lasting effect on the fashions of the elite classes.

Conclusion

With its rich social and cultural history, Mexico presents a fascinating challenge to the study of costume and textiles. The beauty of Mexican artistic expression lies in the unparalleled convergence of cultures, which has created an astonishing mix of traditions, combining indigenous, Asian and European influences. Recent scholarship has celebrated the contributions of Mexico's indigenous people and continues to explore the artistic and technical excellence of these groups. But the colonial and independence periods of Mexico have also presented an exciting opportunity to explore aspects of dress in a society where the population was undergoing rapid miscegenation and "creolization." While hardly a comprehensive study, this essay has begun to explore the wide range of European costume that was available to the different classes. Naturally, those who were more spiritually aligned with Europe conformed to the standards of dress as dictated by that region. *Creoles* and *mestizos* who had lived their entire lives in the Americas felt comfortable enough to adopt those elements of both indigenous and European dress that reflected their experiences and personal history. That these tendencies emerged early in the colonial period signals the importance of costume as an expression of a nascent identity, foretelling the late nineteenth-century concept of *mexicanidad*.

While the upper classes fashioned themselves after Europe, it is not surprising that most foreign visitors found the costumes of the working classes with their blending of Spanish and indigenous elements much more charming and representative of the Mexican people. Despite their preconceptions or orientalist fantasies, most travelers were frank in their admiration of not only the *china poblana* but other types as well. During the French Intervention and the dictatorship of Porfirio Díaz, the French influence reached great heights in the capital, dominating not only fashion, but architecture, interior design and cuisine as well. That the Mexican Revolution of 1910 led to such a fervent embracing of Mexico's indigenous and *mestizo* past is easily understood given the glittering artificiality and social inequalities of the nineteenth century. When the Mexican artist Frida Kahlo abandoned her European fashions, she adopted regional and *mestiza* costumes, in particular the dress of the women of Tehuantepec. When the German army occupied Paris during World War II, the fashion industry of the United States looked to its own hemisphere and found inspiration in Mexico's many costumes. To this day, high fashion periodically revives the embroidered white blouse and sequined skirt, which ultimately stands as a tribute to the enduring creativity of *mestiza* style.

4

Far Eastern Influences in Latin American Fashions

Araceli Tinajero

In 1625, Thomas Gage wrote:

> It is a by-word that at Mexico four things are fair; that is to say, the women, the apparel, the horses, and the streets. But to this I may add the beauty of some of the coaches of the gentry, which do exceed in cost the best of the Court of Madrid and other parts of Christendom, for they spare no silver, nor gold, nor precious stones, nor cloth of gold, nor the best silks from China to enrich them. (Gage 1958: 67)

Gage, an English Dominican friar who lived and traveled throughout Mexico and Guatemala between the years of 1625 and 1637, was not exaggerating. Elaborate apparel made of textiles from the Far East was quite fashionable. In colonial Mexico, clothing underwent several transformations that would influence dress in a multicultural fashion. While scholars have tended to focus on the European influences of Mexican and by extention, Latin American fashions, this chapter demonstrates how Far Eastern fashions (such as textiles, dress, accessories and even interior decoration) have influenced Latin American styles at given historical moments.

Anne Brydon and Sandra Niessen emphasize the importance of changing the way we think about fashion, because its very concept has, until recently, been considered exclusive to "civilized" nations. They explain:

> Clothing systems of the colonial Other were considered to be non-fashion, or fashion in negative image: sign of the child-like mentality of the prototypical "primitive." The category "fashion" was reserved for an industrial, mass-production and consumption system. Thus defined, fashion mirrored the familiar and insidious dichotomies of large- vs. small-scale, literate vs. non-literate, developed vs. undeveloped, and people with history vs. those without. (Brydon and Niessen 1998: xi–xii)

These deceitful dichotomies become even more intricate when we analyze the influences of a region with its own colonial and postcolonial past on another with similar experiences, as in the case of the influences of Asia on Latin America.[1] Aubrey Cannon provides a more inclusive definition by proposing that fashion develops in all societies as the product of a testimony of "self identity and social comparison" (Cannon 1998: 24). Therefore the category of fashion will be applied to the trends of the colonizers *and* to the styles of Latin American natives and practices but also to styles of Latin American traditional societies, for as Andrea Molnar suggests, the concept of the "traditional" does not imply something static and unchanging. Molnar (1998: 41) explains, "Local traditions are dynamic systems and have always accommodated changes by incorporating and localizing adopted from other (or) neighboring groups." In their study of Asian influences in European and North American dress, Valerie Steele and John S. Major (1999: 70) remind us that "fashion is not *about* the accurate historical reconstruction of past styles. To say that fashion involves the creation of *fantasies* is not a valid criticism, although it is certainly true that the fantasies expressed in fashion may be subject to critical deconstruction."

Asian textiles, apparel and accessories began to influence Latin American fashions when both regions were still part of the Spanish Empire's trade routes and territory. While the dynamics of supply and demand often obeyed colonizers' tastes and desires, it also by extension accommodated the taste and needs of the colonized lower classes. Cannon (1988: 25) suggests that the fundamental unity of the fashion process is the "manipulation of appearance to enhance or maintain a positive self-image." To some extent, Spanish colonizers where in charge of "manipulating the appearance" of the colonized people; on the other hand, Spaniards in Mexico and the major cities in Latin America were up-to-date with the latest European fashions that – curiously – embraced Far Eastern ideas of design and utility. This multicultural presentation of fashion had already been witnessed in Europe during the seventeenth and eighteenth centuries, when the closets of the wealthy were filled with the magnificent textiles of the East, a fact that brought a "new pattern and possibility to the Western dress" (Koda and Martin 1994: 12). In Latin America and particularly in Mexico, the same phenomenon occurred except that the fashions also adopted the characteristics and styles of the natives transforming the apparel not only in ostentatious garments but eclectic in all the senses of the word. As Magnus Mörner (1967: 62) writes, "In the seventeenth and eighteenth centuries, the Indians, by imitating the Spanish dress of the day, created the costumes that nowadays are considered to be typically 'Indian'." With these thoughts in mind, this chapter analyzes how Far Eastern fashions influenced the apparel of the upper classes and, in the process, transformed the fashions of the lower classes. If in the colonizers' eyes, Latin America was regarded as the "exotic" Other, what would happen when another "exotic" culture influenced its very ways? Who would remain "exotic"?

The impact of Far Eastern influences in Latin America has long been underestimated. Between 1565 and 1815, ships that belonged to the Spanish empire crossed the Pacific Ocean to established ports and trading posts, carrying merchandise from Manila to Acapulco. In Mexico these goods were resold to buyers from other regions within Latin America. The so-called "Chinese ships," or Manila galleons carried silks, spices and other valuable goods of the East to Acapulco. Manila was a strategic meeting point for silks from the north and spices from the south. Fine cottons were exported from the Mogul Empire in India, namely from Bengal and the coasts of Coromandel and Malabar. Other cotton goods, such as blue *cambayas*, were made in China, while the *mantas* (coverings) were products of the Philippines. When returning to the Far East, the galleons transported silver argosies laden with Peruvian and Mexican pesos (Schurz 1959: 15, 60).

In sixteenth-century Mexico, the demand for products from the Far East, particularly silk, clothes and accessories, was such that a report from 1573 mentions that two galleons that had arrived in Acapulco carried 712 pieces of Chinese silk among other goods. The Manila galleons mainly transported silk to the region. There were silks of every variety, design, and weave: the flowered silks of Canton, gauze, velvets, fine damasks, taffetas, rougher grosgrains, heavy brocades, fine cottons. Shipments of silk apparel, including stockings, petticoats, skirts, velvet bodices, robes, shawls, kimonos and shoes also arrived with these same ships. Accessories from the Far East shipped to Acapulco included fans with ribs of ivory and sandalwood, dressing or grooming combs, ornamental combs, handkerchiefs, small brass bells and scarves. It is important to note, however, that not all silks and textiles were meant for clothing. Galleon chests were also filled with silk bed coverings and tapestries, tablecloths and napkins, as well as handkerchiefs and rich garments for the service of convents and churches (Schurz 1959: 32).

Much of this merchandise was destined only for members of the Spanish aristocracy. A well-enforced caste system forbade others, as illustrated by a 1582 edict, to dress in similar fashions. Furthermore, Chloë Sayer reveals how different castes were required to distinguish themselves along the racial and gender lines. The same edict states that "negro, mulatto, and *mestizo* women were forbidden to dress like Indians unless married to Indians: should they fail to comply they were threatened with imprisonment and one hundred lashes of the whip" (Sayer 1985b: 91). Black and mulatto women could not wear silk, pearls, or gold, unless married to Spanish men. As revealed in the period's caste paintings, women wore different Indian skirts, shawls, blouses, corset-covers and under-doublets. What is most striking, however, is that the apparel does not always obey caste-based dress codes. Some compositions depict fruit stalls run by Indian women and those of other castes. García Sáiz (1989: 42) points out that women of all castes always seem fashionably dressed, with native or foreign skirts and striking shawls, pearl earrings, necklaces and velvet ribbons. Thomas Gage, who seems to have studied the fashions of Mexico City fervently, confirms:

> Their clothing is a petticoat of silk or cloth, with many silver or golden laces, with a very broad ribbon of some light colour with long silver or golden tags hanging down

before, the whole length of their petticoat to the ground, and the like behind; their waistcoats made like bodices, with skirts, laced likewise with gold or silver, without sleeves, and a girdle about their body of great price stuck with pearls and knots of gold (if they be any ways well esteemed of), their sleeves are broad and open at the end, of Holland or of fine China linen, wrought some with coloured silks, some with silk and gold, some with silk and silver, hanging down almost unto the ground. The locks of their heads are covered with some wrought coif, and over it another of network of silk bound with a fair silk, or silver, or golden ribbon which crosseth the upper part of their forehead, and hath commonly worked out in letters some light and foolish love posy. Their bare, black, and tawny breasts are covered with bobs hanging from their chains of pearls. (Gage 1958: 69)

For women – and men, arguably – of the middle and upper classes, silks, linens and lace from the Far East were important commodities. Following a stroll about Mexico City's Alameda, Gage would refer to those gentlemen used to "[having] their train of blackamoor slaves, some a dozen, some half a dozen, waiting on them, in brave and gallant liveries, heavy with gold and silver lace, with silk stockings on their black legs, and roses on their feet, and swords by their sides" (Gage 1958: 73). This description serves as an example of the cultural significance of Far Eastern textiles and motifs among all classes.

In the sixteenth and seventeenth centuries, the upper classes emulated those styles from Spain that were fashioned with Far Eastern materials. Men wore jerkins, shirts, hose, puffed breeches, cloaks, wide-brimmed hats and caps. Close fitting knee-length breeches, higher hats, and velvet caps with feathers became quite fashionable. Women donned dresses, chemises, doublets, underskirts, detachable sleeves, cloaks and bonnets. During the eighteenth century, dresses became even more elaborate and incorporated lace ruffs. Intricate brocades and embroidery also became very popular. This rich splendor in apparel was also evident in the garments of the Church, because the material was embroidered with gold material and silk threads. Nuns wore veils embroidered by indigenous peoples with silk, gold, and pearls (Sayer 1985b: 90–1), a fact that made these fashions not only flamboyant and eclectic but unique.

Indian and *mestizo* artisans seemed enchanted with the hand painted motifs and needlework of Chinese textiles, as their hands imitated these designs enthusiastically and with devotion. According to Chloe Sayer, Spanish needlework already had a diverse series of stitches. Even though indigenous peoples already possessed ancient embroidering techniques, their role in the production of garments led to the appropriation of Spanish techniques to be practiced on imported textiles from China and the Philippines (Sayer 1985b: 84). As Lyman Johnson establishes, "Indian women were actively involved in the production of textiles, ceramics, and other products before the conquest and continued to dominate these fields throughout the colonial period . . ." and adds that "Indian master craftsmen were found among the painters, sculptors, silk weaves, glove makers, and many other artisan groups" (Johnson 1986: 231). Worked with threads of silk, cotton, linen, or gilt, the embroidery was completed on Far

Eastern textiles with a mix of Indian and European designs. A good example of this would have been a broad scope of flat or satin stitches of Mexican flora and fauna.

These textiles and needlework were not the only Far Eastern fashions to appeal to the upper classes. Mexican porcelain provides an interesting example, for as Jean McClure Mudge suggests, large jars of a range of quality from the Far East influenced Mexican potters, particularly those working in Puebla de los Ángeles (Mudge 1986: 46). Colonial monuments such as *riscos* (rocky cliffs or crags) were often decorated with various porcelains from China and Mexico, creating uniquely baroque structures. Mudge adds, "The proximity of these two sorts of ceramics symbolizes the close connection between native wares and their Chinese models over the years" (Mudge 1986: 84). This porcelain or chinaware was extremely fashionable among the aristocracy, its members aspired to own at least one piece and if fortunate, to stockpile an impressive collection. As Gustavo Curiel emphasizes, the varying qualities of china made this fashion accessible to all levels of colonial society, where even "in the humblest dwellings one might find tea cups, plates, or ornaments made of an inferior quality of porcelain" (Curiel 2002: 30).

By the eighteenth century, imports from the Far East were consumed regularly, with silk from China and cotton from India easily obtained. A 1720 Regulation declared that "Chinese goods form the ordinary dress of the natives of New Spain" and Viceroy Revillagigedo declared that "Philippine commerce is acclaimed in this kingdom, because its merchandise supplies the poor folk of the country" (quoted in Schurz 1959: 362). The importation of goods was not limited to Mexico, with items sold in Peru, Panama, and Chile; all Asian goods made their way through Acapulco and on to vessels headed to Peru, Ecuador, Panama, and Nicaragua. The places that traded most of these Asian goods were Mexico and Peru, however, since they even had established markets where people could buy luxurious items, such as Mexico City's San Agustín Street and Lima's Mercaderes Street. Here, much was available for purchase: large quantities of handkerchiefs, women's combs, fans with ribs of ivory and sandalwood, eye glasses, hats, and what are known as bibelots of ivory, jade and jasper; small brass bells, eye thimbles, paper balloons and even toothpicks. Bibelots were available to most of the population; soon after their arrival they were imitated, transformed and reproduced by Indian hands. As José Benítez emphasizes, indigenous natives produced thousands of fans with imported paper from China and also learned and applied a technique used in the Philippines to weave palm hats (Benítez 1946: 146).

The trade of the Manila Galleon would come to an end in 1815, following the outbreak of civil unrest throughout Latin America and the ensuing wars for independence from Spain. In Mexico, fashion was considered a social problem that affected the values of the population at large.[2] In Mexico, like in most Latin American countries, a national form of dress developed that meshed old styles with new ones. Imports from the Far East had for the most part halted, but nostalgia for the Manila galleon and its goods would be represented in the popular literature of the period. The American-born Spaniard protagonist of José Joaquín Fernández de Lizardi's *El periquillo sarniento* (1816), finding himself in Manila for eight years following a sentence that forced him to leave Mexico, would make a fortune by sending goods to his native country for sale.

Among the many accounts and lithographs that illustrate early nineteenth-century apparel,[3] the one that stands out is the series of letters written by Frances Calderón de la Barca during her two years of residence in Mexico (1837–9). In letters to friends and relatives, she details Mexican customs and manners such as the one practiced by the indigenous women of Uruapa:

> They wear "*naguas*," a petticoat of black cotton with a narrow white and blue stripe, made very full, and rather long; over this, a sort of short chemise made of coarse white cotton, and embroidered in different coloured silks. It is called the *sutunacua* – over all is a black *reboso* [sic], striped with white and blue, with a handsome silk fringe of the same colours. When they are married, they add a white embroidered veil, and a remarkably pretty coloured mantle, the *huepilli*, which they seem to pronounce *guipil*. The hair is divided and falls down behind in two long plaits, fastened at the top by a bow of ribbon and a flower. In this dress there is no alteration from what they wore in former days; saving that the women of a higher class wore a dress of finer cotton with more embroidery, and a loose garment over all, resembling a priest's surplice, when the weather was cold. (Calderón de la Barca 1966: 498)

The silk embroidery in the chemise and *rebozo* suggest the early influences of the Far East combined with pre-Hispanic elements. According to scholars, the *rebozo* was first a carrying-cloth of pre-Hispanic origin, or an *ayate*, which was later transformed into an *ikat*-patterned shawl at the time that Far Eastern techniques were introduced. As Sayer suggests through the findings of Donald and Dorothy Cordry, *rebozos* were often *ikat*-dyed, a style of decoration that was already well developed in Southeastern Asian garments. She notes that the fringes of the Mexican rebozo were – and still are – elaborately finger-knotted like the fringed ends of Manila shawls (Sayer 1985b: 107–8).

Calderón de la Barca goes on to describe other modes, including that of the *poblana* (the woman of Puebla). For more than a century, scholars have compared her costume to that of Spanish models. In 1921, Nicolás León suggested that this costume was identical to the one of the Spanish *manola* [a villager] of the beginning of the nineteenth century (León 1971: 68–70). In 1948 Manuel de J. Solís stated that the garment was modeled after Oaxacan indigenous women's clothing (quoted by Carrasco Puente 1950: 108). Chía Bolaños Montiel (1993) emphasizes that the dress was worn since colonial times and that it therefore has Spanish origins but Mexican characteristics.[4] However, few have considered its Far Eastern influences. While the costume's petticoat seems derived from Spanish models, its embroidered gold and silver threads on satin – with designs depicting Mexican landscapes in a symmetrical fashion – are in essence Chinese. If *rebozos* and silk stockings were influenced by Asian designs and techniques, why not the china poblana costume? In later descriptions of *poblana* dress, Calderón de la Barca notes its "gold fringe, gold bands and spangles; an under-petticoat, embroidered and trimmed with rich lace, to come below it" and "a satin vest, open in front, and embroidered in gold; a silk sash tied behind, the ends fringed with gold, and a small silk handkerchief which crosses the neck, with gold fringe" (Calderón de la Barca 1966: 84).

Carefully crafted with silk and gold threads, the dress incorporated accessories like spangles that remit to the Far East. While *poblana* dress remains a symbol of Mexican identity, what is the source of its name? Several scholars have suggested that the first *china poblana* was Catarina de San Juan, an Asian slave taken to Mexico during the seventeenth century, where she would live as a virgin, martyr, visionary and devout Catholic. Born in Delhi, India in 1613, she was seized at the age of ten by Portuguese corsairs. Baptized by Jesuits and sold in the slave market in Manila, she made her way to Puebla, Mexico, where she lived until her death in 1688. While she served as a slave to a Spanish couple, her visions earned her several followers. What we know about her childhood in Delhi and life in Puebla comes from her biographers and confessors José del Castillo Graxeda (1987[1692]) and Alonso Ramos (1689, 1690, 1692).[5] Even though she would never speak Spanish fluently and was illiterate, the religious power of her testimonies was never obscured. Mirra (Catarina's name before she was baptized) claimed that she descended from a great king, although she could not recall his name. Ramos writes that Catarina's father was a holy man who was able to stop the storms and heal the sick. His account also describes the Virgin Mary's appearance before Borta, Mirra's mother, when she gave birth to her princess. The Virgin Mary then took Borta to a hidden treasure trove, the source of Mirra's gold and jewels. When Portuguese captors found her, they stripped Mirra of her regalia and made her a slave.[6]

Her legacy lives on in cultural documents from later centuries. Historian Antonio Carreón studied Catarina de San Juan's testimony of her imperial past in his *Historia de la Ciudad de Puebla de los Angeles* (1896), claiming that the Asian "princess" had invented *china poblana* dress. Decades later, the government of Puebla built a public monument to honor the memory of Catarina, believing that she embodied a national archetype. Even with these commemorations, there are enormous differences between the attire of that first *china poblana* – according to Castillo Graxeda (1987), Catarina often wore a simple dress, shawl and bonnet – and that of the typical nineteenth-century Mexican villager. What cannot be overemphasized is the fact that the legend of Catarina de San Juan and subsequent revisions of this nationalist icon have allowed Mexicans to express an identity that rescues a small part of their past with the Far East. Catarina had been sent to Mexico in a Manila Galleon, one of the same ships that carried Asian textiles, accessories, and clothing to Latin America. Today's *china poblana* has a skirt that resembles the national flag: glittering red, green and white embroidered with spangles that form the eagle devouring the snake atop a cactus. The blouse is usually white and lace-trimmed, although sometimes it is embroidered with silk. A tri-colored rebozo is wound around the waist. Celebrating the diversity of the Mexican nation, the dress of the *china poblana* is an expression of the many faces of Mexico, as intricately complex as the spangled design of her skirt.

During the second half of the nineteenth century there was no direct trade between Asia and Latin America. Because of international trade regulations, Far Eastern textiles, decorative accessories and bibelots made their way to Latin American from Europe and the United States. At this time, as Roberto González Echevarría notes, Cuba (a colony of Spain until 1898) began importing Chinese workers in hopes of ending its African slave trade. May the presence of these workers have influenced modes of dress and customs in Havana? One artifact, in particular, comes to mind: the "Chinese flute," which has played a significant role in musical "fashions" since that period. In the late nineteenth century, Latin American cities imported several items from the Far East: silks from China, Japan, and India; damask; linen and silk handkerchiefs and neckties; silk robes and slippers; cotton; blue and white linen; baskets; straw hats and parasols; paper; artifacts made of ivory, bronze, lacquer, tortoiseshell, porcelain, and bamboo; statues and figurines; vases and flowerpots; serving dishes; chairs, shelves and folding screens; sewing cases; and game sets for checkers, dominoes and chess.[7]

The literature of this period makes several associations between the aesthetic value of these artifacts. Rubén Darío's short story, "The Death of the Empress of China" narrates an unusual love triangle consisting of a sculptor, his wife, and a statue sent as a gift from a friend who travels the Far East (the bust of the Empress of China). The friend writes to Recaredo, the protagonist, "I came and I saw. (I have not yet conquered.) . . . One leap and I landed in China. I'm the agent for a California importing firm that deals in silk, enamels, ivory, and other *chinoiseries*" (Darío 1997: 108). As an intellectual, Recaredo would give anything to speak Chinese or Japanese. Most importantly, he is a sculptor in pursuit of the perfect form and whose passions are these *chinoiseries* and bibelots, but also the authentic works of Yokohama, Nagasaki, Kyoto, Nanking, and Peking: ". . . knives, pipes, weird and hideous masks like faces in drugged dreams; mandarin minidwarfs with bloated bellies and indented eyes; frog-mouthed freaks with big, gaping, toothy grins; tiny, gruff tartar soldiers" (Darío 1997: 107). Recaredo places the *Empress* on an altar that resembles a Buddhist sanctuary, as if she represents a divine power and so that she might be complemented by the motifs of a folding screen complete with rice fields (symbol of life and strength) and cranes (longevity). The sculptor surrounds his new statue with cultural artifacts from China and Japan – a small umbrella and lacquered plate – that might just have easily been purchased in Valparaíso, Chile, Buenos Aires, Havana, or Mexico City. Might Rubén Darío have known that the first American ship to sail East was named the *Empress of China*?[8] Combining the high with the low, his display of Asian artifacts reveals how much these objects were valued at that time.

Darío's contemporaries confirm this great demand.[9] With industrialization and massive immigration in the late nineteenth century, the general public became fascinated with Asian artifacts. It was quite fashionable to acquire statues, all kinds of china, fans, porcelain, ivory figurines, and inexpensive reproductions of small decorative items. Japanese and Chinese robes and slippers indoors were also in vogue. Outdoors, people used fans, shoes and printed garments with the images of Eastern monks, goddesses and pagodas, as well as Asian flora and fauna.[10] Even the *mantilla*, or *mantón de Manila* (Spanish shawl), a garment that had originated in the Philippines during the time of the China trade, was still in style.

The twentieth century witnessed even greater imports of articles alongside the massive immigration of Chinese, Korean, and Japanese people to Latin America. During the early part of the century, thousands of Japanese people arrived in Peru and Brazil. Large groups of Chinese people landed in Mexico.[11] In Cuba, the Chinese migrations halted, but a substantial population still remained. Many of these immigrants remained within their own communities initially but they have been able to integrate themselves economically, socially, and culturally in their new home countries (Baltar Rodríguez 1997: 83). Those foreigners who moved to the countryside have opened small businesses; those who stayed in the cities established small-scale Chinatowns. In her memoirs, Renée Méndez Capote describes how Chinese salesmen went door to door in the Cuban countryside, selling silks, stockings, handkerchiefs, robes, and shoes (Capote 1969: 65).[12] In the city, she remembers, one could buy Asian figurines, lamps, porcelains and all types of articles for interior decoration, as well as gauze, silk, crinoline, cambric and several other materials (Capote 65: 143–4). As the demand for goods increased, new stores were established. Still, the size of Chinatowns (or "Japanesetowns") in cities like Havana, Lima, Mexico City, and São Paulo pale in comparison to those in Los Angeles or London. In most cases, they comprise a few stores and a restaurant on one street.

Although small in size, Chinatowns in Latin America have had a significant impact on the fashion of the times. On occasion, articles sold there become trendsetters, such as jade bracelets, embroidered shoes, amulets, hair clips, robes, dresses, sandals, figurines, incense and so forth. Needless to say, whatever is in vogue is normally mass produced. These trends have influenced the domain of language in the process, as in the case of the Peruvian "Sayonara" sandal, which means "Good-bye." Produced en masse and retaining its Japanese name, this import became all the rage in the late twentieth century. Other influences from the Far East appear in apparel designs and textiles: Nepalese *pershamina* shawls, Indian silk dresses, sari-inspired wraps, and Chinese-inspired patterns.

In Buenos Aires, Santiago and Mexico City, the art of Feng Shui has overtaken trendy sections. Its practitioners believe that the harmoniousness of a room or environment depends on its layout; therefore, one studies the energy flow patterns of rooms as well as the design of exterior landscapes. Given areas of the house require specific furniture, lights, objects and colors to ensure the proper flow of energy in every room and thus create harmony. Like all fashions, Feng Shui will eventually lose its popularity. But sooner or later, it will return with new characteristics that cater to a younger generation's tastes. In this case, the appropriations of Asian themes and designs cannot be considered statements of exoticism, particularly because it represents the appropriation of "exotic" Far Eastern from "exotic" Latin America. As Valerie Steele and John S. Major suggest: "What may be new in our own time is the intention on the part of many designers to integrate Asian shapes, fabrics, iconography, and other design elements into Western fashion, not simply as yet another resurgence of exoticism, but as a genuine expression of broadening cultural horizons around the world" (Steele and Major 1999: 98)

For centuries, Latin American fashions have also represented this fascinating, unwavering multiculturalism thanks to the influences of the Far East.

Part 2

Altered Traditions

5

Ixcacles: Maguey-fiber Sandals in Modern Mexico

Pamela Scheinman

In twentieth-century Mexico many indigenous garments have disappeared or undergone a gradual transition from daily wear to ceremonial costume to a craft produced for an urban tourist market, sometimes inferior in workmanship and denuded of symbolism. Textile scholars and anthropologists have debated repeatedly whether modernization imposes inevitable and irreversible conditions, in effect, coercing conservative subsistence farmers into a cash economy and *mestizo* culture; or whether ethnic groups living in small rural communities can mediate the process, shedding certain traditions and adopting others in order to maintain their cultural identity (Garcia Canclini 1993; Meisch 1996; Sandstrom 1991). As Western clothing increasingly obscures distinctions, important social meaning often can be found in an overlooked detail, like footwear (Hendrickson 1995: 99).

Sandals with characteristic stitched sole, raised heel guard, and ankle ties, handmade entirely from agave fiber, ranked lowest in the elaborate hierarchy of Aztec footwear, only a step above going barefoot (Fernandez Ledesma 1930: 68). Similar humble sandals – called *ixcacles* (from the prefix for *ixtle*, or maguey fiber, and *cacle* for sandal) or *huaraches de ixtle* – still are made and sold by villagers in San Felipe Tepemaxalco, in the mountains of southwestern Puebla, from the spiky *agave* plants that grow wild in the rock-strewn fields and steep ravines of this semi-arid zone (Ávila Blomberg 1997: 113). No one remembers the sandals ever being worn in Tepemaxalco. Instead, the craft provided vital cash income to a population of subsistence farmers. As weaving, it has been considered women's work.

Generations of sandal makers have traversed rough footpaths, within view of the snow-capped volcano Popocatépetl, to supply indigenous women in far-off Hueyapan, Morelos, where *ixcacles* comprised part of the famous hand-woven female attire. Since in the past most Indian women went barefoot, the designation of specific footgear conferred prestige. Today, even when the wearer chooses manufactured clothing, her sandals identify her birthplace, ethnicity and status. Midwives and healers also prescribe their use at home, both during the postpartum period and recovery from serious illness, to restore a woman's vitality. And custom requires every man, woman and child – not just in Hueyapan but commonly among Nahuas throughout central Mexico – to be buried in a new pair of maguey-fiber sandals "to ease the journey" to the afterlife. A single style of *ixcacle* has predominated for these functional, magical and metaphorical purposes.

Remoteness and poverty tended to insulate many mountainous pueblos from change well into the twentieth century. However, from the mid-1950s onward, improved schools, better roads and transportation, job training, penetration of mass media and emigration to cities for employment accelerated the abandonment of indigenous dress and spoken Nahuatl (the Aztec language). Progressive modernization promoted urban, *mestizo* values. In a society whose median age now is twenty-two, *ixcacles* are under threat from plastic flats, leather shoes, rubber thongs and sneakers. A generation of younger women in Hueyepan has never worn maguey-fiber sandals, except perhaps as costume for a school pageant. Fewer families supply the town, and none sells directly at the weekly Tuesday market any more.

As a result, craftsmen recently have modified sandal designs slightly to appeal to tourists seeking items that are natural, handmade and authentic. They also have created miniature versions to clothe saints and hang from key chains or rear-view mirrors. It is unlikely, however, that the souvenir market, the vogue for beach sandals or counterculture fashion or the revival of interest in Nahua culture among assimilated urbanites will replace traditional wearers.

Instead, the widespread and persistent "cult of the dead" continues to sustain this ancient craft. A cycle of Lenten fairs, held at pilgrimage sites in the states of Mexico and Morelos, acts as one distribution point for wholesale buyers, who travel great distances annually, then resell sandals at small groceries and tackle stores (*jarciarías*) throughout central Mexico. A few families maintain sales to small shops in Hueyapan and the city of Cuautla, while itinerant vendors from Tepemaxalco travel more widely throughout the year as wholesalers.

One obstacle to perpetuating traditional burial customs is the spread of evangelism, which discourages or prohibits practices associated with folk Catholicism. Another is the ageing of craftsmen and a growing "generation gap." Virtually every Tepemaxalcan knows how to make maguey-fiber sandals, but fewer young people devote their time to it. Instead, most now attend secondary school and migrate to larger cities or the United States for jobs, at least briefly – opportunities previously unavailable to their parents. Gradually the economy of the village is improving, as dollars wired home fund the construction of new homes and shops, and government aid programs to drought-stricken areas somewhat offset dependence on craft income.

All these factors currently in play lend urgency to the firsthand documentation of *ixcacles*, particularly because a very similar, more finely woven maguey-fiber sandal, worn by Zapotec women of Yalalag and Zoogocho, in the Villa

Alta district of the Sierra of Oaxaca, disappeared by the late 1980s (Ávila Blomberg 1997: 113; Johnson 1992: 365). San Felipe Tepemexalco is the last place in Mexico where *ixtle* sandals of pre-Hispanic design are being fabricated and exchanged. The tradition, though diminished in volume, remains largely intact. This chapter examines the social and economic importance of maguey-fiber sandals among people who still identify with an agricultural cycle and Nahua cosmology.

A Brief History of Mexican Sandals

Ixcacles consist of four elements made in a specific order: 1) a foot-shaped sole (*la suela*) of three layers of fiber, rolled and doubled over, then stitched tightly in a concentric or horizontal pattern; 2) a rectangular heel guard (*el carcañal* or *la talonera*), like the back of a shoe, of weft-faced plain weave; 3) a toe band (*el puente*) woven over three (or up to ten) warps;[1] and 4) two fine, two-ply cords, one of which loops from the outer corner of the heel guard through the center of the toe band and is fastened around the ankle by a slip knot.

Ixcacles are one example of the astonishing diversity of sandals (and shoes) used prior to the Spanish conquest, from which modern peasant huaraches (or *guaraches*) descend. Depictions with a raised heel guard – a feature unique in Mesoamerica – abound on ceramics, bas-reliefs (Palenque and Bonampak), statuary and frescoes (Toltec, Mexica and Maya) and sixteenth-century picture books (Aztec and Mixtec). Despite a paucity of archaeological textiles in Mexico due to climactic conditions, a number of adult and miniature *ixtle* sandals have been found in dry caves, which bear a striking resemblance to modern examples.[2] Richard MacNeish excavated twelve adult sandals or sandal fragments associated with burials from the Coxcatlán Cave in the Tehuacán Valley, Puebla (MacNeish 1961: 26–7; 1967: II: 183–7).[3] The relatively small number of sandals, as compared with yields of other organic materials, and their late-horizon date (1250–1540 AD) led him to speculate that the site may have been a repository for an underclass, many of whom would have gone barefoot (MacNeish 1967: II: 183).

Aztec society enforced strict dress codes. Basic garments were the same for all classes, so the quality of materials, decoration and accessories denoted rank (Johnson 1971: 312). Thus, sandals fashioned from fine cotton or animal skins (doe, jaguar, ocelot and fox) were the prerogative of gods, rulers, priests, warriors and wealthy merchants. At the other extreme, peasants and peons went shoeless, "but as they rose in social scale they might put on *cactli*, sandals with fiber or hide soles," at least for travel (Soustelle 1955: 128). *Ixcacles* ranked relatively low but conferred some prestige. Although females usually are shown barefoot, a few goddesses and elite women did possess sandals.[4]

Immediately after the Conquest, Bernal Díaz del Castillo, a conquistador under Hernán Cortés, discovered vendors at the vast Tlatelolco market, "who sold cloths of henequen and ropes and the sandals with which they are shod, which are made from the same plant" (Diaz del Castillo 1956: lxv, 216). The Spanish imposed new sumptuary laws. During the colonial period cattlemen and tanners arrived in New Spain, forming guilds to produce shoes and boots (Zaldívar 1996: 26–9). Wealthy people and urban *mestizos* distinguished themselves from rural hicks and Indians by adopting European styles, a situation not so different from the Aztecs' disdain for the Chichimec nomads from the northern deserts who arrived in the capital wearing "uncivilized" yucca or palm sandals (Sahagún cited in Berdan and Anawalt 1997: 186). The sale of native footwear, demeaned as *zapatos del indio* (Indian shoes), was restricted in cities. As recently as 1923, a ban on wearing huaraches in downtown Mexico City was legislated and violators threatened with a fine or jail term (Bazan 2001). Although such laws were not enforced in rural areas, bias existed.

As Arnold Bauer points out, the social distance between classes was accentuated in the early twentieth century by *shining* shoes with polish (Bauer 2001: 148). Bauer estimated that in the 1920s, among Mexico City's population of 400,000, only 50,000 wore shoes. After the Mexican Revolution, shoes gradually became a prerequisite for school attendance (Jiménez 1972: 25) and those seeking urban employment, an attitude reinforced by government-organized Cultural Missions sent "to civilize" indigenous pueblos. Footwear was considered such a clear measure of Indianness that beginning with the sixth national census in 1943 data was collected on those who wore shoes and those who wore sandals or went barefoot. However, by 1980 it was becoming increasingly difficult to distinguish *mestizos* from Indians, and this question was dropped (Sandstrom 1991: 65).

Daily and Fiesta Wear in Hueyapan, Morelos

Hueyapan, Morelos, located at the extreme northeast corner of the state, near the Puebla border, lies at an altitude of 2,340 meters above sea level in forests of pine and oak. According to the 2000 census, the population of this predominantly Nahua community numbers 5,681, of whom 3,048 are female. *Ixcacles*, which completed women's costume (*traje tipico*), proved ideal footwear in the extreme climate, with its hot midday sun and cold nights and mornings. Today only *abuelitas* (grandmothers) dress in the traditional ankle-length, indigo-dyed skirt (*chincuete*), pleated and tied with a brilliant red wool belt (*ceñidor*) over a short-sleeved, embroidered white cotton blouse, topped with a matching, blue-black wool serape. Local weavers spin, dye and weave the woolen garments. However, these have become rare and expensive, an example of what textile scholar Lynn A. Meisch calls a "costume survival." (Meisch 1991: 147).

Women in their eighties and nineties continue to wear *ixcacles*, as do many middle-aged women who have adopted Western-style clothing (cotton or polyester dresses and bibbed, gingham aprons) but prefer maguey-fiber sandals for reasons of comfort, cheapness and ethnic identity. As Juanita Rosales insisted: "These are *our shoes*" (personal communication, Hueyapan, 20 March 2002). A few women now reserve *ixcacles* for best. Josefina Hernández, who used to buy a half-dozen pairs at a time to wear around the house, now puts on *ixcacles* "by preference, not necessity" when she goes to sell flowers in the city of Cuautla (personal communication, Hueyapan, 24 June 2001). However, Gabriela Rivera complained that her grandchildren asked her not to wear *ixcacles* or speak Nahuatl outside the pueblo, because Indian ways embarrassed them (personal communication, Hueyapan, 24 June 2001). Younger women and girls reject "scratchy" maguey-fiber sandals in favor of more modern and fashionable footwear. They have been wearing tennis shoes or plastic flats since grade school, but might don *ixcacles* for a school program or to perform the dance of the *Inditas* on 12 December, the feast day of the Virgin of Guadalupe (Elvira Hernández, personal communication, Hueyapan, 25 June 2001).

A single style of sandal was worn daily, not only by women in Hueyapan, but by those in the nearby villages of San Felipe, San Juan, Tlacotepec, Alpanoca, Metepec and in the district center, Tetela del Volcán. Although different classes (and prices) of *ixcacles* still are sold, Hueyapeñas demand a high standard of workmanship. The soles must be firm but pliable, with tight rows of stitching evenly spaced and an outline of chain stitch around the perimeter as a finish. This preference is both aesthetic and practical because

Figure 5.1. A pair of maguey-fiber sandals from San Felipe Tepemaxalco, Puebla.

Altered Traditions

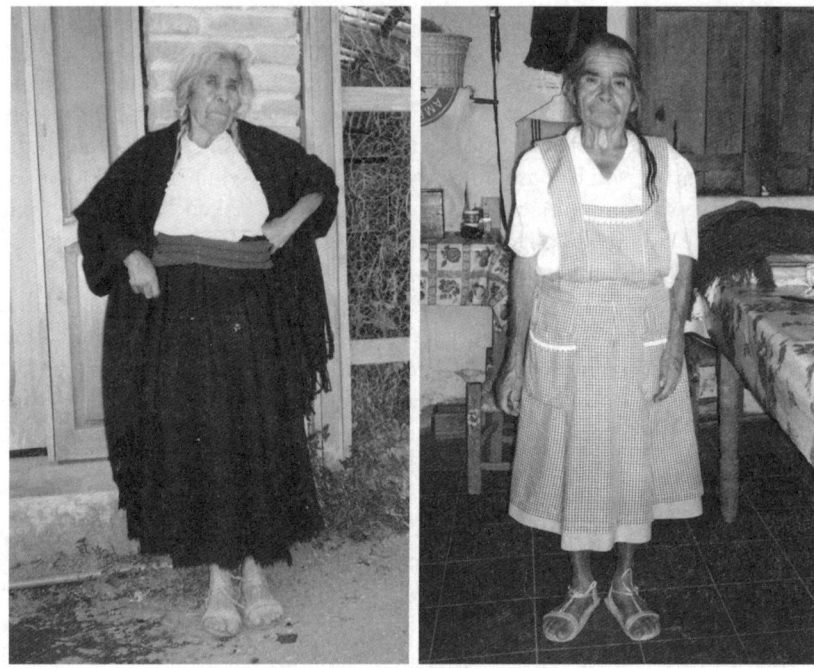

Figure 5.2. On the left: Doña Angela Escobar (age 80) wearing the traditional *traje* of Hueyapan, Morelos. On the right: Hueyapan shop owner Doña Camila Perez Zamudio (age 87) in her *ixcacles*. Photographs by Pamela Scheinman.

the soles must resist puncture, protecting the feet from thorns and stones. The plain finger-weave of the raised heel back and three-warp toe band must be fine, tight, trimmed clean of loose fibers and *bien planchado* (pounded smooth). The top edge of the heel should be finished with three vertical rows of weaving; the bottom edge, sewn flush with the sole back. Finally, the fiber must be sun-bleached to a light color.

The "age of reason" at which a girl received her first pair of sandals varied. Eighty-eight-year-old Doña Augustina reported: "When I was old enough 'to open my eyes,' my mother said, 'You are a señorita now, it's time to buy your first pair of *ixcacles*,' and she took me to Doña Camila's store" (personal communication, Hueyapan, 20 March 2002). Juanita Rosales Rivera, who is twenty years younger, underwent this rite of passage at six or eight (personal communication, Hueyapan, 20 March 2002). *Ixcacles* conferred social status among indigenous women with the means to buy them and symbolized their identity within the community.

Prior to the 1953 construction of roads to Tlacotepec and Tetela, shops in Hueyapan stocked only bare necessities like matches, soap, candles and needles.

Ixcacles were the only women's shoes sold locally. They were very cheap but not durable: a pair worn daily lasted about a month.[5] Roads were prerequisites for establishing the Tuesday market (Friedlander 1975: 63). Tepemaxalcans regularly displayed dozens of sandals in the plaza, then hawked their unsold pairs door-to-door, to shopkeepers and housewives. Wholesalers often bought at the Hueyapan market.

When Donald and Dorothy Cordry, coauthors of *Mexican Indian Costume*, visited this market in 1963 costume change had begun: they noted little girls were dressed in cotton dresses (Cordry and Cordry 1968: 249).[6] The introduction of chemical fertilizers in the 1950s altered the emigration pattern from seasonal work in lowland sugar-cane fields. As farming became more productive, men stayed home, and increasingly, young women moved into more permanent domestic jobs in Cuernavaca or Mexico City. On visits home they brought urban goods and values to the pueblo (Friedlander 1975: 63). Inexpensive shoes of Mexican manufacture were followed by cheap imports from Taiwan and China (Gomez Gonzalez, personal communication, Cuautla, 15 March 2002). An irrigation project supported by Morelos governor Lauro Ortega (1982–8) spurred further growth of commercial orchards (peaches, plums, pears, raspberries) and floriculture (roses, carnations, lilies). Improved education and public transportation also eased some of the restrictions imposed on older generations of women kept at home. Retention of *ixcacles* divides along generational (and class) lines.

Ritual Use of Sandals for Curing and Burial

Comfort and natural fiber are properties that have linked *ixcacles* with traditional healing practices. Nahuas incorporated the Greco-Roman theory of "hot-cold," which dominated sixteenth-century European medicine and was brought to Mexico by the Spaniards, into the Aztec system of complementary opposites (see Foster 1991 and López Austin 1974). According to this theory, everything in the universe "from God to an aspirin tablet" is designated as "hot," "tepid," or "cold," or some degree in between, based on an association with either the sun ("hot"), earth ("tepid") or water ("cold"), rather than its actual temperature (Madsen 1960: 163). To cure an imbalance in the normally temperate body, caused by an extreme emotion or sensation, the healer administered substances of the opposite classification.[7]

Pregnancy heats up the body, but giving birth depletes this energy, making a new mother vulnerable and "cold." In Hueyapan, a woman customarily received a pair of *ixcacles* during the forty-day postpartum period, because the natural *agave* fiber warmed her feet. Prohibited from any work for about a month, she gradually resumed light household chores for another few weeks, until considered healthy again (Elvira Hernandez, personal communication, Hueyapan, 25 June 2001). The prescription usually included eating certain foods, massage and bathing in a *temascal*, the traditional sweat-bath heated by hot stones.[8] Today, many of these dome-shaped chambers lie in disuse, replaced by modern plumbing (Alvarez 1987: 169; Friedlander 1975: 24–5). Likewise the custom of new mothers putting on *ixcacles* has declined.

Older women still wear *ixtle* sandals during recovery from a severe illness, a period that may last from two to six months or more. A patient may order a softer pair with widely spaced stitching on the soles or buy a slightly larger size to provide maximum comfort. Those who suffer from chronic arthritis and poor circulation also find *ixcacles* therapeutic. Even Tepemaxalcans, who claim never to have worn the sandals they make for daily use, occasionally endorse their curative powers or put them on "to relax at home."

Although arguably the use of a warm pair of slippers is universal and commonsensical, by calling their sandals *calientitos* ("hot"), informants ascribe them with medicinal or magic properties. However, wearers frequently praise sandals as *frescos*, or cooling. When asked about this apparent contradiction, they made a distinction between the open design, which ventilates the foot with a flow of air, and the *ixtle* fiber, which comes from nature (from a plant grown in full sunlight) and insulates the foot against the cold ground and atmosphere. Cures for female complaints typically stress hotness. They are administered within the house or family compound, as opposed to outside in the street or larger world.

What will happen as Western values continue gaining credence? Perhaps some belief in the benefits of maguey-fiber sandals may generalize, as suggested by the *mestiza* from Zacualpan, Morelos, a town near Hueyapan, who described wearing a pair of *ixcacles* after undergoing a hysterectomy performed in a hospital (Isabel Cerezo Vargas, personal communication, Zacualpan, 2 March 2002). Recently, aggressive marketing of packaged "natural medicines" (plant derivatives mixed with Vaseline or dispensed in gelatin capsules) by itinerant vendors, who tout their products on local buses, or consult with patients by appropriating the patio of a private residence for a few hours, has met an increasingly enthusiastic reception among both rural and urban residents. Most are either too poor to pay for doctors and prescription drugs, or believe in the efficacy of household remedies but seek the legitimacy a label confers. This trend also would appear to favor wearing *ixcacles*, if they are considered as healthful, natural footwear rather than merely Indian shoes.

However, the most widespread and significant use of *ixcacles* is for burial. This custom persists among several ethnic groups. Nahuas throughout central Mexico, in the states of Mexico, Morelos, Puebla, Tlaxcala and Guerrero (and perhaps in Veracruz, Michoacan and others) ritually place new sandals on the feet of deceased men, women and children before burial. *Ixcacles* owe their survival today largely to this cult of the dead.

The concept of an afterlife fuses Catholic heaven and hell with Aztec Mictlán, the place of the dead. Certain widely accepted beliefs – that death is a natural part of the life cycle in which the soul moves on to another place, that the way to the next world is beset with obstacles, such as rocky roads and ferocious animals, and that a dog leads or swims the deceased soul across a river to reach its destination – appear ancient in origin (Toor 1947: 163; Madsen 1960: 13, 209–13). After a period in purgatory, the majority of souls are consigned to one of the nine underground levels of Mictlán (Smith 1998: 141–2; Vaillant 1962: 30). The choice of a final resting place depends on the manner of death and on the provisions made by living relatives. This amounts to a form of ancestor worship, in which the deceased can be appealed to, like a saint, but also engenders a prevalent fear of vengeful or malicious ghosts. Therefore, a death obligates family members to observe funeral rites and a yearly commemoration. Families celebrate the Days of the Dead (1–2 November) by erecting an altar with offerings of candles, flowers, food and gifts, cleaning and decorating the gravesite and reciting prayers to honor the deceased.

In Hueyapan and the surrounding area a relative runs to buy *ixcacles* while the person is *in extremis*, if possible, before last rites are administered (Consuelo Hernandez, personal communication, Hueyapan, 19 March 2002). Friedlander gives an example of the urgency an individual feels in having a pair of sandals available for burial, quoting her informant Doña Zeferina's description of a near-death experience, in which she fainted in the steam bath and hallucinated that she entered a large church with its doors wide open to receive her: "The only concern Doña Zeferina had as she was going in was that she did not have her sandals on. She knew she was about to meet her Maker and she was bothered by the fact that she was barefoot at such an important moment. She then woke up and realized that she must have been at the Gates of Heaven" (Friedlander 1975: 43).[9] Today, it is common for an individual to purchase and put aside sandals in anticipation of his or her own death.[10]

According to Hernández, burial takes place within twenty-four hours. The corpse is dressed in clean clothes and a new pair of maguey-fiber sandals. *Ixcacles* neither tire the feet nor offend the dog's sense of smell, which would be thrown off by leather (Soustelle 1961: 202). The head is crowned with a colorful wreath of flowers. Children's hands are positioned with palms pressed together in prayer, while an adult's arms are crossed over the chest. A staff of *membrillo* (quince) is tucked under a man's arm as a defense against animals that he might encounter; the fruitwood is thought to generate new roots in the afterlife. The corpse is provided with water in a gourd container and tortillas in a woven shoulder bag for the long journey, just as a *campesino* might set out for his fields. Candles and bouquets of flowers – calla lilies, tuberoses and tiny white *nubes* – fill the room. People gather all night to recite prayers. The next morning guests are served breakfast. Four men bear the casket to the cemetery, accompanied by family members and friends on foot. Prayers recited on nine consecutive evenings conclude the *novenario*, and after forty days a final gathering is held.

The transmission of ancient practices often elicits the simplest explanation. "It's not written down anywhere, it's just the custom" (Andrés Pérez, personal communication, San Felipe Tepemaxalco, 6 January 2002). Froylan Martínez Cuenca, who builds elaborate Day of the Dead altars in the nearby *mestizo* town of Huaquechula, Puebla, echoed this sentiment: "The feet should always be shod with *ixcatles*: ... Sometimes we put them on just before death, sometimes we wait until after death. I don't know why we do this – I only know it's a devotion that we must perform" (Carmichael and Sayer 1990: 95). However, changes do take place, often for practical reasons. Another Huaquechulan, Candido Reyes Castillo, noted that a dead person's possessions, such as a man's machete, no longer are put into the coffin: "Why send a rich man to the grave with all his wealth, when it could help us who are alive?" (Carmichael and Sayer 1990: 100).

A significant change in these burial customs has been spurred by emigration. When young men working in the United States die abroad, certain rituals are not performed because they must be done at the place of death (Carmichael and Sayer 1990: 100). Perhaps this fact accounts for an unconfirmed report by Jaquelina Pérez Tejeda, who saw very crude *ixcacles* for sale in a Brooklyn, New York bodega (personal communication, San Felipe Tepemaxalco, 27 April 2001). Usually the sealed coffin is shipped home for proper burial.

Clearly, not everyone adheres to these religious customs. Early in the twentieth century missionaries began conversions. Several hundred Hueyapeños, especially in the outlying barrios of San Andrés, San Bartolo and San Felipe, belong to one of four Protestant sects – Pentecostals, Universalists, Seventh-Day Adventists and Jehovah's Witnesses. These prohibit or actively discourage "Catholic" rituals, including fiestas, and their numbers are growing (Friedlander 1975: 122). Martínez Cuenca reported the effect on Day of the Dead celebrations in his town: "Sadly, this year in Huaquechula, three new souls were left without *ofrendas*. Their families have broken with tradition ... they have been converted by evangelists" (Carmichael and Sayer 1990: 96). Death rituals reinforce cultural values of family, community and ethnicity. They are an important link with the past, reaffirming the cycle of life and balance in the universe.

Even emigrants to cities, whose lapse might be expected, are reluctant to shed certain beliefs, at least for a generation or two. Many continue to regard *ixcacles* as a remnant of ancient practice, necessary for their cultural continuity.

Lenten Fairs and the Changing Marketplace

The cult of the dead is perpetuated partly through the sale of *ixcacles* at a series of important Lenten fairs. Carnival Sunday (the Sunday preceding Ash Wednesday) marks the onset of one of the holiest periods in the Roman Catholic calendar. During the six Fridays of Lent that culminate in Easter week, masses and processions to venerate a miraculous image take place in many parts of the republic, alongside traditional dances and special markets, organized like ancient Aztec *tianguis* (market) by category of goods. In the region of the volcanoes, pilgrims, craftsmen, wholesalers and tourists from the states of Mexico, Morelos, Tlaxcala, Puebla, Guerrero and Veracruz converge on sacred sites to receive blessings, exchange goods and seek diversion.

Anthropologist Guillermo Bonfil Batalla documented one such cycle, dating to the sixteenth century (Batalla 1971: 167–79). Fairs are held on the first and sixth Fridays at Amecameca, Mexico. The largest falls on the third Friday at Tepalcingo, Morelos, which is famous for the abundant display of crafts, especially lacquer ware from Olinalá, Guerrero (Batalla 1971: 173). Other Lenten markets where *ixcacles* are sold include: Santiago Tecla (Puebla) on the fourth Friday, Señor de Tejalpa (Puebla) on the fifth Friday, Matlala (Puebla) on Palm Sunday and Huazulco (Morelos) or Santo Domingo Ayotlicha (Puebla) on the Tuesday (*martes santo*) before Easter Sunday.

Anticipated throughout the year, these fairs provide a key source of income during the hot, dry season between the late fall harvest and late spring planting, when food supplies run low and subsistence farmer-craftsmen need cash. Working speedily, María Fortina Martínez estimates she can make a dozen pairs of *ixcacles* every two weeks. Like many Tepemaxalcans she stockpiles the individual parts, then assembles them before traveling to a big fair (personal communication, San Felipe Tepemaxalco, 2 May 2001). Members of an extended family arrange to travel together by truck or bus, and are given *posada* (shelter) by local householders, who offer hospitality as a form of religious devotion. Those who attend Lenten fairs also incur an obligation to return year after year, so that a sense of ritual duty tempers purely commercial interests.[11]

A few sandal vendors circulate with no fixed spot, but most return to a designated locale, usually near the church atrium or among vendors of incense or handmade crafts.[12] Male vendors, who purchase sandals for cash from their neighbors in Tepemaxalco and resell at a profit, wait next to feed sacks filled with *ixcacles*. Women vendors spread plastic tarps and arrange displays on the ground. While Tepemaxalcans distinguish between wholesalers and retailers, in fact the two categories overlap because men sometimes produce a few dozen of the sandals they sell, and women pile up consignments from relatives or godparents next to their own merchandise. The visible differences are that resellers make extended sales trips and bring more stock (four to six dozen versus two or three), while women maker-vendors travel round-trip to specific fairs. All vendors expect to sell sandals in quantity, by units of a dozen (300 pesos as of 2002). However, most sales observed were single pairs (25–35 pesos), an indicator of the shrinking demand.

As they wait for customers, women handspin *ixtle* fiber into thread and stitch soles or assemble sandals with an awl or needle. This pastime attracts public attention, and passers by commented to each other, "Para los muertitos" ("For the deceased"). The scene resembles a description by the Spanish chronicler Fray Bernardino de Sahagún (Parsons and Parsons 1990: 288): "The sandal seller is a sandal maker, a maker of sandals who . . . shakes out [the cords] rolls

Altered Traditions

them. He has an awl, a copper awl; he has sandal soles ... He cleans [the threads] twists them, using his teeth; rolls them over his hip. He stitches the sandals, sews them ..."[13] Tepemaxalcans also sell incense, locust beans and other items foraged from the tree-lined slopes around their village to maximize earnings. (Smoking incense is used to cleanse a home of evil spirits, for curing and to propitiate most rituals.) These traditional items can be bartered (*cambio* or *trueque*) for food or goods from other vendors.

When someone points to the sandals, sellers name their price and ask what size. Women's sizes range from 20 or 22 to 25 and men's from 26 to 30. Some print the size on the sole in pen; others urge customers to try a pair on. Variations in width and shape of the foot may affect size. For example, Josefina Hernández wears size 22 *ixcacles*, size 23 huaraches and size 24 shoes (personal communication, Hueyapan, 26 June 2001). Vendors always stress that they must bring a full assortment of sizes in order to sell well, but most display dozens of a single large and small size.

Who buys *ixcacles*? Sales during a full day at Amecameca (Ash Wednesday, 13 February, 2002) indicate how uses and designs are being modified to supplement traditional customers. The latter buy sandals for curing or burial. For example, a woman in crisscrossed leather huaraches arrived limping, supported on either side by family members. Her navy wool skirt and tunic identified her as a Nahua from Tetelcingo, a town just over the border from the state of Mexico and the only place in Morelos beside Hueyapan to retain indigenous dress.[14] She wanted a loose fit to salve a chronic condition. Another customer, a spry old man accompanied by his daughter, declared: "I'm 88, and it's time to prepare for the end." When he questioned whether the narrower three-strand toe band was for women, he was told that both men and women wear the same style. The only wholesaler that day was a merchant from the city of Toluca, an hour's ride west of Mexico City. She bought several dozen pairs to have on hand "when people come looking for them," an allusion to the moment of death. Her son trailed behind her carrying a loaded sack.

Several buyers associated *ixcacles* with an ancestral past and freely interpreted tradition (see Hobsbawm 1994: 4). For example, a wiry young bicyclist, sporting a helmet and the latest Nikes, consulted with his four friends, who feigned punches and joked with each other as he tried on a pair of *ixcacles* to wear for his role as a Nazarene in the Easter pageant in Iztapalapa, at the edge of Mexico City. This famous re-enactment of the Crucifixion draws thousands of spectators on Good Friday. His deliberate choice of rustic *ixtle* sandals might be likened to the attention lavished on uniforms and historic details in restaging Revolutionary or Civil War battles in the United States, although his participation also implied a *manda* or *promesa*.[15] Fulfillment of a sacred vow, often preceded by fasting and prayer, completes an obligation to a saint for a wish granted or serves as penance for some transgression. Similarly, a woman, whose newborn daughter bore the floral crown of a first-time pilgrim, commented that her own mother wore maguey-fiber sandals on a visit to the miraculous shrine at Chalma, in the state of Mexico, where she pleaded for relief from a leg ailment.[16]

Another adapted use is dressing images of the *Niño Dios* (Baby Jesus). During the Roman Catholic feast of Candelaria on 2 February, refurbished and newly dressed religious images from household altars are brought to church to be blessed. This custom – facilitated by temporary booths set up at markets throughout the Republic to repaint statues and sell miniature clothing and tiny gold leather sandals – is now being reinforced by a magazine featuring costumes and by institutions like the Museum of Popular Culture in Coyoacan (Mexico City), which holds an annual competition for the best-dressed *niño*. Since Candelaria marks the onset of Lent, technically buyers must anticipate their needs by a year, but Tepemaxalcans insist that images can be re-shod at any time. In this case, the sandal makers have suggested a religious application. No sales were made.

In their search for a market to replace traditional consumption in Hueyapan, vendors from San Felipe Tepemaxalco now offer *ixtle* sandals in a range of sizes and styles. Several touted sandals for little girls and their dolls. To tempt children, craftsmen make bow-tie-shaped toe-bands (called *rosas*, the Spanish word for the bow tied in shoes), as well as models with three to five thin, radiating toe straps. These are decorated with *figuras*, one or two bright-colored stripes of acrylic yarn. Parents and grandparents attending the fair willingly indulge children, but several girls refused, presumably because they preferred the plastic jelly sandals and Barbie accessories on sale elsewhere. Souvenir sandals, an inch or smaller, had more acceptance, even at a comparable price.

Women craftsmen also make large sizes with widely spaced stitching and coarse weave for casual wear, claiming foreigners consider them softer and more flexible (Celia Díaz, personal communication, San Felipe Tepemaxalco, 10 April 2001). They willingly remove heel guards and comply with other requests considered mere caprice. For example, Flaviana Tejeda described making four tiny round pads, each with a pair of tying cords, for a customer's dog. She tried her prototype out on her own pet, Capulín, but he growled and spun backward in circles, tearing the cords to shreds with his teeth (personal communication).

According to 58-year old wholesaler Benito Romero, women may be better sandal makers, but men innovate more styles (personal communication, San Felipe Tepemaxalco, 1 March 2002). As an example he cited *ixcacles* that fully cover the toes like shoes, available only by special order from Juvencio Pérez, a widower from Tepemaxalco. Pérez travels to markets in three states to sell suede huaraches and *ixtle* sandals. In addition to Hueyapan-style *ixcacles* (with narrow, three-strand toe-bands) his stock includes at least four heelless versions, modeled after plastic beach thongs and slip-ons with horizontal bands of different widths (generically referred to as *chanclas*). One model has crisscross straps.[17] Clearly these designs are calculated to appeal to "tourists," both Mexican and *gringo*, who value novelty, natural materials and handmade crafts.

Romero's comment implies that wholesalers are more worldly, observant and responsive to the market because they sell directly to tourists, shops and other wholesalers (*acaparedores* or *regatones*) in cities that include: Cuautla, Cuernavaca and Tepoztláin (Morelos); Atlixco, Izucar de Matamoros and Puebla (Puebla); Mexico City and Ixtapan de la Sal (Mexico); Taxco and Acapulco (Guerrero), and Oaxaca (Oaxaca). In such places *ixcacles* retail for 55 to 75 pesos a pair. These men are not so much usurping a women's domain as carving a special niche within it that enhances the reputation of the whole town and looks to the future.

Even small amounts of cash, as Sheldon Annis (1987: 50) suggests, represent substantial earnings to artisans with no other options. Tepemaxalcans continue to derive an important sense of ethnic identity from their role as makers and sellers of a unique type of sandal. Their efforts to develop new markets and ceremonial uses for *ixcacles* represent a struggle to keep their heritage alive. Despite the overall decline in sales, a deeply religious sense and powerful cultural attitude about death support their efforts.

Acknowledgements

The author wishes to acknowledge her *maestras*, Irmgard W. Johnson, Flaviana Tejeda and Elvira Hernández Escobar, as well as Mexico City researchers José Luis Alvarado, Elizabeth Cuellar, Cecilia González, Ruth Lechuga, Beatriz Oliver, Fernando Sánchez-Martínez and Claude Stresser-Péan, who shared their expertise and collections.

6

"Why Do Gringos Like Black?" Mourning, Tourism and Changing Fashions in Peru

Blenda Femenías

Embroidered Objects and the Commoditization of Identity

One April afternoon, Nilda Bernal took an order for a black vest from my friend. While Patricia Jurewicz and I were riding the bus from Arequipa to the Colca Valley for *Semana Santa* (Holy Week) of 1992, we had discussed buying embroideries. A textile designer from the United States then living in Peru, Jurewicz was intrigued by *bordados*, the distinctive Colca-style embroidered clothes.[1] To obtain a unique garment, I explained, she should commission it from a workshop rather than buy it in the market. When we reached the village of Coporaque, we visited my friend Nilda and her husband, Juan Condori. As they frequently accepted commissions, they might embroider a *corpiño* (vest) for Patricia. After six years in the *bordado* business, Nilda had developed a good sense about customers' tastes and desires. Patricia, as a professional designer, was hardly a typical tourist. She desired a garment that would exemplify the best in *bordados* and that she might actually wear. Nilda suggested a half dozen garments and colors. Nothing did the trick. Then she got a look in her eye. What about black?

Finding that a partially sewn black vest fitted Patricia well, Nilda and Juan agreed to finish it. They would sew the shoulder seams, perfect the fit, and then apply the embroidered trim, using fiesta colors and designs although the black corpiño had been destined for *luto*, or mourning wear. As we discussed "black," Nilda admitted that she had been puzzled by the foreign taste for the "dark," "sad" color (*osevro, triste*), but now she too was *antojando* black – developing an eye, or taste, for it. And while Patricia knew that "black" meant "mourning" in the Colca Valley, having observed its Good Friday ritual use only the day before, she also saw black as a United States wardrobe basic. When her black vest was completed, the outstanding product satisfied everyone. The central

Altered Traditions

Figure 6.1. Nilda Bernal holds a shawl embroidered by her and Juan Condori, Coporaque, Peru, 1992. Photograph by Patricia Jurewicz.

band of figures and the framing bands using multiple designs were all finely drawn. The garment was far superior to anything that could be purchased ready made.

In this chapter, I examine clothes and identity through exchange, considering a set of practices that produce identities and occur within families, households, and workshops. Black cloth and clothes offer an ideal window for analyzing exchange and identity. "Black" circulates between the realm of death and funerals, and the dominion of tourist fashion. When Nilda and Juan created Patricia's garment, their traditional roles as artisans were maintained but modified by interacting with a foreign tourist. The garment also was entirely traditional in its designs, figures, construction, and technique but nonetheless a novelty in its manner of combining festival and mourning styles. By observing genuine tourists *in situ* in the market and stores in the town of Chivay, and even more by conversing about tourism with artisans such as Nilda, I learned how artisans' multiple means of circulating and obtaining *bordados* are framed by the market.[2] The trading places I discuss are both physical places where exchanges are carried out, such as Chivay market, and social spaces where changes in identity and social relations occur, such as from artisan to vendor. "Trading places" conceptually encompasses goods for other goods, money, or services, and, more broadly, ideas, identities, and categories.

I am particularly concerned with links between the marketing of objects and the marketing of ethnicity itself. Trading places encompasses the idea of the capitalist Indian: the ethnic artisan who promotes and advocates his or her own product and thus simultaneously reauthenticates and folklorizes his or her identity. Because *bordados* are often produced and exchanged by the same person or members of the same family, kinship and gender structure the practices of exchange. The vendor often uses ethnic clothes to gain leverage in commercial transactions in both rural and urban exchange settings, thus trading on her ethnic identity. In the Colca Valley – and in Caylloma, the province which contains it – this embodiment through dress is most potent for women because they, rather than men, wear *bordados*.

Most enterprises that sell *bordados* are small scale, interacting with many customers, middle men, and suppliers, and participating in an economy with many informal characteristics. The urban–rural social and economic networks have points of intersection in Chivay market kiosks, regional and provincial fairs, and the informal street markets of Arequipa – everywhere an artisan must travel to buy and sell, wheel and deal, and keep the ball of commerce rolling. Yet trading places are only partial solutions; each trade and each place only sharpens the contradictions and conflicts in Cayllomino vendors' lives.

Tourist sales in Caylloma have spurred changes in *bordados*. Patricia, who has a degree in design from a United States university and studied fashion in New York, has more appreciation of *bordados* than have typical tourists to the Colca Valley. But like them, she sought the rare, precious, and beautiful, and looked to an artisan to provide it. Peruvian and foreign tourists venture forth from Arequipa, a nearby city of one million, in search of natural wonders and cultural exoticism – towering snow-capped peaks, scenic vistas, condors, vicuñas, picturesque colonial villages, and "native" inhabitants.[3] Caylloma's "Indians" constitute the indigenous Other for white, urban Arequipa in the interest of attracting tourists as well as in regional self-identification. The characteristic, colorful, embroidered clothes seem suitable "authentic" mementos. Shopping in Chivay market, tourists often buy the garments on display. But tourists from the United States and Europe also frequently view black clothes as fashion statements. Sometimes, vendors told me, tourists say the colors are too bright and ask for similar clothes in another color.

Just the same. But black.

Few tourists realize, however, that people in the Colca Valley associate black with death. Black clothes are worn for Catholic mourning rituals: funerals, All Souls' Day, and Good Friday.[4] Even the black garments displayed for sale usually have sacred connotations and their use is largely divorced from fashion. As artisans and vendors stock black garments to meet the tourist demand, this change in production and exchange alters the ritual character of black cloth and clothes, turning sacred cloth into a secular commodity. The multiple uses and transformations have affected the very idea that sacredness is embodied in cloth objects.

Seeing "black" in action as I attended mourning ceremonies sparked my understanding of more general exchange of cloth and clothes. In analyzing the influence of increasing tourism on economy, identity, and ethnicity, I focus on the ways that the simultaneous marketing of objects and of identities juxtaposes sacred and secular uses of cloth. Tourism now drives ritual objects to become commoditized.[5] In the broadest sense, commoditization is capitalist exchange: buying and selling in the marketplace. In particular, I explore commoditization as it proceeds hand-in-hand with changes in identity, because the marketing of image and ethnicity is a component of the successful sale of objects. What happens when a thing is transformed into an object of desire and an object of consumption?

Black Clothes and Mourning in the Colca Valley

The "sacred textiles" I discuss here are mostly new objects expressly made for ritual uses in contemporary society, rather than ancient textiles preserved for such use, which are usually considered heirlooms. In Caylloma, families keep a few antique objects in ritual bundles. Among them are mourning textiles that may be 100 years old or more, but very few if any are pre-Hispanic or colonial relics. In other parts of the Andes, relic textiles have received the lion's share of scholarly and public attention for their religious, political, and economic significance, especially after entering the international art market.[6] My concerns with sacredness relate to the market somewhat differently.

The special kinds of Caylloma textile that are made for ritual uses are also commodities. Cayllomino artisans make all embroidered garments explicitly for sale and their primary consumers are local people. Many potentially sacred cloths are readily available for sale in the market. When such cloths are appropriated for fashionable tourist clothes, they are never used in ritual contexts. But the commoditization of objects has both preceded and followed sale to tourists, with many detours also comprising the sacralization and secularization process. The increasing secularization of sacred textiles cannot be attributed to "outside influences" alone, because local artisans have also initiated change for local consumers.

Mourning customs in many societies prescribe one color to indicate mourning, who should wear clothes of that color, and for how long. In European

Catholic tradition the use of black for mourning dates to the Middle Ages; it is still common in many Latin American and Mediterranean countries (Hollander 1978: 372–4; Freedman 1986).[7] The contemporary use of black mourning clothes in Peru seems to be a Spanish colonial legacy, but it cannot be ascertained when the tradition was established. In the Colca Valley, the association between black and mourning largely holds sway.[8]

The valley's ritual black cloth and clothes are sometimes handwoven and usually embroidered. The garments made in mourning style are: for women, the *phullu* (shawl), *pollera* (skirt), *saco* (jacket), and *corpiño* (vest); for men, the poncho. Extremely similar in form and design to daily and festival garments, mourning garments differ primarily in color and fabric. They are black, but never plain black. All feature small amounts of white, blue, and dark green. Shawls and ponchos have thin color stripes. Polychrome embroidered borders also employ the blue-and-white scheme. The ground fabric of shawls and ponchos is usually handwoven of alpaca or synthetic yarn, whereas vests and skirts use *bayeta* (a rustic, handwoven sheep-wool fabric) or commercial synthetic fabrics. While similar mourning garments are used throughout the valley, their details vary by village, as do those of daily dress. The *phullu* from the town of Cabanaconde is larger than the Chivay version. All Cabanaconde *polleras* are trimmed with *trencilla* ("rickrack"), but on mourning polleras it is blue. Chivay-style mourning polleras use blue or dark green applied yarn.

Combining purchase and commission, a customer often acquires a mourning garment. After obtaining a woven shawl from one artisan, a woman takes it to another to embroider the border. The handwoven piece is generally black with several narrow bands of white and blue woven stripes, and all the edges are trimmed with a wide blue commercial-cloth border, on which the birds and flowers characteristic of the Colca Valley are embroidered.

Men usually wear only one mourning garment, a poncho. All ponchos are roughly five feet square, are handwoven of alpaca or synthetic yarn, and feature next to no embroidery, typically a narrow neck-binding with a simple, one-color swirl. (Men's clothes are not otherwise embroidered.) The mourning poncho resembles the *phullu*: black with white, blue, and occasionally dark green stripes. Daily and festival ponchos are usually tan with pink stripes or pink with green stripes.

People wear black mourning clothes for these events and purposes: all funerals, mourning by immediate family members of the deceased for one year, a memorial mass observed at the end of that year, All Saints' and All Souls' Days, and Good Friday. Although women in mourning should wear black for a year, they rarely wear an outfit of all black garments for that long; rather, a few months after the funeral they usually reduce the number to a few garments. For example, one day I ran into a friend, Felícitas Bernal, whom I had not seen in years. Her white straw hat had a black band, but none of her other garments was black. The black band was for her mother, who had died the previous year. As I learned that even tiny amounts of black signify mourning, I also became accustomed, when I met a woman wearing black, to expressing appropriate condolences for her family's loss.

Observed throughout Latin America, the celebrations of All Saints' Day (Todos Santos) and All Souls' Day (Todas Almas), held on 1 and 2 November are often called the "Days of the Dead."[9] Stemming from the European Catholic heritage, these ceremonies commemorating the dead focus on the physical remains in the cemetery, which are reminders of their continued presence. In the Colca Valley, families visit the village cemetery to offer prayers for the souls of deceased relatives, install crosses over new graves, and clean and decorate existing crosses and graves, often with wreaths (*coronas*) of fresh or paper flowers (Paerregaard 1987). Many of these customs are also carried out in Peruvian cities.

I have been privileged to participate in these ceremonies in Coporaque. People who died during the preceding year receive the most attention. In 1991, one of them was Marcelina Terán, the elderly mother of Agripina Bernal, my friend and neighbor. On All Saints, I arrived in Coporaque on the bus from Arequipa via Chivay. Upon visiting Agripina, I found her home filled with relatives who had come from Arequipa and elsewhere to commemorate her mother. While I shared a meal with them later that day, and accompanied them to the cemetery the next day, Agripina explained the mourning customs carried out by her family and others. I also shared Todas Almas with my *compadres* and close friends, especially several *comadres* and their families: Nilda and her children, and her sister Candelaria and brother-in-law Epifanio and their children. (I am godmother to two of the children.)

Several days before All Saints' Day, the immediate family of the recently deceased installs a cement tomb cover and a cross, usually metal, on the grave. On All Souls' Day, they decorate the grave and pay respects. The elaborate rituals include orations in Spanish and Quechua by *cantores*, or reciters (see Ráez 1993: 283); prayers said in Spanish by the priest; and offerings left on the tomb. Everyone spends the whole afternoon and evening in the cemetery. The year I attended, families decorated graves from about noon until 2 p.m., when the priest from Chivay arrived. Standing near her mother's grave, Agripina and her aunts and uncles discussed and rearranged the wreath on the cross until they agreed it looked proper.

In the cemetery, women wear a black *phullu*, or shawl, around their shoulders. Agripina wore a fairly elaborate shawl and *pollera*, but her aunts wore black shawls with a plain, Western-style skirt or pants. Agripina's shawl was on loan from her mother-in-law. Agripina is from Coporaque and her husband, Dionisio, is from Cabanaconde, 30 miles downriver. She often signified her association with his community through clothes, wearing a Cabana-style *pollera* almost daily. The *phullu* signaled a relationship not just with the community at large, however, but with her mother-in-law directly. Such loans are temporary exchanges, frequently occurring within and between families, which may become permanent as gifts or through inheritance.

A similar but smaller cloth used in the cemetery is also called *phullu*. On this black cloth, spread on Marcelina Terán's tomb, relatives and friends placed offerings. All around the cemetery, a similar ceremony was repeated. Each relative places a different offering on the tomb, typically a small pile of grain (corn, quinoa, or barley) or small breads in animal and human shapes.[10] One relative records each offering. That night, while all contributors attend a feast at the sponsoring relative's home, the offerings are given to the *cantores* or, some say, taken by spirits.

When Father Rafael arrived, he said a lengthy service for the entire assembled village group, then individual prayers requested by families for departed relatives. For the rest of the cool, cloudy afternoon, I made my way around the cemetery with friends and compadres, learning where their family graves were located and creating a personal commemoration for my own deceased family members. People had brought drink as well as decorations and, as day became evening, consumed considerable amounts of alcohol. After a thoroughly drunken man tripped on a grave, went sprawling, and knocked down Nilda's daughter Enadi (my goddaughter), Nilda pronounced it time to go. I bid farewell to Agripina and her relatives, who were heartily drinking and weeping, weeping and drinking. With Nilda and her daughters, I walked slowly to their home.

Remembering the dead is a participatory experience in Latin American communities. Its collective character merges with personal experience, as I learned that afternoon. All the people of Coporaque trouped to the cemetery, and together created a sense of family, lineage, and community by attending to their ancestors' remains. By sharing funerary ceremonies with friends and relatives, community members learn that they belong to a large, living family which also contains the heritage of the dead. By participating in those rituals, I also reflected on the embodied legacy of my own ancestors, who were laid to rest in the United States, Chile, Sweden, Argentina, Spain, France, and other countries unknown to me, as well as the forms of embodiment through objects. Because the ethnographic experience was personal, that All Souls' Day bound me forever to Coporaque.

Another important occasion when Latin Americans wear black clothes is Good Friday, Viernes Santo, a day of mourning for the death of Christ, and the end of Lent. In Catholic churches a special service is held; it is the only day mass is not said. In Caylloma, people wear the same black clothes they use for personal and family mourning. The village of Yanque has an elaborate Good Friday service in its seventeenth-century Franciscan church, which Patricia Jurewicz and I attended in April 1992 at the invitation of the nuns who serve there; also present were several hundred Yanqueños and six Peruvian tourists.

On Friday evening, Patricia and I entered the vast, candle-lit, stone church and sat in a pew. Men and women in black slowly filtered into the church, filling the pews and then sitting on the floor. The black clothes seemed to recede into the dim interior. The altar was draped in plain black cloth, another component of the paschal mourning tradition. Other communities have elaborately woven black altar cloths.[11] The hour-long ceremony includes a sermon by the priest and readings by parishioners. Then everyone focuses on the central activity: the removal of the life-size effigy of Christ from the crucifix. The figure in Yanque's church has articulated limbs. As several men, members of the *cofradía* (church's lay confraternity), remove the figure from the cross, its arms bend at the shoulders. Then more parishioners come forward and wash the effigy, using cotton balls and alcohol. The devotees place it in a glass coffin and, still wearing black ponchos, carry the coffin on a bier through the dark streets, traversing a set course. Finally, they return the coffin to the church.

That evening, the atmosphere in the Yanque church was eerily somber. On the altar, dozens of huge candles, some three meters high, illuminated the image of Christ with compelling, flickering flames, but the church as a whole was dim. Although hundreds of people were there, the darkness of their dress accentuated that of the church and created a sense of absence as much as presence. It was a chilling and impressive experience, diminished only by the presence of tourists snapping flash photographs.

Yanque's Good Friday service has become known outside Caylloma and now attracts tourists. The life-size articulated Christ is apparently unique. The rituals, although central to Cayllominos' experiences, are being altered and commoditized. María Luisa Lobo, a Peruvian film maker, not only profiled the ceremonies in a documentary (1988) but encouraged several modifications to the procedures and the participants' costume. For example, she suggested that small children dress like angels, in white dresses with metal wings (made from United States surplus food aid oil cans), and take part in the procession; they now do so routinely. In 1992, the church's front row of pews was occupied by a group of Peruvian tourists who had come from Lima especially to see the service. Continuously snapping flash photographs, they both commemorated and commoditized the ritual and Cayllominos' life experiences.

Commemorative clothes and ceremonies, as these three cases have shown, are tightly linked. Although Cayllominos commemorate the dead and the ancestors twice a year, we should not forget that death is a somber, omnipresent reality in a nation at war, as Peru was during the years I lived there. That presence pervades human consciousness throughout the year, although the ceremonies crystallize it only twice. Objects are the embodiment of memory. In the context of mourning rituals, black garments provide a physical prompt that encourages the living to remember the dead and, by fulfilling their obligations to the dead, to strengthen their bonds to the living.

Objects that embody memories of the dead are often glossed as "heirlooms." If "heirloom" means a valued, ancient object that has been handed down within a family, then most Colca black mourning clothes are not heirlooms. I gloss "heirloom" differently, as an object that embodies memory and contains meaning about the past, no matter what its age. This interpretation treats "heirloom" as a type of object, similar to other mnemonic devices. What is handed down need not be one specific object; rather, the continuity is in the idea of the past, the meanings that the past holds, and the knowledge to create an object of the type that embodies such memories. Through repeated, multiple uses of such objects, the ideas invested in them are retained, even in the absence of one particular object in which those ideas have been continuously embodied (Hallam and Hockey 2001). For example, a woman attending Todos Santos rituals should use a mourning shawl that conforms to a recognizable type: black with white and blue. The shawl need not be the same one she used last year or even identical to the shawls other women use this year. What matters is that mourning clothes resemble each other today, and resemble those of the past, in certain, condensed aspects of color and/or design. A small emblem, such as Felícitas's hatband, may replace larger ones. The single garment or element assumes the function of synecdoche that the whole ensemble normally fulfills, but expresses that function in even more condensed form: a part of a part stands for the whole. The uses and meanings of mourning clothes are similar to those of other mnemonic devices and discourses that encourage both ongoing habituation and connection with the past and the ancestors, but they are more narrowly configured within the broader domain of Caylloma textile traditions.

Exchange Spaces, Tourism, and the Sale of Ritual Attire

Selling Embroidery, Selling Ethnicity

Anyone can enter a home-shop or Chivay market, speak with a vendor, and purchase or commission a garment.[12] Most vendors sell primarily from home, from Chivay market, or both, and they travel infrequently. A few depend heavily on travel, taking goods from Chivay to other Colca Valley communities and/or to weekly fairs in rural Caylloma and neighboring provinces. Only a few successful vendors make a living primarily from selling rather than making *bordados*. Vendors who earn a living from sales must deploy numerous cooperative strategies within a competitive environment and in different sales venues. The business aspect of selling *bordados* must also accommodate other occupations, identities, and aspects of daily experience. The successful vendor judiciously combines numerous skills, balancing opportunity, risk, security, and social interaction.

"Time," "help," and "knowing" are major considerations. Becoming known, making a name for oneself, and promoting one's art and business are all part of the selling game. Successful individuals who are more entrepreneurial and aggressive than their peers often attribute their success to such personality traits. Men more than women offer such explanations. Despite the appeal of a go-getter ideology, other factors often matter more. Having a larger family business in which artisans delegate many tasks leaves them "time" to travel and sell, and provides the "help" that frees up that time. They "know" the ins and outs of embroidery, making higher-quality garments; using materials efficiently, and innovating new colors, motifs, and objects for different markets. Finally, they sell other people's works on consignment or commission. Vendors do compete with each other for shares of the closed market that Caylloma's female consumers constitute, but they also stress the importance of looking outward, especially by expanding markets through tourism, NGOs, and cooperatives.

The majority of vendors rely on a few standard garments for the bulk of sales. Most vendors sell all the embroidered garments, and in recent years, more are offering embroidered hats. The best sellers are "second-quality" garments, the type worn daily, especially those which wear out fastest – the *camisa* (blouse) and *corpiño* (vest), often sold as a matched set – so vendors try to keep these in stock. Smaller items also cost less to make, in both materials and time, than *polleras*, as the skirts use at least three meters of fabric. The backbone of the *bordado* business is the vendors who rely on higher-volume sales. Most vendors are also artisans and they produce similar quality garments in the mid-price range, thereby remaining competitive with fellow vendors but not undercutting them.

Three businesses exemplify different strategies. Susana Bernal and Leonardo Mejía have operated a workshop together continuously since 1981, when they married. Usually they sewed intensively together for several days before a fiesta (when women wear more elaborate, expensive *bordados*), and then Leonardo traveled and sold in the sponsoring town while Susana stayed with their children. They sometimes traveled together to sell at a distant fair. After Leonardo became a schoolteacher in a distant town, however, more *bordado* work fell to Susana. She owed her success in part to "help" from family and neighbors, which enabled both sales and production in the shop. Also, after years in the bordado business, customers know Susana and her family, and this knowledge encouraged their return. Susana's sales style is not aggressive and her solid reputation is based on reliability and quality goods. During Leonardo's absence, she expanded her sales opportunities by traveling to more fairs and by enlarging her stock of traditional garments, but also by innovating small tourist-oriented items, which she sold in Chivay market or, using intermediaries, in Arequipa tourist stores.

Rosalía Valera works another way. Her workshop in Coporaque produces middle-of-the-road goods and accepts few commissions. Rather than maintain a Chivay kiosk, she sells on the road, spending the vast majority of her time trading at regional fairs. Well known as an aggressive salesperson, she relentlessly promotes her own goods. Rosalía herself no longer embroiders; her adult daughter and a male *operario* (paid employee) do all the construction and embroidery in her shop, and she sells embroideries made by Juan and Nilda, her son and daughter-in-law. These arrangements give Rosalía more opportunity to travel and more goods to sell. She also sells agricultural produce purchased from other farmers. At the higher-altitude fairs, Rosalía also extends credit: customers pay down half the selling price; the next week, Rosalía collects the balance due in cash or in wool, fleece, meat, and grain, all of which have established, but fluctuating, monetary equivalents.

"Why Do Gringos Like Black?"

Nilda Bernal takes a third approach: her sales are dependent both on *bordado* production and her mother-in-law's activities. Nilda and Juan sell their *bordados* out of their home-shop, and she travels to sell. During 1992, Juan was away working at the Caylloma mine and their oldest daughter started school; Nilda began to go occasionally to other towns and regional fairs. For example, one weekend she went to a holiday fair in Tisco, a town 15 miles upriver. Some of the *bordados* she sold were made by her and Juan; others were from Rosalía's shop, on which her mother-in-law paid a small sales commission. Taking the three year old with her, she usually left the five year old with her own mother or Rosalía.

Middlepersons and merchants, both indispensable to *bordado* use and popularity, are linchpins of rural economy. *Bordado* artisans who produce small amounts rarely keep a Chivay market kiosk but seek various outlets for their products. Vendors try to diversify their offerings, especially the Chivay merchants with larger-volume businesses. Melitón Cutipa and his wife, in their seventies, have had a market stand for almost 30 years, where they primarily sell *bordados* but also industrially manufactured clothes and materials for *bordados*. From artisans, Cutipa takes complete garments on consignment more often than he buys outright. For example, he sells local-style hats made by various artisans, taking a small percentage of the retail sale price as a commission. Because consumers know appropriate prices, Cutipa cannot raise them so the artisan absorbs the cost of his service.

There are very few large merchants in Caylloma Province, and the major retail stores are all in Chivay; none is primarily devoted to textile crafts. Eleuterio Mamani has the largest general store, which occupies a corner of the plaza across from Chivay market. In his truck, he or his driver travels to other communities, supplying tiny shops with sundries, kerosene, and alcohol. His store carries only a few embroidered items but several shelves of cloth and other materials.

Bordados use about fifty different materials; the only ones produced locally are sheep-wool fabric (*bayeta*) and alpaca yarn and fiber. Several businesses in Caylloma supply the fabrics imported from outside the province, the region, and the nation, and some of those also sell finished embroideries. Ten such vendors are in Chivay market. Froylán Quinto and his wife own the largest fabric store in Caylloma, located four blocks from Chivay market. They carry several hundred fabrics and a wide variety of fabrics, trims, and yarns used for *bordados*, but no finished garments. Quinto's prices tend to be lower than those of small vendors and he extends credit to regular customers. Some artisans travel to obtain materials, but several said that Quinto's prices are the same as in Arequipa, so combined with the credit, they find no advantage to buying in Arequipa (except wholesale).

Beyond Caylloma, larger forces shape the small-scale social exchanges. One is NGO involvement in marketing. This is largely channeled through cooperatives, which help rural herders and weavers challenge the Arequipa-based alpaca cartel's domination; only a few Chivay-based groups provide loans to embroiderers. Even these organizations apply their programs through the micro-level exchange relationships. Substantial outmigration is another factor. Among the kin who provide the vital "time" and "help," a few relatives and/or *compadres* do the lion's share; those in Lima and Arequipa, and even abroad, often in the United States, may play key roles.

Cabanaconde hats provide a concrete example. Artisans embroider directly onto a purchased wool felt hat. For many years, only one brand, Arrogui, was suitable, as its felt is both high quality and malleable enough for embroidering on the machine. And only the Arrogui factory in Lima makes these hats; the main Caylloma supplier is Juan Tejada of Cabanaconde. Tejada's cousin, who works at the factory, ships several dozen to Arequipa several times a year. Tejada brings them to Caylloma, where he sells them outright to embroiderers or commissions artisans to embroider them, and he then distributes the decorated hats to Chivay market kiosks and stores or sells "direct," meaning from his home, in Cabanaconde. He embroiders other garments but not hats. When I visited his home, he had fifteen finished hats on hand – three times more than any other vendor. The previous year, he exulted, a Japanese tourist bought fifty hats from him![13]

Important *bordado* sale venues outside Caylloma Province are weekly regional fairs in highland locations several hours from Chivay. Some vendors go to all four: Chalyuta on Monday; Ichuhuayco, Tuesday; Chichas, Friday; and Chalhuanca, Saturday. Chalhuanca (in the Department of Apurímac) is the farthest from Chivay, requiring a two-night stay, so fewer Caylloma vendors go there. Modesta Condori, however, does not mind traveling to Chalhuanca, where she was born and has relatives; her immediate family moved to Chivay in the 1970s. On days without fairs, she stays in Chivay and works in her father's shop with her brothers and husband or sells from a sidewalk stand outside the market.

Even vendors like Modesta Condori and Rosalía Valera, who travel constantly and do not have kiosks, remain connected to the Chivay merchants to obtain materials. Especially during peak season, Carnival, in the rush to finish and deliver garments, speed and convenience trump cost. Artisans obtain materials on credit from Quinto's store or weather dry spells through loans. Artisans also try to reduce costs by using their materials prudently. Small garments, accessories, and doll clothes, which use remnants, improve the return on expenditures for fabric. Branching out into souvenirs, artisans both intensify production and diversify their markets.

Selling regular amounts on a daily basis, accessing the usual markets, obtaining materials, and delivering completed orders to customers are crucial to a successful embroidery business. Success depends largely on an individual's ability to maintain simultaneous relationships with others in several exchange networks, which sometimes requires subordinating long-term goals, such as increased travel, to the networks' immediate demands, such as sharing childcare. Entering non-kin credit and consignment arrangements is another strategy. Most artisans say they want to continue embroidering and selling, but they face the future by looking toward a different arena, often expanding from in-home sales to renting a kiosk, or from a kiosk to opening a store. Obtaining loans through NGOs, innovating new products, and locating new sales venues always entail taking risks and often require negotiating the domain of tourism.

Tourism, Identity, and the Promotion of Ethnicity

Around Coporaque, the Mayor was known as "the Tourist" (el Turista). Ricardo Ramos did not live in the village but came and went as he pleased, people said; arriving just as fiestas began, he left once they were over. One day my friend Leonardo Mejía surprised me by saying, "He's like you." As I wondered how a native, male, political authority resembled me, he continued, "He's a tourist."

Was I a tourist or not? Every time a Cayllomino said so, "I'm not a tourist, I'm an anthropologist!" I would protest. Living and studying in Coporaque must be entirely different from sightseeing. However much it went against the grain, I finally conceded their point. I am a foreigner, came and went frequently, and apparently had money without working. Mayor Ramos owned a print shop in Arequipa, which was apparently his primary means of support. He drove around in a pick-up truck. He owned land in Coporaque and his relatives had land in Chivay, where they were active in politics. Not living permanently in Coporaque left him wide open to teasing about being a tourist.

My foreignness, nevertheless, set me apart. It included my distinctly non-local tastes and preferences about clothes – tastes that I never dislodged completely. Vendors assumed that other gringos had similar tastes. Their questions about how to increase sales to tourists helped make me aware of changes in embroidered garments and other objects intended to accommodate tourists' desires. The few times I observed "authentic" tourists in Chivay, I rarely spoke with them. My aversion to tourists, while crucial to defining my identity as an anthropologist, did not noticeably alter Cayllominos' opinions.

An embroidered garment is an exemplary "souvenir of the exotic" if we apply Susan Stewart's (1984: 147) definition, as it is both a specimen and a trophy, both exterior and foreign but also intimate, interior, and personal. In Caylloma, with few exceptions, tourists buy garments through individual transactions with vendors in the same venues where Cayllominos shop. In the city of Arequipa, some stores are geared toward tourists, while others specialize in providing garments for migrants. Tourists traveling to the Colca Valley, though, are buying more than souvenirs. They are consuming ethnicity itself. Thus tourism is affecting the identities of the artisans who make *bordados* and the vendors who sell them, as they clearly have a stake in the marketing of ethnicity. The specific occurrences in the market, shops, and fairs form part of a broader pattern. Identities are exchanged and transformed as ethnicity becomes commoditized and Indian identity becomes a good that can be sold – as is often noted for North America (Meyer and Royer 2001; Phillips and Steiner 1999).

A simplistic discourse about national, regional, and racial identities is sold in the global marketplace to attract foreign tourists to Caylloma and other parts of Peru. An image of the Colca Valley as an archaic survival is promoted both in guidebooks and academic discourses on pre-Columbian and colonial topics. The commoditization of the image goes hand-in-hand with the commoditization of objects that outsiders consider part of it. Tourists buy objects; local ceremonies draw tourists. Even dead bodies are promoted as attractions. The archaized image is both reinforced and contradicted by the modern media that present it, including high-tech formats.[14] The exoticism of the locale is accented through descriptions of an "unspoiled" valley that abounds in natural wonders, especially the Canyon of the Condors, one of the principal Andean condor habitats in South America, adjacent to a large nature preserve where *vicuñas* roam.

Tourism to the valley rose steadily in the 1970s and 1980s, sparked by MACON, a multinational project that diverted the waters of the Colca and Majes Rivers (Benavides 1983; Gelles 2000; Hurley 1978; Treacy 1994). Along with irrigation, a development and expansion program was supported by the Arequipa Chamber of Commerce, the Majes governing authority, and the Peruvian national tourism agency, FOPTUR (de Romaña, Blassi, and Blassi 1987: 195–6), but little investment was made in local infrastructure. In the late 1980s, tourism to Peru in general plummeted, reaching its nadir during the early 1990s. Terrorism and cholera fueled negative United States State Department travel advisories and relentless bad international press. While the overall decline affected Arequipa and the Colca Valley, closing hotels, restaurants, and travel agencies, Arequipa's continued reputation as one of the safest parts of Peru brought tourists who skipped Lima and even bypassed Cusco and Machu Picchu.

All travel to the Colca Valley begins in the city of Arequipa. Tourists may choose a high-priced tour, of which there are only a few, or make their own arrangements for a bus or the *colectivo* (long-distance taxi). Backpacking, ecotourist types enjoy roughing it in the rugged valley. Not only does the high altitude cause discomfort, but there are few amenities and no luxury hotels or tasty regional cuisine. The picturesque appeal provides Gringo Trail war stories of crowded buses, lumpy beds, and real craft bargains.

During two years of fieldwork (1991–3), I saw perhaps 100 foreign tourists and twice that many Peruvian tourists in the valley. While I lived in Chivay, the few couples or small groups who wandered around were quite conspicuous in the market. All the vendors eyed them with interest, but rarely called out to them, knowing that they would buy a few items from one or two stands. Apparently unaware of fiesta days, except for Semana Santa, tourists often arrived on normal weekdays when business was slow, and they quickly descended to the Canyon.

Tourism in the city of Arequipa centers on its Spanish colonial heritage, especially the week around Founders' Day (15 August), when a large folklore festival, Festidanza, is held on the city fairgrounds. Other tourist activities occur year-round: tours to local scenic spots, and shows of "typical Andean" music and dances. Folkloric events in the city often include Colca Valley groups, such as school teams that dance in Festidanza. Not all urban performances are folklore staged for tourists. Festivals for the patron saints of Caylloma villages are usually held in Arequipa neighborhoods inaccessible to tourists and not publicized to them. Such fiestas, although smaller than in home communities, have *mayordomos* (individual sponsors), as well as more general sponsorship by the migrant association (Asociación Provincial de Caylloma), and are not sponsored by tour agencies.

Craft souvenirs are available in Arequipa at several shops on and around the Plaza de Armas, as well as six blocks away in the Fundo de Fierro, a gallery of twenty shops adjoining San Francisco Church. Several Fundo shops sell Caylloma embroideries, usually made in valley workshops, and one is devoted to alpaca crafts woven by members of ADECALC (Asociación de Criadores de Alpaca de Caylloma), a herders' and artisans' group in Callalli. In addition, several artisans who live in Arequipa make garments and dance costumes for Cayllomino migrants and urban dance teams, who buy or rent garments to perform in the city or back home. Walking through downtown Arequipa one day, I was surprised to encounter a Caylloma-style embroidered costume on a mannequin in a huge, new shop window. This display marked the location of Kepicentro, the city's largest costume-rental business, which is not an embroidery workshop. Formerly shoe-horned into a tiny shop on a narrow side street, it had become one of few occupants in a new commercial center, spacious but inordinately overpriced, built as part of the city's modernization campaign. The costume was neither accurate nor complete, featuring a blouse and hat never worn with Caylloma *polleras*. Intrigued, I stepped inside. The walls were festooned with "Latin American" costumes, such as a bullfighter's outfit, and with *polleras* from Caylloma and Cusco, all rubbing elbows with disguises of Mickey Mouse, Bugs Bunny, and other imported icons. Although the commercialization of *polleras* in this novel way seemed incongruous, such transformations are in fact consistent with the folklorization stemming from generations of urban migration. Questions of authenticity in Arequipa's performative domains were entangled with marketing strategies in both urban and rural sales venues.

Black figures prominently in these strategies. Authenticity and innovation shape artisans' and vendors' creation of new objects and quest for new markets. Vendors must keep their eye on the objects themselves, in order to appeal to the customers. Color is a significant factor. Hot pink and lime green, colors beloved by local customers, scream "Gaudy!" and affront the North American aesthetic (Femenías 2002, 2004). Black, however, is a color tourists desire. As sales are altered by tourism, objects formerly intended for purposes of mourning and commemoration are now made and marketed for secular, rather than sacred, contexts. To Caylloma artisans, the foreign taste was far from obvious.

Altered Traditions

So ingrained was the association of black with mourning that it masked aesthetic considerations. "Why do gringos dress so sad?" asked Nilda Bernal.

Taste results from such thorough cultural conditioning that very few people see it as such. "I would just wear it more," one says, or "I have lots of black clothes." The visual preferences that dominate aesthetic choice, naturalized through a process of habituation, are gradually made part of "distinction" (Bourdieu 1984): the selective apparatus people employ when they choose among alternatives in dress and other cultural features. In Western fashion, black has been well established for at least a century but enjoyed a substantial vogue in high art and fashion as early as the Renaissance (Schneider 1978; see also Hollander 1978 and Harvey 1995). What Tierney calls "the black fetish" in New York might hold sway because black is practical, elegant, unnatural, or even satanic (1994: 32–4). Its very austerity lends it the allure of power.

Tourists to Caylloma request black clothes that resemble traditional clothes but feature brightly colored embroidery. While Caylloma artisans continue producing the "authentic" black mourning clothes, to meet tourist demand they now make modified garments, which I term "hybrid" mourning–tourist clothes. On black backgrounds, instead of blue embroidery, hybrid garments feature the polychrome embroidery of daily wear, which contrasts handsomely to the dark ground. One such hybrid garment is the vest Juan and Nilda made for Patricia.

The fabrics used in black clothes have changed as well. It might seem that "natural" fabrics are more "authentic" local elements and that synthetics are cheap substitutes foisted onto tourists, but this is not the case. Tourists tend to prefer "natural" fibers and dyes and thus associate black with undyed alpaca yarn. Such yarn, usually confined to ponchos, carrying cloths, and shawls, is rarely found in *bordados*. Black fabric used in Caylloma is not always hand-woven and is as likely to be imported as locally produced. Imported and luxury fabrics are now widely used in dark colors and black. Most black yarn, except in a few high-altitude communities, is synthetic, usually factory-dyed acrylic. True black undyed wool or fiber is rare. The "black" *bayeta* fabric in *polleras* may be undyed dark brown or over-dyed medium brown. Other black fabrics have crossed into Caylloma from other classes and ethnic groups. Some are luxury fabrics used for special-occasion clothes by elite white Arequipeños. For example, artisan Hugo Vilcape of Cabanaconde made his wife a *pollera* of dark blue velvet printed with metallic designs – a fabric brought to their town, he said proudly, by a cousin who lives in the United States.

While Cayllominos' recent use of black cloth for fiestas apparently contradicts its preferred use for mourning, this paradox highlights the exaggerated dichotomy between "secular" and "sacred" practices. Black clothes do not exclusively connote mourning for Cayllominos. They have additional uses in ritual, and others outside the sacred realm. One way that sacred and secular blur is through use of clothes by widows, especially the elderly, who often continue to wear black after the mourning period ends. Associated with senior age status, their black clothes become acceptable daily wear. More often than black exclusively, old women wear other dark or muted colors. Second, for practical reasons, women of any age also use mourning clothes as daily wear. Susana Bernal acquired a black *bayeta* mourning-style *pollera* after her mother died. One day, three years later, when I noticed she was wearing it, I became alarmed that a relative had died. No one had; rather, it was winter, and Susana wore the wool skirt for warmth. Third, practical utility is a social value that Cayllominos do not take for granted. Yarn and fabric matter not only for aesthetic and economic reasons. Alpaca, if properly spun and woven, is much stronger and more durable than synthetic yarn; an alpaca poncho will sustain heavy use for many years. Farmers deploy many textiles in agriculture. A "mourning" poncho also makes a suitable ground cloth on which to collect produce in the fields. In a farming society, objects too must earn their living, performing their service in the mundane, as well as the sacred, realm. When I saw a mourning poncho on the ground during harvest, I was prompted to consider the numerous gray areas in contextual usage of "sacred" cloth. If a ritual poncho can be pressed into service for the most mundane activity, what gives the object its sacred quality? The meaning of black cloth has become unmoored from mourning. Recall Nilda's recent "eye for black."

While brightly colored *bordados* still rule, black is gaining ground. In Chivay market and artisans workshops, black clothes long constituted a small percentage of those made, displayed, and sold. Recovering from the very low sales in the early 1990s, as sales slowly increased so did the percentage of black garments. The relationship between artisans' expectations of tourists and actual sales is complex. Selling more black clothes could deplete the supply of "authentic" black items, but the more likely effects of tourism are to spur production and create issues of quality. An increase in lower-quality, lower-priced items, a familiar process in craft "development," is often lamented as the epitome of the loss of authenticity. Just as frequently, however, artisans create higher-quality, higher-priced items for more affluent or discriminating buyers, such as Patricia's vest. Increased tourism, such as Caylloma experienced in the mid-1990s, may alter more radically the types of objects produced. Even if authenticity is what tourists want to purchase, sometimes their knowledge of "authentic native costume" is less than expert, such as their preference for "natural" fibers now rarely used.

Still and all, black objects constitute less than half of the total sold. Caylloma garments appeal to tourists not only as garments but as souvenirs to display. At US $35–50, Cabanaconde-style embroidered hats were expensive by local standards; Cabaneños bought them infrequently, but they fell within most tourists' reach. The new types of hats cost $12–25; the lower prices made them even more attractive. When choosing between a hat and a *pollera* at the same price, the tourist often prefers the souvenir that will look good hanging on a wall to the one that will be packed away.

A recent phenomenon, apart from color, is the development of a few retail establishments in Caylloma that actively cater to tourists. They carry a much higher percentage of novelty items, which Cayllominos do not use. Livia Sullca's shop is, hands down, the stellar establishment in this domain. Having built her career as the only Chivay vendor specializing in tourist art, Sullca works hard on the displays and wants to attract more tourists. She asked me to take photographs, featuring her ten-year-old daughter modeling *polleras*, which she would make into postcards/advertisements. Jenny had on typical daily wear, pants and a T-shirt. "Go put on your *polleras*!" insisted her mother. Normally she wears them only for festivals and school dance performances. Because her hair is only shoulder-length, long braids had been made of black yarn and sewn into her hat. Once fully outfitted, she posed holding several heart-shaped bags.

Within Sullca's wonderland of embroidered souvenirs, Colca Valley dolls are the primary specialty. Livia does sell traditional garments, which she and commissioned artisans make. What she particularly enjoys is making and selling tiny things. She has created new styles of bag, purse, belt pouch, and backpack (*ch'uspa, bolsa, kanguro, mochila*). Increasingly, all of these use black background fabric. Nonetheless, dolls dominate her store, in six or eight different styles, 30 cm to 80 cm high.

"Barbie" is the star. The pert plastic doll wears traditional Caylloma-style bordados, modified to fit the miniature form, but sewing-machine embroidered the same way as full-size *polleras*. This popular item sells for $10. Since the unclothed doll costs about 50 cents (wholesale), almost all Sullca's expenditure is for the mini-*bordados*. Barbie™ dolls are marketed globally. The Mattel Corporation itself has produced various "ethnic" Barbies and "black" relatives, but the doll it calls "Native American Barbie," for example, does not present the dress of any specific tribe but reflects outsiders' interpretations of Native American identity (Lord 1994: 186; Urla and Swedlund 1995: 284, 307 n. 4; duCille 1996). Genuine Barbies are sold throughout Latin America, where blondes outsell all other haircolors (Lord 1994: 195–6). Mattel sets prices lower than in the United States because it sees the Latin American market as soft (Lord 1994: 196), but the dolls are still pricey. Most plastic fashion dolls in Peru are bootlegs, called "Barbi" in Spanish but produced in Asia for a fraction of the cost.[15]

Sullca has appropriated the ultimate emblem of the hegemony of fashion and has transformed the chorus-girl silhouette into the woman of substance enveloped in the voluminous local costume. The bootleg Barbie dressed in authentic ethnic garb speaks not only of the commercialization of Caylloma *bordados*. Miniature, souvenir representations of female body image also signify the condensation of ethnicity within gender. Because femaleness is the dominant symbol of Indianness, signified by the comparative paucity of male ethnic dress, Barbie is the ideal symbol for this relationship. For years, Sullca made no Colca "Kens"; no one would buy male dolls, she claimed, because they lack *bordados*. By 2000, however, she had begun to sell male dolls in the Witite role, a transvestite festival dancer (Femenías 2003, 2004). And many of these cross-dressed Kens wore black *polleras*.

Both the overall commercialization and the specialization in different commodities tell us much about broader changes in exchange relations, as

Colloredo (1999), Nash (1993), and Orlove and Rutz (1989) have explored. As marketing, economy, class, and ethnicity intertwine in *bordado* sales, their articulation prompts us to rethink categories. When I began studying commerce in Caylloma, I suspected that class and ethnicity would closely correlate in marketing arrangements. Production and exchange would logically be divided between artisans who make handmade crafts and who are primarily Indian, and merchants, who are primarily *mestizo*. Because Andean communities are well known for their highly developed systems of reciprocal economic and kinship relations, their participation in capitalist society has often been viewed as part of a dual economy. In this model, *mestizos* are the merchants and capitalists, and in those roles, they exploit Indians, who are not capitalists. In practice, however, class and ethnic divisions are far from neat today, and were not clear even in the past (Harris 1995, also Bauer 2001; Jacobsen 1993; Orlove 1997). "Traditional Andean" relations of barter and noncapitalist exchange do operate in Caylloma. Family members make garments for and obtain them from relatives: a godmother provides clothes for the godchild she is baptizing; a mother-in-law lends, then ultimately gives, a *pollera*. I have detailed few such traditional exchanges here, however, largely to emphasize that *bordados* are a business: in market, workshop, and home, over and over it impressed me how thoroughly commercialized is their exchange.

Economic success in Peru often is accompanied by social whitening, but in Caylloma this is rarely the case. Nor does any single class or ethnicity adequately encompass the constantly moving artisans, vendors, or merchants. Most artisans are not only vendors at some point but may become merchants. Their identities do not fit neatly bounded categories because ethnicity is relational and situational. The blurring of boundaries has ideological ramifications. To posit strict divisions between artisans and merchants would reinforce preconceptions that Indians are not capitalists. To review just one case, Rosalía Valera, a woman who was once an artisan is now a successful vendor, at the same time as she wears *polleras*, lives on her land as a peasant farmer, and participates in community religious festivals. Is Rosalía an Indian? Or does her economic activity make her a *mestiza*? Does a change in occupation compel a change in ethnic identity?

The Caylloma situation suggests that we should reconsider the role of Indian identity *in* marketing to encompass identification *as* marketing. Cayllominos are apparently buying into the hegemonic discourse that renders Indian identity exotic; they seem to be folklorizing themselves to market identity. The sale of souvenirs like Barbie dolls, by appropriating notable visual qualities of Caylloma women, markets their identity as a commodity. Does this mean Cayllominos are selling off, or selling out, identity? Perhaps, instead, by selling it they are keeping it.

Caylloma *bordados* embellish many subjects and objects: bodies and representations of them. Embroidery is an object saturated with local cultural value that has been transformed into an object of desire and an object of consumption. The meanings of *bordados* have been altered through circulation in diverse "regimes of value" (Appadurai 1986: 15), in which associations attached to objects are constantly challenged and altered. In analyzing such attachments and detachments, Annette Weiner posits that exchange moves society because an object is not only attached to current values but acts as a kind of reinvestment, endowing contemporary society with the worth of the past; she terms this "the paradox of keeping-while-giving" (Weiner 1992: 6–9). Caylloma vendors are apparently "giving" the representation of their "indigenous" identity to consumers when they sell *bordados* to tourists. Yet these objects must be distinguished from the "inalienable possessions" of which Weiner writes because many are made expressly to be alienated. The alienation of object and that of culture are not the same, however. As Cayllominos participate in capitalist economy, they are challenging a dominant paradigm that relegates their goods, and themselves, to a non-capitalist sphere: They are not giving, but taking; they are selling-while-keeping as they avail themselves of the benefits of the market. Therefore, Indianness is part of what propels them into capitalism. To be capitalists they must be Indians, and to be Indians they must be capitalists, because what they are selling is Indian identity. Andean exchange does not exist in a separate sphere from capitalist exchange. Although Cayllominos participate in an intricate web of reciprocity, Indian identity depends on capitalism.

Conclusion

Caylloma cloth has a dazzling variety of forms and uses. I found it difficult to reconcile that coy plastic Barbies inhabit the same cultural universe as austere alpaca ponchos. Although both objects were used in secular contexts, in my Western cosmogram they could never comfortably coexist. In fact, I drove them apart with labels: "sacred," "secular"; "mundane," "ritual"; "authentic," "tourist." Reconsidering the shifting meanings of ritual objects and commodities, I realized, required analyzing the interpenetrating nature of categories and the transformation of the same object in different contexts.

In this essay, I have examined diverse objects in the social economy where they are consumed. Sale of embroidered garments is part of daily life; loss of relatives to illness and death is part of the mundane world as well. Yet Catholic religious practice and local tradition exhort Cayllominos to separate a time and place for commemoration of personal and communal loss – a space constituted, in part, by black fabric with which people surround their bodies and which they place in churches and cemeteries. The authenticity of their experience and of the objects that represent it is not necessarily discounted by tourism because authenticity shapes the marketing of ethnicity to Cayllominos themselves as well as to tourists. As combined workshops and stores, commercial establishments create ethnic clothes and sell them to the local indigenous consumers. As culture brokers, artisans and vendors promote ethnicity as a cultural good and, at the same time, as one that will earn money. In doing so, they may change roles many times daily and for longer terms.

As Indianness relates to market sales, ethnicity has become commoditized. Ethnic identity has been reified into a thing that is marketable and consumable in the sale of clothes, as they reaffirm and exaggerate Indian appearance, and in the broader realm of folkorization, as one segment of national culture is promoted to foreign and national tourists. Even as they aim to re-authenticate their identity, Cayllominos risk folklorizing themselves. The people who move away and return to the valley only for ceremonial occasions are sometimes mockingly called tourists and their authenticity as natives is questioned by relatives who have stayed home.

The production and use of black clothing in Caylloma are simultaneously continuing along traditional paths and being rerouted by tourist desires. Cayllominos continue to commemorate the dead, observing the responsibilities that the living have to the dead and to each other. In doing so, they involve this fabric in a communal experience made salient at specific annual instances. Through the observation of Catholic rites and customs, tenderness toward the dead helps make life possible for the living in a harsh environment. Participating in those events and attending ceremonies in churches, I was incorporated into the community. Sharing moving experiences with friends and compadres, I learned about the bonds expressed through black. Coporaque is my home only in an episodic way, and part of me has remained a tourist.

"Black" is more than a color that "symbolizes" different cultural values. Black creates boundaries, demarcating ritual space around bodies among Cayllominos. Black also creates communication, establishing shared, though conflictual, grounds for discourse between Caylloma artisan-vendors and foreign tourists. For this new buyer, black is not sad; it speaks not of loss, but of finding; it signifies the novelty of experience. Once the tourist purchases her memento, she participates in a new phase of the cycle, resacralizing the souvenir as an untouchable object to be admired. She will remove it once again from the realm of the mundane, tucking it away in the reliquary of a closet, hanging it on the wall as artwork, or donning it as fancy dress for a cocktail party. In the eyes of others, longing for the unreachable artifact enhances its value. The object of desire becomes an emblem of its owner's exclusivity and, at the same time, of her membership in the secular cult of multicultural connoisseurship.

7

Dressed to Kill: The Embroidered Fashion Industry of the Sakaka of Highland Bolivia

Elayne Zorn

Indigenous Fashion[1]

Almost immediately upon one of her return trips home in 1989 from the Chapare, Bolivia's principal coca-growing region (Leóns and Sanabria 1997), a young unmarried Sakaka woman in the community where I was living set up her loom to weave a new overskirt or *aqsu* for an upcoming festival. Juana (all names are pseudonyms) was stylishly dressed that day in the latest factory-made Cochabamba-style *pollera* or full pleated skirt and sweater set, similar to the young woman on the left in the photograph (Figure 7.1). Like many young Sakaka, Juana alternated between wearing factory-made and handmade clothing, like the clothing worn by the woman to the right in the photograph. Juana's new textile on the loom featured brilliantly hued images of leaping lions and flowers in the latest northern Potosí fashion, contrasted against a shiny black ground. This new overskirt, woven of exuberantly colored synthetic-fiber *lanas* [yarns], would make a striking combination with a new, handmade, synthetic-fiber long black dress or *aymilla*, whose embroidered details were characteristic of her ethnic group.[2] The overskirt, worn only with the long dress, identifies its wearer as Indian. Both garments were starting to go out of fashion among Juana's generation, but her new dress and overskirt were on the cutting edge of modern "traditional" Sakaka fashion, filled with currently fashionable images woven in synthetic-fiber yarns. Juana purchased those yarns with money she obtained by working in the illegal coca/cocaine economy as a cook.

Dressed to Kill: The Mamani Brothers

By mid-January, Andeans are frantically busy, working long hours to prepare for the festivities of Candelaria on 2 February and, more importantly, Carnival in February or March. My neighbor Pastor Mamani – famed as a ritual battle fighter, brawler and, in the town of Sacaca, trouble-maker – and his large brothers were busy in their family's red-stone house getting ready for the upcoming festival and ritual battle. They prepared by embroidering.

Taking turns on the family's hand-operated sewing machine, the young men, in their late teens and early twenties, sewed coordinated outfits of white or black pants, vests, and jackets. The decorated their clothing with embroidered images on the cutting edge of fashion, including double-headed serpents, a devil dancer, the Bolivian national seal, and quantities of vibrantly colored flowers with curling leaves. Siblings or especially close friends sometimes embroider matching outfits, so they can make a particularly attention-getting entrance as they march into Sacaca town to attend mass, and eat, drink, and play music at the festival's sponsors' homes. Later, as the piercing Andean afternoon sun darkened, these young indigenous men looked forward to fighting at a ritual battle, or *tinku*. The excitement of combat, renown as a warrior, the attention of young women, a chance to settle old scores, and the satisfaction of making the opponent's blood flow for Pachamama (the Earth Mother) awaited the winner of each ritual battle that takes place nearly a dozen times throughout the year, in Sakaka territory in highland Bolivia.

Introduction

This chapter examines a fashion system[3] quite distinctive from the familiar commercial system based on clothing and objects designed, produced, and marketed by people unknown to, and typically far distant from, its wearers. The system I analyze here exists in northern Potosí, highland Bolivia, where tens of thousands of members of an indigenous ethnic group are passionately concerned about fashion, but with the difference that they design and produce almost all of their clothing themselves, as the opening anecdotes illustrate. The material basis for their system is a complex and ever-changing mixture of barter and money, encompassing both the "ethnic economy" of trade and the market. Dozens of other parallel systems, of other ethnic groups, coexist and sometimes intersect the one I describe, independent of Western commercial fashion.

Most of the time, many or nearly all the members of most of Bolivia's large indigenous ethnic groups, such as the nearly 21,000 people of Sakaka *ayllu* of northern Potosí, wear a distinctive daily dress, similar to the young women in the photograph. Their clothing, nationally and internationally, is emblematic of the Sakaka's separate and, to many, inferior, identity as Indians. To the wearers such dress marks a division between clothed indigenous humans, or

Figure 7.1. Two young women, from *ayllu* Sakaka, pose in the central plaza of the town of Sacaca on a Sunday market day. Photograph by Elayne Zorn, 1988.

runa, and naked foreign outsiders, *q'ara*. (This interpretation coincides with but reverses ethnocentrism between Indians and non-Indians.)

Dress remains a major creative focus for many Andeans, in which people invest substantial resources of time, materials, money, and labor, with the secondary effect that as people create and wear cloth, they also make statements about themselves. This chapter examines Sakaka dress in relation to issues of identity, since cloth remains a principal medium through which identity is expressed and symbolized, in the Andes as elsewhere. Research was done during the late 1980s, after the height of the coca/cocaine boom, and prior to the neoliberal reforms of 1993 onward that were supposed to result in the re-creation of Bolivia as a multi-ethnic, postmodern state.

The 1980s were a moment of transition in the Andean "ethnic"[4] textile economy, when Sakaka textile production became grounded on money from the coca economy. This occurred because by the 1980s the Sakaka fashion system – including "traditional" textile production – had become increasingly dependent on the market.[5] A shift by young Sakaka to factory-made dress, which many Andeans now wear instead of handmade dress, might have been expected due to "modernization," a general process of proletarianization, homogenization of local cultural differences, and loss of traditional textile technology and knowledge caused by rural-to-urban migration. I expected to find that seasonal peasant laborers such as Juana used money earned in the Chapare to buy Western-style factory-made clothing. Somewhat surprisingly, however, during the boom young Sakaka also spent earnings from the Chapare to buy factory-spun synthetic-fiber yarns, which they used to create handmade, locally-styled "traditional" Andean cloth (Zorn 1977a, 1977b). Why, I wondered, in a country with continued discrimination against its large indigenous population, would young people want to continue to wear "ethnic dress" when they had the money to buy Western-style clothing?

To answer such questions, I carried out anthropological ethnographic fieldwork in Sakaka in 1986 and 1987–9, on the production and uses of cloth by contemporary *runa* (Quechua for people who define themselves as indigenous).[6] Given the historical importance of cloth in Andean societies, and my previous research in southern Peru, I was interested in what people did with, talked about, and thought about cloth, in the context of regional, national, and international macro-economic processes that affect rural people (Zorn 1997a). My research included apprenticeship to several women weavers.

In the late 1980s, the vast majority of Sakaka wore some style, or genre, of "ethnic" dress on a daily basis, though each year this becomes less common for rural Andeans. This is primarily because such dress identifies them as "Indian," a derogatory term. Some like Western fashion, and some hope that by switching to Western-style cosmopolitan dress they will face less discrimination and thus be able to improve their lives. In northern Potosí, Sakaka *runa* and non-*runa* wear a variety of styles or types of dress. The distinctions in dress style fall along a continuum based on the dichotomy of Indian versus non-Indian. In the textile literature, these dress styles are referred to as "ethnic," versus "cosmopolitan" or "Western" (below).[7]

Bolivian society is highly polarized in terms of race and ethnic identity. The tiny minority of Bolivian "whites" is at the top of the social scale, with the majority identifying as *mestizo* (mixed race), and a large percentage (approximately 40 per cent to 50 per cent) considered indigenous. Like many anthropologists, I believe that race is not a valid biological category, but societies such as Bolivia are racialized, and racism remains persistent. The dichotomy of Indian versus white or *mestizo* is reproduced, and contested, daily in multiple ways,

Altered Traditions

including language and residence. The body, through phenotypical variation, plays a defining role, but race remains cultural, not biological.

Since, as Terry Turner (1980: 112) points out, the body surface is "the symbolic stage upon which the drama of socialization is enacted," it is not surprising that many of these "racial" distinctions involve dress, which is a prime marker of "ethnicity." My research showed that Andeans such as the Sakaka selectively choose and use (appropriate) technologies, materials, practices, and images to represent themselves, with fine distinctions, as belonging or aspiring to the statuses of *runa* (Andean) or Indian, *cholita/cholo* (urban Indian), or *mestiza/o* and *boliviana/o* (Bolivian).[8] The Sakaka also use dress to define themselves in relation to other neighboring indigenous Andeans. For women, such differences are crystallized in the distinction between wearing the *aqsu* (handmade woman's overskirt) and *aymilla* (long full dress) or sweater set and *pollera* (full pleated skirt), versus *vestido* (woman's factory-made fitted dress). To dress is to be: *de pollera* (Indian or *cholita*) versus *de vestido* (*mestiza* or white).

To understand Sakaka fashion in terms of identity, I first provide background information on the Sakaka in the context of their region, economy, and textile system. I then examine macro-economic phenomena that have affected the Sakaka textile system, focusing on their dress and fashion system. I analyze distinctions in dress styles ("genres") as a lens to view the complexity of ethnic and class identity in northern Potosí, and how people move between the seemingly fixed categories of Indian and white.

Northern Potosí

The Sakaka live in the northern Potosí region, renowned as the heart of "traditional" indigenous Bolivian highland culture. It is culturally very rich but economically very poor (cf. Ministerio de Desarrollo Humano 1993). This region sits at the top of Potosí Department, bordered by the Departments of Cochabamba, Oruro, and Chuquisaca (Sucre). The city of Potosí, Department capital, was once the richest city in South America and the most populous city in the world, based on silver extracted from the Potosí mine by Indian laborers.

Today peasants and miners live in the region (Harris and Albó 1986). Many of Bolivia's largest indigenous ethnic groups or *ayllus* live in or border northern Potosí, including the Macha, Laymi, and Sakaka. These *ayllus* formed part of extensive pre-Columbian Aymara nations and confederations before their conquest by the Inca (Platt 1982), who subsequently were conquered by Spain.[9] The Sakaka roughly correspond to the "first" nation of the pre-Columbian Charka federation (Abercrombie 1986; Espinoza Soriano 1969; Memorial de Charcas n.d.). The Sakaka are descendents of a warrior nation and they remain proud of their fighting abilities in the contemporary ritual battles (*tinkus*) common in this region. The clothing I describe features predominantly in *tinkus*

(Zorn 2002) – both the outfits embroidered by the Mamanis, and garments made especially for fighting.

The Sakaka

The approximately 21,000 Sakaka (spelled with a "k") form one of Bolivia's largest ethnic groups (Zorn 1997a). Contemporary Sakaka territory roughly corresponds to Alonso de Ibañez province in northern Potosí; *ayllu* lands extend slightly to the east of the province into the valleys. Sakaka call themselves *runa* in Quechua or *jaqi* in Aymara, meaning people.[10] *Runa* is contrasted with *q'ara*, or non-Indians. In Quechua, *q'ara* literally means peeled, like an animal hide that is worn bare. This is a pejorative term implying "non-human" and may refer to those who are "naked" because they do not wear human, handwoven *ayllu*-specific dress.

Sakaka *ayllu* is composed of smaller, minor *ayllus*. The great *ayllu* and its two "halves" (moieties) no longer elect officials (Bustamante 1985; Velasco 1997), and the minor ayllus have become increasingly important as functioning political units.[11] Despite the ongoing destructuring of great *ayllu* Sakaka, the Sakaka still constitute an ethnic group and function as a major *ayllu*. They control a common territory, though this no longer includes the valley fraction; are overwhelmingly endogamous, marrying among themselves at a level higher than 90 per cent; share a particular festival-ritual cycle; perform a distinctive sub-style of northern Potosí music; and wear a distinctive, identifiable style of clothing – a sub-type of the regional northern Potosí style – that proclaims their identity to the textile literate. They also participate in *tinkus* (Zorn 2002).

Tinkus also are practiced in others parts of Bolivia, Ecuador, and Peru. Nowadays, some traditional ritual battles are enacted in subdued forms, as in a soccer rivalry between communities. In northern Potosí, *tinkus* take place most months of the year. They are common but dramatic and violent events. The Quechua word *tinku* can be translated as an encounter or meeting between two opposites, such as two roads that meet, or two opposite colors, such as blue and red, woven side by side. These ritual battles take place between, ideally, matched pairs. *Tinkus* are most common between men, or between boys, but women also fight women, and girls fight girls. The smallest *tinku* is between two people who fight with their fists. The largest pit 200 or 300 men on each side, who fight by using slings to hurl sharp rocks, launched with an accuracy honed by years of practice herding. Almost all *tinkus* take place between indigenous peoples, but in Sacaca there is a "bull *tinku*" (between two animals), and townspeople play a game called *chiwka* between opposing teams.

The capital of Alonso de Ibañez province is the town of Sacaca (spelled with a "c"), founded in the colonial period. Once a stop along the important silver route between Sucre and Cusco, Sacaca – a green oasis amidst eroded pink and brown hills – today is a sleepy town populated year-round by 900–1,000 people.

Sacaca's population quadruples during important festivals, however, and was approximately 6,000 before Bolivia's 1953 Agrarian Reform (Lucio Montesinos, personal communication, 1988.) Nearly all Sacaqueños, or people from the town, classify themselves as *vecinos*. This means "townsperson" and refers to *mestizos* or non-Indians, of higher social status than Indians. *Runa* and *vecinos* live in close, mutually dependent, and sometimes bitter relations. Sacaca is connected by a dirt road to the city of Oruro, four hours away in the dry season; buses and trucks travel daily between Sacaca and Oruro. The town has a teacher's college. The province has three other small towns, mostly populated by *vecinos*.

Runa and *vecinos* are monolingual, bilingual or trilingual in Quechua, Aymara, and/or Spanish.[12] Formerly Aymara speakers, approximately half the Sakaka now speak Quechua as a first language. Many Sakaka (especially men) also speak some Spanish, which they learned in school, the army, or the Chapare. Primarily peasant farmers, the Sakaka live in approximately 500 hamlets scattered at 3,000 m to 4,000 m (9,900 feet to 13,220 feet) above sea level. Sakaka territory ranges from the upper *puna* (high grasslands) through lower *puna*, down to intermontane valleys. Hamlets contain as few as four or five or as many as sixty households. Typical hamlet size is fifteen households, with an average population of seventy-five people.

The Sakaka today are impoverished subsistence farmers, who cultivate potatoes, broad beans, and wheat. Many raise small herds of sheep; some raise chickens or cattle, or herd llamas. Fields are not irrigated, their lands are severely eroded, and farming is subject to frequent frosts and periodic hailstorms. The Sakaka, like other northern Potosí *runa*, are among the poorest in a poverty-stricken nation (UNICEF 1989). Most hamlets lack potable running water, sewer systems, electricity, irrigation, roads, and transportation. Sakaka homes, hand built with stones and adobe bricks, do not have electricity, sinks, bathrooms, heat, or other modern conveniences. Literacy is in Spanish, but many Sakaka are still illiterate. More boys than girls attend school; few attend high school, which requires a long walk or residence in town.

In contrast to other Andean highland regions, however, *ayllus* in northern Potosí and southern Cochabamba still hold title to sizeable territories, and their ethnic groups are much larger than those of other ethnic groups or communities. Northwest of the Sakaka live the Kirkawi (known as the "Bolívar" after the town), an *ayllu* of Quechua-speakers in Arque province, Cochabamba. The Sakaka and the Kirkawi share a general northern Potosi culture but do not intermarry. They have fought over boundaries for centuries and their border remains a site for intermittent conflict (Izko 1992).

While Kirkawi and Sakaka dress appears similar, stylistic features differentiate their textiles and mark the groups' separate ethnic identities. These features include use of an embroidered head shawl; woven and knitted images; width of hat brim; and embroidery style. The Kirkawi have been described as having a unique textile style called *kurti* (Gisbert, Arze and Cajías 1987: figures 229,

231), characterized by double-headed serpents. In the late 1980s, both the Kirkawi and the Sakaka used *kurti* to mean warp-faced double cloth (Zorn 1997a), which I suspect the Sakaka learned from the Kirkawi.

Money and the Sakaka Economy

As in the "ethnic" economy of the Laymi *ayllu* described by the anthropologist Olivia Harris (1987), today most Sakaka products still circulate through the economy of their *ayllu* using forms of non-monetary exchange.[13] The Sakaka barter with members of other ethnic groups and with *mestizo* townspeople to obtain products from outside their *ayllu*: salt, foods from the valleys such as corn and fruit, and wood for agricultural and weaving tools. The Sakaka also need cash to obtain basic necessities that they cannot acquire by barter: matches, kerosene, sugar, agricultural inputs such as fertilizer and pesticides, and an increasing amount of clothing and textile inputs.

Cash, however, is hard to come by. The Sakaka barter or occasionally sell agricultural produce or a sheep in the town of Sacaca. The few well-off Sakaka commercialize surplus produce in Oruro or La Paz. Many Sakaka obtained money by selling heirloom textiles during the 1980s, though old textiles are a clearly limited good (Zorn 1990). Agricultural labor in the town of Sacaca provides some cash, yet in 2001 local wages reached only US $2.10 per day in the countryside, and $3.50 in nearby cities. Much peasant labor is unpaid, yet life is expensive.

Since opportunities to work for money are extremely limited, temporary migration out of the region has always been important. A few Sakaka work in the region's mines. The Sakaka more commonly earn money by seasonal work in Bolivian cities as porters (men) and low-end resellers of produce such as limes (women). Women sometimes peel potatoes in markets, wash clothes in urban homes or, less commonly, beg on city streets. The Sakaka formerly obtained cash through seasonal migration to Bolivia's agricultural regions. By the late 1980s, the major way to earn money was the coca/cocaine economy in Bolivia's Chapare region, where young peasants such as the Sakaka work as seasonal wage laborers or, exceptionally, become full-time colonists (Léons and Sanabria 1997; Sanabria 1993; Zorn 1997b). The increase in temporary migration to Bolivian cities and the Chapare had a significant impact on Bolivian peasant life. Migration introduced new ideas, desires, and influences to some of the Andes' indigenous groups, whose rural isolation and strong cultural traditions mask millennia of historical changes.

Identity in Bolivian Society

I stated that daily wear of a distinctive, ideally handmade, style of dress marks the wearer's identity as *runa*. Is *runa* identity fixed? I believe that people at any specific moment are completely clear about their identity, as compared to others around them and to any other potential identity they could assume, represent, and/or display. Over time, however, any such identity may change, a point that was clear to local users of cloth and observers, though less obvious to me.

By identity I mean one's status in society, as determined by the intersection of the well-known parameters of gender, race, and class, as well as of age. The definition of status depends in great part on situation and social class, and is relative. A member of a small town's middle class may be perceived as poor by the urban elite but as wealthy by rural Andeans. In Bolivia and Peru the terms and concepts of class, race, and ethnicity are used in many ways. I use ethnicity to define a localized group identity, and ethnic group (a social category) for *ayllu*. In this region, class, race, and ethnicity often are conflated or used interchangeably, and inconsistently. The categories slide into one another; highland Indians (an ethnic group), often considered a race, are usually members of the peasant class. Non-Indians, though they may be peasants or workers, often are believed to belong to a separate race and a higher class, and so on.[14]

If dress codes Sakaka identity, what is it coding (Cassandra Torrico, personal communication, 1989)? As noted, the primary Andean social opposition is between Indian and non-Indian or "white"; this dichotomy is mediated by the intermediate groups of *cholos/cholitas* (urban Indians) and *mestizos/mestizas* (Tomoeda and Milliones 1992). Like Peru, at the top of Bolivia's social hierarchy are people who define themselves as creoles, Spanish, white, or Bolivian. The elite wear a national variant or imported cosmopolitan dress, but men or women may use ponchos (worn by male *runa*) to symbolize Bolivianness. Next in status, and sometimes overlapping, are *mestizos/mestizas*. To depoliticize class identity, many or most non-Indians refer to themselves as *mestizos*, a Spanish word meaning "mixed blood" (referring to a mix of Spanish and Indian), although they identify themselves as Bolivians. Saying one is *mestizo* implies or imagines a middle class that in reality exists in ever-dwindling numbers, and masks racism: "we are all *mestizo*, we are all Bolivian." Like the elite, *mestizos* also wear variants of cosmopolitan dress.

Bolivia has the highest percentage of *runa* in South America. In Bolivia to be Indian is usually to be poor and discriminated against by both *mestizos* and whites. The category of *runa* – even highland *runa* – is not, however, homogeneous or necessarily lifelong. There are rich *runa* and poor *runa*, urban *runa* and rural *runa*. Though social mobility is limited and I am not aware of reliable statistics, in rural areas a percentage of *ayllu* members regularly change status and cease being *runa*.

The first step in upward mobility is to become *cholitas/cholos* (*chola* or *cholita* for females; *cholo* for males; this term is problematic, as is this "in-between" category: cf. Wesimantel 2002). This transformation occurs in a fairly predictable way. The usual route is for a Sakaka woman to marry a townsperson, move to the town of Sacaca, change fashion, stop weaving, and learn to speak Spanish, along with changes in behavior, such as denying *runa* origins. Men usually make this change by moving to town or a city on their own; *runa* women marry "up" far more often than men.

To change status, a Sakaka *runa* woman changes her *aqsu* (woven overskirt) and *aymilla* (woven full black dress) (Figure 7.1: woman on the right) for a pleated skirt or *pollera* and sweater set (Figure 7.1: woman on the left). The children of former *runa*, if born and raised in the town of Sacaca, usually are considered *cholos/cholitas* or, in certain circumstances, townspeople, depending upon context. Other routes for changing status also involve a change of residence, such as a move to the mines, the Chapare, or a city, where one learns Spanish, wears factory-made dress, and becomes *civilizado* (civilized, the term used in the highlands for this transformation). Peasants in the Lake Titicaca area typically move to El Alto, the capital's satellite city, where they – or more likely their children – become *cholos/cholitas*. The social category or class of *cholo/cholita* overlaps *mestizos* and Indians. Like other Bolivianist social scientists such as Xavier Albó, I translate *cholita/cholo* as urban Andean (urban "Indian"), as do, I think, most people who consider themselves such.

Cholos usually wear a variant of Western-style dress, typically with a fedora, along with a scarf, knit cap, and/or poncho. *Cholitas* wear a distinctive style of dress, including a shaped felt hat, such as the well known bowler hat (the finest come from Borsalino in Italy), several full-pleated skirts, sweater sets, an apron, a mantle, and jewelry (Ackerman 1991; de Sahonero 1987). Dress is central to defining this group; *mestiza* townswomen also wear *polleras* and bowler hats, but typically of less costly materials. *Cholita* dress is among the most expensive in the Andes: far more so than cheap factory-made or second-hand cosmopolitan dress. Yet even relatively well-off *cholitas* and *cholos*, some of whom manage a relatively large amount of money in their commercial enterprises, continue to suffer discrimination by Bolivia's elite and middle classes. This group has become much more active politically. One political party member – "Comadre" Remedios (Loza) – stunned the Bolivian nation in the late 1980s by continuing to wear *polleras* (dressing "*de pollera*") while serving as an elected representative in La Paz.[15]

The Sakaka Textile System: Cloth in the Andes

The Andean region is heir to one of the world's greatest textile traditions, which has continued, with spatial and temporal variations, for 5,000 years. Textiles were crucial to ancient Andeans – they were *the* single most important medium, encoding meaning and wealth, in multiple ways that it is difficult for us to appreciate today (Murra 1962). Textiles fulfill many of these roles today.

Following the Spanish invasion, cloth no longer was produced by or for the state, but local traditions continued, forming the direct precursor to contemporary production. Cloth is, however, a supremely time-consuming medium for encoding meaning and wealth. A patterned narrow belt may take a week to weave; an elaborately patterned poncho may require three to six months of concentrated daily work, apart from yarn preparation, which takes twice as long.

Among the Sakaka, cloth has multiple functions. Cloth is a paramount sign in the representation – and construction – of identity in its manifold forms. It is a communicative system, with meanings and values that textiles, taken as a whole, evoke, express and constitute for their wearers, and is the most important Andean expressive visual medium ("art"). Cloth also functions poetically, that is, in ways in which the textile refers to itself. Cloth has a significant economic function, including embodying wealth, whether displayed in public, stored in homes, or inherited. Cloth has a profoundly religious function, which permeates the process of creation of certain kinds of handmade cloth. Cloth retains limited military functions. The international handicraft industry, including local tourism, has provided another function for cloth in the Andes, although not necessarily for Andean cloth. Cloth plays an important role in the international market for ethnic art and antiquities, which is, overall, detrimental to Andean society. The international fine arts market provides a potential outlet for high-quality, expensive merchandise although, with very few exceptions, little goes to the producers.

Dress in Bolivia

Andeans such as the Sakaka, as noted, selectively appropriate technologies, materials, and images to represent themselves, with fine distinctions, as belonging or aspiring to a gamut of socioeconomic and racial statuses. Not all Sakaka, however, wear "Sakaka" dress all the time (Zorn 1994). Like members of other large indigenous Bolivian ethnic groups, the Sakaka wear (or strategically deploy) several styles of clothing. Sakaka even sometimes dress as whites (in parody, or when dressed by town godparents on their wedding day). The number of dress styles appears to have increased considerably since about 1950, probably because of increased industrial textile production. Each dress style has its own gender, class, ethnic, and "racial" meanings. Dress also varies by generation and region. Most generally, if the range of styles is conceptualized as a continuum, "hand made" dress is at one pole, and "factory-made cosmopolitan" style dress is at the other. In a nation such as Bolivia, with deep racism towards its indigenous population, the decision to wear one style of dress or another, though constrained by finances, is enormously significant.

Sakaka women weave most of the textiles that mark Sakaka ethnicity, though men also produce textiles. Within the sexual division of labor men make certain textiles, mostly items such as pants, skirts, shirts, and dresses, derived from Spanish peasant-style garments. Women create items derived from Andean-style garments, including coca purses, belts, shawls, and ponchos. In most of Peru and Bolivia, women weave on the Andean-type continuous-warp loom, and men on the Spanish-type treadle loom. The well-known Andean ideals of "reciprocity" and "complementarity" can be seen in textile production, because it takes textiles made by both men and women to clothe an individual.

Dress styles are difficult to describe with precision because, somewhat like Saussurian distinctions between *langue* and *parole*, idealized general rules vary in day-to-day practice. Furthermore, styles and names for dress styles are cross-cutting sign systems that vary regionally and socio-economically. A garment such as the full-pleated skirt (*pollera*) that Juana sometimes wears (Figure 7.1), which indexes urban Indian status (de Sahonero 1987; Mendoza 1992; Paredes-Candia 1992), may – depending on factors such as cut, material, and place of manufacture – polysemously signal higher status to a rural Indian, or lower status to a *mestizo* city dweller. The ironies of this signaling, however, include the fact that the indigenous factory-made *pollera* costs less than handmade ethnic dress, while the more expensive variations of *polleras* cost more – sometimes far more – than factory-made, working-class Western-style dress.

Terms such as hand made and factory made are key to understanding certain distinctions in Bolivian dress. By *handmade* (handwoven, handspun), I mean garments made completely by the user and/or a family member or sweetheart, including the processes of spinning the yarn, weaving the fabric, and sewing the finished garment. Handwoven garments are made inside the ethnic group. *Cottage industry-made* garments or fabric are handmade outside the ethnic group, in indigenous communities, small towns, or provincial cities in rural regions. *Factory-made* (factory-woven, factory-spun, or industrially manufactured) yarns, fabrics, or garments are made in factories of varying dimensions, using heavy machinery; factories are located in large cities. Large cottage industries and small factories overlap in scale, though technology differs. Varying combinations of handwoven, cottage-industry woven, or factory-made dress express, among many attributes, aesthetic preference, identity, social status, and claims to economic prosperity. Cosmopolitan dress requires cash to buy, but ethnic dress, because of its many components, costs far more.

Dress Among the Sakaka

The Sakaka make two major distinctions in dress, between "cosmopolitan," and "traditional" or "ethnic" dress. The Sakaka call cosmopolitan dress *civil p'acha,* meaning civil, civilized, or civilian dress. They contrast this with *runa p'acha,* or human or Indian dress. These terms have many connotations, and the distinction is clearly based on the prevailing racist classification of Western as civilized, and Indian as barbaric.

Cosmopolitan dress is industrially manufactured; "traditional" or "ethnic" dress incorporates items of clothing made in several ways. The core of the "most traditional" ethnic dress consists of garments handwoven by users and their families or *ayllu* neighbors. However, some essential items of ethnic dress are made in cottage industries located outside the local ethnic group. For the Sakaka, these items include the "typical" northern-Potosi-style white felt hat and rubber-tire sandals, worn by young people in the photographs, as well as the embroidered black skirts and jackets that inspired Sakaka's "new" traditional style.

Cosmopolitan dress is a cheap variant of dress worn by much of Bolivian society who self-identify as *mestizo* or elite. Distinctions in the materials, cut, and style help index specific class and regional identities. The Sakaka variant of cosmopolitan dress is roughly equivalent to working-class (*mestizo*) dress. Sakaka men, not women, wear cosmopolitan dress. This gendered difference is not unique to the Sakaka; women worldwide are more likely than men to wear some variant of ethnic dress (Barnes and Eicher 1992). Cosmopolitan dress for Bolivian male peasants such as the Sakaka consists of cheap industrially manufactured synthetic-fiber clothing, including some kind of baseball cap, a tailored shirt, a sweater or zippered jacket, pants, a leather belt, and sneakers, with or without socks. Some items, such as cheap baseball caps, have come to index a "peasant" social status.

Whereas cosmopolitan dress is worn by both working class *mestizo* and urban Andean males (the latter working class or peasant), the styles of working class *mestiza* and urban Andean women usually differ, and sometimes significantly so. Working-class women usually wear cosmopolitan-style dresses, blouses and skirts, or even pants, considered a quintessentially male garment. Urban Andean women (*cholitas*) usually wear regional variants of ethnic dress, whose *sine qua non* is the *pollera* in its nearly infinite varieties; they sometimes wear pants under a skirt, for warmth, practicality, and according to some social analysts, to claim certain masculine prerogatives (Weismantel 2002). (In Figure 7.1, the woman on the left wears generically indigenous urban Indian (*cholita*) style *polleras*, whereas in Figure 7.2, the young woman on the right wears a cottage-industry woven, northern-Potosi "ethnic" style *pollera*.) *Cholita* dress varies regionally; it can index substantial class differences between wealthy and poor *cholitas*.

Ethnic dress, or *runa p'acha*, for the Sakaka encompasses (mostly) locally handwoven garments, based on a mix of pre-Columbian and Spanish peasant-derived styles. Women wear a long pleated black dress, embroidered at cuff and hem, called an *aymilla* (Figure 7.1: right). A woman's ensemble includes one or more handwoven shawls, a white felt hat, multiple braids with hair ties, one or more belts, an overskirt like the one woven by Juana, and rubber-tire sandals. This long dress and, especially, the overskirt (not visible in the photograph), symbolize "*runa*-ness" in many Bolivian regions, especially northern Potosí. The shift from the long dress and overskirt to some type of

Dressed to Kill

Figure 7.2. A young man, playing charango, and two young women singers, perform in the Samkha *ayllu* folklore festival. Photograph by Elayne Zorn, 1989.

pleated skirt (Figures 7.1 and 7.2: left) symbolizes modernity and an urban orientation – except in the case of young Sakaka who during the 1980s developed the "new traditional" style (Figure 7.2: right) which symbolizes "modern Sakaka-ness" and is analyzed here. Sakaka male ethnic dress consists of hand woven and embroidered tailored clothing (pants, vest, jacket), worn over a factory-made shirt, as well as a handmade poncho, knit cap, hatbands, and a coca-leaf purse, and a cottage-industry-made white felt hat, and rubber-tire sandals. In this "new" style of ethnic dress, embroidery is becoming increasingly important and elaborate; earlier embroidery styles were far simpler.

For analysis, I classified the enormous number of variations in dress that I saw while living in northern Potosí into groups, akin to genres.[16] I believe these groupings reflect Sakaka categories, not just the impositions of a Euro-American anthropologist seeking a system. As the anthropologist Nancy Ries argues, creating types and groups runs the risk of imposing categories that may be based on serious misunderstandings, but they may also be structured to reveal culturally constructed, socially valid categories (Ries 1997).

In the late 1980s, the range of Sakaka dress styles included seven types. The Quechua terms that describe them are semantically rich, such as *ñawpa muda*, from *ñawpa*, old or prior or ancient (Quechua) and *muda*, fashion (*moda*, Spanish). Types 1 through 6 – subcategories of the broad "genre" of *runa* (Indian, "ethnic") dress – are opposed to type 7, which is part of the broad genre of *q'ara* (non-Indian, "white" or *mestizo*) dress. I summarize these types here; see Zorn (1999) for full details.

Sakaka Dress Styles

1) Handwoven "classic traditional" Sakaka dress – old-fashioned Indian/ethnic dress (*ñawpa muda runa p'acha*: literally, old-fashioned *runa* dress). This substyle of "classic" Sakaka dress is worn by highland *ayllu* members: primarily middle-aged and elderly Sakaka, teenagers from poorer families, and small children whose parents, especially mothers, are particularly interested in weaving. Women's "classic traditional" dress is characterized and symbolized by the handwoven *aqsu* or overskirt, *aymilla* or full long dress, and *awayu* or mantle. Men's dress is characterized by handwoven pants, vest and jacket, and symbolized by the handwoven poncho. Embroidery is simple, in narrow bands. An important aesthetic feature is images enclosed in separate squares or "boxes" (cf. Gisbert, Arze, and Cajías 1987). This style, made primarily of handspun and handwoven garments, is worn by people for various reasons, including relative poverty, generation, or fashion preference. As noted, some items are purchased or bartered for from outside Sakaka *ayllu*. Use of "classic" or "traditional" Sakaka dress is diminishing, due to the loss of Sakaka heirloom textiles as models, and the breakdown of the agro-pastoral economy.

2) Handwoven "modern traditional" Sakaka dress – new fashion "modern" ethnic dress (*musuq muda runa p'acha*: literally, new-style *runa* dress). This substyle, also called *runa p'acha*, or *muda* (fashion, from the Spanish *moda*), is worn primarily by Sakaka teenagers, and by middle-aged people who are more fashion-conscious and/or better off financially than wearers of substyle 1. This substyle is produced using factory-made materials, and incorporates significant aesthetic changes, including color, image, and the organization of stripes. Juana's overskirt is in this style. Women's dress still is characterized and symbolized by the handwoven overskirt, full long dress, and mantle. Men wear handwoven pants, vests, and jackets, combined with second-hand

factory-made Western-style shirts. Dresses and men's clothing are heavily embroidered by men using sewing machines. Sakaka who dress in this substyle buy white hats and rubber-tire sandals made outside the *ayllu*. These "modern traditional" textiles are plyed (re-spun) and handwoven from factory-spun synthetic polyester yarns. This requires greater access to cash, obtained outside the *ayllu* and mostly outside the province. Changes in this substyle include new images (motorcycles, helicopters), new aesthetic devices (gradated rather than sold-block color stripes between warp-pattern-weave stripes), and new weave structures (warp-faced double cloth and supplementary weft warp patterned weave). Garments in this substyle often imitate substyle 3.

3) Cottage-industry-woven "modern traditional" Indian dress – new fashion "modern" ethnic dress (*muda*, or *runa p'acha*: literally, fashion, or *runa* dress). The Sakaka teenagers and older people I just referred to wore this substyle, also called *muda* and *runa p'acha*. Most of this substyle is made outside the *ayllu*, in a cottage industry developed in the early 1980s. Cottage-produced garments for women include the full long dress or a skirt (a non-traditional item, since highland *runa* women usually wear dresses) (Figure 7.2: right). Garments for men include jackets, vests, and scarves (Figure 7.2: left). These cottage-woven ready-to-wear garments are woven and embroidered in a regional northern Potosí peasant style. This small industry is centered around Llallagua, near Bolivia's former tin mines, though many producers work in their rural hamlets.

Although this substyle appears quite different from Sakaka handwoven dress, this impression is based on only a few garments – the woman's skirt and the man's vest: the best sellers of the industry. The fashionable ready-to-wear synthetic-fiber "traditional" garments of this substyle also are woven from factory-spun synthetic polyester yarns. Male members of this regional cottage industry elaborately embroider individual garments on treadle sewing machines, and come from various non-Sakaka *ayllus*. *Mestizos* who wish to (re-)present themselves as Indians – typically from "norte Potosí" – wear these clothes for masked dances, even in Peru. Elaborate embroidery styles change frequently, which is partly why I characterize its production as an indigenous fashion industry. In substyles 2 and 3, most handmade garments continue to be made by women, while most cottage-manufactured garments are made by men. Handmade garments, and especially the mantle, hatband, and knit cap, mark the wearers as Sakaka – that is, the users' *ayllu*-specific identity – even when combined with factory-woven cloth in pan-Bolivian-peasant or working-class styles (Figures 7.1, 7.2: left), and thus it is women's textile production that produces *ayllu*-specific identity.

4) Hand- and cottage-industry woven "modern traditional" dress – categories 2 and 3 combined (*muda*, or *runa p'acha*: literally, fashion, or *runa* dress) (Figure 7.1: right). This is a household variant of substyles 2 and 3. Sakaka men such as the Mamani brothers purchase handwoven yardage from non-Sakaka-*ayllu* producers, then sew and embroider the garments in their Sakaka

homes, copying the Llallagua dress styles, or working in a Sakaka embroidery style. They also call this *runa p'acha* or *muda*. The Llallagua-based ethnic fashion cottage industry offers, then, four market alternatives with varying mixes of household and cottage production, each with varying implications for the mode of textile production and the identity being marked. Clients such as the Sakaka can buy yarns and weave garments; buy some garments ready-made with Laymi/generic northern Potosí embroidery styles; buy yardage and sew and embroider the garments in the household; or buy an unembroidered jacket and then embroider the garment in the household, providing options depending upon cash, time, and skills.

5) Synthetic-fiber factory-made urban Indian/regional peasant dress – urban Indian "ethnic" dress (*cholita/cholo p'acha*: literally, female urban Indian or male urban Indian dress) (Figures 7.1, 7.2: left). This substyle is worn primarily by Sakaka schoolchildren, an increasing number of teenagers, and some older people who are better off financially and more upwardly mobile (perhaps seeking entry into the *cholo/cholita* class). Young Sakaka, especially, consider this peasant style to be the most "modern," and therefore fashionable. While good quality factory-made peasant-style clothing is expensive, cheap versions cost the same or sometimes less than cottage-woven garments. Men's *cholo* dress looks like Western-style dress, but women's *cholita* dress remains ethnically distinctive. However, with this style many Sakaka typically wear some "Sakaka" style handmade textiles for a complete "fashion," and ethnic, statement. Such mixing allows individuals to symbolize themselves as Sakaka, or as generic peasants, who are not necessarily Indians.

6) Combined handwoven "modern traditional" and synthetic-fiber factory-made urban Indian/regional peasant dress (Sakaka *cholita p'acha*: literally, Sakaka urban Indian dress). This is exemplified by the young woman in Figure 7.1 (left), who combined factory-made urban Indian items of dress (sweater set, *pollera*) with Sakaka-style garments (especially the mantle). Many young Sakaka also wear one or more woven hatbands, which mark them as Sakaka.

7) Synthetic-fiber factory-made cosmopolitan-style national working class dress (*q'ara p'acha*, or *civil p'acha*: literally "white" (non-Indian) dress or civilian dress). This is cosmopolitan dress. Sakaka adults rarely wear this substyle in its complete form, except for the wedding outfit rented by the town's *vecino* godparents for a new Sakaka couple. Elderly male Sakaka authorities who are "warriors," or veterans of Bolivia's Chaco war, commonly wear an old worn Western-style suit at festivals or when traveling, but in the late 1980s the primary wearers of cosmopolitan dress were children attending school, who are required to wear the white Bolivian national school uniform.

In practice, the categories or "genres" I described sometimes overlap. Categories 3, 4, and 5 sometimes are mixed, or crossed (cf. Weismantel 2002). It is worth underlining, however, that peasant use of *any* handwoven Sakaka garments, even in combination with factory-made clothing, marks the wearer not only as runa but also as *Sakaka runa*. (Figure 7.1: the young woman on the left wears factory-made generically indigenous *cholita* dress, but with a handmade Sakaka-style mantle. In Figure 7.2, the man wears factory-made pants with a Sakaka-style knit cap.) Insofar as combining different dress styles crosses, plays with, or challenges established social identities of race and ethnicity, we can analyze these practices as "ethnic cross-dressing," extending the term cross-dressing – across gender boundaries – to dress that crosses ethnic boundaries.[17]

Sakaka sometimes told me they would prefer to wear industrially made Western-style clothing, even if second hand, but they couldn't afford to buy other clothing, so they wove their own. Some poor Sakaka indeed owned no or very few factory-made garments and only wore handmade textiles woven with handspun yarns spun from the sheep owned by the weaver or her family. Handmade clothing woven from sheep-wool yarns could signify, then, either poverty or aesthetic preference. However, many weavers used factory-spun rather than sheep wool yarns, to save on labor or because of poor quality wool. Factory-spun yarns can be obtained by barter or purchase incrementally, but even then the switch to factory-spun yarns raises production costs so much that it always is more expensive to weave and wear such modern "traditional Andean" or even urban Andean dress than cheap factory-made or second-hand cosmopolitan dress. Cholita, or urban Indian dress, uses more garments, with differently styled skirts, usually with more expensive materials, and jewelry, and thus generally costs more than cosmopolitan dress.

Ideally, many Sakaka would prefer to own sets of clothing of different styles: Sakaka ethnic dress, modern ethnic dress, cholita/cholo dress, and factory-made "Bolivian" working-class dress. Since runa can place themselves differently in terms of the identity they claim at a given moment and place, the Sakaka, when economically possible, alternate wearing industrially made or traditional clothing, or combine them. Given Bolivia's prevailing social structure with Indians at the bottom, it is not surprising that Sakaka might want to change ethnic/class affiliation, which can begin with and/or be symbolized by changing from ethnic to cosmopolitan dress. Wearing handmade cloth is an important expression of ethnic group solidarity, a key marker that distinguishes "Indians" from "non-Indians." What is perhaps more surprising is that young peasants such as Juana and the Mamani brothers might instead choose to create a new and fashionable variant of ethnic dress.

A New Style of Sakaka "Traditional" Dress

The creation of a new style of Sakaka ethnic dress that I witnessed in the late 1980s occurred at the tail end of massive sales of heirloom textiles in the ethnic textile market (Zorn 1990). The "new" "traditional" Sakaka style, made and worn primarily by young people, was considered the most fashionable and interesting of other potential styles. New textiles such as Sakaka's lime-green mantles with dancing devils, the leaping lions and flowers in Juana's overskirt, or the multi-colored curling flowers in the Mamani brothers' outfits, were absolutely unappealing to the market and its intermediaries who purchased antique cloth for resale to tourists. However, that fashion satisfied a new generation of young *runa* who wanted textiles that represented modernity, not tradition, but modernity without rejection of Sakaka identity.

The Sakaka's new textile style, both at first glance and to the textile literate, appears very different than earlier "traditional" styles, and distinct from neighboring ethnic group styles, though some colors or images are shared, and the new Sakaka style textiles in many ways are built on the garment types, technologies, and aesthetic principles of their older cloth. Weaving technology continues to be extraordinarily time-consuming, though time is saved by using factory-spun yarns. Levels of skill vary, though there has been a general decline in weaving skills, and certainly in spinning. Few contemporary textiles demonstrate the technical levels found in antique weavings, though the strength of the weavers' aesthetic vision frequently remains evident.

The garments Sakaka weave in the "new" style include women's mantles, men's vests, jackets, pants and ponchos, and hatbands and belts for both sexes. The young women in Figures 7.1 and 7.2 wear similar shawls and hatbands, but combine them with factory-made sweater sets, and non-*ayllu*-made skirts. The new Sakaka style utilizes new aesthetic forms (Aymara-influenced rainbow striping), materials (factory-spun synthetic-fiber yarns), colors (synthetic-fiber DayGlo neons), weave structures (warp-faced double cloth), and images derived from diverse sources outside the *ayllu* (motorcycles, lowland parrots, devil dancers). Both women and men participated in developing this style. In the 1980s, Sakaka women wove textiles and knitted caps in that new style of ethnic dress. Sakaka men wove striped and plaid jackets and, like other northern Potosí *runa*, also developed an increasingly elaborate style of embroidery on plain-colored garments; Sakaka embroidery was inspired by synthetic-fiber skirts and jackets made outside the *ayllu* (Figure 7.2: skirt at right).

Two socioeconomic phenomena – the difficulty of getting traditional materials, and the availability of new materials – underlay the creation of this new style, though they do not explain it. Both phenomena should be understood in the broader context of the Andean textile economy.

Transformations in the "Traditional" Sakaka Textile System and the Agro-Pastoral Economy

The "traditional" Andean textile system, transformed repeatedly during the region's history, faced changes in the second half of the twentieth century that in scale perhaps approached those that of the colonial period. Modernization in the form of economic, social, and cultural changes affected the traditional

Andean textile system in multiple ways (Zorn 1996). Here I discuss the effects of this transformation on the Sakaka, but these transformations occurred throughout the Andes.

Even in the second half of the twentieth century, most Sakaka made their own clothing, with fiber obtained from their own animals or from exchange with other *runa*. They participated in an "ethnic" textile economy, though cash sometimes was needed to purchase chemical dyes, or felt hats. Unlike Andeans who produced textiles for exchange or sale to non-group members, Sakaka textile production circulated within the *ayllu*. However, we do not know if this was the case in the colonial period, because the poverty and barter system of the early twentieth century may be partly a consequence of the impoverishment of *ayllus* following nineteenth-century reforms. During the colonial period, many Indians participated in various markets. Colonial Sakaka nobles sometimes wore fine Spanish cloth (Espinoza 1969), and numerous Andeans were forced to work in Spanish textile sweatshops, though there is no evidence that the Sakaka did so (the Sakaka worked in mines instead).

Traditionally, indigenous weavers could count on obtaining fiber, the most critical material needed to produce cloth, through direct access from their own herds, kinship networks, or barter. While the finest textiles are woven with alpaca fiber, carefully selected llama fiber can be of good quality, though it is best for making slings, ropes, and sacks. One of the world's finest fibers comes from the wild Andean vicuña, a threatened species off-limits to contemporary Andean weavers. Sheep wool is adequate to weave yardage for cosmopolitan clothing, but is inferior to camelid fiber.

Most Sakaka had to obtain camelid fiber from non-Sakaka, since few Sakaka own camelids. Until the 1970s, most Sakaka obtained camelid fiber from Aymara-speaking herders who crossed Sakaka territory with their llama caravans. Herders journeyed from Oruro through Sakaka on their way to the warm valley lands of northern Potosí in search of corn, and even in the late 1980s I saw herders with small caravans walking through Sakaka territory, or even through Sacaca town. Sakaka say they typically traded potatoes for unspun camelid fleece. Most Sakaka can obtain sheep wool for yardage from their own mongrel sheep (raised more for the manure for fertilizer), or from kinsfolks' sheep. When fiber is available, weavers produce "traditional" Sakaka dress.

A series of changes occurred in the Sakaka textile system during the 1980s that affected the system and transformed it irreversibly. The overall effect of these phenomena was to "push" the Sakaka into the market for both the production and commercialization of "traditional" handwoven cloth. There were four principal changes. First, social, economic, and cultural transformations at local, regional, national, and international levels resulted in the collapse of certain sectors of the agro-pastoral economy, whose consequences included declining or non-existent access to textile inputs (primarily wool and dyes). Second, the rise of an international market in ethnic antique/heirloom cloth resulted in the removal of an incalculable number of handwoven textiles from homes, communities, and *ayllus* (Zorn 1990), leaving the technical knowledge and memory but not the physical models for weaving. Third, Bolivia developed a national textile industry that produced yarns and some garments for an indigenous market. Finally, the appearance of two short-term sources for materials and/or cash made it possible to obtain industrially manufactured yarns and garments. These were the antique textile market (where peasants often bartered old textiles for new ones or for synthetic-fiber yarns), and the growth of the coca/cocaine economy in Bolivia (which provided a source for income for purchasing textile inputs).

As a consequence of these phenomena – especially the collapse of certain sectors of the regional agro-pastoral economy – by the late 1980s virtually all Sakaka needed money to purchase the materials needed to create handmade cloth. Some Sakaka could handweave or handknit a few garments from the wool of their sheep, but the fiber and therefore resulting garment quality was poor, and colors were only white or dark brown, as dyes also were of poor quality.

By the late 1980s, Sakaka access to raw materials for producing cloth had declined enormously. Erosion continued to limit pasturage and therefore the wool quality of their sheep. The agro-pastoral economy had declined, according to the Sakaka, by the 1970s. The herders who formerly brought llama fiber to the Sakaka rarely crossed their territory. By the mid-1980s, most herders traveled by truck down to the valleys, or bartered for or purchased corn in the cities, rather than endure the long treks of several weeks or months required to travel from the high puna down to the eastern valleys. "Millma mana kanchu [There's no wool]," Sakaka lamented.

By the second half of the twentieth century, few Andeans still knew how to use, or could locate good sources of, natural plant and mineral dyes. Since the turn of the twentieth century, Andeans imported aniline dyes from Germany, but these became increasingly unavailable by the 1970s. Peruvian dyes, which when first produced in the 1960s were fairly good quality, declined in quality and colors often bled with the first washing. The Sakaka, like many Andeans, were left without access to either fleece or dyes.

For these reasons, as well as the pressures of modernization and an increased opportunity to dress in a way that allowed some peasants to lay stake to higher non-Indian social status, the Sakaka, like other Andeans, found in factory-made clothing – either generically indigenous or cosmopolitan working-class styles – an alternative to handmade clothing that was both available and relatively cheap. Textile manufacture is one of Bolivia's few industrial sectors, providing relatively cheap cosmopolitan-style garments. Industrially manufactured synthetic-fiber clothing is widely available at regional fairs, in the town of Sacaca, and in cities to which Sakaka normally travel. Depending upon fluctuations in the exchange rate, contraband imports from Peru and Brazil sometimes flood Bolivia. Used American clothing is also available relatively cheaply, from sources such as locally based Mothers Clubs run by the Catholic

Church. Garments from the rag trade can be found in markets throughout Bolivia.

Since both fleece for spinning yarn and dyes for adding color were poor in quality, the logical solution for Sakaka who wanted handmade clothing was to turn to synthetic-fiber factory-spun yarns, available in a wide palette of colors, like those Juana and the Mamanis used. Spinning factories based in Bolivian cities produce synthetic-fiber yarns of varying thickness, plys, and colors for the national market, encompassing both middle-aged *mestizas* in La Paz who knit sweaters and young Sakaka teenagers in northern Potosí who weave coca leaf purses. The anthropologist Cassandra Torrico (personal communication, 1986) observed that these factories were quite savvy about Andean demand, producing and marketing yarns that accorded well with the specific colors preferences of different ethnic groups.

Factory-spun yarns also present a significant advantage in terms of saving labor in the most time-consuming phase of textile production: spinning. My research revealed that, surprisingly, young Sakaka used the considerable time saved by buying factory-spun yarns to weave more, thereby increasing productivity, although primarily for use, not sale. I also observed this in other ethnic groups. Yet, the Sakaka could not sell their beautiful synthetic-fiber weavings because the market in ethnic textiles heavily prefers natural, not synthetic-fiber, weavings.

In the late 1980s, a skein of fine two-ply yarn, of appropriate thickness for respinning into a yarn suitable for weaving a northern Potosí-style garment such as a poncho, cost approximately US$1, or half a day's wages in Sacaca town. Sakaka who buy factory-spun yarns generally have greater relative access to cash, obtained outside their *ayllu* and mostly outside their province. In the 1980s, the Sakaka obtained materials (principally machine-spun yarns) from two main sources. They exchanged or sold heirloom textiles for yarns or factory-woven shawls, as part of the international trade in ethnic textiles (early to mid-1980s), or worked as seasonal wage laborers in the coca/cocaine economy in the Chapare (mid-to-late 1980s).

The International Market for Antique "Ethnic" Cloth

The decade of the 1980s saw one "boom" in Andean peasant economies – the rise of an international market for antique handwoven Andean cloth, most of which left indigenous communities for export to Europe and the US, pausing along the way to lie piled in the streets of Bolivia's capital, La Paz (Zorn 1990). This market reflected increased consumer demand from industrial countries for Third and Fourth World "ethnic" art, as part of late capitalist reactions to industrialization manifested in an increasing interest in authenticity and demand for "original" handmade objects. Andean textiles were priced at the very low end of the international antique cloth market. Starting in the mid-1970s, and reaching a peak around 1983 and 1984 (following years of drought and floods), incalculable quantities of heirloom textiles, dating primarily from the nineteenth century, although some may have been much older, left Andean communities.

The Sakaka, unlike ethnic groups such as the Ecuadorian Otavalos (Meisch 2003) and people from Taquile Island, Peru (2004), did not produce textiles for the market; the Sakaka only commercialized antique textiles. Multiple factors account for this, including historical patterns of production and exchange, and the low prices paid for textiles. Even at the rate of local wages in the town of Sacaca, a weaver would need to earn at least US $18 (1.5 weeks' work) for a shawl, excluding the cost of materials, for her labor alone. (The stored labor in antique textiles typically is much greater, with one shawl often requiring three months' labor.) In Sacaca, weavers are paid a tin of grain for weaving a blanket, which takes two weeks' work. Selling a newly woven Sakaka shawl, if possible, earns a weaver US $5–10, which barely covers materials. The Sakaka receive so little for their weaving because they have no direct access to buyers of ethnic textiles; Sakaka sell handwoven textiles to intermediaries, who travel to rural areas seeking antique textiles, then go to La Paz where they resell to dealers who market to tourists (Zorn 1990). This market peaked in 1983–5, although even today mountains of handwoven textiles lie piled for sale on La Paz streets.

While some Sakaka, like other indigenous Peruvians and Bolivians, sold heirloom textiles (usually shawls, woven by women) for small amounts of money to middlemen, others exchanged their older textiles for factory-made synthetic-fiber shawls, or for skeins of factory-spun synthetic-fiber yarns in fashionable colors (Zorn 1990). On La Paz streets, a handmade Sakaka shawl sold for US$10 to $20, and up to $75 for older or more elaborately patterned textiles. A typical exchange in the late 1980s of an heirloom textile for skeins of yarn was one shawl for five or six skeins of yarn, worth US$5 to $6. By the late 1980s, very few old textiles remained in Sakaka communities. I found that young Sakaka were, however, largely unconcerned about this, primarily because they were confident of their productive capabilities and busy creating new and, to them, "more beautiful" textiles, often using the yarns they received in exchange for older textiles.

The purchase of handmade textiles, by foreign dealers and Bolivian intermediaries, slowed in the late 1980s as fewer "good" old pieces remained. Dealers were not interested in the newer Sakaka textiles, produced using synthetic-fiber neon-colored yarns, as these would not sell in the ethnic textile market that demanded older natural-colored or softly colored pieces. The young Sakaka's preferences for synthetic-fiber incandescent colors – lime green in particular – did not appeal to Western buyers, or at least those intermediaries could identify. Such handwoven textiles therefore could not be commercialized. Within the ethnic group, however, those new-style textiles demonstrated the weavers' skills, and served as the markers of an ethnic identity that people still had an important interest in maintaining.

One of the most interesting aspects of the Sakaka style of dress created in the 1980s was, then, its being situated outside the international textile market, responding to internal demands – aesthetic, symbolic, social – within an indigenous fashion system. These attributes form part of the social meaning of the continuity of weaving. Aesthetics has value in and of itself, but also as an index of weaving skill, which indexes and symbolizes economic productivity, including desirability as a potential spouse.

Discussion and Conclusion

Investments by young unmarried Sakaka in ethnic-style cottage-industry-made garments and in materials for creating handmade "ethnic" dress require some explanation. The reaffirmation of "tradition" and the assertion of Sakaka ethnic identity symbolized by creating and wearing Sakaka dress seems somewhat surprising given the forces – modernization, racism, poverty, globalization – that one might expect would make peasants such as Juana and the Mamani brothers want to be anything other than Sakaka.

At the turn of the millennium, fewer Sakaka wore ethnic dress. However, many continue to do so. Wearing ethnic dress expresses an increasingly self-conscious choice in ethnically diverse and polarized Bolivia, where dress can be – but is not always – a form of non-verbal resistance to the political and cultural hegemony of the white and *mestizo* Bolivian state. Style also matters in ways that are hardly trivial (although fashion can be this). Clothes do make the woman and the man. Although cosmopolitan clothing is cheaper than handmade dress, many Andeans still make cloth, and textiles continue to be enormously important in local cultural and social reproduction, as a site for investing money, labor, and materials. Exquisitely woven and embroidered dress proclaims skill, economic resources, and *gusto* (good taste) (Zorn 1997a). These attributes bring high prestige to young *runa* such as Juana and the Mamanis, creating attractiveness and desirability, drawing many potential admirers and suitors. The finest textiles, and the most innovative fashions, are woven by the young unmarried or recently married, who have the eyesight, physical strength, desire, and time to weave, and the economic resources to obtain materials to do so. (Older weavers have a surer sense of taste and aesthetics, and experience, but the demands of married life leave little time for fine weaving.)

The late twentieth-century transformation in Bolivia's "traditional" textile economy occurred at the intersection of an unfortunate combination of regional, national, and international forces. In this process, key materials for producing cloth – wool and dyes – became unavailable through barter in the ethnic and regional economy. The materials to handmake cloth now require cash to obtain, and are frequently factory made.

It is worth emphasizing that the shift from ethnic to generically indigenous to cosmopolitan dress, and from Indian to urban Indian to *mestizo* ethnic/racial/

social categories (and statuses), generally includes a shift from local to regional to urban production, and from natural wool to man-made synthetic fibers. However, these dualistic divisions, between local and natural and Indian on the one hand, and global and synthetic and *mestizo* on the other, are much more complex in daily life. For example, Sakaka ethnic dress has come to rely on synthetic-fiber yarns, while elite cosmopolitan dress uses natural fibers.

Coincident with the loss of availability of natural materials, and a new availability of factory-made substitutes, was the rise and collapse of the international market in ethnic textiles. The loss of heirloom textiles in Sakaka hamlets by the late 1980s was another factor that might have been expected to lead to the demise of cloth production, since the physical models for weaving (the "books" in textile libraries) were lost (Zorn 1990). Yet by the late 1980s the young Sakaka had created a new style of dress, outside of the textile market, which dealers in antique cloth – the only market for Sakaka weavings – refused to buy because the intermediaries considered these weavings impossible to sell.

As Sakaka fine heirloom textiles were becoming depleted, the Sakaka found another means (the coca economy) to obtain the cash needed to buy the materials needed to create local cloth, which continued to proclaim their distinctive identity. Participation in the coca economy ironically took Sakaka such as Juana "back" into the "ethnic" economy, by providing an alternative source of money that "freed" the Sakaka from the minimal returns of the textile market, which they were losing access to anyway as their stocks of antique textiles were depleted. In the 1980s the Sakaka no longer needed to sell heirloom textiles to obtain the inputs required to continue to create handwoven cloth – even though many of these inputs are factory-made and therefore "in the market."

Paradoxically, then, work in the coca/cocaine economy in the late 1980s, which though necessary for landless and impoverished peasants has so clearly been shown to be dangerous, and socially and culturally disruptive, allowed young Sakaka weavers to finance the creation of a new style of dress, and to avoid either weaving textiles for sale, or selling heirloom textiles in the international ethnic arts market, thereby reinforcing the "traditional" Andean textile system of meanings. Willingness to invest meager earnings from the coca/cocaine economy in clothing and weaving materials points to both the continued importance of cloth in the Andes for many young people, and the poor opportunities available to Bolivian peasants to earn adequate wages, and modify their lifestyle in the way adoption of Western-style clothing would signify. This occurred despite the fact that such clothing would be cheaper and would require much less investment of time to obtain.

When Juana returned from the Chapare, she wove a fashionable garment in a "modern" ethnic style of dress, using materials she purchased with cash she earned as a peasant laborer in the global coca/cocaine economy. Similarly, the Mamanis embroidered matching outfits to participate in the region's renowned *tinkus*. The theoretical implications of these apparently idiosyncratic acts can contribute valuable insights to the analysis of larger, global social forces. I argue that Sakaka creation of a new style of dress, financed by seasonal migration to the Chapare, counters the assumption that insertion into the global economy (albeit at the lowest rung as an unskilled wage laborer in the coca/cocaine economy) inevitably homogenizes or eradicates local culture. This is becoming increasingly clear from studies of local interpretations of globalization phenomena (Nash 1993; Rowe and Schelling 1991, and others).

Many of the topics I discuss require further investigation. Research is needed to assess changes in the Sakaka and ethnic fashion system in the twenty-first century; to study factory production of yarns and garments for Andean "traditional" indigenous and peasant markets; to document the international market in Andean ethnic cloth; and to thoroughly investigate the history of transformations in the "ethnic" textile economy, especially during this century. Other issues, which require further research, seem clear.

Modern peasants such as the Sakaka seek changes in the national Bolivian agrarian structure that would provide better prices for their crops, jobs with wages that at least equal what they earn in the Chapare, a market that would pay a fair wage for handmade textiles, and a change in the United States' drug policy, which unfairly shifts the blame to supply, rather than seriously try to control demand. While I do not think that cocaine is the solution some would hope for, ironically, the demand for this product in the global economy – the fact that money from the crack epidemic on United States' streets financed "traditional" Andean textiles (Blenda Femenías, personal communication, September 1994) – makes it possible for Sakaka peasants to create one of the most culturally meaningful local products, their cloth. As long as Bolivian peasants can commercialize neither agricultural products nor handwoven cloth for wages that provide a fair return on their investments of inputs and labor, it should not be surprising that peasants such as Juana and the Mamanis weave only to please themselves, and that they and their relatives migrate to the Chapare to participate in the coca/cocaine export economy to earn cash.

Although dress is, on one level, an activity that is "superfluous to survival," as in the mocking title of an edited volume by Lewin and Cherfas (Turner 1980), the importance of dress can be noted in many ways: in the investment of materials by young Sakaka peasants, the economic weight of the fashion and clothing industry worldwide, or the propensity of many regimes and elites, historically, to try to control what should, or should not, be worn (de Areche 1995; Phipps 1996).

Figure 7.1, which shows two young Sakaka women in the central plaza of Sacaca town, gazing defiantly at me, was taken on an ordinary Sunday market day. I could not have photographed this prior to Bolivia's 1952 nationalist revolution. Sakaka told me that before that time, they were "not allowed" to use the public space of the plaza. How were Sakaka recognized? By their dress. One of the stories that has haunted me since I first heard it in the mid-1980s, from an elderly indigenous man, reminds us that dress and identity are indeed not superfluous. Whether literally "true" or not, the structure and content of the narrative recounts important truths.

Sometime in the 1940s, that man returned from work in a Chilean mine to his home in southern Peru. He went from his rural hamlet to a nearby town in the Department of Puno, where he bought some items with money he had earned. He then went to the plaza to do as all others do: stroll or sit, rest, watch people. He was wearing, he emphasized, a new, Western-style shirt (perhaps imported), rather than handmade ethnic dress. He told me he was harassed, beaten up, stripped of his shirt, and thrown out of the plaza. His "crime," to the town *mestizos*, was to be an Indian in the town's public space, and to dare to "cross-dress" in Western-style fashion. (If his shirt was from Chile, local elites would not have had access to it.)

Within the crosscutting parameters of social identity of gender, class, race, and ethnicity, fashion enters in a variety of ways. My discussion of different styles ("genres") is a start towards illustrating the complexity of identity in the south-central Andes. Yet whereas identity is clear at any given moment, dress does not always neatly line up with the identity being demonstrated or claimed. Textiles from one substyle may be worn with another. A Sakaka woman wearing a dress of substyle 2 (made from synthetic yarns) may also wear an overskirt made from sheep wool (substyle 1) and/or a mantle woven in a factory (substyle 5). A Sakaka man may handweave a jacket from synthetic yarn (substyle 2) that imitates a jacket purchased from the Laymi cottage industry (substyle 3). Fashion is not a fixed semiotic code like language.

Dress in Sakaka, as in much of the Andes and many other parts of the world, remains profoundly important for the formation of both individual and group identity. I think that what we see today has been going on for a very long time. Precise use of combinations of elements such as the ones I illustrated makes it possible for the Sakaka to differentiate themselves – or not – from their non-Indian neighbors, other peasants, and their indigenous *ayllu* neighbors, in clear ways, with conscious (re)presentation. Distinctions in styles of dress remain important in the Andes as powerful semiotic indexes and symbols of gender, ethnic, class, and racial identities. Dress codes the experiences of the Sakaka. They fashion their dress, using diverse materials from varied sources, into many styles, which help them construct not one "essential," but rather multiple, Sakaka identities, within a distinctive indigenous fashion system.

Acknowledgments

I am grateful to the funding sources whose generous support made it possible for me to conduct Ph.D. dissertation research in northern Potosí, Bolivia during summer 1986, and September 1987 to August 1989: the Cornell University Latin American Studies Program (Travel Grant); the Joint Committee on Latin American Studies of the Social Science Research Council and the American

Council of Learned Societies (with funds provided by the William and Flora Hewlett Foundation and the Andrew W. Mellon Foundation); the National Science Foundation (Grant No. BNS08712056); Fulbright-Hays; and the Inter-American Foundation. Black and white photographs were printed with support from the Research Council of Colgate University, by Warren Wheeler.

Many colleagues and friends in Latin America, the United States, and Europe have contributed to this project. Because they are so numerous, and they know who they are, I thank them here *en grupo*. I also would like to thank Regina Root for her invitation to contribute a chapter to this volume, and for her patience and excellent comments.

The research on which this article is based was possible due to the generosity and assistance of members of *ayllu* Sakaka, and residents of the town of Sacaca, as well as many Bolivians. I would like to particularly acknowledge the hospitality and help of the community of Totoroqo, Sakaka, who fed me, taught me to weave, accompanied me, put me up, and put up with me.

8

Representations of Tradition in Latin American Boundary Textile Art

Elyse Demaray, Melody Keim-Shenk and
Mary A. Littrell

Theoretical discussions on both tradition and boundary textile art reveal the complexities involved in defining these terms and their relationships to each other. In the past, scholars such as Kroeber (1948) viewed tradition as static and firmly fixed in the past, while others more recently have challenged this definition (Moreno and Littrell 2001; Cohen 1988, 1992; Graburn 1979; Handler and Linnekin 1984; Shils 1981). Theorists such as Handler and Linnekin (1984) see tradition as totally abstract, as a symbolic act that carries on the *meanings* of tradition for people in the present while the actual form of material goods, behaviors, or beliefs from the past might change. While definitions of tradition shape scholars' understanding of all textiles, they become particularly complicated and important in regards to boundary textile art which "crosses the boundary where ... two cultures meet"[1] (Baizerman 1987: 5). Produced for the "ethnic art market" (Wade quoted in Lucero & Baizerman, 1999: 179), boundary art revolves around the ongoing, dynamic interactions between artisans and consumers and the mediators who bring them together. In this process, mediators or cultural brokers often advise artisans on how to alter existing textile forms to meet market demands. Thus, as Jules-Rosette (1984: 229) notes, works produced for the ethnic art market become "at once a statement about the identity of the artists and a commentary on the audience for which it is produced."

This chapter looks at two apparel companies that sell Latin American boundary textile art but use different approaches to tradition as the basis for their business concepts and decision-making: Maya Traditions, a fair trade, not-for-profit company and Peruvian Connection, an upscale for-profit business. We analyze how the companies' differing goals determine their approaches to tradition; how these approaches, in turn, shape design decisions, marketing strategies and interactions with artisans; and, finally, how the companies' working definitions of tradition do or do not corroborate current academic theories.

Scholarship on the history of Maya and Andean textiles, the expression of ethnic identity through textiles, and discussions of tradition and boundary art informed our study. Field research in Panajachel, Guatemala and Tongonoxie, Kansas enabled us to conduct on-site interviews with the respective company owners and observe business practices. Content analysis of online catalog sales, moreover, provided insights on products, presentation, and narrative texts about the cultures from which products are sourced.

Textiles and Tradition

"Tradition," is an elusive term that scholars understand in different and often conflicting ways. Some of the primary questions involved in determining the precise meaning of tradition as it relates to boundary textiles include the following: when we speak of traditional textiles, are we referring to designs, colors, fibers, the means of production or all of these elements from the past? How can we determine when a "tradition" began? How long does a design, color, fiber, or technology have to persist to be considered traditional? How do these concrete elements relate to their meanings for the producers and the consumers? To what degree does tradition "refer to a core of inherited culture traits"? Or is tradition "a wholly symbolic construction" that relies on individuals' interpretations of what physical objects signify (Handler and Linnekin 1984: 273)?

As scholars have shifted their perceptions of epistemology from positivism to postmodern relativism, their understanding of tradition has also taken this turn. As Handler and Linekin (1984: 276) note, some theorists believe that "a real, essential tradition exists apart from interpretations of that tradition," while others understand tradition as the changing symbolic meanings that individuals attach to specific cultural objects, such as textiles. Classic definitions of tradition, like that of A. L. Kroeber (1948: 411) rely on the positivist view that meaning can be found in observable phenomena that remain the same over time. Thus, for Kroeber, tradition involves an "internal handing on through time" of unchanging elements that help define a specific culture. Like Kroeber, Shils (1981) defines tradition as the transmission of objects, beliefs, practices, or institutions from the past to the present. Yet, his theory of tradition also includes the idea of change. Shils holds that both cultural elements from the past and interpretations of them in the present can and do change over time.

While Shils moves away from a view of tradition as static, and he recognizes that the meanings of objects can change over time, identifiable elements from the past remain essential to his definition. Similarly, textile theorist Susan

Baizerman (1987: 7) views tradition in a "process-oriented manner, as that which is passed along from one generation [of artisans] to the next." Yet she is very clear about which specific aspects of boundary art must stay under the control of the artisans producing the textiles in order for the boundary art to "remain firmly rooted" in tradition (Baizerman 1987: 7). As long as artisans carry on the "process of production" (for example, backstrap weaving or knitting techniques and their development) mediators can alter formal elements of a textile, such as "color, designs, materials and forms of weaving" (Baizerman 1987: 9), without severing its vital relationship to the past. In contrast, Cohen (1992: 20) states that "motifs and designs are . . . the most important ethnic *markers*."

Handler and Linnekin (1984) focus their examination of tradition on the present rather than the past, concluding that "Traditions thought to be preserved are created out of the conceptual needs of the present. Tradition is not handed down from the past, as a thing or collection of things; it is symbolically reinvented in an ongoing present" (Handler and Linnekin 1984: 280). In their relative, poststructuralist perspective, the meanings of tradition reside outside of the concrete characteristics of historical objects, behaviors or beliefs. Instead, meaning is generated in the "context and meanings of the present" (Handler and Linnekin 1984: 281): "Juxtaposed to other objects, enmeshed in new relationships of meaning," they state, "they [objects] become something new" (Handler and Linnekin 1984: 280). If we apply Handler and Linnekin's concepts to textiles from the past, the source of meaning and, thus, its designation as traditional no longer depend on concrete characteristics such as color and motif, but rather on individuals' perception of specific textiles in their current context. Finally, Glassie (1995) furthers Handler's and Linnekin's relativist view by explaining how individuals "negotiate" or determine meaning depending on their overall goals or desires as well as their particular circumstances.

But how do textile companies, such as Maya Traditions and Peruvian Connection, understand the meaning of tradition? Do they, like academic theorists, view tradition from a relativist postmodern perspective? Or do they depend upon concrete characteristics embedded in textiles of the past? More importantly, what are the consequences of the companies' working approaches to tradition?

Boundary Textiles and Tradition

Boundary art is most often connected to, but not identical with, art made by artisans for use in their own communities. By their very nature, then, boundary textiles problematize definitions of tradition because artisans create them expressly to sell to individuals outside of their ethnic communities, whether local, regional or international. Artisans and/or mediators, therefore, must consider consumer demands in order to sell their goods. Mediators familiar with fashion trends often suggest or require changes intended to produce more salable textiles. As mediators make decisions about product changes, moreover, their choices necessarily incorporate their personal beliefs about what constitutes tradition (Moreno and Littrell 2001). In the past, a weaver or knitter controlled the whole creative process, choosing the materials, designs, colors, production methods, and the products made. Today, the mediator or intermediary, in the role of designer or retailer, takes on many of these decisions when textiles are made for sale. Therefore, the same textile could be perceived by an artisan as non-traditional but identified by a mediator as traditional as she anticipates consumer needs.

For the purposes of this study, we conceive of boundary textile art very broadly so that any textile produced by an individual by hand, with the intent of selling it to others beyond their ethnic community, "counts" as boundary textile art. We do not distinguish boundary textile art from "tourist" art or "airport" art, or from other similarly labeled subcategories identified within the larger body of works we designate as boundary art. Mass-produced objects made by machine for sale to outsiders fall outside the scope of this essay, however, since this massive group of commercial goods has its own history and trajectory of development, despite the fact that some overlap still exists. Including the whole spectrum of works produced by artisans by hand for sale beyond their ethnic communities enables us to examine companies as diverse as Peruvian Connection and Maya Traditions. Both companies identify their goods as traditional at the same time that they acknowledge that the products are not identical to those that artisans make or have made in the past for themselves. Most salient, perhaps, is that *the companies'* understandings of what constitutes boundary art and tradition, rather than our own, serve as the focus of this study.

Only recently have scholars begun to discuss boundary art, despite the fact that most artisans have traded or sold their goods to outsiders from early times (Cohen 1992). One of the first academics to write in these terms, Graburn (1979) produced a typology of arts and crafts that includes "popular art," "commercial traditional arts," "souvenir art," "reintegrated art," and "assimilated fine arts." While other writers have generated terms to identify somewhat differently defined categories, Graburn began an academic conversation that continues to identify and distinguish between the needs and ideas of the producers, audience/consumers, commercial mediators, and businesses who make decisions about the formal attributes of a finished art object.

Cohen, for example, (1988) created a typology that presents a continuous variable to identify the distance between the artisan and the consumer of the product. Similarly, Moreno and Littrell (2001) present a model based on nine variables of both concrete and abstract characteristics to determine a textile's level of "traditionality." "Concrete levels of tradition" measure high or low along the specific continua of "producers," "original intended consumer," "function," "age," and "production," while "abstract levels of tradition" include "rate of change," "visibility of change," "number of changes," and "source of change." Levels of tradition for producers, intended consumer, function, and production, for example, are identified with who makes and uses textiles, Indians (high) or "foreigners" (low).

In contrast, Lucero and Baizerman (Baizerman 1987; Lucero and Baizerman 1999) look at all textiles produced for sale outside of artisans' ethnic communities and shaped by mediators as boundary art. Moreover, Baizerman (1987: 5) considers boundary art as "part of a continually emerging and unfolding tradition." Therefore, all boundary textile art counts as traditional in her thinking.

When objects that artisans historically have created for their own use become commodities, that is, objects for sale, the basis for their value shifts from the use value of the object for its creator to the exchange value for both producer and consumer (Moreno and Littrell 2001). This shift, moreover, establishes a connection between "people who live profoundly different lives but who can respond to the symbols, textures, and forms that express distinct cultural traditions" (Nash 1993: 1). Thus, the "culture of the artisan is packaged along with the product" (Nash 1993: 12). Interestingly, the textile characteristics that artisans associate with their culture and historical past do not always correspond to those that consumers consider "traditional". Some individuals make purchase decisions without previous knowledge of an artisan's culture or the history and nature of a community's arts. Ironically, in some situations, consumers come to identify a particular motif or design as traditional even though artisans have always created the motif solely for the tourist market (Cohen 1992).

Consumers do not form a homogenous group, moreover, so one person's criteria for determining whether or not a textile is traditional can differ considerably from those of another individual, thereby generating a wide range of perspectives among consumers and adding another layer to the question of who determines a textile's value and meaning. Most consumers of boundary textiles gauge the "authenticity" of a specific textile with two primary criteria: it must be handmade, and/ or it must incorporate a "traditional" motif or design (Cohen 1988; Littrell 1990). If people do not begin with a clear understanding of tradition, determining an object's authenticity with these criteria becomes an impossible task. In a similar way, some buyers distinguish "authentic" textile art from "tourist art", another vague label most often used to designate mass-produced goods or poor quality work more generally (Baizerman 1987; Littrell 1990). Moreover, some consumers make purchase decisions based on other criteria such as current aesthetics or fashion trends in their home country. However a consumer determines if an object is traditional or authentic (terms often conflated by consumers), these designations come from individuals who belong to a culture that differs from the producer's culture. Artisans might very well perceive their own work very differently. As Cohen (1992: 26) notes, "in some cases the cultural group of the producers may not possess such concepts as *authenticity*, *originality* or *fakery*."

With all of these perspectives and changes, can boundary textile art ever be traditional? If so, which elements of a community's textiles can change before tradition is lost? Or does the consumer ultimately determine if a textile is traditional? Consumers and companies that sell "traditional" textiles must take these types of criteria into consideration as they make concrete decisions about the boundary textiles they market and sell. Using their company goals as a starting point, businesses negotiate between their desire to sell products and the characteristics of textiles from the past.

Maya Backstrap Weaving

For more than 3,000 years, the indigenous Maya women of Latin American have woven their clothing on backstrap looms. According to ancient Maya mythology, Ixchel, the goddess of weaving, wove the cosmos and gave the backstrap loom to her people. Even today, with each new creation, weavers pray to Ixchel for a successful outcome. Thus, for a Maya woman, weaving is an act of remembrance, one she identifies with her heritage and culture each time she kneels down at her loom. In the twenty-first century, mothers and grandmothers continue to teach their young daughters how to weave their clothes when they are eight or nine years old (Maya Traditions 2003).

The long history of backstrap weaving in Guatemala and its association with indigenous cultures, means that women's *traje* (traditional clothing) remains a vibrant symbol of Maya identity. As anthropologist Carol Hendrickson (1995: 43) observes, "traje can be taken as an active, enduring cultural object – one that summarizes and symbolically maps some cultural core of the people with whom it is related." *Traje* consists of a particular style of clothing for both women and men that differs in certain aspects from village to village. The colors, styles, and decorative designs, on women's huipiles, hair ribbons, and belts distinguish individuals as members of a specific highland village (Hendrickson 1995: 51). In Tecpan, for example, a specific set of motifs appears in women's *huipiles*: "a curl, star, comb, scissors or lightening, and flag" (Hendrickson 1995: 158), while red *huipiles* with embroidered necklines signal the village of Patzun (Hendrickson 1995).

Each village identifies the *vero traje* (real traje) as "a unique form of dress that has been handed down from pre-conquest times to the present" (Hendrickson 1995: 38). The clothing that individuals actually wear day to day, however, depends more specifically on each person's unique history, the specific occasion, and available options. For example, a woman who marries a man from a different village will continue to wear the *traje* from her birth-town, while her daughter will most probably wear the *traje* typical in her father's birthplace (Henrickson 1995).

For females, the parts of traje that women and girls weave on backstrap looms include a long hair ribbon (*cinta*), a loose blouse (*huipil*) with designs, motifs, and colors specific to her town, and a belt (*faja*), and, in some areas, a shawl (*rebozo*). The only part of men's *traje* woven on backstrap looms is the belt, generally identical to women's (Hendrickson 1995: 34). Most men, however, now wear *traje* only for special occasions, while others wear *vestido* (commercially made shirts and trousers) exclusively. In contrast, most women continue to wear *traje* on a daily basis.

Although the use of the backstrap loom has remained a consistent means of production, women's *traje* has never remained completely static. Weavers express their individual creativity within the parameters of their village colors, designs, and motifs through slight alterations such as the placement or size of a design element, or the striping pattern in the base fabric. In addition, some motifs wax and wane as current village fashion dictates. Within this context, a Maya woman's daily dress visually announced her village, marital state, age, and socio-economic status until the 1960s (Hendrickson 1995). As a consequence of Maya exposure to the world beyond their village parameters, however, women's *traje* had become less specifically tied to individual villages by the 1970s (Kennedy 1993). Today, young girls often mix *traje* from a variety of regions. Despite constant changes, however, *traje* continues to serve as a central symbol of Maya identity.

While Maya women still weave their own clothing, they also use their backstrap looms to make products specifically for outsiders. Textiles woven for tourists rarely include the specific pieces of *traje* women typically weave and wear, and they range widely in the colors, motifs, and fibers. In addition, natural colors and darker hues replace the highly saturated colors and high contrasts that characterize Maya aesthetics. Weavers make items such as wallets, passport carriers, hair "scrunchies", backpacks, and Western-style jackets, some with the motifs used in Maya *huipiles*, others without.

In some communities, backstrap weavers work in weaving co-operatives formed by women who lost their husbands and sons in the violence of Guatemala's civil war in the 1980s. Weaving enables them to bring in much needed income to clothe and feed their often large families. Some of these cooperatives deal directly with companies based in Guatemala who provide design and marketing help and sell textiles both locally and through Fair Trade or Alternative Trade venues. Maya Traditions and Ruth y Naomi, an organization located near Chichicastenango, fall into this category. Other weavers sell their boundary textiles through local businesses in the tourist town of Antigua (Moreno and Littrell 2001). Still others work with mediators representing off-site companies that sell products through retail catalog sales (Hendrickson 1996).

Many of these businesses tie Maya textiles to Maya history, especially their victimization during the Spanish conquest and the more recent civil war in Guatemala during the 1980s. Scholars debate the value of this approach. In a study of twenty-seven United States mail-order catalogs, for example, Carol Hendrickson analyzed the narratives used to generate a connection between consumers and producers. One third of these companies focused their texts around "political missions" that "express concern for the lives of the producers, and these concerns are tied to 'the sell'" (Hendrickson 1996: 116). Hendrickson bemoans the fact that the only medium for communication between the consumers who buy from these catalogs[2] and the women who weave the textiles centers around commodities. By buying products primarily for their leisure use, United States consumers can simultaneously signal support for Guatemalan war victims. Yet, as Hendrickson further comments, "in each case Maya causes need to be tailored to sell to foreign audiences, and individual products cannot become too connected with the horror of the country of their origin" (Howes 1996: 119). Maya weavers, therefore, alter their textiles in order to cater to much more affluent individuals who, ironically, salve their consciences by purchasing items for their own use.

While Hendrickson focuses on consumers' motives and economic affluence as well as artisans' willingness to "tailor" their goods for American's leisure, Cohen examines artisans' motives for changing and selling textile art to outsiders: "Such production in turn opens for members of the group [artisans] a new channel of communication ... Aesthetic or cultural or even political motives for the production of tourist arts thus tends to accompany the dominant economic ones" (Cohen 1992: 10). In addition, Cohen's assessment, unlike Hendrickson's, considers what options exist for artisans who live in severe poverty. "In any evaluation of the impact of commercialization," he states, "the alternative has to be taken into account – and in many cases that alternative is not the preservation of pristine ethnic arts, but their complete disappearance as they succumb to modern industrial mass consumer goods" (Cohen 1992: 25). Carlsen (1993) corroborates Cohen's ideas in his discussion of Maya textiles in particular: "It is evident that the decision by weavers to make changes [in their textiles] has allowed the continuity of highland Maya textile production" (Cohen 1992: 201). Finally, Nash (1993: 20) views commoditization of ethnic textiles as an opportunity for new forms of creativity: "In this postmodern world of amalgamated cultures and the search for identity through consumerism, the strange alliance of a politically conscious consuming elite and culturally rooted producing communities may continue to generate new and beautiful forms and textures in artisan products."

Maya Traditions

In 1988, Jane Mintz began working with Maya weavers in the highlands of Guatemala. A native of the United States, Mintz combined her skills as a weaver and her education as a social worker to establish her business, Cosas Hermosas de Guatemala. Mintz bought handmade textiles from small family businesses and sold them at fairs and flea markets back in the United States. In 1994, Mintz shifted her focus to work solely with groups of Maya backstrap weavers, and she changed her business to a fair-trade[3] wholesale enterprise in order to provide income for more individuals. Now named Maya Traditions, the company works with five established groups of backstrap weavers, around 100 indigenous women who live in small highland communities. With the marketing aspects of the business in San Francisco and an operational base in Panajachel, Guatemala, Mintz shuttles between the two locations several times a year.

The goals of the business are twofold. "We are committed," says Mintz, "to renewal and preservation of Maya textile traditions while providing consistent economic sustenance for the women" (Special Projects 1998: 1). Mintz's definition of tradition centers on the means of production, or Maya weaving techniques. "My particular focus is on the weaving traditions," says Mintz. "Back-strap weaving is symbolic of the traditions of generations of Maya women, passed down from mother (or grandmother) to daughter" (Mintz, personal communication, 2 May 2002). Not only does each community identify itself through specific colors and motifs, as women do with their *huipiles*, but also through unique backstrap weaving techniques and styles intimately intertwined with the local history of each group. Maya Traditions strives to maintain these distinctive methods in the products they sell, yet the colors and products change to conform to market demands. Mintz elaborates, "We have tried to work with the traditional craft, continuing the basic techniques of the particular weaving regions but expanding the color range and encouraging excellence in the quality and presentation of the work, creating new products while preserving the skill and knowledge of generations" (Mintz, personal communication, 2 May 2002). Thus, company decision-making rests on a difficult balancing act: weighing the need to succeed in the international market with a desire to preserve Maya traditions without losing the "integrity of the weavings" (Lynd 2000: 81). Martha Lynd, a United States native who works as business and design facilitator at Maya Traditions in Panajachel, understands the significance of asking Maya weavers to make new products in new colors. "We acknowledge," says Martha Lynd, "that introducing new designs and color combinations is a delicate issue" (Lynd 2000: 71).

The second goal of Maya Traditions and the primary reason for the company's existence is "to help improve the quality of life for the weavers" (Maya Traditions 2003). By paying the weavers a fair wage, running health clinics, and donating funds for the weavers' children to attend school in Guatemala City, Maya Traditions functions as a socially responsible fair trade entity as well as a business enterprise. In addition, the company makes a conscious effort to preserve backstrap weaving as a part of village life, thereby enabling Maya women to integrate their weaving into their daily routine of child care and household duties. As they comment on the Maya Traditions Web site, "This service component is at the heart of our efforts at Maya Traditions and creates personal relationships with the women in the weaving groups" (Maya Traditions 2003).

Maya Traditions' target customers also reflect the company's mission. They initially sold their products retail to the general public at markets and fairs, but they now sell wholesale almost exclusively to museum shops and stores that share their fair trade commitment. "These are the shops," says Mintz, "interested in high quality weaving and the quality of life for the people who make the product" (Mintz, personal communication, 2 May 2002). In addition, their wholesale status has increased sales, a change needed to provide consistent work to a substantial number of weavers.

Maya Traditions' business goals, and thus their target market, shape product development and their product lines. The advice of mediators familiar with current fashions and customer demands guides Mintz and Lynd at the Guatemala headquarters. In addition, the designers work with the best weavers from each community collaboratively to develop products and color palettes. Then, these weavers create colorways with the established palettes and produce samples of each new product. In tandem with these weavers, the designers fine-tune color combinations, measurements, and techniques to provide a visual reference for each weaving cooperative. The sample makers then take the company's work orders back to their villages along with an adequate supply of first quality cotton thread provided by Maya Traditions. Women weave as they are able amidst their daily tasks, using the specifications of each sample as a guide and paying careful attention to the size and quality of the weaving.

As we indicate above, indigenous women in Guatemala historically have woven huipiles, hair ribbons, and belts on their backstrap looms, for themselves and other family members. But the women who weave for Maya Traditions produce a variety of textiles that are incorporated into products for the international market: accessories such as bags, hats, scarves, and passport holders; household items such as cushion covers, wall hangings, and table runners, but also tapestries and huipiles. Many of the products combine small pieces of backstrap weaving with plain-colored cloth, zippers, buttons, and Velcro closures.

New color combinations come from several sources. At times, a few of the colors women use in their own huipiles are used for boundary textiles. At other times, subdued hues, pastels, or over-dyed fabrics replace the electric pink, lemon yellow, and bright orange typical in Maya *huipiles*. The motifs and designs woven into the textiles, however, reflect those in the weavers' own *huipiles*, although they may showcase a single design. For example, the women from the group in Chichicastenango make a small, women's shoulder bag with velcro and zipper closings and slots to hold credit cards. The central geometric design on this contemporary purse mirrors one that appears on the huipiles from Chichicastenango. Muted versions of the greens, blues, and purples in the *huipiles* color the small bag.

The five weaving groups also participate in The Doll Project that the company identifies as "an economic development project, designed to create a unique product for the groups to develop and sell" (Maya Traditions 2003). The doll begins with a body made from brown, foot-loomed fabric. Then the women weave a miniature set of their distinctive village *traje* for each doll on their backstrap looms. Afterwards, the five weaving groups meet at Maya Traditions in Panajachel to stuff the dolls, attach yarn hair, sew on eyes, noses, and mouths and then dress the dolls in their distinctive attire. This project has given the women new levels of self-confidence, pride in their Maya heritage, and additional income.

When the weaving groups complete their orders of woven items, they take them to the Panajachel staff for closely monitored quality control. They compare each weaving to the original sample, evaluating them on their adherence to the designated colors, size, and shape as well as a lack of twisting and the tightness of the weaving. While some companies refuse to pay for items that contain any problems or inconsistencies, Maya Traditions takes a different approach. They evaluate each item, noting problems and deducting a specified amount from the total price they agreed to pay for each weaving. In this way, the weavers receive much-needed money for their work, even if Maya Traditions decides not to use a specific piece. Weavers can learn from their mistakes so as to receive the full price for items in the following round of orders. Deductions for repeated inconsistencies increase from order to order, and if a specific weaver does not improve, she is eventually dropped from the group (Lynd 2000).

The company reaches wholesale customers through trade shows, a Web site (www.mayatraditions.com), and a printed catalog. Mintz regularly attracts customers through exhibits at the San Francisco Gift Show, the Museum Store Association Exposition, and connections with like-minded businesses in the Fair Trade Federation. The wholesale mini-catalog consists of eight glossy pages measuring 8 1/2" × 11". The four-color booklet highlights images of the company's goods as well as photographs of the women from each of the five weaving groups named according to the home communities where they live: Chichicastenango, Sololá, Santa Catarina-Nahuala, San Jaun la Laguna, and Santa Clara. The weavers appear in their *traje* with the motifs, designs, and colors of their *huipiles* clearly visible. Beneath each group photograph, the catalog shows the specific items that the group makes, emphasizing their use of the motifs from their huipiles. Wholesalers can order a limited-range of products from a catalog or from the company Web site that presents images of their full-line of products. These include non-woven items such as crochet and embroidery work found in baby hats, booties, and bibs; beaded, ceramic and cloth jewelry; and toys, including dolls, masks, wooden animals, ceramics, and musical instruments. Products range from $1.50 to $70. In addition, the Web site provides clear descriptions of Maya Traditions' goals, the women who produce the goods, and the company's specific health and education projects for the weavers and their families.

Peruvian Textile Traditions

Because of their long history, cultural significance, technical sophistication and artistic beauty, Peruvian textiles count among the most valued in the world. Textiles discovered in tombs near Huaca Prieta (in current-day Peru) date back almost 4,000 years, making them some of the oldest found to date. Woven textiles have given Peru its prized position in art and anthropology. These textiles show their creators' superior artistic abilities; weavers regularly used every weaving technique known today and dyed their yarns in over 200 colors and shades to produce bright, intricately detailed textiles (Anton 1984).

Not until 600–800 AD did precursors to knitting come into existence (Anton 1984), and current-day knitting techniques arrived in Peru with the Spanish and Portuguese in the mid- to late sixteenth century. LeCount finds support for this in tombs where the oldest Peruvian textiles were previously found: "The lack of knitting needles and knitted cloth in the tombs indicates that knitting as we know it did not exist in Peru and Bolivia before European contact. Nor has anything resembling a crochet hook been discovered in the ancient gravesites" (LeCount 1990: 23). Knotting, along with a technique called "simple looping" or "cross-knit looping," notes LeCount, "are two single-element fabric structures related to knitting techniques, and considered antecedents to modern knitting" (LeCount 1990: 23).

The two primary ethnic groups in the Andean mountains of Peru and Bolivia, the Quechua and Aymara, took up knitting. How soon after the Spanish conquest the Andeans adopted knitting, however, remains unknown. The European artisanal practice of men as knitters, rather than women, also came to Peru and Bolivia along with knitting needles and knitting techniques, and today men continue to knit items for family use, such as hats, socks, and leggings. "Not only do men create most Andean knitting," says LeCount, "they create the pieces with superior workmanship and unbelievably complex design arrangements" (LeCount 1990: 2).

The oldest surviving examples of Andean knitting include the colorful, woolen hats called *ch'ullus*. Knitted and worn by men, boys, and sometimes girls, the colors and motifs of Andean *ch'ullus*, like those in Maya huipiles, signal specific cultural information about the wearer's home region, ethnic identification, status, and sometimes age (LeCount 1990: 2). In addition to *ch'ullus*, knitted items handed down from the past include armwarmers (*mangas*), leggings (*polainas*) and socks (*medias*) for men and boys, as well as women's purses (*monederos* or *bolsitas*) and small bags for ceremonial occasions. In some rural areas, Andeans still wear these apparel items, although the younger people who move into more urban areas abandon them in that setting (LeCount 1990).

Motifs and design elements in early Andean knitting came from the intricate images and shapes on Andean woven textiles. Some scholars believe that Peruvian textiles, in particular, contained a type of pictorial language for communication because an abstract written language did not exist in pre-Columbian times (Anton 1984). Some pre-Hispanic motifs and designs have survived, and knitters continue to use them today. Typical geometric shapes include "triangular stairsteps, interlocking waves, stars, zigzag-edged triangles, and diamonds," whereas images from the natural world center on animal shapes: "stylized birds, felines, llamas, fishes, snakes and foxes, plus egg- or seed-like symbols" (LeCount 1990: 43). With the advent of the Spanish, however, new motifs appeared in woven textiles and the knitted items the Andeans began to create as they encountered new sights and influences. For example, horses and cattle, both introduced by the Spanish, found their way into textiles along with lions, eagles, and the distinctive eight-pointed Spanish Burgos Star (LeCount 1990: 44).

Unity and balance of motifs and designs through the use of a single background color such as white or black is a common characteristic of Andean aesthetics, as is a striped background. Brilliant, naturally dyed colors such as reds, yellows, and oranges formed the motifs and abstract designs until the advent of synthetic dyes in the mid-nineteenth century. Prior to the arrival of the Europeans, fibers consisted of cotton or the fine camelid wool produced from alpaca, llama, and vicuna. The Spanish brought sheep to the region, and their coarser wool has now become commonplace in the Andes (LeCount 1990).

Today, men continue to knit *ch'ullus* for themselves and their children, while women almost exclusively knit goods for the tourist trade, including knit caps that resemble *ch'ullus* but "are not of the same quality" as the ones men make for themselves and their families (LeCount 1990: 37–8). In addition, women knit sweaters, ponchos, and gloves for the market, sweaters and socks for their families, and purses for themselves.

Large numbers of women began knitting sweaters for upscale markets in the 1960s when family ownership of land began to diminish and men's work options in certain regions of the Andeas, such as the Cochabamba valley, were limited to demeaning jobs like day labor for the cocaine industries (Page-Reeves 1998). Most women work for privately owned companies doing piecework in putting-out systems for very low pay because other alternatives provide unstable or limited work opportunities. Alternative trade organizations (ATOs) such as SELF HELP Crafts and Oxfam Trading provided secure work and pay for knitters in the past, but their markets are limited, and they have not been successful in selling sweaters to up-scale companies. As a result, a glut of handknits in ATO outlets has diminished their ability to hire knitters. Peruvian Connection remains one of the few companies able to command high prices in the retail market, and with it, the ability to pay the knitters more than subsistence wages. However, it cannot provide work for the large numbers of women who both want and need employment (Page-Reeves 1998). A few women have formed knitting co-operatives, but most often, the lack of knowledge about designs that will sell elsewhere, the inability to penetrate outside markets, and unrealistic expectations for remuneration have hampered their long-term success. As Page-Reeves (1998: 92) summarily notes, "Co-operation at the local level is not sufficient to affect the structural position of knitters in the global markets for handknits. Nor is grassroots participation a prescription in and of itself for the challenges of producing and selling in the competitive knitwear market." Thus, self-sufficiency remains an illusive goal for most Andean hand-knitters.

Peruvian Connection

Taking Peru's unusual textile tradition as a starting point for a business venture, Annie Hurlbut began Peruvian Connection in 1976. As an anthropology student, Hurlbut lived in Peru for several years and fell in love with ancient Peruvian textiles. The extraordinary fibers and intricate knitting techniques she witnessed in Peru gave rise to the company's signature sweaters. For several years, Hurlbut sold her unique, upscale knitwear out of her old car, targeting exclusive boutiques such as Henri Bendel in New York and Washington, DC. In 1979, a *New York Times* article on the fledgling company gave Hurlbut her big break. Orders rushed in, and Hurlbut swiftly changed her business from a wholesale business to a retail catalog company. Now a multi-million dollar business, owned jointly with her mother, Biddie Hurlbut, Peruvian Connection employs ninety-two workers at their base in Tonganoxie, Kansas, plus five in New York city, five in Lima, Peru, and in-store employees at four outlet locations. Catalog sales have moved beyond the US to include Germany, the UK, and Japan.

Hurlbut presents her company's goals in broad terms. "Our catalog's mission," she says, "[is] to knit the world's most beautiful sweaters in two of its most precious natural fibers [pima cotton and alpaca]" (Peruvian Connection catalog, Spring 1995). In addition, she ties the sweaters they sell to Peru's distinctive textile history. In an early catalog (undated), for example, Hurlbut describes Peru's textile tradition in this way: "From the dawn of history in Peru, textiles have been a primary form of cultural expression. Six thousand year old graves have yielded fragments of tapestry unequalled in beauty or complexity. Andean weaving has held its own in both ancient and modern worlds" (inside cover). In addition, she emphasizes the unusually fine and complex knitting techniques that the Quechua and Aymara women use to knit the company's sweaters by hand. "The knitters we work with in the Andes have an age-old textile tradition that dates back 3,000 years or more," says Hurlbut. "They are equal to any knitting challenge" (Peruvian Connection catalog, Spring 1995). Yet, Hurlbut remains intentionally vague about the specific historically based similarities between her products and those from the Andean past to provide flexibility in the products they sell:

We didn't want to limit our concept so much that people felt like, "Oh, I think I'll dress Peruvian today". We wanted people to have a sensibility for native art forms and cultural expressions as they are expressed in textiles. We wanted our customers to have a range of things that they could select from. We do try to have a connection with Peru. First of all, the products are made there. The fibers are Peruvian fibers. So we might do an English tapestry that has nothing to do with Peru, but it's made in the fibers. So, there is still that connection with the Andes, with Peru. (personal communication, February 1999)

Peruvian Connection strives to make and sell exquisite "art-knits" that carry an exotic feel rather than historically specific Andean knitting techniques, motifs, colors, or practices (for example, men knitting). Thus, as Hurlbut notes, the company's goals shape their definition of tradition.

Peruvian Connection's upscale sweaters sell primarily to consumers who make $100,000 or more a year (Hurlbut, personal communication, February 1999), and retail for $200 to $500. In addition to sweaters, Peruvian Connection offers a wide range of apparel items for women: skirts, trousers, Capri pants, dresses, coats, hats, scarves, and vests – some knitted, others woven commercially by machine in many different countries. The company also has added several new product lines over the years, including men's sweaters, scarves, polos, and ties; children's sweaters, coats, dresses and nightgowns; women's jewelry with a Latin American flare, and a few decorative products for the home.

Product development is carefully controlled by the company from palette selection to prototype analysis. To produce the intricate sweaters, Hurlbut depends first on the United States design team. Inspired by textiles from all over the world, the designers create stitch-by-stitch diagrams for the women who knit the sweaters in Peru. When the design details reach the knitters, they collaborate with the Peruvian Connection designers by recommending specific knitting stitches particularly suited to each project. Color palettes follow United States fashion; they have changed from "classic shades" such as magenta and mallard green in the 1980s, to the current trend of black and more muted hues. After the raw materials suppliers in Peru develop the yarns in the colors and fibers chosen by the design team, they distribute the yarn to the 20 to 30 cottage industries that produce the finished sweaters. Peruvian Connection works with these small businesses strictly on a contract basis. They do not own the companies who produce the yarns nor the cottage industries who produce the sweaters. "We hand them [the cottage industries] the blueprint," says Hurlbut, "and we give them the tools to make it. The only thing we don't do is we do not ever own that yarn, and we do not hire those knitters" (Hurlbut, personal interview, 1999).

Quality control resides with both the cottage industries and Peruvian Connection employees. Selling "the most beautiful sweaters in the world" to an upper middle-class market requires near perfection. If items do not meet Peruvian Connection's high standards, the company will not accept them. After the company approves them for quality, sweater samples or prototypes are sent back to Kansas where Annie Hurlbut and Biddie Hurlbut, the design team, and one or more valued customers review them. Each person rates every product to decide which specific styles and colors will appear for sale in the Peruvian Connection catalog.

Peruvian Connection's catalog has developed over the years from a small pamphlet produced in a studio in Kansas City to the current full-sized 8 1/2" × 11" glossy catalog of just under fifty pages. Professionals model the company's clothing in scenic areas of Peru, posing in front of an ancient arched doorway or walking on a cobblestone street. Peruvian Connection's Web site (www.peruvianconnection.com) shows the merchandise from each catalog in a user-friendly format that is easy to navigate. Outlet store Web sites show past-seasons' sweaters at reduced prices. Like the catalog, Peruvian Connection's web sites reveal the hand of experienced professionals at work, upholding the near perfection of every aspect of the company.

Peruvian Connection functions as a retail, for-profit company, so the needs and desires of its customers drive the company's decision-making, rather than those of the artisans who produce the hand-knitted sweaters. Orders from Peruvian Connection do, however, provide much-needed work for knitters in Peru. In addition, the cottage industries compete for the best knitters by offering them attractive perks in addition to their regular wages. With a portable craft, the knitters can also integrate their knitting into their everyday tasks at home. Both Hurlbut and the knitters acknowledge their situation with pride. "They [the knitters] are so proud of being a Peruvian Connection knitter. It's like [being] a Cordon Bleu knitter," says Hurlbut (personal communication, 1999). While Peruvian Connection ties itself to Peru through the knitting techniques and the fibers it uses, and it gives a nod to the ancient history of the knitters who make many of their sweaters, the company's mission does not center on sustaining Peruvian motifs, colors, or products from the past or helping the Andean women maintain their cultural heritage. Rather, dramatic photographs of an idyllic-looking countryside and close-ups of the Andean women who knit their sweaters provide a symbolic identification with Peru and its people, one that customers can carry with them as they don a Peruvian Connection sweater.

Conclusions

Can boundary textiles ever be traditional? As a fair-trade organization, Maya Traditions strives to perpetuate Maya weaving methods and motifs in order to help weavers maintain their culture in Guatemala where they live as a non-dominant people among the more dominant Ladinos. "Our primary focus," states owner Jane Mintz, "is the creation of high-quality weaving and hand crochet products while preserving the integrity of traditional crafts" (Mintz, personal communication, 2 May 2002). The company does this by selling small items made from high-quality backstrap weaving (for example, bags, hats and scarves) with motifs that tie Maya weavers to their ethnic and local community identities. While the items they sell and the colors of the weavings change from time to time, the method of production – backstrap weaving – and the motifs handed down among the Maya women remain the same.

In contrast, Peruvian Connection highlights traditional Peruvian fibers and knitting techniques to sell unique, up-scale knits. The company does not focus on particular clothing items, motifs, or colors from the past, so its knitted goods often do not resemble those that Andeans wear now or ever have worn in the past. With company profits as its primary goal, moreover, Peruvian Connection focuses on consumer demand rather than the knitters' understanding of and relationship to their textile traditions. Because of this, Peruvian Connection ties its unusually beautiful and intricate sweaters to Peru in more abstract ways. The catalogs promote the company's goods through extraordinary photographs of the Peruvian countryside and close-ups of Andean women in their native costumes. In addition, catalog pages devoted to a description of Andean art tie the women broadly to ancient textile traditions. In this way, their catalogs and Web site promote an idea of Peruvian exoticism that attracts buyers to sweaters that most often look more European than Peruvian.

As the above descriptions show, neither company fits into Kroeber's (1948) positivist definition of tradition as a passing on of objects, beliefs, or practices unchanged through time. Despite their differences, both Maya Traditions and Peruvian Connection alter the textiles that the Maya and Andean people, respectively, have made for themselves in the past and those they make for their own internal use today. At the other end of the theoretical spectrum, both companies do, as Glassie (1995) describes, "negotiate" between the concrete characteristics of textiles from the past and their business goals in the present. Maya Traditions strives to sustain backstrap weaving and its ties to Maya identity in order to help Maya women support their families through sales profits. At the same time, however, Maya Traditions changes the colors of the weavings and the actual objects the women make from the weavings in order to assure sales to individuals from other countries, like the United States. Thus, the business defines tradition in a way that enables them to achieve their mission, exactly Glassie's point.

Similarly, Peruvian Connection maintains the knitting techniques the Andeans developed after the Spanish conquest and the fibers indigenous to Peru, pima cotton and alpaca. But they freely change the colors, motifs, and products they design. In order to sell upscale goods to people in Westernized countries, the actual appearance of their sweaters remains quite removed from Andean aesthetics. Peruvian Connection's knits look more European than Peruvian.

However, in this process of negotiation, both companies *do* retain some concrete aspects of textiles from the past and present, a fact that places Maya Traditions and Peruvian Connection into a theoretical position more aligned with Shils and Baizerman. Both companies tie their boundary art to the past through the one feature that Baizerman finds essential: the means of production.

Backstrap weaving has been handed down from mother to daughter among the Maya for over 3,000 years, even though colors and motifs have shifted, albeit subtly, in the weavings the Maya have made for themselves and dramatically for boundary art. Peruvian Connection's commitment to Andean knitting links its knitwear to the past in a similar, though not identical, way. Because knitting arrived in the Andes with the Spanish, this craft has a shorter history with the Andean artisans than weaving does with the Maya, and knitting did not originate with the Andean peoples. Peru's distinctive weaving remains its oldest form of indigenous textile production, predating knitting by thousands of years. However, the means of production provides a concrete connection to the historical past for both companies, placing them squarely in line with Shils and Baizerman who hold onto the idea that tradition involves objects, beliefs, and/or practices handed down from the past, though they might change over time.

On a strictly abstract level, Peruvian Connection relies more heavily on symbolic connections to Peru than Maya Traditions does to Guatemala. This fact aligns Peruvian Connection with the purely symbolic view of tradition held by Handler and Linnekin (1987: 280): "Traditions thought to be preserved are created out of the conceptual needs of the present . . . [Tradition] is symbolically reinvented in an ongoing present." While Maya Traditions visually ties many of its products to the Maya through distinctive motifs that connect the women to their home communities, Peruvian Connection establishes a symbolic relationship to Peru and its textiles through current, romantic photographs of the country and its people and through catalog pages that describe "ancient" Andean textile traditions in very general terms. Precisely how the "ancient" Peruvian weaving traditions have influenced the Andean women who knit Peruvian Connection sweaters remains unclear, for Hurlbut's primary concern centers on the exotic aura that the text and photographs create for catalog readers – one they will carry with them as they wear a Peruvian Connection sweater.

In their differing ways, the products that both Maya Traditions and Peruvian Connection develop and sell hold meanings that they and their customers identify with tradition. Through constant negotiation, each company, in its own specific context, defines and redefines tradition to achieve its business goals, a process Glassie (1995) defines. In addition, both companies maintain the means of production that artisans have used for centuries or millennia, a concrete connection that Baizerman considers essential. Yet, an abstract, symbolic relationship to Peru and its ancient textile traditions remains central to Peruvian Connection's image and marketing strategy, a condition that aligns the company to Handler and Linnekin. Clearly, Maya Tradition's and Peruvian Connection's approaches to tradition do not fall under one definition or theory of tradition. In practice, the concept of tradition continues to contain unexpected or yet undefined complexities unique to each situation. Perhaps these slippery and elusive qualities themselves continue to fuel academic theories on the precise nature of tradition and keep consumers longing for an indefinable past that brings them back for more.

Part 3

Fashion and the Cultural Imaginary

9

Ponchos of the River Plate: Nostalgia for Eden[1]

Ruth Corcuera

The poncho is a simple and functional article of clothing that, confectioned with diverse materials, appears on various sites across the globe. A simple and comfortable garment, it has been rediscovered today by the great tailors. In a world where the great urban conglomerates dominate with all their tensions, this garment is associated with the image of freedom and space – an association that perhaps, subconsciously, renders it especially attractive. The poncho protects us and covers us. As any textile, it acts as a second skin.

A Bit of History

Rooted in elements that define the Argentine patrimony, the poncho is present in our art, our literature, our songs. It speaks to us of Creole customs and its recollection fragments into infinite images. The poncho is, as is well known, a rectangular garment generally measuring 1.8 m by 1.4 m; it has an opening in the center enabling the wearer to pull it over his head and leave it resting on his shoulders, from which it falls in harmonious and baggy folds, amply covering the body and arms. Depending on its color or size, this garment receives different names. The small poncho, called *ponchillo* and often *calamaco*, is short and has rounded borders. It is thought that its form must have been very popular at the beginning of the nineteenth century; historical documents suggest that 5,000 *ponchillos* arrived in Buenos Aires from the Peruvian highlands. In contrast, the *balandrán* – a poncho that resembles a chasuble[2] – was a large poncho like the ones from the pampas and those worn in contemporary Argentina.

The simplicity of its form contrasts with its rich symbolism. For us, inhabitants of the American continent, it is a testament to integration because it has indigenous roots and was adopted and popularized by Europeans. It is a *mestizo* garment, as its story reveals. The chronicles of the conquest tell us that in the sixteenth century a new generation of Americans was born. They were the young *mestizos*, born of Spanish and Native American unions that with time affirmed the foundations of new forms of being and feeling. They shared the heritage of two worlds that either confronted each other or reconciled their differences through wayward expressions or ambitious dreams. Soon they were joined by others, the children of Europeans, Creoles who adopted the clothes that their circumstances indicated as appropriate for long journeys and rural life. Thus, the poncho acquired its emblematic character.

The poncho became known across the continent, and its characteristics conformed to its owners' preferences and climate. In order to cross barren plains and cold steppes, the wearer chose ponchos made of the wool of vicuña, alpaca, guanaco, llama or sheep. And for tropical climates, ponchos made of silk, linen and cotton prevailed.

Ponchos of Vicuña wool

The most prestigious poncho was made of the wool of vicuñas, considered sacred animals for the Incas. The vicuña was thought to be the Daughter of the Sun and the Mountain. Only the Inca and his *ayllu*, or great family, could use these weavings. Breaking this tradition was punishable by death.

Traditionally women were the select weavers of the vicuña ponchos. The women of the *allachuasi*, or Inca textile establishments, wove vicuña cloths for members of the nobility. At the beginning of the seventeenth century, manual labor by Spanish women brought the stigma of dishonor to a family. By the end of that century, however, this was no longer the case given that economic necessity obligated individual communities to assume the functions that could palliate the absence of clothing from Spain. In many regions, Creole groups – particularly women of all ages, including the elderly – carried out the work of artisans, spinning wool and weaving with noted ability. From the gathering of *grana* – a seed that produced a scarlet hue – in the forests to the exhausting workday at the spindle, or the weaving on the stretcher in order to make ponchos and blankets, women became members of a kind of artisan's proletariat. Around this same time, every rural house would have a weaving loom.

At the end of the eighteenth century, the most prestigious ponchos were those confectioned with the precious vicuña wool of Belén, the more thickly spun vicuña wool of the Peruvian highlands, wool from the Córdoba plains, sheep wool from San Luis, and cotton and wool from Santiago del Estero. In the first decades of the nineteenth century, Córdoba and San Luis were the sites that provided cloth and ponchos needed for uniforms during the war for Independence, while La Rioja provided soldiers with cotton shirts. Whereas men, often between the ages of twenty-six and forty, joined the war effort, women stayed home to spin and weave for the troops.

Linen and Silk Ponchos

South American ponchos were woven of silk, of vicuña and silk, of alpaca and silk, or of cotton and silk. The use of silk and linen was introduced and made popular by the Europeans. The adaptation of silk, from Mexico to the South Andean regions, was of particular concern to the Spanish government, a fact that is evident in the laws passed to privilege peninsular political and economic interests. Under Moorish rule, Spain had developed a high level silk industry with Asian contacts, especially in the warmer regions to the South, one of its main centers being in Murcia. Following the Conquest, establishments were created to import the silk worm to the Americas. While the American silk industry eventually rivaled that of China's, peninsular politics interfered with the stability of production. Our weavers were very adept at using the environment to take advantage of natural fibers – such as the cotton of the *palo borracho* tree and diverse vegetable fibers that appear in the wild – to make ponchos. But the low cost of Chinese and European silk restricted the emergent industries that otherwise would have enriched a large expanse of the Andean region.

The new Americans who modeled their daily lives after the Metropolis, quickly imported silks from Europe and the Orient via shipping routes between Manila and Acapulco. The mining boom of Potosí brought to the Andean region, at the end of the sixteenth century and during the first decades of the seventeenth century, luxuries from around the world; alongside the import of Bohemian crystal, that of Chinese, Spanish, French and Italian silk did not lag far behind. The draw of Potosí rivaled that of present-day New York. Men wore vicuña ponchos while women dressed in Chinese and European silks and the finest laces.

Southern Ponchos: The Last Andean Dwellers

Immense plains, perfectly circumscribed by a blue horizon; deserts, *cangrejales*, a pampa populated by birds will hear the first gallops defying the wind. This is the poncho's true habitat.

Toward 1870 Lucio V. Mansilla, a well-known Argentine writer and military careerman, embarked upon his famous *Visit to the Ranquel Indians*. The seminomadic Ranquel Indians were dispersed throughout the pampas, from the Andean mountain range to what is today modern Buenos Aires. They exchanged ponchos and it is quite likely that the Argentine cowboy known as the *gaucho* used ponchos woven by Ranquel women. These tribes – descendants of the Tehuelche, infamous and feared for their raids – established their communities in the environs of the Leovuco Lagoon and to the south of San Luis. Excellent weavers of ponchos, they began to assimilate elements of Araucan culture due to their trans-Andean relations. Ranquel designs suggest that their incursions in other territories – namely the South and Northeast – resulted in the appropriation and utilization of textiles in their own weavings. The nomadic nature of the Ranquel Indians and their proximity to North Andean traditions present a range of opportunities for further research. Mansilla would leave behind a wealth of information about their lives, detailing the everyday role played by the cult of the horse, equestrian accessories and weavings when describing indigenous leader Caniupán and forty individuals who appeared

> in parade dress; that is to say, mounted on fiery steeds whose trappings displayed every luxury of the Pampas – silver-trimmed brow bands, tailpieces, breast leathers, stirrups, and headstalls, all in the Chilean taste. The riders had put on their best ponchos and hats; some wore sewn boots of tanned leather, some soft colt's-foot boots, many the spur on the naked foot. (Mansilla 1997: 102)

The descriptions in other first-person accounts vary depending on which tribes the travelers encountered. The belongings of the Pampean Indians can be divided into three groups: clothing; home furnishings, in spite of the fact that they were nomadic and lived in straw huts; and the horses' accessories, which were highly esteemed. In regards to this last item, chiefs made sure that their saddles were beautifully adorned and, to the extent that they were able, used bronze, iron, or silver stirrups and spurs. The cushion was woven with blue, scarlet, or white wool.

It is Mansilla's narrative that would give the *cacique* (Indian chief) poncho its prestige in late nineteenth-century Argentine culture. As Mansilla makes clear, the poncho was an identity-invested garment with emblematic designs. Today its languages are for the most part ignored. The superb confection of a poncho invested the weaver and her social group with prestige. Its value for the Ranquel Indians is evident in the dialogue between Mansilla and Chief Mariano Rosas, who gives the author his most prized possession in order to protect him from harm:

> "Take it, brother; wear it in my name; my chief wife made it."
>
> I accepted this very significant gift and reciprocated it by presenting him with my rubber poncho. Receiving it, he said, "If ever we're not at peace, my Indians won't kill you, brother, if they see that poncho on you."
>
> "Brother," I answered, "if ever we're not at peace and we meet, I'll know you by that garment."
>
> The great significance of Mariano Rosas' poncho, however, was not that it could shield me in danger, but that the poncho woven by the chief wife is, among Indians, a love token, like the wedding ring among Christians.
>
> When I emerged from the tent and they saw me wearing the chief's poncho, an expression of surprise was painted on every face. (Mansilla 1997: 326)

Almost 10 years after the publication of Mansilla's *Visit to the Ranquel Indians*, from 1879 to 1880, Argentine political debates centered on ways in which to resolve a perceived "Indian problem." A push for territorial expansion similar to the Manifest Destiny of the United States opened the Patagonia region to new settlers. In the brutal fight that separated Indians and Argentine soldiers during the Conquest of the Desert, certain coincidences are worth highlighting: a loyalty to the earth, for some arising from their nomadic way of life and for others from their experience with territorial expansion; and their common love for the horse. The soldier had to understand his adversary, be as skilled a horseman, and familiarize himself with how the Indian dominated his horse.

During the Conquest of the Desert two ideologies and ways of life collided. As Niella, a modest soldier anticipating battle with the Ranquel Indians expressed it:

> To whom did the air belong? And the water of the lagoons and the rivers, the salt, the firewood, the guanacos, ostriches, wild horses, the cattle? To one element of the tribe, or to another tribe, or to everyone so that people could breathe, drink, and eat in order to survive? Who would destroy the cattle? In their raids, had they not found the countryside covered with animals slain for their hides while their flesh was left there to rot? (Martínez Sarazola 1992: 266)

The map of 1876 indicates the defeat of the indigenous way of life, signaling how far the ancient dwellers of the plain had been able to expand. By then, the territory of the Pampan Indians had been fractioned, and had extended itself South instead. The humid Pampa took up again the ancient craft of leather, and weaving became a Creole art. A few years later, when the French explorer H. Armaignac visited the Catriel tribe, he verified that Indian women traded their weavings daily, in the marketplace of Azul, in exchange for tea, sugar, ginger and other products; and he signaled that Catriel dress "was more or less like that of the gauchos, but the poncho and the *chiripá*, generally blue with white and red designs, were the workmanship of women" (Armaignac 1974: 67). The women of these tribes remain expert weavers today. The textile patrimony of the province of Buenos Aires must recognize in their work and in the Tehuelche contribution the source from which emerged the poncho that today makes Argentines so proud.

Pampean ponchos

Ornamental motifs, like colors, did not appear in traditional societies by accident. In the Pampean weaving of the nineteenth century, we find a wide range of designs and color linked to traditional Andean origins, as well as elements originating in Mapuche culture that manifest themselves more strongly in the nineteenth century. By this time, the Mapuches had displaced other groups in the area, like the Tehuelches. Nevertheless, in both ethnic groups and in different garments we find similar designs. If we pause to observe a Tehuelche *quillango*[3] and a double-sided Pampean poncho with banded cruciform designs, we will see that they appear very similar because both are based in a concept of space divided into four large zones, which in turn correspond to places and sacred colors, a "cosmology of the Andean world." Warriors wore ponchos with red backgrounds and those of Mapuche tribal leaders were deep blue.

Cruciform designs predominate in Pampean ponchos. In *La cruz en América*, Adán Quiroga suggests that this motif was a common theme throughout many centuries, from the designs found at the Paracas archeological site (on the Peruvian coast) to those cultures that developed during the first millenium after Christ, like the Nazca along the Southern Peruvian coast and the Wari in Tiahuanaco who would disseminate the designs from the Bolivian high plateaus. While the unity of Pampan ponchos' design is similar to that of the Wari-Tiahuanaco, its composition is not; in the former, the woven bands of crosses are joined, accentuating their difference from traditional pre-Hispanic designs. Héctor Greslebin, an architect from the 1930s, studied a series of weavings from the Chilean provinces of Cautín and Valdivia. His point of departure is the simple cross, to which other crosses circumscribing previous ones are associated. While he does not negate their symbolic connotations, he emphasizes that textile production was limited, given that the right angles of the weft and warp forced the geometry of the design.

In the 1960s, Osvaldo Menghin and Alberto Rex González signaled the relationship between Rupestrean paintings and intaglios that are plentiful in the Patagonia as well as designs of textile origin. Marcelo Bórmida concurs that many Patagonian designs are clearly textile based, assigning them the term "histomorphic." For Menghin the fretwork style is a Patagonian phenomenon related to what some archeologists call "linear labyrinthian designs." Its center is the Northern Patagonia, from which they may have radiated along the Andean range, taking over the Chilean Patagonia and reaching the South of Mendoza and San Juan. González does not doubt that this Rupestrean art form shares decorative motifs with Araucan weavings. He affirms that their complex composition results from the combination of "minimal units," among which predominate the "graded motif" used in South American, and especially Andean, art beginning with the oldest cultures of the continent, particularly the Condorhuasi.

Menghin elsewhere signals the similarity between these designs and motifs in the pottery of Barreales in today's San Juan region of Argentina, noted for its predilection for crosses, rhombi, triangles, stairs, labyrinthine lines and suns. These designs appeared around 500 AD, and therefore, according to Menghin, they precede the Araucan phenomenon, as Juan Schobinger had previously indicated. The labyrinthine frets, contrary to real labyrinths, do not converge in a point of departure. We must remember that these designs adhere to South American art norms. Not only was the frets' geometric style Patagonian; as Raoul d'Harcourt's path-breaking studies in the field of pre-Hispanic textiles suggest, they were the design that defined South American art. The fret is related to the serpent motif in Mexico and the Andean world, and to beliefs about ascent to the afterlife.

The Gaucho's Poncho

The gaucho of the nineteenth century did not emerge spontaneously, but rather came to be in the course of various decades. Gauchos emerged as a social group among young men as wild as the environment they inhabited – a world altered only by the presence of the Argentine Rhea, who would scatter at the sound of their approach. These dwellers of the infinite horizon were racially diverse – they could be *mestizos* or mulattos – but shall be considered a social type, not an ethnic group. These first gauchos rejected the order the Spanish sought to impose on the population at large. Wide open spaces, a world of displaced people, indigenous women tied to Spanish settlers of modest backgrounds all gave origin to the gaucho. The disappearance of indigenous villages and the absence of concentrated indigenous groups that could be organized to labor on the plains – excepting Jesuit reservations – led to a population comprised of sometimes illegitimate families characterized by their adaptation to this inhospitable environment.

Toward 1773, Alonso Carrió de la Vandera, better known as Concolorcorvo, initiates a long journey, from Lima to the River Plate region. It is in his *Lazarillo de ciegos caminantes* that we find a first mention of wild young men inhabiting what is present-day Uruguay. According to Concolorcorvo, they dressed poorly, drove cattle, played the guitar, and possessed nothing more than one or two ponchos that at times did double-duty as their sleeping quarters. These predecessors of the gaucho were known as *gauderíos*, a term derived from the Latin word "gaudium," signifying joy, and probably introduced by Jesuit priests. Among their principle gifts was their ability thrive in their natural environment. These young men, in their travels between plains and mountain ranges, joined the coastal cultures of the River Plate with those of the Rio Grande do Sul. Visible in early nineteenth-century iconography, we find the gauchos of the River Plate's shores dressed in striped ponchos, most likely woven with rudimentary indigenous techniques.

As the nineteenth century progressed, it became clearer that, insofar as clothing was concerned, the population of the River Plate region was divided in terms of its preferences also denoting the kind of nation it desired. If there is one being above all to whom the poncho belonged, it was the gaucho, who proudly wore his poncho at the close of the eighteenth century, during the nineteenth and part of the twentieth centuries. As a historically Argentine prototype, he adopted this garment, along with his horse and dagger, into his semi-nomadic existence, which later included cattle driving and serving on the large *estancias*.

The poncho, light, simple, discreet and useful, is one of the gaucho's few material possessions. Argentine literature and iconography register the poncho, which accompanied the gaucho night and day, as his source of protection, a bed, pillow, sometimes shelter, a shield, his card table. In the *Martín Fierro*, an Argentine literary classic, we can see that this garment was omnipresent in the austere life of the gaucho. His modest belongings are thus described, "The poncho could even be his house." The cult to valor is another of the typical characteristics of the gaucho. One of his principle tests was the Creole duel, fought with a dagger rather than a sword. In this encounter, the poncho, wrapped around his arm, acted like a shield. As a semi-nomad, the gaucho tied the four corners of his poncho together to transport his scarce belongings. Sleeping and covering himself with the poncho under the open sky below the Southern Cross, no material obstacle could keep the gaucho from exercising his liberty. Toward 1822 Felipe Senillosa would describe the austerity and archaism of the gaucho in the 15 June issue of *La abeja argentina* (*The Argentine Bee*): "On the whole, our rural population has relatively few needs. A horse, the bit, a poncho or a few yards of woven cloth are the principle elements on which they rely for their migrations."

The Spirit of Nineteenth-century Ponchos

The gaucho, inhabitant of the pampa, is a product of a pastoral economy. His equestrian lifestyle influences his dress, making the poncho the ideal garment since it enables his arms to move freely while providing him with cover. According to travel writings of the late eighteenth and early nineteenth century, we find the following articles among the gaucho's dress: *bombachas* (a baggy, white pant) covered with the *chiripá* (a colored cloth tied around the waist), a hat, a poncho and calfskin boots. When the Italian writer Pablo Mantegazza visited Argentina in the second half of the nineteenth century, he described the gaucho and the poncho as synthesizing in their essence the search for the principle of liberty:

> To compose his dress, the gaucho has searched for everything that might make his way of life most comfortable. Pants restrain him; the tie oppresses him, for he needs air and freedom. Instead, he cuts a piece of cloth in the middle and passing his head through this gap, he makes a kind of chasuble that he calls a poncho. He ties another piece of cloth, the *chiripá*, around his waist, which falls in ample folds over his thighs, leaving his legs naked, which he then covers with calfskin boots or another type of foot covering made with the un-tanned hide of the horse's legs. This elemental mode of dress does not require sewing or artistic cuts and is the most simple and comfortable that can be improvised when one disposes solely of cloth and a knife. This Argentine form of dress has later been modified by European fashions that slowly infiltrate, demonstrating the leveling and omnipotent influence of the dominant races. But against the introduction of the pant, the Argentine of the plain will fight a long time because

many centuries have yet to pass before he abandons his poncho. (Mantegazza 1867: 71)

Gauchos gathered in *pulperías*, where they would drink alcohol, play cards and trade.[4] In 1718 there were ninety *pulperías* in Buenos Aires, around 1749 there were 224, and finally in 1826, they had increased to 464. Those on Victoria Street – Hipólito Yrigoyen in present-day Buenos Aires – to Patagones Street were the most famous, averaging roughly nine per block. During Spanish rule, the gauchos' nomadic lifestyle and continuous presence in the *pulperías* (local taverns or general stores) irritated political leaders who applied what was common law not only in Spain as in other European countries. They would punish "idleness," or according to a 7 January 1716 edict, "those who [did] not work or have a known profession, those who attended song and guitar sessions." Thereafter the labelling of the gaucho as "lazy and poorly entertained" will anticipate the military draft and their destiny on the frontier during what was called the Conquest of the Desert. Every gaucho needed to carry a document signed by the *estancia* boss and a judge certifying that he was not a "vagabond."

The first images of the gaucho were undoubtedly those of an individual that society feared. For urban dwellers, the Indian and gaucho constituted a somber image as the following description from the late eighteenth century reads:

> The savage was worrisome. He had to be destroyed, or at the very least, sent far away, very far, toward Chile or Patagonia, from whence he would never return. For months their likely invasion was the talk of the town, until the initial fright subsided and another concern typical of rural life replaced it. At this time the gaucho outlaw, with his measured speech and fearsome actions, roaming about the plain, already existed. The bandit and his infinite variety of fighters, while not as abundant as during war periods, already disturbed the small general stores of the pampas, with their adventures being disseminated widely.

Outside Buenos Aires, in the town of Luján, a gaucho stole a slave belonging to Don Manuel Gil Moreno in 1758. The authorities were unable to apprehend him. To demonstrate his boldness, he returned a few days later to Gil Moreno's ranch to take a horse. Popular stories such as these confirmed the gaucho's astuteness and, like the slave with him, he now sought refuge in the Pampa. A century later, this type of gaucho was the most likely to be drafted to defend the frontier, his reaction being to flee.

Not all gauchos were equal, but all wore ponchos. There were as many human types of gauchos as there were regions in the country. Numerous sociological and historical studies have been dedicated to them, but it is useful to look at the gaucho from a more contemporary perspective. Bonifacio del Carril dedicated many pages to defining types of gauchos and their various forms of behavior. For example, he mentions the gaucho *paisano* who imitates the city dweller in his dress and customs. Another type of gaucho, while shirking

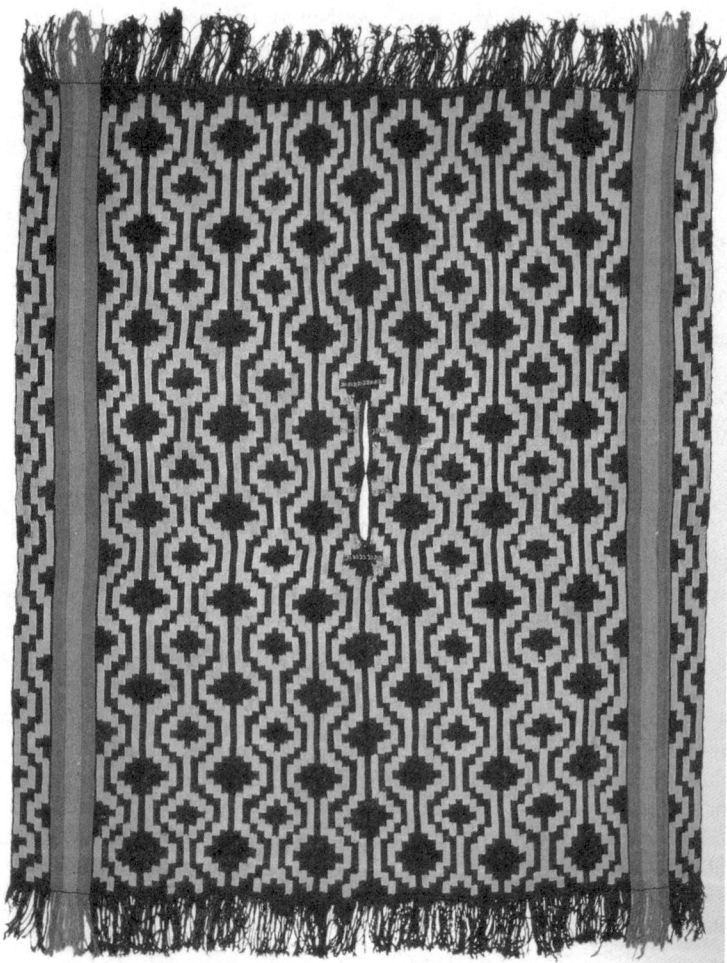

Figure 9.1. Nineteenth-century poncho from the Argentine Pampas that belonged to Chief Cayupán. Poncho stitch with the ikat and its lines. Note that the warp helps shape the Spanish flag. Made of sheep's wool, it measures 1.95 m long and 1.54 m wide. Courtesy of the José Hernández Museum.

"civilization," carries with pride his silver equestrian accessories, complete with dagger and good poncho. Del Carril explains:

> The first takes off his poncho to enter town, while the second enters showing off all his accoutrements. The first is a worker, a horse breaker, cattle driver, cowboy, manual laborer. The second hires himself out as an ironsmith. The first has been a soldier many times. The second at some point formed part of a contingent from which he deserted as soon as he was able. The first makes up the Argentine social mass and the second is disappearing. (Del Carril 1978: 36)

It has also been said that:

> The gaucho of the Banda Oriental [present-day Uruguay], Santa Fe, Corrientes or the province of Buenos Aires, a gaucho of wool and cotton ponchos, is joyful and well disposed although also uppity and disdainful with foreigners: If one should appear on his ranch and ask for a cigarette light, he replies dryly "Dismount and light" because he believes that granting the request would be akin to service. (Del Carril 1978: 57)

Del Carril also writes,

> The gaucho of the interior – of Salta, Tucumán, Jujuy, Córdoba – is more adept and savage. A traveler will say, "Friend, how many leagues from here to there?" The gaucho will reply with the same question, "How many might there be, then?" "Is such and such a place close?" "Yes," the gaucho responds without looking at the man who asks. And he does not speak more than necessary because, between them, the biggest compliment that can be paid a man is to say that he is a "silent chap". (Del Carril 1978: 57–8)

The spread of *estancias* throughout the countryside altered the nomadic lifestyle of the gaucho. The *estancia* would become the new world modifying some of their ways and leaving others, like their sleeping habits, unchanged. The gaucho loved sleeping beneath the stars and desperately tried to maintain his traditional way of life, including his habitual form of dress, despite the strong current of change that permeated the pampa. As Uruguayan writer Francisco Bauzá would suggest in 1855, the traditional attire of the gaucho and his own herd represented his guarantee of freedom. With riding equipment and a herd of horses, the gaucho could be self-sufficient, feeding himself by killing animals and selling rhea feathers and leather in the *pulpería* to buy tea and tobacco. As Bauzá explains, the Argentine liberal elite represented the gaucho's attire as being politically significant, with some intellectuals identifying their ways with the emergence of *caudillos*, local bosses who ruled the provinces with military force, and *montoneras*, or mounted rebels.

Observing the advance on Buenos Aires of his gaucho cavalry in order to overthrow the regime of Juan Manuel de Rosas (who held power from 1829 to 1852), future president General Justo José de Urquiza lamented the presence of the *chiripá*, poncho and other traditional garments. If Argentine soldiers did not alter their mode of dress, he reflected, the country would be destined for military rule by *caudillos*. The transformation of the most basic elements of life meant more than superficial, cosmetic alterations; it signified the loss of a dear and traditional way of life. The once formidable *facón* (larger dagger) was reduced to a modest knife to flay animals and castrate bulls. The new garments mass-produced in European factories displaced hand woven native cloths, *bombachas* replaced the *chiripá*, and industrially manufactured boots replaced those made of calfskin. In their dress, *estancia* workers came to resemble the immigrant colonist or urban worker, except in the most traditional regions.

The customary long hair and curled beard subsisted, but the external appearance of the peasant changed as drastically as did life on the Pampas.

The Poncho or the Dress Coat

The gaucho, horse and poncho come together most forcefully for Argentines at a particular historical moment, a time of the lance, gallop and poncho; of road travel during a period of anarchy and *caudillo* rule. Two options, the poncho or dress coat, appeared to signal a destiny that should be shared. Domingo Faustino Sarmiento, educator and Argentine president from 1868 to 1874, described this dichotomy between different forms of understanding of what were sometimes opposing series of values. Resistance to men immersed in nature, to the cult of valor and courage; and an urban culture that advanced along other lines. Thus he portrays the gaucho in his *Facundo*:

> We must see these heavily bearded faces, these grave, serious countenances like those of Asian Arabs, to judge the pitying disdain inspired in them by the sight of a sedentary city dweller, who may have read many books but does not know how to pull down a fierce bull and kill it; who would not know how to provide himself with a horse in the open country, on foot and without help from anyone; who has never stopped a tiger, facing it with a dagger in one hand and a poncho wrapped around the other to stick in its mouth, while he runs it through the heart and leaves it lying at his feet. (Sarmiento 2003: 57)

These were two worlds difficult to reconcile, as suggested by the many stories and popular songs from the period, full of mourning and tears that extend throughout the Argentine territory.

This image of individualism, with the melancholy and nostalgia that are associated with the nation's Edenic past, fed a romanticism that animated daily life in many South American cities. In Argentina, this was expressed in the work of Esteban Echeverría and in the clothes of those who read him. If Echeverría was appalled by the barbarity of the Indian, a common theme in the nineteenth century, the exaltation of the gaucho's freedom proved no less romantic. This admiration appears in José Hernández, author of the *Martín Fierro*, and in most travel narratives. During the course of this century, the mounted *gaucho* with his silver trappings, horse, and poncho came to synthesize the Creole. But this romantic archetype emerged at the very time when the real *gaucho* was fading away into the horizon, unable to negotiate the new forms of life that the option of a fenced-off Pampa imposed. The gaucho thus appears as a free man, a spontaneous reader of natural law, neither Indian nor citizen "domesticated" by the use of a Dress Coat.

Today, in the country's interior, there are still Creole women who weave ponchos and men who wear them. Yet the garment that they create is more than an element of fashion amongst us. This icon of the Argentine cultural imaginary unites the diverse personal histories of Argentina. Pre-Hispanic ponchos reflected the most ancient American testimony. Following the conquest, newcomers and *mestizos* would appropriate the poncho and its designs. From this America of the first cultural and racial mixing we have legends and nostalgias that will forever envelop the men and women who encountered for the first time the Andean majesty with its magical forests and harsh, ascetic deserts. In the decades following independence the poncho reflected the tensions at play in the creation of an Argentine nation. Towards the end of the nineteenth century, men and women from diverse nations would arrive from the Atlantic to the South American continent through the door that is the River Plate. They were inspired by intimate promises and hopes of realization. At this second great instance of *mestizaje* in these lands, many of these men and women adopted the poncho, leaving behind testimonies of another time past. Into the twenty-first century, many versions of the poncho have made their way into collections around the globe, far from the vision of the land that inspired them. Nevertheless, in the hands of its Creole weavers, the poncho still retains the resonances of archaic rites and inspires in our imagination a memory of Eden.

10

Mappin Stores: Adding an English Touch to the São Paulo Fashion Scene

Rita Andrade

The opening of an English department store in São Paulo was the consequence of urban modernization. From the nineteenth century until the first decade of the twentieth century, the major capitals of Latin America were Rio de Janeiro and Buenos Aires. In 1913, Mappin Stores allowed the members of an aspiring middle class and the bourgeoisie of São Paulo to experience "Englishness" – in a way that only the upper classes had previously – through the consumption of luxury goods.

English Influences in the Tropics

It has been said that the first external evidence of the advent of real civilization in what has hitherto been virgin territory is supplied by the erection of a saloon, then by the establishment of a church, and lastly by the founding of a newspaper. That statement however, was made some years ago, and today it would be correct to amend it by saying that modern folk cannot live in comfort until they have been afforded the facilities provided by a department store. ("Store in São Paulo a Credit to British Enterprise," *Times of Brazil*, 18 July 1919)[1]

The decision to choose São Paulo for the site of a new English department store stemmed from the fact that commercial relations had existed between Brazil and England since the eighteenth century, during the colonial period and following independence from Portugal. European influences had been prevalent since 1763, when Brazil's capital was transferred to Rio de Janeiro in order to accommodate expanding commercial activities. This shift began the development of the southeast and, a few decades later, its inhabitants had assimilated to the new modes of European-style consumption. Rua do Ouvidor (Ouvidor

Street) in Rio de Janeiro reflected the eagerness of Brazilians and wealthy immigrants who desired to further their socioeconomic status. In spite of this ideology, which deemed European culture superior to native ways, the Rio de Janeiro of the nineteenth century was a far cry from the cities that served the population as a cultural and architectural model (Mauad 1997: 207). Photographs from the period reveal a dirty city with a chaotic series of street vendors, trolley cars and buildings.

The opening of Brazilian ports to "friendly nations" in 1808 would initiate a unique link between Brazil and Europe, especially the United Kingdom. In 1815, Dom João IV declared Brazil a kingdom and established a series of administrative measures that gave the former Portuguese colony the status of a nation (Basbaun 1968: 103). Rio de Janeiro's aristocracy, eager to imitate the Portuguese in habits and titles, began to create a metropolis with commercial establishments, including fragrance stores, jewelry bazaars, and fashion showrooms. With the defeat of Napoleon in Portugal, Dom João IV returned to Portugal and left in his place Prince Dom Pedro, who declared Brazilian independence from Portugal in 1822, thus becoming the first Emperor of Brazil (Basbaun 1968: 104–6). With this relatively peaceful emancipation from Portugal, Brazil began to trade with the United Kingdom (Boris 2001: 78).

During the colonial period, a prohibition of the production of manufactured goods had slowed this commercial exchange. Exports of raw materials, like coffee and cotton, facilitated the import of manufactured goods, such as fabrics (Dowbor 1994: 33–56). At this time, injunctions from 1785 had ordered the closing of all existing factories in the colony, a move that hindered Brazil's ability to produce fine textile articles that would compete with other markets (Basbaun 1968: 102). Only the manufacture of thick cotton fabrics to dress slaves was permitted, thereby forcing inhabitants to import fine fabrics from Portugal. Despite emancipation and a shift in power, the challenges were great. England delayed the nation-building process. Giroletti writes

> The modern textiles mills were created during the second half of the nineteenth century. Many factories were established, from the Maranhão state in the north to Rio Grande do Sul in the south. The greatest concentrations of these factories were in the Rio de Janeiro, São Paulo, Bahia and Minas Gerais provinces. Most of them were owned by small companies with less than one hundred employees, producing goods for local markets. Few had more than three hundred workers and they were mainly located in Rio de Janeiro and São Paulo. Rio mills produced for wider markets and used a commercial network to sell imported industrial fabrics. (Giroletti 1995: 215)

While many owned tobacco, cotton and coffee fields at the end of the nineteenth century, some entrepreneurs established industries that made fabrics, ceramics, hats, and shoes. Gold mining was a resource for a few of the Brazilian provinces. In 1874, a textile factory using domestic raw materials was founded in Rio Grande do Sul. The following year, more than twenty-five silk, felt, and straw factories had opened (Basbaun 1968: 108).

Large landowners who supported slavery, as well as obstacles imposed by Portugal, delayed Brazil's industrialization. Following independence, the elite of São Paulo and Rio de Janeiro contributed to this delay by continuing the dependency on manufactured goods. England supplied Brazil with prime materials, which natives assembled. The submission to the interests of England on behalf of the leading Brazilian classes evolved into a kind of subaltern culture that found its expression in the imitation of the habits, dress and patterns of consumption of the European upper classes.

São Paulo: Its Origins and Its Modernization

By the first half of the twentieth century, *paulistas* (people born in the city of São Paulo) and *paulistanos* (those born in the State of São Paulo) already exhibited the influences of modernity and industrialization. Casa Mappin would play a pivotal role in the dissemination of the customs and styles proper to this experience. As Mappin's seventieth anniversary book reads, "Mappin, besides being a place to shop, was a habit in the Paulistanos's lives. One did not go there only to buy clothing or to obtain the last novelty in home ware. Above all, the store was a place to meet and to be entertained" (Alvim and Peirão 1985: 113). As a backdrop, the modern city favored the advent of equally modern goods. But why did Mappin Stores open its doors in São Paulo, especially when Rio de Janeiro and Buenos Aires were more renowned internationally? Was São Paulo more like a modern European city? The differences between Rio de Janeiro and São Paulo were quite apparent at the time:

> ... Around 1870, particularly in São Paulo, the socio-economic transformations had generated a new class based upon coffee production that assumed, with all its consequences, one of the main aspects of decentralization: the defense of provincial autonomy. At the same time, a new sort of conviction was emerging amongst groups from a diversity of social basis, such as that of the coffee bourgeoisie and the urban middle class. It consisted of the disbelief that decentralizing reforms or enlargement of political representation could take place in such a frame as the Monarchy. The republican movement was then born. (Fausto 2001: 99)

Western *paulista* plantation owners were often more receptive to the idea of abandoning slavery in order to support Brazil's entry into the modernization process.[2] This generated a new coffee bourgeoisie that promoted the growth of urban centers. Spurred on by late nineteenth-century immigration, São Paulo emerged with capitalist practices and consumption patterns that mirrored those of Europe's greatest centers. In its consumption of imported goods, the new bourgeois class began to compete with the royal court (Mauad 1997: 211), a fact that led to industrial growth in São Paulo and which ultimately helped defeat the economic hold of Rio de Janeiro, the site of the Empire's capital.[3]

The role of Rio de Janeiro in the adoption of European-style consumption patterns, however, cannot be denied. Mauad writes:

> The link with the Parliament was not limited to the visits of dignitaries of the Empire. The royal court was always a highly held reference of excellence to the farmers. This included the coffee negotiations, health treatment, shopping on *Rua do Ouvidor*, as well as, comings and goings to the theater and ballrooms. The economic prosperity of the region, besides deepening the ties with the royal court, guaranteed the coffee barons a social representative appropriate to the ladies' class. Among such forms of representation which stand out is the consumption of products and the idioms of the royal court and the exterior. China, furniture, bed linens and dress were acquired frequently through catalogs from the great stores of the royal court or even from France, especially Lafayette Gallery, as noted in the accounting books of the Baron of Vassouras. (Mauad 1997: 211–12)

Into the first decade of the twentieth century, Rio de Janeiro was Brazil's capital and commercial center. Novelties from Europe arrived at the city's port and Ouvidor Street became a popular marketplace for these items. According to Cohen (2001: 31), French influences prevailed as evidenced by a large group of French traders who "specialized in fine textiles, millinery, perfumes, fashion and costumes objects, jewels, books and many other items." This may explain the hesitation on the part of the English to direct business there, but as Cohen illustrates, it might have more to do with the fact that British investments have often been associated with the industry trades rather than retail. But that did not stop British entrepeneurs from inaugurating their Mappin & Webb store at 100/101 Ouvidor Street in 1911 (Cohen 2001: 99; Alvim et al. 1985: 22). Built like its London flagship model, one of which the company had already installed in Buenos Aires, the store would later become known as Casa Mappin.

Given the fact that Buenos Aires had more English inhabitants, it seemed more plausible to initiate a store in Argentina. But Nicolau Sevcenko reminds us that "Rio de Janeiro and Buenos Aires could be temporarily bigger, but the growth compass and resources magnitude of São Paulo were such that its triumph over the two closest rivals was unavoidable and pointed to even higher fates" (Sevcenko 2000: 37). This might explain why São Paulo, and not Rio de Janeiro, was chosen for the second site. Mario de Andrade confirms that the dynamic nature of this city would transform European ideas – and fashions – into *Brazilianness*. He writes:

> São Paulo was much more updated than Rio de Janeiro ... There was a profound difference, only now less sensitive, between Rio and São Paulo. Rio was much more international, as a norm of foreign lifestyle. It is clear: the country's capital, a port city, Rio has an innate internationalism. São Paulo was much more "modern" though; it was the necessary product of coffee economy and consequent industrialism. Innocently provincial, keeping even now a servile provincial spirit, São Paulo denounced it through its politics. Either through its updated trading or its industrialization, if less social,

more spiritual (I am not saying "cultural") and technical, São Paulo was simultaneously in contact with the world's current news.[4]

For Andrade, the spirit of São Paulo aligned itself with the interests of intellectuals and the aristocracy. Rio de Janeiro, which Andrade perceives as being tied to a national form of "exoticism," was not in a position to liberate itself from a recent monarchical past.

Fashion and the Modern City

One can still recognize the British influences on São Paulo's cityscape. Urbanization campaigns in the nineteenth and early twentieth centuries incorporated English-style buildings, as evidenced by the façades of banks and trade houses. In 1899, Canadian Light, the first power company in the city, allowed a series of developments that included the illumination of public spaces, the establishment of a trolley car system, and electricity for industrial use. At the onset of the twentieth century, São Paulo had also been transformed by the wealth amassed by coffee plantations and invested in the city. The affluent coffee barons moved their families from the countryside to mansions in the city, their new urban lifestyle bringing them in close proximity with fine European goods and services. In 1910, the Estação da Luz (Station of Light) was imported in its entirety from England, still serving residents today. Modern methods of transportation and the importation of red bricks for stations and other buildings gave the city its English appearance. Social customs soon followed: five o'clock tea, theater concerts and daily promenades were part of the lives of elegant *paulistanos*, although their habits were not influenced by those of London alone. As the city sought all things English, immigrants from Portugal to Turkey and from all social backgrounds helped reshape city life.

By the 1920s, both immigrants and the new coffee aristocracy enjoyed a sort of European lifestyle. The city boasted teahouses, car rides and the City Hall Theatre (Teatro Municipal). So what better place than São Paulo, with its population that viewed "Englishness" as a synonym of elegance, to launch an English department store? There was misery, but also a promise of sophistication. Paulistas were thirsty for the styles of Europe and they had the buildings and means of transportation with which to make a department store feasible in their city.

That a department store appeared in São Paulo almost eighty years after its appearance in Europe might suggest that this city possessed a subaltern culture. According to Homi Bhabba, relationships between the North and the South can be viewed in light of their established specifications (Bhabba 1994). The Mappin Store did not just launch a branch in São Paulo; instead, it carefully synchronized its appearance with the modernity – and social hybridity – experienced in the Brazilian city. Was, then, the launch of this department store a confirmation of the elite's readiness to consume or had a new consumer-based culture with particular fashion tastes already been established?

São Paulo, it is worth highlighting, was a city preoccupied with its own industrialization, as some of its inhabitants had abandoned the coffee and other agricultural production that still persisted in much of South America. Its industrial growth was so rapid that São Paulo became known as a "Brazilian Manchester." Mappin Stores was at the heart of the city, or the Triângulo, at which point the XV de Novembro, São Bento and Direita Streets met. Sevcenko writes: "From 4 p.m. on, many paraded by the circuit of fine stores in the Triângulo, its apex the five o'clock tea salon at the Mappin Store prior to the six o'clock rush hour. The city's center smelled of perfume and skirt ruffles communicated feminine waves, a hustle and bustle, circumscribing the Triângulo in a desirable space" (Sevcenko 2000 [1992]: 51).[5] One located English influences in the education, culture, tastes and habits of wealthy *paulistanos*. Most of all, this influence was evident at the level of material culture, in those very luxury items coveted by São Paulo's high society.

The Department Store and Modern Life

A product of the late nineteenth century, the department store catered to clients who desired to experience and consume luxury in a seemingly private but yet so public atmosphere. The concept had first emerged in France and England of the 1830s and 1840s.[6] In Paris, as well as in the north of England, a change in architecture and urban planning all contributed to the birth of a business that gathered various articles under one roof. In this initial phase, production was usually determined by demand. In England in the 1830s, the majority of goods were still produced in sweatshops or small workshops.

Two department stores that appeared in the north of Britain claimed to be the first: Bainbridge's of Newcastle upon Tyne and Kendal; and Milne & Faulkner of Manchester (Lancaster 2000: 7). In France, the *magasin des nouveautés* preceded the opening of Paris's Bon Marché, anticipating its sales, customer service, and luxurious spaces. As Aristide Boucicaut, the founder of Bon Marché would declare, this store had been "specially constructed and entirely intended for a great trade in *nouveautés*" (Miller 1981: 20). All stores marked a shift in the shopping patterns and behaviors of their clients. Lancaster describes what might have happened on any given day: a lady visits the store to buy fabric to make a dress but she also needs thread, bows, ribbons. As she looks for the right ones, she comes across other novelties that might match her first purchase, like a pair of gloves or socks (Lancaster 2000: 10–11). With all her needs and desires in one place, the client hardly ever left with just one item. The Mappin Store of São Paulo would market similar novelties, although it would soon find the need to shift its marketing strategies.

Mappin Stores: The Height of Sophistication

Mappin Stores first opened its doors in São Paulo on 29 November 1913. The main newspapers, like *O Estado de São Paulo*, assigned whole pages to the big event (see Figure 10.1). It was not only the opening of another English shop; it was Brazil's first department store. The origins of the business dated back to eighteenth-century Sheffield, England where since 1774 the store Mappin & Webb had sold silver, ceramics and other fine goods (Alvim et al. 1985: 21). When contemplating the market overseas, São Paulo did not immediately come to mind. Late nineteenth-century Buenos Aires had the reputation of being the Paris of South America and it was home to the largest English community outside Great Britain. Mappin and Webb was thus established in Buenos Aires and Rio de Janeiro before the setting up of São Paulo's branch in 1912. The nature of the business in São Paulo was, however, very different from that of the shops in Europe, Buenos Aires and Rio de Janeiro, as it did not just specialize in silver and crystal but instead branched out to become a true department store.

In a short period of time, Mappin was a place where one could find fine clothes, fabrics, trimmings, accessories, furniture, and household appliances. It was the very experience of elegance, the perfect meeting point for afternoon tea or a ladies fashion show. Salespeople (usually women) attended to the needs and requests of loyal customers and served coffee. A client could sit down as goods were brought to her. Attendants picked out the latest arrivals. Because items purchases were noted in notebooks with information about family accounts, one's socioeconomic status was noted at the time of payment. Thus, the Mappin shopping experience adapted the desire for that certain "Englishness" to particular class-based hierarchies that predominated in Brazilian culture.

Soon after the launch of Mappin & Webb in the three South American cities, São Paulo was the one chosen to house Mappin Stores, an English anonymous society formed by Mappin & Webb and Debenhams. The Brazilian undertaking, called Mappin & Webb (Brazil) Ltd., consisted of three English partners: Walter John Mappin, Herbert Joseph Mappin, and Henry Portlock. In 1913 those three partners joined Sir John Kitching, manager for the English shop Debenhams, to found Mappin Stores in São Paulo (Alvim et al. 1985: 21–4). Mappin Stores and Mappin & Webb were housed in the same building at XV de Novembro Street, in the very heart of the city and they stayed there until 1919, when Mappin Stores moved out to the Praça do Patriarca (where it existed until 1936). The launch of this new branch attracted the following note from the English newspaper *Times of Brazil*, published on 1 August 1919:

> When the prefect [Mayor] arrived, shortly before 9.30 p.m., the ground floor and the upper galleries were thronged with visitors. Dr. Washington Luiz was met at the Rua Direita entrance by Mr Kitching, managing director of the Stores, ... The prefect [Mayor], in a brief address congratulated Mr. Kitching on the enterprise which had

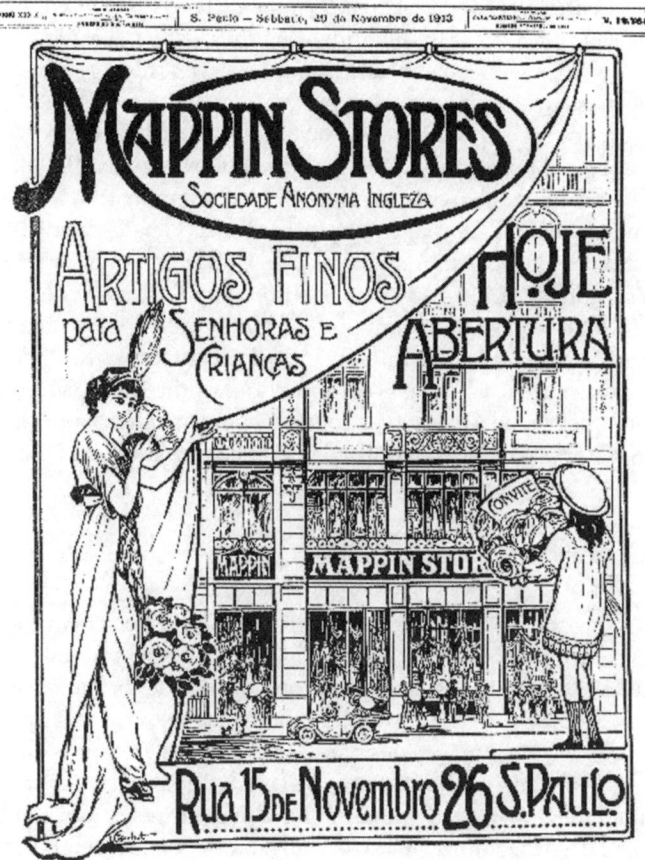

Figure 10.1. Advertisement for the opening of Mappin Stores. From the 29 November 1913 issue of *O Estado de S. Paulo*.

given São Paulo such a magnificent establishment and wished that it might meet with the success that it undoubtedly deserved.

As this description suggests, the Mappin Stores inaugurated a much welcome establishment that far surpassed others in its elite clientele. Similar store concepts, such as the Casa Alemã (German House) launched by Daniel Heydenreich and located on 25 de Março Street since 1883, targeted a less economically privileged consumer (Alvim et al. 1985: 35).

During the first two decades of the twentieth century, the coffee baron families settled in new mansions on what had been farmland previously (Rolnik 2001:

26–7). Today's Paulista Avenue, on which one finds São Paulo's business center, gave way to rows of European-style mansions with more "Latinized" features. The new residential areas were called Campos Elíseos (the French Champs Elysées) and Garden Cities. By building them in clusters, São Paulo's streets took on the feel of European sophistication; however, this push marginalized the working class to the city outskirts.

The interests of skilled immigrants, businessman and wealthy *paulistanos* were at the core of Mappin Stores' early years. Following the 1929 depression and the sale of Mappin shares to an English tradesman in 1936 there was an attempted name change. The Casa Anglo-Brasileira (Anglo-Brazilian House) concept, however, proved impractical as the Mappin name was fixed in the *paulistano* imaginary. The 1940s witnessed the popularization of the department store, a reflection of the boom in the region's industrial and commercial infrastructure. The increasing influence of the United States brought new businesses and an emphasis on mass consumption. By the 1950s, Mappin Stores saw an end to its elevated status as the company implemented a more aggressive marketing-style approach that paralleled that of businesses in the United States.

Mapping Fashion

When consulting the Mappin Historical Archive, the wide array of advertisements that the store placed in São Paulo's main newspapers stands out.[7] With these images and descriptions, Mappin proposed its own brand of modernity – one that made its way to the consumer (and hence, the city at large) at every instant. Furthermore, it is a fashionable identity targeting a cosmopolitan society with the elegance of European social circles. It also appears to be quite French, using French words to name colors, styles, garments and emphasizing the praised Parisian fashions of *Vogue* magazine – even though there is no evidence to suggest that these garments actually came from France.[8] While there is ample evidence to document that these fashionable goods were imported from England, Mappin preserved its use of English terms only to denote types of fabrics. In the imaginary of the time, this approach preserved the fashionable crowd's sense of elitism grounded in that center of fashion, Paris; while maintaining a certain Englishness. The profusion of fashion magazines in São Paulo counted on these associations, especially as more and more members of the middle and upper classes traveled to Europe to purchase these fashions on their own account.

Richard Sennett explains that the term "sophistication" was first used in nineteenth-century France and Britain as a compliment amongst the bourgeoisie, denoting "the one who could [be] recognize[d] as 'well educated', or as one who has 'good manners', in spite of any language, national customs or age barriers" (Sennett 1988: 175–6). Sophistication was indeed one of Mappin Store's most marketable qualities, as this testimony by Olga Rubião,[9] a middle-class woman born in the 1920s, indicates. She told me during an interview on 23 March 2002:

> When I was a child, I remember my Mom coming home with a big box filled with porcelain that she had just bought at Mappin. It was sale time and I think she spent all of our family's savings to buy it. It was so elegant and we all were overwhelmed with happiness. Mappin was chic and we felt great to be able to own something from the store.

As her testimony indicates, the items sold at Mappin did not possess the same aura as the store itself. Although Mappin's advertisements linked its goods to modernity and sophistication, the styles it marketed were quite conventional if compared to those appearing in the French issues of *Vogue*. Brazilian columnists for nationally circulated fashion magazines sometimes criticized French fashion styles (even those sold at Mappin) to promote American sports styles.

Rubião remembers the kinds of clothes sold at Mappin, saying: "I preferred Mappin's ready-made clothes that had been imported from England, such as cashmere pullovers and overcoats. But the dresses were so unfashionable. British women had no taste and some of their garments seemed a bit too conventional." Her statement reflects a distancing effect that Mappin's marketing department would promote rather than downplay. A lecture room included a bookshop that sold mainly foreign English titles. Mappin placed its advertisements in the English-language newspapers of São Paulo, such as the *Anglo Brazilian Chronicle*. In October 1937, Casa Mappin announced the arrival of new book titles available at the department store; of the 35, all titles were in English.[10] Another popular section of the store was its Tea Salon, where the elite – politicians, plantation owners, bankers and writers like Mario de Andrade – enjoyed meeting. The Tea Room, or Salão de Chá as it was also known since its inauguration in 1919, was also the site of the more popular fashion shows in Brazil. As a result, the salon's events received wide press coverage, such as this review of a fashion show in December 1933:

> Surrounding tables decorated with flowers, illustrious ladies and lovely young ladies anxiously waited the announcement of a live mannequins' fashion show for Mappin's twentieth Christmas celebration. The twentieth Christmas celebration . . . Twenty years, then? Yes, twenty years . . . How many sweet young ladies have ignored that fact? Nonetheless, Mappin Stores is more than twenty years old. In a woman's life, twenty years represents spring, the dawn of the future. In a "department store's" life, twenty years reflects a very slow, long, and almost secular existence.[11]

Mappin's Tea Room, which took up the store's first floor of the XV de Novembro Street section, was later moved (along with the rest of the store) to Praça Ramos de Azevedo in 1959. Its popularity, however, had seen its peak in previous decades and it was transformed into a new banquet-style Sala Verde

(Green Room) with an "American spirit" and visited by secretaries of state and military officers.

In a short period of time, Mappin had transformed its fine goods reputation into a place for "being seen" by other elegant members of society during a fashion show or afternoon cup of tea. Mappin's storefront displayed those items that were transforming the lives of elite Brazilian households. The department store simultaneously marketed the exclusivity of the upper classes, when announcing in 1915, for example, the option to tailor for its clients Carnival costumes. Other fashions, such as an advertisement for women's blouses indicates that same year, implied that wealthy *paulistanos* also possessed the best of France and England. The May 1915 advertisement categorizes these washable – read as "modern" – garments with Parisian chic and British design: "New model in washable white silk, modern collar"; "Modern blouse in washable white silk"; "Chic blouse in silk taffeta, modern style"; and "Shirt Blouse in sheer wool and silk, English cutting, various colors" . . .[12] The Mappin of the 1920s would leave an indelible mark on the cityscape and an impression on the customs of São Paulo's inhabitants. The pursuit of an English chic style would persist in the Brazilian cultural imaginary for decades, even after the Mappin brothers sold their company shares to Alfred Sim following the 1929 stock market crash (Alvim et al. 1985: 94–7).

In the end, Mappin conquered both its Brazilian and European clientele with the distribution of catalogs and by furthering its advertisement campaigns. Each time a new product arrived in Brazil, Mappin Stores was at the forefront, publishing notes that invited its customers for a private showing. Gradually, some Brazilian craftsmen and newly arrived immigrants were hired to produce specialty items. Mappin also added well-known tailors to its staff so as to expand its repertoire of services. To best appeal to the Brazilian client, these nationally produced goods and garments still possessed British style and design. The department store continued to import fashions from France and England, especially fabrics that could be tailored into individualized designs.

From the moment that Mappin integrated its sale of imported fabrics with a growing local clothing industry, it became more like an American department store. Mappin's catalogs expanded its city-based clientele to the countryside and thus initiated a special delivery system to provide its products to customers who could not enter its store as frequently. Each catalog contained instructions on made-to-fit measurements and suggestions regarding sizes for newly introduced ready-to-wear clothing. By 1939, Mappin had relocated to a new building at Praça Ramos de Azevedo, opposite the City Hall Theatre, where it still stands as a landmark in the downtown area (Alvim et al. 1985: 104).

Grounded in São Paulo's Anglo-Brazilian identity, Mappin department stores would continue to disseminate fashionable forecasts and news of newly arrived goods. Well educated in British modes, the Brazilian elite relished in Mappin's presentation of their status and relationships with other classes. Although the founding partners had long left Brazil, a new group of shareholders appropriately named the Casa Anglo-Brasileira Society expanded on and promoted what many perceived as that certain "Englishness" in Brazilian society. With its rising middle-class clientele and a locally based staff, the store deepened its presence in the cityscape, only to be concluded by the announcement of Mappin department store's bankruptcy on 29 July 1999. Today, the name Mappin continues to represent a small part of Brazil's national heritage, a symbol that remains uniquely *paulista*.[13]

Acknowledgments

I am very grateful to Teresa Cristina Toledo de Paula, Textiles Curator at the Museu Paulista in São Paulo, Lesley Miller of the University of Southampton, Regina Root, and Iraci Santos of the Mappin Historical Archive, whose guidance contributed greatly to the development of this project.

11

As She Walks to the Sea: A Semiology of Rio de Janeiro[1]

Nizia Villaça

In 1964, Antônio Carlos Jobim's song *The Girl from Ipanema* would inspire the world to think about the beach fashions of Rio de Janeiro, a complex and multivalent city with a mythical image often displayed on Brazilian postcards. Because of tourism and media packaging, Rio de Janeiro has emerged as a culturally constructed landscape of bikini-clad women in the narratives of music, literature and the social sciences. Due to continued media coverage of its inhabitants, known as the *Cariocas*, the images that circulate are easily recognized in Brazil: of Rio's colonial architecture and its dilapidated, multicultural forms; of its lascivious excesses that contrast greatly with metropolitan consumption patterns; of its promotion of natural beauties. Most recently, Brazil has experienced an explosion of political discourses and newspaper chronicles about the violence in this same city, now shattered by misery. Still, it is impossible to determine the type of image that prevails. The fashionable Rio de Janeiro of beautiful tourist destinations is also a place of beach assaults and robbery. Here, "there are more killings over Reebok tennis shoes than love," writes Patrícia Melo (1994: 31).

This chapter connects the fashionable and media discourses that have touched on the Marvelous City since the 1950s, focusing on a series of behaviors specifically connected to Rio's southern zones. Postcard images reveal a magnificent tropical landscape in which women walk toward the sea in utter sensuousness, as if to reinvent time and space. In my chapter, I will demonstrate how the relationship between the body and clothing in Rio de Janeiro has changed over time, tracing prosthesis fashion of the 1960s and 1970s, fetish fashions of the 1980s, and alibi fashion of the 1990s and the beginning of the twenty-first century.[2] In the process, we will see how Brazilian beach fashions respond to specific social, political and economic considerations.

In this study, I propose that we consider the multiple clothing codes that appear on the beach by adding a vertical space/time axis to the horizontal one related to the space of tribes and behaviors. In the window of being and seeming, fashion is a kind of record keeper that reveals aspects of one's individual and collective appearance. If fashion can be considered a mask that hides and disguises the body, as Jennifer Craik (1993) suggests, we can view clothing as an active statement or technical construct that represents the *self*. In the realm of capitalist enterprise, Western fashion serves to express ideas, wishes and beliefs predominant in society, putting into dialogue the elements of a global existence through the cult of the individual: Jewish-Christian morality, gender identity, imperialism and multiculturalism. As Zygmunt Bauman[3] (1998) asserts in O *mal-estar da pós-modernidade*, the fashion world and its symbolic order supply the elements necessary for the negotiation of identity as they relate to social, political and economic change.

The Little Sea Princess of the 1950s

The sandy expanse of Copacabana, known as Sacopenapã to the indigenous population and noted for its cashew, *pitanga* and iamb trees, was discovered around 1886. By the 1950s, one of its neighborhoods exhibited a particular Carioca style, made immortal by the musical composition *The Little Sea Princess*. This score drastically altered the reputation of Copacabana as a resort for the sick, creating an image of glamor and consumption-oriented cosmopolitism. The neighborhood would become a glowing example of the "marvelous city," and by extension Brazil, at a time when television was still a novelty. In his ethnographic essay on Carioca identity, anthropologist Fabiano Gontijo writes that Copacabana, as a cultural center, generates and threads together diverse situational identities (Goldenberg 2000: 83). Lúcia Benedetti points to the singular features of Copacabana inhabitants in her image of this community. In a December 1949 essay published in the *Revista de Copacabana*, she writes, "Observe our differences... We have a body just like anyone else's. Not taking a break to exercise is as common as eating breakfast in the morning... Riding a bike is an obligation, to avoid rolls of fat that show up in unconventional places. It is imperative to exhibit a body that others do not find shocking." In the formation of a discourse about Copacabana, the popular imaginations quickly turned to the city's "body cultural capital."

Until 1922, Copacabana permitted sea bathing only for those with medical conditions and, in those cases, only until 8 a.m. in the morning. In general, the city had its back turned to the sea until the inauguration of Hotel Copacabana Place in 1923. As Ricardo Boechat (2002) reminds us in *Copacabana Palace*, this hotel would introduce Brazil to its sun culture. As in other parts of the world, the pursuit of outdoor activities contributed to a change in women's clothes. Even if not generally practiced, golf, tennis, bicycle riding, sea bathing, hunting and other sports brought about slow changes to women's fashions, which then accelerated after the First World War. Golf had introduced the cardigan. Bicycle riding had brought about the fashion of bouffant pants tied down under the knees around 1890. In 1934, a summer short was introduced. Around the 1920s, the sleeveless and round swimsuit with a neckline became the swimwear of choice. In the 1930s uncovered backs accompanied the two-piece swimsuits. By the 1940s, the bikini had made its first appearance (Queiróz Valda 2002: 109).

30 June 1946 would mark the eruption of so-inspired swimwear along the South Pacific's Bikini Archipelago. The name of the archipielago had long fascinated French entrepreneur and stylist Louis Réard. Five days later, at a Paris fashion show that featured conservative swimsuit collections, he threw his petard: a skimpy bathing suit, composed of panty and bra to which he gave the name – *bikini*. According to Gilda Chataigner, the first bikini was made of cotton tissue with prints consisting of contemporary world news headlines. The scenery was the Molitor public swimming pool in Paris at 40 °C. The public considered Réard's creation so indecent that even the professional models refused to wear it. Only Micheline Bernardi, a strip-tease dancer, accepted it. Despite its strong impact in the realm of popular culture, the Frenchman's creation was no gunpowder discovery, signals Chataigner. In the fourth and fifth centuries, she writes, women of southern Italy and Greece wore very similar models. Curiously, those garments were not intended for sea bathing (as everyone swam naked) but rather for gymnastics. Not until the beginning of the nineteenth century did Monsieur Maillot create the maillot beachwear that retains his name. This first swimsuit was comfortable and allowed for fast movements since it was made of woolen jersey or silk meshed tricot.

In the 1950s there emerged a certain "Copacabana *way of life*," a slogan that remitted to a special atmosphere made from the ideals of renovation and liberation proper of modernity. A new model quite different from the "Belle Époque" style appeared, characteristic of Rio's aristocratic neighborhoods known as Downtown and Botafogo. From then on, Copacabana initiated a kind of democratizing process. As the world media stressed luxurious consumption and leisure activities, the city developed a beach culture of hedonist juveniles on a massive scale. The *tijucanos* (Tijuca residents)[4] and beach dwellers often found their lifestyles juxtaposed in the pages of O *Cruzeiro*, as illustrated by this 20 January 1951 essay that describes the beach dwellers as: "People who conquered the right to adorn their body with thin straps of technicolor cloth. Whoever sees them in the bus with their breasts showing through the open blouses, their gypsy-like skirts swinging in the wind, silk-colored scarves tied around their heads, will understand the definition."[5]

At the beach, various beauty contests helped promote summer fashion tendencies. Catalina, the American swimsuit brand, widely advertised its designs through contests that judged young women with similar smiles and standard measurements. Many contestants aspired to achieve the measurements of 35-23-35 inches for the breasts, waist and hips, a skirted one-piece suit, and a flawless hairstyle stiffened with thick coats of spray. The objective was to inspire a guitar-shaped body and thick legs that could help advertise new products such as *helanca*, a thick mesh that rendered wool obsolete. Influences from abroad determined to a great extent what one should wear at a given time and place, a first stage in Brazilian fashion that lasted into the 1950s. These proposed fashions represented a larger project of standardization, correction and perfection. And in Copacabana, the public turned to those dictates issued by the French masters of *haute couture*. By the end of the decade, matching bra and panty suits appeared everywhere, with Brazilian showgirls Carmem Verônica and Norma Tamar being among the first to wear them. From that period forth, bikinis became an integral part of the history of Rio de Janeiro, emergent trends in turn influencing the beach fashions worn throughout Brazil.

Fashion as Prosthesis

The 1960s were quite revolutionary years for Brazilian beach fashions. At this time, the prestigious status of *haute couture* in general found itself transformed as television and popular consumption-oriented inventions changed the lives of middle-class women. *Prêt-a porter* fashions would market the aura of *haute couture* at affordable prices. In the West, young people involved in the student movements of May 1968 became a social force with which to be reckoned. In Brazil, a so-called *prosthesis fashion* emerged, its name an allusion to the garment as an extension of a body in search of greater expressivity. Unisex fashions, blue jeans, the T-shirt and the mini-skirt all helped break the rigid barriers of sexual and behavioral differentiation.

Beginning in 1964, when the Brazilian military initiated a repressive dictatorship, fashion took a leading role in the protests against authoritarianism. The spirit of *tropicalismo* (a cultural movement from the late 1960s that fused the modern and traditional elements of Brazilian culture) dominated the airwaves and attributed fashion attitudinal and behavioral aspects that would play out in future decades. Legs, thighs and bodies were displayed openly with the use of mini-skirts, mini-blouses, and micro-dresses. Freedom was the only unchangeable commandment, as represented by mini- and macro-limits.

Fashion magazines presented an independent woman lifting her head as if endowed with a sense of purpose. Ipanema, the beach by Montenegro Street, became the spot where the muses of Bossa Nova would parade. Nearby, at Veloso Bar, Vinicius de Moraes and Tom Jobim would compose the famous song *Garota de Ipanema* (*Girl from Ipanema*) as they watched a slender, long-haired Heloisa Pinheiro march toward the sea. Besides the still discrete bikini, often made of printed cotton with little frills around the hips, the 1960s also witnessed a very popular model called the "Mom-deceiver," with the front of a regular swimsuit and a bikini behind linked by a strap. It was the paradoxical time of military dictatorship and *tropicalia*, the combination of rigid political control and delirious cultural fantasy.

In the late 1960s and the early 1970s, Brazilian collections threatened the supremacy of French *haute couture* by incorporating daring social spaces that put into dialogue sexual, racial and political divisions. Instead of being held at the usual *haute couture* salons, designers showed their collections in metro stations and bars, creating spectacles that attracted photographers, foreign industrialists, department-store buyers, journalists, social climbers, among others. It was the time of *flower power* and *hippie* culture, of big *rock* festivals with unbelievably large audiences who wore long skirts, tassels, embroidered corsets, Indian tunics, and the faded blue pants synonymous for freedom.

At this juncture, a daring blond actress named Maria Zilda reduced the size of her bikini by lifting and rolling it up to her waist. Thus was created the thong that gave Rio its prestige and creative edge in the realm of beach fashion. Due to the counterculture spirit of the time (as it was influenced by rebellious youth movements, rock music concerts, and social unrest), any artificial element that placed pressure on the body was discarded.[6] In Rio, this meant that men dressed in leather innovations and crochet thongs, and women reduced the sizes of their bikinis and gave up shaving. Brazilian celebrity Leila Diniz surprised everyone when she exposed a very pregnant belly while wearing a bikini, making her a symbol for the women's movement. Artists and intellectuals such as Gal Costa, Caetano Veloso, Regina Casé, Luis Melodia and others often met at Ipanema Pier in their swimsuits to "try to reinvent a good time" and forget the sinister reality of dictatorship. Luiz Carlos Maciel, a cultural critic known for his countercultural stances, provides a particular glimpse into this period in his book *As quatro estações* (*The Four Seasons*):

> 1972. I am at Ipanema beach, Rio de Janeiro, in front of the pier. I am not wearing shorts. I am wearing Celia's Zazá panty. It represents a unisex attitude that I have adopted to make its sufficiently innocent message clear. It marks my assent to the behavior revolution. I remember I had an . . . erection the first time I wore a woman's panty . . . I didn't feel like I was a woman wearing panties; rather I felt as if a woman's flesh, and not a piece of cloth, were touching my penis . . . I and others who come often to the pier like to think that this is a free territory in our dictatorial country. The lack of political freedom is replaced by other kinds of freedom – sexual, drug-induced or of any delirium . . . (Maciel 2001: 13)

Beach styles often included their own critique of national politics and Ipanema Beach became a site from which to transgress repression (Santiago, 19 September 2001: 8). In Copacabana, beach goers listened to Bossa Nova; whereas at the Ipanema Pier, a rock-and-roll sound track with the rhythms of the *Novos Baianos* prevailed.[7] When the Pier was dismantled following the installation of a new drainage system, young people migrated to Posto 9, located between the streets of Montenegro and Joana Angélica. The fashionable said that it was always evening at Posto 9, a place to discuss art and politics, but also to peruse the Indian gowns, necklaces, flip-flops and leather bags with tassels and stones for sale at boutiques. Most importantly, this was the place to purchase *cocotas,* tiny, crocheted bikinis worn low on the hips. As the 1970s came to a close, those incarcerated for political reasons during dictatorship were granted amnesty, an event also marked by Brazilian beach fashion. Fernando Gabeira, returning to Brazil from exile, paraded on the beach in his crocheted mini-thong, an image of mythical proportions for many Brazilians. For this period, as Henri-Pierre Jeudi suggests in another context, the ideology of body liberation paralleled a resistance to authority thereby creating a "pressure to liberate" the body from the trappings of traditional society.

Fetish and Alibi Fashions

If body culture of the 1970s – with its jogging and natural foods – was rebellious, the 1980s witnessed a more sophisticated relationship between the body and beachwear, in part due to the sedimentation of the market. At this time, the body and swimsuit seemed made for each other. Fashion demanded "perfect" bodies molded by aerobic exercise and Lycra wear. So began fetish fashion, in which the body inscribed in a consumer society became sign. Surfers launched their own fashions, emphasizing long and colorful pants. Their girlfriends would toast the friends flying over the beaches in Delta wings, a sport that began with flights from Pedra da Gávea, right on Pepino beach. The minute bikini triangles of the 1970s grew with pronounced curves that mirrored these very wings. Men preferred pants worn loosely, with surfers adhering to neoprene, a version of the black armour worn by sea divers but splashed with bright colors. The delta wing for women was short-lived, however. The decade ended with a G-string fad that has been documented for posterity in the thousands of postcards with tanned *Carioca* bottoms lying on the sand. For the more sport-conscious, especially for beach volleyball, the period also introduced a *sunkini* with a more generous top and bottom. For young surfers, tattoos also became popular at this time, especially at the Pepê and Barra da Tijuca beaches. Fashion spectacles on the beach, or so it seemed at the time, helped define consumption patterns, with a boom in beachside shopping centers and the establishment of a fashion calendar to parallel the beach vacation periods.

In the 1990s, beachwear inscribed the body in a process of displacement, as so-called *alibi fashions* associated the wearer with certain ethical stands. Inspired by police terminology, the term alibi remits to two spaces: one in which the crime was committed and the other in which the presumed perpetrator exists. In such a fashion, a T-shirt that voices support for breast cancer research would imply that the wearer is in some way "ethical." In other words, fashions from this period were used to justify one's participation in various social spaces. Such logic justified the sale and purchase of fetish merchandise and designer labels while omitting their tainted underpinnings. Seduced by images, the fashionable body dramatized the contradictions of contemporary life. The process of fashion production and merchandising accelerated and mixed influences with increasing speed, extending the spaces of intervention and thus making the fashion world more complex. The influence of fashion journalism as disseminated by cable television networks such as GNT (a channel of Globosat) and CNN (Cable News Network), as well as the Internet, cannot be overemphasized.

In alibi fashions, the frontiers of art, science, technology, and politics merged, transforming previous notions of acceptable behavior according to gender, class, race and age. To a large degree, fashionable intervention has replaced revolutionary political action in this neoliberal age in which conglomerates dictate an increasingly global market. From the beginning, the Internet-based *Moda Brasil* (http://www.modabrasil.com.br) worked to place Brazil on the map as one of the world's great centers of fashion, marketing both national designs and academic analysis. In February 2002 the French fashion periodical *L'Officiel* presented the innovations of "Dossier Brésil" (Brazilian Dossier) and Brazilian summer fashions received positive press in the United States. A communicative circle had been formed and fashion cultural production reflected this shift.

In Brazil, the early 1990s were marked by an economic and political crisis that slowed down the fashion industry. Fernando Collor de Mello, Brazil's first democratically elected president following dictatorship in January 1989, was later impeached for corruption in 1992. Despite these setbacks, an expanding market allowed for the textile industry to update their factories in record time. While many factories closed, new ones were created despite civil strife throughout the nation. From these challenging moments, however, the fashion world became a more professional venture. Events such as Morumbi Fashion, Brazil's fashion week, received outstanding media coverage. In Brazil, the fashion world created elite projects that were aimed at more diverse markets. The rhythms of the fashion industry in some ways mirrored those of the population at large. The hierarchical, codified model of fashion, like that of the pyramid, transformed itself into a kind of archipielago-inspired system. Clothing styles as well as social class divisions would seem to have pulverized the pyramid into small islands, with limitations and characteristics increasingly difficult to define. In the 1970s, beachwear was a good value that offered presence. In the 1980s, it also offered status. By the 1990s, one's entire lifestyle was key in fashion merchandising. The product, marked by a designer's label, had always implied a certain amount of value, quality, status, customer service. The added focus of lifestyle added pedigree and soul, thus communicating succinct messages aimed at increasing one's knowledge of the self and the other. Alibi fashions helped create a new system of mobile messages and messengers. As Warren Susman (1979) states, everything – or so it would seem – could be discussed on the beach.

The 1990s emphasis on *lifestyle*[8] would help bring about alibi fashions. Subjectivity became a mobile celebration.[9] As Warren Susman (1979: 220) writes in another context, this historical period marked the displacement of the virtues of character in favor of more personality-based traits, a shift that transformed the body into an object of cultural capital. Truth, goodness and beauty became performative acts in a process of fashionable self-making rather than confirmations of an already existing subjectivity. On the beaches of Rio de Janeiro, this meant that the focus on fashion and body care increased with the arrival of liposuction and silicone prostheses. As Miriam Goldenberg points out, the individual became accountable for the policing of his or her youth, beauty and health. This attitude perceives ugliness as a choice, as the good-looking body is an investment (both temporal and economic) as well as a sign of personal success, as the popular phrase "There are no fat and ugly individuals, just lazy ones" suggests. And as would be expected, cotton Lycra shorts and skirts have replaced the *cangas* of yesteryear. As a result, beachwear is more suited to extensive aerobic activity, allowing the skin to breathe.

Vogue fashion journalist Erika Palomina confirms that a plurality of fashionable plots appear on today's Ipanema beach (*Vogue* 2002: 15).[10] The brand *Água Doce* narrates an earlier chronology in Brazilian beachwear. Inspired by the 1970s, one finds its crocheted brassieres; *batinhas* or short, light beach robes; and tie-dyed gear. The Zoomp brand appeals to elegant but elite sports fanatics. The stylists for the *Água de Coco* (*Coconut Water*) line allude to the calls of tropical wildlife. Young people who don the *Cia. Marítima* (Maritime Company) label display their support of multiculturalism with Che Guevara stamps on their bikinis. The designs of *Rosa Chá* bring to fore the images, colors, and songs of a well-known Carnival figure, Rosa Magalhães. "The Sea will roll," a popular Carnival song, and a remix of the Brazilian national anthem had blasted on its fashion runway. With state-of-the-art technology, designers with an eye on the beach incorporate flashes of memory and in the process create new fictions for their consumers. The *Vide Bula* line, for example, dramatizes a fictional history of five foreigners who discover Brazil and its many beauties, representing this aesthetic diversity with its use of cuts, shapes and prints.

New Tribes

On today's beaches in Rio de Janeiro, one finds a variety of styles. There are hermudas, *cangas*, one-piece swimsuits, all on a variety of bodies. Fat, thin, old, young, short, tall ... One need only walk along the Copacabana beach promenade in the morning to see this. After 11 p.m., however, call girls and transvestites overtake this space, congregating in front of hotels, on the lookout for tourists. In the morning, towards Ipanema Beach, we find the beach divided according to age, social status, aesthetic persuasions and gender. Before most have arrived, discreet and affluent retirees walk the eight kilometers of the beach, with no shrill colors or shine to their tennis shoes, bermudas and shirts. In the afternoon, the young and athletic take their turn burning calories and posing in aerodynamic Lycra fabrics. After exercise, some go on to shop, removing their shirts as they walk about.

Ipanema's Posto 9 is still a place where artists, intellectuals and *neo-hippies* of varied ages meet, with quite a few sporting audacious beachwear. In front of the elite Country Club, the very young members of the middle and upper classes parade by in the latest productions: high-heeled shoes, purses, and *cangas*, but nothing considered vulgar. At Barra da Tijuca a similar mapping of space occurs. Yuppies religiously tan on Pepê beach, amidst personal trainers and beautiful body worshippers. The Prainha gathers surfers whose boards, swimming fins, and shirts seem united for the preservation of nature.

When most think of Rio de Janeiro beach fashions, they imagine the southern part of Rio de Janeiro, with its Ipanema, Leblon, Copacabana and Recreio beaches. Here, the bikini represents a part of the whole, an almost naked synecdoche for Brazilian beauty. In the northern part of the city, one finds a big swimming pool that has taken the place of a polluted section of the beach. The people who go there are often subject to ironic humor on the *TV Globo* soap operas, which depict them as individuals with bad taste, wearing big straw hats with ribbons, Hollywood-style sunglasses, extremely high-heeled shoes and bikinis that fail to contain their voluminous shapes.

When looking at Rio de Janeiro through the lens of fashion, one inevitably finds a varied and fragmented city. Groups are formed out of their preferences for certain styles of clothing and accessories. And these predilections for certain foods, books and music come together in the Brazilian cultural imaginary, even as the media emphasizes the differences among tribes. During the first summers of the twenty-first century, Brazilian networks announce a new fashion for beach parties, recommending that the viewer take a bag filled with sophisticated clothes while on vacation. Bars, nightclubs and even multibrand stores hire DJs, put on shows, and serve beer and *prosecco* (an Italian wine like champagne). "The afternoon will be good, anything may happen" one Rio Show magazine announces. "We want Ipanema to be the great corridor to Carioca behavior and not a neighborhood crowded with banks and drugstores," states one of the enthusiasts of this fashionable programming.

The culture of Rio fixates on particular regions of the body to sculpt every season. In 2000 the most valorized region was the gluteus, intensively worked on with the help of localized exercises, massage and aesthetic surgery. The media considered this phenomenon a metaphor for the new millennium. No longer a taboo, the behinds became totems. Many commented on the gulf between this fetish and the concern for political, economic, and social life. Today, the new area of focus is the breast, which has led to larger brassiere models in magazines and specially enhanced bikini tops for the beach. Ruffled triangles nicknamed "little curtains" now share the scene with a variety of other tops that frame the craft of the silicone experts.

In effect, the beach fashions and especially the bikini have evolved alongside the Carioca spirit and their notions of a *tropicalized* sexuality. Because the city of Rio de Janeiro is perceived in Brazil as the continuous site of transformations in the cultural field, these influences are not imposed but rather developed there. It is as if the dynamics of dress emerged "from the waves of the sea," to remember the title of Jobim's music. And as she walks, the emblematic narrative about the tropical beauty of Ipanema comes to mind, a myth that has survived to represent the hospitable and lively ways of the *Carioca* people.

12

"Every girl had a fan which she kept always in motion":[1] Puerto Rican Women's Dress at a Time of Social and Cultural Transition

Dilia López-Gydosh and Marsha A. Dickson

In 1898 the island of Puerto Rico was an offspring of Spain and its language and customs. Having dominated Puerto Rican society for over 400 years, the presence of Spain was reflected through a paternalistic and patriarchal mode of thinking. As a result of this type of culture, the condition of Puerto Rican women at the end of the nineteenth century was one of subordination and inferior status. "The only career for the woman was matrimony. The culture of adornment was the bachelor degree for this career," María L. Campo Alange (1964: 26) writes of this period. But with the Spanish-American War of 1898, the influence of American culture in Puerto Rico brought meaningful changes in the roles and social status of Puerto Rican women at the turn of the twentieth century.[2] Improvements in education, industry, commerce and the recognition of divorce were very influential in modifying the role of Puerto Rican women. They took the necessary steps to unwrap themselves from seclusion and ignorance, emerging as independent and educated contributors to society and developing a voice that could not be ignored. The women of Puerto Rico became teachers and nurses, organized civic groups, and became involved in the suffragette movement.[3]

Clothing, as an important aspect of material culture, plays a symbolic role in the mediation of the relationship between people, nature, and the socio-cultural environment (Schwarz 1979: 31). Just as their American counterparts, Puerto Rican women's dress after 1898 reflects the wide variety of fashions that became more simple and practical as women's roles in society took them from the internal "home" sphere to an external "professional/work" sphere.[4] This chapter explores the manner in which Puerto Rican women's appearance and dress was affected by the economic, social, and cultural changes brought about by American sovereignty of the island at the end of the nineteenth century and for the first two decades of the twentieth century.[5]

Historical and Cultural Overview of Puerto Rico

Christopher Columbus encountered the island of Borinquén in 1493 during his second voyage to the New World. Columbus claimed the island for the Spanish crown by right of discovery and named it San Juan Bautista. After 1521, the capital came to be known as San Juan and the island as Puerto Rico. For the next 400 years following Columbus' "discovery," Puerto Rico was neglected under the control of the Spanish regime. It was under a cloud of disenchantment with the Spanish government that Puerto Ricans came to be involved in the Spanish-American War at the end of the nineteenth century. The bombing of the United States' ship *Maine* at port in Havana, Cuba, sparked a four-month war between Spain and the United States, which included an American invasion of Puerto Rico.[6]

The 1898 Spanish-American War concluded with the signing of The Treaty of Peace by both Spain and the United States in August of the same year. With this treaty, "Spain ceded to the United States the island of Puerto Rico and other islands now under Spanish sovereignty in the West Indies" (Fernández García 1923: 11). Puerto Rico went from 400 years of Spanish rule, to the commercial, political, and moral influence of its North American neighbor, the United States. In the opinion of Guy S. Métraux (1952: 62), the American plan for Puerto Rico was the following:

> The Americans, unhindered by rebellion and overt opposition, set themselves to the task of transforming Puerto Rico. They were persuaded that they had brought with them "the advantages and blessings of enlightened civilization" and were bound ultimately to give the Puerto Ricans the American way of life which implied of those methods that have resulted in the success of the American nation.

The Americans were received cordially and enthusiastically by Puerto Ricans who were overtly empathetic with their cause, thus allowing the United States immediately to put its plan into progress.[7] Over the years Puerto Rico has been transformed by contact with the United States (Fernández Mendez 1973: 605; Scarano 1993: 571–2, 596). An elected civilian government replaced military rule. Trade between the United States and Puerto Rico increased dramatically after 1898, with United States imports averaging $9 out of every $10 by 1914. The agricultural system of production changed "from the period of family-style haciendas to that of [United States owned] corporate land combines," with the production of sugar becoming the number one priority, and *la industria de la aguja* (the manufacturing of embroidered cotton textiles) and tobacco following

(Cripps Samoiloff 1984: 106; Scarano 1993: 585–95). Roads and railroads opened throughout the island connecting all the island's people (Cripps Samoiloff 1984: 111 and Fernández García 1923: 193). United States influence brought about the celebration of American holidays, the introduction of the eight-hour work day, trial by jury and the right to divorce. The latter was established in Puerto Rico in 1902, earlier than in other countries of Latin America (Cripps Samoiloff 1984: 126; Suárez Findlay 1999: 111–12).

English became the official language in the schools, which tripled in number. In 1903, the University of Puerto Rico was founded (Scarano 1993: 605, 609).[8] Taking into account the constant cross-cultural contact between Puerto Rico and the United States since 1898, potential for one or both of the cultures influencing the rate and direction of change as well as shaping specific cultural details was very probable (Harris 1987: 12).

Dress and appearance are aspects that can be influenced by cross-cultural contact. An understanding of the life and situation of Puerto Rican women during the nineteenth century and beginning of the twentieth provides context for examining how dress and appearance communicated the economic, social, and cultural changes resulting from American sovereignty over the island.

The Status and Appearance of Puerto Rican Women, 1895–1920

The End of the Spanish Regime in Puerto Rico

At the end of the nineteenth century, the world of the Puerto Rican women was the result of elements from the different cultures, *Tainos*, African, and Spanish, which have intermingled throughout the island's history (Christensen 1979: 53). These elements include religious beliefs, position or role in the family structure, and form of dress, to name a few. Spanish social customs prevailed on the island in the late 1890s. In Frederick Ober's (1899: 168) words, "scratch a Puerto Rican and you find a Spaniard underneath the skin, so the language and home customs of Spain prevail here . . ." Puerto Rican women of the higher and middle classes were considered Spaniards on the island. These women belonged to the commercial, professional, and planter classes, being reared in affluence and luxury. Several writers, including Americans and Spanish, at the end of the nineteenth century described the Puerto Rican women of the elite classes as:

> . . . sweet and amiable, faithful as wives, loving as sisters, sweethearts, and daughters, ornaments to any society in the world, tasteful in dress, tactful in conversation, graceful in deportment, and extremely elegant in their carriage. In truth, visitors from Old Spain have often remarked their resemblance to the beautiful *doncellas* of Cadiz, who indeed are world famous for their beauty, grace, and loveliness! (in Ober 1899: 174–5)[9]

In 1898, Ober would observe the following on his second visit to Puerto Rico:

> The type [of beauty] here is also that of Spain the mother country. Brunettes prevail and blondes are a rarity. The large eyes, black as night; the peachblow complexion; hair abundant, dark and glossy as a raven's wing; gracefully moulded, voluptuous form – these attributes of Spanish beauty have not changed during all the 300 years of Spanish domination. (Ober 1899: 173)

As with other Latin American societies, the lives of the Puerto Rican women of the elite classes were molded by ideals derived from the "old European legacies of patriarchy" resulting in their own subjugation to the male-dominated society (Jiménez de Wagenheim 1998: 251 and Acosta-Belén 1986: 3). The condition of women in Puerto Rico at the end of the nineteenth century was one of an inferior status. If the woman was unmarried, the social rule that "little children must be seen and not heard" also applied to them (Hamm 1899: 131). Another example was seen at the dinner table, where guests and males were placed in the seats considered most honorable, while the women were all grouped at less distinguished seats of the table (Dinwiddie 1899: 153). Margherita Hamm interpreted the relationship between men and women of the island in this way: "The men treat women with exquisite courtesy, both in speech and action. They foresee every want, and they bestow attention with tact and delicacy, but it is the master pleasing the slave, and not one human being treating his equal" (Hamm 1899: 99).

With this type of culture, the life of the Puerto Rican women of the middle and upper classes was essentially secluded and conducted inside the home. As a newspaper correspondent for *The Evening Post* during the months of August, September, and October 1898, Albert Robinson noted this seclusion by "the absence from the streets [cities and towns] and stores of ladies whose apparel and demeanor would indicate them as of well-to-do families" (Robinson 1899: 57). The seclusion of women of the elite classes was attributed to their Spanish heritage, education, and habits, as well as lethargy produced by the climate, where staying indoors was preferred over more physical activities.[10] By the end of the nineteenth century, the situation of the women of the island was being questioned by a few progressive minds (both male and female), who argued that their subjugation and confined conditions had a created a "deplorable state of ignorance" that could be improved with education (Jiménez de Wagenheim 1998: 252).

As well as being restrained in their social life, at the end of the nineteenth century, the educational level of women in Puerto Rico was described as "pitiably behind." An observer in 1898 recounted how 75 per cent of middle class women were illiterate; the higher classes had similar low levels of literacy. William Dinwiddie stated that "one never sees a book or a magazine in these [well-to-do] houses, though in two or three of the larger cities there are many literary men. Reading is not a strong point of the island population." This notion of a lack of reading is supported by Robinson who stated the "Porto

Rican generally are not a reading people." However, this generalization obscured the fact that some well-bred Puerto Rican women had a reading knowledge of French, and sometimes Italian. This knowledge was achieved through the home teachings of governesses or tutors (Hamm 1899: 131–2; Dinwiddie 1899: 153, Robinson 1899: 188; Bryan 1899: 383).

Besides their formal education with a governess or tutor, many Puerto Rican women displayed more informal achievements in the 1890s. Nearly every woman played an instrument and sang. Some painted and drew while others made lace, embroidered, or crocheted. Other activities Puerto Rican women excelled in were floriculture, fruit culture, herbaria, and cultivation of aquariums (Hamm 1899: 131). In addition, Dinwiddie described the well-to-do Puerto Rican woman as being far more assiduous in her interest in household economy than her sisters of other Spanish-speaking territories of North America.[11]

The "bourgeois spirit" that characterized England, France and the United States, had not yet fully developed in the Puerto Rican woman.[12] During the 1890s in Puerto Rico there was an obvious absence of the "grisette and shop-girl class, and of women professors, doctors, lawyers, dentists, typewrites and bookkeepers." Not only were women not employed in stores, but not until 1900 were there female typists on the island. As a consequence of the lack of "bourgeois spirit" within the general female population in Puerto Rico, positions such as nurses, invalid's companions, readers, preceptors, book agents, art critics, garden directors, and advisors in household economics were held by members of the religious sisterhood. (Hamm 1899: 138; Bryan 1899: 303).

Among Puerto Rican women, there had always been a great interest in dress and a great deal of money, when available, went into the purchasing of clothing (Cripps Samoiloff 1984: 173). From the seventeenth century on, information on women's fashion came to Puerto Rico in fashion journals and fashion plates that would trickle slowly from the European continent (Babín 1958: 145). Fashion was so important to Puerto Rican women that sometimes it overrode other social considerations. For example, when French fashion at the beginning of the eighteenth century dictated the low, round neckline, as seen on Madame de Maintenon in the 1711 portrait of *Louis XIV and his Family* by Nicolas de Largillière, the Catholic Church considered it too low for decent women. The Bishop of San Juan condemned their provocative dress "llevando las sayas tan sumamente cortas y los pechos tan descubiertos, que no sólo escandalizan sino que al mismo tiempo son causa de graves pecados" (with skirts so extremely short and bosoms so bare, that they are not only scandalous but also cause of grave sins).[13] Even with the threat of a monetary fine by the Bishop, the convenience of the neckline for the warm climate and its fashionability won over the women.[14]

Puerto Rican women's tastes and habits at the end of the nineteenth century, according to Hamm, were a combination of Spanish culture, French influences, and the tropical climate (Hamm 1899: 154). These fashion preferences were detected from the wide variety of items imported into the island in the 1890s, such as woolens, laces, embroideries, fans, perfumery, cosmetics, boots, shoes, linens, watches, jewelry, ribbons, umbrellas, parasols, and cotton goods (Hamm 1899: 152).

Dry-goods stores were a common sight in Puerto Rico in the last years (1895–8) of Spanish rule and the shopper could buy in the same store a yard of calico or a saddle, a *mantilla* (lace or silk headdress) or a *machete* (cane knife). Importing and exporting was big business in Puerto Rico, and there was more or less regular contact with ships from Spain, England, Cuba, Santo Domingo, St. Thomas, Martinique, Guadalupe, South America, and New York (Robinson 1899: 173).[15] A Spanish customs report from the 1890s accounting the goods that Puerto Rico imported from the United States listed the major items as cotton fabrics, yarn and thread, and paper products such as stationary and books. Puerto Rico also imported similar goods from other countries, as well as boots and shoes (mainly from Spain) and watches from other countries. In addition, they acquired from these nations (Spain, England, Cuba, Santo Domingo, and so forth) such goods as laces, embroideries, fans, perfume, cosmetics, linens, eyeglasses, jewelry, ribbons, umbrellas, and parasols (Hamm 1899: 151, 152). "Good" dress clothes tended to be higher priced than in the United States and woolen goods were quite limited. Additionally, it was less expensive to buy Spanish or French made shoes on the island than to buy United States-made shoes (Dinwiddie 1899: 66, 75; Robinson 1899: 169).

Robert Hill and Charles Morris described the Puerto Rican ladies of the higher classes at the close of the nineteenth century as petite in form, with small hands and feet, and dressed in what they characterized as Parisian styles although these styles were usually a year or two old by the time they reached Puerto Rico (Hill 1898: 66; Morris 1899: 205). Additionally, the hairstyles, jewelry, shoes and *los afeites* (adornments) also followed Paris and Madrid (Babín 1958: 147). Through the late nineteenth century, high society in Puerto Rico would follow the fashion trends of Paris and Madrid through such fashion journals as *El Salón de la Moda* or magazines for the "fairer sex" such as the *Guirnalda Puertorriqueña* (Santaliz 1985: 23; Jiménez de Wagenheim 1998: 251).[16]

Based on photographs of Puerto Rican women of the time, their fashionable appearance in the three years prior to the 1898 Spanish-American War and the ensuing United States takeover of the island was to an extent parallel to the fashionable appearance of United States women. The bell shape silhouette in vogue was supported by a pulled-up hairstyle, fitted or shirtwaist bodice, high stand/band collar, long full or narrow sleeves with shoulder puffs, belted narrow waistline, and a full "bell shape" skirt. These garments were embellished with lace bertha collars, pleating, embroidery, and flowers.[17] Within their "Western" manner of dress, the examination of these same photographs reveal certain aspects of Puerto Rican women's dress and appearance that could be constituted as particular to the island and its Spanish heritage when comparing to United States women's dress. These particular aspects of their dress included clothing ornamentation, shirtwaists, jewelry and accessories.

A type of surface embellishment seen in Puerto Rican women's dress at the end of the nineteenth century can be described as eyelet "lace" with ribbon trim. Eyelet cutwork is one of the simplest and most common ways of achieving a lacy look. It is produced by patterns of cut holes, which the edges are stitched to prevent unraveling, in a woven fabric creating a design (Kurella 1998: 22). In this particular case, the eyelet lace had a darker color ribbon woven through and it was used as trim for the skirt of a daywear ensemble.

Another aspect of the Puerto Rican ladies' dress was the "untucked" shirtwaist look. This was represented in two styles – tailored and loose fit. The tailored style was form fitted to the body and ended right above the hips. It was paired up with a matching skirt. The loose fit style did not define the body, took more fabric, ended at the hips or lower and it did not seem to be part of an ensemble. These styles of shirtwaists were observed in casual settings both outdoor and indoor. Because the climate in Puerto Rico is extremely warm and humid, it could be deduced that this "untucked" look was a way for the Puerto Rican women to adapt their manner of dress to the weather and to become more comfortable. This style would have increased the airflow under the women's garments alleviating the hot sticky feeling of closely fitted clothing against the body. This is supported by Hamm's (1899: 154) observation that the Puerto Rican women's mode of dress was influenced by the tropical climate. In addition, the tailored "untucked" look and the loose fit style were seen in pictures of Cuban and Philippine women respectively, countries with a tropical climate, during the same period of 1898.[18]

Other aspects of Puerto Rican women's appearance include jewelry and headwear. The women of the island tended to wear jewelry frequently and in a variety of quantities. Earrings, necklaces, brooches, bracelets, and finger rings were common items with Puerto Rican ladies. Often the jewelry was worn in multiple quantities or combinations. When it comes to headwear, unlike their American counterparts at the beginning of the period 1895–98, hats were not common to Puerto Rican women's dress. Hamm attributes the absence of hats to the Puerto Rican women's preference for the *mantilla*. The *mantilla* (lace headscarf), of Spanish descent, was commonly worn to church (Cripps Samoiloff 1984: 173). The wearing of *mantillas* explains the lack of hatwear adopted by Puerto Rican women and reflects an interest in the Spanish heritage of Puerto Rico.[19]

Lastly, Puerto Rican women carried a folding fan or a *porta-abanico* (long chain necklace with a folding fan) as part of their dress. Even though fans from time to time were considered fashionable items in the United States, they never became such a consistent identifying aspect of dress as with these Puerto Rican women. For these ladies, the folding fan was not just an item used to cool off from the heat; it became a fashionable accessory for their dress. The review of photographs showed the *porta-abanicos* on Puerto Rican women outdoors, indoors, in casual and formal social functions, as well as in photographs taken in studios. The way these *porta-abanicos* were worn gives the impression that they were considered another piece of jewelry or an adornment. The

Figure 12.1. Left: "Untucked" shirtwaist look, porta-abanico and eyelet "lace" with ribbon trim, circa 1898. Reprinted from W. S. Bryan, *Our Islands and Their People as Seen with Camera and Pencil* (St. Louis, 1899, p. 269). Right: Extremely wide flat brim hats trimmed with feathers and flowers, porta-abanico and eyelet "lace" with ribbon-trim, circa 1909–10. From *La moda en Puerto Rico, una mirada al pasado.* Museo de Arte de Ponce, Puerto Rico.

"necklaces" were of beads, pearls, chain link, or black double link material, and the women matched them with the outfit worn.

Puerto Rican women's dress and appearance while still under Spanish rule paralleled Western fashion with elements of Spanishness. How did their manner of dress reflect Puerto Rico's changing status from a Spanish to an American colony?

The "Splendid Little War"[20] and American Takeover

The position of Puerto Rican women was to shift in the early 1900s with the economic and social changes brought under United States rule. Gone were the days of illiteracy, ignorance, and seclusion typical of their lifestyle under the Spanish regime. Opportunities for education allowed Puerto Rican women to enter the teaching market. They also became nurses, organized civic groups, and became involved in the suffragette movement.[21]

During the first decades of the twentieth century the main concern of Puerto Rican women of the middle and upper classes was to achieve an education. Acquiring an education paved the way for women to participate in professional services, such as teaching and nursing, and clerical occupations, which would be the basis for their economic independence (Ribes Tovar 1972: 187; Pico Vidal 1980: 206). This desire for education was reflected in an increase in the number of schools and number of students in attendance on the island. In 1899, immediately after the United States takeover of Puerto Rico, there were 528 public schools with an attendance of 18,243. By 1914, the island's schools had multiplied to 3,000 with an attendance of 118,000 (Boyce 1914: 439).

The "soft rumbles" of an emerging feminist movement in the late nineteenth century did not take off until the beginning of the twentieth century due to a wider availability of education and professional jobs for the women of the middle and upper classes (Suárez Findlay 1999: 54; Pico Vidal 1980: 210). With their education in hand, not only were Puerto Rican women able to participate in the professional workforce, the "murmurs" of the 1890s bourgeois spirit became a full fledge "roar" with the creation of civic and women's organizations and the right to vote as a key fight in their new position as emancipated women in society. Through their involvement with women's organizations and civic groups, the women of Puerto Rico contributed to the American war effort during the First World War by making bandages and other work for the Red Cross in Puerto Rico (Clark 1975: 37). The feminist movement in Puerto Rico was composed of two factions: labor and professional. Both desired the improvement and equality of Puerto Rican women's lives both at home and work, but each spoke to a different level of society – working, and middle and upper class correspondingly.[22] Even though both factions desired the right to vote for women, it was the professional faction with its membership of middle and upper class Puerto Rican women, which made it its mission. In 1917, the first feminist organization was established under the name of Liga Femenina Puertorriqueña.[23]

Even though the first two decades of the twentieth century saw major improvements in the lives of Puerto Rican women, the first couple of years (1899–1900) after the United States became sovereign over Puerto Rico were characterized by economic and social instability. This period saw the decline of international commerce and the devaluation of the Spanish coin that reduced the wealth of many Puerto Ricans. In addition, merchants and plant owners of Spanish descent throughout the island became victims of a violent anti-Spanish movement known as *partidas sediciosas*. As a climax to this period, on 8 August 1999, Puerto Rico was hit by a very powerful and destructive hurricane, San Ciriaco, which completely demolished plantations, factories, and houses, leaving thousand of Puerto Ricans, including many of the well to do, in poverty and beggary (Bryan 1899: 382).

The takeover of Puerto Rico by the United States after the Spanish-American War of 1898 altered the importation of goods to the island. Puerto Rico began to trade less with Spain and more with the United States. For example, in 1896, 18 per cent of Puerto Rico's trade was with the United States, but with the Organic Act of 1901, the percentage rose to 71 per cent. This law guaranteed free trade between the United States and Puerto Rico. Thus, American merchandise entered the island and Puerto Rican merchandise was exported without payment of customs duties. After 15 years under the American government, Alpheous Verrill remarked on how the Americanization of the island could be seen in commerce, social life and manner of dress. The Puerto Ricans who adopted American ideas replaced aspects of Spanish life, still prevalent in places such as Cuba and other Spanish-American lands. The transformation was visible in the up-to-date stores stocked with American and European goods (Boyce 1899: 448; Verrill 1914: 11, 17).

In 1914, the dry goods stores of earlier times were being replaced by department stores, such as González Padín. In the shops and stores of Puerto Rico, a visitor could buy anything that could be found in a New York store and the prices were as low or lower than in the United States. Not only was American merchandise found in Puerto Rican stores – it could also be found in the American-owned stores such as Gillie & Woodward, that had opened retail locations on the island. When walking down the shopping arcade in San Juan, Verrill noted that "the large plate-glass windows of the stores in this section are filled with an attractive display of the latest... Parisian, Spanish, and American wearing apparel, musical instruments, furniture, kitchen utensils, curios and every article known to American stores" (Verrill 1914: 39, 20, 30, 40).

Women of the island could not only follow fashion through the wide variety of retailers, but also by perusing through weekly publications such as *El Carnaval, Gráfico* and *Puerto Rico Ilustrado*. These publications included information on the latest fashion, in the form of style features, fashion columns, advertisements and illustrations. In a particular style feature for a shirtwaist (or blouse) in the 15 November 1903 issue of *Los Domingos del Boletín*, the caption describing the blouse states "Publicamos hoy un precioso modelo de la blusa para señoras y señoritas, más popular en los Estados Unidos..." ("Today we publish a precious style for a woman's blouse that is all the rage in the United States."). Sometimes the fashion columns would include advice on how to adapt the featured mode to the Puerto Rican climate. Magazine advertisements included information about local and United States retailers. Some examples of local clothing retailers include *Los Muchachos, La Favorita, González Padín Co.* and Paris Bazaar. An example of an advertisement for a retailer in the United States was Bertha Gowns mail order. In many instances, the fashion illustrations featured in the weekly magazines would include the original English caption describing the styles.[24] Even with the noticeable move toward a more American culture and a less Spanish one, Verrill noted that the women of Puerto Rico were very much still attached to their fans. This aspect of Hispanic culture was also common to Cuba and other Latin American countries (Verrill 1914: 104).

Fashion in Puerto Rico at the beginning of the twentieth century varied across the major cities of the island. In San Juan, the capital, fashion was said to be more Spanish than in the southern city of Ponce, where a bigger French influence existed. In the western city of Mayagüez the beginnings of a local mode of dressing was making its mark (Santaliz 1985: 22). But by 1914 these differences may have become less evident. While traveling through Puerto Rico in that year, Verrill came in contact with all levels of the island's population, and came to the conclusion that the Porto Ricans have few local or unique habits and no national costume, and many of the interesting mannerisms and Spanish-American customs have been destroyed by the Americanisation of the island: . . . *mantillas* are no longer in evidence and even the beautiful silken shawls worn by the women of Havana, Central and South America, and San Domingo are scarcely ever seen on Porto Rican shoulders. (Verrill 1914: 104)

After the Spanish-American War of 1898, the mode of dress in Puerto Rico did not change dramatically until 1902, when the S-curve mono-bosom look made its appearance.[25] This fashion consisted of the popular "pompadour" hairstyle, very ornate shirtwaist with "pouter-pigeon blousing," long sleeves with bottom fullness, high stand collars, S-bend waistline, and a smooth over the hips skirt with flared fullness at the bottom. A modified version of the S-curve but without a mono-bosom followed around 1906. This style of fashion consisted of a softer waved and full hairstyle, bodice with all around fullness and high stand collar and long sleeves, natural small waistline, and either a full gored skirt or a stitched down pleated one. During 1898–1905, ornamentation (lace, pin-tucks, ruffles, and so forth) first appeared heavily but began to diminish with time.

Later during the time period of the S-curve-no mono-bosom (1906–11), the princess style dress made its appearance. This silhouette was based on one-piece garments with a full-length front panel and no waistband. Style features of the dress included lower necklines, long narrow sleeves, and gored full skirts or more A-line form-fitting skirts. As a continuation of the move toward a less full silhouette, the empire style came into fashion in Puerto Rico around 1911. With the narrower silhouette, the hairstyle became sleeker; it was waved and molded closer to the head. The empire silhouette was manifested through semifitted or fitted bodices or a shorter length, a higher waistline, and with skirts of the A-line look or the straight look. With the complementing lower necklines and kimono style sleeves, the empire look was one of modest embellishment. With the emergence of all these silhouettes, the use of hats increased. Even Verrill (1914: 17) noticed the fact that the "graceful *mantillas* have given way to outlandish . . . hats."

Even though the dress of the Puerto Rican women was losing some of its Spanish elements, such as the use of the *mantilla*, other Spanish elements from the end of the 1890s were still included in their dress. The eyelet "lace" with ribbon trim embellishment was seen in the daywear of Puerto Rican women in images from 1900, 1903, 1906, 1911 and 1912. The eyelet cutwork embellished necklines, princess seams, shoulders and skirts. Also, jewelry and the folding fan or *porta-abanico* seemed constantly present in the period between 1899 and 1917. Such a key item was the fan to the Puerto Rican women's dress, which a 1912 photograph featured with a mannequin "wearing" a *porta-abanico* as part of the dress it displayed.[26]

By the year 1917, the Puerto Rican woman had made great strides in carving a new position and role for herself in society. Comments or observations concerning the seclusion of the women of the middle and higher classes by visitors to the island were not to be found in their writings anymore. Puerto

Rican women had taken to the streets, armed with education and desire for emancipation, and their dress and appearance reflected that. What would the next three years reveal about this "new" woman and her manner of dress?

The Puerto Rican Woman as an American Citizen

By the end of the 1910s (1918–20), the 1917 "Jones Act" (which gave United States citizenship to all Puerto Ricans) was already a year old. In addition, the First World War, which had started in 1914, was coming to an end. In 1919, the first bill to grant suffrage to Puerto Rican women was introduced in the local legislature unsuccessfully (Clark 1975: 42).

As the United States maintained its presence in Puerto Rico, stability was seen in government and trade. As the women were given new opportunities (education, professional careers), they continued to follow the fashions in vogue in Europe, and in particular the United States. Verrill wrote about the "Americanization" of the island, noticing how the Puerto Ricans were adopting American ideas that were reflected in their social life, business, and clothing attire (Verrill 1914: 17). Examples of this "Americanization" of clothing can be seen in advertisements from weekly publications. If a Puerto Rican happened to be visiting New York City, she could stop at B. Altman & Co., where "Hallaran . . . todo lo necesario para el más completo aprovisionamiento de sus guardarropas" (You will find . . . all that is necessary to complete your wardrobe.") Or she could purchase a pair of "Keds: zapatos con suelas de gomas" ("Keds: shoes with rubber soles") from Pietrantoni & Sojo retailers, with locations in San Juan and Mayaguez.[27]

The professionalization of middle and upper class women was a reflection of the cultural changes that Puerto Rico had been experiencing since 1898, a date which connotes the saying "out with the old [Spaniard], in with the new [American]."[28] With important social, economical and cultural happenings at the end of the 1910s Maritza Díaz Alcaide in her article "Piernas al descubierto: Trayectoría de la moda en Puerto Rico" ("Exposed legs: a trajectory of fashion in Puerto Rico") states that "the Puerto Rican woman would go out to the street. She would become an important figure in production and because of this, gained the right to a more practical and simple dress . . . which she adores" (Díaz Alcaide 1993: 110). Characterized by the pear-shape silhouette and the tubular barrel, this manner of dress became the dominant look for the last four years of the period in question (1895–1920). These simple and uncluttered looks were completed with a short hairstyle and high crown hats worn low over the eyes, a baggy bodice, low necklines, simple sleeves, loose waistline, and plain mid-calf skirts. Trims were either non-existent or kept to a minimum and the amount of jewelry worn at one time was reduced. Yet, with all this simplicity and functionality to their dress, the Puerto Rican women's appearance still included the eyelet with ribbon trim embellishment and the folding fan or the *porta-abanico*.

Conclusion

When two cultures meet, as in the case of the American and Puerto Rican, changes in the original cultural structure may involve the reorganization of one or both groups within a short period of time.[29] Clothing serves as a transmitter of social signals and distinct components of a culture, and this is also valuable for understanding cultural change. The "Americanization" of the economy and education system (Scarano 1993: 582, 604) helped the women of Puerto Rico to leave the seclusion and ignorance of the 1890s and become "modern" women of the early twentieth century, while still maintaining an interest in fashion and their appearance.

The first two decades of the twentieth century saw a time of "great reforming fervor" in the United States. Some of these reforms, including American women's suffrage, influenced developments in Puerto Rico during the same period of time (Suárez Findlay 1999: 174). What was realized was a widening of both Puerto Rican and American women's spheres. With changes in their social roles came a variety of fashions reflecting their new positions within their worlds (Cosbey et al 2003: 103). For the Puerto Rican woman, having more access to clothing from the United States, as well as the cultural influence of the colonial status of the island, increased the opportunity for their manner of dress to reflect a more American style. In adopting aspects of American fashion, the women of Puerto Rico reinforced their new status in Puerto Rican society. Caroline R. Milbank, who defined the new American woman of the first two decades of the twentieth century as independent and professional, a view reflected in the United States fashion for the time, supports this notion. Simplicity became an element of American fashion and style. Fashion reflected this new professionalism, prioritizing the working woman's needs for simple, unrestrictive clothing that could be worn all day (Milbank 1989: 13, 46, 48).

Even though Puerto Rican women embraced a more "American style" of dress, they did not relinquish all of the Spanish aspects of their dress. They may have exchanged their *mantillas* for hats, but the constant sight of the folding fan or *porta-abanico* and the continuity of the eyelet "lace" with ribbon trim throughout the 25 years covered by this study tells us that these women did not want to leave their entire Spanish heritage behind. So dominant are these aspects of their clothing that Verrill reported how even with the obvious Americanization of the island, the women of Puerto Rico were very much still devoted to their fans (Verrill 1914: 104). In addition, the eyelet "lace" with ribbon trim seen from 1895 through 1920, is now a part of the ornamentation of contemporary Puerto Rican folkloric dance costumes and the Puerto Rican Barbie® Doll by Mattel®.[30] The dress and appearance of the Puerto Rican women throughout the cultural and social transitional period of 1895 to 1920 communicated their Old Spanish roots and at the same time expressed their New American identity as newly independent and educated women in society.

Part 4

Mediation and Consumption

13

Guayaberismo and the Essence of Cool

Marilyn Miller

Of all animals, man is the only one who has not been granted a natural suit.

Francisco Ichaso

Introduction: Anecdotal Evidence

Ladies and gentlemen, with your kind permission . . . Cubans, countrymen, it is now time for us to give a warm hand to our clientele in the courtyard, who have welcomed with the proverbial generosity and typical courtesy of the Criollos, so typically ours, typically Cuban as these palm trees which you see at the end of the salon and these *guayaberas* (with a black tie, eh?) Which is the typical dress of the elegant habanero, with that typical hospitality as always – our typitality, ho ho ho! – you have allowed us to present to you first our international clientele. Now, as is only fitting, it is the turn of the more familiar spectators of our social, political and cultural life. (Cabrera Infante 1971: 5)[1]

In the first scenes of Guillermo Cabrera Infante's dazzling *Tres Tristes Tigres* (*Three Trapped Tigers*), considered by many to be the quintessential novel of twentieth-century Cuban experience, the emcee at the Tropicana nightclub has just introduced the noteworthy international guests in the audience, and is now about to start with the hometown VIPs. In a club that is itself emblematic of the skillful exploitation of the island's natural beauties and talents in a prodigious display of Cuban showmanship, the guayabera *invests* its wearer with Cubanness. Though the Tropicana has passed through many changes since the timeframe of Cabrera Infante's novel, it continues to offer an unparalleled show of music, dance, and cabaret, despite shortages, embargoes and the absence of many of Cuba's finest performers. Remarkably, the garment of choice for many watching the show is still the *guayabera*, as Cuban as the palms that frame the marquee. Or is it? Nowadays, more *guayaberas* are worn outside Cuba than in it, in distinct corners of the world where devoted fans purchase the cool and comfortable shirts from private tailors, major retail chains like Banana Republic, and even over the Internet. But current market indicators aside, the *guayabera* is still a topic of fierce national pride in Cuba, one of the few cultural products that has signified and continues to signify *cubanía* despite the radical changes implied by the Cuban Revolution of 1959, and despite Cubans' individual or collective responses to those changes inside and outside the island.

The symbolic weight of the *guayabera* is surprising, since it's just a shirt, after all. Nor is it an especially elaborate, technically complex, or exaggerated garment that takes weeks or even months to weave, sew, or construct, as is the case with Latin American fashion markers ranging from an indigenous *huipil* woven in highland Guatemala, to a Carmen Miranda hat. In fact, one of its many attractions is its free-flowing cut, which drops straight from the bottom of the armholes and provides a roomy alternative to the strictures of the dress shirt. Designed with a straight hem to be worn untucked, the guayabera is beloved as a way to counteract the tropical heat or camouflage an expanding waistline.

But despite its seeming simplicity and innocuousness, the guayabera has arguably come to represent Latin American identity more thoroughly than any other garment in the American hemisphere. It has been a notoriously shifting or free-flowing signifier of social or political affiliation, with a profile that has moved from its incorporation as part of the military uniform of Cuban soldiers fighting for national independence at the end of the nineteenth century, to its condemnation by the upper-crust ladies of the Lyceum Lawn Club of Havana in the mid-twentieth century (for its "savage" qualities), to its rebirth in the twenty-first century as the garment of choice amongst "Generation Ñ" Cuban-Americans – male and female – dancing in the nightclubs of Miami.[2] At least, that's one trajectory of the guayabera, the one that takes it from the central Cuban provinces to Havana (where it was refashioned as the *guayahabana*) and then on to Little Havana in Miami.

This particular history vouches for the *guayabera*'s essential Cubanness, even in its many different settings, but leaves us with several interesting dilemmas. One of the most provocative of these conundrums is how the *guayabera* can so unequivocally denote *cubanía* when its wearers in the island and elsewhere differ so radically on how such a concept should be defined. Two anecdotes illustrate this extremely divergent enlistment of the *guayabera* in the defense of Cuban culture. The first took place in the summer of 1994, when Fidel Castro met with other Latin American leaders at the Fourth Annual Ibero-American Summit in Cartagena, Colombia. For the first time in over 30 years, Castro donned a *guayabera* over his military attire, at the request of conference organizers who had asked the visiting dignitaries to appear at certain events *enguayaberados*. The vision of Castro in the notorious shirt prompted a Cuban reporter to later note that "Some said you were half civilian, half military," to which Castro responded,

My guayabera and my uniform, however, are the Latin America of which Bolívar and Martí dreamt. As I said today to our friends, we are not worthy of speaking about Martí and Bolívar until we attain a united, politically and economically, integrated Latin America. This is my dream, and I believe, the dream of every progressive and revolutionary man of Latin America.[3]

While Castro's inclusion of the *guayabera* in an ideal vision of Latin American cooperation that included the names of nineteenth-century revolutionaries Simón Bolívar and José Martí may seem hyperbolic, it follows, to a certain extent, a conception of Cuban history in which the shirt has been tied to key liberation struggles. This association is perhaps most succinctly recalled in poet Raúl Ferrer's famous *décima* which includes the line "Porque Patria es un mambí de machete y guayabera," ("Because the fatherland is a Mambí wielding a machete and dressed in a guayabera").[4]

This image is particularly potent if we take into account Roberto Fernández Retamar's discussion of the *mambí* in his seminal *Caliban and other Essays*. "The most venerated word in Cuba – *mambí* – was disparagingly imposed on us by our enemies at the time of the war for independence, and we still have not totally deciphered its meaning," he points out. "It seems to have an African root, and in the mouth of the Spanish colonists implied the idea that all *independentistas* were so many black slaves – emancipated by that very war for independence – who of course constituted the bulk of the liberation army" (Fernández Retamar 1989: 16). Fernández Retamar notes that what the colonists intended as insult, revolutionary Cubans used with pride, thus remeaning the demeaning so that even today, the word has tremendous power in the Cuban imaginary. "To offend us they call us *mambí*, they call us black; but we reclaim as a mark of glory the honor of considering ourselves descendents of the *mambí*, descendants of the rebel, runaway, *independentista* black – never descendants of the slave holder" (Fernández Retamar 1989: 16). Within this refashioning of the term *mambí*, the guayabera takes on a special significance in its relationship to revolutionary struggles, an association that extends not only into the Castro years in Cuba, but also into socialist or left-leaning political struggles elsewhere in Latin America, to the extent that from the 1960s on, it was de *rigueur* to see other world leaders from the Americas appear at public events in a *guayabera*. Claiming during the Summit that the shirts are "truly comfortable and cool," the Cuban president again appeared in a *guayabera* in June 2002 alongside former United States President Jimmy Carter, who also wore the quintessential "Cuban" uniform. That meeting was the first visit of a United States President to the island since the Revolution, and the choice of both leaders to wear a *guayabera* was taken by many as a sign of their mutual desire to relax entrenched antagonisms and work towards improving relations between the two countries.

In a second anecdote, we see – paradoxically, it would seem – members of the Cuban "exile" community in the United States and elsewhere choosing a *guayabera* for their militant anti-Castro activities – or for just relaxing over a Cuban-style coffee or a game of dominoes. A seminal representative of this second *guayabera*-wearing camp is Pepe, the grocery store and bar owner in Roberto Fernández's (1997) ribald novel of Cuban American life, *Raining Backwards*. Pepe's store wall is adorned with a set of "before-and-after" photos of himself. In the first, he appears naked, covering his private parts; the caption reads, "Thank you, *gracias*! I came with one hand in front and one behind." The second picture, captioned "Only in America," shows "a radiant Pepe dressed in an embroidered *guayabera*, with mother-of-pearl buttons, and white linen pants, posing next to his Monte Carlo parked in front of his store" (Fernández 1997: 161). Here, the *guayabera* is the shining uniform of an "authentic" Cubanness that has only been recognized, harbored, and allowed to flourish *outside* Cuba, in a geographically nearby but politically distant United States. The implication is that only after his United States makeover was Pepe able to purchase or put on the coveted shirt, whereas in Cuba he didn't even have the shirt on his back.[5]

The contradictions encapsulated in such anecdotes threaten to erase or render neutral the political weight of the *guayabera* in the identification of its wearers with an essential *cubanía*. But even if we put aside the hotly debated issue of *cubanidad* and the relationship of the *guayabera* to its sometimes diametrically opposed appropriations, the fact remains that the *guayabera* is now worn in so many different parts of the planet, by so many different kinds of people, that its Cuban character is at the same time repeatedly appropriated and questioned by non-Cubans. The shirt has appeared and continues to reappear as the garment of choice in places as disparate and disconnected from contemporary Cuba as the Maya towns of the Yucatán, the fashion catwalks of Paris and Milan, and the barrios of East Los Angeles. In all these spaces, the shirt flirts with various and even mutually exclusive forms of identification, sometimes that of the landowner or *hacendado*, of the laborer or freedom fighter, of the *mestizo* official or functionary, of the ethnic "other," the world traveler, or the fiercely nationalistic Cuban, Dominican, Colombian, Puerto Rican or Nuyorican, Venezuelan, or United States Latino or Latina. Clearly, the *guayabera* plays a surprisingly important role in the literary and cultural histories of both Latin America and the United States, where it is frequently employed by writers (both in their texts and in their attire) to portray national or regional norms, as in Cabrera Infante's previously mentioned portrait of the Tropicana, Fernández' satire of Cuban America, or when Colombian novelist Gabriel García Márquez, considered by many to be the author most representative of Latin American literature for an international reading public, wore one in 1982 to accept the Nobel Prize for Literature.

All this suggests an irresoluble dilemma in terms of what a *guayabera* means or signifies in the twenty-first century. Its popularity is growing rapidly at an international level, even though it has been scorned by the younger populations in the countries most associated with its use, particularly Cuba. There's no denying its staying power in the Spanish American fashion imaginary for at least a century, despite intermittent declarations of its status as *pasada de moda*. And while the shirt's basic contours have changed very little, except to incorporate worldwide trends in fabric choices and assembly practices, the myriad appropriations of the quintessentially "Cuban" *guayabera* constitute, I believe, a particularly convincing example of how "national" or "local" cultural phenomena in Latin America often reveal complex negotiations and movements across national borders, social classes, terrains of cultural identity, languages, generations, and the machinations of history. Such movements ultimately prove just how susceptible or suspicious the concept of local cultural "autonomy" can be in the Americas.

In Search of Lost Origins

A first step away from the anecdotal towards an archeology or material history of the *guayabera* might be to find a satisfying definition, which includes information as to its origins, etymology, and historic usage. Ana López has provided the following thumbnail sketch in the *Encyclopedia of Contemporary Latin American and Caribbean Cultures*:

> Amply-cut, lightweight cotton shirt, with front pockets, vertical pleating and fancy embroidering worn untucked by men. Its origins are uncertain, but known to be in Cuba, where a wealthy *hacendado* fell in love with his wife's lightweight cotton fabric called *batista* (batiste) and asked her to make him a shirt with multiple pockets. His workers also liked it and copied the style; they called it the yayabera, after the nearby Yayabo river. The named turned into *guayabera* for the *guayaba* or guava trees, where workers sat for lunch to avoid the midday sun. Once worn only by *campesinos* – for various occasions that required dressing up, from playing a game of dominoes to attending church on Sundays – the *guayabera* has again become chic, not only in the Caribbean and Central America, but in the USA as well. The June 1999 issue of the magazine *Cigar Aficionado*, dubbed it the "historical apparel piece of Cuba". (Balderston et al. 2000: 688)

Other sources dispute this definition, suggesting that the garment arrived in Cuba worn by Philippine workers; thus the early collarless version of the shirt, known in Mexico and other countries along the Caribbean rim as the *filipina*. While *guayaberas* are still commonly worn in the Philippines, it is now perhaps impossible to ascertain whether the shirts became popular there as a result of the Spanish presence and shipping trade with the islands, or if Philippine tailors had an early influence on the development of the garment later associated with the Caribbean. As Arturo Chang notes, histories of the *guayabera* have been transmitted orally for the most part, allowing for embellishments and adornments along the way, and making a definitive account of origins elusive. Even within Cuba, the origins of the *guayabera* are variously traced back to the eighteenth, nineteenth, or twentieth centuries, to Spanish tailors who came from Seville, Granada, or the Canary Islands, or to the Chinese who brought in thousands of laborers when slavery was abolished in the late 1800s.

There is also little documentation explaining how *guayaberas* circulated throughout the circum-Caribbean area to become so ubiquitous by the middle of the twentieth century. In Veracruz, Mexico, the long-sleeved *guayabera* is an essential part of the costume of the *jarocho* dancer, and local legend has it that the *jarocho* inherited it from black slaves who arrived in the region, probably from Cuba (see Carrillo Vasquez). This would suggest, of course, that the *guayabera* was already being worn by many agricultural workers in the last quarter of the nineteenth century, before slavery was abolished in Cuba in 1886. However, Juan Carlos Rodríguez, a reporter for a newspaper in Mérida, Mexico, wrote in a 1995 article that the word "guayabera" appears for the first time in a Cuban dictionary in 1921, where it is described as a man's shirt, decorated with pleats, and worn untucked, without a jacket, typical of the Cuban *campesino*. While further investigation shows that Rodríguez was wrong about the first dictionary entry, he may have been right about this as the first documented reference to "guayabera" as a certain kind of shirt. Argelio Santiestaban, in his collection of Cuban popular speech from 1985, also asserts that the *guayabera* could not have existed for more than a century, since there is no known mention of it in earlier sources (Santiestaban 1985: 246).

Indeed, the reigning authority on such usage, *Pichardo's Diccionario provincial casi razonado de vozes y frases cubanas*, published in four editions from 1836 to 1875, includes the word *guayabera* only in the last of these editions, but *not* to mean a special kind of shirt. For Pichardo, *guayabero/a* is first "the person or thing that is native to or from the town of Santi-Espíritu, for the abundance of the guayabito plant in the region," and second, "the tricky person, disposed to telling lies of no great consequence." But as Rodríguez notes, fashion has a strong semantic content that is not always recorded in official sources, and the *guayabera* is an exemplary case in point. "The guayabera has come to express nonchalance and happiness, rural simplicity and a festive spirit. It has survived for its obvious advantages: comfort, freshness, simplicity and economy. If it didn't have a nationalist meaning in the moment it appeared; later it has taken on this meaning," he explains.

Various political leaders – former presidents Carlos Prío in Cuba (1948–52) and Luis Echeverría Álvarez in Mexico (1970–6), the late farmworker activist Cesar Chavez in California, and presidents Hugo Chávez in Venezuela and Vicente Fox in Mexico, for example – have all conducted much of their most important national and international business dressed in a *guayabera*.[6] In most of these cases, the *guayabera* has been read as an indicator of a commitment to local concerns and a populist or socialist politics. In this way, the breezy shirts call attention to their wearers' roles as mediators between economic classes, between local and global economies, between mass production and custom preparation, between national and transnational ideologies, and between negotiations of cultural difference and belonging. Fernando Chavez, son of the famous farmworker organizer, hopes that when new generations of Latino and non-Latino children in the United States ask "Who is the guy in the guayabera shirt?" they will be told Chavez was "just a man who dedicated his life to making everyone else's better."[7]

This strong identification of the Mexican-American community with the *guayabera* signals the extent to which the shirt has been an inveterate border crosser, showing up not just in Havana and Mexico City, but in Little Havana and New Mexico as well. Along the Pacific as well as along the Atlantic, the *guayabera* often marks the retention and defense of cultural elements from the home country, including dress. In the classic Mexican film *Primero soy mexicano* (*I am a Mexican First and Foremost*), from 1950, a *pocho*, or Mexican immigrant in California, sings that while he may have learned to eat hotcakes and to say hello without shaking hands, his attire will still mark him as a Mexican:

> Ancho charro y no texano
> Guayabera y no chamarra;
> La moda a mi no me agrada
> ¡Primero soy mexicano!

> A wide charro's sombrero and not a cowboy hat
> A guayabera and not a dress shirt
> Fashion means nothing to me
> I am a Mexican first and foremost!

Not only does the "Mexicanness" of the *guayabera* go unquestioned in this declaration, but the shirt is marked as unfashionable, a reputation that, as we have seen, will be turned inside out in the following decades in yet another re-dressing of this versatile garment.

Despite local and national appropriations of the *guayabera* like the *pocho's*, many fans insist it is undeniably and irrevocably Cuban. In an article titled "Porque la Guayabera es Puramente Cubana" ("Why the Guayabera is Purely Cuban"), Ruben Díaz-Abreu sets out to prove that the *guayabera* originated in Cuba, the "Pearl of the Antilles" (alluded to, perhaps, in a kind of fashion metaphor, in the mother-of-pearl buttons that adorn Pepe's *guayabera*). His version recounts an often-repeated story of the arrival in Sancti Spíritus of José Pérez Rodríguez and his wife Encarnación. He even includes the conversation that took place between "Joselillo" and his wife – right down to the Andalusian idiomatic expressions – when he asks her to sew him a shirt from a lightweight fabric that has just arrived from Spain, with pockets for his tobacco and other knickknacks. Soon, his tale continues, the *guajiros* or Cuban campesinos saw the practicality of the garment and began to use the shirt as well. And because either a) the town lies along the Yayabo River, or b) these *guajiros* used to fill up their pockets with *guayabas* (guavas), the pleated, pocketed, cool, and comfortable shirt became known as a *yayabera* or (perhaps later) a guayabera. According to Díaz-Abreu, this history is documented in several *décimas*, songs in verse which commemorate local history, including this one:

> ¡Oh guayabera! Camisa de alegre botonadura. Cuatro bosillos, frescura, de caña brava y de brisa. Fuiste guerra mambisa con más de un botón sangriento cuando el heroico alzamiento, y por eso la Bandera tiene algo de guayabera que viste al galán del viento.

> [Oh guayabera! Shirt of festive buttons. Four pockets, the coolness of the sugar cane and the breeze. You were a *mambi* fighter with more than one button bloodied during the heroic fight, and that's why the Flag seems like a guayabera that clothes the hero of the wind.]

Although this highly romantic *décima* does not connect the shirt to a specific birthplace, it does link it to several other keywords in the Cuban national imaginary: sugarcane, *mambis*, the flag. In a text delivered during the First Provincial Symposium on the Culture of Sancti Spíritus in 1982, Esbértido Rosendi Cancio also characterized the shirt "amidst our most national elements" such as the flag, flower, tree, and national anthem.[8] He urged listeners that the "elegant, pure, simple and *cubanísima* guayabera" should be regarded as a motive for pride and admiration, a garment that has appeared the world over, leaving "in the most diverse sections of the planet a note of the happiness that is an inseparable element of the Cuban character." Nonetheless, Rosendi Cancio noted that "what we can be sure of is that it is not the patrimony of anyone in particular, but the product of a long process of adaptation in which climate, tradition, and economic and sociopolitical situations intervene." In 1955, the mayor of Sancti Spíritus had even decreed the first of July as "Guayabera Day," signaling the extent to which the humble shirt had come to stand for local civic pride.

Rosendi Cancio's suggestion that "an interesting aspect for another study would be the possible interdependence that exists between our garment and others which are used in places like Panama and Mexico," hints, nonetheless, at the enormous trajectory the *guayabera* would have outside the island, becoming to some extent the uniform of Caribbeanness and/or Latin Americanness in all the countries along the Caribbean (Spanish-speaking or not), in Central America, in Mexico, and finally in the United States. The *guayabera*'s growing fame was not only a motive for pride for mid-century Cubans, however. It was also the subject of an extended and heated debate in Havana on appropriate standards for male dress, questions imbedded in concerns with class, democratizing influences in the island, and Cuba's reputation within an accelerating tourist market.

Use and Abuse of the *Guayabera*

On four Thursdays in August of 1948, the members of the Lyceum Lawn Tennis Club of Havana heard four different speakers present their views on the growing popularity of the *guayabera* in Cuba, a "problem" so widespread and accelerated that the term "guayaberismo" emerged as a label for the alarming phenomenon. Rafael Suárez Solís, the first of the four speakers, titled his talk "El guayaberismo," and his intonations, along with the comments of the three other presenters, were collected and printed together in a book titled *Uso and Abuso de la Guayabera* (*Use and Abuse of the Guayabera*) later that same year. At the beginning of this curious document, the reader is advised that it was at this very moment in the middle of the twentieth century that "the guayabera became more a subject of conversation than of dress."

In his talk, Suárez Solís expressed his dismay at the wholesale adoption of the shirt at all hours of the day and evening by rich and poor alike, and he advocated for a "dividing line" of 6 p.m., before which it was appropriate to appear in a *guayabera*, but after which it was uncivilized and in bad taste. Suárez Solís didn't dispute the shirt's association with Cuba's hard-won independence, but he cautioned, "When we remember that the liberators used the guayabera as a military uniform, we can respond as well that they ate roots and wild animals, because heroism and duty submit us to any number of bothersome elements" (Suárez Solís et al. 1968: 11). No one can respectably attend the theatre, appreciate a sophisticated menu, an intelligent conversation, or even the smile of a discreet woman, dressed in a *guayabera*, he argued (Suárez Solís et al. 1948: 15), warning that civility and good taste should not be sacrificed to comfort.

The second speaker, Isabel Fernández de Amado Blanco, similarly shuddered when confronted by the "grave sin" the *guayaberistas* had committed by converting all of Havana "into an immense warehouse of *guayaberas* that threaten to displace any other style of manly dress" (36). But she showed little concern that such a practice would spread outside the island. The two motors for influencing fashion, she pointed out, were first, the potential for creating sexual attraction and second, economic demand. The *guayabera* couldn't be considered a forerunner in either category, Fernández (erroneously) concluded.

In the third talk, presenter Francisco Ichaso drew a comparison between Havana and Miami. Ichaso maintained the "vulgarity" of the clothing in Miami, and considered the sad state of affairs in Havana a result of Miami's pernicious influence on the island. "Miami is a city at the service of a beach. Havana is a city at the service of civilization," he admonished (Suárez Solís et al. 1948: 63). Ichaso's talk also demonstrated the degree to which a humble shirt could stimulate reflection about national identity at a number of levels, pointing to the "inevitable resonance" that such "negligence" could have for social, ethical, aesthetic, and even civic standards (Suárez Solís et al. 1948: 63). "The guayabera is the minor concern. What's worse is the *guayaberismo*, that is, the attitudes, habits, states of conscience, even the ideas which this systematic use or abuse of the garment produces" (63). Concerned that the country might develop overnight into a "guayabera republic," Ichaso maintained that the *guayabera* was fine for the *guajiros* in the countryside, but an imminent and "carnivalesque" danger in the city.

> Do you know what this would signify? Simply that we renounce civilization and the culture to which we have always belonged and which we have chosen, in order to create in the future art, literature and politics that are exclusively guayaberistic. Or what amounts to the same: art, literature and politics without universal aims, lacking in rigor, bearing the seal of laziness, backwardness, not amounting to anything. (Suárez Solís et al. 1948: 64)

Even though this was 1948, in his conclusion Ichaso appealed directly to the classic nineteenth-century Latin American obsession with proving it was a civilized, rather than barbaric territory. He equates civility with maintaining the stifling attire of a shirt (buttoned at the neck and tucked in), coat, and tie, even though the *guayabera* might be infinitely cooler and more comfortable. "There are occasions," he determined, "in which there's no choice left but to sweat out the privilege of not being savages" (Suárez Solís et al. 1948: 72). At least for the members and friends of the Lyceum Lawn Tennis Club, *cool* and casual had not yet become synonyms in the lexicon of fashion, nor was there a consensus that the *guayabera* should represent Cuban style, ingenuity or ease in an international context.

Herminia del Portal de Novás Calvo, the last speaker, was the only respondent to seriously consider the admittedly cloudy origins of the tendentious garment. Del Portal remarked that it was undoubtedly the landed class in the region of Trinidad and Sancti Spíritus that first paraded in *guayaberas* (Suárez Solís et al. 1948: 89), since its fancy pleating and pearl buttons would make it impractical for laborers. Having performed this rescue of its class origins, she adopts a more mild position toward the shirt, noting that for better or for worse, the *guayabera* has become "the only typically Cuban garment, rooted in the history and tradition of the best part of our people" (Suárez Solís et al. 1948: 96). Besides, she consoled her audience, "this guayabera style which has devolved into 'guayaberismo,' according to Suárez Solís, won't last long. It won't last because nothing lasts in Cuba . . . So the guayabera will go out of style, no matter how cool, economical, or historical it might be" (Suárez Solís et al. 1948: 98). Time would pass, and eventually, not even *guajiros* would wear the shirt, del Portal predicted, but perhaps "some pious museum will display the guayabera, pleated with history" (Suárez Solís et al. 1948: 100). Along with her colleagues, she enormously underestimated the staying power and fashion moxie the *guayabera* would demonstrate in the ensuing years.

This series of talks on the increase of *guayaberismo* produced such a stir that various newspaper and magazine editors also entered the fray, including the editor of *Bohemia*, who commissioned Dr. Raúl Gutiérrez, "Director del

Departmento de 'Surveys'," to conduct a survey throughout greater Havana that would assess the "social problem" in all its varied aspects. The results, printed on 5 September 1948, were situated in a context that mentioned the "alert ladies of the Lyceum" as well as intellectuals, writers, news directors and publishers, but which also drew on responses from Cubans across a wide spectrum of professions and presumably, social classes. The survey showed that 80 percent of all men interviewed used the shirt, regardless of age. Of these, 61 percent cited "coolness" as a reason for adopting the *guayabera*, and another 48 percent mentioned *comodidad* or comfort. Another 85 percent reported they wore a *guayabera* because it was more economical than traditional attire. Only 0.5 percent of respondents chose the *guayabera* "por moda" or for its fashionability. *Bohemia* also interviewed women in greater Havana, in order to answer the equally pressing question, "Do women like to see men dressed in a guayabera?" Although the answers varied according to age, most women answered in the affirmative, with only 15 percent opposed to men wearing *guayaberas* in general. Despite the signals of alarm that had been voiced in the Lyceum lectures, *Bohemia* concluded that "men use the guayabera because it's cool, comfortable and Cuban, and with its use, they please women who for the most part enjoy seeing a man so dressed" (Suárez Solís et al. 1948: 71).

The influential *Diario de la Marina* offered another forum in which opinions alternately scourged and defended the *guayabera*. In a letter to the editor from October 1949, Ramón Rivero objected to a campaign in the newspaper to combat the use of the *guayabera* because it was inappropriate and "anti-aesthetic," since it was country-wear. "I don't understand why you intellectuals see in the guayabera so much ugliness and ignobility, as it's a garment of elegant and discreet lines, when it's worn well." "Precisely because the guayabera is a *campesina* creation, we should use it with pride, as a glorification of our blessed Cuban land, and impose it as a style in other countries, whose customs, good or bad, we insist on copying," Rivero argued (Gutiérrez 1948: 13).

Rarely has a mere shirt generated such sustained controversy, and amongst the writers and pundits who responded from a variety of positions, there was a consensus that the significance of the *guayabera* went well beyond considerations of function or fashionability. In September 1949, university professor Filiberto Rodríguez Angulo published an article in *Carteles* titled "La guayabera no es un producto de la moda" ("The guayabera is not a product of fashion"). The professor argued that its growth in popularity was a function of the need for comfort and economy, rather than the exigencies of fashion – and thus the *guayabera* should be viewed as a clear sign of progress, rather than an index of backwardness (Gutiérrez 1948: 73).

Amazingly, the momentous events of the late 1950s, and the ultimate triumph of the Castro regime in 1959 did not silence discussions of the *guayabera* and its connection to national culture. It was in fact due to its murky class background and association with populist expression that the *guayabera* became *the* everyday professional garment of government officials charged with implementing the policies and reforms of the revolutionary government. For these functionaries, the *guayabera* embodied the new ideals of *compañerismo* and classless cooperation. In 1961, the well-known writer Nicolás Guillén, who by this time was famous as Cuba's National Poet, voiced his own opinions in a short and characteristically pithy piece in *Trabajo*. Responding to a Dutch visitor's query as to whether the *guayabera* was Cuba's national dress, Guillén responded that while local politics may have undergone a thorough transformation, the *guayabera* had been a constant indicator of Cuban culture and customs since the beginning of the twentieth century. "We've created our own form, a way of dressing 'a la cubana,' as valid as the rumba in dance," he noted (Gullén 1961: 86). Guillén indeed alludes to the "difficult days" of the *guayabera* in the late 1940s, when the members of the Lyceum Lawn Tennis Club, and even President Carlos Prío himself, prohibited its use during certain hours and in specific spaces. But while former governments and protocols had toppled, the simple shirt had triumphed, proving once again that its inimitable freshness, comfort and *cool* superceded the instabilities and volatilities of wide-scale political change.

Border *Bordados*

As Cubans in the island continued to take a stand for or against the *guayabera* and its relation to national identity, manufacturers elsewhere had caught on to its possibilities as a garment that combined creature comforts and style. *Esquire's Encyclopedia of Twentieth Century Men's Fashions* notes that the Philadelphia shirtmaker John Wanamaker had introduced a *guayabera* in 1936 that was advertised as "an authentic copy of the garment worn by sugar planters in Cuba" (obviously revising historical accounts that associated the shirt with the field laborers, rather than the planters). This acknowledgment of the soaring popularity of and market for the shirts was the result of at least two factors: an increase in United States tourism in Cuba, where visitors discovered the comfort and practicality of the garment, and the growing population of Cubans living in Florida and other parts of the United States where the shirt also made good fashion sense. The North American version was made of high-quality linen in light colors and dark blue, dark brown, and yellow. Wanamaker sold the shirts for $10, and they were so popular, he had to expand the line to include matching and contrasting trousers cut from the same fabric. His *guayabera* "maintained its popularity and was seen in many different fabrics and patterns throughout the decade." It would be updated in the late 1960s "with the addition of front and back panels and buttoned patch pockets," and sewn in the 1960s and 1970s on polyester-cotton blends (226).

Wanamaker, other United States manufacturers, and shirtmakers in Cuba, Mexico, and other parts of Latin America were soon competing for customers in a transnational market. Although the exotic-sounding *guayabera* remained the most common name, the same garment became popular in the English Caribbean islands and British Guyana as a "shirtjacket" or just "shirtjac." The *guayabera* also found an eager market in countries throughout the Caribbean basin, particularly along the Gulf Coast of Mexico and in the torrid Yucatan Peninsula, where locals pride themselves on producing, if not inventing, the best *guayaberas* in the world, often referred to there as Mexican wedding shirts. Articles in Yucatecan newspapers from the 1960s, 1970s, and 1980s, and private interviews conducted more recently with small manufacturers and retailers in Merida, recall the rise and subsequent demise of the *guayabera* throughout Mexico. During the apogee of local production in the 1970s (due in large part to the shirt's popularization by then President Luis Echeverría), more than 200 workshops were dedicated to their production in Mérida alone, with the shirts being shipped throughout the country and exported to Santo Domingo, Miami, New Orleans, and other markets.

One of the most famous of these producers was Pedro Cab, whose indigenous last name is a clue that in the Yucatan, the *guayabera* would often be enhanced and enriched with embroidery and other elements borrowed from the *huipil*, the traditional blouse of Indian women in the region. In fact, another famous tailor with an indigenous surname, Jorge Alberto Pech, invented the hybrid *guayahuipil*, a women's garment that featured "counted-thread" Mayan embroidery instead of the typical pleats, thus taking advantage of the skills of employees who specialized in the embroidery of the traditional Indian garments (Ramírez Aznar). The *guayahuipil* soon gained such popularity that Pech developed versions for men, including austere models in gray and white, embroidered with Maya motifs. He presented these shirts to Presidents Luis Echeverría and José López Portillo y Pacheco (1976–82), who not only wore them with obvious pride, but in fact promoted the garment in Mexico and beyond. It's possible that Echeverría, who insisted on appearing in his Yucatecan *guayaberas* even in high-level government meetings and international tours, is the figure most directly responsible for the shirt's widespread adoption throughout Latin America. Journalist Luis A. Ramírez Aznar recalls that in an international convention of 350 UPI reporters that took place during his presidency, Echeverría presented each attendee with a commemorative *guayabera*.

While Pech was known for his *guayahuipiles* (and later *minihuipiles* and *maxihuipiles*), Cab's *guayaberas* were famous for their outstanding workmanship and *alforza fina*, or fine pleating. According to Pedro Cab's daughter-in-law Marta Arrazate, who still works in the Cab *guayabera* store in Veracruz (Guayaberas Cab maintains a solid clientele base in Mérida and Mexico City as well), Mexicans acknowledge the garment's roots in Cuba, but also proudly point out adaptations and innovations by Yucatecan artisans. In the early years of production in the late 1930s and 1940s, Mexican *guayaberas* were usually cut from high-quality linen and sometimes with silver- or gold-plated buttons known as *bolitas*. According to Arrazate, tightly woven linen was preferred because it was resistant to the spines of the henequen agave, which was cultivated on huge expanses of land in the region during the late eighteenth and early nineteenth centuries, usually by Mayan peons who worked in conditions approximating slavery.[9] Cab's *guayaberas* were popular, however, with a much broader audience than Merida's henequen growers. On the wall of her store, Arrazate still displays two letters received from Washington DC in May of 1956, one from John Foster Dulles, then Secretary of State, and the other, from President Dwight Eisenhower. Both praise the quality, comfort, and style of the *guayaberas* produced in Cab's workshop.

The massification of clothing production in Asia in the 1970s and 1980s produced a marked drop in demand in the Yucatan for the locally produced *guayabera*, as most younger men preferred to purchase the more trendy styles of *ropa casual*, including t-shirts and other sport shirts. News articles from the period lament this usurpation of the *guayabera*, their authors worrying that the typically "Yucatecan" garment would be forgotten. But as was the case in Cuba, the *guayabera* wasn't necessarily abandoned, it was just reappropriated by a different kind of customer. In a situation reminiscent of changes in the shirt's fortunes in Cuba, most Yucatecan *guayaberas* are now purchased by tourists from other states and by non-Mexicans. Men and women buy them for their comfort value, but also because they provide a cool and hip alternative for an evening at a cocktail party or nightclub – or even for a wedding, thus proving that the *guayaberismo* so feared by Cuban talking heads in the 1950s had not disappeared, but rather changed places and faces, and perhaps a few features as well.

Neotribal Negotiations

Alison Lurie has suggested that "When persons of foreign origin or ancestry deliberately adopt native dress, they tend to wear outmoded styles, those that they or their forefathers wore when they left the homeland" (Lurie 1981: 93). The last section of this chapter considers the *guayabera's* popularity and significance outside Latin America, especially as the uniform of Cubans, Dominicans, Puerto Ricans, Mexicans, and all these groups' children and grandchildren living in the United States. I want to argue that while there is once again an enormous range of meanings attached to the garment, in most of these appropriations, personal identity as tied to perceived ethnocultural affiliation is the key issue. The tremendous power of the *guayabera* to signify, so threatening to the Lyceum speakers in the middle of the twentieth century, is both expanded and dissipated in the vast marketplace of signs it occupies at the beginning of the twenty-first. As Caroline Evans (2000: 96) has noted,

> Now the fashioned garment circulates in a contemporary economy as part of a network of signs, of which the actual garment is but one. From its existence primarily as an object, the fashion commodity has evolved into a mutant form with the capacity to

insert itself into a wider network of signs, operating simultaneously in many registers. Whereas it used to exist as, for example, a dress, which preceded its single representation in the form of an advertisement or fashion photograph, it is now frequently disembodied and deterritorialised. As such, it can proliferate in many more forms, within a larger network of relations: as image, as cultural capital, as consumer goods, as fetish . . .

The insertion of the *guayabera* in this new register, which may reappropriate it as a costume, does not, however, do away with its connections to Cuba, the Caribbean, or Latin America. The *guayabera's* "deterritorialization" signifies a reterritorialization of the United States by members of a wide range of ethnic and cultural groups who use it to add the Latin back to their (Latin) American identity.

In Oscar Hijuelos' semi-autobiographical novel *The Mambo Kings Play Songs of Love* (1986), a child raised in the United States reflects on the way his Cuban family members negotiated the complex process of assimilation and the persistent longing for a return. Of course, one strategy was to bring the home culture along, as did the narrator's father and Uncle Cesar as the Mambo Kings, musicians who provided the new community with their own brand of Cuban dance music. The novel both opens and closes with a reference to the episode of *I Love Lucy* in which the Mambo Kings were asked to appear, invited to the show by the famous Desi Arnaz himself. Hijuelos' first-person narrator recalls that the Mambo Kings were to play "Ricky Ricardo's singing cousins fresh off the farm in Oriente Province, Cuba" (Hijuelo 1986: 3). When the Mambo Kings knock on Mrs. Ricardo's (Lucille Ball's) door in the novel, they are wearing "white silk suits and butterfly-looking lace bow ties." But in the film version of the novel, the Mambo Kings, played by Armando Assante and Antonio Banderas, stroll onto the set of Lucy's living room dressed in crisp white *guayaberas* with a traditional knotted scarf around their necks and a straw hat in their hands. Lucy soon discovers just how connected to the homeland they are when she tries to carry on a conversation with the two, whose attempts at gracious repartee are hindered by their shaky dependence on a handful of words quickly consulted in an English phrasebook one carries in his pocket. Nonetheless, Lucy's interpretive resourcefulness produces laughs instead of embarrassment, as well as an identification on the part of the viewer with the essentially comic situation of being either the immigrant *or* the immigrant's host. The scene inscribes the *guayabera* as the sign of true Cubanness, now transported to the United States, an authenticity reinforced by the wearers' linguistic difficulty. It demonstrates how the Cuban in America is reinterpreted for television viewers as a romanticized version of the *guajiro*, a figure infinitely simpler, less threatening, and much funnier than the immigrant they are likely to encounter on the street.

The film version of *Mambo Kings* suggests the various ways in which *guayaberas* perform a Latin identity that has been nuanced, if not invented, on North American soil. Sure, the shirts may be worn by immigrants from the

Caribbean and Mexico because they're comfortable and practical, or because that's what they brought with them, but they also assume another level of signification, marking the wearer as somehow connected to the other Americas. The shirt has been especially prevalent in the Cuban "exile" community, where it is stacked alongside other symbols that immediately evoke the irretrievable homeland and provoke an insatiable nostalgia. This symbolic value is apparent in a May 2000 advert for a party at the Miami nightclub CubaNostalgia, which announced that the evening would begin with a *mojito* or *cubalibre*, quintessential Cuban cocktails, and continue with a buffet of Cuban food, along with a full night of dancing on a floor in the shape of the map of Havana to the beloved Cuban rhythms of boleros, mambos, and chachachas. The dress code called for *guayaberas* for the gentlemen, but pointed out that the ladies could now wear them as well, since Donna Karan had recently featured women's *guayaberas* in her *pret a porter* line. The cost to attend, $150 per person, or $1,500 for a table of ten, suggested that the *guayabera* had once again been reinvented, this time as a costume of the financially successful but perpetually nostalgic Cuban American. Evans suggests the following:

> The haunting of contemporary fashion design by images from the past is a kind of return of the repressed, in which shards of history work their way to the surface in new formations and are put to work as contemporary emblems. The fragmented and episodic traces of the past that surface in contemporary designs are traces of instability and transience. These traces come back as fragments under the weight of some cultural trauma... In particular, contemporary fashion has fastened on the themes of instability and alteration, selecting past images of mutability which resonate in the present. Fashion imagery, itself semiotically unstable, thus fixes images of instability and change, but in ways that destabilise conventional history, and run counter to the idea of coherent narrative. (Evans 2000: 16)

This destabilization provides for the adoption of the *guayabera* as a sign of Cuban integrity in the face of exile as a form of national disintegration, and as such, it turns older ideas of inappropriateness inside out.

This reinvention of the *guayabera* as classy rather than country, as *cool* rather than common, has occurred in other North American scenarios as well. Agustín Gurza has written about a similar scene across the country in West Los Angeles, where a young man dons his best *guayabera* for a night of feverish salsa dancing. "Jamie González thought he looked cool in his tropical shirt, jet black with white embroidery. He felt cool too. His traditional guayabera was made to fit loosely, worn outside the pants so heat escapes and breezes get caught underneath," explains Gurza's article in *Hispanicvista*. "Perfect for salsa dancing, which makes Jamie sizzle. The shirt is roomy enough for those fancy spins and dips. Stylish and sensible." While researching the piece, Gurza explored the outer reaches of his own closet, and found a *guayabera* made in the Yucatan and sporting delicate, multicolored embroidery. Though the focus is more on coolness – in both its senses – than on nostalgia, the Hispanic names of both author and protagonist suggest that once again, the *guayabera* offers its wearer a United States identity filtered through or enhanced by some essential or fundamental link to Latin America. Gurza argues, however, that "guayaberas transcend humidity and politics," noting that his most recent acquisitions of the pleated shirt were produced for Perry Ellis in Korea, and sold at the huge Macy's department store in Costa Mesa, California.

Alison Lurie (1981: 96) wrote that "On a Cuban or Mexican-American, the guayabera shirt is merely a sign that he is dressed up for dinner, a party or an evening out. On a non-Latin, however, such a shirt suggests familiarity with Latin America and/or makes a claim to such stereotypical Latin qualities as relaxation, spontaneity and a sense of rhythm." While Lurie may have been right for the most part, she clearly did not foresee the shirt's tremendous crossover potential. In the late 90s, the *guayabera* became the symbol of Nuevo Latino identity as well as an important player in a burgeoning aesthetic of neo-ethnic chic. *The Princess and the Barrio Boy* (2000) is a Hollywood teen movie which recounts the coming-to-culture saga of a rich Latina high-schooler from West Los Angeles who falls in like with the humble but handsome boy who serves *hors d'oeuvres* at her lavish *quinceañera* party. In a key scene that shows how the "princess" has crossed (over) Los Angeles to attend a party in the lower income *barrio*, many of the musicians who let loose with the Tex-Mex-laced salsa music are wearing *guayaberas*, as are several of the men – Hispanic and non-Hispanic – throwing down on the dance floor. Viewers are encouraged to see the shirt for its textual value, as a document of pan-Latin or Latin-sympathetic identity that has been comfortably assumed or embraced.

As Diana Crane (2000: 13) has noted, "Fashion contributes to the redefinition of social identities by continually attributing new meaning to artifacts," a process that is evident in the refashioning of the *guayabera* from the outmoded garment of the *abuelos* to the choice of the younger performers of Latinity in United States urban centers. The *guayabera* is thus consumed and exhibited in efforts to differentiate from, and belong to, "neotribal" groups or subcultures. Within this fashion(able) discourse, the *guayabera* simultaneously functions to construct, deconstruct, and reconstruct narratives of personal history, and to transform and contest hegemonies. We recall Pamela Gibson's observation that "Fashion itself supplies the constituent elements of an indeterminate number and range of social performances or self-constructions. Fashion is a storehouse of identity-kits, of surface parts which, assembled, determine the 'interior essence' which is subsequently taken to determine the assemblage itself" (Gibson 2000: 356).

Post-*guayaberismo*

In twenty-first century Cuba, there seem to be three kinds of *guayaberas*. First, there are a few new shirts being produced in small lots by a handful of seamstresses, many in state-owned workshops whose market is composed almost entirely of tourists. Government-owned retailers such as Quitrín that cater to this market specialize in reproducing a pristine version of the *guayabera* sewn in white *hilo,* lightweight cotton. Their customers buy the garment in order to negotiate the tropical heat and humidity, and as an "authentic souvenir" of their visit to Cuba. One also sees a few *guayaberas* worn by Cubans on the streets, usually well preserved shirts that have been in circulation for as long as twenty years or more. It's not uncommon to see older men wearing threadbare versions in lime green, lavender, or chartreuse.

Nowadays, however, *guayaberas* are no longer really everyday wear in Cuba, but instead a specialty garment, most frequently seen in bars, nightclubs, and restaurants, where either the waiters or the musicians – and sometimes both – wear the shirts as they cater to a clientele dominated by international tourists, who themselves display fancy, expensive versions bought in Miami, Havana, or elsewhere. This suggests that within the island, the *guayabera* has become something of a costume worn in the production of Cuban or Caribbean identity, not necessarily the costume worn by those attending the Tropicana, but by those *performing* there. One thing hasn't changed though: within Cuba, the *guayabera* remains so firmly classified as masculine attire, that Cuban women find it surprising and strange that for women in the United States and elsewhere, "It's not your *papi's* guayabera anymore," as a fashion spread in the bilingual United States women's magazine *Latina* proclaimed in the late 1990s.

In fact, outside Cuba, the shirt in question often *is* the property of a dad or an *abuelo*, but it's now being worn in a very different way, in tandem with other looks and fashion trends such as tattoos and body piercings that sometimes make their earlier wearers cringe. Retro *guayaberas* have become so popular that they now appear in flea markets in Los Angeles and Mexico City, as well as in the crafts market in Havana. At the same time, designers continue to reinvent the *guayabera* for the twenty-first century. At a 2001 fashion show in Terepaima, Venezuela, models graced the runway in transparent silk, organdy, and linen *guayaberas*, reinvented "for feminine curves" by the Dominican designer Arcadio Díaz. Reporter Igor Molina judged that "Arcadio must have had a great time creating them, since the changes that he's made to the guayabera – without losing its original structure of rows of pleats in the front and simple pockets, either double or quadruple – have transformed it into a most original, playful, and elegant garment."

Despite these new (tr)ends, there is still the question of its history and contemporary significance in Cuba. In Sancti Spíritus, long regarded by many as the birthplace of the shirt, designer Georgina Martínez continues to sew *guayaberas*, mostly for sale to European, Canadian and American tourists. When I visited her home and studio in the summer of 2002, she was glad to talk about theories of the shirt's origins and show me several examples of her own fine handiwork, but was much more interested in examining the *guayabera* I was wearing, a woman's shirt adorned with typical Yucatecan embroidery that I had bought in Mérida. Once I had convinced the perspicacious Doña Gina that *guayaberas* were now being designed for and worn by women in Mexico, the United States, and Europe, she asked me to sell her the hybrid shirt off my back, so she could use it as a model – to once again reformulate and reinterpret this most "Cuban" article of attire.

14

Transvestite Pedagogy: Jacqueline and Cuban Culture

James J. Pancrazio

> That things are not always what they seem – or that seeming itself, the mirage or camouflage, was all there was to see . . .
>
> Marjorie Garber

The topic of this essay suggests a relationship between transvestism and fashion; my overall contention is that both are representative of representation. That is, they are emblematic and necessary signs of signification itself.[1] Thus, far from emanating from capitalist excess, fashion is very much part of the symbolic order; it is structured like a language. My analysis follows Marjorie Garber's claim that "the transvestite makes culture possible, that there can be no culture without the transvestite because the transvestite marks the entrance into the Symbolic" (Garber 1992: 34). I make much the same claim regarding fashion. Indeed, the fashion writer is analogous to the transvestite. Both presupposed that clothing, styles, accessories and cosmetics depend largely on the combination of structures that produce the image of a complete (textual) body. While there is a lengthy history of fashion writing in colonial and post-colonial Cuba, the keystone of this essay is a little-known fashion column entitled, "De la moda femenina" ("On Feminine Fashion") and "S.M. La moda" ("His/Her Majesty: Fashion"), which appeared in the Havana magazine *Social* from 1925 until 1927.[2] Although the signature that appears on these articles is that of Jacqueline, those familiar with the biography of novelist Alejo Carpentier will recognize these works as part of his vast journalistic production.[3] However, Carpentier's "writing the feminine" should come as no surprise. He dedicated most of his career to the creation of narrators and implicit authors that performed numerous subject positions.[4] In this respect, I am more interested in what the "Jacqueline texts" tell us about representation, fashion, and the formation of Cuban culture than anything that one could derive by speculating about the author himself.[5] My central questions are: What does this textual transvestism tell us about the symbolic order? What kind of pedagogy does transvestism and fashion present?

In his 1964 interview with César Leante, Carpentier describes his early years as a writer by stating "I was even the 'Jacqueline' from the fashion section of the magazine *Social*" (Leante 1974: 59–60). However, what does it mean for him to claim that "he used to be" Jacqueline? What are the implications of a male writer claiming he was a woman? Does it infer that Carpentier himself somehow saw himself as a woman? Does it suggest that his notion of self was feminine? Or, does this suggest that the concept of the author is an empty construct, a figment of reading that can embody any number of forms?[6] I believe that authorship is very much the latter. This is not far from Roland Barthes contention that the author does not speak in the text, but rather it is "language which speaks" and "to write is, through a prerequisite impersonality . . . to reach that point where only language acts, 'performs' . . ." (Barthes 1988: 143). Barthes adds that "writing is the destruction of every voice, of every point of origin. Writing is that neutral, composite, oblique space where our subject slips away, the negative where all identity is lost, starting with the very identity of the body writing" (Barthes 1988: 142). Writing, nonetheless, creates the illusion of authorship by forgetting that it is writing, and by assuming that there must be a speaker whose text is his or her reflection.

This is not to suggest that all will agree with my approach to transvestism and fashion. Doubtless, many will fixate on the (closeted) image of the male writer who passes himself off as a woman to impose male authority by controlling the sartorial norms. These issues cannot be simply obviated without some discussion. Thaïs Morgan, a critic who has studied "men writing the feminine," asks, "What does it mean to say that a male author writes the feminine? Is he writing as (identifying with) a woman? Or writing like (mimicking, and perhaps mocking) a woman? Or writing through a woman (an Other that confirms his own identity as the Same)?" (Morgan 1994: 1). What these questions presume is that the self that writes always corresponds to (or is a reflection of) the self that is represented. This logic of identity grants a privileged space to the "I" that writes and presumes that it also must be the "I" that is the subject of the discourse. Language, however, involves symbolic substitutions. As Joël Dor observes, "the subject can be made present in it only if he is absent from it in his essence" (Dor 1997: 136; the emphasis is Dor's). Therefore, the subjects that appear in the texts are always already sutures, stand ins for the missing subject. This is especially the case for the fashion writer in postcolonial Cuba, a period in which one self was lost while another was actively being fashioned.

To focus on Carpentier as the author, I believe, tells us little about the conditions within language and culture that makes transculturation possible. Before fixating or falling prey to a biographical reading, one might consider that such a claim is already "begging the question." Indeed, it proves what is already known. Moreover, such a focus may actually eschew a thorough reading of the texts in favor of a narrative that explains away the anxiety associated with cross-dressing. Marjorie Garber, in *Vested Interests*, refers to this tendency among many writers and critics to "look through rather than at the cross-dresser," and avoid the face-to-face encounter with the transvestite (Garber 1992: 9). One of the principal means of ameliorating the anxiety is the "escape" or "employment" narrative. In most cases, the he-to-she cross-dresser is represented as obligated by social and economic forces to disguise himself to get a job, escape repression, or gain political freedom (Garber 1992: 70). A second problematic area is the tendency to collapse transvestism into homosexuality. Judith Butler, in *Bodies That Matter*, notes that "not only are a vast number of drag performers straight, but it would be a mistake to think that homosexuality is best explained through a performativity that is drag" (Butler 1993: 235).[7] While Garber herself concedes that "the conflation of 'transvestite' with 'gay and lesbian' is itself a matter of historical contingency," she argues that there have been numerous moments in Western, Far Eastern, Near Eastern, African and other areas, in which sexual orientation has had "little or nothing to do with transvestite representation, and vice versa" (Garber 1992: 131).

This is not to say that all agree with Garber and Butler's positions. Ben Sifuentes Jáuregui, in *Transvestism, Masculinity and Latin American Literature*, affirms that "transvestite," in Latin America, is synonymous with "homosexual" (Sifuentes 2002: 46–7). His point is that in popular culture there is only one type of homosexual, the effeminate one.[8] Thus, the male who is penetrated sexually is already transvested by virtue of his positioning as feminine. For Sifuentes, critics like Garber and Butler are guilty of universalizing their constructs and of neglecting the relevance of the cultural context. While it is true that Latin American popular culture images male homosexuality as effeminate, this is a far cry from actual cross-dressing. Conflating the two constructs may, in fact, reify the masculine and feminine binary as the only possible subject positions. However, Sifuentes's observation is nothing new in Latin American cultural studies. Octavio Paz, in *El laberinto de la soledad*, refers to this same phenomenon and notes that the "active" male homosexual in Mexico is treated with a certain "indulgence" (Paz 1985: 35). However, his framing of male-homosexuality in terms of "indulgence" and "tolerance" suggests that there is much more "passing" involved here than Sifuentes would have us believe. That is, the critic's deployment of popular culture functions as a means of explaining away the active male's homoerotic desire, even when it is most salient. Despite the fact that homosexuality and transvestism share not only the performative but also a similar positioning in regard to the primary identification as an object of desire, they are not synonymous. Transvestism, I believe, seeks to disavow the primary signifier's lack while homosexuality represses the desire for the primary signifier by identifying with its object of desire.[9] The disavowal of lack, a structure common to both fetishism and transvestism, is not limited to questions of a sexual body. For this reason, cross-dressing often exhibits a tendency to cross social, class and racial borders as well.[10]

Jacqueline, the dramatized author, is not Carpentier's fabrication, but rather she is a continuation of a highly conventionalized image that evoked the modernity that Cubans desired. A brief review of the magazine *Social*'s fashion history would reveal that, from the onset of its publication in 1916, authorship, authority, and legitimacy were almost always of dubious origins. It was common practice in *Social* for writers to publish on a variety of themes without bylines. Moreover, in an epoch of rampant intercultural appropriations, authorship, authority, and authorization were the least of the editors' concerns. Often, the magazine's editors even poked fun at the anonymity of their writers by signing with the name "Godknows" in English. The first "dramatized author" on women's fashion appears in July 1917. She is known only by her first name "Henriette." The language, as well as the place of authorship, is very similar to those which appear in the "Jacqueline texts." Invariably, the Cuban-fashion writer positions the self with a French-derived name, outside of Cuba (Paris or New York). The world of fashion is also represented as superficial, capricious, and as one of the most delightful and tempting vanities of the modern era. This is particularly important to our notion of fashion pedagogy; because pedagogy is a style of teaching, fashion writing is a style of styles. Invariably, the fashion writer approaches modern style as if it were not important or relevant to the development of the symbolic order. These stylistic disclaimers, however, attest to the presence of social scrutiny that ascribes the utmost importance to appearances. Otherwise, there would be no need to present a disclaimer.

The next regularly featured column on women's fashion in *Social* appears in the summer of 1920; its implicit author signs with the name "Mademoiselle D'Arles." Her column, entitled "Crónicas de París" runs until December 1923 when it is replaced by Ana María Borrero's "S.M. La moda" in January 1924. There is a marked similarity in the language used by all three writers. The Cuban-fashion writer is characterized by a Janus-faced double gaze, one that looks outward to Paris or New York and the other with an eye on the cultural reality of the island. This writer shares the same penchant for geographical displacement and translation that Gustavo Pérez Firmat finds as characteristic of the Cuban writer in general (Pérez Firmat 1989: 11–15). Fashion is always represented in terms of its instability; without exception; it is characterized by references to power shopping, frustration, and the anxiety of not knowing what to wear. The French vocabulary of fashion is also highly conventional: by-words like "Ville Lumiere," "chiffones," "paniers," "pendant," are common. Moreover, French style was ubiquitous in early Republican Havana; El Encanto, the largest and most important department store in Havana, ran advertisements that informed Cuban readers that "if you want to have 'chic,' spirituality, distinction . . . there's no two ways about it, you have to shop at El Encanto" (*Social*, August 1920, 101). My point here is that the language of fashion already constructs its own image of authorship as well as authority. Fashion was something to be "had"; if it was not just across the border it was because the fashion writer knew how to detach it to the island.

While the notion of cross-dressing as a metaphor for cultural formation may seem far-fetched in a discipline that tends to favor metanarratives of identity, nation, and resistance, transgression, I think, is written into the foundational codes of Cuban culture itself. A brief review of its literary and cultural history finds a plethora of instances of transvestism. Cuban writers and historians from the nineteenth century to the present have shown a remarkable fascination for the cross-dresser. One prominent example is Enriqueta Faber, the ninteenth-century transvestite and practicing physician who resided in Cuba until it was discovered that he was a she. Faber's story gave rise to no fewer than three historical novels: Francisco Calcagno's *Don Enriquito* (1895), Andrés Clemente Vázquez's *Enriqueta Faber* (1894), Antonio Benítez Rojo's *Mujer en traje de batalla* (2001), as well as essays by Emilio Roig de Leuschenring (1965) and Emilio Bacardí (1972). The cross-dresser also appears in the streets during the Carnival celebrations, in the *appataki*, or Afro-Cuban legend, about the gods Changó and Oyá (Efundé, 1978), and throughout much of Severo Sarduy's work: *De donde son los cantantes* (1969), *Escritos sobre un cuerpo* (1969), *Cobra* (1972), *La simulación* (1982) and *Colibrí* (1983). Further, the recent documentary "Mariposas en el Andamio" ("Butterflies on the Scaffold") (1995) clearly attest to the ubiquity of the transvestite in Cuban popular culture and history. However, showing existence is a far cry from elucidating significance. The transvestite stands in camouflaged contrast to the militarist-political imagery often associated with island, and sheds light on the processes by which Cuban culture emerges. As Leví Marrero observes, Cuba has traditionally been an open island (Marrero 1995: 1–7). Its history has always involved the narratives of other nations, and this co-penetration has converted the island into a cross-roads and *bodega* (warehouse) of cultures. Thus, the fixed notion of an inside and outside of Cuban culture has always been problematic. In *Tropics of History*, Alan West adroitly notes that "transvestism [in Severo Sarduy's work] is a metaphor for transculturation because it resolutely opposes paternalistic, logocentric and rigid thinking about culture, gender and class" (West 1997: 152). However, there may be more to West's observation than meets the eye. The concept of transculturation, I think, shares common structures with transvestism and fashion. Both are governed by rules of substitution, combination, and abrogation; breaking the rules, so to speak, proffers innovative possibilities for cultural identification.

This notion of transculturation, however, is slightly different than Fernando Ortiz's original conception, which involved a process of deculturation, acculturation, and culminated in a synthetic culture. Deeply embedded in Ortiz's vision of cultural development was a progress narrative that implied a "weaker" culture's acceptance of a dominant culture's practices, languages and rituals (Ortiz 1987: 96). Ortiz's model presumes that the subaltern always appropriates elements from the dominant culture, and not visa versa. His model fails to address how or why white *criollos* would also appropriate African-derived music, words, and belief systems into their own self imagery. Passing, transvestism, and cultural border crossing formed the body of Cuban culture by constituting a process of substitution and recombination of cultural elements.[11]

Along with the gendered borders, the ethnic, national, and racial borders were crossed frequently. Robin Moore, in *Nationalizing Blackness*, refers to this period as a "critical decade" whose importance is often overshadowed by the First World War, the Machado dictatorship, and the economic crisis of 1929 (Moore 1997: 1–5). This was the epoch of the tango, jazz, the Harlem Renaissance, and "primitivism," all of which converge in the Afro-Cuban movement when white writers and musicians begin to express themselves through African-derived music. Border crossing was so rampant that strictly defined categories of identification highly questionable. In this sense, it is important to underscore that the "Jacqueline texts" appear in the midst of Cuba's postcolonial renovation. While writers, intellectuals, and urbanized Cubans are attempting to break with the Spanish colonial past and bring themselves culturally, politically, and economically into the twentieth century. Fashion played a large role in this process of postcolonial formation because it provided an instantaneous visual referent of modernity.

Further, in the wake of Cuban independence, women began to participate in national culture in forms never before seen. Upon first glance, it would be tempting to assume that the readers of magazines like *Social* in the 1920s were well-to-do Cubans. Fashion writers typically refer to their readers as "elegant and refined women." Nonetheless, it is unlikely that the Cuban upper class would seek advice from popular magazines. On the contrary, during the colonial period, wealthy *criollos* often traveled directly to the United States to make their fashion purchases (Pérez 1999: 69). However, almost thirty years of war left the economy of post-colonial Cuba virtually destroyed. Those same wealthy *criollo* families, who once enjoyed frequent travel, were forced to sell off valuable property at a fraction of its worth. Many from the upper class descended while others moved into the positions created by United States intervention in the Cuban economy. In this regard, the fashion writer's comments are directed to a readership that desires to appropriate models from other classes, cultures, and nationalities. Louis A. Perez, in *On Becoming Cuban*, writes that this new group of "secretaries, sales clerks, telephone operators, and teachers, among others, led the transition to new styles and inevitably to new ways" (Pérez 1999: 315).

Women entered the work force, offices, universities, and golf and tennis clubs in numbers never before seen (Pérez 1999: 155–7). Women leaving the confines of the house challenged the strict *criollo* sensibilities as fashion presented itself as one of the fundamental means through which Cuban women could express their modernity. However, these transformations, as Pérez's correctly observes, were not limited to the privileged classes; the importation of cheap copies of European fashion also offered the working class female an affordable means to project status and demonstrate social mobility. He adds, "under some circumstances, clothes could facilitate the invention of a usable self by which mobility might even be realized" (Pérez 1999: 315). Ana María Borrero, an important fashion editor of the period, noted that even poor single women could maintain the illusion of being well dressed. She adds that even her washerwoman could afford inexpensive copy of a Jean Patou dress and Reboux hat to take on the appearance of a lady (Borrero 1936: 41–2).

In *La simulación* Severo Sarduy theorizes that transvestism manifests itself as a "lethal sexual drive" that "emanates however from camouflage, that is a disappearance, a factitious loss of individuality that dissolves and is no longer recognizable" (Sarduy 1982: 16). Moreover, Sarduy contends that this mimetic drive does not respond to any practical function derived from natural selection or from competition among the species, but rather these mimetic drives demonstrate that a law of pure disguise exists in the living world, a practice that consists of passing (Sarduy 1982: 16). That is, simulation is a drive to insert the self into space, to merge with it either through camouflage or display. Jacqueline's function as a fashion writer is pedagogical because she provides insights into the artful manipulation of the symbolic order. This process is allegorized in the May 1927 article, when Jacqueline discusses the problem of a distinguished woman who, while vacationing in France, commits the grave error of purchasing an entire collection from a single designer. According to Jacqueline, the principal problem is that the woman fails to understand that designers create styles for all types of women. Buyers need to consider only those items that conform to their type of beauty, stature, complexion and silhouette (May 1927: 91). She adds, "our women that travel ignore, in large part, the true meaning that Parisian designers give to the word 'collection' . . . No *genuine* Parisian woman acquires her dresses for a *saison* in a single fashion house" (May 1927: 90; the emphasis is mine). The authentic Parisian woman, according to Jacqueline, is not a "being" but rather she is a way of "dressing." Further, the logic of performance suggests that the genuine and the authentic do not refer to a biological or historical gender, but rather to the knowledge of representation as a combination and recombination of codes. In no way do these lessons imply the facile imitation of hegemonic models, but rather they suggest that all cultures constitute themselves by assimilating disconnected parts and suturing them to a single body.

Because I am not focusing on questions of authorial intention, my task is to demonstrate that transvestism is a textual act. In this regard, what is most significant is how the narrator maintains the categories of gender – that is, gender as an appearance and the appearance of gender – in an atmosphere in which she frequently crosses gendered borders. This category maintenance constitutes itself as a caveat, an excuse or a justification, that indicates the presence of another's critical gaze. Pamela L. Caughie, in *Passing and Pedagogy*, writes that the caveat is "an effort to protect ourselves from being accused of doing precisely what we are doing . . ." (Caughie 1999: 30). It is a textual excess that appears to prevent misinterpretation, but, more tellingly, it serves to explain away or mitigate the social anxieties and guard against the total collapse of the categories of identification. Often, these caveats consist of a self-deprecating terminology like "fashion frivolity," "weaker sex," or outright disavowals of a feminist agenda. These disavowals, however, appear just as Jacqueline advocates greater access to the symbolic order for women. Thus, her avocation of the new lifestyles was made possible by a feigned concern about the possible loss of femininity. While her terminology is unpalatable in today's day and age, self-deprecation functions as a textual consolation to the conservative reader (both male and female) by reassuring him or her that although women are dressing like men (for example, pants, ties, suit coats), performing the same activities as men (for example, voting, smoking, working paid jobs outside the home), and are found in the same social spaces as men (for example, streets, offices, universities), they are not becoming manlike. In terms of gender as a linguistic, social, sartorial, sexual performative, these caveats (performatives) are precisely what maintains the notion of gender in the text.

To illustrate this conventionality in the representation of women, it would be difficult to find a better example than that of Ana María Borrero, a well-known fashion writer of the Republican period in Cuba. In this example, she suggests that a woman's desire to dress *à la mode* was far from an issue of vanity, but rather it was a matter of a "profound need to create beauty, to exteriorize our interior garden; to remain if even for a day, in another's memory... And in its essence, divine instinct of maternity with which the woman vivifies and nourish all that surrounds her" (Borrero 1925: 55). Thus, for Borrero, the drive toward fashion stems from a desire to become a mother; it is similar to Sigmund Freud's nineteenth-century narrative of female subjectivity. According to Freud, this trajectory moves from the so-called castration complex and penis envy toward the eventual possession of the phallic object in the form of a male child. Freud argues that nineteenth-century women move along a symbolic equation that links the desire for the penis to a baby (Freud 1989: 665). Thus, the castration complex is constantly displaced in a trajectory that moves from a lack, to the supplement of the penis, that is, from father to husband, and from husband to son. For Borrero, it is the maternal desire that drives the fashion world. Traditionally, the symbolic economy constitutes itself through the exclusive positions of "having" the phallus, that which man possesses, and "being" the phallus, that which the woman is (Butler 1990: 56). That is, being the phallus is being the signifier of the other's desire and appearing as that signifier. Judith Butler affirms that "it is to be the object, the Other of a (heterosexualized) masculine desire, [and] also to represent or reflect that desire" (Butler 1990: 56).

Despite the conventionality of this representation, this is not to say that there is no slippage from one position to another in the symbolic register. Indeed, symbolic substitution implies the possibility of comic inversion, parody and surreptitious manifestations of desire. Jacqueline as "representative of representation" is the figure who instructs her readers on the artfully positioning of desire in the symbolic register. When she comments that fashion has historically fluctuated between the extremes of tyranny and slavery, she is referring to nineteenth-century mores that restricted the possibilities of symbolic substitution to the assimilation of a single model. Under fashion tyranny, she writes, "the woman has been a true slave. Corsets, whalebones, pompous hoop-skirts, sizes reduced to their minimum expression, almost chimerical hairstyles, have not sufficed to make the tyranny more effective . . ." (April 1927: 90). However, nineteenth-century practices stand in sharp contrast to the 1920s. Postcolonial nation building, postwar Europe, the Jazz Age, and the vogue of primitivism, were the telltale signs of a dynamic in which the means to produce new images of the self corresponded with new means of positioning desire. The predominance of detail and excess in fashion accessories permits women to "turn the tables," so to speak, on men by taking a passive-aggressive role in sexual relations. Jacqueline writes:

> The woman at all times, plagued by her inexhaustible desire to please, to make herself more attractive, has used her wardrobe like Orpheus's lire – to enchant those difficult and willful little beasts, very weak at times, that are called men. For that reason, the refinements that have surrounded her have multiplied; she has perfected to the smallest detail the mass of exquisitenesses used to maximize the exquisite qualities of her persona. And, in her eagerness to appear ever more beautiful, more suggestive, in her desire to highlight the airy lines of her silhouette or the grace of her face, she has created that ever dangerous monster called: Fashion. (April 1927: 89; the emphasis is mine)

The transvestite marks the point in which the "Oedipus complex" gives way to the allure of "Orpheus's lire." Fashion is now the servant that calms and enchants. It is a metaphor for the entrance into the symbolic order through the acquisition of a language that is both concealment and articulation of desire. Jacqueline writes, "We live in an epoch in which all freedoms are permitted to us. Never, like now, have fashions submitted to the all powerful will of the woman" (April 1927: 90). She adds that fashion is now a servant, an "enchanting ally of her life and of her pleasures, complimenting her existence instead of complicating it" (April 1927: 90).

Moreover, this notion of "Orpheus's lire" marks the intervention of seeming into the traditional binary of "having" and "being" the phallus. Jacques Lacan refers to the intervention of a third category of appearances or "seeming," as one that "replaces the 'to have, in order to protect it on the one side, and to mask its lack in the other" (Lacan 1977: 289). This intervention not only conceals lack but also maintains the symbolic economy of the phallus by protecting the subject against the anxiety of loss. Fashion, thus, serves the compensatory need for a display that hides lack. The driving force behind women's fashion is the desire to be the object of desire. That is, she expresses and camouflages her desire by positioning herself as the object of another's gaze. This positioning not only replicates the pleasure associated with the "mirror stage," but it also suggests that all positions in the symbolic economy derive pleasure through a similar positioning. This is especially the case for masculinity as well, because he who supposedly possesses must lack the object to experience desire. In short, one cannot desire if one already possesses, and one cannot "possess" if one already is that object. Hence, the dynamic of sexual attraction depends on seeming (fashion) to hide the fact that no one really possesses the phallus.

Returning to our earlier notion of the caveat, it is important to note that the function of the transvestite is not to inaugurate a category collapse, but rather to stage pedagogy of cultural formation, and the artful management of the symbolic. Because of this, there is a necessity to maintain difference and conceal transgressions, even when the transgressions were quite obvious. Some of the most striking examples of cross-dressed fashions are found in the emergence of the sport lines. These styles not only appropriated elements of male attire, but they also mark the entrance of women into what was considered masculine space. In July 1926, Jacqueline comments

> Few things please a woman as much as feeling herself free of hindrances for a little while, dressing herself lightly with those enchanting sport dresses, those with an aspect of masculine style, more than any other, those dresses grant those of the weaker sex the just sensation of the ground gained in the privileges from the eternal "strong" of the opposite sex. (July 1926: 68)

The casting of men as the "eternal strong" and women as the "weaker sex" does not function as an essential definition of sex or gender, but rather as an ironic attempt to conceal the fact that the borders marking the gender terrain were arbitrary and shifting. If women had recently gained terrain from men, men were obviously not eternally strong. Although the dynamics of "having" and "being" remained as the anchoring points in relations between men and women, fashion was something to be possessed and displayed. Thus, the avenues for pleasure could become numerous. Further examples of the shifting grounds registered in fashion were the jumper, a masculine outfit for playing golf (January 1926: 69), trousers, and a tuxedo designed for women (July 1926: 67).

Because of the tuxedo's notoriety as a sign of masculinity, its status merits special attention. Cuban advertising in the first several decades of the Republic invariably presented a chain of signifiers that linked the tuxedo to cigar smoking. Thus, both became icons of masculinity. Cigar smoking provides a visual sign of masculinity that condensed images of virility, power, pleasure, social status, with a narrative of initiation. Men were supposed to smoke. To this day, the tuxedo in many Spanish-speaking countries is still referred to as an *esmoquin* or a smoking suit. The *esmoquin* was supposedly what one wore when one smoked; at least it was in the world of Cuban advertising. The typical images of the cigar smoker were highly eroticized. Most prominently, the Larrañaga advertisements visually reproduced the image of a fully erect masculinity, puffing on a cigar, either in an army officer's uniform or in a gentleman's tuxedo.[12] After the First World War, the military uniform disappeared from the full-page advertisements and Larrañaga Nacionales made the tuxedo synonymous with cigar smoking. Like the cigars themselves, the men were either "long and thin" or "short and stout." One such image is a full-frontal depiction of a tall tuxedo-clad man exuding cigar smoke, standing with his legs slightly apart and the slit of his coat-tails marking an empty space between his legs (March 1921: 2). The Larrañaga company also ran tersely stated slogans with sexual innuendos that alluded to the postcoital bliss of smoking. These advertisements exhorted Cuba males to "Conserve su sonrisa" ("Conserve your smile") (April 1921: 2); or they told them that "Kipling tenía razón" ("Kipling was right") (March 1921: 2), in other words that there was peace in smoking. The tuxedo linked cigar smoking to high society, to masculinity, to peace, and to sexuality itself. Even in our day and age, smoking a torpedo-style cigar like a Gran Corona or a Montecristo is still considered a masculine activity par excellence.

Havelock Ellis, one of Freud's contemporaries, observes that sexual inversion in women often is characterized by a notable desire to smoke tobacco (Ellis 1895: 152–4). It should come as no surprise, then, that smoking appears in the "Jacqueline texts" as one of the prevailing new feminine trends. She writes

> Ever since the Parisian woman acquired the habit of smoking – controversial although undoubtedly enchanting –, the objects that have as their purpose the gratification of that vice . . . have multiplied. I have seen in the shop windows of the Rue de la Paix an enchanting display of cigarette holders, cigarette lighters, and above all, cigarette cases in an almost overwhelming variety . . . It's also worth mentioning a certain little model of cigarette case with a small lighter hanging on a chain . . . And for this time, that will do for temptations. After enumerating so many trifling and exquisite objects, I almost feel an uneasy conscious. (April 1926: 67; the emphasis is mine)

However, what is really hanging from the chain she describes? Is it the cigarette lighter? Or, is it the chain of signifiers that link smoking to masculinity? If tobacco is the object of desire, then the object itself is always already detachable. It is no wonder that this leaves Jacqueline feeling uneasy. Also, the emphasis on "seeming" in the Larrañaga tobacco advertisements also calls into question the essential relationship of men to masculinity. If a man was, in fact, masculine, why was there a need to supplement his masculinity with the visual images of the cigar and the tuxedo? Perhaps the most significant example of the phallus as a multifarious signifier of the object of desire appears in the October 1919, edition of *Social*. In this full page advertisement, Larrañaga producers state that their brand of cigars are good "hasta la última chupada" ("to the last puff/suckle") (March 1919: 2). The graphic design presents the man's profile in the lower left-hand corner. The face is looking slightly upward toward the right at the cigar as if it were a woman's breast. The notion of disconnectability and substitution also appears in another advertisement in which the tuxedo-clad man, sporting an apron, while packing his bags for a lengthy voyage. Like the English word "sack," "bags" is an argot expression in Spanish for the scrotum and testicles. The caption reads, "a gentleman will forget everything . . . but his Larrañaga cigars" (April 1922: 62). If cigars point to masculinity, it is a masculinity that can be lost or one that is lacking. Further, if the cigar could also double as the breast, an object lost in the waning of the Oedipal complex, then the ostensible signs of masculinity come to represent the negation of the loss of the primary signifier. How else can one "possess" the object, if the object itself is not already detached or lacking.[13]

Cigarette smoking in the early twentieth century was a sign of sophistication. Actresses like Marlene Dietrich, Joan Crawford, and Lauren Bacall glamorized the already eroticized notions of tobacco use. In contrast, however, to the image of hypervirility evoked by the cigar, the cigarette bore the mark of social grace, elegance, and suaveness. Although Ellis considered smoking a sign of feminine inversion, the diminutive cigarette suggests that it is a practice that is already ambiguous, undefined, and, to some extent, effeminate. That is, men who sought to project an image of elegant masculinity did so by opting for the feminized cigarette. One of the words that came to designate the cigarette was the fag, a term that condensed a series of images related to social status, size, and male effeminacy. Cigarette smoking per se was so ambiguous that society quickly established special places in which men and women could smoke without intermingling. Tobacco companies later remasculinized the cigarette by creating the Marlboro Man as well as the so-called feminine cigarettes like Virginia Slims with its memorable slogan, "You've come a long way baby," to further cater to both gender distinctions.

Due to the metonymic relation between smoking and the *esmoquin*, it is logical to assume that if women were smoking publicly in the 1920s, those changes would be reflected in feminine attire. This is the same period in which the female tuxedo makes its appearance on the fashion scene. Jacqueline employs a series of caveats to mitigate the social anxiety of cross-dressed fashion. In place of referring to the visual signs of border crossings, she deliberately uses the understatement, "masculine touches" to describe the latest styles. She writes:

> Many women contemplated these dresses with justifiable fear: in effect, if we add short hair, to the extra plain silhouette of the latest fashions, masculine looking suits, what would be left of our enchanting femininity? . . . But fashion is adaptable. *An insignificant detail* suffices to modify the whole character of the ensemble. Furthermore, the shirt which tends to complete the female tuxedos lends itself to an infinity of delicious combinations. One can enrich it with a ruff made with Chinese crêpe or pleated lace. A straight jacket, bois de rose color, worn with a plaid skirt the same color would be the least masculine-looking as possible. (June 1926; 67–80, the emphasis is mine)

The rhetorical question, "what would remain of our enchanting femininity?" inserted into the commentary, marked by the ellipsis, is what Bakhtin refers to as a "sideways glance at the others' language." This heteroglossic fluctuation indicates that Jacqueline's style is not determined solely by her words, so to speak, but also by another's words, point of view, and conceptual system (Bakhtin 1981: 375–6). This fluctuation demonstrates that she anticipates social condemnation and circumvents criticism by retracing the line she has just crossed. In doing so, she suggests that femininity may be at times a strategy of feigned frailty as opposed to essential or historical position of subordination. Furthermore, her retracing the border of gender reveals the arbitrariness and utility of the category itself. If the objects of desire were not prohibited, how else could one derive pleasure? Successful border-crossing, then, depends on a justification that, in part, insists that no borders have been crossed. The transvestite's reconstruction of the category entails the rhetorical shift from the whole to the part (for example, a different color, a ruff, or a pleat). In this regard, Jacqueline's "insignificant detail" is sufficient to mark the totality; its insignificance is what produces the necessary difference for gendered signification. Thus, in this case, the most insignificant detail is what is most significant.

Although women's fashion acquired masculine touches in the 1920s and 1930s with the addition of trousers, tuxedos, and sport styles, Jacqueline suggests that cosmetics also function to retrace the borders. While it will come to no surprise that femininity could be described as a cosmetic mask, the cigar, the tuxedo, the walking stick, and the facial scar suggest that masculinity is also an appearance. Sander L. Gilman, in *The Jew's Body*, notes that even as late as 1912, men ceremoniously challenged each other to sword duels for the express purpose of leaving a scar on the duelist's face. "The more marginal you were the more you wanted to be scarred" (Gilman 1991: 181). The scar stood for masculinity itself. Hence, cosmetics, often considered as a means of beautifying the hair, body or face, are also the means by which lack is camouflaged and ambiguity is displayed. That is, the subject inscribes or erases gender from his or her face. Womanhood, in this sense, is a "coming of age" story because it is age that writes the signs of gender on the face (wrinkles, crow's feet, sagging eyelids, and so forth). This is precisely the defining narrative that both cosmetics and the transvestite seek to suspend to maintain the illusion of indefinition.

In Jacqueline's review of Lucie Delarue Mardus book, *Seducir*, she affirms that "a woman's *authentic* youth is due to many details of her persona, but there is one, very small, that appears insignificant and says much about the *true* age of its owner: the edge of the nose" (June 1926: 64–5; the emphasis is mine). Authenticity and true age are not only the products of insignificant details, but also they are detachable parts. Much like prefixes or suffixes, which function to alter meaning, these parts can be altered to arrest the definitive narrative of age. Youth is effectively simulated by adopting the model of a "niño" (male child). Jacqueline adds, "look at it in a *niño*. Smooth, intact, without greasy dirt, attached to the cheek without shining, without the streaks of small veins nor full of imperceptible cavities, nor covered with minuscule black dots" (June 1926: 65). Like the Larrañaga advertisement that alludes to breastfeeding, the subject's object of desire is always another's body part. Modeling the woman's nose on that of a boy, however, does not suggest that the male nose is the ideal of feminine beauty. On the contrary, it suggests that beauty is constituted as agelessness. It is the lack of definition that permits one to become the other's object of desire.

Jacqueline's textual transvestism, in my mind, points to the mask of the author as a side effect of language, a figure of reading, which creates the illusion of a speaker behind the words. Because writing is representation in its most codified form, the subject who creates the discourse becomes necessarily absent so that the stand-in can be represented. Therefore, transvestism in these texts is not a question of the male author's transgressions, but rather it is a question of the "dramatized" author's border crossings within the text itself. To demonstrate that Jacqueline is a transvestite, my task is to prove that there is a fluctuation in her own positioning as a subject. Like the transvestite, this illusion must not only be "identical to itself" and "different from others," but it must be "different from its identity" and "identical to its difference." In this regard, subject positioning in the "Jacqueline texts" always points to the liminal space of representation itself. This is most evident at the opening of the Fall 1926 season, when Jacqueline asks, "¿Qué líneas nuevas aportará la próxima moda? ¿Qué colores y telas *usaremos*? . . . Toda parisiense *se plantea* estas preguntas actualmente" ("What will the lines of the next style bring? What colors and fabrics will *we use*? . . . Every Parisian woman *is asking herself* these questions now") (October 1926: 69; the emphasis is mine). I have left the original Spanish to illustrate how the grammatical subject pronouns mark a fluctuation between several different positions. Literally, Jacqueline moves from one point to another in a continuum that extends from Havana to Paris. For example, in the second phrase in the citation above, she uses the first-person plural subject pronoun, and thereby suggests that she is a part of the group inquiring about the colors and fabrics that designers will use in the following season. The third phrase, however, marks a transition in which the narrator locates herself outside the collective by specifying that the previous subjects were Parisian women. However, could this imply that if Cuban women are asking the same question, are they too somehow Parisian? Bakhtin refers to this stylistic phenomenon as the inclusion of another language in concealed form because it is not marked with the formal markers that accompany that language (Bakhtin 1981: 303). "This is not just another's speech in the same 'language' – he writes – it is another's utterance in a language that is itself 'other' to the author as well" (Bakhtin 1981: 303). The Parisian woman's language is itself a foreign language, as is Jacqueline's Spanish. The transvestite narrator is both inside and outside of the collective body she represents. As Marjorie Garber observes, the transvestite always points "toward a place where it is not" (Garber 1992: 37).

This vertiginous play of masks also appears in the first article of the series in August, 1925. In the vast majority of the fashion articles that appeared in *Social*, writers conventionally address their readers with the familiar *vosotras* or the inclusive *nosotras*. The pronoun marks a space that the dramatized author shares with the implied reader. In this case, the "we" is a collective subject pronoun that bonds implied author to the implied reader. For this, Jacqueline refers to her readers as "nosotras, las mujeres" (us, we women) (August 1925: 51) to emphasize that the "we" in the text does in fact refer to women. Despite the fact that the gendered Spanish pronoun already conveys that the group is composed of women, the supplemental phrase, "we women" inadvertently suggests that there could be a "nosotras" that does not really refer to women.

The presence of the supplement not only suggests that the feminine pronoun lacks self-sufficiency, but it alludes to a femininity that is different from women. The textual excess is a sign for lack and the detachability of the signifier from what it apparently designates. Textual gender is a detachable part, a sign of the missing link written into signification itself. It is plausible to assume that the supplement is necessary to distinguish between women and girls. However, this marks a difference within sameness, and implies that womanhood is not given but rather it is a product of a definitive age narrative. It is likely for this reason that Simone de Beauvoir writes, "one is not born a woman, but rather becomes one" (cited in Butler 1990: 141). Many feminist theorists, likewise, question any notion of the essentiality of women (and men) as subjects. Although Beauvoir was willing to affirm that one is born with a sex, Monique Wittig contends that one not only becomes a gender but also that one becomes sexed because both sex and gender are politically and culturally charged categories and products of the symbolic register (cited in Butler 1990: 141–63). Jacqueline's supplement, thus, implies that gender is a free-floating sign, a detachable part, distinguishable in Spanish often by the mere substitution of an "o" for an "a." In this case, the grammatical "we" and its supplement allude to a space of ambiguity: the difference between the masculine and the feminine and the difference within the feminine itself. The undefined body, that which is not man or woman, is a self-referential sign of representation itself. Because of this, the transvestite is a sign of a self that is different from other and the same as its difference. As Marjorie Garber observes, "the transvestite is both a signifier and that which signifies the undecidability of signification. It points toward itself – or, rather, toward a place where it is not" (Garber 1992: 37).

My point throughout this chapter has been that Jacqueline's textual transvestism has little to do with male authorship. Indeed, a critical reading of the texts themselves should bring us to question a number of our "common sense" assumptions about what authorship is. If the prerequisite for representation is the absence of the real and its replacement with a symbol, then a "dramatized" author should bring us to contemplate the illusions of a self, rather than the self. Hence, this textual transvestism speaks to the intervention of "seeming" that is inherent in the symbolic order. Fashion, much like language, is structured by rules that govern substitution. It compensates for lack through display and camouflage. In this sense, the transvestite and the fashion writer do not represent themselves, but rather they are representative of representation. Both stage the performative and present a pedagogy that proffers the artful management of the symbolic order through creative identifications and appropriations. Jacqueline, in this regard, typifies the deauthorized writer of the period; the illegitimate figure that finds a part of herself on another's body. This cross-over identification is, I believe, the condition for transculturation, without which there would be no Cuban culture. Indeed, this lends credence to Marjorie Garber's contention that "the transvestite makes culture possible, that there can be no culture without the transvestite because the transvestite marks the entrance into the Symbolic" (Garber 1992: 34).

15

Evita and Frida: Latin American Icons for Export

María Claudia André

It has become apparent that the nineteenth-century Republican ambition to educate and civilize all members of society has been replaced by a great project of commercialized seduction in which both the scientific and the humanistic are presented as marketable curiosities for the passive entertainment of an affluent consumer. The search for apparent truth, social utility and moral values have been displaced by a more practical and utilitarian world order geared to match the demands of growing independent markets with that of the society in which consumption in itself defines each individual's place within a given social order. Such process of individualization or identification, as Jean Baudrillard notes, is built upon a system of floating signifiers in which the sign not only functions as a commodity, but also as an inexhaustible source that perpetually incites the consumer's desire.[1] Both the desire to consume and the desire to belong are key components of a *postmodern condition* that, according to François Lyotard, promotes a pluralistic and open democracy over coercive totalizing regimes. Contemporary socio-cultural reconfiguration, in Lyotard's opinion, has placed an emphasis on multiple individual and social identities that vouch for the invention of a personal, private style, born out of the principle of universal consumerism. Among the many features associated with postmodernity, Lyotard distinguishes first the distinctive concern for style over depth or content, and second, the constant reformulation of reality through a wide variety of devices – parody, pastiche, fragmentation, montage, repetition and collage of images – intended to efface cultural, ethnic and social boundaries, thus creating the illusion of the world is a global village. Under this encompassing scenario, all systems of artistic and intellectual expression become assimilated and rearticulated for the benefit of society as a whole.

Since the mid-1980s, the consumerist machine has extended beyond the world of cultural artifacts and objects into the realm of contemporary and historical personalities, many of whom, due to their lives, talent and/or looks, have become marketable commodities and iconographic symbols of popular consumption. Significantly, two of the most outstanding names from the vast gallery of personalities in circulation within the circles of mass media and cultural production are the Mexican painter Frida Kahlo de Rivera (1907–54)[2] and the controversial figure of Eva Duarte de Perón (1919–52). In spite of – or perhaps, due to – their political ideology and non-orthodox conduct, these women have become popular Latin American icons whose fame has by now overshadowed that of their own husbands. Embracing Baudrillard's theories on postmodernity and the consumer society, this essay explores the implications and processes through which the images of these notorious women have been have transformed into marketable products regardless of their anti-imperialist discourse and active militancy within left-wing segments of their respective countries. Furthermore, this study analyzes the ways in which these outstanding personalities, through the constant reproduction of their image, sought to construct an ideal of themselves that paradoxically both matches and mismatches most of the consumer theories and practices that have made icons out of them.

Partly as a result of the changes introduced by the world's transition to democracy and globalization, culture as a factor that shapes people's lives and sense of identity is today appreciated as one of the main ideological instruments of society – along with law, education, family and religion – for it provides a conceptual framework through which individual and collective identities may be interpreted and progressively incorporated into the socio-political agenda of hegemonic institutions.

In contrast, the transition from modernity to postmodernity has also altered traditional distinctions and hierarchies based on class struggle, gender and race in favor of new paradigms based on multicultural, neoliberal and global migrations promoting a system of cultural hybridization that neutralizes differences and social conflicts behind a mask of equality. The dissolution of an organic unity, the rejection of totalitarian discourses and further technological developments have given priority to the illusion that Western and non-Western societies form an homogeneous compound living in pluralistic harmony. Such illusion, however, is supported over a series of essentialist referents and paradigms that are non-responsive to economic, historical and social differences and simply restricted in their capacity to produce cultural expression only in terms defined or accepted by the West.

The restructuring of modern culture into postmodern implies a radical reformulation of the relationship between tradition and modernity as well as between "high" and popular culture. The complexities of such a process go far beyond the concerns of the market; they affect not only individual and collective identities but also national and foreign articulations of culture (García Canclini 1996: 46). Whereas some of these articulations may associate the popular with a wide variety of contemporary or avant-garde discourses, others link the popular to the primitive, indigenous or imagined communities, ethnically identified for their exoticism and their relation to an idyllic past. Yet, this fascination with the past has a straight relation to the postmodern experience and the advancement of socio-economic interests. As a result of this experience, according to Baudrillard, the postmodern subject has grown increasingly incapable of retaining its own past and its own history, and is apparently living a perpetual present. Moreover, as Homi K. Bhabba notes, this process of cultural reconditioning, in itself, serves to empower the minority subject, since the emergence of a hybrid national narrative – that displaces the historical present – opens up the nostalgic past to 'other histories and incommensurable narrative subjects' (Bhabba 1984: 318). These shifts have legitimized the inclusion of some revolutionary movements and underground sectors within the spaces of debate, and as García Canclini examines, 'In short, the ideological veneer of pluralism admits difference without that difference constituting a threat to state and market systems' (García Canchini 2001: x).

Baudrillard understands that hybridity, pluralism and ethnicity of non-Western cultures may serve as a panacea to "present-day multinational capitalism" (Sarup 1993: 181) but other socio-critics, like Mirko Lauer condemn: "Indigenism is the fixed point against which modernity is measured" (Lauer 1996: 111). In other words, the value of indigenous art and culture is only limited to its primitivism and exoticism in relation to the Western perspective, and consequently, subjected to this cultural dichotomy, indigenous societies are forced to remain genuine, traditional and stuck in the past.

In Latin America, however, hybridity has forever been a part of the historical continuum; as Norma Alarcón explains, "We live in incomplete and mixed times of premodernity, modernity and postmodernity, each of these linked historically in turn with corresponding cultures that are, or were, epicenters of power. Our identity is ambiguous multiple and metamorphic" (Canclini 2001: 55). Affected by its own multiplicity and the daily interaction of subaltern groups, Latin American societies are somehow able to resist cultural pollution and confront the transformations of their national identities – without having necessarily to substitute their traditions – as through the years of colonialism, they have developed different methods of balancing the dynamics between the neoliberal mode of globalization and their own ethnic and regional particularities. Yet, as Renato Ortiz argues, several decades of transnational symbolic construction have created "'an international popular culture' with a collective memory made from garments of different nations" (Canclini 2001: 44).

Art and culture are neither consumed nor produced in equal proportions because within a consumerist society not all consumers have the same buying power or the same access to production. In Latin America, as in most underdeveloped or developing countries, consumption and production are limited to those who can either afford the value of a cultural commodity or have access to the knowhow, the data and the technology to create it. Furthermore, García Canclini and Baudrillard agree that the mass media have contributed to the formation of a cultural citizenship, one in which consumers/citizens are constantly sharing codes that refer less to the ethnicity, class and nation into which they were born. Particularly for García Canclini (2001: 45) the definition of nation is less determined by its geographical limits or by its political history, "It survives, rather, as an interpretive community of consumers whose traditional – alimentary, linguistic – habits induce them to relate in a particular way with the objects and information that circulate in international networks."

The expansion of the cultural market developed by international centers of artistic, scientific and communicational production at work that condition audience's cultural development, have made out of indigenous or native artifacts a commodity and marketable items through the homogenizing practice of exotization, "a system of exotic representation that commoditized the colonials to suit imperial consumption" (Savigliano 1995: 2). In this process, rather than establishing the intrinsic diversity and complexities of subaltern cultures and non-Western societies, Western interpretations only accentuate those elements of the exotic and the primitive that mirror their own aesthetic perception and pathological stereotypes, therefore perpetuating the colonialist legacy of exclusion, incorporation and domination.

Against the argument of cultural elitism that sustains that artwork and cultural capital may elevate the masses to a higher spiritual level and invoke their critical consciousness, Baudrillard argues that the socialization of cultural systems of representation does not contribute in providing more information but, to the contrary, it erases any real significance or meaning, for only a partial identity and fictionalized interpretation of the artwork or group in question is indeed articulated. In addition, aware that only the elites may possess or acquire cultural capital – the ability to read and appreciate a work of art – silent majorities passively consume commodities and mass-produced simulations of the original, without trying to make sense of the cultural objects. For them there is no meaning, but only a virtual transference of the objects' essence, a simulation, and floating signifier through which they are able to either make an impression or gain a certain status (Sarup 1993: 166).

If García Canclini's (2001: 22) argument that "To consume is to make more sense of a world where all that's solid melts in the air" is true, then it is worth considering what ideological or conceptual premises Latin American icons bring to the Western consumer? How do Westernized representations of legendary figures such as Ernesto "Che" Guevera, Carmen Miranda, Pancho Villa, Evita Perón and Frida Kahlo among others,[3] enrich the saturated gallery of fictional and real characters mass produced for the United States consumer mainstream? What lies at the heart of this phenomenon, and how – if at all – do such articulations ascribe or counteract the hegemonic discourse of the West?

From the vast repertoire of personalities, Frida Kahlo and Eva Perón render themselves as the quintessential paradigms through which we may explore the complexities of cultural iconography. Apart from the coincidence that both were married to exhibitionistic and charismatic men of genius, who loved women and who also created a sense of mystique about themselves, the similarities between them are, indeed, many. Both challenged the patriarchal mold of their times that limited women to space of the domestic: Kahlo was the first female artist to ever sell a painting to the Louvre Museum and the first Latin American artist to present her artworks in a Parisian art gallery (1939), and under similar social circumstances, Evita was the first woman to be nominated for a vice-presidential candidacy in Latin America (1951).[4]

For Frida as well as for Evita, the personal was political: the first one fully embraced the Marxist ideology and supported the Mexican revolution, the latter passionately embodied the fight of the proletariat for equality and justice. Through their lives, both developed their own distinctive styles, public images, verbal and non-verbal behavior (gestures, hairstyle, clothing, jewelry, attitude), not only as a means to exercise power and express their own sense of identity, but more importantly, as tools for survival. Whereas Frida Kahlo emphasized her *mexicanidad* strictly wearing traditional Mexican costumes to challenge the predominant "normalized" Eurocentric fashion of her time, Evita Perón adopted such fashion to construct a public image with which to cross class and social boundaries, and to identify herself with both sectors of the population. Ironically, these two women, whose figures stood out for the exuberance of their clothing, jewelry and style, were physically affected by a process of corporal decay, which ultimately led, in both cases, to a premature death. These sexually contradictory figures who fit the prototype of the fallen woman – Frida for her bi-sexuality and extramarital affairs and Evita for the many men she used to gain access to stardom – still today, stand as legendary symbols for those who dare to dream and to be different. In the United States and in Latin America, both women have achieved the status of role models, cult figures and martyrs venerated to the point of sanctity as they stand as symbols of physical pain, social struggle and gender or political oppression.

Frida for Export

In the early 1970s, Frida Kahlo was mostly known outside of Mexico among a few art critics and small academic groups, but within the last decade, the increasing popularity of her life and art have added to her fame, making out of her figure one of he most extraordinary pop icons and cult phenomena of the twentieth century.[5] Art critics and biographers Margaret A. Lindauer, Hayden Herrera and Martha Zamora to name a few, concur that the key to Kahlo's magnetism lies, on one hand, in the versatility of her image – as seen in commercial advertising and a wide range of consumer objects such as cards, jewelry, clothing and art – and on the other, in her ability to convey in each painting a "potent mixture of personal history, cultural inheritance, political commitment and sheer self-conscious myth-making."[6]

Posing as the model and main focus of her pictorial narrative, Kahlo's self-referential paintings cast an aura of feminine sensuality reminiscent of that of Renaissance icons in which the play of light and shadow, anatomy and dramatic action are used to accentuate the intensity of facial expressions. In particular, the graphic quality of her portraits combines modern influences of expressionism and surrealism with the imagery and the color palette characteristic of indigenous Mexican art. Still, despite the artist's obvious attraction for the female form, her portrayals never fall into the traditional objectification of the feminine as frequently seen in masculine renditions, but to the contrary, Kahlo's body stands as a mythical presence and ethnic signifier, physically devoid of social conditioning. Her artistry reveals sensually charged images of pain and martyrdom projected through an aura of mysticism, at times sexually suggestive and whimsically related to primordial cycles of existence: birth, life and death. Kahlo's female figure is biologically and emotionally brought into full light, thus subjecting her intimacy to the dynamics of erotic, exotic and cultural encounters in which both Western and non-Western traditions are in constant dialog with each other.

Upon positioning herself within the role of the "other" in relation to the West, the artist sustains a clear argument against the silent consensus regarding the Westernization by the vast majority of Mexican society of her times. Still, what remains problematic when analyzing her pictorial discourse at first glance, as Milner argues, is that while she wanted her art to reflect her Mexicanness and to serve the communist revolution, her paintings are so individualistic and "*so palpably egocentric, that even after making allowances for her contextuality, prevailing ideology, or any of the various 'determinants' that might have circumscribed her vision, the pictures simple do not speak strongly of much other than Frida Kahlo*" (Milner 1995: 86).

Indeed, the general audiences' perception of the Mexican painter's creative skills is very much reduced to her market value as an icon of emotional and physical endurance in relation to the pain and the tragic narrative of her life, other than appreciated – like Rivera – for her artistic talent. Such misinterpretation of Kahlo's artistry lies in the fact that while her self-taught, almost naïve technique and style may seem overly simplistic to the trained art critic, in the world of mass-produced cultural industry, the symbolism in her paintings does not incite rationalist criticism. As such, her paintings may be interpreted at face value, requiring no further critical consciousness or deeper intellectualization from the consumer culture. Additionally, in Lindauer's opinion, the overall perception of Kahlo's artwork exemplifies how women are confined to feminine commodity prescription and locked out of certain parameters determined by capitalist and patriarchal discourses that aim to suppress all counter hegemonic expressions of the feminine that may challenge or question the *status quo* (Lindauer 1999: 151).

Underscoring her femininity through art, one of the most frequently depicted symbols in Kahlo's pictorial vocabulary is her Tehuana dress, the characteristic costume of the Tehuantepec region of Mexico. Milner is one of the many critics who sustain that Kahlo's attire selection was not a means to hide her physical imperfections and/or to please Diego as other critics suggest but a way of asserting her cultural identity and her individuality.[7] Recent studies, however, argue that her attraction to the Tehuana dress has some relation to the fact that in the indigenous regions of the Isthmus of Tehuantepec, through the centuries, women have managed to sustain a matriarchal social structure where women hold high rank economic and political positions. In her excellent study of Kahlo's fetishization, Lindauer indicates that the dress in itself is a particularly rich symbol of cultural difference and defiance to colonialist imposition, which stands as a reference of a matriarchal society that was known for resisting cultural assimilation as well as European and patriarchal ruling. "In other words, according to myth, they represented a past that had escaped European rule, thereby sustaining a 'true,' uncorrupted Mexican society" (Lindauer 1999: 126). The Tehuana dress was also a political statement of the nationalist project fueled by socialist revolutionaries whom, after the Mexican Revolution, sought to create a government of national unity through land and social reforms. As Milner indicates, this ethnic attire "conformed with similar efforts by other metropolitan middle-class women to emphasize the Mexican uniqueness" (Milner 1995: 11). Kahlo adopted such fashion not only when traveling abroad, but also among the Mexican middle-upper class and other social circles where most people aspired to wear Western clothes as an indicator of prestige. In fact, to most Mexicans, her costume represented an exaggerated Mexicanization of Mexico as it both challenged the dominant culture's consensus regarding fashion and style as much as it defied the traditional conventions of her times.

Self-Portrait on the Border between Mexico and the US (1932) and *My Dress Hangs There* (1933) are perhaps two of the most well-known allegorical representations in which the painter manifests, through clothing and background, an explicit critique towards socioeconomic corruption and exploitation systems brought along by American capitalism. In *Self-Portrait*, Kahlo stands as the physical border between Mexico and the United States holding the Mexican flag on one hand and a cigarette in the other. Conveying the idea that both countries and cultures are, in fact, "two worlds apart," in the Mexican side – to the left of the canvas – flowers and plants rooted on fertile ground grow amidst the ruins of a Mayan temple that reflects the echoes of a past still obedient to the pre-Columbian cosmological order. Shockingly depleted of natural elements, in the United States – to the right – roots and plants have been replaced by cables and electric cords. Machinery and buildings rise like tombstones into a sunless sky covered with a thick veil of smog out of which the silhouette the American flag stands as a symbol of capitalism and industrialization. In this painting, Kahlo is not wearing her traditional Tehuana costume, but a pink colonial-style dress, its color matching the tone of the American skyscrapers.

Apart from the obvious contrast between both cultures, the symbolism in this painting has led art critics to consider the artist's own ambivalence regarding her *mestiza* identity, product of her Indian and European heritage.[8] For Oriana Baddeley, "In those paintings where Kahlo wears European dress she is passive, weak and unable to control her own destiny, but in the Tehuana costume she is strong, powerful, hopeful" (Baddeley 1991: 14). On the other hand, as Lindauer observes, in this portrait she depicts an image that is not an expression of her identity "... she is not herself, she is Carmen Rivera, identified by the border marker upon which she stands, a masquerade, a theatrical role, one that does not necessarily project her own political views, but rather uses her own image as a signifier" (Lindauer 1999: 130). Such a deployment of power or dramatization of her own persona may also be interpreted as a mechanism of passive resistance, a stance and a statement to redefine herself. Cultural, national and gender ambiguous references in Kahlo's allegorical paintings portray many of the persistent social and political issues dealing with by-standard notions of domination and oppression, present and past, and primitive and modern, as complex points of tension that define as much as perpetuate the dynamics between Western and non-Western societies.

Another example of such a contradictory and yet symbolic significance is *My Dress Hangs There*. In this complex representation of American society, Kahlo overtly critiques the advance of capitalism, overwhelmingly sympathizing with the oppressed masses, which, as portrayed, are invited to enjoy the products of the corporate imperialism only to become exploited by it. The typical Tehuana dress hangs between a toilet and a trophy, while cables, telephones, gas pumps and buildings rise over a uniformed colorless mass of workers marching into New York City, the core of the capitalist machine. The allegorical representation of the Tehuana dress has been interpreted by critics Milner and Herrera, as an ethnic signifier of her *mexicanidad* and statement of economic freedom; for others, like Lindauer, the dress stands as a symbol of socio-economic corruption and exploitation, as it does not rise above the corporate, but stands as the procreator of the laborers who will later become exploited. In other words, the dress it embodies "the benefits of capitalism's drive toward lucrative modernization and its costs to the human social body and psyche. The dress is giving birth to the immigrants that are coming to the US to be exploited by the system" (Lindauer 1999: 127). Through wires, cords and representative objects – a telephone, a gas pump, Mae West's portrait, churches, commercial buildings – Kahlo also seems to mock mass communicational, political processes and socioeconomic systems that reorganize the rules of hegemony and subordination for the benefit of market expansion, regardless of their effects or their impact over individual and collective identities.

It is ironic that Kahlo herself was unable to escape that same consumerist machine that she so fiercely critiqued. Deemed as the quintessential icon of Mexican surrealism, her paintings nowadays fetch the highest prices of any Latin American artist. Most likely, such an overwhelming popularity is related to the fact that Kahlo's peculiarities and "looks" were captivating and intriguing. In her visit to Paris, when she was invited by André Bretón in 1939 for the opening of the surrealist exhibition *Mexique*, the originality of her Tehuana dress caused a great sensation among the European elites. Franco-Italian designer, Elsa Schiaparelli designed a *couture* line and a dress that she baptized "la Robe de Madame Rivera." To promote such a style, Kahlo's hand, covered with jewels, appeared on the monthly cover of French *Vogue* magazine. In his spring 1998 collection, French designer Jean Paul Gaultier once again revamped the Mexican artist's image and *Mexique* look in a successful collection that still today can be appreciated on the Web.[9] In his collection, Gaultier deconstructs the original figure, presenting a postmodern Kahlo whose marked androgynous look combines European, Latin American and traditional Mexican fabrics, costumes and styles. Fully stripped from its original meaning as cultural signifier, Kahlo's Tehuana dress, hairdo and jewelry are reinterpreted within a carnivalized fashion under the label of "primitiveness" and "exoticism" that caters to the demands of novelty seeking consumers.[10]

Dale Bauer's interpretation of the Bakhtinian carnival may be helpful to clarify the issues of empowerment that appear in the crass "commoditization" of Kahlo's status as fashion icon and cult figure. For Bauer, the carnival may be defined as "The realm of unmasked desire, taken out the law of culture and involved in a economy of difference. While the authoritative discourse demands conformity, the carnivalized discourse renders invalid any codes, conventions, or laws which govern or reduce the individual to an object of control" (Bauer 1991: 679). During carnival, the temporary suspension of all barriers creates a world unrestricted by authoritative discourse and in which desire is freed from its mask. This suspended time or fantasy world provides the opportunity for those who do not traditionally hold power to do so, if only for a limited amount of time. It is only then, through carnivalization and cannibalization of the exotic Other, both Westerners and non-Westerners are able to relate and participate in an egalitarian society in which racial, social and cultural differences become erased. Engulfed by this process, historical and political events surrounding Frida Kahlo's life are then subordinated in favor of those themes that accentuate her individuality, femininity and Mexican style. Such elements counterbalance the totalizing discourse of globalization, capitalism and neo-liberalism and become, in Shifra Goldman's view, part of the "long history of utilizing art works and art exhibits as symbolic carriers, as mediators for political ideologies and economic transactions – particularly between Mexico and the United States" (Lindauer 1999: 175).

The carnivalization and rearticulation of the "Frida-look" as a fashion commodity that sells individuality and style has led fashion magazines to downplay the artist's physical condition through the depiction of Kahloesque looking models who only accentuate the exoticism of Kahlo's costumes and the seductiveness of her persona. Indeed, as Lindauer observes, while some aspects of Fridamania accommodate the masculinist reduction of the individual Frida Kahlo to the category "woman" by accentuating the sensual and feminine kahloesque look, others project Kahlo's figure as the personification of gender resistance by emphasizing the artist's facial hair and physical deformities (Lindauer 1999: 162). Baddeley notes that these fashion magazines all share "the emphasis on 'her,' as an encapsulation of stereotypical images of Mexico rather than her work. It is her body as the canvas, her appearance as art. The art of self-expression becomes self-expression as art" (Baddeley 1991: 12).

Within this frame, the market value of the Frida phenomenon has also become associated with some underground countercultures and extreme cultural tendencies, such as the cyborg culture. In *Simians, Cyborgs and Women* (1991), Donna Haraway introduces the idea of the cyborg culture as a powerful critique to science and technology. Cyborg, as defined by Haraway, is a condensed image of both imagination and material reality. As such, Frida Kahlo's deconstructed body incarnates a postmodern archetype of the cybernetic or cyborg counterculture playing upon the idea of deformity, pain and suffering as a commodity, the results of which appeal to those fascinated by the perverse mixture of natural impulses and technology. Endorsing Haraway's views, Daniela Falini argues that Frida stands a forerunner of postmodern extreme cultural tendencies as her artworks deal with the limits between the invisible and visible, transformation, fragmentation and mutations of several kinds, thus representing a collective biography of human emotional and physical upheaval characteristic of contemporary society.

Kahlo's life and art still continue to be portrayed in operatic plays – like Migdalia Cruz's show *Frida*, which opened in Brooklyn Academy of Art in 1992 – as well as in a variety of documentaries and films.[11] The first cinematic production of Frida's biography, *Vida y Muerte de Frida Kahlo según fue referida a Karen y David Crommie,* was released in 1965 and presented in San Francisco's International Film Festival in 1966. The second, directed by the Mexican cinematographer Paul Leluc, *Frida, Naturaleza Viva* was produced in 1985, and gained worldwide recognition for its remarkable rendition of the artist's life. The third, under the direction of Julie Taymor with the Mexican actress Salma Hayek in the role of Frida, Alfred Molina as Diego de Rivera and the Australian actor Geoffrey Rush as Leon Trotsky was released in October 2002.[12] While *Frida* was well received among American audiences and film critics, for Mexican viewers, Hayek renders a superficial, passionless and misleading interpretation of Kahlo's character. According to film critic Perla Ciuk:

> The script, written by five irresponsible ignorants, barely refers to the history of the Muralist movement, and surrealism, when in fact, Diego and Frida are its history . . . . Everything is superficial in this narration, Frida suffers, paints, loves and deceits in the same light tone in which the great comrade Diego Rivera (Alfred Molina) – character without which Mexican communism is inexplicable – is portrayed as a "fatso," womanizer, drunkard and irresponsible.[13]

Originally, singer-actress Madonna intended to play the role of Kahlo out of her sheer admiration for the Mexican artist's work. In the October 2002 issue of *Vanity Fair,* Madonna confesses to interviewer Steven Daly her love for Kahlo's painting *My Birth,* a piece that she proudly displays "propped on a shelf" at her house. "Ah, my Frida Kahlo," says Madonna, sweeping into the room. "I carry it with me everywhere in bubble wrap, in a Sainsbury's [supermarket] plastic bag. Just so no one thinks I'm carrying anything valuable." As posed by Madonna, her consumption and cannibalization of Kahlo's art "for my eyes only," denotes on one hand a superficial appreciation of the artist's work, and on the other, the commodification of a recognizable painting, covered in plastic wrap not to protect the artwork, but to conceal its market value to the otherwise "ignorant" masses. For Janice Bergman-Carton, the Madonna/Kahlo connection is a ploy by

> Hollywood publicists, art world entrepreneurs and Madonna herself to exploit an old and reliable advertising device, the artist/celebrity validation code. By this measure, Kahlo is a better artist (investment) because Madonna collects her work, and Madonna is a more serious and respected celebrity (investment) because she collects Kahlo paintings. This reciprocity resonates in box offices, museum coffers, record companies and the art market. (Lindauer 1000: 173)[14]

To crown Kahlo's popularity, in 2001 the United States Postal Service honored the artist with a commemorative 34-cent image "Self-Portrait with Necklace" (1930s), at a ceremony held at Phoenix Art Museum, Arizona, an event that coincided with the Nineteenth Annual Convention of the National Association of Hispanic Journalists. It is noteworthy to point out that whereas white American consumers revere Kahlo's image as a signifier to gain the acceptance of the social elite to which they aspire to belong, for the Hispanic-American community – and particularly for women – Kahlo is a symbol of femininity and inner strength. Under this light, the artist stands as an empowering icon for the Latina agenda in the United States because her art illustrates, at best, the conflictive experience of growing and surviving in what Chicana poet Gloria Anzaldúa calls, "the Borderlands": a meeting ground for all divergent people who live and share the joy of being part of more than one culture, language, class and race (Anzaldúa 1987: 28). Anzaldúa's perception is shared by Chicanas and Mexican women alike who, bread within borderland cultures, struggle to deconstruct misogynist and/or racist representations of minority sectors of society. For them, Kahlo's work is symbolic of the process of restoration and decolonization of the feminine subject; a process that begins with the recognition of their roots and their historical past, and ends with the reinscription of their right to participate and become socially and politically integrated within a community as a whole.[15]

Evita or Madonna?

The charismatic figure of Eva Duarte de Perón and her capacity to attract both the attention of the mass media and the admiration of the masses, merits at least a brief analysis in this study, as even today, some forty years after her death, the legendary story of Evita and her social climb from rags to riches remains very much alive. Current theories of gender construction and performance are appropriate to explain the ways in which Evita's theatricality and performance became a political strategy not only for the empowerment of her own persona, but also, as Silvia Pellarolo notes, "a political strategy for claiming public space and political visibility for the empowerment of traditionally erased sectors of society" (Pellaroio 2000: 35). Indeed, Evita's acting training along with her radio, film and stage performances, helped her develop a melodramatic style that later became a powerful tool of seduction in her political career as the First Lady of Argentina.[16] As most of her biographers concur (Taylor 1994; Navarro 1994; Dujovne 1995), her short career as an actress was only a dress rehearsal for the future role she was to play in the history of her country and once given the chance to finally be herself Evita became the performer of her own political agenda making out of the mass media her medium and of the country her stage. Significantly, her popularity grew in straight proportion to the control she exerted over the press and the radio, means of communication that she exploited to her advantage, extracting the last possible drop of propaganda from bureaucratic functions, charity acts, public speeches and political rallies. In 1947, she purchased the newspaper *Democracia* and later, *El Mundo* to promote her own activities and those of the Eva Perón Foundation. As Joan Barnes examines, "Evita owned or controlled the four principal radio stations in Buenos Aires, and through her influence over the Ministry of Information, exercised virtual censorship rights over the news contents all of Argentina's thirty three radio stations" (75).

Even before becoming the president's wife during her acting career, Evita carefully tailored her image to project both the glamor and the sex appeal of famous silver screen divas of the times – such as Joan Fontaine, Lana Turner, Jean Harlow and Marilyn Monroe – with a touch of local flair as the incarnation of "the new model of Argentine beauty: a blend of Hollywood screen allure with the earthy nature of vernacular melodrama heroines" (Pellarolo 2000: 29). Moreover, aware of the powerful influence of the mass media over popular audiences, from the very first moment Evita became Argentina's First Lady, she hired a personal entourage of fashion designers, makeup artists, image consultants, speech writers, ghostwriters and publicity men to work "for the same goal: to create a legend" (Wilkie and Menell-Kinberg 1981: 134).

Soon after her marriage to Perón, Evita became one of Christian Dior's main customers, and "By 1948 she owned more than 100 furs and her jewel collection was said to rival that of Cleopatra. Her critics blasted her for being so extravagant. Evita knew that dressing up was a way of saying to the people, 'I was once like you, but look at me now. You too can be like me'" (Wangemann n.d. 3). As Marysa Navarro and Nicholas Fraser examine, the couture houses of Christian Dior and Marcel Rochas would send her clothing sketches through the French Embassy in Buenos Aires or would send her clothes that they would consider appropriate for the First Lady (Navarro and Fraser 1994: 98). It is interesting though that Elsa Schiaparelli who was so enthusiastic about making Kahlo's acquaintance refused to meet Evita. In her autobiography, the designer writes that she could have met her at The Ritz in Paris, "Evita, in spite of her political interests, loved jewels and clothes, but instead of going out to look for them she summoned them to her. I was invited to wait on her, but did not go. A number of other *couturiers* and jewelers were asked to go to her on a specified day" (Schiaparelli 1954: 228).

Placing herself as a symbol of social conscience and a role model to which Argentine women could aspire, Evita became the embodiment of desire serving as catalyst to the hopes and needs of the lower class. Modeled after Mussolini's fascism, the Peronist discourse sought to take advantage of the dynamics between the classes. Its ideology promoted a new model of a rising class born out of the popular weave, in opposition to oligarchic and capitalistic regimes, which, as Evita perceived, collaborated with foreign powers. Peronism considered that while capitalism exploited the workers, communist party sought to build a nation of a single class, "of former proletarians who will live and work worthily" (*Evita by Evita* 83). The First Lady's public image and luxurious clothing, however, reflected her ambivalence towards poverty and wealth. As Eva Perón, the president's wife, she adopted upper class, fashionably elegant European clothing, and as Evita, the Patron Saint of the Poor, she limited her wardrobe to a simple chignon and plain double-breasted suit with a velvet collar, which finally became her uniform. In her biography *La Razón de mi Vida*, published in 1951, she intends to disclaim her ostentatious gowns and jewelry on the grounds that she was only following the protocol as required to the First Lady, "I am Eva Perón, the wife of the President, whose work is simple and agreeable, a holiday job of receiving honors, of gala performances; I am also Evita, the wife of the leader of a people who have deposited in him all their faith, hope and love." Publicly, Evita disregarded public criticism by claiming that most of her jewelry did not belong to her as they were mainly tokens of appreciation given to her by friends, and foreign governments. Even on her deathbed she requested her jewels be returned to the people. "I don't want to them to fall into the hands of the Oligarchy and that is why I want them to stand . . . as a permanent source of credit which banks, may then use for the benefit of the people."

The actual status of her possessions is unknown, yet the myth behind the woman and her social legacy has been kept alive in the works of several biographers, documentarists, cinematographers and composers, who, inspired by the South American Cinderella, have further contributed to the perpetuation of the legend.[17] The most popular of all biographical renditions of Evita's life to date has been the hit musical *Evita* composed by Andrew Lloyd Webber and Tim Rice (1978), winning seven Tony Awards and eight Los Angeles Drama Critics Awards.[18] In 1996, years after its London premiere, the musical was finally adapted into film and produced by directors Oliver Stone and Alan

Parker with pop icon Madonna in the role of Evita, Antonio Banderas as revolutionist Ernesto "Ché" Guevera acting as narrator, and Jonathan Pryce in the character of Juan Domingo Perón. Despite cinema critics' negative reviews, the film received an Oscar for best film score and as well as three Golden Globe Awards, cashing in $160 million dollars profit over the $60 million originally invested in production.

Among the many factors that added to the film's immediate popularity was the much-promoted conflict behind Madonna's performance as Argentina's First Lady, for both sectors of society opposed the idea of having the controversial actress incarnate Evita. While the upper classes and military sectors preferred to keep the myth of Evita subdued or dormant, Peronist audiences perceived that Madonna's overt sexuality would not only hinder Evita's memory, but also would misrepresent Evita's true character. But, above all, as Silvia Pellarolo notes, Argentine audiences opposed the idea of having Madonna impersonate Evita because such metonymic twist would perhaps, "demystify the flat 'saint-whore' dichotomy that pro- and anti-Evita sectors had grudgingly accepted as a safe way of immortalizing and disembodying her memory" (Pellarolo 2000: 35). Despite the Argentines' criticism, Madonna, enthused by the role, jumped at the opportunity to take part in the production assuring both Argentines and producers that she had much more in common with Evita than her humble origins and her ambition for power and success: "I am the only one to deserve the role of Evita. I am the only one to understand her passion and pain."[19]

While it may be true that Evita and Madonna share common lifes' experiences and were originally guided by an incredible ambition for success and popular recognition, their most outstanding similarity is their ability to transform, update and stage their public image through the effective manipulation of the media as a mobilizing force to seduce audiences worldwide.[20] Posing as the reflection of the sinner/saint dichotomy, Madonna, as a pop icon, accentuates her physical attributes and overt sexuality to break taboos and destroy patriarchal constructs of gender, whereas Evita, as a political figure, constructs out of her image a social symbol and political body with which to mythologize herself as the leader, martyr and patron saint of the proletariat.[21] According to James Wilkie and Monica Menell-Kinberg, such calculated manipulation behind the figure of Evita may be clearly understood in terms of the "elitelore," which as the critics note represents a refined method of self-justification for the elite to stand as the ruling class and a way to influence as well as to gain the appreciation of the folk. "Elitelore mixes with folklore, then, when the elite create their own 'reality' from what they understand to be the lore of the people. The result is a fictionalized folklore that may have results unintended by the author" (Wilkie and Menell 1981: 101).

As elitelore is passed down over the time, the folk gradually begin to collectively accept and incorporate the fictionalized interpretation of their own lore as represented by the political elite. This concept is relevant for it helps us understand how the dynamics behind the restructuring of culture today are subtle and easy to overlook. In the same fashion that Evita's public figure was disruptive to the ruling class and the institutionalized armed forces because it challenged and carnivalized traditional notions of propriety in political practices, Madonna also became a dangerous sign that threatened Evita's narrative memory as constructed by the elitelore as a bipolar figure, accepted by both rival political fractions. Such transference of popular tradition to the culture industry – or from folklore to elitelore – in relation to Evita's identity as impersonated by Madonna not only creates an interesting mirror effect out of which several analogies may be drawn, but also helps envision the intricacies behind the net of symbols and signifiers hurled at us by the mass media industry.

Along with the process of identity transference, the visual metaphor of Evita/Madonna sacrifices Evita's political persona and the contents of her ideological message in favor of those melodramatic aspects of her personality that seem to appeal to mass audiences (such as her ambition for power, her physical seduction and her social and political ascension). On the other hand, the commodification of the Argentine leader through Madonna's portrayal ironically contributes to fulfill Evita's dream of becoming an acclaimed Hollywood star. Paradoxically, for Evita, that fame comes at the cost of surrendering her identity and idealized self-image to Madonna's performance and characterization of herself, as it is the American singer and not the Argentine activist that audiences view in the hundred of clips and advertising campaigns launched to promote the film's release. We just have to wonder how many people, when thinking of Evita, draw upon the image of Madonna.[22] Indeed, as Marta Savigliano points out, 'Madonna the superstar shapes the ways in which Evita's image and story reach the film audience . . . No one seems to doubt that the Evita that Argentine children will know will be the one represented by Madonna in Alan Parker's Hollywood film, and they resent it" (Savigliano 2002: 357).[23]

Significantly, Savigliano's excellent analysis on the Hollywood romanticized and unthreatening interpretation of Eva Perón also applies to that of Frida Kahlo's; "Have you seen *Evita*?" Savigliano questions, "Not Eva, not Eva Duarte, not Eva Perón, but a version of her historical mythical character in the diminutive; not just a foreshortening but a downsizing, right from the beginning, to situate spectators comfortably, to help them take a close look at the tamed Eva, an Eva made familiar" (Savigliano 2002: 344). Such controlled remythologization, as the critic notes – and which I sustain is equally applicable for both figures – underscores their personal traits and desires while neutralizing their ideology and politics. In this process, not only are Kahlo and Evita's inner strength and autonomous character subdued and softened, but also the controversial role they played in the history and society of their own times is presented in a dramatically undisturbing way as their "public, political figure is thoroughly personalized and thus banalized" (Savigliano 2002: 344).

Fredric Jameson believes that the restructuring of culture and the random cannibalization of the past brought along by postmodernity has produced a transcultural and transhistorical world market project in which distinctive cultural and social expressions as well as artistic techniques – like surrealism and magic realism so popular in Latin American literature and art – have already become objects of mass consumption. Adding to this comment, Valentine Moghadam believes that contemporary societies – including Third World – are all suffering from Westoxication or Westitis, "a plague from the West, a phenomenon of excessive Westernization that renders members (usually those with a Western education) of the community alienated from their own culture" (Moghadam 1994: 120).

Paradoxically, upon the realization that Western ethnographic curiosity in other cultures is based on a superficial interest to cannibalize folk themes and techniques, exotic others – subaltern cultures, minorities, non-Westerners – who struggle to inhabit within the realm ruled by postmodern standards, fuel the Western desire by accentuating their passionateness, primitivism and exoticism so as gain global recognition, inclusion and representation. In this cultural exchange, the civilized, postmodern colonizer constitutes his own progressive identity on the basis of this confrontation with exotic colonized others, thus granting the colonized-exotic-Other a certain level of social-cultural recognition that provides both a locus of identity and a source of contestation against the colonizing-civilized desire (Savigliano 1995: 3).

Acting as a global kaleidoscope in which all cultures converge, postmodernity comprehends and reshuffles a wide spectrum of cultural symbols, myths and imagery in order to convey the idea of total liberation and self-expression "organically linked to the conception of an authentic self and private identity which can be expected to generate its own unique vision of the world and to forge its own unmistakable style" (Sarup 1993: 146). In the postmodern universe where everything is a simulacrum or simulation of reality, there are no incentives to return to the social or to generate new ideals at the collective level, and therefore, passively consuming and wrapped in what Jameson calls "consumer schizophrenia," people forget traditional politics and the problems afflicting society and the world as a whole. As Baudrillard's writings on cultural imperialism indicate, and Latinamericanists John Beverley and José Oviedo further concur, "the production of a postmodernist 'sublime' in relation to Latin America may involve the aesthetic fetishization of its social, cultural and economic status quo. Thereby attenuating the urgency for radical social change and displacing it into cultural dilettantism and quietism" (Beverley and Oviedo 1995: 3). If we tend to agree with Marxist critic Antonio Gramsci's concept that everything is political, then we should perhaps ask ourselves if the vocation of achieving an absolute social, economic and political ideal is still a possibility or if we should just surrender and worship the new paradigm of multiple freedoms that the market and mass media has to offer.

16

Fashioning United States Salvadoranness: Unveiling the Faces of Christy Turlington and Rosa Lopez

Claudia M. Milian Arias

> It's an apparition that causes even jaded Manhattan pedestrians to halt midstep and gape: Christy Turlington, in the flesh, is strolling up Madison Avenue. Because the iconic model is enshrined in the popular imagination as a two-dimensional Venus in Calvin Klein skivvies, seeing her walking and talking seems more shocking than encountering a movie star or even a President; it's as jarring as if the Mona Lisa had come to life . . .
>
> Handelman

> . . . And follow her they did. Reporters staked out the Salvadoran international airport throughout the weekend, then on Monday traveled two hours to Sensuntepeque, where they mobbed [Rosa] Lopez outside her home. Then they followed her in a convoy as she fled to a farm deep in the Salvadoran countryside.
>
> Wilkinson

United States Salvadorans are configured in the United States neocolonial imaginary through civil war discourse and social dependency. Submerged in rhetoric reminiscent of the Vietnam War, they are positioned as silent, impoverished, hallucinatory and unmeltable ethnics bringing chaos to the United States (see Rogin 1999). Propelled by a kind of Salvadoran nationality exclusively understood through the problematic lifestyles of Salvadoran (Central) Americanness in opposition to white (North) Americanness, this study interrogates two contrasting visual representations, as reported in the national press, that surfaced during the 1990s. The short-lived image of domestic servant Rosa Lopez, a Salvadoran who lived in the United States for 30 years, is juxtaposed with the lingering profile of supermodel Christy Turlington, the daughter of a retired white American pilot and a former Salvadoran flight attendant for Pan American Airlines.

Although the signifiers behind each face had its distinctive moment in United States popular culture, this work starts with the premise that the poverty-stricken, recognizable illegality of Lopez and the undecipherable, "Latin" Salvadoranness of Turlington operate as forms of American consumption that eliminate, thereby delocalizing Salvadoran subjectivities in the United States, from the "American" imaginary. The ways that these women experience, articulate and identify with Salvadoranness varies, as are the lenses through which the media – supermarket tabloids, television talk shows, daily newspapers and weekly magazines – construct their respective fashionable, or unfashionable, roles in the United States social and economic world. Yet, Turlington and Lopez are unified by the larger implications of their respective occupations: Hollywood productions of brownness through deportability and assimilability. These oppositional expectations oversimplify United States Salvadoran existence. They point to a depersonalization of Salvadoran identities that does not allow for an adequate exploration of their complex lives in the United States.

Despite the fairly obvious associations that may surface from depictions of the undesirable maid versus the sexy supermodel, or the drudgery of household work against the fantasy world depicted in fashion, these images contain a social intensity that intermixes the cultural politics of everyday life. As employed hereafter, fashion does not exclusively connote the world of *haute couture* or clothing behavior in capitalist systems. In *The Face of Fashion*, Jennifer Craik elaborates that the meanings of these cultural phenomena relate "to particular codes of behavior and rules of ceremony and place. It denotes and embodies conventions that contribute to the etiquette and manners of social encounters" (Craik 1993: 10). In this chapter, notions of fashion operate as a "technique most available to women" (Bhattacharyya 2002: 417). As a form that dresses bodies "everywhere," fashion activates a communicative power that, from Elizabeth Wilson's perspective, "links beauty, success and the city" (Wilson 1985: 9). The role of the invisible, but visibly useful maid in a major city like Los Angeles, a location that Henry Giroux, in his analysis of popular culture, classifies as the embodiment of "the changing nature of the metropolitan urban terrain and the cultural politics that appear to besiege it," chronicles how the United States public imagines Salvadorans (Giroux 1994: 80). Turlington's cosmopolitanness in metropolitan centers provides a revealing glimpse of the cultural luxury behind color and economic blindness. The idea of Turlington as picture-perfect, however, is subverted by her ability to link her subject position to "real" life situations.

Lopez's notoriety surged as a defense witness in *The People of the State of California v. Orenthal James Simpson*, or in public terms, the Trial of the Century. Her declarations were seemingly significant for the defense strategy of O. J. ("the Juice") Simpson, an African American National Football League

Hall of Famer, 1968 Heisman Trophy winner while at the University of Southern California and television personality. Lopez was the only person to testify that she had seen Simpson's car outside his home around the time prosecutors believed the crime – multiple stab wounds that resulted in the murder of two white Los Angeles residents, Simpson's ex-wife, Nicole Brown Simpson, and her friend, Ronald Lyle Goldman – had occurred, 10.15 p.m. Put more succinctly, Lopez "flickered briefly in the paparazzi's flashes" during the 1995 trial, as the *Chicago Sun-Times* deemed it (Zwecker 1995: 33). Interest in her personal life paradoxically reveals an accessible figure: the servant with the replaceable occupation who needs to be uncovered with an unspecified, yet foreseen, wrongs.

By contrast, the deracializing popular discourse that surrounds Turlington's face alludes to a contradictory unattainable, yet accessible, white American reality. This conception of facile, visual Americanness is fashioned, defined and disseminated by systems of power that reinforce asymmetrical relationships within dominant understandings of the nation. Turlington's commodified Americana is portrayed through her advertisements for Camay soap, Kellogg's Special K, Shalimar, Maybelline and Calvin Klein products, including CK's underwear and swimwear lines as well as the fragrances Eternity and Contradiction. Decades after the 1980s United States-financed civil conflict in Central America, the media coverage surrounding Turlington, one of the Big Six Supermodels of the 1990s and recipient of the Face of the Twentieth Century Award by the Metropolitan Museum of Art, illustrates the unplaceability of certain United States Salvadoran subjects outside the social pathologies of a "collective" downtrodden refugee population.[1]

Given the hypervisibility and marketability of the contemporary (textual) Latin in United States urban landscapes – for example, Univision, a leading Spanish-language television network, represents itself as "American as *flan*" (Albacete 2001: 23) and Mike Davis's introductory volume, *Magical Urbanism* (2000), acquaints America with the ways that Latinas and Latinos "reinvent the United States city" – Turlington's and Lopez's representations are examined so as to revisualize and reconceptualize a (distant) Salvadoranness that does not discursively exist in dominant United States as well as in Latina and Latino cultures. As the last decades of the twentieth century indicated, the projected growth of the Latina and Latino population led the corporate media to emphasize and warn about a "brown lump" that remains on the margins of United States culture (see Milian Arias 2000–1). Despite this parenthetical state, a temporary hypervisibility surfaced during the spring and summer of 1999 through a quick succession of Latin profiles. Some of these feature stories explicated a Latina and Latino homogeneous culture to a mass audience. The media's ethnoracial and cultural "whatever-ality" was evoked via the "Latin Music Goes Pop" issue of *Time* (May 1999); *Newsweek*'s "Latin USA" (July 1999); *George*'s "Latin Heat" motif (July 1999); and *New York*'s tribute, "The Latin Explosion" (September 1999). The latter's homage to Latinness exceeded previous configurations: *New York* was transformed into *Nueva York*. Indeed, there is a New York for everyone. Standard staples in newsstands, however, maintained their boundaries when it came to issues of intellectual capital and United States politics. *Time*, which chronicles middle America, did not become *Tiempo* and *George*, with its short-lived celebrity coverage of Capitol Hill, did not become *Jorge*. Unlike its popular counterparts, literary outlets like the *New Yorker* did not commemorate United States Latina and Latino letters through issues as *El Nueva Yorker*. The question remains: do Latinas and Latinos, as writers, matter?

While many Latina and Latino nationalities are eliminated through the rubric of exoticized Latinness, mainstream representations of this overdetermined appearance – what sociologist Clara Rodríguez identifies as recognizable, if not phenotypically random and democratic "Latin looks" (Rodríguez 1997) – rearticulate a static Latina and Latino triad of Mexican American, Cuban American and Puerto Rican. These ethnoracial categories, alongside the lived realities behind them, are eliminated through the enigmatic expectation of *what* Latin constitutes. Based on recent coverage, Latin signifies Hollywood, celebrity stature, musical rhythms and food – cultural signifiers open for consumption. But as Américo Paredes's novel from the United States–*Tejano* borderlands, *George Washington Gómez*, attests, Latin is also a pejorative state of being; one that awaits absorption into the melting pot. "The little Latins," proclaims the narrator, "must learn the English language . . . the little Latin is thinking in English" (Paredes 1994: 148–9). To this literary observation, one could effortlessly add that the little, accented Latin learns the English language, but is not supposed to talk back. This act, not of rebuttal but of symmetrical conversation, constitutes what feminist theorist bell hooks references as "empowering, defiant speech" (hooks 1989: 5). These *fashioned* dialogues respond – in hooksian terms, "back talk" or "talk back" – to an authority figure on equal grounds, rather than meekly accepting, from the sidelines, declarations on the structural order of civil and social life (hooks 1989: 5–9).

As this work untangles popular configurations of "new" United States Latins – Turlington and Lopez – it also signals how these women construct a self-authorship that responds to stereotypical expectations of their occupations as mindless and irrelevant. Their oppositional but interlocking roles – Lopez as woman of color, Turlington as un-colored woman of color – emerged in 1995. These antithetical mainstream locations converged as Lopez's Salvadoran peculiarities were widely interpreted and Turlington's Salvadoran racializing and deracializing ties were exposed and dissected. (Some articles positioned Turlington in a "passing" narrative. *Hispanic* bestowed upon her the title of "closet Hispanic" – "Newsmakers" 1995a: 2.)[2] This investigation of ambiguous Latin signifiers that demand Salvadoran authenticity thus explores Lopez's national body, a site of labor and exploitation that signified "credibility problems" to the United States gaze, in relation to Turlington's face, a site of beauty and glamour devoid of political, ethnoracial and cultural specificities

(Price and Lovitt 1995: 9). Turlington's un-Latinized face, coupled with Lopez's overly accentuated, but domesticated, Latinness, serve as points of departure that explore the meanings of Salvadoranness in popular culture. How is Salvadoranness consumed in the United States? In Turlington's case, what does it mean to supposedly communicate "non-Salvadoranness"? In what ways does Lopez reflect an "authentic" Salvadoranness discursively opening a space for deportability, ridicule and dehumanization?

The mass media's exclusive focus on Turlington's face – illustrated in *Time*, *Esquire*, *Latina* and *Hispanic* – reproduces the value of her highly lucrative good looks and a *doubt* concerning the existence and recognizability of United States Salvadorans. This uncertainty forces the public not so much to simply unmask Turlington as a Salvadoran, but to question rigorously the unvarying and too often predictable assumptions about the significations of Salvadoranness. United States Salvadoran, through Turlington, echoes Latin, but with an emphasis on a white Americanness devoid of Latina and Latino "brownness." Ideological and material brownness, in relation to Latina and Latino, is framed and understood in the context of ethnoracial, cultural and linguistic signifiers that mark un-Americanness. Sociologist Agustín Laó-Montes appropriately notes that "one of the main racial ideologies of *latinidad* defines Latinos as a third race, as it were, in between black and white – the bearers of an allegedly new *mestizaje* and hybridity, the so-called browning of America" (Laó-Montes 2001: 9). Turlington's face intimates an unbrowning of America, which through popular configurations, becomes a rewhitened, rehegemonized face that conceals the intricacies of racial mixing in America, what has been identified elsewhere as "the land of miscegenation" (Senna 1998: 11).

If Turlington represents the ideal, assimilable American body, does Lopez emphasize the apologetic existence domestic workers are supposed to feel when inserting their undocumented, untranslatable lives into a law-abiding, English-speaking United States audience? These extremes of domestic labor and glamour are a platform that theorizes the particular locations of United States Salvadorans, alongside their points of entry and exit from United States popular institutions: the dark, illiterate maid, soap opera style and the light-skinned supermodel pointing toward whiteness. Further exploration of these concerns illustrate how American sociopolitical anxieties are transmitted and projected into visible and invisible Salvadoranness; established and recent Latina and Latino migrations; common and uncommon citizen/subject; and authentic and illegitimate stories.

Because Latinas and Latinos oftentimes think of themselves by or through their particular cultural group, United States Salvadoran "anything" seldom emerges in critical discourses by Latinas and Latinos. Voices representing United States Salvadoran spaces are dwarfed through an internal Latina and Latino ethnoracial paradigm. With these dominating and normative voices, a Latina and Latino project, outside Mexican Americans, Puerto Ricans and Cuban Americans, is sidelined. Yet, Salvadorans exist. Their existence is confirmed in the United States, the borderlands, Central America, Latin America and elsewhere. Salvadoranness does not equate to Latina and Latino because, as presently situated, United States Salvadoran identities pose a Latina and Latino problem through their presumed unifying refugee status, segregated enclaves and scarce political clout.

This chapter begins by looking at disparaging depictions of United States domestic workers through Lopez's characterization. Reading the markers around Lopez's body require an exploration of how the maid and "her" nation are referenced in the United States terrain. Such examination exposes the ways that El Salvador operates in United States popular culture and how this rhetoric demands the relocation of these aliens from regions that are invariably positioned as "tropicalized" (see Aparicio and Chávez-Silverman 1997).[3] A cursory glance at United States cultural productions including documentaries about El Salvador and Guatemala as Patricia Goudvis's *If the Mango Tree Could Speak* (1993) and Paul Theroux's novel about Honduras, *The Mosquito Coast* (1982), confirms Central America's steamy location through the region's meteorological character and its affinity for armed conflict. El Salvador's climate contributes to this first world differentiation – a tropicalization that also includes geographically specific identifiers as banana republics, coffee plantations and lawless terrains long regarded as physically, culturally and politically outside the realm of United States democratic principles.

Next, this chapter explores the making of the un-Salvadoran cultural figure by way of Turlington. The visibly invisible mixedness of Turlington is advanced as one that is not simply informed by the popular media's tendency to valorize whiteness. Turlington's location, rather, shows the unwillingness and negation of the mainstream to address issues of (mixed) whiteness of a different color: Salvadoran mixed-race. The discussion concludes with an analysis of United States Salvadoran subjectivities that remain "new" and "unexplored." By doing so, this study points to how United States Salvadoran transculturation contributes to transformative interpretations that redirect normative notions of Americanness, Latinaness and Latinoness.

The Service Industry Talks Back: The Nation, the Maids and Other Stories[4]

> "You know, your job is really not so bad when you think about it. You should smile more." – Mikey, a fifth grade suburbanite, to Consuelo, his Salvadoran maid, in Todd Solondz's film, *Storytelling* (2002)

The role of the Salvadoran maid in United States popular culture touches upon issues of race, class, illegality and gender. The latter signifies agreeable service, with a touch of loyalty, by the Salvadoran woman and by implication Latina. In *Doméstica*, Pierrette Hondagneu-Sotelo notes that in Los Angeles, "Central

American workers are hugely over-represented in these jobs" (Hondagneu-Sotelo 2001: 53). Central American domestic servants, in spite of embodying the pathologies of indigence, become indispensable to the United States labor force. Mary Romero's study, *Maid in the USA*, contributes to this growing body of literature by detailing the vulnerability of certain women of color, who are regularly employed under humiliating circumstances and poor working conditions. Romero speaks of the invisibility relegated to domestic servants and attests to the "constant supervision and condescending observations" consistent with the occupation (Romero 1992: 5). As Romero highlights a devalued form of employment inhabited in ethnoracial, gender and class terms, she clarifies that the existence of Latinas as domestics only turns "visible when an order [is] given" (Romero 1992: 4).

Yet, the value of the Salvadoran maid seems to increase through complete submission. In praise of his live-in Salvadoran nanny, an employer recently admitted that: "Central American nannies are not like Alice on *The Brady Bunch*. They do exactly what you tell them" (Darling 1999: 3). From this viewpoint, Central American maids – in contrast to fictional Alice, a vocal (white) woman who is almost on par with the Brady family – are cast through the lens of service and compliance. In calculating the "worth" of a maid, journalist Alma Guillermoprieto publicly inquired: "How much does a servant cost? By definition, a housekeeper must not cost much, because if she did we would be uncertain of her neediness and therefore of her loyalty" (Guillermoprieto 2000: 74). Guillermoprieto's admission indirectly references the social dependency of the illegal Salvadoran maid not only on the household where she works, but ultimately, on the national implications of such dependency. If "the" illegal Salvadoran refugee is fired, she may turn to state agencies for assistance. Someone in that situation should be grateful for being employed.

Such was the case in Simpson's double murder trial, featuring a housekeeper turned-into-overnight-celebrity Rosa Lopez, described by the *Los Angeles Times* as "another Salvadoran maid with a sad story" (Darling 1995: 2). Through this expected narrative of Salvadoran economic and political sadness, a predictable subtext of comic relief surfaces – ranging from the maid's appearance (she wore a new sea-green jacket, the *New York Times* delighted; Margolick, 1995: 8) to how she would fare as a witness in a case that "fleshed out its multicultural cast of a black defendant and mostly black jury, white victim and white police officers, Japanese-American judge and a single-working mother prosecutor" (Seigel 1995: 4).

Lopez's testimony, which was videotaped without a jury present, was dismissed as gossipy, contradictory and delusional. Her declarations about the June 1994 killings offered time frame variations. At first, it was reported that she had seen Simpson's white Ford Bronco parked outside his home around 10.15 p.m., the presumed time of the murders. When asked during cross-examination about concrete time lines by Deputy District Attorney Christopher Darden, Lopez was less precise, acknowledging, "All I said was that it was after

10" (Newton and Ford 1995: 1). Darden proceeded to illustrate Lopez's inconsistencies by playing a tape-recorded interview she had with a defense investigator, Bill Pavelic. Darden insinuated that Pavelic proposed a cluster of acceptable times that would coincide with Simpson's story: that he was home at the time of the crime. Pavelic's recommendations are heard on the tape, "10:15, 10:20, 10:30, okay." Lopez follows with the confirmation, "Yeah" (Ford and Newton 1995: 1). Ultimately, Lopez agreed with Darden's assessment, that she had seen Simpson's car "shortly after 10" (Newton and Ford 1995: 1).

Darden continued to question Lopez about her foggy sense of time. The *New York Times* reported that:

> Mr. Darden ridiculed her for not knowing how long she met with Mr. Cochran last Saturday. "You're not very time conscious correct?" he said.
> "Yes," she shot back, through an interpreter. "I'm conscious about the time I waste here." (Margolick 1995: 8)

Darden's cross-examination of the indigent Salvadoran maid from affluent Brentwood, California reveals a struggle for truth as much as moments of tension that, from a subaltern standpoint, defy authority. Lopez appears reverent in court, answering the series of questions with "no, sir," "yes, sir," and "if you say so, sir." These courtesies seem to keep her interrogators at arm's length, while digressing from the definitive and linear statements her inquisitors expect. This dynamic became evident when Lopez, tired of the media frenzy, informed the court that she had already scheduled a flight to El Salvador and could not continue to testify in court. Darden challenged Lopez's claim about the supposed airline reservation. Requiring a straightforward response, Darden queried, "That was a lie, correct? And you knew that?" (Margolick 1995: 8). Lopez replied "yes," but would not concede to Darden's version of a "lie." On the contrary, Lopez's revision insisted on amplifying her intentions. "I am going to reserve it, sir," she announced. "As soon as I leave here, I will buy my ticket and I will leave. If you want to, the cameras can follow me" (Toobin 1996: 299).

Departing from mainstream interpretations of Lopez's story as "shadowy," Jeffrey Toobin's intricate chronicle of Simpson's trial provides noteworthy observations of her declarations. Toobin remarks that "Lopez brought a survivor's instincts to the witness stand ... as well as a considerable reservoir of street smarts" (Toobin 1996: 298). Lopez, Toobin continues, "was never rattled" despite the contradictions before her (Toobin 1996: 299). On the creative front, Edwidge Danticat's novel on Dominican–Haitian relations, *The Farming of Bones*, illuminates other ways to contextualize Lopez's agency. The narrator, Amabelle Désir, testifies about the role of domestic labor, adding an excerpt that dialogues with Lopez's predicament. Amabelle admits: "Working for others, you learn to be present and invisible at the same time, nearby when they needed you, far off when they didn't, but still close enough in case they changed their minds" (Danticat 1998: 35).

To the United States public Lopez's account remained, in the words of *USA Today*, a "zigzag testimony" (Holland 1995: 3). The *New York Times* added that Lopez "said 'I don't remember' in Salvadoran Spanish at least 50 times" (Margolick 1995: 8). Lopez and her country become interchangeable subjects that demand clarification. Joan Didion's journalistic endeavor, *Salvador*, a three-week travelogue published in the early 1980s, suggests fascinating insights into the positioning of that nation and its citizens. "The place brings everything into question," she declares early in the narrative (Didion 1982: 35). Didion's point extends to Lopez. The message: Lopez, like her country, is absent of reason. "In the absence of information (and the presence, often, of disinformation)," Didion proceeds, "even the most apparently straightforward event takes on, in El Salvador, elusive shadows, like a fragment or retrieved legend" (Didion 1982: 67).

Making sense of Lopez's proclamations requires an understanding of what becomes "non-sense," Salvadoran ways. On the one hand, Lopez was instructed by defense attorney Johnnie Cochran to speak "en Español, por favor" in order to avoid any misunderstandings in the courtroom (Seigel 1995: 4). Yet, on the other, Judge Lance Ito, who presided over the Simpson case, requested "a new interpreter because several television viewers had called or written and said the [translator] had used a Mexican dialect rather than El Salvadorean" (Toobin 1996: 309). These linguistic preoccupations and cautionary notes rigidly situate Lopez to her monolingual, non-English speaking origins.

What is at stake when that "other" life from Central America is performed, one where Salvadoranness, as vocalized and embodied by a third world subject, inverts tropicalized views of the American neocolonial imaginary? Consider, for a moment, Lopez's elaboration, if not altered embellishment, that her phrase "I don't remember" – "no me recuerdo" in Salvadoran Spanish, as the *New York Times* specified – is equivalent to "no." The explanation of this Lopez particularity, what shifts to a Salvadoran peculiarity, performs a formidable task fleetingly posed in a Victor Hernández Cruz poem. That is: "Can you sound Salvadoran" (Hernández Cruz 1997: 40)? Lopez's rendition of this Salvadoran Spanish incident was acted out thus:

"In my, in our Latin countries, we speak different dialects," Lopez said. "When I'm saying I don't remember, I am saying no."
"Is that something that's common to your particular country, El Salvador?" Cochran asked.
"Yes, sir," Lopez said. (Ford and Newton 1995: 1)

Lopez's linguistic modification and subsequent innovation in terms of Salvadoran linguistic folklore warrants parallels with what literary theorist Carlos Monsiváis classifies, in *Mexican Postcards*, as "cantinflismo." Expanding on Mario Moreno's popular Mexican character, Cantinflas, the above concept submits to a visibility of "the outcast's vocation for the absurd – in part disdain and annoyance for a logic that condemns and rejects him – which finds its raw material in the rapid fire of words, where the objects are lost long before getting to the verb" (Monsiváis 1997: 96). Within the realm of Lopez's recollection, as activated and mediated in the courtroom, what matters is not the maid's verb tense – the action – but her monosyllabic affirmatives or negatives. Additional disclosures from the maid thus become forms of *cantinflismo*, a fashion of the statement. This fashioning of the statement highlights what Salman Rushdie ingeniously communicates, from a migratory viewpoint, in *The Satanic Verses*. Rushdie warns, "most migrants learn, and can become, disguises" (Rushdie 1997: 49). Lopez's verbal disguises, made to fit digressions, unsettle the orderly spectator to the point that Lopez herself becomes the joke.

Lopez provided entertainment materials for dining experiences as well as latenight programming. Facetiously speaking, one could consume Lopez before, during and after dinner. In Santa Monica, California, Abiquiu Restaurant introduced the Rosa Lopez chicken tamale. The manager explained, "It's chicken because people had the feeling she wasn't telling as much as she knew. When we first put it on the menu after she testified, people would say 'Oh, you guys. That's naughty.' But now a lot of people say, 'Who was she again? A character on *Dallas*?' It's like she was just one more TV character" (Harvey 1996: 4). Lopez's selection as a feathered creature fulfills a linguistic duality of United States outsider. Whereas chicken, in English, signifies cowardly behavior, the employment of *pollo*, in Spanish, connotes a disparaging reference to undocumented border crossers and migrant workers. By way of late-night television, Jay Leno took a crack at Lopez on the *Tonight Show*, proposing her name as President Clinton's nominee for CIA director in 1995. Leno's punchline: "She speaks several languages, her hobby is spying on the neighbors and if she's ever captured she won't say a straight answer" ("Newsmakers" 1995b: 2). This knee-slapper ironically validates the dehistoricization of the CIA's role in that nation and the implications of its inherently covert operations.[5]

Lopez phenomenally inverts her imposed narrative of a contradictory duality, celebrity and social pariah, a binary that echoes the temporary eminence granted to the trial's procession of witnesses like Simpson's houseguest, Brian "Kato" Kaelin. Lopez overturns the social significance of her stereotype by distorting the character of the agreeable maid. After her testimony, several newspapers and magazines as *Vanity Fair* mockingly reported the "weird tidbit," as the *Baltimore Sun* dubbed it, that Lopez was engaged to Mike Gabriel, a twenty-eight year old part-time candy store clerk and ventriloquist, who is also "primarily a teacher of cat yoga" (Shapiro 1996: 3). Unbeknownst to these publications was the knowledge that the engagement was a hoax. *Vanity Fair* soon corrected the inaccuracy, as Lopez's media savvy faux fiancé clarified: "I think she has a great sense of humor" (Shapiro 1996: 3). To Lopez's humor one need also add intelligence and determination, aspects that journalists clearly missed. Positioning her through the specter of prosecutor Marcia Clark's conviction, that "Rosa Lopez is living better now than she ever may have in her entire life," columnists neglected to hear Lopez talking back (Seigel 1995: 4). She complained to Judge Ito, in Caliban's English, that: "the reporters won't leave me alone. I'm tired of looking at them. They have been harassing me" (Toobin 1996: 298).

After her testimony, Lopez relocated to Sensuntepeque, El Salvador, where the United States media's fascination with her continued (its brevity notwithstanding). As reporters crowded Lopez, she proceeded to demonstrate diasporic elements of New World Salvadoranness. She discharged, from Central America, a fusion of North Americanness that is informed by processes of becoming a United States Latina. While in Sensuntepeque, the *Los Angeles Times* cited an articulate Lopez. Her effective messages were conveyed in the following way:

> "Get away from my house!" she yelled in English. . . . "I'm coming here tired of the courts. I'm coming here tired of so much injustice. Don't bother me. I don't want to see you."
> That was followed by a curse uttered in Spanish, a reference to the reporters' mothers. (Wilkinson 1995: 14)

Another remarkable example of Lopez's quotable dissent illustrates her physical and economic hardships on the job. Her doubts and hesitations about United States ethnoracial politics are echoed as well:

> "I have worked with much honor, I have cleaned bathrooms, I have cleaned houses . . . but always with honor, and the few cents I have cost me much sweat and many tears," she said.
> In response to a reporter's question about whether she was a victim of racism in the United States, Lopez said: "You go there and try it. They don't like us there; they discriminate against us in everything." (Wilkinson 1995: 14)

The social commentary surrounding Lopez outlast Simpson's televised trial. Such perceptions punctuate a form of "alienization" Salvadorans experience through marginal roles that often parallel El Salvador's underdevelopment. Alienization refers to the countering of variations of national, political, racial and cultural marginalizations imposed upon certain subjects who are consistently rendered as "illegal," metaphorically and in legal terms, by United States hegemonies. While processes of alienization underscore notions of proximity (the United States) and distance (Central America), alienization points, as well, to a greater awareness that surfaces because of the distorted locations of a denied humanity. Amidst this alienization, Lopez's tailored responses indicate, like Franz Kafka's Joseph K. in *The Trial*, that despite irrationality and absurdity, one's intelligence must be kept "calm and analytical to the end" (Kafka 1992: 225).

Making Face, Making Latin: Decoding the "Un-Latina"

While Lopez signified explicit Salvadoranness, different aspects of United States Salvadoranness in United States popular culture demonstrate a displacement with that ethnicity. Representations of Turlington in popular discourse explain how United States Salvadorans become racially and ethnically ambiguous. Turlington is portrayed as someone who is out of reach by virtue of her face, which is often compared to that of Audrey Hepburn. *Time* describes her as "the exquisitely patrician beauty who never lived next door" (Bellafante 1992: 85). *Esquire* adds, "the skin on her slender hands is heartbreakingly transparent" (Miller 1997: 80). London's *Financial Times* writes, "You will have seen those exquisite features a thousand times: as the face of Calvin Klein's Eternity, her limpid doe eyes have gazed from billboards and magazines for more than a decade – but nothing prepares you for her beauty" (Sissons 2001: 3). Through such elaborations on her face and skin tone, Turlington is deemed as "not of the physical world" (Miller 1997: 80). Even though her "face has been churned out, processed, assimilated – plastered on billboards, bus stops, magazine covers, [and] the small screen," Turlington's position is interpreted through her unplaceable, but plasterable face (Miller 1997: 80). It is a face that has been whitened twice over via its *ideological* content. Her Salvadoranness without the geographic location of El Salvador is dislocated in popular culture, leaving no room for fashioning and recreating diasporic versions of El Salvador within the United States. Turlington's profitable career as a supermodel, not to mention racial "ambiguity," may have something to do with the neutrality of her non-Latin sounding name. Had Christy's equally impartial first name been followed with last names like González or Pérez, the explanations of what she is may differ. Likewise, the expectations may vary had a first name like Guadalupe, Consuelo, or Juana, succeeded the Turlington. A name such as Guadalupe can work in this divine supermodel context, verified in the explorations of this religious turned feminist and popular culture icon catalogued in Ana Castillo's anthology, *Goddess of the Americas/La Diosa de las Américas*.

Because of the discourse surrounding Turlington, one must invariably turn to the emphasis on her face. *MediaWeek* called this phenomenon "Christy-turlingtonicity," after *Esquire* celebrated the supermodel with several articles, photographs and 43,681 mentions of her name (Grossberger 1997: 50). Such continuous efforts to dissect her features – descibed across the Atlantic by London's *Daily Telegraph* as "a set of perfectly geometric features that can look exotic or wholesome, waif-like or sophisticated, whichever is required" – suggest a subtext by reporters to decode her face and tell us what lies (racially) "underneath" (Slater 1998: 22). These different, yet racially punctuating visions of Turlington illustrate social processes that, as feminist theorist Elizabeth Grosz confirms, render the body solely on textual grounds. Grosz maintains: "The body becomes a 'text' and is fictionalized and positioned within myths and belief systems that form a culture's social narratives and self-representations" (Grosz 1994: 119–20). In *Hispanic*, Turlington's facial characteristics, or her "unique looks," are regarded as "a true combination of her mother's olive skin and her father's bone structure" (Moscoso 1995: 26).

The above observation "unracializes" – if not "re-racializes" – its audience as well as ethnic category by accentuating Turlington's (non-Hispanic) difference.

Her "unique face," through "her mother's olive skin and her father's bone structure," requires biological explanations of "her race." Turlington's Central American genealogy, when traced to her mother, is also minimized. Journalist Michael Gross attributes Turlington's mother, Elizabeth, as being of "Salvadoran extraction" (Gross 1996: 464). *Hispanic* reveals that Turlington is "aqua-eyed." *Esquire* discloses that her hair was "sort of reddish" as a little girl. Turlington's racial inheritance of her mother's "olive skin" and father's "bone structure" are denationalized, de-ethnicized and deracialized, since she is "not of the physical world." When she was featured on the January 1999 cover of *Latina*, the *Chicago Sun-Times* asked: "What's the supermodel doing on the cover of the bilingual women's magazine" (Kim 1999: 31)? Turlington's difference is rendered through an uncertainty concerning the function of languages in the United States other than English. It should be noted, however, that Turlington does not speak Spanish.

As *Time* suggests, her "fine-boned visage" led the Metropolitan Museum of Art in 1993 to use Turlington as a model for 120 fiber glass mannequins at the Met's Costume Institute, which displays "more than 200 years' worth of gown, dresses and tweeds" (Bellafante 1992: 85). Her United States and Salvadoran compositions are represented as a "unique" mixture that concocts a lucrative (yet ethnically unplaceable) Latin face. Turlington told *Hispanic*: "people find it difficult to pinpoint exactly what my background is, from my looks. They can tell I'm of an ethnic background, but uncertain of what that background may be" (Moscoso 1995: 26). A fascinating inversion, the beheading of Turlington's ("white") face, occurred in 1995, when Disney's animated feature on Pocahontas used Turlington's *body* (sans payment) as a model for the Native American character. According to the *Toronto Sun*, Disney paid

> $700 to the women who served – wittingly or not – as models for *Pocahontas*: $0 to supermodel Christy Turlington, whose fashion-mag spreads inspired the body; $200 for four modeling sessions to Dyna Taylor, a California college student of Filipino descent who shaped the face; and $500 for consulting to Powhatan historian Shirley Little Dove Custolow, who inspired the "dignity," according to *Entertainment Weekly*. (Penfield III, 1995: 68)

Disney's marketing knows no (racial) bounds as it severs Pocahontas' body to "ethnic" and "unethnic" parts for a multicultural "whole" granting primacy to whiteness. This fashioning of Pocahontas' white body points to a whiteness en route. That is: a body that walks in and out of Americanness, one that can possibly pass. At this moment, it is a "native" whiteness that begins with the body and can then be fulfilled with the face. The irony is that unbeknownst to most spectators, Turlington indigenizes "the rest of" Pocahontas by virtue of her Salvadoran background. In the world of fashion such particularities are often eliminated. A momentary view of perhaps the only time Turlington has textually appeared as part of the economically and racially downtrodden occurred in 1998 by way of Calvin Klein's advertising campaign. The ads depicted the millionaire model laboring in a rustic skirt while picking potatoes. The campaign, according to the weekend pages of the *Guardian* in London, advocated a peasant chic approach to clothing and made it possible to call someone a peasant without offending them. Although the *Guardian* encouraged the farm worker aesthetic, the newspaper also cautioned, "Those of a more urban leaning . . . might still approach the look with trepidation. How, then, to avoid looking like an extra from *Little House on the Prairie*? The safest way to indulge your rustic side without getting into fancy-dress territory is to keep things minimal – go easy on the accessories" (Brown 1998: 44).

The persistent focus on Turlington's face blends the ways that United States Salvadoranness does, does not, or should not look like. In *Mythologies*, Roland Barthes uncovers popular constructions of language, symbols and objects by closely scrutinizing how these forms of *organized* communication – in effect, objectification – mask, or speak, their meanings to a mass audience. He notes:

> Viewed as a transition the face of [Greta] Garbo reconciles two iconographic ages, it assures the passage from awe to charm. As is well known, we are today at the other pole of this evolution: the face of Audrey Hepburn, for instance, is individualized, not only because of its thematics (woman as child, woman as kitten) but also because of her person, of an almost unique specification of the face, which has nothing of the essence left in it, but is constituted by an infinite complexity of morphological functions. As a language, Garbo's singularity was of the order of the concept, that of Audrey Hepburn is the order of the substance. The face of Garbo is an Idea, that of Hepburn, an Event. (Barthes 1998: 57)

In the context of Turlington, Barthes's observation is appropriate for various reasons. His excerpt provides insight on the facial tradition from which Turlington's appearance works. (*Time* has drawn comparisons between Turlington and Hepburn.) Barthes's comments complicate the ways that reality is not only dressed and decorated, but how the "essence" of the face generates a seemingly unquestionable, "natural" state for the larger social world (Barthes 1998: 11). Barthes signals how Turlington becomes both an Idea (personified by Garbo) and an Event (exemplified by Hepburn). Yet Turlington's face, as an Idea, differs from Garbo's. It offers a socio-cultural transition between diasporic Salvadoranness (where, in all its variations and combinations, Salvadorans contribute to the changing nature of this experience inside and outside El Salvador) and homogenizing Salvadoranness (where the reigning accuracy of that identity is dictated by misrepresentations based exclusively on violence, poverty and illegality).

Turlington's unplaceable Salvadoranness indicates how her "mixture" has no comparison or reference point among other mixed race celebrities in United States popular culture. The mixed race compositions of performers like Cameron Diaz, Linda Ronstadt and Mariah Carey, among others, are not solely explained through the uniqueness of their faces or fine-boned visages. Their Cubanness (Diaz), Mexicanness (Ronstadt), Venezuelanness and blackness

(Carey) is referenced within the United States popular culture imagination; they contextualize their particular roles in the entertainment industries. A short list of additional celebrities from a more recognizable Latin American, yet United States-based entertainment camp might include: Desi Arnaz, Gloria Estefan, Celia Cruz, Anthony Quinn, Ricardo Montalban and María Conchita Alonso. Turlington's Salvadoranness challenges the mainstream gaze, even though the ways she is read minimize her racial compositions.

Larger perspectives on re-reading Turlington are also provided in Barthes's *The Fashion System*. Barthes informs us that fashion is entirely a system of signs that make and transport meaning. Turlington is thus thrown into a language that attempts to decipher what is intelligible in fashion. Barthes contends: "it is not the object but the name that creates desire; it is not the dream but the meaning that sells" (Barthes 1990: xii). Emphasis on Turlington's racial and facial compositions reflects how garments are illustrated in the fashion world. Clothing in general, Barthes writes, "constitute[s] an excellent poetic object; first, because it mobilizes with great variety all the qualities of matter: substance, form, color, tactility, movement, rigidity, luminosity" (Barthes 1990: 236). Through this construction, Turlington is supposed to embody the deracialized and celebratory aspects of consumerism.

Despite the dislocation of Turlington's Salvadoranness, she publicly shifts and politicizes Salvadoran aspects of her identities within the corporate media realms that give primacy to her face. W. E. B. Du Bois's comments about Nella Larsen's novel, *Passing*, hold relevance here, for Turlington "is deceiving no one" (Du Bois 1995: 522). Unlike Larsen's book, where a "white" body maintains its status through covert blackness, the rhetoric applied to Turlington's face infers a shift in narratives of ethnoracial passing. Emphasis on Turlington's face suggests a discursive purpose, of putting one's best *American* face forward. A white face *can* pass, but not if it is attached to a non-white body.

The silence surrounding Turlington's Salvadoranness is the mass media's – not hers – especially as she debunks pathologies about Salvadorans. Turlington, who graduated *cum laude* from New York University with a degree in philosophy and comparative religion, inserts a primacy to her intellectual interests that exceeds modeling. As an undergraduate, she maintained, "I don't have a sense of pride and completion after a modeling shoot – whereas I do when I've written an essay, because it's much harder for me" (Slater 1998: 22). Turlington is also actively involved in various social causes. Journalist Ian Halperin describes her as "one of the most outspoken models in the business" (Halperin 2001: 90). The *Financial Times* lists her campaigns as "breast cancer, animal rights, El Salvador (her mother's homeland), and anti-smoking crusades on both sides of the Atlantic" (Sissons 2001: 3). She clarifies, somewhat modestly, that: "I'm just one person out there trying to do my small part. I enjoy working with people who are committed to changing injustice" (Halperin 2001: 90).

Turlington also discussed United States policy towards El Salvador with former Vice President Albert Gore, Jr. The proceeds of her 1995 Christy

Turlington calendar, shot in El Salvador, were donated to the Salvadoran American Health Foundation. She serves as chairwoman for the International Committee for Intercambios Culturales of El Salvador. The non-profit organization, based in San Salvador, includes a public library, a community technology center and a gallery. Her efforts are an attempt "to help restore El Salvador" after the civil war (Moscoso 1995: 26). Turlington utilizes her position with the fashion industries and politicizes Salvadoranness within the representational realms that subdue and distort it. The circuitous route taken by the "white" and "ethnic" media concerning Turlington's "unrealness" must be framed through a Du Boisian double consciousness that emanates from the measuring of one's sociopolitical location and soul through the dominant gaze (Du Bois 1996: 5). While challenging the senses, Turlington's Salvadoran and United States-informed duality uncovers spaces for new forms of diasporic Salvadoranness. She looks and answers back. In so doing, Turlington highlights Grosz's observation that, "The body is not simply a sign to be read, a symptom to be deciphered, but also a force to be reckoned with" (Grosz 1994: 120). Turlington supports Grosz's comments, declaring, "I've always tried really hard not to follow the cliches that come with this job" (Sissons 2001: 3).

Like Rosa Lopez, Turlington understands and speaks to the industry for which she works. The problematic placing of these two women can be seen in a wider framework that dialogues with black cultural productions responding to material and metaphorical locations of blackness as a problem. From Du Bois's century-old, non-fictional observation on the ways that "the other world" demands a response from African Americans centered on the question, "How does it feel to be a problem?" (Du Bois 1996: 3) to Toni Morrison's novel, *Sula*, where life in Medallion, Ohio – "the Bottom" – discloses "A shucking, knee-slapping, wet-eyed laughter that could even describe and explain how they came to be where they were" (Morrison 1982: 4), the model and the maid convey an act and agency that are not altogether visible or discernible to the outside world. Turlington's infamous (lovely) face and Lopez's well-known (Salvadoran) looks communicate the importance of fashioning one's responses, as Gloria Anzaldúa notes in *Making Face, Making Soul*, through "political subversive gestures, the piercing look that questions or challenges" (Anzaldúa 1990: xv).

From El Salvadorean to United States Salvadoran: Toward a More Expansive Intersection of Salvadoran Experiences

The United States has become a material and conceptual space that houses and informs the construction and assertion of United States Salvadoranness. In 1993, a year after the Salvadoran peace accords were signed between the military and the guerrillas, the *San Francisco Chronicle* ran a front page story announcing: "it appears that most of the 1.5 million Salvadorans who came to the United States do not intend to return . . . Salvadorans are trying to shed the refugee status that distinguishes them from ordinary immigrants – and that brought them sympathy from Americans who disagreed with United States policy in El Salvador" (Espinoza 1993: 1). This article points to a new North American location for Salvadorans. The Mayor of Los Angeles, Richard J. Riordan understands that there is a political constituency in this population, or generally speaking, a United States component to Salvadorans. Riordan inaugurated 6 August 2000 as "El Día del Salvadoreño," Salvadoran Day, a recognition that will continue in subsequent years ("Salvador del mundo en E.U.": 2000). United States Salvadorans have concentrated in five American cities: Houston, Los Angeles, New York, San Francisco and Washington. These settlements prove that urban landscapes have been influenced by the presence of other ethnicities outside an internal Latina and Latino racial hierarchy.

Turlington's and Lopez's representations may be the closest one can get to these popular extremes of United States Salvadoran configurations – refugees or exotics – that allude to diametrically opposed distortions. As conveyed through these women, United States Salvadorans are not all consequences of the 1980s civil war, nor are they all cosmopolitan deracialized thermometers of bourgeois tastes. Rather, Turlington and Lopez prompt the consideration that United States Salvadorans express multiple modes of existence. They verify that diasporic Salvadoranness must be intersected within the intertexual meanings and conceptualizations of Americanness, multiple mappings that negotiate a sense of place away from the physical geopolitical spaces that are exclusively designated as "theirs." The tensions emanating from the positions of these two figures mark the pressing need to actively engage with actual processes that provide insights on Salvadoran experiences intimately linked and situated within United States surroundings.

Part 5

In Search of Fashion

17

Scattered Bodies, Unfashionable Flesh

Fabricio Forastelli

I arrived in Buenos Aires in the late evening on 18 December. It was hot. And I am not just talking about the weather. Over the next two days popular demonstrations would commemorate the social and economic collapse of the country two years ago. In 2001, thirty-four people died during popular protests against the Argentine government, most of them killed by police or paramilitary forces called on to defend a collapsing order. Good-bye Social Democracy and welcome back again, Peronism. The tailored Gianni Versace suits of the late 1990s have disappeared; now the candidates emerge with the more discreet, even national, styles of Gino Bogani and the like. At the airport everyone seems to be wearing uniforms: private guards, police officers, military personnel, taxi drivers, stewardesses, the brightly robed *cumbia* singers on the television screens in the lounge. After opening my suitcase for customs, I rush downtown to meet Silvia D, a queer activist who also teaches at the University of Buenos Aires. Interestingly enough, she wears her own style of uniform, dressing only in black, as journalist María M observes in a witty article entitled "Argentine Intellectual Performances." Describing the fashion trends of the Argentine *intelligentsia* as some sort of savvy narcissistic projection, María M posits that the way the intellectual dresses has become a euphemism for the connection between who you are and what you think. Fashion as euphemism resembles the art of discretion, overwritten by personal guilt, political activism and public calumny. Well, the article is bold but let's not make this sound personal. After all, boldness is a way to make a living. In describing Argentine fashion she turns to intellectual performances, quoting at the same time the nineteenth-century tradition in Latin America that mixes – and confuses – the garment with one's political ideas and remitting to a postmodern spleen that bemoans lost unity. If polite conversation in England focuses on the weather, in Argentina it is all about job precariousness. I guess it is a universal truth that you talk about what you do not have. Fashion in Argentina, to the scandal or amusement of everyone who is not Argentine, points to the failure of politics. However, as I keep telling myself, for us it is not a singularity; it is a destiny.

During my journey downtown, I begin to think that I should look around in order to catch up with fashion trends, to note what is particular to Buenos Aires and even to Latin America. Many Argentines would agree that their country does not link itself easily to the rest of Latin America, as the nation has represented a privileged point of intersection between the economic modernity of Europe and "native" cultural complexity. One can only imagine the kind of variations in fashion that such a crossing point produces, as it breaks down not only the idea of purity of taste, but also the very limits traced by hybridism. To the scandal of my friends in Paris, I would argue that everyone has their own ideas about matters of taste, even if the outfit and the occasion seem misplaced. All of a sudden I feel blind to the differences I am trying to detect. Even worse, it feels like my vision of Latin American fashion is just too broad and blurred, as today's fashion connects issues of poverty, social protest and economic discourse to a dimension that goes beyond its traditional academic boundaries. At least I am relieved to see that there is no fashion police in the streets. My first memories of fashion date back to 1970s, precisely the moment when fashion becomes "moda"; that is, a statement that unveils the repetition and the triviality always present in the nature of violence. Back then, people wearing their pants too tight or their hair too long would be stopped by the police and publicly punished. I am very tired after a long flight and, having arrived downtown, I reflect about fashion in Buenos Aires. In a city overtaken by Christmas shoppers, *cartoneros*, *piqueteros* and political activists, fashion is still extremely relevant. Even though there is rampant unemployment – around 25 percent – government officials announce that the GDP has grown eight points or so this year. Where has the money gone? It is interesting to me that one of the areas of economic growth has to do precisely with fashion. Nowadays, Argentina has a thriving garment industry that copies international fashion brands and fosters the feeling of "there is no way I could afford this."

In the past 24 hours I have been in Miami and Río de Janeiro, and Buenos Aires still looks special. Despite being impoverished, Buenos Aires is still interesting, which is a rather unusual combination. At my hotel, I retire for the evenings and sleep into the next morning. Feeling the heat and the humidity of December, my body seems programmed to perspire. There is no way for anyone to walk outside dressed to the nines and look good fifteen minutes later. By mid-afternoon Argentines are out in the streets full force. Silvia and I spend half an hour trying to find a cab with air conditioning. Looking through the window of a half destroyed taxi, yet another reminder that there is no such thing as a fashion industry, we hop in. And I think: It is 2003 and the very concept of fashion is unfashionable, but in the Paris of Latin America it all looks so well placed and so appropriate. Could style be right, as my friend Roberto E claims, but fashion wrong? Then I wish I was within a more controlled academic environment, where I could study Mexican *maquiladoras* along the border of Mexico and the United States, or the relationship between slavery, plantations and textiles during the eighteenth century; or the strategies used by wealthy Mexican women of the postcolonial period who imported fashionable garments from Europe just to complicate them with silver details. Must our study of dress always corroborate an unjust social hierarchy? Perhaps, as Angel Rama once posited, we have worried too much about the symbolic consequences of our material practices when we should have been engaging a materialist analysis of the body as regulated by culture all along. Looking at Lucrecia E's volume on fashion in *DeSignis*, the journal of the Latin American Association of Semiotics, reminds me of the gap between street fashion and cultural analysis. In the back of the taxi, I wonder how long a culture can go on reconfiguring its practices of poverty and wealth. Later, in a hushed tone, Silvia D muses: it is not the same to do cultural studies *about* poverty and *from* poverty, is it?

By now I am completely lost in fashion. We are at the Congress building, where protesters have gathered for what seems to be the daily national supply of social resistance. In the past, only politicians walked the area, with ties and tailored suits *de rigueur*. With the political class in hiding or under house arrest, demonstrators have since overtaken the area. Today the streets are filled with retirees and young people, and, of course, the Secret Service. Tomorrow, it might be some members from the middle classes banging pots and singing "All politicians must go," participating in a type of activity that is not strictly political nor what one might consider non-political. I guess this is what Naomi K calls "experiments in direct democracy" and Beatriz S calls "populism." The choreography is strange; people circulate from one corner of the square to the other, refusing to stand in any place for long, making for a surreal and ephemeral atmosphere, extremely open and paranoid at the same time. I feel dizzy for five seconds and then react. Nobody is looking at my new Specsavers or my rather trendy English shoes. I feel better. There are uniforms everywhere again. To be honest, I expected more emphasis on "guerrilla fashion," but everyone seems dressed down for the occasion. The fact that the Left gave up their beards, Che Guevara's black beret and khaki pants makes everything more confusing. In a city where one out of every two people is unemployed or underemployed, dressing like a Subcomandante Marcos would be a bit of an overstatement. We are obviously far from the now almost forgotten Chiapas; we are in a "white" country where according to official ideology everybody fits into the melting pot or at least within the seams of fake Calvin Klein jeans.

Further ahead, we meet up with Lohana B and other friends from the Argentine Transvestite Association, who are there for a demonstration with students and workers. The body Trans takes to the streets, leaving city suburbs and the underground. You would expect Argentine transvestites to dress with glamour, Lohana points out, but that's just not the case. In Argentina, transvestites make up a critical presence in everyday life; they are not only some exotic aspect of a sexual experience nor are they the ugly sisters you hide behind the closet of gay liberation. One would characterize Trans fashion in Latin America as a process that mimics and improves upon the contours of the female, a "creole" mixture of street fashion and hopelessness. "Wrong," says Lohana. "Now we dress without glamour, like any other sweaty worker in the streets." I try to imagine an argument over poverty and queerness, but everything goes wrong, or becomes more elusive. We kiss and meet the other girls – one of whom has just been released from the hospital after being trashed by police, her flesh reshaped by power. The body Trans is one who has lost its material support. It is, first of all, an unemployed body or a body engaged in some sort of slightly illegal activity. And second, it is slightly illegal not only because nobody knows for sure where legality starts, but also because without material support the body becomes illegal in itself. It is a void.

In addition to being such a fascinating fashion experience, the *piqueteros* are another instance of that void. During the twentieth century social organization and coherence have been articulated by work, not by unemployment and violence. Traditionally, the Ministry of Economy used to regulate unemployment in order to maintain social order. But this assumption collapsed after the 1980s, when economic theory declared full employment not only impossible but also undesirable. As Argentina would find out, the goal of full employment went against the process of capital accumulation and, within that framework, fashion not only represented economic deregulation, but also freedom. Ironically, as this freedom grew, so did the economic emergency programs. Sipping an *espresso*, Silvia and I discuss a recent intervention by Gayatri Spivak that implies that experience in the vanishing present is defined by the entry into a web of "text-ility" woven into the social fabric. Rather than grounding oneself in a notion of reality, she writes, it is more important to interrogate the languages we construct to formalize our perceptions and build up social resistance. For Spivak, architecture and fashion are the very symptoms of a new transnational order, sites at which the symbols of economic growth (the building, the body) are placing an understanding of the economic under erasure. After her celebrated visit to Buenos Aires, during which she became known as "Calláte piba" ("Shut up, girl!"), it should not surprise anyone that, in the highly politicized circuits of cultural criticism in Latin America, Spivak never looks quite so radical as she does in the United States. Her critique of the postmodern is so insightful that it has become obligatory. What a pity that as soon as something becomes obligatory in Buenos Aires it is considered suspicious or irrelevant. Anyway, we left Gayatri and the Congress after failing to join the demonstration. We could not find it, or maybe it was just happening in front of us, or maybe even we were the demonstration. Before leaving we had a coffee in one of the many coffeehouses often visited by the *botones* of the Secret Service, certainly the kind of place that would notice a transvestite. The word for *informant* comes from *button*; in today's usage it denotes a person who spies over the social fabric not attending to security but to a new context of poverty and crime. Outside, the transvestite. Inside, the *botones*. Buenos Aires, I think, is out of joint with its own material representation; it cannot be any other way.

Scattered Bodies, Unfashionable Flesh

Figure 17.1. On the sidelines of the Argentine Worker's Movement mobilization on 6 September 1996. Photograph by Regina A. Root.

Leaving the square of the Congress, we drove to the University of Buenos Aires for a reading on memory and epitaphs, finding literary critic Jorge P dressed in black as one would expect. Strange, María M does not mention him on her list, thus creating a strange dilemma: What type of intellectual performance is required to clinch a spot on the fashion list? Jorge talks of the erasing epitaphs from discourse, because an epitaph is a way to kill someone a second time. It is now 7.30 p.m. and I am sticky, tired, confused. My confusion is alarming until I realize that, in a sense, I am pleasantly naked in this room full of ideas.

It might seem like a gratuitous moment in my story, but Jorge Luis Borges once described the very history of fashion in modern Latin America when recounting the story of Teodelina Villar. An upper-class socialite obsessed with fashion (her goal was "perfection" not "beauty," writes Borges), Villar is deceived by an unscrupulous man who professes that odd-shaped hats are all the rage in Paris. Because it is the onset of the Second World War, there is no way for Teodelina to check the information. In her hunger for the fashionable she dons the odd-shaped forms, only to discover that no one had ever worn such a thing in Paris. For Teodelina Villar, this marks the end of her leadership in fashionable circles. She is banished to an impoverished neighborhood, as a pariah of her own class and of all classes, where she dies without note. This story seems almost prophetic if one thinks of the Versace fever of Argentine politicians and movie stars in the 1990s. Showing up to events in Miami fashion mistakes, many ended up in jail a few years later, ostracized and forced to leave their expensive penthouses. Others escaped at midnight under a bizarre blitz of media coverage, their bags full of the not-so-wearable-now Versaces. Such has been the epitaph for fashion in Latin America, one that would seem to offend everyone as it pushes fashion discourse to a new dimension. If the fashion authorities are forced to leave – as once did Teodelina – the rest are left to their own devices.

Together with Carolina Herrera and Oscar de la Renta, a so-called Latin American Fashion Council based in Miami has made the claim that Latin American designers need to move away from those exotic, native fabrics – so colorful and nice but so dated – in order to engage the modernization of an industry that had already disappeared by the 1980s. Lost in fashion. In the meanwhile, Lohana and her friends work the streets, live in shantytowns and attend the university. After the conference on epitaphs, Silvia turns to me and says, "Fashion is a way to regulate social and economic performances. Fashion interrogates what makes authority possible. It explores the questions: To whom do we owe our obedience? How do we go about obeying social codes?" As economic recipes after Argentina's deluge become more and more unintelligible in the discourses of transnational financial bodies, dress may be the very performance that helps us calculate the ruins of the local amidst the ashes of the economic global market. Scattering evidence over unfashionable flesh, we also find that fashion discourse dislocates identities and boundaries. If fashion today exists only as a superficial register of ethnographic relevance, then hopefully we will turn to the ethnography of fashion to understand some of the goals of human equity.

Another taxi. We're on our way to a Trotskyist center in front of the Brukman factory to discuss ethics and aesthetics. Brukman is a garment factory that was abandoned by its owners and reclaimed by its women workers. In April 2003 six hundred police officers arrested the fifty-four workers (almost all female) of the factory who decided to appropriate the means of production collectively. In an insight shared with me by Francine M, I found out that the workers did not appeal for higher salaries, but wanted instead the right to work and to control production as a means for survival. The workers wanted to control their work experiences and not just the means of production or the surplus. As one of the dozens of factories taken over by the government and handed over to workers' cooperatives, the actions of those who work at Brukman defended the value of the place of work in itself, and not what it represents to the owner. Furthermore, the experience highlighted the limits of neoliberal capitalism in the Third World: a state where economic growth is only possible on the base of connecting the defense of private property to the repression of workers. In moralistic terms, the problem with neoliberal ventures in Latin America is that they rely on economic growth at the expense of another. The struggle for power, as in the case of the Brukman protests, can be found under the label of fashion. Fashion thus becomes a discourse of authority that distributes taste and possession, time and space, masters and subalterns, the symbolic and the material. Fashion is the name we give to the ever-working machine of cultural distinction that is replacing the old factory. At the Trostykist center, the debates centered on the efficacy of testimonial devices in the creation of art and protest (the word "revolution" long left behind, a remnant of history in the vocabulary of the Left). Afterwards I viewed an exhibition of photographs of street demonstrations, which seemed to critique the process of packaging the democratic process under the guise of "law and order." The images in one corner attracted my attention: Bolivian women dressed in their traditional, elaborately woven outfits of bright colors. The artist had left their faces out of the frame, and what is disturbing about them is that the wearer could have been anywhere: in La Paz, in a shanty town in Jujuy, or in downtown Buenos Aires. It was all about the color of the Bolivian woman's dress, colors not usually worn in the streets of Argentina, where black and beige dominates. Just as the transvestite body at the plaza near the Congress announced an unexpected body, so these photographs disrupted the ideological frame of the exhibit. The photographs played with the notion of what most threatens popular unity – divisions based on race, gender and class – while at the same time asking each spectator to reconsider his or her own quest for consistency.

A friendly reception followed the exhibition. We even drank Coke, which has now replaced the bomb-cocktail made of fernet, coke and rophynol as the drink of choice, or the more traditional red wine. We did not reach a consensus about the value of realism and protest propaganda. Leaving the center at around 11.30 p.m., we found the outdoors overtaken by garbage pickers whose trucks were beginning the return to the shantytowns that lie on the outskirts of the city.

Then we went to the *Angel* behind the morgue ... An uncertain epitaph. Into the morning, we danced village-style *cumbias* while dressed for a rave. By 7 a.m. I went back home to shower before joining the mass demonstrations at the Plaza de Mayo. Pure flesh and bones, the toothless *piqueteros* now represent the very antithesis of the optimistic – and relatively healthy – Peronist *shirtless* from the 1940s and 1950s. A hot but clear morning in polluted Buenos Aires. In the elevator, I remember Cuban writer Severo Sarduy, who living in Paris during the French May 1968, said: "Revolution, yes. But you have to dress up for Revolution." Today revolution seems closer and distant at the same time, covered and uncovered by the tenets of fashion but never quite making it. By the early evening my friends and I had left the Plaza de Mayo, minutes before a bomb exploded and wounded dozens of people. Silvia rushed to the telephone to call the people who had stayed at the demonstration. Through the shredded T-shirts with political slogans designed by the collective art group "Arte y confección," we found the price of freedom on the lacerated flesh of a friend who may never return to a factory.

Notes

Introduction

1. Segments of this introduction have appeared previously in the Scribner's *Encyclopedia of Clothing and Fashion* by Regina A. Root, © 2005 Gale Group. Reprinted by permission of the Gale Group.

Chapter 1

1. I would like to thank the editors of *Revista de Estudios Hispánicos* for granting permission to reprint portions of Meléndez (1995).
2. Lawrence Langner (1959: 22) suggests that the invention of clothes by prehistoric men was promoted by a desire to cover certain parts of their bodies and to establish a sign of distinction.
3. This chapter does not pretend to be an exhaustive examination of all colonial texts in which the topic of clothing is used to construct representations of otherness. I try to incorporate a myriad of well-known documents in the field and others that are less studied by critics to offer a general idea of how pervasive the theme of clothing was throughout this period. For a more exhaustive study on this topic see Meléndez (1999: 166–92).
4. Tom Conley (1992: 110) argues that in the famous engravings made by Théodore de Bry between 1590 and 1634 included in his *Grand Voyages*, the fully clothed Spaniards versus the naked Indians "underscore the relation of power held between the colonizer and the natives."
5. As Margarita Zamora (1992: 184) argues, that "sort of what's missing" is what enabled Colón to present the other as a docile subject ready for conversion.
6. Fray Ramón Pané was a Catalan who came to the Americas in the second voyage of Christopher Columbus. He was ordered by Columbus to record the customs and antiquities of the Indians of La Española. He is considered the first missionary to learn the language of the natives in the island in order to interpret their history.
7. A.P. Maudslay does not translate this passage. All translations that do not include a page number are mine unless otherwise specified.
8. Rolena Adorno (1986: 83) underscores the important role that pictures played in Guaman Poma de Ayala's text. As a rhetorical device, the drawings aimed "to please, to teach, and, most important, to persuade." The drawings related to the Inca lineage served as good examples of the importance of clothing as a social denominator.
9. Descola's study centers mainly on the Viceroyalty of Peru.

Notes

10. One must bear in mind that the preoccupation with clothes as a sign of social status and its material value was also a common feature in Europe. France, for example, began to be recognized inside and outside Europe as the center of fashion. Many newspapers in the eighteenth century were devoted to teaching women how to dress, what to wear, how to achieve a good appearance, what kinds of fabric and colors were more valuable and where to buy them. As Daniel Roche (1994: 187) explains, these newspapers were crucial discursive vehicles where a "new philosophy of taste" was born.
11. In the Spanish it reads: "herradores, zurradores, esparteros, especieros y de otros cualesquier oficios semejantes a éstos o más bajos, y obreros, labradores y jornaleros no puedan traer, ni traigan vestidos de seda, ni de otra cosa mezclada con ella, y que solo puedan vestir y traer vestidos de paño" (Konetzke 1962: 130). In the eighteenth century, the word "paño" could refer to fabrics such as wool, cotton, linen or silk. See the *Diccionario de autoridades* (1990: 111).
12. Magali M. Carrera (2003: 6) explains that in the eighteenth century, the word *calidad* was used to demarcate individuals. She adds that *calidad* could be understood "as the differentiating, defining, and ordering of diverse people . . . by kind or type." It included "references to skin color" but also encompassed "occupation, wealth, purity of blood, honor, integrity, and place of origin."
13. Richard Boyer and Geoffrey Spurling (2000: 314) explain that, in colonial times, the word *fábrica*, referred to a "mill, factory, business, sumptuous building; [and could] refer both to a physical structure and to its upkeep or operation."
14. Peter Flindell Klarén (2000: 102) reminds us that in the River Plate region, especially in colonies controlled by the Portuguese government, "substantial contraband, including quantities of British textiles, penetrated the Spanish trade monopoly in southern South America." As Klarén (2000: 105) adds, in the late eighteenth century "the level of contraband trade throughout had reached overwhelming proportions." On the impact of contraband on the crown's trade monopoly see Klarén (2000: 105–7.
15. Marita Sturken and Lisa Cartwright (2002: 10) establish a difference between the act of seeing and the act of looking at. The first implied an arbitrary "process of observing" whereas the second, constitutes a process in which people "actively make meaning of the world" in order 'to communicate, to influence and be influenced."

Chapter 2

1. A previous version of this chapter appeared in Spanish in 1999 in *Folios* 35(6): 3–11. Courtesy of Monte Ávila Editores.
2. In 1998, the most popular songs in the United States included "Zoot-Suit Riot," by Cherry Poppin' Daddies, and "Hey Pachuco!" by Royal Crown Revue. The *New York Times* would publish several articles celebrating the new *Zoot-suiters* at swing clubs.
3. Because Unitarians had a predilection for French fashion, this term referred to them.
4. This relationship between objects, especially if one chooses an item of clothing in order to refer to its wearer or the system he or she supports, could also be considered

a synecdoche, defined by J. A. Cuddon as, "A figure of speech in which the part stands for the whole, and thus something else is understood within the thing mentioned" (Cuddon 1979: 676). The boundaries between metonymy and synecdoche can be so marvelously blurred that one might easily mistake them for examples of what they signify. Because of this ambiguity, there is nothing that might impede us, to cite Le Guern, from considering the metonymy of dress for a person as an example of synecdoche (Le Guern 1973: 33). To simplify matters, I will refer to metonymy exclusively.

5. The veiled history of this linguistic play helps explain why scholars have dedicated volumes to the study of metaphor but surprisingly little to the complexities of metonymy. For more regarding the metaphoric and metonymic poles, see the essay by Roman Jakobson, "Aspects of Language and Types of Aphasic Disturbances" (Jakobson 1990: 116–33). Also see Michel Le Guern's historical presentation and annotated bibliography in *La metáfora y la metonimia*.

6. See Marcela Taletavicius' (1995) analysis of late twentieth-century fashion.

7. For more on this theory, see López and Botalla (1983).

8. The *mantilla* was worn by the women of high society. For cold days, servants used *rebozos*, which although identical in appearance to the *mantilla*, were considerably more ornate because they were often the most elegant piece of clothing that they possessed.

9. See *El Monitor* (1834) 152: 2–3.

10. A war with Brazil over land entitlement led, ultimately, to the conception of Uruguay in 1828, when a British treaty proposed the creation of the Republic in order to create a buffer zone between Argentina and Brazil (Rock 1987: 103).

11. Sizable hair accessories appeared in other regions of the Southern Cone, from neighboring Montevideo to mountainous Mendoza. The symbolic value of each has not been studied, but one might argue that the emergence of these styles parallel that of the *peinetón*. The headdress from the mountainous region of Mendoza, for instance, possessed the vertical height, though not the horizontal span, of the Buenos Aires *peinetón*.

12. The fashion column highlighted recipes for homemade products that promised hair growth and the aesthetic improvement of hair follicles. Women appear to have expressed concern over the heaviness of their *peinetón*, which sometimes pulled out otherwise healthy hair. Usually, these recipes required staple goods available in most homes: eggs, milk, vinegar, broth. A few concoctions involved a lengthy creation and application process. To create the most popular recipe, for hair growth, follow these directions:

> *To make the hair grow.* Take four ounces each of chicken broth, hemp seed oil and honey. Melt the mixture in a pot and beat it until it has the consistency of a pomade. Nourish the crown of the head for eight days straight.

Unfortunately, there is little information regarding the effectiveness of this recipe. One can only imagine the horrific reactions produced by recipes that describe mixtures of aged eggs and vinegar (*El Iris* (1833) 4: 3–4).

13. I borrow this concept of being dressed to kill and prey to the Look from Shari Benstock and Elizabeth Ferris. See the introduction to their volume *On Fashion* (Benstock and Ferris 1994: 1–17).

Notes

14. See Barbara Creed's analysis of the vagina dentata in *The Monstrous Feminine: Film, Feminism and Psychoanalysis* (Creed 1993).
15. The article appears in *The British Packet*, 312: 2–3.
16. See the article in *The British Packet*, 474: 3.

Chapter 4

1. I use the term "postcolonial" in the ways suggested by Ashcroft, Griffiths, and Tiffin (1989: 2) in *The Empire Writes Back*: "We use the term 'post-colonial', however, to cover all the culture affected by the imperial process from the moment of colonization to the present day."
2. This "social problem" in explained in detail by Jean Franco in her essay on "Women, Fashion, and the Moralists in Early-Nineteenth-Century Mexico."
3. Among the most outstanding works are the following lithographs and accounts: Carlos Nebel's *Viaje pintoresco y arqueológico sobre la parte más interesante de la República Mejicana en los años transcurridos desde 1829 hasta 1834*; Claudio Linati's *Trajes civiles, militares y religiosos de Mexico (1828)*; Guillermo Prieto's *Memorias de mis tiempos. 1828 a 1840* and Manuel Payno's *Un viaje a Veracruz en el invierno de 1843*. For caste paintings, see María Concepción García Sáiz's *Las castas mexicanas: un género pictórico americano*.
4. See *Recopilacion de la vida y leyenda de Catarina de San Juan y la China Poblana*.
5. See José del Castillo Graxeda's *Compendio de la vida y virtudes de la Venerable Catarina de San Juan* (1692) and Alonso Ramos's *Primera Parte de los Prodigios de la Omnipotencia. y milagros de la Gracia En la Vida de la Venerable Sierva de Dios Catharina de S. Joan. Natural del Gran Mogor, y difunta en esta imperial ciudad de Puebla de los Angeles, en la Nueva España* (1689); the *Segunda Parte de los Prodigios de la Omnipotencia, y milagros de la Gracia En la Vida de la Venerable Sierva de Dios Catharina de S. Joan. Natural del Gran Mogor, y difunta en esta imperial ciudad de Puebla de los Angeles, en la Nueva España* (1690); and the *Tercera Parte de los Prodigios de la Omnipotencia. y milagros de la Gracia En la Vida de la Venerable Sierva de Dios Catharina de S. Joan. Natural del Gran Mogor, y difunta en esta imperial ciudad de Puebla de los Angeles en la Nueva España* (1692).
6. Recent historical and literary studies include Francisco de la Maza's *Catarina de San Juan. Princesa de La India y Visionaria de Puebla*; Kathleen Myers's essay on "The Mystic Triad in Colonial Mexican Nuns' Discourse: Divine Author, Visionary Scribe, and Clerical Mediator"; and Jeannie L. Gillespie's essay on "Gender, Ethnicity and Piety. The Case of the *China Poblana*."
7. For more examples, see María Elena Ota Mishima's *México y Japón en el siglo XIX: la política exterior de México y la consolidación de la soberanía japonesa* (Mishima 1976: 54–6).
8. *Chinese Export Porcelain in North America*, one of the most lucid studies on the influences of Chinese porcelain in United States and Mexican culture, provides more information about this first ship.
9. Here I refer to *modernista* writers like Julián del Casal, José Asunción Silva, Enrique Gómez Carrillo, and José Juan Tablada. For a more detailed analysis, see my *Orientalismo en el modernismo hispanoamericano*.

10. See in particular the writings of Julián del Casal in *Prosas. Edición del Centenario* and his *Obra poética*. Robert Jay Glickman also mentions these fashions in *The Poetry of Julián del Casal: A Critical Edition*.
11. See *El movimiento antichino en México (1871–1934): Problemas del racismo y del nacionalismo durante la Revolución Mexicana*; Zuleika Alvim's "Imigrantes: a vida privada dos pobres do campo" (222–35) and Cesar Angeles Caballero's *Japón en la literatura peruana*.
12. I owe this source to Roberto González Echevarría's groundbreaking research, as found in his introduction to *De donde son los cantantes*.

Chapter 5

1. Oaxacan sandals had a plied cord loop as a toe thong (*la correa* or *la pata del gallo*, i.e, rooster's claw (see de Avila Blomberg 1997: 114).
2. Sandals were found in the Cuicatlán Canyon (de Avila Blomberg 1997: 114), at Atzcala, in the Balsas River area of Guerrero (Johnson 1971: 301) and in the caves of El Gallo and La Chaguera near Ticumán, Morelos (Sánchez-Martínez 1994: 131–46; 1997: 40–1; Alvarado 1997: 35; Mornett 1999: 70–1).
3. The sandals "differ fundamentally from sandals of the Southwest and other regions" (MacNeish 1967: 184). MacNeish described the most complete sample as having a "heel support . . . a small rectangular piece of one-over-one woven cloth of fine *agave* fiber, with the longer sides of the rectangle attached to ankle loop and sole" (MacNeish 1967: 187).
4. These include a large stone statue of Chalchiuhtlicue, the Toltec water goddesss, and a drawing of the Respectable Women of the Mat Shield following three Venerable Men on the journey of the Mexica people to found Tenochtitlan (Mexico City) in the *Codex Boturini*, also known as the *Story of the Pilgrimage*. Both items are in the collection of the National Museum of Anthropology and History in Mexico City.
5. Initial scratchiness softens with wear, much like newly washed blue jeans. In damp weather soles cake with mud. Moisture yellows the *ixtle*, which turns warm amber like manila rope. Eventually, mildew blackens the fiber or it shreds.
6. Slung over the shoulder of a man from Tepemaxalco, pairs of sandals in one size only cost the equivalent of 28 cents in United States money (Cordry and Cordry 1968: 250).
7. Nahua cosmology attributes a number of diseases to supernatural forces – *aires* (winds), *susto* (fright), *mal de ojo* (the evil eye) and *hechizos* (spells) – which require intervention by specialists, who perform ritual cleansing and recite incantations. Today residents of Hueyapan have a choice of herbalists, midwives, bonesetters, homeopathic healers, spiritualists, shamans and doctors trained in Western medicine (Alvarez 1987: 77).
8. Carol Hendrickson (1995: 99–101) chronicles very similar postpartum treatment – diet, ritual bathing and restricted activity – among Mayan women in Tecpán, Guatemala, but no mention of footwear, which must be a local adaptation.
9. In Hueyapan, Morelos, a "return from the dead" is considered a prerequisite for a traditional healer.

Notes

10. Mexican burial rituals vary widely. Elsewhere sandals of plaited palm, yucca or cardboard, with cords from toe to either side of sole and no heel guard.
11. Beside the Lenten fairs, craftsmen from San Felipe Tepemaxalco sell at neighboring markets and fiestas in the Puebla region. Most limit their sales to the dry months, so they are available to work in their fields, still their primary occupation. Women aid their husbands in sowing, weeding and harvesting.
12. The Cordrys observed dozens of sandals piled up for sale at Amecameca in the early 1940s (Cordry and Cordry 1968: 250).
13. Cited from Dibble and Anderson (1961: 73–4).
14. The Tetelcingo costume is sewn from store-bought fabric, formerly imported English woolens (Cordry and Cordry 1968: 251).
15. Surprisingly, despite a strong Indian revivalist movement since the 1970s in urban areas – where classes are taught in Nahuatl, traditional dance and pre-Hispanic music – *ixcacles* have not been adopted, perhaps because they prove less durable than leather huaraches. Historic disdain for peasant footwear may give way to nostalgia, as rural men rapidly switch to running shoes, and urbanites revaluate huaraches as national costume.
16. In the past pilgrims frequently approached a holy site crawling on their knees and/ or barefoot as a sign of humility and suffering. The prickliness of new sandals may add to the person's penance (Andrés Pérez, personal communication, San Felipe Tepemaxalco, 6 January 2002).
17. Ten years ago, Gabriela Rivera, who returned to Hueyapan after living in Cuautla, asked a Tepemaxalcan vendor to make her a backless pair of sandals with two crossed toe straps and a padded heel underneath the sole. Two other women saw this model and wanted pairs, but the vendor refused because he doubted the style would sell (personal communication, Hueyapan, 24 June 2001). A decade later sandal makers mention such design modifications to interest potential buyers.

Chapter 6

1. My writings about Peruvian dress, especially Colca *bordados*, include Femenías 1996, 1997, 2001, 2004, and n.d.
2. There are no book-length studies of Peruvian rural town markets. Micro-level studies of Peruvian marketing usually address large urban markets and the informal sector; see Babb (1998: 57–60) and Seligmann (2004). On highland markets in Bolivia, see Larson and Harris with Tandeter (1995) and Sikkink (1994). On markets and women traders in Mexico, other areas of Mesoamerica, and Central America, consult Cook and Binford (1990), Chiñas (1976), Smith (1986), and Nash (1993); Seligmann (2001) presents global concerns.
3. In addition to my work, the extensive scholarship on the Colca Valley, including its lifeways and relationship with Caylloma and Arequipa, includes works by Benavides (1983, 1988); Cook (1982); Denevan (2001); Denevan (1986, 1988); Gelles (1990, 2000); Gelles and Martínez (1993); Guillet (1992); Hurley (1978); Manrique (1985); Markowitz (1992); Paerregaard (1997); Pease (1977); Ráez (1993); Stoner (1989); Treacy (1989, 1994); Valderrama and Escalante (1988, 1997); and Wernke (2003).

Notes

4. *Luto*, Spanish for mourning, applies to the period, rituals, and clothes (Ráez 1993: 268).
5. My concern with objects' cultural and economic meanings resonates with discussions about circulation, especially regarding the commoditization of the sacred (Appadurai 1986; Cook 1993; Geary 1986; Kopytoff 1986; Marcus and Myers 1995; Myers, ed. 2001; Phillips and Steiner, eds. 1999; Thomas 1991; Weiner 1992). Schneider's (1978) nuanced analysis of the political economy of European colored cloth has been especially influential.
6. One case created an international legal scandal: Sacred ancient textiles were not merely removed from the sacred context but stolen from their community of origin (Coroma, Bolivia) and sold for exorbitant prices on the international art market; they were subsequently repatriated as cultural patrimony (Bubba 1993; Healy 2001; Lobo 1991).
7. During the Crusades, Christians suppressed white as the mourning color in Europe; black replaced it to indicate funerals, graveyards, and churches (Schneider 1978: 414–15, 422; Harvey 1995: 44–50).
8. In many South American rural communities, black is customary daily dress and not particularly associated with mourning, for example, Cusco and Taquile, Peru, and Sakaka, Bolivia (Allen 1988: 81; Seibold 1995: 323–5; Zorn 1997a).
9. On All Souls in Cusco, see Allen (1988) and Meyerson (1990), and in Bolivia, Harris (2000). The extensive literature on Mexico includes Brandes (1988); Carmichael and Sayer (1992); Garciagodoy (1998); Nutini (1988); and Sayer (1994).
10. During this period, face-shaped rolls called *wawas* ("babies" in Quechua and Peruvian Spanish) are given to children (Harris 2000: 36, n. 18). One Arequipa bakery featured *Tortuninjas* (Teenage Mutant Ninja Turtle) *wawas*.
11. Coporaque has an enormous altar drape which may date to the colonial period. After Holy Week, I saw it laid it out on, and completely covering, the church steps before villagers rolled and stored it for another year. Beneath perhaps a hundred repairs and patches, the original textile is tapestry-woven, probably of alpaca fiber, and features skulls and symbols of the Passion. Little is known about Caylloma colonial textile practices and only a handful of objects survive, mostly in churches (Stastny 1987: 173).
12. The language of exchange is usually Quechua but with outsiders it is Spanish. Migrants from Puno who are native speakers of Aymara also may use Spanish as their trade language. I met no vendors who spoke English or any language other than Spanish, Quechua, and Aymara.
13. During my 2002 visit, many more artisans were embroidering hats. Another factory had begun producing different color, and much cheaper, blanks; using them lowered the final sales price.
14. In the mid-1990s, several frozen bodies, probably Inka, were removed from Sabancaya glacier and publicly displayed in the United States (Conklin 1996; Fowler 1996; Gelles 2000: 79; Fine-Dare 2002). *National Geographic* then substantially expanded its coverage of the Colca Valley. June 1996 brought both an article in the magazine (Reinhard 1996) and a cable TV special. Several Web sites include references to the valley: www.yachay.com, www.peru.org.pe, and www.perucultural.org.pe; they are also linked to Peru's official site, Red Científica Peruana.

15. Mattel's exploitative practices in Asian factories, especially the use of child labor, contrast starkly with the high price of a "real" Barbie (Press 1996).

Chapter 7

1. An earlier version of this chapter was published in 1999 as "(Re)Fashioning the Self: Dress, Economy, and Identity among the Sakaka of Northern Potosi, Bolivia," in *Revista Chungará* 30(2): 161–96. Permission for re-publication is gratefully acknowledged.
2. I use the term "ethnic group" as a shorthand for *ayllu*. *Ayllu* is the basic Andean unit of social organization; it can be translated as ethnic group, polity, community, or kin group, in part depending upon the level of social organization discussed. An abundant literature exists on this topic (Zorn 1997a).
3. My use of "fashion system" plays off Barthes' (1983) application of the concept to the late capitalist West.
4. This term deliberately echoes Olivia Harris' (1987) formulation of the "ethnic" economy of the Laymi of northern Potosí, where products circulate throughout the totality (highland and lowland) of the Laymi ethnic group.
5. While in a postmodernist world it appears that the adjective "traditional" can only be used ironically, within Peru and Bolivia traditional, as used here, refers to cultural practices conceptualized as having pre-Conquest, indigenous origins, such as Sakaka handmade dress.
6. By cloth, I mean all textiles. On the meanings and classification of dress, see Eicher and Roach-Higgins (1992: 15), who support the "use of the word 'dress' as a comprehensive term to identify both direct body changes and items added to the body": specifically, "as an assemblage of body modifications and/or supplements displayed by a person in communicating with other human beings."
7. Eicher and Sumberg (1995) suggest the term cosmopolitan dress, because of this style's worldwide use.
8. I use the term *cholita* (female urban Indian) here, rather than *chola*, because this is how people in the Sakaka region referred to urban Indians (sometimes referring to themselves); *cholita* was considered a more respectful term than *chola* (see Paredes Candia 1992; Weismantel 2002).
9. Significant anthropological and ethnohistorical research has been carried out with *ayllus* in the northern Potosí region; see among others Godoy (1990); Harris (1987); Harris and Albó (1986); Izko (1992); and Platt (1976, 1982). On *ayllus* in Oruro, see Abercrombie (1986, 1998); Arnold (1988); Arnold, Jiménez, and Yapita (1992); and Arnold and Yapita (1999).
10. Most indigenous people in Bolivia do not call themselves *indio*, the Spanish word for Indian, preferring the term *campesino* (peasant); in Bolivia *indio* is used self-consciously by a few small but significant political parties with an Indianist agenda, and its use is increasing.
11. Padre José Antonio Bustamante C.M.F. was the first to study the Sakaka (1985). I am indebted to him and to Enrique Tandeter for copies of Bustamante's important work.
12. Quechua is the Peruvian Spanish spelling of the Inca language; Aymara is Bolivia's other principal highland indigenous language. Most Aymara-speakers in northern

Notes

Potosí also speak Quechua, which is the *lingua franca* of the zone and the language spoken in the region's towns.

13. In addition to geographic and historic differences between the Laymi and the Sakaka, the Sakaka's increasingly limited access to valley lands, and therefore the products from that ecological level, explains a greater need for cash in the Sakaka economy.
14. The complex interplay of ethnicity and race in Bolivia, with its kaleidoscopic variations, are clearly beyond the scope of this chapter. Social identity is somewhat simplified within the *ayllu* since precise identity – Sakaka or non-Sakaka – basically determines access to land and other *ayllu* resources (Zorn 1997a).
15. The category of the *cholita* is highly charged semiotically in Andean society, bearing many strongly held, often contradictory, meanings, such as sensuality, fecundity, astuteness, and rebelliousness; see Paredes-Candia (1992); Mendoza (1992); and Weismantel (2002).
16. The analysis of dress as a semiotic form clearly has the potential to draw on linguistics and semiotics, as the insightful work of Cereceda demonstrates (Cereceda 1978, 1992); while I borrow from linguistics, I do not analyze dress as a text.
17. Enrique Mayer, discussant for the 1997 session on "Popular Strategies of Ethnic Representation," at the Annual meeting of the American Anthropological Association, challenged our panel to do this. Blenda Femenías and I are preparing a volume on this topic.

Chapter 8

1. We use the term "boundary art," following Baizerman (1987), to denote the body of work produced by artisans for sale to external markets, whether local, regional, or global. Related terms such as "tourist art" generally carry negative connotations that we do not share and often refer to one part of artisans' larger output designated for trade or sale to individuals outside of the artisans' ethnic group.
2. Hendrickson includes a full list of the twenty-seven mail-order catalogs she analyzed on pages 119–20 of her article.
3. "Maya Traditions is a member of the Fair Trade Federation (FTF), which is an association of fair trade wholesalers, retailers, and producers whose members are committed to providing fair wages and good employment opportunities to economically disadvantaged artisans and farmers worldwide" (Mintz 2002, www.mayatraditions.com).

Chapter 9

1. Translated by Regina A. Root and Silvia Tandeciarz. A previous Spanish-language version of this essay appeared in *Ponchos de las tierras del Plata* (Buenos Aires: Verstraeten Editores, 1999).
2. In Spanish, a *casulla* refers to the outer garment worn by priests during Mass or Holy Communion.

Notes

3. Made of guanaco leather, this covering was worn in reverse so that the skin faced outward. The designs on the exterior were at times identical to those found on ponchos.
4. Creole men would enter these *pulperías* with their horses. This custom, out of necessity, led to the introduction of a practical element known as the *palenque*, a stake driven into the ground in front of the *pulpería* so that horses could be tied.

Chapter 10

1. This newspaper advertisement announcing the launch of Mappin's new store at Praça do Patriarca in 1919 is available at the Mappin Historical Archive.
2. Slavery was abandoned in 1888 (Fausto 2001: 113 and Bakewell 1997: 355). At the same time, the number of immigrants coming to São Paulo from other countries increased from 6500 people in 1885 to 92,000 in 1888 (Fausto 2001: 115).
3. As suggested previously, the 1880s were marked by massive immigration. By the time a republic had been created, following the defeat of the Emperor, São Paulo could boast stable jobs for immigrant workers and former slaves. In 1891, approximately 30 percent of the factory workers in crafting and manufacturing workshops were black. In 1893, 84 percent of all industrial jobs belonged to immigrants (Fausto 2001: 124).
4. See his essay on "O movimento modernista" as republished in the 10 February 2002 issue of *O Estado de São Paulo*. This is a facsimile edition of the essay, originally written in 1942.
5. The translation is mine.
6. William Lancaster (2000: 7) gives this early version the name of "proto-department store."
7. The Mappin Historical Archive has a strong section of documents pertaining to the years period between 1913 and 1940.
8. My master's thesis for the MA history of textiles and dress at the University of Southampton studies the presence of couture in *Vogue* (French, American and British editions) and other fashion magazines from 1920 to 1938. See *The House of Louiseboulanger: An Insight into Couture and its Commercial Practices in Paris of the 1920s and 1930s*.
9. Personal interview conducted by Rita Andrade in São Paulo, 23 March 2002 with Mrs Olga Rubião. Mrs Rubião was reluctant in saying her exact date of birth. She is a *paulistana* and grew up in the wealthy area of São Paulo at the time Mappin was at the height of its popularity.
10. The Mappin Historical Archive also houses these announcements.
11. See the article entitled "'Mais um aspecto do dinamismo Bandeirante' – S. Paulo, centro irradiador da elegância e da beleza" in the 17 December 1933 edition of the *Jornal da Manhã*.
12. Newspaper advertisement from 12 May 1915. Newspaper clippings, such as the one cited, were untitled. All clippings can be found at the Mappin Historical Archive.
13. At this time, the store was owned by the Ricardo Mansur Group, which also declared bankruptcy one year later (24 March 2000). See http//:www.estado. estadao.com.br/edicao/pano/00/03/23/eco/929.html.

Notes

Chapter 11

1. Translated by Regina A. Root and Cândida Bordenave.
2. For more information about these categories see "Alta, média e baixa costura: moda e semiologia cultural" in Kathia Castilho and Diana Galvão's edited volume on *A moda do corpo, o corpo da moda*; and "Menos corpo, mais fetiche?" in Nizia Villaça's volume on *Em pauta: corpo, globalização e novas tecnologias*.
3. See pp. 160 to 176 in particular.
4. Tijuca residents belong to a neighborhood located far from the sea and thought of as more conservative.
5. *O Cruzeiro*, 20 January 1951, p. 35.
6. For more on Brazilian counterculture see Carlos Alberto Messeder Pereira's *O que é contracultura* (São Paulo: Brasiliense, 1983) and Luiz Carlos Maciel's *Geração em transe; memórias do tempo do tropicalismo* (Rio de Janeiro: Nova Fronteira, 1996).
7. This group comprised of singers from Baia emerged on the Brazilian musical scene after a first generation of "baianos" like Caetano Veloso, Gal Costa, and Gilberto Gil.
8. This notion of an egocentric lifestyle brought to the fore of publicity is discussed in Anthony Giddens' "Tribulações do eu" in *Modernidade e identidade* (Rio de Janeiro: Jorge Zahar Editores, 2002).
9. See Stuart Hall's *A identidade cultural na pós-modernidade*, translated by Tomaz Tadeu da Silva and Guaraciara Lopes Louro (Rio de Janeiro: DP&A, 2000).
10. See her essays in *Vogue Magazine*, in particular the special edition for summer 2002/2003 entitled, "Cinqüenta e Oito Estilistas – São Paulo Fashion Week/ Fashion Rio" (São Paulo: Carta Editorial, 2002).

Chapter 12

1. The quote "Every girl had a fan which she kept always in motion" is part of an observation made by an American writer who attended an aristocratic ball in Puerto Rico in 1899. See Samoiloff (1984: 101).
2. Even though the reforms and improvements in fields such as education and commerce brought about by the American government affected, on one or many levels, all classes of Puerto Rican women, this essay focuses on the women of the middle and higher classes.
3. For more on the Puerto Rican women's emergence into society see Vidal (1980: 202–13).
4. In a more general context, see Sarah Cosbey, Mary Lynn Damhorst, and Jane Farrell-Beck (2003: 101–9) on the relationship between American women's daytime clothing styles in relation to their roles in a changing society.
5. In order to analyze the appearance and dress of affluent Puerto Rican women from 1895 through 1920, the authors relied on photographs from the period.
6. See in particular the work of Arturo Morales Carrión (1983: 6, 8); Guy S. Métraux (1952: 60) and Francisco A. Scarano, (1993: 556).

Notes

7. Even though Métraux (1952: 59–62) does not elaborate on the reason for the gleeful welcome, others have explained it in their writings. See Olga Jiménez de Wagenheim (1998: 206) and Eileen J. Findlay (1998: 139).
8. Also see William Boyce (1914: 439) and Fernández García (1923: 193). Spanish as the primary language of instruction was reinstated in 1946. In 1898 there were 528 public schools in Puerto Rico with an attendance of 18,243 by 1914 there were
3,000 schools with an attendance of 118,000 students. Originally, the University of Puerto Rico was exclusively an institution for the preparation of teachers.
9. This is the opinion of a nineteenth century Spanish writer on the "fair sex" of the island.
10. For views on Puerto Rican society, including the seclusion of elite women, at the end of the nineteenth century, see Bryan (1899: 383); Hamm (1899: 121); and Charles Morris 1899: 205); and Ober (1899: 169).
11. It is not clear if Dinwiddie (1899: 153) was referring just to Mexico or his statement also includes the Spanish speaking territories of the west and southwest United States.
12. Pico Vidal (1980: 202) argues that the lack of "both a feminist movement and a strong feminist consciousness" for most of the nineteenth century in Puerto Rico was due to the "precarious educational and employment situation of women of the island."
13. This early eighteenth century quote by Bishop Fray Jimenez Pérez can be found in the *Boletin Histórico de Puerto Rico*, volume 1, page 162 and reproduced in María Cadilla de Martínez, (1938: 153).
14. A color image of the Largillière portrait can be found in François Boucher (1987: 264). For more on this fashionable neckline, see Doreen Yarwood (1992: 51).
15. For information on imports and exports in Puerto Rico at the end of the nineteenth century, also see Robert Hill (1898: 159); Morris (1899: 189); Ober (1899: 235).
16. Coqui Santaliz, "Entre historias, encajes y una isla vestida," *El Reportero*, 18 May 1985, Viva section; Jiménez de Wagenheim, (1898: 251).
17. For an image of "an accomplished young Spanish lady of Mayaguez, Puerto Rico" in 1898 see Bryan (1899: 322).
18. Images of Puerto Rican women wearing the fitted and loose "untucked" look, as well as Cuban and Philippine can be seen in Bryan (1899: 116, 269, 270, 552).
19. Susannah Worth and Lucy R. Sibley (1994) examine the use of Andalusian imagery, including the *mantilla* and fan, to define Spanishness.
20. These are the words of Truman R. Clark (1975: 3).
21. For more information, see Edna Acosta-Belén (1986: 276). Ribes Tovar (1970: 194). Teaching became a "female" occupation with 74.5 percent of teachers female in 1930 versus 30 percent in 1899. See also Vidal (1980: 206).
22. Key leaders in the women's movement from both the labor and professional factions include Luisa Capetillo and Ana Roqué de Duprey. Capetillo was involved in the labor movement, established a journal devoted to women's issues and it is considered the first woman in Puerto Rico to wear pants in public. Among her many accomplishments, Roqué de Duprey was a teacher, wrote academic textbooks, founded several female oriented journals, as well the *Liga Femínea Puertorriqueña* and *La Asociación de Mujeres Sufragistas de Puerto Rico*. For more on these extraordinary women see Norma Valle Ferrer (1990) and Sarah

Notes

Vazquez Graziani, "'Flor nueva' en viejos quehaceres masculinos" (master's thesis, Universidad de Puerto Rico, 1985).

23. The suffragists try to get the right-to-vote bill passed in 1919, 1921, 1923 and 1927 before it was finally approved in 1929. The bill only gave literate women the right to vote. After voting for the first time in 1932, the law was changed in 1935 to include all Puerto Rican women in the electoral process. See Scarano (1993: 650–4).

24. An example of a fashion column can be found in "Modas," *Gráfico*, 15 March 1913. For a local retailer see *Puerto Rico Ilustrado*, 18 November 1916; Bertha Gowns are found in *Puerto Rico Ilustrado*, October 1911. Other fashion illustrations can be found in "Últimas Modas," *El Carnaval*, 31 January 1907.

25. Conclusions for the mode of dress between 1899–1917 are based on the analysis of photographs of Puerto Rican women and local magazines including fashion images, articles, and advertisements.

26. The photograph features the dress made at the dress shop of Mr. and Mrs. de Frontera for Miss. Estrella Bianchi of Mayaguez, who was to wear it for the season. See in particular the 11 February 1912 edition of *Gráfico*.

27. For a B. Altman & Co. advertisement, see the 6 March 1920 issue of *Puerto Rico Ilustrado*; for Keds, see the 28 September 1918 issue of the same magazine.

28. Suárez Findlay (1999: 123) mentions how for many Puerto Rican women, the institution of divorce by the United States in 1902, distinguishes the "*epoca de los americanos* (time of the American) from *los tiempos aquellos, cuando los españoles* (that time long ago, when the Spaniards ruled)."

29. For a more general theoretical approach, see David L. Sills (1972: 22); Clyde M. Woods (1975: 28); Grant D. McCraken (1988: 60), (1979: 7).

30. The Puerto Rican Barbie® Doll was introduced by Mattel® in 1997 as part of the company's "Dolls of the World" collection. The Institute of Puerto Rican Culture was consulted about the costume, which is similar to a type of folkloric dance dress. The eyelet "lace" with pink ribbon trim (representation of the real trim) of the doll's costume embellishes the neckline, sleeves, and skirt.

Chapter 13

1. Bilingual readers will notice that *Three Trapped Tigers* (on which Cabrera Infante collaborated with the talented translator and translation critic Suzanne Jill Levine) is a somewhat free and definitely playful translation, which nevertheless retains the untranslatability and thus "essential" nature of the *guayabera*, which appears italicized, as a word foreign to English. The Spanish version reads: ". . . Damas y Caballeros, cubanos todos, nos toca ahora hacer las presentaciones de nuestros favorecedores del patio, que han sabido acoger con la generosidad proverbial y la típica caballerosidad criolla, tan nuestra, tan cubana como esas palmas que se ven al fondo y esas guayaberas (con su lacito, ¿eh?) que visten los elegantes habaneros, con esa misma hospitalidad de siempre, han permitido ustedes que presentáramos primero a nuestros parroquianos internacionales. Ahora, como es debido, les toca a los espectadores más connotados de nuestra vida social, política y cultural" (Cabrera Infante 1967: 17).

Notes

2. All of these contexts will be taken up at more length in the chapter, but for general reference, see Suárez Solis et al. 1948 and Rosendi Cancio 1982.
3. Castro reportedly told reporters after the Summit, "To tell you the truth, I did not have a single guayabera. I had to borrow some and try them on to see if they would fit, but none did. They made some guayaberas for me in a few hours ... This guayabera made history. Many praised it. Some people were against it." The comments are included in an exchange between Castro and his advisors on 16 June 1994, recorded by the Havana Cuba Vision Network, available at http://lanic.utexas.edu/la/cb/cuba/castro/1994/19940619.
4. A longer version of Ferrer's ultra-nationalistic *décimas* can be found in the June 1966 issue of *ANAP*, pages 28–9.
5. In Pablo Medina's *Exiled Memories: A Cuban Childhood* (1990: 39), the *guayabera* is invoked in the production of nostalgia as writer recalls strolling with his family along Havana's famous seaside boulevard, the *malecón*, the kids playing, the mothers chastising, and "the fathers walking imperturbably on in their white *guayaberas*."
6. The fact that Vicente Fox often wears a *guayabera* with cowboy boots has been interpreted by some as a sign of political ambivalence. In a September 2000 article in the Mexico City daily *La Jornada*, columnist Julio Hernández López wrote that "Vicente Fox ... parece dispuesto a combinar las botas puntiagudas con la guayabera echevarrista. Ni izquierda ni derecha, sino todo lo contrario." ("Vicente Fox ... seems ready to combine his cowboy boots with the guayabera of Echeverría. Neither the left nor the right, not one or the other.")
7. Quoted in "Knowing the father behind the legend. How to bask in adulation wasn't one of dad's lessons." San Jose Mercury News, Friday 31 March 2000, http://www.ufw.org/sjm33100a.html.
8. At the time of publication, Rosendi Cancio was Director General del Consejo de Artes Plásticas in Sancti Espíritus. The text in question is a manuscript version housed in the Rubén Martínez Villegas Library in Sancti Espíritus, Cuba.
9. In the nineteenth century, a collarless long-sleeved shirt similar to a *guayabera* was customary attire for the *hacendados* or landed gentry on the Yucatan's *henequen* plantations, the garment that distinguished them from their Mayan laborers. This difference in costume was at no time more pronounced than after the so-called Caste War of 1847, an unsuccessful struggle for Mayan autonomy that lasted five years, and is considered by many to be more bloody and cruel than the conquest itself in this part of Mexico (Berunza Pinto 1997: 70). Following the Caste War, which was really a class war, the Mayans were once again forced to work on large plantations owned by mestizos and *criollos*, and some were even transported to Cuba to work on sugar plantations. In the years that followed, and especially after the Mexican Revolution in 1910, landowners in the Yucatan strove to maintain their neocolonial practices – which included the famous *pernada*, or *droit de seigneur* over the Mayan women on the haciendas – in the face of increased demands for land reform and Mayan autonomy. In a scene from Julián Pastor's 1976 film *La casta divina*, a wealthy landowner and his family have just finished saying mass for the death of his brother. He then addresses his Mayan servants, informing them that they will have to fight for him and the interests of Yucatecan separatism, and against the forces of revolutionary reform. Both he and his son are dressed in the pocketless, collarless linen version of the *guayabera* called a *filipina*, free of the fancy embroidery later associated with the shirt in both Cuba and Mexico.

Notes

Chapter 14

1. This concept is derived from Jacques Lacan's reading of Freud's *Fort-Da*. He observes how children play with a nursery rhyme by exchanging the sounds produced by one animal with those produced by another. Upon observing children stating "dog goes miaow, cat goes woof-woof," Lacan writes, "the child by *disconnecting* the animal (dog) from its sound (woof-woof) suddenly raises the sign to the level of the signifier" (*Écrits* 303–4). This play converts signs into signifiers that are, in Freud's words, an example of *vorstellungsrepräsentanz*, that is, representative of representation. Henry Krips, in *Fetish: An Erotics of Culture*, suggests that what is attained is the apprehension of language as a "signifying system governed by rules of substitution and combination, and that, by breaking the rules, word sense is lost" (Krips 1999: 16).
2. For a discussion on the role of fashion in Cuban culture, see Norman Holland's essay, "Fashioning Cuba."
3. See Klaus Müller-Bergh's *Alejo Carpentier: Estudio Biográfico-Crítico* (Madrid: Las Américas, 1972), Roberto González Echevarría and Müller-Bergh's *Alejo Carpentier: Bibliographical Guide/Guía Bibliográfica* (Westport and London: Greenwood Press, 1983), and Araceli García-Carranza's *Biobibliografía de Alejo Carpentier* (La Habana: Editorial Letras Cubanas, 1984). It is interesting to note that all three bibliographies change the spelling of the dramatized author from the French "Jacqueline" to the more Hispanic sounding "Jaqueline" without the "c." Further, none of these texts document the entire collection. The series ran uninterruptedly from August of 1925 until July of 1927 when Carpentier was apparently detained by the Cuban police for signing the manifesto of the *Grupo Minorista* against then dictator Gerardo Machado.
4. Specifically, I am thinking specifically about Vicky Unruh's lucid essay "The Performing Spectator in Alejo Carpentier's Fictional World". She argues convincingly that performative dynamics emerge through a constant fluctuation between conflictive ontological and cultural positions. Like many of the playwrights of the early twentieth century – she contends – Carpentier uses *performance* as a point of departure in his theoretical inquiry into ontology (Unruh 1998: 58).
5. It is tempting to conclude that Jacqueline is a transvestite, as Ben Sifuentes Jáuregui does, for the simple fact that *she* is the product of masculine creation. The only serious treatment of the "Jacqueline texts" to date appears in Ben Sifuentes-Jáuregui's *Transvestism, Masculinity and Latin American Literature* (Sifuentes-Jáuregui 2002). Sifuentes opts to focus on questions of the author's motivations for writing the feminine and, as a result, accuses Carpentier of colonialism, homosexual panic, and sadomasochism for not claiming paternity. Nonetheless, his major point is that the texts have "remained hidden for seven decades" (Sifuentes-Jáuregui 2002: 55) fails to take into account the fact that Carpentier claimed the texts in his 1964 interview with Leante precisely at a moment in Cuban history when there was a clear and present danger in being labeled as a homosexual.
6. Here I am referring to essays like Paul de Man's "Autobiography as De-Facement," *The Rhetoric of Romanticism* (New York: Columbia University Press, 1984) 67–81.
7. Nonetheless, Butler does not entirely discount or dismiss a relationship between homosexuality and drag. She adds, "it is important to underscore that drag is an effort to negotiate cross-gendered identification, but that cross-gendered identification

Notes

is not the exemplary paradigm for thinking about homosexuality, although it may be one" (Butler 1993: 235). The multiplicity of paradigms for thinking about homosexuality in the Cuban context is found in Reinaldo Arenas's discussion of four categories of homosexual, only two of which (the *loca de argolla* and the *loca regia*) would seem to have resonances in the drag model (Arenas 1992: 103–4).

8. Indeed, Sifuentes-Jáuregui's monograph provides little if any insights into female transgression. Characterizing she-to-he cross-dressing as an issue of political and social empowerment, he views transvestism as male-centered. Hence, under this logic, female transgression becomes invisible precisely because masculinity is the norm. In this case, it seems that Sifuentes equating transvestism with homosexuality reifies the dialectic of the *open* and the *closed,* the *chingón* and the *chingada*, that Octavio Paz describes in *El laberinto de la soledad* (Paz 1985: 69–70). This construct assumes, as Marjorie Garber concludes, that "wishing to be or act like a man is considered 'normal' or 'natural'" (Garber 1992: 105).

9. Cruz-Malavé, in his innovative work on the works of José Lezama Lima, contends that the novel *Paradiso* bears a homosexual logic that manifests itself through the protagonist's simultaneous identification with his mother and his repression of his incestuous desire for her. José Cemí apprehends maternal absence by identifying himself with her lack, the absent father. Cruz-Malavé notes that the son identifies with the mother, and upon identifying himself with her, he identifies with her desire (Cruz-Malavé 1994: 91). Homosexual transgression in this case is produces the image of the paternal metaphor and ushers the subject into the symbolic order. It becomes, as Cruz-Malavé insightfully adds, "the only means of accessing paternal succession of the adolescent poet, the family and the nation" (Cruz-Malavé 1994: 93; the translation is mine).

10. Garber suggests that cross-dressing emerges in a category crisis which marks "displacements from the axis of *class* as well as from *race* onto the axis of gender" (Garber 1992: 17).

11. Gustavo Pérez Firmat, in his insightful essay on the poetics of José Lezama Lima, "The Strut of the Centipede," refers to this process as a hermeneutics of creative assimilation. He writes that this "involves the rearrangement of cultural blocks—natural phenomenon, historical events, works of art, or myths – into novel configurations" (Pérez Firmat 1989: 318).

12. See the full page Larrañaga advertisement in the March 1919 issue of *Social* (issue number 2).

13. It is important to underscore Lacan's insistence in the difference between the penis as organ and the phallus as a structure (1977: 285).

Chapter 15

1. For further information consult Jean Baudrillard (1981), *For a Critique of the Political Economy of the Sign* translated by Charles Levin (St. Louis MO: Telos Press). Also Baudrillard (1994) *Simulacra and Simulation* translated by Sheila Faria Glaser (Ann Arbor: University of Michigan Press), and Baudrillard (1990) *Seduction* translated by Brian Singer (New York: St. Martin's Press).

2. Born Magdalena Carmen Frieda Kahlo Calderón, the artist later adopted the name Frida and changed her birth year to 1910 to match that of the Mexican Revolution.

Notes

3. The legend of Ernesto "Che" Guevara has not only been kept alive in documentaries and in the film Evita, but also his name and his face continue to be reproduced in posters, T-shirts, and other novelty products worldwide. Antonio Banderas (an actor who coincidentally played the character of Guevara in the film Evita) will play Mexican revolutionary Pancho Villa in a new film produced by HBO. *The Life of Pancho Villa* will be directed by Bruce Beresford. *Pancho Villa* (1972) is an older version of the revolutionary's life played by actor Telly Savallas. Carmen Miranda's life was reenacted as a documentary in *Bananas Is My Business* (1994). Starring Carmen Miranda and Alice Faye under the direction of Helena Solberg. See http://www.reel.com/movie.asp?MID=11876.
4. On 2 August 1951, the Confederación General del Trabajo (National Confederation of Workers) proposed the Perón-Evita formula; however, due to her cancer and the opposition of military sectors, Eva later declined this nomination.
5. According to Margaret A. Lindauer, the commercial promotion of Kahlo's self portrait used by the Metropolitan Museum in New York to advertise *Mexico: Splendors of Thirty Centuries*, a traveling exhibit on Mexican art in 1991, was responsible for promoting her name and figure throughout the United States (Lindauer 1999: 1). A blatant example of Fridamania is the following advertising on the Web, "Frida Kahlo Paintings on Personal Checks. Order check designs featuring the artwork of Frida Kahlo. The next time you write a check, make it a masterpiece on www.checkworks.com."
6. See Frank Milner's *Frida Kahlo*, front cover.
7. See Andrea Kettenman (1993), *Frida Kahlo 1907–1954: Pain and Passion* (Cologne: Bendikt Taschen, 1993), p. 26.
8. Social and racial dualism are, in fact, the essence of the *mestizo* identity. The double is a fairly common trope in Latin American literature and arts, as the divided self-alternative networks or possibilities of exchange can produce.
9. For a reinterpretation on Kahlo's fashion style consult: *Elle* (May 1989), *Mirabella* (Nov. 1990), *New York Times* ("Frida report," February 1990), *Vogue* (April 1990), *Time Magazine* (October 2001), *Elle* (November 2001), *Harpers Bazaar* and *Vogue* (both in December 2001).
10. For Gaultier's site go to www.fridakahlo.com. Interestingly enough, even in 1933 women in the United States tried to imitate Kahlo's style, something that the painter herself commented upon, "some of the gringa women are imitating me and trying to dress 'a la Mexicana,' but the poor souls only look like cabbages and to tell you the naked truth, they look absolutely impossible."
11. This play has been edited in *Puro Teatro: A Latina Anthology,* Alberto Sandoval and Nancy Saporta-Sternach (2000) (Tucson: The University of Tucson), pp. 337–90. Other plays are *Helen and Frida* (1998), based on a short story by Ann Finger and Naomi Goldberg's play; it depicts a fictional love affair between Helen Keller and Frida Kahlo. Also *Goodbye, My Friduchita* (1999) by playwright Dolores C. Sendler. *Frida, un retablo* by Dañel Malán (2002), *La Casa Azul* by Robert Lepage and Sophie Faucher (2002), *Recuerdo* by Rosanne Ramos (2002), and "Tres Vidas" chamber music theater work for a singing actress and trio of musicians. This play is based on the lives of Kahlo, Argentine poet Alfonsina Storni and Salvadoran activist Rufina Amaya, written by Chilean author and scholar Marjorie Agosín. Consult http://www.fridakahlo.it/teatro.html.
12. Consult *Salma Hayek is Frida Kahlo* at http://hayekheaven.tripod.com/frida/news.html. The site contains information on Hayek's publicity as Kahlo. *Time*

Notes

Magazine in its 10 October 2001 issue published a special edition titled "The New Mexico" with Salma Hayek as Frida Kahlo on the cover.

13. My translation. See Perla Ciuk's review, *"Frida" Entre palomitas y Coca light* ["Frida" Between Popcorn and Light Coke) in www.noticine.com/noticine/secciones/critica_film.asp. Other reviews in English by American critics agree: "I doubt if the results would have satisfied Kahlo, whose originality in matters of life, art, and ideas was vastly more far-reaching" (David Sterrit in the *Christian Science Monitor*); "Though *Frida* is easier to swallow than Julie Taymor's preposterous *Titus*, the eye candy here lacks considerable brio" (Ed Gonzalez in *Slant Magazine*); "An old-fashioned, Hollywoodish biopic, oddly unimaginative in everything but its visuals" (Frank Swietek in *One Guy's Opinion*); "Gorgeous to look at but emotionally flat" (Laura Clifford in *Reeling Reviews*); "A technical triumph and an extraordinary bore" (Walter Chaw in the *Film Freak Central*). For further comments consult www.rottentomatoes.com.

14. In fact, *The Two Fridas* is another version of Kahlo's life, produced and interpreted by singer-actress Jennifer López. As Hayek's film was released first, López's production was suspended until further notice.

15. Sandra María Esteves' poem *Raising Eyebrows* dedicated to Frida Kahlo, is a perfect example of such admiration. "Here we are Frida/Sisters face to face/You hanging on museum walls/Your canvass singing/Familiar womansongs/In bramble bush hair/Eagle eyebrow wings/Blood-stained wedding dress/Cloudy sky fan/Unspeakable man-suit/Where we met /Thru different times/Finding each other at last/Your colored visions seeing/Into my magic world/Under the surface/Where nothing much has changed ... I offer you this time/The way your brushstroke sacrifices/Offers your soul to us/Some called you crazy/What did they really know?/Opinionated woman/Shut into wrenching poems/Silenced into speaking paintings/Where I imagine/More than sisters/Seeing what you see/Seeing myself thru you/Clear as crystal/Drinking water from your brushstrokes/Reflections in the mirror." In Roberta Fernández (ed.) (1994), *In Other Words: Literature by Latinas of the United States*, Houston, Texas: Arte Público Press, p. 124.

16. After arriving in Buenos Aires, she had minor parts in the following plays: *La señora de los Pérez* (1935), *Cada casa es un mundo, Mme. San Gene, La dama, el caballero y el ladrón* (1936), Los inocentes (1937), and *La nueva colonia* (1937). Apart from several second rate roles in commercial theaters and films, her most relevant cinema performances were: *La cabalgata del circo* (1944) and *La pródiga* (1945), but this last film was never released to the public. In 1939 Eva's radio soap programs aired in *Radio Argentina, El Mundo*, and from 1943 to 1945, she began a series on the biographies of illustrious women in Radio Belgrano.

17. See *Eva Perón* (1951). For an excellent discourse analysis of Evita's narrative consult, David W. Foster (1985) "Narrative Persona in Eva Perón's a razón de mi vida," in Carmelo Virgilio and Naomi Lindström (eds), *Woman as Myth and Metaphor in Latin American Literature*, Columbia: University of Missouri Press). As Foster argues, being more than a biography, *Razón* may be interpreted as "a serious political statement of a fictional narrative, artfully designed to strike responsive cords in a sympathetic audience, *Razón* deserves its important role as an eloquent example of literature produced by popular Peronist culture." Also consult. J.M. Taylor (1981), *Eva Perón: The Myths of a Woman* Chicago: University of Chicago Press), and Alicia Dujovne Ortiz (1995), *Eva Perón* trans. Sean Fields, New York: St. Martin's Press.

Notes

18. Andrew Lloyd Webber and Tim Rice (1979), *Evita: The Legend of Evita Perón (1919–1952)*, New York. Patti Lupone and Elaine Paige are among the many successful actresses and singer to impersonate Evita since its debut in 1978. Some of the original film productions are: Marvin Chomsky's *Evita Perón, First Lady* (1981) an NBC's movie for television with Faye Dunaway and James Farentino, and Carlos Pasini's, *Queen of Hearts*, produced for Thames Television in England.
19. According to Michael Warren this statement is part of an eight-page letter written by Madonna to Alan Parker begging him to play Eva Perón. See www.wbr.com or www.madonna/journey-on.com/evita/. Moreover, *Eva Perón – La tumba sin paz*, in http://www.servicenet.com.ar/mbarbera/evita displays photos of the embalmed corpse of Evita and provides details on her posthumous odyssey.
20. For an interesting analysis on the similarities of these women see Michael Warren's "Eva and Madonna: Parallel Lives?" (http://www.journey-on.com/evita/art2.html). I concur with Savigliano (2002: 346) that Madonna's best skill is "her lack of depth. Her flatness is precisely what allows her image to shine brightly as an icon. Rather than inhabiting or playing different characters, she appropriates them. Her ability to put on whatever suits her at the moment imbues her with an aura of power signaled by success and manipulation."
21. Seeking to keep her wife's memory alive, Juan Domingo Perón proclaimed 18 October Saint Evita Day. According to Paul L. Montgomery, Evita had planned the construction of a 449-foot high tomb, project for which she placed two conditions: "that the architect be a Peronist and that the structure be taller than the statue of Liberty (305 feet high)" (Wilkie and Mennell-Kinberg 1981: 114).
22. For example, Jimmy Wilson comments, "Madonna's performance was her best yet. I never once felt that I was looking at Madonna, I was watching Eva. Madonna has, with this movie, proven herself to be an actress" http://www.geocities.com/Broadway/2804/frame.htm.
23. Upon Madonna's arrival to Buenos Aires, several posters plastered across the city read: "Evita hay una sola, y es nuestra" (there is only one Evita, and she is ours) (Savigliano 2002: 357).

Chapter 16

1. Additional members of the Big Six included Naomi Campbell, Cindy Crawford, Linda Evangelista, Elle MacPherson and Claudia Schiffer, who *USA Today* described as "the cusp of what's being seen as a likely stampede of long-legged lovelies" (Snead, 1990: 5). In 1992, the *Chicago Sun-Times* explained the notoriety and significance of these models to the general public. "What distinguishes the world's supermodels [sic] from other merely successful models?" the newspaper inquired. "For one, they're as easily recognized in Paris, Texas, as in Paris, France – thanks to magazine editorials, advertisements, billboards and music videos. They often date, marry or bear the children of famous men – who usually happen to be rock stars. They're profiled in magazine articles and on shows like MTV's *House of Style*. In short, they're celebrities" (Brooke 1992: 41).
2. This article, commenting on *Hispanic*'s "Gringo of the Year" selections, reported: "Christy Turlington was chosen closet Hispanic – her mother is from El Salvador" (Newsmakers 1995a: 2).

Notes

3. Literary theorist Arturo Arias warns about the representational uniformity suggested in the concept of "tropicalization." He notes: "I do not believe that [tropicalization], marked by its Caribbeanness, should be extended to embrace all of Latin America. There is too much risk of homogenizing and grouping what is in reality a very heterogeneous array of cultural experiences and effects. The Guatemalan, Salvadoran, or even Central American experience as a whole is independent and irreducible to large unities that seek to discipline its singularity" (Arias, 2003: 171).
4. The title of this subheading borrows from and is indebted to Jean Genet's play, *The Maids*, where the protagonists, Solange and Claire, convey their desires and contradictions of loving and hating themselves as maids and simultaneously of loving and hating Madame, their mistress. In one instance, Solange declares: "But what if you're only a maid? The best you can do is give yourself airs while you're doing the cleaning or washing up. You twirl your feather duster like a fan. You make fancy gestures with the dishcloth. Or... you treat yourself to historical parades in Madame's apartment" (Genet 1954: 52).
5. See Walter LaFeber, *Inevitable Revolutions: The United States in Central America* and Lloyd S. Etheredge, *Can Governments Learn? American Foreign Policy and Central American Revolutions*.

Bibliography

Abercrombie, T. A. (1986), *The Politics of Sacrifice: An Aymara Cosmology in Action*. Dissertation, University of Chicago.
—— (1991), 'To Be Indian, to Be Bolivian: "Ethnic" and "National" Discourses of Identity', in G. Urban and J. Sherzer (eds), *Nation-States and Indians in Latin America*, Austin: University of Texas Press.
—— (1998), *Pathways of Memory and Power: Ethnography and History Among an Andean People*, Madison: University of Wisconsin Press.
Ackerman, R. (1996), 'Cloth and Identity in the Central Andes: Province of Abancay, Peru', in M. B. Schevill, J. C. Berlo and E. B. Dwyer (eds), *Textile Traditions of Mesoamerica and the Andes: An Anthology*, Austin: University of Texas Press.
Acosta-Belén, E. (1980) 'Women in Twentieth Century Puerto Rico', in A. López (ed.), *The Puerto Ricans: Their History, Culture, and Society*, Cambridge, MA: Schenkman.
—— (1986), *The Puerto Rican Woman: Perspectives on Culture, History, and Society*, New York: Praeger.
Adorno, R. (1986), *Guaman Poma: Writing and Resistance in Colonial Peru*, Austin: University of Texas Press.
Albacete, L. (2001), 'America's Hispanic Future', *New York Times*, 19 June: A:23.
Allen, C. (2002), *The Hold Life Has: Coca and Cultural Identity in an Andean Community*, Washington, DC: Smithsonian Institution Press.
Altman, I. (1991), 'Spanish Society in Mexico City after the Conquest', *Hispanic American Historical Review*, 71(3): 413–45.
Alvarado, J. L. (1997), 'La magia de las cuevas', *Artes de México: Cestería*, 38: 32–5.
Álvarez Heydenreich, L. (1987), *La enfermedad y la cosmovisión en Hueyapán, Morelos*. Serie de Antropología Social #74, Mexico City: Instituto Nacional Indigenista.
Alvim, Z. (1998), 'Imigrantes: a vida privada dos pobres do campo', in N. Sevcenko (ed.), *História da vida privada no Brasil*, Sao Paulo: Companhia das Letras.
—— and Peirão, S. (1985), *Mappin setenta anos*, São Paulo: Editora Ex Libris.
Anawalt, P. R. (1981), *Indian Clothing before Cortés: Mesoamerican Costumes from the Codices*, Norman: University of Oklahoma Press.
Andrade, M. (1942), 'O Movimento Modernista', republished in *O Estado de S. Paulo* (10 February 2002).
Andrade Pereira, S. (1994), 'Cultura sem estilo ao sol de Copacabana', in N. Villaça and B. Jaguaribe (eds), *Rio de Janeiro, cartografías simbólicas*, Rio de Janeiro: Diadorim.
Ángeles Caballero, C. (1999), *Japón en la literatura peruana*, Lima: San Marcos.
Annis, S. (1987), *God and Production in a Guatemalan Town*, Austin: University of Texas Press.
Anonymous (1919), Advertisement, Larrañaga Nacionales, *Social*, 3: 2.
—— (1920), Advertisement, 'El Encanto', *Social*, 8: 101.

—— (1921), Advertisement, Larrañaga Nacionales, *Social*, 3: 2.
—— (1921), Advertisement, Larrañaga Nacionales, *Social*, 4: 2.
—— (1922), Advertisement, Larrañaga Nacionales, *Social*, 4: 62.
Anton, F. (1987), *Ancient Peruvian textiles*, London: Thames & Hudson.
Anzaldúa, G. (1987), *Borderlands/La frontera: The New Mestiza*, San Francisco: Aunt Lute.
—— (1990), 'Haciendo caras, una entrada: An Introduction', in G. Anzaldúa (ed.), *Making Face, Making Soul/Haciendo caras: Creative and Critical Perspectives by Feminists of Color*, San Francisco: Aunt Lute Books.
Aparicio, F. R. and Chávez-Silverman, S. (eds) (1997), *Tropicalizations: Transcultural Representations of Latinidad*, Hanover: University Press of New England.
Appadurai, A. (ed.) (1986), *The Social Life of Things: Commodities in Cultural Perspective*, Cambridge: Cambridge University Press.
Areche, J. A. de (1995), 'All Must Die!', in O. Starn, C. I. Degregori and R. Kirk (eds), *The Peru Reader. History, Culture, Politics*, Durham: Duke University Press.
Arenas, R. (1992), *Antes que anochezca*, Barcelona: Tusquets Editores.
Arias, A. (2003), 'Central American-Americans: Invisibility, Power, and Representation in the U.S. Latino World', *Latino Studies*, 1: 168–87.
Armaignac, H. (1974), *Viajes por las Pampas Argentinas*, Buenos Aires: Eudeba.
Armella de Aspe, V. and Castelló Yturbide, T. (1988), *La historia de México a través de la indumentaria*, Mexico: INBURSA.
Arnold, D. Y. (1988), *Matrilineal Practice in a Patrilineal Setting. Rituals and Metaphors of Kinship in an Andean Ayllu*. Dissertation, University College London.
——, Domingo Jiménez, A. and Yapita, J. de D. (1992), *Hacia un orden de las cosas*, La Paz: HISBOL/ILCA.
—— and Yapita, J. de D. (1999), *Rio de vellón, río de canto. Cantar a los animales, una poética andina de la creación*, La Paz: HISBOL.
Arrom, S. M. (1985), *The Women of Mexico City, 1790–1857*, Stanford: Stanford University Press.
Arróniz, M. (1858), *Manual del viajero en Méjico*, Paris: Librería de Rosa y Bouret.
Ashcroft, B., Griffiths, G. and Tiffin, H. (1989), *The Empire Writes Back. Theory and Practice in Post-Colonial Literatures*, London: Routledge.
Ávila Blomberg, A. de (1997), 'Threads of Diversity: Oaxacan Textiles in Context', in K. Klein (ed.), *The Unbroken Thread: Conserving the Textile Traditions of Oaxaca*, Los Angeles: Getty Conservation Institute.
Azara, F. (1969), *Viajes por América Meridional*, Madrid: Espasa-Calpe.
Babb, F. (1998), *Between Field and Cooking Pot: The Political Economy of Marketwomen in Peru*, revised edition Austin: University of Texas Press.
Babín, M. T. (1958), *Panorama de la cultura puertorriqueña*, New York: Las Américas.
Bacle, C. H. (1947), Trajes y costumbres de la provincia de Buenos Aires, facsimile edition, Buenos Aires: Viau.
Baerga, M. C. (1993), *Género y trabajo: La industria de la aguja en Puerto Rico y el Caribe hispánico*, San Juan: Editorial de la Universidad de Puerto Rico.
Bailey, G. A. (1997), 'A Mughal Princess in Baroque New Spain', *Anales del Instituto de Investigaciones Estéticas*, 71: 37–73.
Baizerman, S. (March 1987), 'Textile Tourist Art: Can We Call It Traditional?' Paper presented at the Symposium on Current Issues in Ethnographic Costume and Cloth: Middle America and the Central Andes of South America, Brown University, Haffenreffer Museum of Anthropology.

Bakewell, P. (1997), *A History of Latin America: Empires and Sequels, 1450–1930*, Oxford: Blackwell.
Bakhtin, M. (1984), *The Dialogic Imagination*, C. Emerson and M. Holquist (trans.), Austin: University of Texas Press.
—— (1984), *Problems of Dostoevsky's Poetics*, C. Emerson (ed.). Minneapolis: University of Minnesota Press.
Balderston, D., González, M. and López, A. (eds) (2000), *Encyclopedia of Contemporary Latin American and Caribbean Cultures*, London: Routledge.
Baltar Rodríguez, J. (1997), *Chinos en Cuba: Apuntes etnográficos*, La Habana: Fundación Fernando Ortiz.
Baretti, J. (1770), *A Journey from London to Genoa; Through England, Portugal, Spain, and France*, London: printed for T. Davies and L. Davis.
Barker, N. N. (1979), *The French Experience in Mexico, 1821–1861: A History of Constant Misunderstanding*, Chapel Hill: University of North Carolina Press.
Barnes, J. (1978), *Evita: A Biography of Eva Perón, First Lady*, New York: Grove.
Barnes, R. and Eicher, J. B. (1992), 'Introduction', in R. Barnes and J. B. Eicher (eds), *Dress and Gender. Making and Meaning*, New York: Berg.
Barthes, R. (1983), *The Fashion System*, M. Ward and R. Howard (trans.), New York: Hill & Wang.
—— (1988), *Image-Music-Text*, S. Heath (trans.), New York: Noonday.
—— (1990), *The Fashion System*, M. Ward and R. Howard (trans.), Berkeley: University of California Press.
—— (1998), *Mythologies*, A. Lavers (trans.), New York: Hill & Wang.
Basbaun, L. (1968), *História sincera da república – das origens à 1889*, São Paulo: Alfa-Omega.
Bauer, A. J. (2001), *Goods, Power, History: Latin America's Material Culture*, New York: Cambridge University Press.
Bauer, D. (1991), 'Gender in Bakhtin's "Carnival" from *Feminist Dialogics*', in R. Warhol and D. Price Herndl (eds), *Feminisms: An Anthology of Literary Theory and Criticism*, New Brunswick, NJ: Rutgers University Press.
Bauman, Z. (1998), *O mal-estar da pós-modernidade*, Rio de Janeiro: Zahar.
Bazan Longi, H. (2001), 'La ciudad de ayer: de chilapastrosos a entacuchados', *El Universal*, 31 March.
Beaufoy, M. (1828), *Mexican Illustrations*, London: Carpenter & Son.
Bellafante, G. (1992), 'Face of Grace', *Time*, 7 December: 85.
Benavides, M. A. (1983), *Two Traditional Andean Peasant Communities under the Stress of Market Penetration: Yanque and Madrigal in the Colca Valley, Peru*. MA thesis, University of Texas at Austin.
—— (1988), 'Grupos del poder en el Valle de Colca, Siglos XVI–XX', in R. Matos Mendieta (ed.), *Sociedad andina pasado y presente*, Lima: Fomciencias.
Benítez, J. R. (1946), *El traje y el adorno en México 1500–1910*, Guadalajara, Mexico: Imprenta Universitaria.
Benstock, S. and Ferris, E. (1994), *On Fashion*, New Brunswick, NJ: Rutgers University Press.
Berdan, F. F. and Anawalt, P. R. (1997), *The Essential Codex Mendoza*, Berkeley and Los Angeles: University of California Press.
Bernal, I. (1969), *100 Great Masterpieces at the Mexican National Museum of Anthropology*, New York: Harry N. Abrams.

Berzunza Pinto, R. (1997), *Guerra social en Yucatán. Guerra de castas*, Mérida: Maldonado Editores.
Beverley, J., Oviedo, J. and Aronna, M. (eds) (1995), *The Postmodern Debate in Latin America*, Durham: Duke University Press.
Bhabba, H. (1990), *Nation and Narration*, New York: Routledge.
—— (1994), *The Location of Culture*, London: Routledge.
Bhattacharyya, G. (2002), 'Fashion', in D. Theo Goldberg and J. Solomos (eds), *A Companion to Racial and Ethnic Studies*, Malden: Blackwell.
Boechat, R. (2002), *Copacabana Palace*, Rio de Janeiro: DBA.
Bolaños Montiel, C. (1993), *Recopilación de la vida y leyenda de Catarina de San Juan y la china poblana*, Puebla, Mexico: Comité de la Feria de Puebla.
Bonfil Batalla, G. (1971), 'Introducción al ciclo de ferias en la región de Cuautla, Morelos', *Anales de antropología*, 8, Mexico City: UNAM.
Borrero, A. M. (1925), 'S.M. La Moda', *Social*, February: 55.
—— (1936), 'Nueva York vs. París', *Carteles*, 30 August: 41–2.
Boucher, F. (1987), *20,000 Years of Fashion: The History of Costume and Adornment*, New York: Harry N. Abrams.
Bourdieu, P. (1984), *Distinction: A Social Critique of the Judgement of Taste*, R. Nice (trans.), Cambridge, Massachusetts: Harvard University Press.
Boyce, W. (1914), *U.S. Colonies and Dependencies*, Chicago: Rand McNally.
Boyd-Bowman, P. (1973), 'Spanish and European Textiles in Sixteenth Century Mexico', *Américas*, 29(3): 334–58.
Boyer, R. and Spurling, G. (2000), *Colonial Lives: Documents on Latin American History, 1550–1850*, New York: Oxford University Press.
Braddeley, O. (1991), 'Her Dress Hangs Here': De-Frocking the Kahlo-Cult, *Oxford Art Journal*, 14(1): 10–17.
Brandes, S. (1988), *Power and Persuasion: Fiestas and Social Control in Rural Mexico*, Philadelphia: University of Pennsylvania Press.
Braun-Ronsdorf, M. (1964), *Mirror of Fashion; A History of European Costume, 1789–1929*, O. Coburn (trans.), New York: McGraw-Hill.
Brooke, R. (1992), 'The Supermodels: '90s Glamour Queens Dictate Standards of Beauty', *Chicago Sun-Times*, 8 March: B: 41.
Brown, S. (1998), 'Fashion: Land Rites; Folksy Is Back, But It's Learned to be Cool', *Guardian* (London), 2 May: 44.
Bruzzi, S. and Church Gibson, P. (eds) (2000), *Fashion Cultures: Theories, Explorations and Analysis*, London: Routledge.
Bryan, W. S. (ed.) (1899), *Our Islands and Their People as Seen with Camera and Pencil*, St. Louis: N. D. Thompson.
Brydon, A. and Niessen, S. (eds) (1998), 'Adorning the Body' in *Consuming Fashion. Adorning the Transnational Body*, Oxford: Berg.
Buarque de Hollanda, H. and Gonçalves, M. A. (1987), *Cultura e participação nos anos 60*, São Paulo: Brasiliense.
Bubba, C. (1993), Presentation of 'Los textiles ceremoniales de Coroma', American Anthropological Association Annual Meeting.
Bullock, W. (1824), *Six Months' Residence and Travels in Mexico*, London: John Murray.
Bustamante, P. J. A. (1985), *Apuntes para una historia de la iglesia en Sakaka (1560-1985)*, Karipuyo, Bolivia: Misión Norte de Potosí.
Butler, J. (1990), *Gender Trouble: Feminism and the Subversion of Identity*, New York: Routledge.

—— (1993), *Bodies that Matter*, New York: Routledge.
Cabrera Infante, G. (1967), *Tres tristes tigres*, Barcelona: Seix Barral.
Cabrera Infante, G. (1971), *Three Trapped Tigers*, D. Garnder and S. J. Levine (trans), New York: Marlow.
Cadilla de Martínez, M. (1938), *Costumbres y tradicionalismos de mi tierra*, Puerto Rico: Imprenta Venezula.
Calderón de la Barca, F. (1966), *Life in Mexico*, H. T. Fisher and M. H. Fisher (eds), New York: Doubleday.
—— (1982), *Life in Mexico*, Berkeley: University of California Press.
Calvino, I. (1990), *Seis propostas para o próximo milênio*, I. Barroso (trans.), São Paulo: Companhia das Letras.
Campo Alange, M. L. (1964), *La mujer en España: Cien años de su historia, 1860–1960*, Madrid: Aguilar.
Canavesi de Sahonero, M. L. (1987), *El traje de la chola Paceña*, Cochabamba: Los Amigos del Libro.
Cannon, A. (1998), 'The Cultural and Historical Contexts of Fashion' in A. Brydon and S. Niessen (eds), *Consuming Fashion. Adorning the Transnational Body*, Oxford: Berg.
Carlsen, R. (1993), 'Discontinuous Warps: Textile Production and Ethnicity in Contemporary Highland Guatemala' in J. Nash (ed.), *Crafts in the World Market: The Impact of Global Exchange on Middle American Artisans*, Albany: State University of New York Press.
Carmichael, E. and Sayer, C. (1992), *The Skeleton at the Feast: The Day of the Dead in Mexico*. Austin: University of Texas Press.
Carone, E. (2001), *A evolução industrial de São Paulo (1889–1930)*, São Paulo: Senac.
Carpentier, A. (pseud. Jacqueline) (August 1925), 'S.M. La Moda', *Social*, 8: 51–3, 66.
—— (1926), 'S.M. La Moda', *Social*, 1 (January): 69–72.
—— (1926), 'S.M. La Moda', *Social*, 2 (February): 63–5.
—— (1926), 'S.M. La Moda', *Social*, 4 (April): 65–7.
—— (1926), 'S.M. La Moda', *Social*, 6 (June): 67–70.
—— (1926), 'S.M. La Moda', *Social*, 7 (July): 67–70.
—— (1926), 'S.M. La Moda', *Social*, 10 (October): 69–72.
—— (1927), 'S.M. La Moda', *Social*, 4 (April): 89–91.
—— (1927), 'S.M. La Moda', *Social*, 5 (May): 89–91.
Carrasco Puente, R. (ed.) (1950), *Bibliografía de Catarina de San Juan y de la china poblana*, Mexico City: Secretaría de Relaciones Exteriores.
Carrera, M. M. (2003), *Imagining Identity in New Spain: Race, Lineage, and the Colonial Body in Portraiture and Casta Paintings*, Austin: University of Texas Press.
Carrillo Vasquez, R., 'Mexican Folk Dances', *Instituto Cultural 'Raices Mexicanas'*: http://www.folklorico.com/folk-dances/veracruz/sintesis-veracruz.html.
Carrió de la Vandera, Alonso (1980), *El lazarillo de ciegos caminantes*. Madrid: Editorial Nacional.
Carrión Cachot, R., 'La indumentaria en la antigua cultura de Paracas', *Wira Kocha*, I: 1.
Castelló Yturbide, T. and Mapellia Mozzi, C. (1998), *La chaquira en México*, Mexico City: Museo Franz Mayer, Artes de México.
Castilho, K. and Garcia, C. (2001), *Moda Brasil. Fragmentos de um Vestir Tropical*, São Paulo: Editora Anhembi Morumbi.
Castillo, A. (ed.) (1996), *Goddess of the Americas/La Diosa de las Américas: Writings of the Virgin of Guadalupe*, New York: Riverhead.

Bibliography

Castillo Graxeda, J. (1692/1987), *Compendio de la vida y virtudes de la Venerable Catarina de San Juan*, Biblioteca Angelopolitana III, Puebla, Mexico: Gobierno del Estado de Puebla.
Caughie, P. L. (1999), *Passing and Pedagogy: The Dynamics of Responsibility*, Urbana: University of Illinois Press.
Cerecceda, V. (1978), 'Sémiologie des tissus andins: les talegas de Isluga', *Annales* (Paris), 33(5–6): 1017–35.
—— (1992), 'Notas sobre el diseño de los textiles "Tarabuco"' in J. Dávalos, V. Cereceda and G. Martínez (eds), *Textiles Tarabuco*, Paz: ASUR/CORDECH.
Chang, A. 'La guayabera', http://www.vanguardia.co.cu/costumbres/GUAYABERA.htm.
Chataigner (1996), *Manchete* (Rio de Janeiro), 24 August: 84.
Chavez, F. F. (2000), 'Knowing the Father Behind the Legend. How to Bask in Adulation Wasn't One of Dad's Lessons', *San Jose Mercury News*, 31 March, http://www.ufw.org/sjm33100a.html.
Chertudi, S. and Nardi, R. (1961), 'Tejidos araucanos de la Argentina', *Cuadernos del Instituto Nacional de Investigaciones Folklóricas*, Buenos Aires: T.1.
Chiñas, B. (1976), 'Zapotec *Viajeras*' in S. Cook and M. Diskin (eds), *Markets in Oaxaca*, Austin: University of Texas Press.
Christensen, E. W. (1979), 'The Puerto Rican Woman: A Profile' in E. Acosta-Belén (ed.), *The Puerto Rican Woman*, New York: Praeger Publishers.
Cieza de León, P. (1540–50/2000), *La crónica del Perú*, Madrid: Dastin S.L.
Ciuk, P. *'Frida' Entre palomitas y Coca light*, www.noticine.com/noticine/secciones/critica_film.asp.
Clark, T. R. (1975), *Puerto Rico and the United States, 1917–1933*, Pittsburgh: University of Pittsburgh Press.
Clausell, M. A. et al. (1998), *Intimidad, moda y diseño: México entrañable*, Mexico City: Patronato Museo de la Ciudad de México, Fomento Cultural y Deportivo Covarra.
Cohen, A. A. (2001), *Ouvidor, a rua do Rio*, Rio de Janeiro: AA Cohen.
Cohen, E. (1988), 'Authenticity and commoditization in tourism', *Annals of Tourism Research* 15(3): 371–86.
—— (1992), 'The Impact of Tourism' in C. P. Cooper and A. Lockwood (eds), *Progress in Tourism, Recreation and Hospitality Management*, vol. 4, London: Belhaven.
Colloredo-Mansfeld, R. (1999), *The Native Leisure Class: Consumption and Cultural Creativity in the Andes*, Chicago: University of Chicago Press.
Colón, C. (1978), *Four Voyages to the New World: Letters and Selected Documents*, R. H. Major (trans. and ed.), Gloucester, MA: Corinth.
—— (1989), *Textos y documentos completos: Relaciones de viajes, cartas y memoriales*, C. Varela (ed.), Madrid: Alianza.
Conklin, W. J. (1996), 'The Ampato Textile Offerings', in *Sacred and Ceremonial Textiles*, Proceedings of the Fifth Biennial Symposium of the Textile Society of America, Chicago, Illinois, pp. 104–10.
Conley, T. (1992), 'De Bry's Las Casas', in R. Jara and N. Spadaccini (eds), *Amerindian Images and the Legacy of Columbus*, Minneapolis: University of Minnesota Press.
Cook, N. D. (1982), *The People of the Colca Valley: A Population Study*, Boulder: Westview.
Cook, S. (1993), 'Craft Commodity Production, Market Diversity, and Differential Rewards in Mexican Capitalism Today', in June Nash (ed.), *Crafts in the World Market: The Impact of Global Change on Middle American Artisans*, Albany, State University of New York Press.

—— and Binford, L. (1990), *Obliging Need: Rural Petty Industry in Mexican Capitalism*, Austin: University of Texas Press.
Cook de Leonard, C. (1971), 'Minor Arts of the Classic Period in Central Mexico', in G. F. Ekholm and I. Bernal (eds), *Archaeology of Northern Mesoamerica, Part One*, Austin: University of Texas Press.
Cope, R. D. (1994), *The Limits of Racial Domination: Plebeian Society in Colonial Mexico City, 1660–1720*, Madison: University of Wisconsin Press.
Corcuera, R. (1987), *Herencia textil andina*, Buenos Aires: Impresores S. C. A.
—— (1993), 'Antecedentes prehispánicos del *poncho* en la Argentina', *Revista Andina: Número dedicado al V Coloquio Internacional 'El siglo XVIII en los Andes'*.
—— (1996), 'El Poncho', *Revista ARTINF (Buenos Aires)*, 21: 20–27.
—— (2000), *Ponchos de las tierras del Plata*, Buenos Aires: Fondo Nacional de las Artes and Verstraeten Editores.
Cordry, Donald and Cordry, Dorothy (1968), *Mexican Indian Costume*, Austin: University of Texas Press.
Cortés, H. (1520/1962), *Five Letters to the Emperor*, J. B. Morris (trans.), New York: Norton & Company.
—— (1985), *Cartas de relación*, Mexico City: Porrúa.
Cortina, L. (1994), 'Transplanted Theater: Gesture and Appearance', *Artes de Mexico*, July–August: 73–5.
Cosbey, S., Damhorst, M. L. and Farrell, J. (2003), 'Diversity of Daytime Clothing Styles as a Reflection of Women's Social Role Ambivalence from 1873 through 1912', *Clothing and Textiles Research Journal*, 21(3): 101–19.
Craik, J. (1993), *The Face of Fashion: Cultural Studies in Fashion*, New York: Routledge.
Crane, D. (2000), *Fashion and Its Social Agendas. Class, Gender, and Identity in Clothing*, Chicago: University of Chicago Press.
Creed, B. (1993), *The Monstrous Feminine: Film, Feminism and Psychoanalysis*, London: Routledge.
Cripps Samoiloff, L. (1984), *Portrait of Puerto Rico*, Cranbury, NJ: Rosemont.
Croce, P. and Vitale, A. (1993), *Los cuerpos dóciles. Hacia un tratado sobre la moda*, Buenos Aires: La Marca.
Cruz, H. F. (1997), *São Paulo em Revista*, São Paulo: Arquivo do Estado.
Cruz de Amenábar, I. (1996), *El Traje. Transformaciones de una segunda piel*, Santiago: Ediciones Universidad Católica de Chile.
Cruz-Malavé, A. (1994), *El primitivo implorante: El 'sistema poético del mundo' de José Lezama Lima*, Amsterdam: Rodopi.
Cuddon, J. A. (1979) *A Dictionary of Literary Terms*. Harmondsworth: Penguin.
Cunningham, P. and Lab, S. V. (1991), *Dress and Popular Culture*, Bowling Green, Ohio: Bowling Green State University Popular Press.
Cunninghame Graham, R.B. (1984), *Temas criollos*, Buenos Aires: Emecé.
Curiel, G. (2002), 'Customs, Conventions, and Daily Rituals among Elites of New Spain: The Evidence from Material Culture', in H. Rivero Borrel, G. Curiel, A. Rubial García, J. Gutiérrez Haces and D. B. Warren (eds), *The Grandeur of Viceregal Mexico: Treasures from the Museo Franz Mayer*, Houston: Museum of Fine Arts.
Daly, S. (2002), 'Madonna Marlene', *Vanity Fair* 506 (October): 308–13.
Dana, R. H. (1992), *Two Years Before the Mast*, New York: Westvaco.
Danticat, E. (1998), *The Farming of Bones*, New York: Soho.
Darío, R. (1997), 'The Death of the Empress of China', in R. González Echevarría (ed.), *The Oxford Book of Latin American Short Stories*, New York: Oxford University Press.

Bibliography

Darling, J. (1995), 'The Simpson Legacy: Los Angeles Times Special Report; Twist of Fate/How the Case Changed the Lives of Those it Touched; Spying Bronco Put Her in Spotlight', *Los Angeles Times*, 11 October: 5: 2.

—— (1999), 'Latina Nannies Rear a Generation En Español: The Influx of Central Americans Starting in the 1980s Has Changed; Caregiving Habits of the Nation. But Parents Retain Their Influence', *Los Angeles Times*, 19 September: A: 3.

Davis, M. (2000), *Magical Urbanism: Latinos Reinvent the U.S. Big City*, London: Verso.

De Gamez, T. and Pastore, A. R. (1954), *Mexico and Cuba on Your Own*, New York: R.D. Cortinz.

Del Carril, B. (1978), *El gaucho*, Buenos Aires: Emecé.

Del Casal, J. (1963–4), *Prosas*, La Habana: Consejo Nacional de Cultura.

Delpar, H. (1992), 'The Enormous Vogue of Things Mexican', in *Cultural Relations Between the United States and Mexico, 1920–1935*, Tuscaloosa: University of Alabama Press.

Denevan, W. M. (ed.) (1986), *The Cultural Ecology, Archaeology, and History of Terracing and Terrace Abandonment in the Colca Valley of Southern Peru*, Technical Report to the National Science Foundation, Madison: University of Wisconsin Department of Geography.

—— (ed.) (1988), *The Cultural Ecology, Archaeology, and History of Terracing and Terrace Abandonment in the Colca Valley of Southern Peru*. Vol. 2. Technical Report to the National Science Foundation, Madison: University of Wisconsin Department of Geography.

—— (2001), *Cultivated Landscapes of Native Amazonia and the Andes*, Oxford: Oxford University Press.

De Romaña, M., Blassi, Jaume, and Blassi, Jordi (1987), *Descubriendo el Valle del Colca/Discovering the Colca Valley*, Barcelona: Patthey e Hijos.

De Sahonero, M. L. C. (1987), *El traje de la chola Paceña*, Cochabamba: Los Amigos del Libro.

Descola, J. (1968), *Daily Life in Colonial Peru 1710–1820*, M. Heron (trans.), New York: Macmillan.

Díaz-Abreu, R., 'Porque la guayabera es puramente cubana', http://www.autentico.org/oa09148.html.

Díaz Alcaide, M. (May 1993), 'Piernas al descubierto: Trayectoría de la moda en Puerto Rico', *Imagen*, pp. 110–15.

Díaz del Castillo, B. (1568/1969), *The Discovery and Conquest of Mexico*, G. García (ed.) and A. P. Maudslay (trans.), New York: Farrar, Straus & Giroux.

—— (1984), *Historia verdadera de la conquista de Nueva España*, Madrid: Espasa-Calpe.

Didion, J. (1982), *Salvador*, New York: Simon & Schuster.

Dinwiddie, W. (1899), *Puerto Rico: Its Conditions and Possibilities*, New York: Harper & Brothers.

Di Primo, R. (2002), *Do brilho à luz*, Rio de Janeiro: Independente.

División territorial del estado de Puebla de 1810–1995 (1997), Mexico City: INEGI.

Dor, J. (1997), *Introduction to the Reading of Lacan: The Unconscious Structured Like a Language*. Northvale: Aronson.

Duarte de Perón, Eva (1980), *Evita by Evita: Eva Duarte de Perón Tells Her Own Story*, New York: Proteus.

Du Bois, W. E. B. (1995), *W. E. B. Du Bois: A Reader*, D. L. Lewis (ed.), New York: Holt.

—— (1996), *The Souls of Black Folk*, New York: Penguin.

DuCille, A. (1996), 'Toy Theory: Blackface Barbie and the Deep Play of Difference', in *Skin Trade*, Cambridge, MA: Harvard University Press.
Echagüe, J. O. (1947), *España: Tipos y trajes*, Madrid: Editorial Mayfe.
Echeverría, E. (1995), *La Cautiva. El matadero*, Buenos Aires: Kapelusz.
Efundé, A. (1978), *Los secretos de la Santería*, Miami: Ediciones Universal.
Eicher, J. B. (ed.) (1995), *Dress and Ethnicity. Change Across Space and Time*. Oxford: Berg.
—— and Roach-Higgins, M. E. (1992), 'Definition and Classification of Dress: Implications for Analysis of Gender Roles', in R. Barnes and J. B. Eicher (eds), *Dress and Gender. Making and Meaning*, New York: Berg.
—— and Sumberg, B. (1995), 'World Fashion, Ethnic, and National Dress', in J. B. Eicher (ed.), *Dress and Ethnicity. Change Across Space and Time*, Oxford: Berg.
Ellis, H. (1895), 'Sexual Inversion in Women', *Alienist and Neurologist*, 16(2): 152–4.
Emery, I. and King, M. E. (1957), 'Additional Examples of an Unusual Peruvian Shirt Type', *American Antiquity*, 23: 1.
Espinosa, C. (1970), *Shawls, Crinolines, Filigree. The Dress and Adornment of the Women of New Mexico, 1739 to 1900*, El Paso: Texas Western.
Espinosa, S. (1993), 'El Salvador's Civil War Is Over – But Refugees Say U.S. Is Home', *San Francisco Chronicle*, 30 August A: 1.
Espinoza Soriano, W. (1969), 'El "memorial" de Charcas. "Crónica" inédita de 1582', *Cantuta* (Revista de la Universidad Nacional de Educación), Chosica, Peru, pp. 117–52.
Etcharren, P. (1993), *El bordado en Yucatán*, Mérida, Yucatán: Casa de las Artesanías.
Etheredge, L. S. (1985), *Can Governments Learn? American Foreign Policy and Central American Revolutions*, New York: Pergamon.
Evans, C. (2000), 'Yesterday's Emblems and Tomorrow's Commodities: The Return of the Repressed in Fashion Imagery Today', in S. Bruzzi and P. C. Gibson (eds), *Theories, Explorations and Analysis. Fashion Cultures*, London: Routledge.
Falini, D. 'Kahlo's Disturbing Art', http://www.fridakahlo.it/distart2.html.
Femenías, B. (1996), 'Regional Dress of the Colca Valley: A Dynamic Tradition', in M. B. Schevill, J. C. Berlo and E. Dwyer (eds), *Textile Traditions of Mesoamerica and the Andes: An Anthology*, Austin: University of Texas Press.
—— (1997), *Ambiguous Emblems: Gender, Clothing, and Representation in Contemporary Peru*. Dissertation, University of Wisconsin at Madison.
—— (2002), 'Ethnic Artists and the Appropriation of Fashion: Embroidery and Identity in the Colca Valley, Peru', in D. Heath (ed.), *Contemporary Societies and Cultures of Latin America*, Prospect Heights, IL: Waveland.
—— (2004), *Gender and the Boundaries of Dress in Contemporary Peru*, Austin: University of Texas Press.
—— (n.d.), 'Dancing in Disguise: Transvestism and Performance in a Peruvian Festival', manuscript submitted to *American Ethnologist*.
Fernández, R. G. (1997), *Raining Backwards*, Houston: Arte Público.
Fernández de Lizardi, J. J. (1987), *El periquillo sarniento*, La Habana: Editorial Arte y Literatura.
Fernández García, E. (1923), *El libro de Puerto Rico*, San Juan, PR: El Libro Azul.
Fernández Ledesma, G. (1930), *Calzado mexicano: Cactlis y huaraches*, Serie de Arte, Mexico.
Fernández Mendez, E. (1973), *Crónicas de Puerto Rico: Desde la conquista hasta nuestros días (1493–1955)*, Barcelona: Manuel Pareja.

Fernández Retamar, R. (1989), *Caliban and Other Essays*, E. Baker (trans.), Minneapolis: University of Minneapolis Press.

Fernández Velasco, L. (1997), '¿Beneficiarios o víctimas? Proyectos de desarrollo como factores de cambio socio-cultural en los ayllus de Sacaca', BA Licenciatura, Universidad Mayor de San Andrés.

Ferry, G. (pseud.) (1856), *Vagabond Life in Mexico*. New York: Harper & Brothers.

Findlay, E. J. (1998), 'Love in the Tropics: Marriage, Divorce, and the Construction of Benevolent Colonialism in Puerto Rico, 1898–1910,' in G. M. Joseph, C. C. LeGrand and R. D. Salvatore (eds), *Close Encounters of Empire: Writing the Cultural History of U.S.-Latin American Relations*, Durham: Duke University Press.

Fine-Dare, K. S. (2002), *Grave Injustice: The American Indian Repatriation Movement and NAGPRA*. Lincoln: University of Nebraska Press.

Ford, A. and Newton, J. (1995), 'The O. J. Simpson Trial; Lopez Ends Her Testimony; 2 Simpson Lawyers Fined', *Los Angeles Times*, 4 March: A: 1.

Foster, G. M. (1960), *Culture and Conquest: America's Spanish Heritage*, New York: Wenner-Gren Foundation for Anthropological Research.

—— (1994), *Hippocrates' Latin American Legacy: Humoral Medicine in the New World*, Langhorne, PA: Gordon & Breach.

Fourt, L. and Hollies, N. R. S. (1970), *Clothing Comfort and Function*, New York: Marcel Dekker.

Fowler, B. (1996), 'Should Just Anybody Be Allowed to Stare?' *New York Times*, 16 June: 2: 5.

Franco, J. (1984), 'Women, Fashion and the Moralists in Early-Nineteenth-Century Mexico', in L. Schwartz and I. Lerner (eds), *Homenaje a Ana María Barrenechea*, Madrid: Castalia.

Freedman, D. C. (1986), 'Wife, Widow, Woman: Roles of an Anthropologist in a Transylvanian Village', in P. Golde (ed.), *Women in the Field*, second edition, Berkeley: University of California Press.

Freud, S. (1989), *The Freud Reader*, P. Gay (ed.), New York: Norton.

Friedlander, J. (1975), *Being Indian in Hueyapán: A Study of Forced Identity in Contemporary Mexico*. New York: St. Martin's.

Fuente, J. (1977), *Yalalag: Una villa zapoteca serrana*, Mexico City: INI (Colección #2, Clásicos de la Antropología Mexicana).

Fuentes, C. (1992), *The Buried Mirror: Reflections on Spain and the New World*, Boston: Houghton Mifflin.

Gage, T. (1958), *Thomas Gage's Travels in the New World*, E. S. Thompson (ed.), Norman: Oklahoma University Press.

Gambier, M. (1993), *Prehistoria de San Juan*, San Juan, PR: Ediciones E.F.U.

Garber, M. (1992), *Vested Interests: Cross-dressing and Cultural Anxiety*, London: Routledge.

García Canclini, N. (1993), *Transforming Modernity: Popular Culture in Mexico*, Austin: University of Texas Press.

—— (1996), 'Modernity After Postmodernity', in G. Mosquera (ed.), *Beyond the Fantastic: Contemporary Art Criticism from Latin America*, London: Institute of International Visual Arts.

—— (2001), *Consumers and Citizens: Globalization and Multicultural Conflicts*, Minneapolis: University of Minnesota Press.

García Carranza, A. (1984), *Bibliografía de Alejo Carpentier*, Havana: Editorial Letras Cubanas.

Garciagodoy, J. (1998), *Digging the Days of the Dead: A Reading of Mexico's Días de Muertos*, Niwot: University Press of Colorado.

García Sáiz, M. C. (1989), *Las castas mexicanas: un género pictórico americano*, Milan: Olivetti.

Geary, P. (1986), 'Sacred Commodities: The Circulation of Medieval Relics', in A. Appadurai (ed.), *The Social Life of Things: Commodities in Cultural Perspective*, Cambridge: Cambridge University Press.

Geijer, A. (1982), *A History of Textile Art*, London: Pasold Research Fund and Sotheby Parke Bernet.

Gelles, P. (1990), *Channels of Power, Fields of Contention: The Politics and Ideology of Irrigation in an Andean Peasant Community*. Dissertation, Harvard University.

—— (2000), *Water and Power in Highland Peru: The Cultural Politics of Irrigation and Development*, New Brunswick, NJ: Rutgers University Press.

—— and Martínez, W. (1993), *Transnational Fiesta*, film distributed by the University of California at Berkeley.

Genet, J. (1954), *The Maids*, New York: Grove Weidenfeld.

Gibson, P. C. (2000), 'Redressing the Balance: Patriarchy, Postmodernism and Feminism', in S. Bruzzi and P. C. Gibson (eds), *Fashion Cultures. Theories, Explorations and Analysis*, London: Routledge.

Giddens, A. (2002), 'Tribulações do eu'. *Modernidade e identidade*, Rio de Janeiro: Jorge Zahar.

Gillespie, J. L. (1998), 'Gender, Ethnicity and Piety: The Case of the China Poblana', in E. P. Bueno and T. Caesar (eds), *Imagination Beyond Nation: Latin American Popular Culture*, Pittsburgh: University of Pittsburgh Press.

Gilman, S. L. (1991), *The Jewish Body*, New York: Routledge.

Giroletti, D. (1995), 'The Growth of the Brazilian Textile Industry and Transfer of Technology', *Textile History*, 26(2): 215–31.

Giroux, H. A. (1994), *Disturbing Pleasures: Learning Popular Culture*, New York: Routledge.

Gisbert, T., Arze, S. and Cajías, M. (1987), *Arte textil y mundo andino*, La Paz: Gisbert y Compañía.

Glassie, H. (1995), 'Tradition', *Journal of American Folklore*, 108(430): 395–412.

Glickman, R. J. (1976), *The Poetry of Julián del Casal: A Critical Edition*, Gainesville: University Press of Florida.

Godoy, R. A. (1990), *Mining and Agriculture in Highland Bolivia. Ecology, History, and Commerce Among the Jukumanis*, Tucson: University of Arizona Press.

Goldenberg, M. (2000), *Nu vestido dez antropólogos revelam a cultura do corpo carioca*, Rio de Janeiro: Record.

Gómez Izquierdo, J. J. (1991), *El movimiento antichino en México (1871–1934): Problemas del racismo y del nacionalismo durante la Revolución Mexicana*, Mexico City: Instituto Nacional de Antropología e Historia.

González Echevarría, R. and Miller-Bergh, K. (1983), *Alejo Carpentier: Bibliographical Guide/Guía Bibliográfica*, Westport: Greenwood.

González Echevarría, R. (1993), Introduction to *De donde son los cantantes*, Madrid: Cátedra.

Graburn, N. H. (ed.) (1979), *Ethnic and Tourist Arts: Cultural Expressions from the Fourth World*, Berkeley: University of California Press.

Greslebin, H. (1932), 'Sobre la unidad decorative y el origen esqueiomorfo de los dibujos del instrumental lítico de Patagonia prehispánica', Publicaciones del Museo Antropológico y Etnográfico de la Facultad de Filosofía y Letras, Seria A:II, Buenos Aires.

Gross, M. (1996), *Model: The Ugly Business of Beautiful Women*, New York: Warner Books.

Grossberger, L. (1997), 'Christy Almighty', *MediaWeek*, 27 October: 50.

Grosz, E. (1994), *Volatile Bodies: Toward a Corporal Feminism*, Bloomington: Indiana University Press.

Guaman Poma de Ayala, F. (1615/1993), *Nueva corónica y buen gobierno*, Mexico: Fondo de Cultura Económica.

'The Guayabera', http://www.edel2000.it/club/CURguayaE.htm.

Gudiño Kieffer, E. (1986), *El peinetón*, Buenos Aires: Ediciones de Arte Gaglianone.

Guillén, N. (1961), 'La guayabera', *Trabajo*, 1 July: 86–7.

Guillermoprieto, A. (2000), 'Personal History: My Servant Problem', *New Yorker*, 8 May: 74.

Guillet, D. (1992), *Covering Ground: Communal Water Management and the State in the Peruvian Highlands*, Ann Arbor: University of Michigan Press.

Gutiérrez, R. (1948), 'El problema de la guayabera', *Bohemia*, 5 September: 52–4.

Guy, D. (1991), *Sex and Danger in Buenos Aires: Prostitution, Family and Nation in Argentina*, Lincoln: University of Nebraska Press.

Guzmán, E. (1959), 'Huipil y Maxtlatl', V: La vida diaria, in Jorge R. Acosta (et als), *Esplendor del México antiguo*, Vol. II, Mexico City: Centro de Investigaciones Antropológicas de México.

Hall, S. (2000), *A identidade cultural na pós-modernidade*, T. Tadeu da Silva and G. Lopes Louro (trans.), Rio de Janeiro: DP&A.

Hallam, E. and Hockey, J. (2001), *Death, Memory and Material Culture*, Oxford: Berg.

Halperin, I. (2001), *Bad and Beautiful: Inside the Dazzling and Deadly World of Supermodels*, New York: Citadel.

Hamm, M. (1899), *Porto Rico and the West Indies*, New York: F. Tennyson Neely.

Handelman, D. (1997), 'The Billboards of Madison Avenue', *New York Times*, 6 April: F: 50.

Handler, R. and Linnekin, J. (1984), 'Tradition, Genuine or Spurious', *Journal of American Folklore*, 97(385): 273–90.

Haraway, D. 'Frida Kahlo: A Postmodern Icon of the Cyborg', http://www.fridakahlo.it/CYBORG2.HTML.

Harcourt, R. d' (1934) *Les textiles anciens du Perou et leurs techniques*, Paris: Les Editions d'Art et d'Histoire.

Harris, M. (1987), *Cultural Anthropology*, New York: Harper & Row.

Harris, O. (1987), *Economía étnica*, La Paz: HISBOL.

—— (1995), 'Ethnic Identity and Market Relations: Indians and Mestizos in the Andes', in B. Larson and O. Harris (eds) with E. Tandeter, *Ethnicity, Markets and Migration in the Andes: At the Crossroads of History and Anthropology*, Durham: Duke University Press.

—— (2000), *To Make the Earth Bear Fruit: Ethnographic Essays on Fertility, Work and Gender in Highland Bolivia*, London: University of London, Institute of Latin American Studies.

—— and Albó, X. (1986), *Monteras y guardatojos. Campesinos y mineros en el norte de Potosí en 1974*, La Paz: CIPCA.

Harvey, J. (1995), *Men in Black*, Chicago: University of Chicago Press.

Harvey, S. (1996), 'Only in L.A.', *Los Angeles Times*, 3 October, B: 4.

Hays-Gilpin, K. A. et al. (1998), *Prehistoric Sandals from Northeastern Arizona: The Earl H. Morris and Ann Axtell Morris Research*, Anthropological Papers #62, Tucson: University of Arizona Press.

Healy, K. (2001), *Llamas, Weaving, and Organic Chocolate: Multicultural Grassroots Development in the Andes and Amazon of Bolivia*, Notre Dame: University of Notre Dame Press.

Heibling, G. and Castilla, A. (2000), *Morelos hecho a mano*, Cuernavaca: Instituto de Cultura de Morelos.

Hendrickson, C. (1995), *Weaving Identities: Construction of Dress and Self in a Highland Guatemala Town*, Austin: University of Texas Press.

—— (1996), 'Selling Guatemala: Maya Export Products in US Mail-Order Catalogues', in D. Howes (ed.), *Cross-Cultural Consumption: Global Markets, Local Realities*, London: Routledge.

Heringhaus, R., *History of Department Stores*, http://www.acs-web.de/magazine/magazine_mmm_dep_stores.htm.

Hermer, C. and May, M. (1941), *Havana Mañana. A Guide to Cuba and the Cubans*, New York: Random House.

Hérnandez, J. (1959), *'Martín Fierro'*, Buenos Aires: Ediciones Kraft.

Hernández Cruz, V. (1997), 'It's Miller Time', in *Panoramas*, Minneapolis: Coffee House.

Hernández López, J. (2000), 'Astillero', *La Jornada*, 26 September, http://www.jornada.unam.mx/2000/sep00/000926/004a1gen.html.

Herrera, H. (1983), *Frida: A Biography of Frida Kahlo*, New York: Harper & Row.

Herrick, J. (1957), 'Periodicals for Women in Mexico during the Nineteenth Century', *The Americas: A Quarterly Review of Inter-American Cultural History*, 2: 135–44.

Hijuelos, O. (1992), *The Mambo Kings Play Songs of Love*, New York: HarperPerennial.

Hill, R. (1898), *Cuba and Porto Rico with the Other Islands of the West Indies: Their Topography, Climate, Flora, Products, Industries, Cities, People, Political Conditions, etc.*, New York: Century.

Hobsbawm, E. and Ranger, T. (eds) (1994), *The Invention of Tradition*, Cambridge: Cambridge University Press.

Holland, G. (1995), 'Rosa Lopez No Slam-Dunk for Defense', *USA Today*, 6 March: A: 3.

Hollander, A. (1978), *Seeing Through Clothes*, New York: Avon.

—— (1999), *Feeding the Eye*, New York: Farrar, Straus & Giroux.

Hondagneu-Sotelo, P. (2001), *Doméstica: Immigrant Workers Cleaning and Caring in the Shadows of Affluence*, Berkeley: University of California Press.

hooks, b. (1989), *Talking Back: Thinking Feminist, Thinking Black*, Boston: South End.

Huepenbecker, A. L. (1969), *Pre-Columbian Peruvian Costume: Characteristics and Variations in the Poncho-Shirt*. Dissertation, Ohio State University.

Hurley, W. (1978), *Highland Peasants and Rural Development in Southern Peru: The Colca Valley and the Majes Project*. Dissertation, Oxford University.

If the Mango Tree Could Speak: A Documentary about Children and War in Central America (1993), Hohokus, NJ: New Day Films.

Instituto Moreira Salles (2003), *Guilherme Gaensly e Augusto Malta: Dois mestres da fotografia brasileira no Acervo Brascan*, São Paulo: IMS.

Iriarte, I. (1993), 'Las túnicas incas en la pintura colonial', in *Mito y simbolismo en los Andes*, H. Urbano (ed.), Cuzco: Centro "Bartolomé de Las Casas": 53–85.
Isabelle, A. (1943), *Viaje a Argentina, Uruguay y Brasil en 1830*, Buenos Aires: Editorial Americana.
Izko, X. (1992), *La doble frontera. Ecologia, política y ritual en el altiplano central.* La Paz: HISBOL/CERES.
Jacobsen, N. (1993), *Mirages of Transition: The Peruvian Altiplano, 1780–1930*, Berkeley: University of California Press.
Jakobson, R. (1990), *On Language*, L. R. Waugh and M. Monville-Burston (eds), Cambridge, MA: Harvard University Press.
Jameson, F. (1986), 'On Magical Realism in Film', *Critical Inquiry*, 12 (Winter): 311.
Jeudy, H. P. (1998), *Le corps comme objet d'art*, Paris: Armand Colin.
Jiménez de Wagenheim, O. (1998), *Puerto Rico: An Interpretative History from Pre-Columbian Times to 1900*, Princeton: Markus Wiener.
Jiménez, Doña L. (1972), *Life and Death in Milpa Alta: A Nahuatl Chronicle of Díaz and Zapata*, F. Horcasitas (trans. and ed.), Norman: University of Oklahoma Press.
Johnson, G. (1992), *Indigenous Clothing of Oaxaca: Continuity and Change*. MA thesis, San Diego State University.
Johnson, I. (1971), 'Basketry and Textiles', in G. F. Ekholm and I. Bernal (eds), *Archaeology of Northern Mesoamerica, Part One*, Austin: University of Texas Press.
—— (1977), *Los textiles de la Cueva de la Candelaria, Coahuila*. Mexico City: Instituto de Antropología e Historia/Secretaría de Educación Pública, Colección Científica, #51 (Arqueología).
Johnson, L. (1986), 'Artisans', in L. S. Hoberman and S. M. Socolow (eds), *Cities and Society in Colonial Latin America*, Albuquerque: University of New Mexico Press.
Jules-Rosette, B. (1984), *The Messages of Tourist Art*, New York: Plenum.
Kafka, F. (1992), *The Trial*, W. Muir and E. Muir (trans.), New York: Schocken.
Kamen, H. (1997), *Philip of Spain*, New Haven: Yale University Press, 1997.
Kandell, J. (1988), *La Capital: The Biography of Mexico City*, New York: Random House.
Kankainen, K. (ed.) (1995), *Treading the Past: Sandals of the Anasazi*, Salt Lake City: University of Utah Press and Utah Museum of Natural History.
Kany, C. (1932), *Life and Manners in Madrid, 1750–1800*, Berkeley: University of California Press.
Kelemen, P. (1965), 'Folk Textiles of Latin America', *Textile Museum Journal*, 2–19.
Kennedy, S. S. J. (1993), 'Guatemalan Costumes and Textiles: Collecting a Living Culture', *Ornament*, 16(3): 40–3, 75–6.
Kicza, J. E. (1995), 'The Social and Political Position of Spanish Immigrants in Bourbon America and the Origins of the Independence Movements', *Colonial Latin American Review*, 4(1): 105–28.
Kim, J-H. (1999), 'Celebs Fill Black Book Debut', *Chicago Sun-Times*, 12 January: 31.
King, M. E. (1965), *Textiles and Basketry of the Paracas Period, Ica Valley, Peru*. Dissertation, University of Arizona.
Klarén, P. F. (2000), *Peru. Society and Nationhood in the Andes*, New York: Oxford University Press.
Koda, H. and Martin, R. (1994), *Orientalism. Visions of the East in Western Dress*, New York: Metropolitan Museum of Art.
Konetzke, R. (1962), *Colección de documentos para la historia de la formación social de Hispanoamérica 1493–1810*, vol. 3, Madrid: Consejo Superior de Investigaciones.

Bibliography

Kopytoff, I. (1986), 'The Cultural Biography of Things: Commoditization as Process', in A. Appadurai (ed.), *The Social Life of Things: Commodities in Cultural Perspective*, Cambridge: Cambridge University Press.
Krips, H. (1999), *Fetish: An Erotics of Culture*, Ithaca: Cornell University Press.
Kroeber, A. L. (1948), *Anthropology*, New York: Harcourt Brace.
Kurella, E. M. (1998), *Guide to Lace and Linens*, Norfolk, VA: Antique Trader Books.
Lacan, J. (1977), *Ecrits: A Selection*, Alan Sheridan (trans), New York: Norton.
LaFeber, W. (1983), *Inevitable Revolutions: The United States in Central America*, New York: Norton.
Lancaster, W. (2000), *The Department Store: A Social History*, Leicester: Leicester University Press.
Langner, L. (1959), *The Importance of Wearing Clothes*, New York: Hasting.
Laó-Montes, A. (2001), 'Introduction', in A. Laó-Montes and A. Dávila (eds), *Mambo Montage: The Latinization of New York City*, New York: Columbia University Press.
Larson, B. and Harris, O. (eds) with Tandeter, E. (1995), *Ethnicity, Markets, and Migration in the Andes: At the Crossroads of History and Anthropology*, Durham: Duke University Press.
Lavin, L. and Balassa, G. (2001), *Museo del traje mexicano, vol. I: El mundo prehispánico* and *vol. 2: El siglo de la conquista*, Mexico: Editorial Clio.
Leante, C. (1974), 'Confesiones sencillas de un escritor barroco', in S. Arias (ed.), *Recopilación de textos sobre Alejo Carpentier*, Havana: Casa de las Américas.
Leask, N. (2002), *Curiosity and the Aesthetics of Travel Writing, 1770–1840*, New York: Oxford University Press.
Lechuga, R. D. (1982), *El traje indígena de México: Su evolución desde la época prehispánica hasta la actualidad*, Mexico City: Panorama Editorial.
LeCount, C. (1990), *Andean Folk Knitting: Traditions and Techniques from Peru and Bolivia*, St. Paul, Minnesota: Dos Tejedoras Fiber Arts Publications.
Le Guern, M. (1973), *La metáfora y la metonimia*, Madrid: Cátedra.
León, N. (1971), *Catarina de San Juan y la China Poblana: Estudio etnográfico-crítico*, Puebla: Ediciones Altiplano.
Leóns, M. B. and Sanabria, H. (eds) (1997), *Coca, Cocaine, and the Bolivian Reality*, Albany: State University of New York Press.
Levey, S. (1983), *Lace: A History*, London: Victoria and Albert Museum and W.S. Maney & Son.
El Liceo Mexicano (1844), Mexico: Imprenta de J.M. Lara.
Linati, C. (1956), *Trajes civiles, militares y religiosos de México*, J. Fernández (trans.), Mexico City: Imprenta Universitaria.
Lindauer, M. A. (1999), *Devouring Frida: The Art History and Popular Celebrity of Frida Kahlo*, New England: Wesleyan University Press.
Littrell, M. A. (1990), 'Symbolic Significance of Textile Crafts for Tourists', *Annals of Tourism Research*, 17(2): 228–45.
Lobo, M. L. (1988), *Perú – cuando el mundo se oscureció*, Film distributed by Arawak, S.A.
Lobo, S. (1991), 'The Fabric of Life: Repatriating the Sacred Coroma Textiles', *Cultural Survival Quarterly*, 15(3): 40–6.
Logan, I. et al. (1994), *Rebozos de la Colección Robert Everts*, Mexico City: Museo Franz Mayer and Artes de México, Colección Uso y Estilo.

Bibliography

López Austin, A. (1974), 'Sahagún's Work and the Medicine of the Ancient Nahuas: Possibilities for Study', in M. S. Edmonson (ed.), *Sixteenth-Century Mexico: The Work of Sahagún*, Albuquerque: University of New Mexico Press.

López, C. and Botalla, H. (1983) 'El peinetón en Buenos Aires, 1823–1837', *Boletín Histórico del Instituto de la Ciudad de Buenos Aires*, 8: 9–47.

Lord, M. J. (1994), *Forever Barbie: The Unauthorized Biography of a Real Doll*, New York: William Morrow.

Loyola Brandão, I. (1996), 'Um ícone histórico', in *Vogue – Grandes Marcas 3* (Brazilian special issue), no. 224.

Lucero, H. and Baizerman, S. (1999), *Chimaya Weaving*, Albuquerque: University of New Mexico Press.

Lurie, A. (1981), *The Language of Clothes*, New York: Random House.

Lynd, M. (2000), 'The International Craft Market: A Double-Edged Sword for Guatemalan Maya Women', in K. M. Grimes and B. L. Milgram (eds), *Artisans and Cooperatives: Developing alternative trade for the global economy*, Tucson: University of Arizona Press.

Lyon, Captain G. F. (1828), *Journal of a Residence and Tour in the Republic of Mexico in the Year 1826*, London: J. Murray.

Lyotard, J. F. (1984), *The Postmodern Condition: A Report on Knowledge*, Manchester: Manchester University Press.

Maciel, L. C. (1996), *Geração em transe; memórias do tempo do tropicalismo*, Rio de Janeiro: Nova Fronteira.

—— (2001), *As quatro estações*, Rio de Janeiro: Record.

MacNeish, R. S., Neiken-Terner, A. and Johnson, I. W. (1967), *The Prehistory of the Tehuacan Valley. Vol. II: Non-Ceramic Artifacts*, Austin: University of Texas Press for the Robert S. Peabody Foundation.

'Mais um aspecto do dinamismo bandeirante – S. Paulo, Centro irradiador da elegância e da beleza' (1933), *Jornal da Manhã* (São Paulo), 17 December.

Major, J. S. and Steele, V. (1999), *China Chic: East Meets West*, New Haven: Yale University Press.

Manrique, N. (1985), *Colonialismo y pobreza campesina: Caylloma y el Valle del Colca, Siglos XVI–XX*, Lima: DESCO.

Mansilla, L. V. (1955), *Mis memorias (Infancia-Adolescencia)*, Buenos Aires: Hachette.

—— (1997), *A Visit to the Ranquel Indians*, E. Gillies (trans.), Lincoln and London: University of Nebraska Press.

Mantegazza, P. (1867), *Rio de la Plata e Tenerife. Viaggi e Studi*, Milano: Gaetano Brigola Editore.

'Mappin's British Library' (1937), *Anglo Brazilian Chronicle*, 29 October.

Marcus, G. E. and Myers, F. R. (eds), *The Traffic in Culture: Refiguring Art and Anthropology*, Berkeley: University of California Press.

Margolick, D. (1995), 'Maid's Memory Is Target of Prosecutors in Simpson Trial', *New York Times*, 3 March: B: 8.

Markowitz, L. (1992), *Pastoral Production and Its Discontents: Alpaca and Sheep Herding in Caylloma, Peru*. Dissertation, University of Massachusetts at Amherst.

Marrero, L. (1995), *Cuba: Isla abierta*, San Juan, PR: Ediciones Capiro.

Marryat, F. (1843), *The Travels and Romantic Adventures of Monsieur Violet, Among the Snake Indians and Wild Tribes of the Great Western Prairies*, London: Longman, Brown, Green & Longman's.

Martínez Carreño, A. (1995), *La prisión del vestido: aspectos sociales del traje en América*, Santa Fe de Bogotá: Planeta Colombiana Editorial.
Martínez Sarasola, C. (1992), *Nuestros paisanos los indios*, Buenos Aires, Emecé.
Martins, A. L. (2001), *Revistas em Revista – imprensa e práticas culturais em tempos de república, São Paulo (1890–1922)*, São Paulo: Editora Universidade de São Paulo.
Masiello, F. (1991), *Between Civilization and Barbarism: Women, Nation and Literary Culture in Modern Argentina*, Lincoln: University of Nebraska Press.
Mauad, A. M. (1997), 'Imagem e auto-imagem do segundo reinado', in L. F. Alencastro (ed.), *História da vida privada no Brasil. Império: a corte e a modernidade nacional*, vol. 2, São Paulo: Companhia das Letras.
Maza, F. de la (1971), *Catarina de San Juan: Princesa de la India y visionaria de Puebla*, Mexico City: Libros de México.
McClure Mudge, J. (1986), *Chinese Export Porcelain in North America*, New York: Clarkson N. Potter.
McCracken, G. D. (1988), 'Clothing as Language: An Object Lesson in the Study of the Expressive Properties of Material Culture', in G. D. McCracken (ed.), *Culture and Consumption: New Approaches to the Symbolic Character of Consumer Goods and Activities*, Bloomington: Indiana University Press.
Medina, P. (1990), *Exiled Memories. A Cuban Childhood*, Austin: University of Texas Press.
Meisch, L. (1996), 'We Are Sons of Atahualpa and We Will Win: Traditional Dress in Otavalo and Saraguro, Ecuador', in M. B. Schevill, J. C. Berlo and E. Dwyer (eds), *Textile Traditions of Mesoamerica and the Andes: An Anthology*, Austin: University of Texas Press.
—— (2003), *Andean Entrepreneurs: Otavalo Merchants and Musicians in a Global Era*, Austin: University of Texas Press.
Meléndez, M. (1995), "La vestimenta como retórica de poder y símbolo de producción cultural en la América meridional: de Colón a *El lazarillo de ciegos caminantes*", *Revista de Estudios Hispánicos*, 29: 411–39.
—— (1999), *Raza, género e hibridez en El lazarillo de ciegos caminantes*, Chapel Hill: North Carolina Studies in the Romance Languages and Literatures.
Melo, P. (1994), *Acqua Toffana*, São Paulo: Companhia das Letras.
Memorial de Charcas (n.d. [1582]), transcribed by Margarita Suárez, London.
Méndez Capote, R. (1969), *Memorias de una cubanita que nació con el siglo*, La Habana: Instituto Cubano del Libro.
Mendizabal, M. O. (1947), 'Las artes textiles en la época prehispánica', in vol. VI of *El Mezquitál, Obras completas*, Mexico City: n.p.
Mendoza L., G. (1992), 'Hacia la identificación historiográfica de la chola boliviana', in A. Paredes-Candia (ed.), *La chola boliviana*, La Paz: Ediciones ISLA.
Mercurio peruano. 1791–1795 (1964 facsimile), vol. 1, Lima: Biblioteca Nacional del Perú.
Messeder, P. and Alberto, C. (1983), *O que é contracultura*, São Paulo: Brasiliense.
Métraux, G. S (1952), 'American Civilization Abroad: Fifty Years in Puerto Rico', *Américas* 7: 59–76.
Meyer, C. J. and Royer, D. (eds) (2001), *Selling the Indian: Commercializing and Appropriating American Indian Cultures*, Tucson: University of Arizona Press.
Meyerson, J. (1990), *'Tambo: Life in an Andean Village*, Austin: University of Texas Press.

Michieli, C. T. (1994), *Textilería de la cultura de Calingasta*, Facultad de Filosofía, Humanidades y Artes, Instituto de Investigaciones Arqueológicas y Museo, Universidad Nacional de San Juan, San Juan, Puerto Rico: Publicaciones 21.

Mignolo, W. (1992), 'When Speaking Was Not Enough: Illiterates, Barbarians, Savages and Cannibals', in R. Jara and N. Spadaccini (eds), *Amerindian Images and the Legacy of Columbus*, Minneapolis: University of Minnesota Press.

Milbank, C. R. (1989), *New York Fashion: The Evolution of American Style*, New York: Harry N. Abrams.

Milian Arias, C. M. (2000–1), 'Affirmative Access: Compassion Illusion in Mike Davis's Magical Urbanism', *Harvard Journal of Hispanic Policy*, 13: 109–12.

Miller, A. (1997), 'The Bearded Lady Wants to Be One of Us', *Esquire*, November: 80.

Miller, M. B. (1981), *The Bon Marché: Bourgeois Culture and the Department Store 1869–1920*, London: Allen & Unwin.

Miller-Bergh, K. (1972), *Alejo Carpentier: Estudio biográfico-crítico*, Madrid: Las Américas.

Milner, F. (1995), *Frida Kahlo*, London: PRC Publishing Ltd.

Ministerio de Desarrollo Humano (1993), *Mapa de pobreza*, La Paz: Instituto Nacional de Estadística.

Mirzoeff, N. (1999), *An Introduction to Visual Culture*, London: Routledge.

Moghadam, V. M. (1994), *Identity. Politics and Women: Cultural Reassertions and Feminisms in International Perspective*, Boulder: Westview.

Molina, Fray A. de. (1944), *Vocabulario en lengua castellana y mexicana (1571)*, vol. IV, Col. de Incunables Americanos. Madrid: Ediciones Cultura Hispánica.

Molina, I. (2001), 'Curvas en guayabera', *El Nacional*, http://128.241.247.116/ediciones/2001/11/16/pB8s1.htm.

Molnar, A. K. (1998), 'Transformations in the Use of Traditional Textiles of Ngada (Western Flores, Easter Indonesia): Commercialization, Fashion and Ethnicity', in A. Brydon and S. Niessen (eds), *Consuming Fashion: Adorning the Transnational Body*, Oxford: Berg.

Monsiváis, C. (1997), *Mexican Postcards*, J. Kraniauskas (trans.), London: Verso.

Montandon, G., *L'Ologenése Culturelle: Traité d'Ethnologie Cyclo-Culturelle et d'Ergologie Systématique*, Paris: Payot.

Moore, R. D. (1997), *Nationalizing Blackness: Afrocubanismo and the Artistic Revolution in Havana, 1920–40*, Pittsburgh: University of Pittsburgh Press.

Morales Carrión, A. (1983), *Puerto Rico: A Political and Cultural History*, New York: Norton.

Moreno, J. M. and Littrell, M. A. (2001), 'Negotiating Tradition: Tourism Retailers in Guatemala', *Annals of Tourism Research*, 28(3): 658–85.

Morett Alatorre, L., Sánchez-Martínez, F., Alvardo, J. L. and Marín, A. M. P. (1999), 'Proyecto arqueobotánico Ticumán', *Arqueología Mexicana*, 4(3) (March–April): 66–71.

Morgan, T. (1994), 'Literature and the Question of Genders', *Men Writing the Feminine: Literature, Theory, and the Question of Genders*, Albany: State University of New York Press.

Mörner, M. (1967), *Race Mixture in the History of Latin America*, Boston: Little, Brown & Company.

Morris, C. (1899), *Our Island Empire: A Handbook of Cuba, Porto Rico, Hawaii, and the Philippine Islands*, Philadelphia: J. B. Lippincott.

Morris, D. (1979), 'Clothing Signals: Clothing as Display, Comfort, and Modesty', in L. M. Gurel and M. S. Beeson (eds), *Dimensions of Dress and Adornment: A Book of Readings*, Dubuque, IA: Kendall/Hunt.

Morrison, T. (1982), *Sula*, New York: Plume.

Moscoso, E. (1995), 'Classic Christy', *Hispanic*, April: 26.

Mota, J. P. (2002), 'A tarde vai ser boa, de tudo vai rolar', *O Globo, Caderno Rio Show*, 20 December: 20–3.

Murra, J. V. (1962), 'Cloth and Its Functions in the Inka State', *American Anthropologist*, 64(4): 710–28.

Murrieta, R. O. (1994), 'Colonial Attire in New Spain', *Baroque Mystique: Women of Mexico-New Spain Seventeenth and Eighteenth Centuries*, San Antonio: Instituto Cultural Mexicano.

Museo del Calzado (c. 1990), brochures on 'El borceguí', 'El *cactli*: El primer calzado en América', and 'El zapato mexicano'.

Myers, F. R. (ed.) (2001), *The Empire of Things: Regimes of Value and Material Culture*, Santa Fe, NM: School of American Research.

Myers, K. (1997), 'The Mystic Triad in Colonial Mexican Nuns' Discourse: Divine Author, Visionary Scribe, and Clerical Mediator,' *Colonial Latin American Historical Review*, (Fall): 479–524.

Nash, J. (ed.) (1993), *Crafts in the World Market: The Impact of Global Exchange on Middle American Artisans*, Albany: State University of New York Press.

Navarro, M. and Fraser, N. (1994), *Evita*, Buenos Aires: Editorial Planeta.

Nebel, C. (1963), *Viaje pintoresco y arqueológico sobre la parte más interesante de la República Mejicana en los años transcurridos desde 1829 hasta 1834*, Mexico City: Porrúa.

Newburgh, L. H. (1968), *Physiology of Heat Regulation and the Science of Clothing*, New York: Hafner.

New Princeton Encyclopedia of Poetry and Poetics, The (1993), A. Preminger and T. V. F. Brogan (eds), Princeton: Princeton University Press.

'Newsmakers' (1995), *Houston Chronicle*, 11 January: A: 2.

'Newsmakers' (1995), *Houston Chronicle*, 22 March A: 2.

Newton, J. and Ford, A. (1995), 'Key Simpson Witness Admits Contradictions', *Los Angeles Times*, 3 March A: 1.

Novaes, C. E. et al (2002), '100 anos de praia', *Todos os verões do Rio*, Rio de Janeiro: RioArte.

Núñez Cabeza de Vaca, A. (1542/1999), *Alvar Núñez Cabeza de Vaca: His Account, His Life, and the Expedition of Pánfilo de Narváez*, R. Adorno and P. C. Pautz (trans and eds), Lincoln: University of Nebraska Press.

Nutini, H. G. (1988), *Todos Santos in Rural Tlaxcala: A Syncretic, Expressive, and Symbolic Analysis of the Cult of the Dead*, Princeton: Princeton University Press.

Ober, F. A. (1899), *Puerto Rico and its Resources*, New York: Appleton & Company.

Olivera, R. (1991), *Life in Mexico under Santa Anna, 1822–1855*, Norman: University of Oklahoma Press.

O'Neal, G. S. (1999), 'The Power of Style: On Rejection of the Accepted', in K. P. Johnson and S. Lennon (eds), *Appearance and Power*, Oxford: Berg.

O'Neale, L. (1935), 'Pequeñas prendas ceremoniales de Parakas', *Revista del Museo Nacional* 4(2).

Orlove, B. (ed.) (1997), *The Allure of the Foreign: Imported Goods in Postcolonial Latin America*, Ann Arbor: University of Michigan Press.

—— and Rutz, H. J. (1989), 'Thinking About Consumption: A Social Economy Approach', in H. J. Rutz and B. Orlove (eds), *The Social Economy of Consumption*, Lanham, MD: University Press of America and Society for Economic Anthropology.

Ortiz, F. (1987), *Contrapunteo cubano del tabaco y el azúcar*, Caracas: Biblioteca Ayacucho.

Ota Mishima, M. E. (1976), *México y Japón en el siglo XIX: la política exterior de México y la consolidación de la soberanía japonesa*, Mexico City: Secretaría de Relaciones Exteriores.

Paerregaard, K. (1987), 'Death Rituals and Symbols in the Andes', *Folk* 29: 23–42.

—— (1997), *Linking Separate Worlds: Urban Migrants and Rural Lives in Peru*. Oxford: Berg.

Pagden, A. (1995), *Lords of All the World: Ideologies of Empire in Spain, Britain and France c.1500-c.1800*, New Haven: Yale University Press.

Page-Reeves, J. (1998), 'Alpaca Sweater Design and Marketing: Problems and Prospects for Cooperative Knitting Organizations in Bolivia', *Human Organization*, 57(1): 83–92.

Pancake, C. M. (1995), 'Gender Boundaries in the Production of Guatemalan Textiles', in R. Barnes and J. B. Eicher (eds), *Dress and Ethnicity: Change Across Space and Time*, Oxford: Berg.

Pané, F. R. (1984), *Relación acerca de las antigüedades de los indios*, Mexico City: Siglo XXI.

—— (1498/1999), *An Account of the Antiquities of the Indians*, J. J. Arrom (ed.) and S. C. Griswold (trans.), Durham: Duke University Press.

Paredes, A. (1994), *George Washington Gómez*, Houston: Arte Público.

Paredes-Candia, A. (1992), *La chola boliviana*, La Paz: ISLA.

Parsons, J. R. and Parsons, M. H. (1990), *Maguey Utilization in Highland Central Mexico: An Archaeological Ethnography*, Anthropological Papers #82, Ann Arbor: Museum of Anthropology, Unversity of Michigan.

Paul, A. (1990), *Paracas Ritual Attire. Symbols of Authority in Ancient Peru*, Norman: University of Oklahoma Press.

Payno, M. (1984), *Un viaje a Veracruz en el invierno de 1843*, Xalapa, Mexico: Universidad Veracruzana.

Paz, O. (1985), *El laberinto de la soledad*, México: Fondo de Cultura Económica.

Pease, F. (ed.) (1977), *Collaguas I*, Lima: Pontificia Universidad Católica.

Pellarolo, S. (2000), 'The Melodramatic Seductions of Eva Perón', in C. Fusco (ed.), *Corpus Delicti: Performance Art of the Americas*, New York: Routledge.

Penfield, W., III. (1995), 'By the No.s', *Toronto Sun*, 15 June: 68.

Perez, L. A., Jr. (1999), *On Becoming Cuban: Identity, Nationality and Culture*, Chapel Hill: University of North Carolina Press.

Pérez Firmat, G. (1989), *The Cuban Condition*, London: Cambridge University Press.

—— (1990), 'The Strut of the Centipede: José Lezama Lima and New World Exceptionalism', in G. Pérez Firmat, *Do the Americas Have a Common Literature?*, Durham: Duke University Press.

Perón, E. (1951). *La razón de mi vida*. Buenos Aires: Ediciones Peuser.

Phillips, R. B., and Steiner, C. B. (eds) (1999), *Unpacking Culture: Art and Commodity in Colonial and Postcolonial Worlds*, Berkeley: University of California Press.

Phipps, E. (1996), 'Textiles as Cultural Memory: Andean Garments in the Colonial Period', in D. Fane (ed.), *Converging Cultures. Art and Identity in Spanish America*, New York: Brooklyn Museum/Harry N. Abrams.

Pico Vidal, I. (1980), 'The History of Women's Struggle for Equality in Puerto Rico', in J. Nash and H. I. Safa (eds), *Sex and Class in Latin America: Women's Perspectives on Politics, Economics and the Family in the Third World*, South Hadley, MA: J. F. Bergin.

Platt, T. (1976), *Espejos y maíz: Temas de estructura simbólica andina*, La Paz: CIPCA.

—— (1982), *Estado boliviano y ayllu andino. Tierra y tributo en el norte de Potosí*, Lima: Instituto de Estudios Peruanos.

Pratt, M. L. (1992), *Imperial Eyes: Travel Writing and Transculturation*, London and New York: Routledge.

Press, E. (1996), 'Barbie's Betrayal. The Toy Industry's Broken Workers', *The Nation*, 30 December: 10–16.

Price, R. and Lovitt, J. T. (1995), 'O. J.'s Alibi: Time Means Everything', *Los Angeles Times*, 10 July: A: 9.

Prieto, G. (1906), *Memorias de mis tiempos. 1828 a 1840*, Paris and Mexico City: Vda. De C. Bouret.

Proal, M. and Charpenal, P. M. (1998), *Los Barcelonnettes en México*, Mexico City: Clio.

Puiggarí, J. (1886), *Monografía histórica é iconográfica del traje*, Barcelona: J. y A. Bastinos.

Queiróz Valda, M. (2002), *O eterno no transitório . . . um estudo sociológico da moda*. Dissertation, Brasília/UnB.

Ráez Retamozo, M. (1993), 'Los ciclos ceremoniales y la percepción del tiempo festivo en el Valle del Colca (Arequipa)', in R. Romero (ed.), *Música, danza y máscaras en los Andes*, Lima: Pontificia Universidad Católica and Instituto Riva-Agüero.

Ramírez Aznar, L. A. (1992), 'La guayabera yucateca. Prenda que se hizo a partir de los años veinte, hasta convertirse en gran industria', *La ciudad (¡Por Esto!)*, 10 October: 16–17.

Ramos, A. (1689), *Primera Parte de los Prodigios De la Omnipotencia y Milagros de la Gracia En la Vida de la Venerable Sierva de Dios Catharina de S. Joan. Natural del Gran Mogor, y difunta en esta imperial ciudad de Puebla en los Ángeles, en la Nueva España*, Puebla, Mexico: Fernández de León.

—— (1690), *Segunda Parte de los Prodigios De la Omnipotencia y Milagros de la Gracia En la Vida de la Venerable Sierva de Dios Catharina de S. Joan. Natural del Gran Mogor, y difunta en esta imperial ciudad de Puebla en los Ángeles, en la Nueva España*, Puebla, Mexico: Fernández de León.

—— (1692), *Tercera Parte de los Prodigios De la Omnipotencia y Milagros de la Gracia En la Vida de la Venerable Sierva de Dios Catharina de S. Joan. Natural del Gran Mogor, y difunta en esta imperial ciudad de Puebla en los Ángeles, en la Nueva España*, Puebla, Mexico: Fernández de León.

Reinhard, J. (1996), 'Peru's Ice Maidens: Unwrapping the Secrets', *National Geographic*, June: 62–81.

Rex González, A. (1997), 'Arte precolombino de la Argentina: Introducciones a su historia cultural', Buenos Aires: Filmediciones Valero.

Ribeiro, A. (1999), *Ingres in Fashion: Representations of Dress and Appearance in Ingres' Images of Women*, New Haven: Yale University Press.

Ribeiro, D. (1975), *Configurações histórico-culturais dos povos americanos*, Rio de Janeiro: Editora Civilização Brasileira.

Ribes Tovar, F. (1970), *Enciclopedia puertorriqueña ilustrada*, San Juan, Puerto Rico: Plus Ultra Educacional.

—— (1972), *The Puerto Rican Woman: Her Life and Evolution Throughout History*, A. Rawlings (trans.), New York: Plus Ultra.

Bibliography

Ries, N. (1997), *Russian Talk. Culture and Conversation During Perestroika*, Ithaca: Cornell University Press.

Rivero, R. (1949), 'Sección Cultural' (Letter to the Editor), *Diario de la Marina*, October: 13.

Robertson, W. P. (1853), *A Visit to Mexico by the West India Islands, Yucatán and United States: With Observations and Adventures on the Way*, London: published for the author.

Robinson, A. G. (1899), *The Porto Rico of To-day: Pen Pictures of the People and the Country*, New York: Charles Scribner's Sons.

Roche, D. (1994), *The Culture of Clothing: Dress and Fashion in the 'Ancien Régime'*, Jean Birrell (trans), Cambridge, Great Britain: Cambridge University Press.

Rock, D. (1987) *Argentina 1516–1987: From Spanish Colonization to Alfonsín*. Berkeley and Los Angeles: University of California Press.

Rodríguez, C. E. (ed.) (1997), *Latin Looks: Images of Latinas and Latinos in the U.S. Media*, Boulder: Westview Press.

Rodríguez, J. C. (1995), 'La guayabera y sus orígenes', *Novedades Yucatán*, 17 January.

Rodríguez, J. E. (1994), *Mexico in the Age of Democratic Revolutions, 1750–1850*, Boulder, CO: Lynne Rienner.

Rodríguez Angulo, F. (1949), 'La guayabera no es un producto de la moda', *Carteles*, 4 September 4: 72–3.

Rogin, M. (1999), 'Healing the Vietnam Wound', *American Quarterly*, September 51: 702–8.

Rolnik, R. (2001), *São Paulo*, Coleção Folha Explica, São Paulo: Publifolha.

Romero, J. L. (1999), *Latin America: Its Cities and Ideas*. Washington, DC: Organization of American States.

Romero, M. (1992), *Maid in the U.S.A.*, New York: Routledge.

Root, R. A. (October 1999), 'La moda como metonimia', *Folios*, 35(6): 3–11.

—— (March 2000), 'Tailoring the Nation: Fashion Writing in Nineteenth Century Argentina', *Fashion Theory*, 4(1): 89–118.

—— (October 2001), 'Vestidas para matar: la mujer, la moda y el espíritu de la independencia', *DeSignis*, 1: 239–52.

—— (2005), 'Latin American Fashion', in V. Steele, J. S. Major and J. B. Eicher (eds), *Encyclopedia of Clothing and Fashion*, New York: Thomson/Gale.

—— (2004), 'Searching for the *Oasis of Life*: Fashion and the Question of Female Emancipation in Late Nineteenth-Century Argentina', *The Americas: A Quarterly Review of Inter-American Cultural History* 60(3): 363–90.

Rosendi Cancio, E. (1982), 'La guayabera: consideraciones generales', Primer Simposio Provincial sobre Cultura Espirituana, Ms. Biblioteca Rubén Martínez Villegas, Sancti Espíritus, Cuba.

Rousso, K. (2003), 'Maguey Textiles in Guatemala Today', unpublished manusript.

Rowe, A. P. (1977), *Warp-Patterned Weaves of the Andes*. Washington, DC: Textile Museum.

Rowe, W. and Schelling, V. (1991), *Memory and Modernity. Popular Culture in Latin America*. London: Verso.

Rushdie, S. (1997), *The Satanic Verses: A Novel*, New York: Picador USA.

Sahagún, Fray B. de (1974), *Florentine Codex: General History of the Things of New Spain. Book 10: The People*, C. E. Dibble and A. J. O. Anderson (trans.), Santa Fe, NM: Monograph of The School of American Research and The Museum of New Mexico.

Saldana Fernández, M. C. (1995), 'Nahuas de Morelos', in *Etnografia contemporánea de los pueblos indígenas de México: Centro*, Mexico City: INI.

'Salvador del mundo en E.U.' (2000), Nacionales section of *El Diario de Hoy* (San Salvador), 29 June, http://www.eldiariodehoy.com.

Samoiloff, L. C. (1984), *Portrait of Puerto Rico*, Cranbury NJ: Rosemont.

Sanabria, H. (1993), *The Coca Boom and Rural Social Change in Bolivia*, Ann Arbor: University of Michigan Press.

Sánchez-Martínez, F. and Alvarado, J. L. (1997), 'Cestería prehispánica', *Artes de Mexico: Cestería*, 38: 36–43.

—— et al. (1998), 'Las cuevas del Gallo y de la Chaguera: Inventario arqueobotánico e inferencias', *Arqueología*, January/June 19: 81–90.

Sandstrom, A. R. (1991), *Corn is Our Blood: Culture and Ethnic Identity in a Contemporary Aztec Indian Village*, Norman: University of Oklahoma Press.

Santamaría, F. J. (1959), *Diccionario de mejicanismos*, Mexico City: Porrúa.

Santamaría Ochoa, J. (1998), *Mujeres de Morelos: una etnografía*, Cuernavaca: Instituto de Cultura de Morelos.

Santiago, S. (2001), 'Zazá? A vida como obra de arte', *Folha de São Paulo*, 19 September: 3.

Santiesteban, A. (1985), *El habla popular cubana de hoy. Una tonga de cubichismos que le oí a mi pueblo*, La Habana: Editorial de Ciencias Sociales.

Sarduy, S. (1982), *La simulación*. Caracas: Monte Ávila.

Sarmiento, D. F. (2003), *Facundo. Civilization and Barbarism*, K. Ross (trans.), Berkeley: University of California Press.

Sartorius, C. C. (1859), *Mexico and the Mexicans*, London: Trübner.

Sarup, M. (1993), *An Introductory Guide to Post-Structuralism and Postmodernism*, Athens: University of Georgia Press.

Savigliano, M. E. (1995), *Tango and the Political Economy of Passion*, Boulder: Westview.

—— (2002), '*Evita*: The Globalization of a National Myth', J. Abbassi and S. L. Lutjens (eds), *Rereading Women in Latin America and the Caribbean: The Political Economy of Gender*, New York: Rowan & Littlefield.

Sayer, C. (1985a), *Costumes of Mexico*, Austin: University of Texas Press.

—— (1985b), *Mexican Costume*, London: British Museum.

—— (ed.) (1994), *The Mexican Day of the Dead: An Anthology*, Boston: Shambhala Redstone.

Scarano, F. A. (1993), *Puerto Rico: Cinco siglos de historia*, San Juan, Puerto Rico: McGraw-Hill.

Schaeffer, C. (1992), *Textured Lives: Women, Art and Representation in Modern Mexico*, Tucson: University of Arizona Press.

Schiaparelli, E. (1954), *Shocking Life*, New York: E. P. Dutton & Company.

Schneider, J. (1978), 'Peacocks and Penguins: The Political Economy of European Cloth and Colors', *American Ethnologist*, 5: 413–48.

Schurz, W. L. (1918), 'Mexico, Peru, and the Manila Galleon', *Hispanic American Historical Review*, 1(4): 389–402.

—— (1959), *The Manila Galleon*, New York: E. P. Dutton.

Schwarz, R. A. (1979), 'Uncovering the Secret Vice: Toward an Anthropology of Clothing and Adornment', in J. M. Cordwell and R. A. Schwarz (eds), *The Fabric of Culture*, New York: Morton.

Bibliography

Seed, P. (November 1982), 'Social Dimensions of Race: Mexico City, 1753', *Hispanic American Historical Review*, 62: 569–606.

Seibold, K. (1990), *The Last Incas: Social Change as Reflected in the Textiles of Choquecancha, Cuzco, Peru*. Dissertation, Indiana University.

Seigel, J. (1995), 'Spanish Has the Upper Hand: L.A.'s Latinos Rapt as One of Theirs Testifies', *Toronto Star*, 5 March: A: 4.

Seligmann, L. J. (ed.) (2001), *Women Traders in Cross-Cultural Perspective: Mediating Identities, Marketing Wares*, Stanford: Stanford University Press.

—— (2004), *Peruvian Street Lives: Culture, Power, and Economy Among Market Women of Cuzco*, Urbana: University of Illinois Press.

Senna, D. (1998), *Caucasia*, New York: Riverhead.

Sennett, R. (1988), *O declínio do homem público – as tiranias da intimidade*, São Paulo: Companhia das Letras.

Sevcenko, N. (2000), *Orfeu extático na metrópole. São Paulo sociedade e cultura nos frementes anos 20*, São Paulo: Companhia das Letras.

Shaeffer, C. (1992), *Textured Lives: Women, Art, and Representation in Modern Mexico*, Tucson: University of Arizona Press.

Shapiro, S. (1996), 'Glare of Publicity Irresistible; Interview: Recall the Guy Who Supposedly Got Engaged to O. J. Simpson's Housekeeper? He's Back, and This Time It Has Something to Do with James Earl Ray', *Baltimore Sun*, 17 November: J: 3.

Shils, E. (1981), *Tradition*, Chicago: University of Chicago Press.

Sifuentes-Jáuregui, B. (2002), *Transvestism, Masculinity and Latin American Literature*, New York: Palgrave.

Sikkink, L. (1994), *Household, Community and Marketplace: Women as Managers of Exchange Relations and Resources on the Southern Altiplano of Bolivia*. Dissertation, University of Minnesota.

Sills, D. L. (ed.) (1972), *International Encyclopedia of the Social Sciences*, New York: Macmillan.

Sissons, S. (2001), 'Perspectives: Beauty, Brains, and Business', *Financial Times* (London), 24 February: 3.

Slater, L. (1998), 'Christy: Student and Supermodel; So Why Did a Millionaire Fashion Icon Give Up the Catwalk and Go Back to School?', *Daily Telegraph* (London), 24 January: 22.

Smith, C. (1986), 'Reconstructing the Elements of Petty Commodity Production', *Social Analysis*, 20: 29–46.

Smith, M. E. (1998), *The Aztecs*, Malden, MA: Blackwell.

Snead, E. (1990), 'MTV: A Model Route to Hollywood', *USA Today*, 12 November: D: 5.

Solís A., Manuel de J. (1950), 'Origen verdadero del traje nacional de 'china poblana'', R. Carrasco (ed.), *Bibliografía de Catarina de San Juan y de la china poblana*, Mexico City: Secretaría de Relaciones Exteriores, Departamento de Información para el Extranjero.

Soustelle, J. (1964), *The Daily Life of the Aztecs*, New York: Penguin.

Stark, L. R. (1980), 'Acerca de los huilliches. Documento de la primera mitad del siglo XVII', *Estudios Filológicos* (Facultad de Letras y Educación, Universidad Austral de Chile [Valdivia]), 15: 193–213.

Stastny, F. (1987), 'The Art of the Colca Valley', in M. de Romaña, J. Blassi and J. Blassi (eds), *Descubriendo el Valle del Colca/Discovering the Colca Valley*, Barcelona: Patthey e Hijos.

Stayton, K. L. (1996), 'The Algara Romero de Terreros Collection: A Mexican Aristocratic Family in the Colonial Era', in D. Fane (ed.), *Converging Cultures: Art and Identity in Spanish America*, New York: Harry N. Abrams.

Steele, V. and Major, J. S. (1999), *China Chic: East Meets West*, New Haven, Connecticut: Yale University Press.

Steele, V. (ed.) (2004), *Encyclopedia of Clothing and Fashion*, Detroit: Charles Scribner's Sons.

Stewart, S. (1984), *On Longing: Narratives of the Miniature, the Gigantic, the Souvenir, the Collection*, Baltimore: Johns Hopkins University Press.

Stinetorf, L. A. (1960), *La china poblana*, Indianapolis: Bobbs-Merrill.

Stoner, B. (1989), *Health Care Delivery and Health Resource Utilization in a Highland Andean Community of Southern Peru*. Dissertation, Indiana University.

Storytelling (2002), Los Angeles: New Line Home Entertainment.

Sturken, M. and Cartwright, L. (2002), *Practices of Looking: An Introduction to Visual Culture*, New York: Oxford UP.

Suárez Findlay, E. J. (1999), *Imposing Decency: The Politics of Sexuality and Race in Puerto Rico, 1870–1920*, Durham: Duke University Press.

Suárez Solís, R. et al. (1948), *Uso y abuso de la guayabera*, Havana: Lyceum Lawn Club of Havana.

Susman, W. (1979), *Culture and Commitment 1929–1945*, New York: Braziller.

Taiara, C. T., Liner notes for *Word Descarga* by Los Delicados, www.calacapress.com/wd-linernotes.html.

Taletavicius, M. (1995), *Aventuras y desventuras del mundo de las modelos 90-60-90*, Buenos Aires: Espasa Calpe.

Taullard, A. (1949), *Tejidos y ponchos indígenas de Sudamérica*, Buenos Aires: Editorial Guillermo Kraft.

'Tepemaxalco' (1988), in *Los municipios de Puebla*, Mexico City: Secretaria de Gobernación y Gobierno del Estado de Puebla, Col. Enciclopedia de los Municipios de México: 897–901.

Teixeira Rainho, M. do C. (2002), *A Cidade e a Moda: novas pretensões, novas distinções – Rio de Janeiro, século XIX*, Brasília: UnB.

Theroux, P. (1982), *The Mosquito Coast*, New York: Houghton Mifflin.

Thomas, N. (1991), *Entangled Objects: Exchange, Material Culture, and Colonialism in the Pacific*, Cambridge, MA: Harvard University Press.

Thompson, C. J. and Haytko, D. L. (1997), 'Speaking of Fashion: Consumers' Uses of Fashion Discourses and the Appropriation of Countervailing Cultural Meanings', *Journal of Consumer Research*, 24 (June): 15–42.

Tierney, J. (1994), 'Color Blind', *New York Times Magazine*, 18 September: 32–4.

Tinajero, A. (2004), *Orientalismo en el modernismo hispanoamericano*, Lafayette: Purdue University Press.

Tomoeda, H. and Millones, L. (eds) (1992), *500 años de mestizaje en los Andes*, Osaka: National Museum of Ethnology.

Toobin, J. (1996), *The Run of His Life: The People v. O. J. Simpson*, New York: Random House.

Toor, F. (1947), *A Treasury of Mexican Folkways*, New York: Crown Publishers.

Townsend, M. A. (2001), *Here and There in Mexico: The Travel Writings of Mary Ashley Townsend*, Tuscaloosa: University of Alabama Press.

Bibliography

Treacy, J. (1989), *The Fields of Coporaque: Agricultural Terracing and Water Management in the Colca Valley, Arequipa, Peru*. Dissertation, University of Wisconsin at Madison.

—— (1994), *Las Chacras de Coporaque: Andenería y riego en el Valle del Colca*, M. A. Benavides, B. Femenías, and W. M. Denevan (eds), Lima: Instituto de Estudios Peruanos.

Turner, T. S. (1980), 'The Social Skin', in *Not Work Alone: A Cross-Cultural View of Activities Superfluous to Survival*, J. Cherfas and R. Lewin (eds), Beverly Hills: Sage Publications.

UNICEF (1989), *Vida para los niños. Programa de Cooperación Gobierno de Bolivia – UNICEF 1989–1994 (Versión resumida)*, La Paz: UNICEF.

Unruh, V. (1998), 'The Performing Spectator in Alejo Carpentier's Fictional World', *Hispanic Review*, 66: 57–77.

Urla, J. and Swedlund, A. C. (1995), 'The Anthropometry of Barbie: Unsettling Ideals of the Feminine Body in Popular Culture', in J. Terry and J. Urla (eds), *Deviant Bodies: Critical Perspectives on Difference and Science in Popular Culture*, Bloomington: Indiana University Press.

Valderrama, R. and Escalante, C. (1988), *Del Tata Mallku a la Mama Pacha: Riego, sociedad y ritos en los Andes peruanos*, Lima: DESCO.

—— (1997), *La doncella sacrificada: Mitos del Valle del Colca*, Arequipa: Universidad Nacional de San Agustín/Instituto Francés de Estudios Andinos.

Valle Ferrer, N. (1990), *Luisa Capetillo: Historia de una mujer proscrita*, Puerto Rico: Editorial Cultural.

Vega, G. de la ("El Inca") (1609/1984), *Comentarios reales*, Mexico: Porrúa.

Verrill, A. H. (1914), *Porto Rico, Past and Present*, New York: Dodd & Mead.

Vidal, E. E. (1820), *Picturesque Illustrations of Buenos Ayres and Monte Video Consisting of Twenty-Four Views: Accompanied with Descriptions of the Scenery and of the Costumes, Manners, &c. of the Inhabitants of Those Cities and Their Environs*, London: R. Ackermann.

Vidal, I. P. (1980), 'The History of Women's Struggles for Equality in Puerto Rico', in J. Nash and H. I. Safa (eds), *Sex and Class in Latin America: Women's Perspectives on Politics, Economics and the Family in the Third World*, South Hadley, MA: J. F. Bergin.

Villaça, N. (1999), 'Menos corpo, mais fetiche?', in *Em pauta: corpo, globalização e novas tecnologias*, Rio de Janeiro: Mauad.

—— (2002), 'Alta, média e baixa costura: moda e semiologia cultural', in K. Castilho and D. Galvão (eds), *A moda do corpo, o corpo da moda*, São Paulo: Esfera.

—— and Góes, F. (eds) (1998), 'Moda: prótese e proposta', in *Em nome do corpo*, Rio de Janeiro: Rocco.

Villanueva, M. A., 'Veracruz Totonaca/Illinois Jarocha: espacio, comida, memoria', http://www.inroads.umn.edu/articles/villanueva.html.

Vogue Magazine (2002), Special Edition: Summer 2002/2003 – Cinqüenta e oito estilistas, São Paulo Fashion Week/Fashion Rio, São Paulo: Carta Editorial.

Wangemann, G., 'Evita: The Woman (Part 3)', http://execp.com/~reva/html73.htm.

Ward, H. G. (1828), *Mexico in 1827*, London: H. Colburn.

Wasserman, M. (2000), *Everyday Life and Politics in Nineteenth Century Mexico: Men, Women, and War*, Albuquerque: University of New Mexico Press.

Weiner, A. B. (1992), *Inalienable Possessions: The Paradox of Keeping-While-Giving*, Berkeley: University of California Press.

Weismantel, M. (2002), *Cholas and Pishtacos: Stories of Race and Sex in the Andes*, Chicago: University of Chicago Press.
Wernke, S. A. (2003), *An Archaeo-History of Andean Community and Landscape: The Late Prehispanic and Early Colonial Colca Valley*. Dissertation, University of Wisconsin at Madison.
West, A. (1997), *The Tropics of Discourse: Cuba Imagined*, Westport: Bergin & Garvey.
Wilkie, J. and Menell-Kinberg, M. (1981), 'Evita: From Elitelore to Folklore', *Journal of Latin American Lore*, 7(1): 99–140.
Wilkinson, T. (1995), 'The O. J. Simpson Murder Trial; Still Spotlighted; Lopez, Hounded by Media, Holds Press Conference', *Los Angeles Times*, 8 March: A:14.
Wilson, E. (1985), *Adorned in Dreams: Fashion and Modernity*, Berkeley: University of California Press.
Winant, H. (1994), *Racial Conditions: Politics, Theory, Comparisons*, Minneapolis: University of Minnesota Press.
Wise, H. A. (1850), *Los Gringos: Or, An Inside View of Mexico and California, with Wanderings in Peru, Chili, and Polynesia*, New York: Putnam.
Woods, C. M. (1975), *Culture Change*, Dubuque, IA: Wm. C. Brown.
Worth, S. and Sibley, L. R. (1994), 'Maja Dress and the Andalusian Image of Spain', *Clothing and Textiles Research Journal*, 12(4): 51–60.
Wroth, W. (1999), *Sarape Textiles from Historic Mexico. The Mexican Sarape: A History*, St. Louis: St. Louis Art Museum.
Yarwood, D. (1992), *Fashion in the Western World*, London: Batsford.
Zaldívar Guerra, M. L. L. (1998), *De maestros, oficiales y aprendices a maquiladores: Los talabarteros de Yucatán en 1978*, Mexico City: INAH (Colección Regiones de México).
Zamora, M. (1992), 'Reading in the Margins of Columbus' in R. Jara and N. Spadaccini (eds), *Amerindian Images and the Legacy of Columbus*, Minneapolis: University of Minnesota Press.
Zamora, Martha (1991), *Frida Kahlo: The Brush of Anguish*, San Francisco: Chronicle.
Zorn, E. (1990), 'Modern Traditions: The Impact of the Trade in Traditional Textiles on the Sakaka of Northern Potosí, Bolivia', in *Textiles In Trade*, Proceedings of the Textile Society of America Second Biennial Symposium, September 1990.
—— (1994), '(Re-)Fashioning Identity: Late Twentieth-Century Transformations in Dress and Society in Bolivia', in *Contact, Crossover, Continuity*, Proceedings of the Textile Society of America Fourth Biennial Symposium, September 1994.
—— (1997a), *Marketing Diversity: Global Transformations in Cloth and Identity in Highland Peru and Bolivia*. Dissertation, Cornell University.
—— (1997b), 'Coca, Cash, and Cloth in Highland Bolivia: The Chapare and Transformations in a 'Traditional' Andean Textile Economy', in M. B. Léons and H. Sanabria (eds), *Coca, Cocaine, and the Bolivian Reality*, Albany: State University New York Press.
—— (1999), '(Re)Fashioning the Self: Dress, Economy, and Identity among the Sakaka of Northern Potosí, Bolivia', *Revista Chungará* 30(2): 161–96.
—— (2002), 'Dangerous Encounters: Ritual Battles in Andean Bolivia', in D. E. Jones (ed.), *Combat, Ritual, and Performance: Anthropology of the Martial Arts*, Westport, CT: Praeger.
—— (2004), *Weaving a Future: Tourism, Cloth, and Culture on an Andean Island*, Iowa City, IA: University of Iowa Press.
Zwecker, B. (1995), 'Trial and Tribulation: It Was a Very Weird Year', *Chicago Sun-Times*, 27 December: 33.

Index

Note: "*f*" following page number indicates figure.

accessories, 3, 45, 48–9, 68; *see also* specific accessories (ie jewelry, *peinetón*, etc.)
Ackermanns' fashion plates, 50
advertisements, for Mappin Stores, 183*f*, 184, 186
African influence, in Latin America, 200
afterlife, concept of, 86–7
agro-pastoral economy, 132–5, 139
Água de Coco, 195
Água Doce, 195
Aguilar, Jerónimo de, 21
The Alameda, 46, 69
Alarcón, Norma, 249
alibi fashions, 193–5
All Saint's Day (Todos Santos), 97–8, 101
All Souls' Day (Todos Almas), 97, 99
alpaca fiber, 133
altered traditions, 1–2, 5–7
Alternative Trade, 148
alternative trade organizations (ATO), 154
Altman, Ida, 47
America Occidentalis (De Bry), 19*f*
American clothing, used, 134–5
American influence, in Puerto Rico, 198, 199–200, 203; *see also* United States
Anawalt, Patrica, 23
Andalusian dress, 51, 54, 59, 60
Andean knitting, 153–4
Andean societies, clothes in, 22–3, 116–17
Andean textiles, 117, 123–4, 134
Andean women, dress of, 126
Andrade, Mario de, 179–80, 185
Andrade, Rita, 7–8
André, María Claudia, 10–11
Anglo Brazilian Chronicle, 185
Anglo-Brazilian House, 184, 187
Annis, Sheldon, 92
anti-fashion, socialist, 12
antique "ethnic" cloth, 135–7
Anzaldúa, Gloria, 257, 278
appearance, physical, 21, 46, 67
Argentina
 fashion in, 11–13, 283–4
 First Lady of, 258–9; *see also* Perón, Eva

and the *peinetón*; *see peinetón*
and the poncho; *see* ponchos
postcolonial, 31–43
Argentine Transvestite Association, 285
Argentine Worker's Movement, 287*f*
Argentinian women, and the *peinetón*, 33; *see also peinetón*
aristocracy; *see* elites
Armaignac, H., 167
Arnaz, Desi, 227, 277
Arrazate, Marta, 225
Arrom, Silvia, 61
Arróniz, Marcos, 57–8
art
 boundary; *see* boundary art
 as commodity, 146
 "ethnic," 135
 in Latin America, 249–50
artisans
 Andean, 159
 producing for tourism, 95, 149
 as vendors, 111
As quatro estações (Maciel), 192
Asian textiles, 47, 69, 226; *see also* China
Assante, Armando, 227
"authentic" mourning clothes, 108; *see also* mourning clothes
authoritarianism, fashion as protesting, 191
ayllu (indigenous ethnic groups), 118–19
aymilla (long black dress), 114, 126
Aztec society, clothes in, 23, 81
Azurduy, Juana de, 3

B. Altman & Co., 209
Baby Boomers, 1, 185
Baca, Micaela, 62
Bacall, Lauren, 243
Bacardí, Emilio, 236
backstrap weaving, Maya, 147–9, 157–9
Bacle, César Hipólito, 36–7, 37*f*–38*f*
Baddeley, Oriana, 253–4, 255–6
Bailey, Gauvin, 52–3
Bainbridge's of Newcastle, 181
Baizerman, Susan, 143–4, 146, 158

Index

Bakhtin, M., 243, 245
balandrán (type of poncho), 163
Baltimore Sun, 272
Banana Republic, and the *guayabera*, 9
Banderas, Antonio, 227, 260
barbarism, and lack of clothing, 20, 23–4
"Barbie" dolls, "ethnic," 110, 112, 210
Baretti, J., 59
Barker, Nancy Nichols, 61
Barreales, pottery of, 168
bartering, vs. cash, 121
Barthes, Roland, 233, 276–7
battle, ritual (*tinku*), 115, 118–19
Baudrillard, Jean, 247, 249–50, 262
Bauer, Arnold, 82
Bauer, Dale, 255
Bauman, Zygmunt, 189
Bauzá, Francisco, 173
beach fashions, 8, 191–3, 195–7
beauty contests, and the bikini, 190–1
Beauvoir, Simone de, 246
"being," and "seeming," 188–9
"being seen," 20, 186; *see also* recognition
"Belle Époque" style, 190
Bellemare, Louis de, 58–9
Bendel, Henri, 155
Benedetti, Lúcia, 189
Benítez, José, 62, 70
Benítez Rojo, Antonio, 236
Berbardi, Micheline, 190
Bergman-Carton, Janice, 257
Berkins, Lohana, 13
Bernal, Felícitas, 97
Bernal, Juan, 102–3
Bernal, Nilda, 93, 94f, 102–3, 108
Bernal, Susana, 102, 109
Bertha Gowns mail order, 207
Beverly, John, 262
Bhabha, Homi K., 21, 180, 249
bikinis, 190–2, 196–7
black clothes
  and Good Friday, 99–100
  as mourning garments, 108
  tourists buying, 107–10, 113
black (color); *see also* colors
  signifying mourning, 93–113
  in Spanish attire, 50–1
  symbolism of, 6, 113
  and tourism, 93–113
  in Western fashion, 108
black slaves, 19f
black women, fashion items denied to, 68
blouses, 3, 54
Bodies That Matter (Butler), 234
the body, and fashion, 188, 193–6
Boechat, Ricardo, 189–90
Bogani, Gino, 283
Bohemia (magazine), 222–3

Bolaños, Chía, 71
bolitas (silver plated buttons), 225
Bolívar, Simón, 3, 215
Bolivia
  dress in, 124–5
  identity in, 117–8, 122–3, 140
  the Sakaka in; *see* Sakaka
bombachas (baggy white pant), 170, 173
Bon Marché (France), 181
Bonfil Batalla, Guillermo, 89
bordados (Colca-style embroidered clothes), 93, 224–6
  materials used in, 103
  meaning of, 111–12
  selling of, 95, 101, 104, 112
"Borderlands," 257
Borges, Jorge Luis, 287
Bórmida, Marcelo, 168
Borrero, Ana María, 235, 237–9
Boucicaut, Aristide, 181
boundary art, 142–59
  marketing of, 6–7
  means of producing, 158–9
  scholars on, 145–6
boundary textile art, 144–7
  consumers of, 146
  defined, 145
  selling of, 142–59
  as traditional, 144–7, 157
Bourbon reforms, 47–8
Bourdieu, Pierre, 17
Braun-Ronsdorf, Margarete, 63
Brazil
  American influence in, 184
  beach fashions in, 191–3, 195–7
  and the bikini, 190–2, 196–7
  English influence in, 8, 182
  French influence in, 185
  independence from Portugal, 177
  Mappin Stores in; *see* Mappin Stores
  opening of ports in, 177
  underwear from, 1
Brazilianness, 179–80
Bretón, André, 254
The British Packet, on the *peinetón*, 33–4, 36, 39–40
Bry, Theodore de, 19f
Bryan, W. S., 205f
Brydon, Anne, 66
Buenos Aires, Argentina, 283
  English community in, 182
  fashion in, 283
  Feng Shui in, 74–5
  Mappin Stores in, 176, 179
  and Miami, 284
  and the *peinetón*; *see peinetón*
Bullock, William, 50, 59
Bündchen, Giselle, 1

Index

bureau (desk, office), 32
burial customs, 80–1, 85–8
Butler, Judith, 234
"Butterflies on the Scaffold" ("Mariposas en el Andamio"), 236

Cab, Pedro, 225
Cabanaconde hats, 104
Cabeza de Vaco, Álvaro Núñez, 17, 20
Cabrera Infante, Guillermo, 213
Calcogno, Francisco, 236
Calderón de la Barca, Frances, 49, 51–3, 55–62
Caliban and Other Essays (Fernández Retamar), 215
call girls, in Rio de Janeiro, 195
camelid fiber, 133
Campo Alange, María L., 198
Canadian Light, 180
Cancio, Rosendi, 220
Candelaria, feast of, 91
Cannon, Aubrey, 67
Cano, Cruz, 60
Canyon of the Condors, 106
capitalism, critique of, 254
Carey, Mariah, 276
Caribbean, and the *guayabera*, 9, 225
Cariocas (Rio's beach inhabitants), 188–9
Carlsen, R., 149
Carnival Sunday, 88
Carpentier, Alejo, 10, 232–45; *see also* "Jacqueline"
Carreón, Antonio, 72
Carrió de la Vandera, Alonso (Concolorcorvo), 169
"Carta a Santángel" (Columbus), 18
Carter, Jimmy, 215
Casa Alemã (German House), 183
Casa Anglo-Brasileira (Anglo-Brazilian House), 184, 187
Casa Mappin; *see* Mappin Stores
Casé, Regina, 192
cash, vs. bartering, 121
caste system, 2–3, 46, 68–9
Castelló Yturbide, Teresa, 54
Castillo, Ana, 274
Castillo Graxeda, José del, 72
Castizo Child (Magón), 53
Castro, Fidel, and the *guayabera*, 9, 12, 214–15, 223–4
Catalina (swimsuit brand), 190
Catarina de San Juan (Mirra), 53, 72
Catholicism, folk, 80
Catriel tribe, 167
caudillos (wealthy Argentinian soldiers), 31
Caughie, Pamela L., 238
caveat, category maintenance as, 238–9, 241
Caylloma, Peru, 100, 103

color black in, 6
identity of people from, 113
textiles from, 96
tourists in, 108, 109
Cayupán (chief of Pampean Indians), 172*f*
celeste (light blue), 32
cellular phone purse (*funda*), 31
ceñidor (belt), 82
Central America, domestic workers from, 269; *see also* López, Rosa
ceremonies, and commemorative clothes, 100
Chang, Arturo, 217
charango, 127*f*
Chataigner, Gilda, 190
Chavez, Cesar, 218
Chavez, Fernando, 219
Chávez, Hugo, 218
La Chaquira en México (Castelló Yturbide and Mapellia Mozzi), 54
Chiapas, handwoven bags from, 1
Chicago Sun-Times, 265, 275
chignon (French hair style), 33–4
Chile, Far Eastern goods in, 70
China, imports from, 47, 70, 85
china poblana (Mexican costume), 4, 44–66, 52–60, 55*f*
  admirers of, 59, 65
  components of, 44–5, 54
  as disguise for fashionable women, 57
  as dress of *mestiza*, 56
  history of, 52–4
  influences on, 71–2
  name of, 53, 72
  petticoat in, 56, 60
  rebozo in, 54, 56
  republican manifestation of, 53–4
  sexual character of, 57, 59
  skirt in, 54–5
  today's, 72–3
  travel writers on, 52–3
La china poblana (Stinetorf), 54
Chinatowns, in Latin America, 5, 74
chincuete (skirt), 82
"Chinese flute," 73
Chinese immigrants, in Latin America, 73, 74
chiripá (colored cloth tied around waist), 167, 170, 173
Chivay market, 101, 103
cholita dress, 126, 131
cholita p'acha (urban Indian "ethnic" dress), 130
cholos/cholitas (urban Indians), 122–3
ch'ullus (Andean knit hats), 153–4
Cieza de León, Pedro, 17, 22
cigar smoking, 241–3
cigarette smoking, 242–3
Ciuk, Perla, 256
civil p'acha ("cosmopolitan dress"), 125, 130

Index

Clark, Marcia, 272
class
　distinction of, 82
　and Eva Perón, 259
　and marketing, 111
"classic traditional" Sakaka dress, 128
Clavé, Pelegrín, 64
Clemente Vázquez, Andrés, 236
climate, influence on fashion, 202–3
clothing, as symbol
　and barbarism, 17–24
　of civilization, 20
　of difference, 18–19
　of distinction, 22, 30
　of native identity, 18–19
　of power, 18–19
　of the "self," 189
　of social status, 17, 24–5
　of superiority, 19
clothing codes, 188–9
co-operatives, knitting, 154–5
Cobra (Sarduy), 236
Cochran, Johnnie, 271
coffee baron families, 183–4
Cohen, E., 144–5, 149
Colca Valley, 101, 106
　dolls in, 110
　mourning in, 96–101
　tourism in, 106–107
Colibrí (Sarduy), 236
Collor de Mello, Fernando, 194
Colloredo-Mansfield, R., 111
Colón, Cristóbal, 2, 17–19, 199
colonial Spanish America, 3–4, 17–30, 24, 28
color (skin), and social status, 25–6
colors; *see also* black (color)
　in *china poblana* skirt, 55–6
　of Maya Traditions' products, 151
　of Peruvian Connections products, 156
　symbolism of, 41
　and tourists' tastes, 107–8
Columbus, Christopher; *see* Colón, Cristóbal
Comentarios reales (Inca Garcilaso de la Vega), 21
commodities, ritual textiles as, 6, 96
commoditization, of identity, 93–6, 255
Compendio de la Vida y Virtudes de la Venerable Catarina de San Juan (Toussaint), 53
Conchita Alonso, María, 277
Concolorcorvo (Alonso Carrió de la Vandera), 169
Condori, Juan, 93, 94f
Condori, Modesta, 104
Confederate power, and the *peinetón*, 40
Conquest of the Desert, 167, 171
conquistador, identity of, 3
consumers; *see also* tourists

　of boundary textiles, 146
　of "ethnic" cloth, 135–7
　of historical personalities, 247–8
consumption
　and cultural mediation, 9–11
　European-style, 178–9
cool, essence of, and *guayaberismo*, 213–32
Copacabana, 8, 189–90
Copacabana Palace (Boechat), 189–90
Corcuera, Ruth, 7
Cordry, Donald, 71, 85
Cordry, Dorothy, 71, 85
corset, 58
Cortés, Hernán, 20, 23–4, 81–2
Cosas Hermosas de Guatemala, 149
cosmetics, 244
"cosmopolitan" dress (*civil p'acha*), 125–6, 130, 137–8
Costa, Gal, 192
Costume Institute, 275
Costumes of Mexico (Sayer), 52, 54
cottage industry-made garments, 125, 129
cotton, exporting to Latin America, 68
Coxcatlán Cave, 81
Craik, Jennifer, 189, 264
Crane, Diana, 229
Crawford, Joan, 243
La crónica del Perú (León), 22
creoles, 47–8
　in caste system, 46
　clothing as status symbol of, 24–5
　dress of, 47, 65
　personality of, 49
cross-dressing, as metaphor, 235–6; *see also* transvestism
Crucifixion, reenactment of, 90–1
cruciform designs, 168
Cruz, Celia, 277
La cruz en América (Quiroga), 168
Cruz, Migdalia, 256
Cuba; *see also* Havana, Cuba
　Chinese immigrants in, 73–4
　Columbus claiming, 2
　and the *guayabera*, 9, 213–14, 219, 226
　independence in, 3
　and "Jacqueline," 232–46
　revolutionary movements in, 12
　women in, 237
Cuban Revolution, 214
"cult of the dead," 80, 88
cultural formation, cross-dressing as metaphor for, 235–6
cultural imaginary, 2, 7–9
cultural mediation, and consumption, 9–11
Cultural Missions (Mexico), 82
culture, Latin American, 249–50
culture, popular vs. "high," 248–9
Curiel, Gustavo, 70

340

Index

curing, ritual use of sandals in, 85–8
Cutipa, Melitón, 103

daily wear
  ethnic dress as, 117
  in Hueyapan, Morelos, 82–5
  Mayan, 148
  mourning clothes as, 109
  of the Sakaka, 115, 122
Daly, Steven, 256
Dama Joven (Linati), 51
Dana, Richard Henry, 48, 49
Dandicat, Edwidge, 270
Darden, Christopher, 269–70
Darío, Rubén, 5, 73–4
Davis, Mike, 265
Days of the Dead, 87–8, 98
De donde son los cantantes (Sarduy), 236
"De la moda feminina" ("On Feminine Fashion"), 232
De La Renta, Oscar, 288
the dead, remembering, 99–101
Del Carril, Bonfacio, 171–3
Del Portal de Novás Calvo, Herminia, 222
Delarue Mardus, Lucie, 244
Demaray, Elyse, 6–7
department stores, 181, 207; *see also* Mappin Stores
Descola, Jean, 25
designer, as creator, 145
DeSigniS, 285; *see also Journal of the Latin American Association of Semiotics*
designs, Patagonian, 168
desire
  being object of, 240–1
  and "Jacqueline," 239–40
D'Harcourt, Raoul, 168
Díaz, Arcadio, 230
Diaz, Cameron, 276
Díaz, Porfirio, 45, 61, 65
Díaz-Abreu, Ruben, 219–20
Diaz Alcaide, Maritza, 209
Díaz del Castillo, Bernal, 17, 19, 21, 24, 81–2
Dickson, Marsha, 8–9
Didion, Joan, 271
Dietrich, Marlene, 243
difference, clothing as symbol of, 18–21, 29–30
Diniz, Leila, 192
Dinwiddie, William, 201, 202
Dior, Christian, 11, 258
Disney, and Christy Turlington, 275–6
display of clothing, "excessive," 28–9
The Doll Project, 151–2
dolls
  Colca Valley, 110
  "ethnic" Barbie, 110, 112, 210
domestic workers, 268–73; *see also* López, Rosa

Doméstica (Hondagneu-Sotelo), 268–69
Dominican Republic, 2
  and the *guayabera*, 226
Don Enriquito (Calcagno), 236
Dor, Joël, 233
D'Orleans, Louise, 63
D'Orvigny, Alcides, 33
dress, long black (*aymilla*), 114, 126
dress coat, and the poncho, 174–5
dress codes, in Aztec society, 81
dress styles, of the Sakaka, 124–5
dressing habits, and social hierarchy, 25–6
Du Bois, W. E. B., 277
Duarte de Perón, Eva; *see* Perón, Eva
Dulles, John Foster, 226
dyes, in Andean textiles, 134

Echeverría, Luis, 225
Echeverría, Rosario, 64
Echeverría Álvarez, Luis, 218
economy
  agro-pastroal, 132–5
  Puerto Rican, 206–7
  rural, 103
  of the Sakaka, 121
Ecuador, Asian goods in, 70
Eisenhower, Dwight, 226
"El que paga el peinetón" ("He Who Pays the Peinetón"), 41–2
El Salvador, 271–2, 273, 277–8; *see also* "Salvadoranness"
elderly women, wearing *ixcacles*, 82–3, 86
elites
  Brazilian, 186–7
  cultural, 250
  Mexican, 60–1
  Puerto Rican, 200–1, 205–6, 208–9
Ellis, Havelock, 242–3
embroidered clothes
  and commoditization of identity, 93–6
  Far East influence on, 71–2
  for mourning rituals, 97
  for ritual battles, 115
  of the Sakaka, 114–41
  for tourists, 95, 101–5, 104–5, 105, 112
emigration, and burial customs, 88
"empire" dress, 8
Encyclopedia of Contemporary Latin American and Caribbean Cultures (López), 217
English influence; *see also* Mappin Stores
  in Brazil, 8, 176–8, 180–2, 187
  in Mexico, 52
Enriqueta Faber (Clemente Vázquez), 236
Escobar, Angela, 84f
Escritos sobre un cuerpo (Sarduy), 236
esmoquin (smoking suit), 241, 243
Espinosa, Carmen, 62

341

Index

Esquire, 274–275
Esquire's Encyclopedia of Twentieth Century Men's Fashions, 224
Esquivel, Antonio María, 49
Estação da Luz (Station of Light), 180
estancia workers, 173–4
Estefan, Gloria, 277
"ethnic" art, 135
"ethnic" Barbie and Ken dolls, 110, 112, 210
"ethnic" cloth, antique, 135–7
"ethnic" dress, 125, 126
  as daily wear, 117
  and globalization, 5
  of the Sakaka, 6, 127–8, 131, 137–8
  urban Indian, 130
  young people wearing, 117
ethnic groups, indigenous (*ayllu*), 118–19
ethnic identity
  in Bolivia, 117–18
  and clothes, 113
  of Kirkawi, 120–1
  of Sakaka, 120–1
ethnicity, marketing of, 95, 101–12
European influence
  in Brazil, 184, 186
  in colonial Mexico, 46, 65–6
  on the *peinetón*, 33
  in postcolonial Mexico, 44–66
  on style of consumption, 178–9
  on wealthy people, 82
Eva Perón Foundation, 258
evangelism, and burial customs, 80
Evans, Caroline, 226–8
The Evening Post, 201
"Evita"; *see* Peròn, Eva
Evita (film), 260–1
Evita (musical), 259
"exotic"
  embroidered garments as, 105
  Far East as, 75
  Latin America as, 75
  and tourists, 106
"Extravagances of 1834" (Bacle), 36–7
"eyelet" lace, 8, 204, 205f, 208–10

Faber, Enriqueta, 236
The Face of Fashion (Craik), 264
Face of the Twentieth Century Award (Metropolitan Museum of Art), 11, 265
factory-made clothes, 125, 131
  Sakaka wearing, 114, 117, 134–5
factory-spun yarns, 135, 138
Facundo (Sarmiento), 174
Fair Trade, 148
Fair Trade Federation, 152
Falini, Daniela, 256
Far East immigration, 74
Far East imports, 68, 70–1, 73

Far Eastern influence
  on Latin American fashion, 4–5, 66–75
  on Mexican porcelain, 70
  on silk embroidery, 71–2
The Farming of Bones (Dandicat), 270
fashion
  and the cultural imaginary, 7–9
  as expressing independence, 3
  language of, 235
  and politics, 194
  and postcolonial formation, 237
  reason for development of, 67
fashion, women's; *see* women's fashion
fashion magazines, 63–4, 194, 207; *see also* specific magazines (i.e. *Social*, *Vogue*, etc.)
The Fashion System (Barthes), 277
Federals, clothing identifying, 31–2
Femenías, Blenda, 6
feminine, smoking as, 242
feminist movement, in Puerto Rico, 206
feng shui, in Latin America, 74–5
Ferdinand VII, 47, 50
Fernández, Roberto, 216
Fernández de Amado Blanco, Isabel, 221
Fernández Retamar, Roberto, 215
Ferrer, Raúl, 215
ferronerie (Mexican brow ornament), 48–9
Ferry, Gabriel (Louis de Bellemare), 58–9
Festidanza, 107
fetish fashions, 188, 193–5
fiber, used by Sakaka weavers, 133
fiesta wear, in Hueyapan, Morelos, 82–5
Financial Times, 274, 277
Fontaine, Joan, 258
footwear, 79–80, 82; *see also* ixcacles
Forastelli, Fabricio, 11–13
foreigners, wearing *guayabera*s, 213–14; *see also* tourists
Fortina Martínez, María, 89
Founders' Day, 106–107
Fourth Annual Ibero-American Summit, 214–15
Fox, Vicente, 218
Fraser, Nicholas, 258
The French Experience in Mexico (Barker), 61
French influence,
  in Argentina, 33–4
  in Brazil, 185, 186
  in the fashion press, 63–4
  in Mexico, 50–1, 52
  in Puerto Rico, 202
  in Rio de Janeiro, 179
  in vocabulary, 184, 235
fret, labyrinthine, 168–9
Freud, Sigmund, 239, 242
Frida, Naturaleza Viva (dir. Leluc), 256
Frida (film), 256

Index

Frida (play), 256
Friedlander, J., 87
funda (cellular phone purse), 31

Gabeira, Fernando, 193
Gabriel, Mike, 272
Gage, Thomas, 66, 68–9
Garber, Marjorie, 232–4, 245–6
Garbo, Greta, 276
García Canclini, Nestor, 249–50
García Márquez, Gabriel, 216
Garota de Ipanema (*The Girl from Ipanema*) (Jobim), 188, 191
gaucho (Argentine cowboy), 167
　lifestyle of, 173
　as symbol, 170–1, 174
　wearing ponchos, 7, 165–6, 169–72
Gaultier, Jean Paul, 11, 255
La Gazeta Mercantil (*The Mercantile Gazette*), 34, 38
gender, textual, 246
"Gender, Ethnicity, and Piety: The Case of the China Poblana" (Gillespie), 53
gender roles, 35–6, 40–1
Generation of 1837 (literary society), 35–6
George Washington Goméz (Paredes), 266
German House, 183
Gil Moreno, Manuel, 171
Gillespie, Jeanne, 53
Gillie & Woodward, 207
Gilman, Sander L., 244
Giordano, Roberto, 33
The Girl from Ipanema (*Garota de Ipanema*) (Jobim), 188, 191
Giroletti, D., 177
Giroux, Henry, 264
Glassie, H., 144, 158–9
Goddess of the Americas/La Diosa de las Américas (Castillo), 274
Godey's Lady's Book, 64
Goldenberg, Miriam, 195
Goldman, Ronald Lyle, 265
Goldman, Shirfa, 255
Gontijo, Fabiano, 189
González, Alberto Rex, 168
González Padín Co., 207
Good Friday (Viernes Santo), 97, 99–100
Gore, Jr., Al, 277
Goudvis, Patricia, 268
gown, white muslin, 61–3
Goya, Francisco, 51
Graburn, N. H., 145
Gramsci, Antonio, 262
green (color), symbolism of, 41
Greslebin, Héctor, 168
"gringos," and the color black, 93–113
Grisette (Parisian costume), 4
Gross, Michael, 275

Grosz, E., 278
Guaman Poma de Ayala, F., 17, 23
Guatemalan women, 150–1
guayabera (Cuban embroidered cotton shirt), 9
　in the Caribbean, 9, 218
　Castro wearing, 214–15, 223–4
　in Cuba, 214, 216–17, 219
　demand for, 226
　Donna Karen's, 228
　foreigners wearing, 213–14
　García Márquez wearing, 216
　history of, 214
　and identity, 229
　kinds of, 229–31
　in Mexico, 219, 225–6
　origins of, 217–22
　of Pedro Cab, 225
　in the Philippines, 217
　political leaders wearing, 218–19
　popularity of, 221–4, 226–9
　as sign of progress, 223
　as specialty garment, 230
　symbolic weight of, 214
　in the United States, 215–16, 220, 224–5
　use and abuse of, 221–4
guayaberismo, 213–32
guayahuipil (*guayabera–huipil* hybrid), 225
Guerrero, Gonzalo, 21
Guevara, Ernesto "Che," 10, 250, 285
Guillén, Nicolás, 224
Guillermoprieto, Alma, 269
Gurza, Agustín, 228
Gutiérrez, Raúl, 222–3
Guy, Donna, 40–1

hair designs, French, 33–4
Halperin, Ian, 277
Hamm, Margherita, 201, 202, 204
Handler, R., 142, 143, 144, 159
handmade clothes, versus factory made, 125
handwoven Sakaka garments, 128–31
Haraway, Donna, 256
Harlow, Jean, 258
Harris, Olivia, 121
hats, 104, 153
haute couture, and middle-class women, 191–2
Havana, Lyceum Lawn Club of, 214, 221–2, 224
Hayek, Salma, 256
head coverings, 56, 204; see also *rebozo* (scarf)
healing, *ixcacles* as aiding, 85–6
heirloom textiles, 6, 100–1, 136, 138
"help," and selling, 101, 104
Hendrickson, Carol, 148–9
"Henriette," 245
Hepburn, Audrey, 274, 276

Index

Hernández, José, 174
Hernández, Josefina, 83, 87, 90
Hernández Cruz, Victor, 271
Herrera, Carolina, 288
Herrera, Hayden, 251, 254
Herrick, Jane, 64
Heydenreich, Daniel, 183
Hijuelos, Oscar, 227
Hill, Robert, 203
"His/Her Majesty: Fashion" ("S.M. La moda"), 232; *see also* Carpentier, Alejo
Hispanic, 266, 274–5
Hispanicvista, 228
Hispaniola, black slaves in, 19f
Historia de la Ciudad de Puebla de los Angeles (Carreón), 72
Historia verdadera de la conquista de la Neuva España (Castillo), 20–1
homosexual, and "transvestite," 234
Hondagneu-Sotelo, Pierrette, 268–9
"hot-cold" theory, and healing, 85–6
huaraches de ixtle (maguey-fiber sandles), 79, 82
Hueyapan, Morelos
  burial rituals in, 87–8
  daily and fiesta wear in, 82–5
  shops in, 84–5
  traditional dress of, 84f
  younger women in, 80
huipiles, Maya, 3, 151, 152, 225
Hurlbut, Annie, 155, 157
Hurlbut, Biddie, 155, 157
husbands, symbolism of clothing for, 28–9

"I am a Mexican First and Foremost" ("Primero soy mexicano"), 219
I Love Lucy, 227
Ichaso, Francisco, 221, 222
icons, Latin American, 10–11; *see also* Kahlo, Frida; Perón, Eva
identity
  commoditization of, 93–6
  construction of, 17, 29–30
  dress as defining, 116–18
  and ethnicity, 105–12
  and writing, 233
ideology, and style of dress, 31–2
If the Mango Tree Could Speak (Goudvis), 268
immigration, to Latin America, 73–4, 180
Incas, clothing of, 22–3, 164
India, exports from, 68
Indian ethnic dress, 130, 137–8; *see also* specific peoples (i.e. Pampean Indians, Sakaka, etc.)
indianilla criolla de algodón, 63
Ingres in Fashion (Ribeiro), 63
International Committee for Intercambios Culturales of El Salvador (Cultural Exchanges), 11, 278
Ipanema Beach, 191, 195–6
Isabelle, Arsène, 33
The Itching Parrot (Lizardi), 49
Ito, Lance, 271–2
ixcacles (maguey-fiber sandals), 5, 79–92, 83f–84f
  and ancestral past, 90–1
  in Aztec society, 81
  cost of, 92
  and "cult of the dead," 80, 88
  documentation of, 80–1
  elements of, 81
  healing properties of, 85, 86
  history of, 81–2
  making of, 5, 89–91
  selling, 88–92, 90
  and social status, 84
  for tourists, 80, 91–2
  who wears, 82–3, 86, 90
  workmanship of, 83–4
Ixchel (goddess of weaving), 147

jacket, in *china poblana* costume, 59–60
"Jacqueline" (Alejo Carpentier), 10
  and articulation of desire, 239–40
  and Cuban culture, 232–46
  as image, 234–45
  and symbolic order, 238–40
  textual transvestism of, 244–46
Jameson, Fredric, 261
Jeudi, Henri-Pierre, 193
jewelry, 3, 204
The Jew's Body (Gilman), 244
Jobim, Antônio Carlos, 188, 197
Jobim, Tom, 191
Johnson, Lyman, 69
"Jones Act," 209
José de Uruquiza, Justo, 173
Journal of the Latin American Association of Semiotics, 285; *see also* DeSigniS
Jules-Rosette, B., 142
Jurewicz, Patricia, 93–4, 95, 99

Kaelin, Brian "Kato," 272–3
Kafka, Franz, 273
Kahlo, Frida, 9, 247–62
  dress of, 10–11, 65, 251–5
  expressing Mexican identity, 252
  films on, 256–7
  image of, as product, 10–11, 248
  and Marxism, 251
  as myth, 261
  paintings of, 251–2
  physical condition of, 255–6
  as pop icon, 251–7
  popularity of, 254–5, 257

Index

Karen, Donna, 9, 228
Keim-Shenk, Melody, 6–7
"Ken" and "Barbie" dolls, "ethnic," 110, 112, 210
Kieffer, Eduardo Gudiño, 34–5
Kirkawi (people), dress of, 120–1
Kitching, John, 182
Klein, Calvin, 275–6
knitting, Andean, 153, 158, 159
knitting co-operatives, 154–5
"knowing," and selling, 101
Kroeber, A. L., 142–3, 158
kurti (Kirkawi textile style), 120–1

El laberinto de la soledad (*Labyrinth of Solitude*) (Paz), 234
Lace: A History (Levey), 50
lack of clothing, and barbarism, 2, 19–20, 22–4
Lagartera, Spain, 54, 59, 60
language
   in El Salvador, 271–2
   of fashion, 235
   and the *peinetón*, 39–40
   of *runa* and *vecinos*, 120
   symbolic substitutions in, 233
Laó-Montes, Agustín, 267
Largillière, Nicolas de, 202
Larrañaga advertisements, 241–2, 244
Larrañaga Nacionales, 241–2
Larsen, Nella, 277
Las Casas, Bartolomé de, 2
Latin America; *see also* specific countries (i.e. Cuba, Mexico, etc.)
   art and culture in, 249–50
   caste system in, 2–3
   historical overview of, 2–5
Latin America: Its Cities and Ideas (Romero), 58
Latin American fashion
   defined, 1
   history of, 1–2
   influence of, 9
   messages of, 13
Latin American Fashion Council, 288
Latin American icons, 10–11; *see also* Kahlo, Frida; Perón, Eva
Latina/Latino nationalities, representations of, 266
Lauer, Mirko, 249
Le Guern, Michel, 32
Leante, César, 233
Lecomte, Hippolyte, 51
LeCount, C., 153
Leluc, Paul, 256
Leno, Jay, 272
Lenten fairs, 88–92
León, Nicolás, 71

Levey, Santina, 50
Lewin. R., 139
Linati, Claudio, 51, 62
Lindauer, Margaret A., 251–4
Linnekin, J., 142–4, 159
literature
   differentiation of the "other" in, 18–24
   on Far Eastern imports, 73
   postcolonial Argentinian, 32–3, 36, 41–3
   transvestism in, 236
The Little Sea Princess, 189–91
Littrell, Mary, 6–7, 145
Lizardi, José Joaquín Fernandez, 49, 71
"Lo que cuesta un peinetón" ("What a Peinetón Costs"), 41
Lobo, María Luisa, 100
López, Ana, 217
López, Rosa, 263–79
   as defense witness, 264–5
   as entertainment material, 272
   image of, 263–4
   narrative of, 272–3
   relocation of, 273
   representing domestic workers, 267, 268, 278
   "Salvadoranness" of, 11, 264–7, 271, 279
   social commentary surrounding, 273
   testimony of, 269–70, 270, 271
López-Gydosh, Dilia, 8–9
Lords of All the World (Padgen), 45–6
Louis XIV and his Family (De Largillière), 202
Lucero, H., 146
Lurie, Alison, 226, 229
luto (mourning wear), 93; *see also* mourning wear
Lyceum Lawn Club of Havana, 214, 221–2, 224
Lynd, Martha, 150–1
Lyon, G. F., 49
Lyotard, Françoise, 247

Maciel, Luiz Carlos, 8, 192
MacNeish, Richard, 81
Madonna
   as Eva Perón, 11, 257–62, 260–1
   as Frida Kahlo, 256–7
Magalhães, Rosa, 195
Magical Urbanism (Davis), 265
Magón, José Joaquín, 53
maguey-fiber sandals; *see ixcacles*
maid, Salvadoran, 268–273
Maid in the USA (Romero), 269
Maillot, Monsieur, 190
maja (Spanish costume), 4, 51, 59
Major, John S., 67, 75
Making Face, Making Soul (Anzaldúa), 278
Mamani brothers, 103, 115, 119, 137

Index

The Mambo Kings Play Songs of Love (Hijuelos), 227
Manila Galleon trade, 68, 70–1
Mansilla, Lucio V., 165–7
Mantegazza, Pablo, 170–1
mantilla (shawl), 8, 34, 45
   Puerto Rican women wearing, 204, 208, 210
Manual del Viajero en Méjico (Arróniz), 57–8
Manuel de Rosas, Juan, 173
Mappin, Herbert Joseph, 182
Mappin, Walter John, 182
Mappin Historical Archive, 7–8, 184
Mappin Stores, 176–87
   advertisements for, 183f, 184
   "being seen" at, 186
   and Brazilian elite, 186–7
   items sold in, 182, 185–6
   in São Paolo, 176–82
   social impact of, 7–8
   and sophistication, 182–5
"Mariposas en el Andamio" ("Butterflies on the Scaffold"), 236
marketing
   and class, 111
   ethnicity, 95, 101–2
   and NGOs, 103–4
   to tourists, 107, 109–10, 112
marketplaces, 58, 88–92
Marryat, Captain, 48
Martí, José, 215
Martín Fierro (Hernández), 170, 174
Martínez, Georgina, 230
Martínez Cuenca, Froylan, 88
Martínez de Compañon, Baltazar, 27f
Marxism, 251
masculinity, symbols of
   scars as, 244
   smoking as, 241–3
   tuxedo as, 241–2
   in women's fashion, 244
Masiello, Francine, 35–6
Mauad, A. M., 179
Mayan
   backstrap weavers, 147–50, 158
   history, 148–9
   huipiles, 3, 151, 152
   traje, 147–8
Maya Traditions, 7, 149–52, 157; *see also* Peruvian Connections
   as company, 148
   customers of, 151
   goals of, 150–1
   products of, 152
   sales approach of, 142–3, 152
   tradition for, 144–5, 159
   wages of weavers at, 150
Maya women, traje of, 147–8

Mayagüez (Puerto Rico), 207
Meisch, Lynn A., 82
Mejía, Leonardo, 102, 105
Meléndez, Mariselle, 3
Melo, Patrícia, 188
Melodia, Luis, 192
men; *see also* women
   Asian influences on, 69
   as *ixcacle* makers, 91
   knitting *ch'ullus*, 154
   Mayan, 148
   mourning garments for, 97
   Sakaka, 125–9
   on women's clothing, 27–9
Méndez Capote, Renée, 74
Menell-Kinberg, Monica, 260
Menghin, Osvaldo, 168
mestizaje (racial mixing), 2–3
mestizo/mestiza (Spanish-Indians), 27f
   in caste system, 46
   dress of, 47, 56, 65
   identity of, 122
metonymy, 32
Métraux, Guy, 199
Metropolitan Museum of Art, 11, 265, 275
Mexican dress
   of elite, 60–1
   European influences on, 65, 66
   and fashion press, 63–5
   and the *guayabera*, 219, 225–6, 226
   Kahlo wearing, 10–11, 65, 251–5
   travel writers on, 45
Mexican fashion publications, 64
Mexican Indian Costume (Cordry, Cordry), 85
Mexican porcelain, 70
Mexican Postcards (Monsiváis), 271
Mexican women, 4, 48–9, 58, 63–4
Mexico
   china poblana in; *see* china poblana
   Chinese immigrants in, 74
   colonial, 46–9
   French retail trade in, 61
   independence of, 48
   ixcacles (sandals) in, 5, 79–92
   national form of dress in, 70
   postcolonial, 44–6, 50–51
   Spanish settlers in, 45–6
   textiles in, 62–3
   working class women in, 4
Mexico City, 51–2, 74–5
Mexique (exhibition), 254
Miami, Florida, 221–2, 284
Miele, Carlos, 12
Mignolo, Walter, 18
Milbank, Caroline R., 210
Miller, Marilyn, 9
Milne & Faulkner of Manchester, 181

Index

Milner, F., 252, 254
Mintz, Jane, 149, 151–2, 157
Miranda, Carmen, 250
"modern traditional" Sakaka dress, 128–30
modistes, French, 60–1
Moghadam, Valentine, 262
Molina, Alfred, 256
Molina, Igor, 230
Molnar, Andrea, 67
"mom-deceiver," 191
Monroe, Marilyn, 258
Monsiváis, Carlos, 271
Montalban, Ricardo, 277
Montezuma, 23, 24
Moore, Robin, 237
Moorish influence, on Mexican fashion, 54
Moraes, Vinicius de, 191
Moreno, Mario, 145, 271
Morgan, Thaïs, 233
Mörner, Magnus, 67
Morris, Charles, 203
Morrison, Toni, 278
Morumbi Fashion, 194
Mothers Clubs, 134–5
Mothers of the Plaza de Mayo, 12
motifs
  in Andean knitting, 153–4
  Asian, 69
mourning, black as signifying, 93–113
mourning clothes
  "authentic," 108
  and black (color), 93–4
  and customs, 96–7
  as daily wear, 109
  phullu as, 98–9, 101
  tourists desire for, 108
Mudge, Jean McClure, 70
"A Mughal Princess in Baroque New Spain" (Bailey), 52–3
Mujer en traje de batalla (Benítez Rojo), 236
Mulattos, dress of, 26, 46, 68
Museum of Popular Culture (Mexico City), 91
Museum Store Association Exposition, 152
muslin gown, white, 61–3
My Birth (Kahlo), 256–7
My Dress Hangs There (Kahlo), 253, 254
Mythologies (Barthes), 276

Nahua society, 5, 82–6
nakedness, as sign of barbarism, 2, 19–20, 22–4
Nash, J., 111, 149
Nationalizing Blackness (Moore), 237
natives, "nakedness" of, 2, 17–18, 67; *see also* nakedness, as sign of barbarism
Naufragios (Cabeza de Vaca), 20
Navarro, Marysa, 258

Nebel, Carl, 55–6, 55f
The New Princeton Encyclopedia of Poetry and Poetics, 32
The New York Times, 155, 270–1
NGOs, and marketing, 103–4
Nicaragua, 12, 70
Niessen, Sandra, 66
North American Free Trade Agreement (NAFTA), 12
northern Potosí, the Sakaka in; *see* Sakaka
Nueva Coronica y Buen Gobierno (Poma de Ayala), 23

O Estado de São Paolo, 182, 183f
Ober, Frederick, 201
O.J. Simpson trial, 264–5, 269
  and Rosa López; *see* López, Rosa
Olivera, Ruth, 57
"On Feminine Fashion" ("De la moda feminina"), 232
order, symbolic, 232, 238–40
Organic Act (1901), 206
Orlove, B., 111
Ortega, Lauro, 85
Ortiz, Fernando, 236
Ortiz, Renato, 249
the "other"
  differentiating, 18–24, 19–20
  Latin America as, 67
  and physical appearance, 21
  recognition of, 30
  "seeing" as containing, 25
Oviedo, José, 262
Oxfam Trading, 154

Padín, González, 207
Pagden, Anthony, 45–46
Page-Reeves, J., 155
Palencia, Isabel de, 59
Palomina, Erika, 195
Pampean Indians, 166–9, 172f
Panajachel, Guatemala, 150
Panama, Far Eastern goods in, 70
Pancrazio, James, 9–10
Pané, Fray Ramón, 17, 19
Paredes, Américo, 266
Parker, Alan, 259–60, 261
Passing and Pedagogy (Caughie), 238
Passing (Larsen), 277
past, ancestral, and *ixcacles*, 90–1
Patagonian designs, 168
patillas (sideburns), 32
paulistas (São Paolo inhabitants), 7–8, 178–80
Pavelic, Bill, 270
Paz, Octavio, 234
"Pearl of the Antilles" (Díaz-Abreu), 219
Pech, Jorge Alberto, 225

peinetón (Argentinian hair comb), 4
  The British Packet on, 33–4, 36, 39–40
  and the *chignon*, 34
  criticism of women wearing, 37–9
  emergence of, 33–4
  as metonym, 32–3
  social codes regarding, 37–8
  and space, 34–9, 42
  symbolism of, 33, 41
  as term, 40, 42–3
  in the arts, 36–7, 41–3
"Peinetones on the Street" (Bacle), 38f
Pellarolo, Silvia, 258, 260
peninsulares (European-born Spaniards), 46–8
The People of the State of California v. Orenthal James Simpson, 264–5
Pérez, Juvencio, 91
Pérez, Louis A., 237
Pérez Firmat, Gustavo, 235
Pérez Tejeda, Jaquelina, 88
Perez Zamudio, Camila, 84f
El periquillo sarniento (*The Itching Parrot*) (Lizardi), 71
Perón, Eva, 9, 250, 257–62
  dress of, 11, 251, 258
  as First Lady, 258–9
  image of, as product, 10–11, 248, 259
  Madonna portraying, 260–1
  and Marxism, 251
  as myth, 261
  possessions of, 259
Perón, Juan Domingo, 260
Peru, 25, 70
Peruvian Connections, 7, 154, 155–7, 158; see also Maya Traditions
  customers of, 156
  goals of, 155–6
  products of, 156–7
  sales approach of, 142–3
  tradition for, 144–5, 159
Peruvian textiles, 153–5
petticoat, in *china poblana*, 56, 60
Philippines, 47, 68, 70–1, 217
phullu (shawl), 98–9, 101
physical transformation, and recognition, 20–2
Pichardo's *Diccionario provincial casi razonado de vozes y frases cubanas*, 218
Pinheiro, Heloisa, 191
Pocahontas, 275
poetry, on the *peinetón*, 41–2
politics
  and beach fashions, 192–3
  and fashion, 12, 40, 194
  and the *guayabera*, 3, 218–9
"pompadour," 208
Ponce, Puerto Rico, 207
ponchillo (small poncho), 163

ponchos, 7, 163–75
  described, 163
  and the dress coat, 174–5
  gauchos wearing, 165–6, 169–72
  history of, 163–4
  as mourning garment, 97
  nineteenth-century, 170–4, 172f
  of Pampean Indians, 167–9
  Southern, 165–7
  symbolism of, 163–4, 170–171
  in travel writings, 170–1
popular culture, vs. "high" culture, 248–9
porcelain, Mexican, 70
porta-abanico (necklace with folded fan), 8–9, 205f, 209
  in Puerto Rican women's dress, 204–5, 208, 210
Portillo y Pacheco, José López, 225
Portlock, Henry, 182
postmodern condition, 247, 248–9
Potosí, Northern (Bolivia), 115, 118–19
  the Sakaka in; see Sakaka
"pouter-pigeon blousing," 208
power, clothing as symbol of, 18–19
pregnancy, and *ixcacles*, 85–86
prestige, of the poncho, 164, 166
Primero soy mexicano (*I am a Mexican First and Foremost*), 219
The Princess and the Barrio Boy, 229
princess-style dress, 208
Prío, Carlos, 218, 224
"Pro-Family Mothers," 38
prosthesis fashion, 188, 191–3
prostitution, and gender roles, 40–1
Pryce, Jonathan, 260
public space
  and the *peinetón*, 34–9, 41–2
  women's mobility in, 27
Puerto Rican women
  achievements of, 202
  American influence on, 209–10
  dress of, 202–4
  education of, 201–2, 205–6
  influences on, 200
  jewelry and headwear of, 204
  and the *porta-abanico*, 204–5
  professionalization of, 209–10
  social role of, 208–9
  travel writers on, 200–1, 203
Puerto Rico
  American influence in, 199–200, 203, 210
  feminist movement in, 206
  the *guayabera* in, 226
  historical overview of, 199–200
  independence in, 3
  reading in, 201–2
  Spanish influence in, 198
  variety of fashion in, 207–8

Index

Quinn, Anthony, 277
Quinto, Froylán, 103
Quiroga, Adán, 168

racial categories
 "appropriate" dress for, 26
 and caste systems, 46
 role of clothing in maintaining, 29–30
Raining Backwards (Fernández), 216
Rama, Angel, 285
Ramírez Aznar, Luis A., 225
Ramos, Alonso, 72
Ramos, Ricardo ("The Tourist"), 105
Randall, Kimberly, 4
Ranquel Indians, 165, 167
La Razón de mi Vida (Eva Perón's biography), 259
Real Pragmática (1716), 25
Réard, Louis, 190
rebozo (scarf)
 and the *china poblana*, 45, 54, 56, 73
 influences on, 71–72
 and social status, 3
 recognition; *see also* "being seen"
 clothes as symbolic tool of, 17
 of the "other," 30
 and physical transformations, 20–2
 and Sakaka dress, 139–140
The Regional Costumes of Spain (Palencia), 59
Relación acerca de las antigüedades de los indios (Pané), 19
representation
 clothing as system of, 29–30
 of Latina/o personalities, 266
 of the *peinetón*, 40–3
Revista de Copacabana (Benedetti), 189
Reyes Castillo, Candido, 88
Ribeiro, Aileen, 63
Rice, Tim, 259
Ries, Nancy, 128
Rio de Janeiro, Brazil
 beach fashions in, 8, 188–197
 and the bikini, 191
 discourses on, 188
 French influence in, 179
 Mappin Stores in, 176
 nineteenth-century conditions of, 177
 and São Paolo, 178–9
 today's styles in, 195–7
Riordan, Richard J., 279
ritual attire, 101–5; *see also* mourning clothes
ritual battles (tinku), 115, 118–19
rituals, use of sandals in, 85–8
River Plate region, ponchos of, 163–75
Rivera, Diego, 252, 256
Rivera, Gabriela, 83
Rivera, Juanita Rosales, 84
Rivero, Ramón, 223

Robinson, Albert, 201–2
Rochas, Marcel, 258
Roche, Daniel, 25
Rodríguez, Clara, 266
Rodríguez, Juan Carlos, 218
Rodríguez Angulo, Filiberto, 223
Roig de Leuschenring, Emilio, 236
Romero, Benito, 91, 92
Romero, José, 58
Romero, Mary, 269
Rondstadt, Linda, 276
Root, Regina A., 287f
Rosales, Juanita, 83
Rosas, Juan Manuel de, 31–2, 40
Rosas, Mariano, 166
rose-colored gowns, in Mexico City, 63
Rua do Ouvidor, 176–7
Rubião, Olga, 184–5
runa (indigenous people), garments of, 117–18, 120, 122, 125–6, 130–1
rural economy, 103
Rush, Geoffrey, 256
Rushdie, Salman, 272
Ruth y Naomi, 148
Rutz, H. J., 111

S-curve mono-bosom look, 208
Sacaca, Alonso de Ibañez, 119–20
sacred practices, and secular practices, 108–9
Sahagún, Fray Bernardino de, 89–90
Sáiz, García, 68
Sakaka (people), 119–21
 background of, 118–19
 bartering among, 121
 commercializing antique textiles, 136
 dress of, 6, 116f, 115–7, 122, 125–31, 139–40
 economy of, 121
 as farmers, 120
 function of cloth for, 124
 and Kirkawi, 120–1
 new traditional style of, 127, 131–2, 139
 sexual division of labor of, 124–5
 textiles of, 123–4, 132–5
 wages for weaving, 136
 wearing factory-made clothing, 134–5
 wearing Western-style dress, 131
Salvadoran American Health Foundation, 278
Salvadoran maids, 268–73
"Salvadoranness"
 of Lopez, 264–5, 271, 279
 in popular culture, 267, 273–4
 of Turlington, 264, 265, 276–7, 279
 in the United States, 11, 263–79
Samkha *ayllu* folklore festival, 127f
San Felipe, Tepemexalco, 79, 81
San Francisco Chronicle, 278–9
San Juan, Puerto Rico, 199, 207

Index

San Martín, José de, 3
Sancti Spíritus, 219–220, 230
sandals, 81, 85–8; see also ixcacles
Santiago, Chile, 74–5
Santiestaban, Argelio, 218
São Paolo, Brazil
   European influences in, 180–1, 184
   immigrants in, 180
   Mappin Stores in, 7–8, 176–82
Sarduy, Severo, 236, 238
Sarmiento, Domingo Faustino, 174
The Satanic Verses (Rushdie), 272
Satorious, Carl, 64
Savigliano, Marta, 261
Sayer, Chloë, 52, 54, 68, 71
scars, as masculine, 244
Scheinman, Pamela, 5
Schiaparelli, Elsa, 11, 255, 259
Schobinger, Juan, 168
secular practices, and sacred practices, 108–9
Seducir (Delarue Mardus), 244
"seeing," and containing the "other," 25
"seen, being," 20, 186
Self-Portrait on the Border between Mexico and the US (Kahlo), 253
Self-Portrait with Necklace (Kahlo), 257
selling, strategies of, 101–4
Senillosa, Felipe, 170
Sennett, Richard, 184
Sensuntepeque, El Salvador, 273
Serrano, Pedro el, 20, 21, 22
service industry, 268–73
Sevcenko, N., 181
Sex and Danger in Buenos Aires (Guy), 40–1
sexuality
   and the bikini, 196–7
   and the *china poblana*, 57, 59
Shawls, Crinolines, Filigree (Espinosa), 62
Shils, E., 143, 158
"shirtjacket" (*guayabera*), 225
shoes, shining, 82
Sifuentes Jáuregui, Ben, 234
silk, importing, 68, 165
Simians, Cyborgs, and Women (Haraway), 256
Simpson, Nicole Brown, 265
Simpson, O.J., 264–5
La simulación (Sarduy), 236, 238
sistema de castas; *see* caste system
skin color, and social status, 25–6
skirt, in china poblana, 54–5
slaves, black, 19f
"S.M. La moda" ("His/Her Majesty: Fashion"), 232, 235
smoking
   as feminine, 242, 243
   as masculine, 241–3
smoking suit (esmoquin), 241, 243

social hierarchy
   clothing as threatening to, 26
   in colonial Spanish America, 24
   for the Incas, 23
   maintaining, 25
   in the marketplace, 58
   and status, 3, 24–6, 84, 122
   and upward mobility, 30
Social (magazine), 10, 232, 242, 245
socialist anti-fashion, 12
Solís, Manuel de J., 71
sophistication
   and Mappin Stores, 182–4
   smoking as sign of, 243
   as term, 184–5
souvenirs, clothes as, 109–10; see also tourists
Spain, 52, 18–21; see also Lagartera, Spain
Spanish-American War, 8–9, 198–9, 203, 208
Spanish aristocracy, 24–5
Spanish attire, in Mexico, 50–1
Spanish culture, head coverings in, 56
Spanish influence, in Puerto Rico, 8, 198, 200, 202
Spivak, Gayatri, 13, 286
sports, and fashion, 189–90, 241
Steele, Valerie, 67, 75
Stewart, Susan, 105
Stinetorf, Lousie, 54
Stone, Oliver, 259–60
stores, dry-goods, in Puerto Rico, 203, 207
Suárez Solís, Rafael, 221
Sula (Morrison), 278
Sullca, Livia, 110
superiority, clothes as sign of, 17, 19, 29–30
surfers, and beach fashions, 193
Susman, Warren, 194

Taiwan, imports from, 85
Tamar, Norma, 191
Taymor, Julie, 256
Tehuacán Valley, Puebla, 81
Tehuana dress, of Frida Kahlo, 252–3, 253, 254–5, 255
Tejada, Juan, 104
Tejeda, Flaviana, 91
Tenorio, Josefa de, 3
Tepemaxalco, 79, 80, 81
Terán, Marcelina, 98
tertulia (weekly gathering), 52
textile art; *see* boundary art
textiles
   Andean, 117, 123–4, 134
   Asian, 67, 69
   heirloom, 136, 138
   Mayan, 148–9
   in Mexico, 62–3
   from the past, 144
   Peruvian, 153–5

Sakaka, 123–4, 132–5
  and tradition, 143–4
textual transvestism, 232, 238–9, 244–6
"The Death of the Empress of China" (Darío), 73
The Mosquito Coast (Theroux), 268
Theroux, Paul, 268
thong, 192; *see also* bikini
Tierney, J., 108
Time, 274–6
"time," and selling, 101, 104
Times of Brazil, 182–3
Tinajero, Araceli, 4–5
tinkus (ritual battles), 118–19
Tlatelolco market, 81–2
Todas Almas (All Souls' Day), 97–8
Todos Santos (All Saint's Day), 97–8, 101
The Tonight Show, 272
Toobin, Jeffrey, 270
Torrico, Cassandra, 135
tourists
  artisans producing for, 6, 80, 91–2, 95
  and black (color), 93–113, 94, 113
  and exoticism, 106
  and the *guayabera*, 224–5
  and promotion of ethnicity, 105–12
  and sale of ritual attire, 79, 101–5
  marketing to, 109–10, 112
  tastes of, 105, 107–8
  textiles for, 148
Toussaint, Manuel, 53, 54
Townsend, Mary Ashley, 64
Trabajo (Guillén), 224
tradition
  and boundary textiles, 144–7
  marketing of, 6–7
  meaning of, 142
  representations of, 142–59
  as term, 143–4
  and textiles from the past, 144
"traditional"
  concept of, 67
  dress, 125–6
  and the Sakaka, 127–8, 131–2, 139
  and world trade, 2
traje (traditional Mayan dress), 3, 147–8
Trajes civiles, militares y religiosos de Mexico (Linati), 51
Trajes y costumbres de la provincia de Buenos Aires (Bacle), 37f, 38f
transvestism
  in Argentina, 285–6
  and fashion, 9–10, 232–46, 285–6
  in literary and cultural history, 236
  textual, 232, 238–9, 244–6
Transvestism, Masculinity and Latin American Literature (Sifuentes Jáuregui), 234

transvestites, and Rio's beaches, 195
travel writers
  on the *china poblana*, 52, 53
  on Mexican fashion, 45, 65
  on ponchos, 170–1
  on Puerto Rican women, 200–1
The Treaty of Peace (Spanish-American War), 199
Tres Tristes Tigres (Three Trapped Tigers) (Cabrera Infante), 213
The Trial (Kafka), 273
Trotsky, Leon, 256
Trujillo del Perú (Compañon), 27f
Turlington, Christy, 263–79
  and assimilation, 267
  calendar of, 277–8
  and Costume Institute, 275
  face of, discourse surrounding, 265, 267, 274–6
  image of, 264
  and Pocahontas, 275–6
  racial ambiguity of, 274, 277
  representations of, 273–8
  Salvadoranness of, 11, 264–5, 276–7, 279
Turlington, Elizabeth, 275
Turner, Lana, 258
Turner, Terry, 118
tuxedo, 241–2, 243

uniforms, and the *guayabera*, 9; *see also guayabera*
Unitarians, 31–2
United States
  Cuban "exile" community in, 215–16
  domestic workers in, 268–73
  Frida Kahlo stamp in, 257
  guayabera in, 220, 226
  influence in Brazil, 184
  influence in Puerto Rico, 210
  Latin American fashion in, 9
  "new" Latins in, 266
  and Puerto Rican women, 205–9
  Salvadoranness in, 263–79, 267–8, 278–9
unkus (tunics), and caste system, 3
"untucked" shirtwaist, 8, 204, 205f
upper classes; *see* elites
urban Indian "ethnic" dress (*cholita p'acha*), 130
Uruapa, Mexico, 71
Uso and Abuso de la Guayabera (Use and Abuse of the Guayabera) (Suárez Solís), 221

Vagabond Life in Mexico (Bellemare), 58–9
Valera, Rosalía, 102–4, 111
Vega, Inca Garcilaso de la, 17, 21
Veloso, Caetano, 192
vendors

Index

artisans as, 111
earning a living, 101
selling strategies of, 89, 102–3, 112
Verônica, Carmem, 191
Verrill, Alpheous, 207, 208, 209
vest, in *china poblana*, 59–60
Vested Interests (Garber), 233–4
Viaje pintoresco y arqueológico sobre la parte más interesante de la República Mexicana (Nebel), 55f
Vida y Muerta de Frida Kahlo según fue referida a Karen y David Crommie, 256
Vidal, E. E., 34
Vide Bula (fashion line), 195
Viernes Santo (Good Friday), 97, 99–100
Vilcape, Hugo, 108
Villa, Pancho, 250
Villaça, Nizia, 8
Villar, Teodelina, 287–8; *see also* Borges
Visit to the Ranquel Indians (Mansilla), 165, 166–7
visual arts, and the *peinetón*, 36–37
Voyage pittoresque et archeologique dans la partie la plus interessant du Mexique (Nebel), 55f

wages, for weaving, 136, 150
Wanamaker, John, 224
Ward, H. G., 50
Wars of Independence, 47–8, 49
weavers/weaving
  Mayan, 148–50, 158
  Pampean, 167–8
  Peruvian, 159
  social meaning of, 137
  wages for, 136
  women, 167
weaving co-operatives, 148
Webber, Andrew Lloyd, 259
Weiner, Annette, 112
Western-style dress, 138
  black in, 108
  and social status, 6
  worn by *cholos*, 123
  worn by Sakaka, 131
"What a Peinetón Costs" ("Lo que cuesta un peinetón"), 41
white muslin gown, 61–3
wives, symbolism of clothing for, 28–9
Wilkie, James, 260
Wilson, Elizabeth, 264
Winterhalter, François-Xavier, 63
Wise, Lieutenant, 58

Wittig, Monique, 246
"Woman from Buenos Aires: Ball gown" (Bacle), 37f
"Woman from Buenos Aires: Summer Dress" (Bacle), 37f
women
  Andean, 126, 154
  Argentinian, 33
  black, 68
  consumption of clothes by, 27–9
  Cuban, 237
  elderly, 82–3
  Far Eastern influences on, 69
  Guatemalan, 151
  as *ixcacle* makers, 91
  Mayan, 147–8
  Mexican, 44, 48–9, 58, 63–4
  middle-aged, 82–3
  middle-class, 191–2
  mulatto, 68
  and the *peinetón*, 4; *see also peinetón*
  Puerto Rican; *see* Puerto Rican women
  representation of, 239
  Sakaka, 125, 126, 128–9
  weavers, 164, 167
  working class, 4, 237–8
  younger, 80, 83
women's fashion
  and being object of desire, 240–1
  masculine touches in, 244
  and sports, 189–90
working class, and the *maja*, 51
working class women, 4, 237–8
writers, travel; *see* travel writers

Yalalag, women of, 80
Yanque, Good Friday ritual in, 99–100
yarns, factory-spun, 135, 138
youth, Latin American, 83, 117, 131–2, 216–17
"Young Woman" ("Dama Joven") (Linati), 51
Yrigoyen, Hipólito, 171

zambos (black-Indians), 46
Zamora, Martha, 251
Zapotec women, 80
Zilda, Maria, 192
Zoogocho, women of, 80
Zoomp brand, 195
Zoot suit, 31
Zoot-suiters, 9, 31
Zorn, Elayne, 6